D0780093

THE
CAMBRIDGE EDITION OF
THE LETTERS AND WORKS OF
D. H. LAWRENCE

THE LETTERS OF D. H. LAWRENCE

*Vol. I: September 1901 – May 1913
James T. Boulton

*Vol. II: June 1913 – October 1916
George J. Zytaruk and James T. Boulton

*Vol. III: October 1916 – June 1921
James T. Boulton and Andrew Robertson

*Vol. IV: June 1921 – March 1924
Warren Roberts, James T. Boulton and Elizabeth Mansfield

*Vol. V: March 1924 – March 1927
James T. Boulton and Lindeth Vasey

Vol. VI: March 1927 – November 1928
James T. Boulton and Margaret H. Boulton, with Gerald M. Lacy

Vol. VII: November 1928 – February 1930
Keith Sagar and James T. Boulton

* Already published

THE LETTERS OF D. H. LAWRENCE

THE LETTERS OF
D. H. LAWRENCE

VOLUME VI
March 1927 – November 1928

EDITED BY
JAMES T. BOULTON
AND
MARGARET H. BOULTON

WITH
GERALD M. LACY

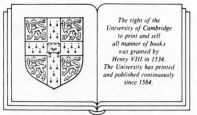

*The right of the
University of Cambridge
to print and sell
all manner of books
was granted by
Henry VIII in 1534.
The University has printed
and published continuously
since 1584.*

CAMBRIDGE UNIVERSITY PRESS

CAMBRIDGE

NEW YORK   PORT CHESTER

MELBOURNE   SYDNEY

Published by the Press Syndicate of the University of Cambridge
The Pitt Building, Trumpington Street, Cambridge CB2 1RP
40 West 20th Street, New York, NY 10011, USA
10 Stamford Road, Oakleigh, Melbourne 3166, Australia

First published 1991

Printed in Great Britain at
the University Press, Cambridge

Library of Congress cataloguing in publication data

Lawrence, D. H. (David Herbert), 1885–1930.
The letters of D. H. Lawrence.
(The Cambridge edition of the letters and works of D. H. Lawrence)
Includes indexes.
Contents: v. 1. September 1901–May 1913 edited by James T. Boulton. –
v. 2. June 1913–October 1916 / edited by George J.
Zytaruk and James T. Boulton. – v. 3. October 1916–
June 1921 / edited by James T. Boulton and Andrew
Robertson. – [etc.] – v. 6. March 1927–November 1928 /
edited by James T. Boulton and Margaret H. Boulton, with
Gerald M. Lacy.
1. Lawrence, D. H. (David Herbert), 1885–1930 –
Correspondence. 2. Authors, English – 20th century –
Correspondence. I. Boulton, James T.   II. Zytaruk,
George J.   III. Robertson, Andrew, 1945–
IV. Vasey, Lindeth.   V. Series: Lawrence, D. H. (David
Herbert), 1885–1930. Works. 1979.
PR6023.A93Z53   1979   823'.9'12   78-7531

British Library cataloguing in publication data

Lawrence, D. H. (David Herbert) 1885–1930
The letters of D. H. Lawrence – (The Cambridge edition of
the letters and works of D. H. Lawrence).
Vol. 6, March 1927–November 1928
1. Fiction in English. Lawrence, D. H. (David Herbert)
1885–1930
I. Title   II. Boulton, James T. (James Thompson) 1924–
III. Boulton, Margaret H.   IV. Lacy, Gerald M.   V. Series
823.912

ISBN 0 521 22147 1 (V.1)
0 521 23115 9 (v.6)

SE

CONTENTS

ILLUSTRATIONS

ACKNOWLEDGEMENTS

The generosity of manuscript holders is acknowledged with gratitude once again: their co-operation is a *sine qua non* of the edition. Their identities will be found in the list of cue-titles.

The volume editors have benefited greatly from the advice and assistance of Michael Black, Warren Roberts, Lindeth Vasey (not least for her meticulous sub-editing) and John Worthen. They have also cause to be grateful to the University of Birmingham which, through its Librarian and his staff, has continued to accommodate and to support the project. The staff of Cambridge University Press have been, as always, very helpful.

Thanks for particular kindnesses are due to Cornelia Rumpf-Worthen and John Worthen for translating Lawrence's letters written in German, and to Simonetta de Filippis and Elena Tognini-Bonelli for translating those written in Italian; to Jim Davies for photographic work; and to Elma Forbes who is responsible for the published index.

As in earlier volumes, many individuals have put their expertise at the disposal of the editors; those who specially merit acknowledgement include: Sir Harold Acton; Sigrid Adickes; Guy Alchon; Armin Arnold; Ben Benedikz; K. V. Bligh; David Bradshaw; Robert C. Brandeis; John P. Carswell; L. D. Clark; Desmond Costa; Pascal Covici Jr; E. C. D. Crossley; Christopher Date; Michael Davidis; T. R. Davis; Georgina Dobrée; Elizabeth A. Falsey; W. Forster; Margaret Glassey; Shirley Mott Graef; John R. Hammond; Bonnie Hardwick; Lilace Hatayama; Cathy Henderson; Ida Hughes-Stanton; Penelope Hughes-Stanton; Lady Juliette Huxley; R. D. S. Jack; Dorothy Johnston; Mara Kalnins; Saki Karavas; Annette Lawson; George Lazarus; Ian Ledsham; Derek Lomax; May Ellen MacNamara; Dieter Mehl; Heather Metcalf; Patricia Middleton; Elizabeth Mills; Jaime Peart; Wendy Perkins; Gerald Pollinger; Christopher Pollnitz; Hans Popper; Elizabeth Powis; Siegbert Prawer; Frederic Raphael; Beth A. Roads; Anthony Rota; Waltraud Rumpf; Sheila Ryan; Keith Sagar; Wilbur Scott; C. Sheppard; Sylvia Sherwill; Michael Silverman; Richard Simmons; Linda Sitterding; Gerry Slowey; Judith Speed; Madeline Spitaleri; W. E. Stober; Saundra Taylor; William B. Todd; W. van der Will.

For permission to use copyright material in annotation, thanks are expressed to the Clerk of the Records of the House of Lords and Trustees of the Beaverbrook Foundation (for use of Beaverbrook manuscripts), to Doris B. Mason (for Harold Mason's correspondence) and to the University of Illinois (for use of the Secker Letter-Book).

For illustrations in this volume the editors are indebted to: Sybille Bedford; Georgina Dobrée; Enid Hilton; Penelope Hughes-Stanton; Lady Juliette Huxley; Matthew Huxley; Philadelphia Museum of Art: Gift of Paul Strand; Gerald Pollinger; Schiller-Nationalmuseum, Deutsches Literaturarchiv; Southern Illinois University; Harry Ransom Humanities Research Center, University of Texas at Austin; David J. Wilkinson.

NOTE ON THE TEXT

A full statement of the 'Rules of Transcription' and an explanation of the 'Editorial Apparatus' are provided in Volume I, pp. xviii–xx. The reader may, however, like to be reminded that the following symbols are used:

[   ]   indicates a defect in the MS making it impossible even to conjecture what Lawrence had written. Where a reconstruction can be hazarded or a fault corrected, the conjecture or correction is shown within the square brackets.

[. . .]   indicates a deletion which cannot be deciphered or a postmark which is wholly or partly illegible.

MSC   = autograph manuscript copy
TMS   = typed manuscript
TMSC = typed manuscript copy
TSCC = typescript carbon copy

Maps are provided to show the location of places which Lawrence visited for the first time during the period covered by this volume. No attempt has been made fully to repeat information given on the maps in earlier volumes.

CUE-TITLES

Cue-titles are employed both for manuscript locations and for printed works. The following appear in this volume.

A. Manuscript locations

BBK Papers	House of Lords Record Office, Historical Collection 184, Beaverbrook Papers B/30
BL	British Library
Bonsignore	Signora Silvia Carenzio Bonsignore
BosU	Boston University
BraU	Brandeis University
Brill	Dr Edmund R. Brill
Brotherton	Brotherton Collection, Leeds University Library
Clarke	Mr W. H. Clarke
ColU	Columbia University
Deasey	Mr Denison Deasey

DeGruson	Mr Gene DeGruson
Edmunds	Mr Vincent E. Edmunds
Eton	Eton College School Library
Forster	Mr W. Forster
Foster	Mrs Leona Foster
HMohr	Mrs Eva Humbert–Mohr
HU	Harvard University
Hughes-Stanton	Mrs Ida Hughes-Stanton
Huxley	Lady Juliette Huxley
IEduc	Iowa State Education Association
Jeffrey	Mr Frederick Jeffrey
Lazarus	Mr George Lazarus
Martin	Mr John Martin
Mason	Mrs Doris Mason
Moore	Mrs Beatrice Moore
Needham	Mrs Margaret Needham
NL	Newberry Library
NWU	Northwestern University
NYPL	New York Public Library
Picard	Mrs Harwood B. Picard
PM	Pierpont Morgan Library
Roberts, W. H.	Mr William H. Roberts
Sagar	Dr Keith Sagar
Schlaefle	Mrs Susan Schlaefle-Nicholas
SIU	Southern Illinois University
StaU	Stanford University
SVerlag	Suhrkamp Verlag
Teale	Mrs Christine Teale
UCB	University of California at Berkeley
UCin	University of Cincinnati
UCLA	University of California at Los Angeles
UIll	University of Illinois
UInd	University of Indiana
UN	University of Nottingham
UNYB	State University of New York at Buffalo
UT	University of Texas at Austin
UTul	University of Tulsa
WHist	State Historical Society of Wisconsin
YU	Yale University

B. *Printed Works*

(The place of publication, here and throughout, is London unless otherwise stated.)

Brewster   Earl Brewster and Achsah Brewster. *D. H. Lawrence: Reminiscences and Correspondence*. Secker, 1934

Bynner   Witter Bynner. *Journey with Genius: Recollections and Reflections Concerning the D. H. Lawrences*. New York: Day, 1951

Carswell   Catherine Carswell. *The Savage Pilgrimage: A Narrative of D. H. Lawrence*. Chatto and Windus, 1932

Centaur   *The Centaur Letters*. Austin: Humanities Research Center, 1970

DHL Review   *The D. H. Lawrence Review*. Fayetteville: University of Arkansas, 1968–83; Newark: University of Delaware, 1984–

Frieda Lawrence Frieda Lawrence. *"Not I, But the Wind . . ."*. Santa Fe: Rydal Press, 1934

Gransden   K. W. Gransden, 'Rananim: D. H. Lawrence's Letters to S. S. Koteliansky', *Twentieth Century*, clix (January–June 1956), 22–32

Huxley   Aldous Huxley, ed. *The Letters of D. H. Lawrence*. Heinemann, 1932

Irvine, Brett   Peter L. Irvine and Anne Kiley, eds. 'D. H. Lawrence and Frieda Lawrence: Letters to Dorothy Brett', *D. H. Lawrence Review*, ix (Spring 1976), 1–116

Lacy, *Escaped Cock* Gerald M. Lacy, ed. *D. H. Lawrence: The Escaped Cock*. Los Angeles: Black Sparrow Press, 1973

Lawrence–Gelder Ada Lawrence and G. Stuart Gelder. *Young Lorenzo: Early Life of D. H. Lawrence*. Florence: G. Orioli, [1931]

Letters, i.   James T. Boulton, ed. *The Letters of D. H. Lawrence*. Volume I, September 1901–May 1913. Cambridge: Cambridge University Press, 1979

Letters, ii.   George J. Zytaruk and James T. Boulton, eds. *The Letters of D. H. Lawrence*. Volume II, June 1913–October 1916. Cambridge: Cambridge University Press, 1981

Letters, iii.   James T. Boulton and Andrew Robertson, eds. *The Letters of D. H. Lawrence*. Volume III, October 1916–

	June 1921. Cambridge: Cambridge University Press, 1984
Letters, iv.	Warren Roberts, James T. Boulton and Elizabeth Mansfield, eds. *The Letters of D. H. Lawrence*. Volume IV, June 1921–March 1924. Cambridge: Cambridge University Press, 1987
Letters, v.	James T. Boulton and Lindeth Vasey, eds. *The Letters of D. H. Lawrence*. Volume V, March 1924–March 1927. Cambridge: Cambridge University Press, 1989
Luhan	Mabel Dodge Luhan. *Lorenzo in Taos*. New York: Knopf, 1932
Mohr, Briefe	'Briefe an Max Mohr von D. H. Lawrence', *Die Neue Rundschau*, xliv (April 1933), 527–40
Moore, *Intelligent Heart*	Harry T. Moore. *The Intelligent Heart: The Story of D. H. Lawrence*. New York: Farrar, Straus, and Young, 1954
Moore, *Poste Restante*	Harry T. Moore. *Poste Restante: A Lawrence Travel Calendar*. Berkeley and Los Angeles: University of California Press, 1956
Moore	Harry T. Moore, ed. *The Collected Letters of D. H. Lawrence*. 2 volumes. Heinemann, 1962
Nehls	Edward Nehls, ed. *D. H. Lawrence: A Composite Biography*. 3 volumes. Madison: University of Wisconsin Press, 1957–9
Phoenix	Edward McDonald, ed. *Phoenix: The Posthumous Papers of D. H. Lawrence*. Heinemann, 1936
Roberts	Warren Roberts. *A Bibliography of D. H. Lawrence*. 2nd edition. Cambridge: Cambridge University Press, 1982
Sagar, Wilkinsons	Keith Sagar, 'The Lawrences and the Wilkinsons', *Review of English Literature*, iii (October 1962), 62–75
Schorer	Mark Schorer, 'I Will Send Address: Unpublished Letters of D. H. Lawrence', *London Magazine*, iii (February 1956), 44–67
Secker	Martin Secker, ed. *Letters from D. H. Lawrence to Martin Secker 1911–1930*. [Bridgefoot, Iver] 1970
Tedlock, *Lawrence MSS*	E. W. Tedlock. *The Frieda Lawrence Collection of D. H. Lawrence Manuscripts: A Descriptive Bibliography*. Albuquerque: University of New Mexico, 1948
Zytaruk	George J. Zytaruk, ed. *The Quest for Rananim: D. H. Lawrence's Letters to S. S. Koteliansky 1914 to 1930*. Montreal: McGill–Queen's University Press, 1970

MONETARY TERMS

    tanner = sixpence (6d) = $2\frac{1}{2}$p.
    bob = one shilling (1/-) = 5p.
    half-a-crown = 2/6 = $12\frac{1}{2}$p.
    quid = £1.
    guinea = £1/1/- = £1.05.

LAWRENCE: A CHRONOLOGY, 1927–1928

6 May 1926–10 June 1928	Lawrences' home is Villa Mirenda, San Paolo Mosciano, Scandicci, near Florence
21–8 March 1927	Stays with Brewsters at Palazzo Cimbrone, Ravello
28 March 1927	Sets off on walking tour with Earl Brewster along coast towards Rome (via Sorrento and Termini)
April 1927	Review of Carl Van Vechten's *Nigger Heaven*, Walter White's *Flight*, Dos Passos' *Manhattan Transfer* and Hemingway's *In Our Time*, together with two poems, 'The Old Orchard' and 'Rainbow', in *Calendar*; 'Two Blue Birds' in *Dial*
4–5? April 1927	In Rome; stays in Christine Hughes's flat
6–11 April 1927	To Cerveteri, Tarquinia, Vulci and Volterra, with Brewster, looking at Etruscan remains
11 April 1927	Arrives at Villa Mirenda (Frieda there on 5 April from Baden-Baden)
12 April 1927	Barbara Weekley arrives (with Mrs Seaman as chaperone); stays till 3 May
13 April 1927	Corrects proofs of *Mornings in Mexico*
16 April 1927	'Fireworks' in *Nation and Athenæum* (in *Forum*, May 1927)
c. 25 April 1927	Writing *The Escaped Cock*
26 April 1927	Sends 'Making Love to Music' to Nancy Pearn at Curtis Brown's
27 April 1927	Sends review of S. S. Koteliansky's translation of V. V. Rozanov's *Solitaria* to Kot
ante 29 April 1927	Has begun 'essays on the Etruscan things'
29 April 1927	Returns proofs of 'The Man Who Loved Islands' and 'More Modern Love' ('In Love') to Marianne Moore for publication in *Dial*
ante 5 May 1927	Sends three 'Flowery Tuscany' sketches to Nancy Pearn
5 May 1927	Sends *The Escaped Cock* to Nancy Pearn
ante 9 May 1927	Has sent introductory essay to Verga's *Mastro-don Gesualdo* to Curtis Brown for Cape (for

	publication in _Travellers' Library_, March 1928)
12 May 1927	Shortened version of 'The Lovely Lady' and review of W. Wilkinson's _Peep Show_ to Nancy Pearn
13 May 1927	Has been 'malarial and down in the mouth for about ten days'
19 May 1927	In Florence, lunches with Nellie Morrison _et al._ and visits exhibition of modern Florentine painting in the Belle Arti
22–3 May 1927	_David_ performed at Regent Theatre, London
23 May 1927	Edith and Osbert Sitwell at Villa Mirenda
27 May 1927	Finishing _Resurrection_ picture (begun ante 8 March 1927); sends 'None of That' to Nancy Pearn
June 1927	_Mornings in Mexico_ published in England by Secker (5 August 1927 in USA by Knopf)
6 June 1927	Has written about eighty pages of 'the Etruscan book' including 'Cerveteri' and two of 'Tarquinia' essays
8 June 1927	Visits the Uffizi with Christine and Mary Christine Hughes
9 June 1927	The Hugheses visit Villa Mirenda
c. 11 June 1927	Painting 'a smallish picture' (_The Finding of Moses_)
12 June 1927	Maria Huxley, Baron Luigi and Yvonne Franchetti at Villa Mirenda
14 June 1927	Sends 'Cerveteri', with photographs, to Nancy Pearn
15 June 1927	Goes by car to Forte dei Marmi with Maria Huxley; returns (probably on 16/17 June) by car to Lucca and train to Florence
19 June 1927	Anna di Chiara visits Villa Mirenda
July 1927	Review of Wilkinson's _Peep Show_ and Rozanov's _Solitaria_ in _Calendar_; 'The Man Who Loved Islands' in _Dial_ (and in _London Mercury_, August 1927)
2 July 1927	Sends six Etruscan essays to Millicent Beveridge in search for illustrations
6–17 July 1927	In bed suffering from 'bronchials and haemorrhage'; Dr Giglioli, from Florence, in

	almost daily attendance
19–27 July 1927	Further haemorrhages and confined to bed
23 July 1927	Six Etruscan essays, with 'all the photographs', sent to Curtis Brown
29 July 1927	'Up and creeping round a bit'
31 July 1927	Orioli visits; Wilkinson family spend the evening at Villa Mirenda
c. 3 August 1927	Writes review of Trigant Burrow's *The Social Basis of Consciousness*, to be sent to Nancy Pearn
4 August 1927	Lawrences go briefly to Orioli's flat in Florence, then take night train to Villach in Austria
5–30 August 1927	At Hotel Fischer, Villach
6 August 1927	To Lake Ossiacher
7 August 1927	To Lake Worther
8 August–3 September 1927	Frieda's sister Johanna, with her husband Emil Krug, at the Grand Hotel, Annenheim
17 August 1927	To Lake Faaker; translating Verga's *Cavalleria Rusticana* stories and sends three to Nancy Pearn before 23 August
26 August 1927	Returns corrected proofs of article on John Galsworthy to Nancy Pearn's secretary
30 August 1927	Lawrences leave for Munich; stay overnight there
31 August 1927	To Irschenhausen with Else Jaffe
31 August–4 October 1927	At Villa Jaffe, Irschenhausen
September 1927	'The Nightingale' in *Forum* (in *Spectator*, 10 September 1927)
5 September 1927	Johanna Krug arrives in Irschenhausen; three Richthofen sisters are together until 8 September when Johanna leaves for Baden-Baden; Else leaves 12 September for Heidelberg
ante 10 September 1927	Paints 'a little water-color of flowers'
c. 15 September 1927	Visited by Franz Schoenberner
16 September 1927	More translations of *Cavalleria Rusticana* stories sent to Nancy Pearn's secretary; finishes whole volume, except for Introduction, by 25 September
17 September 1927	Barbara Weekley arrives in Munich; in

	Irschenhausen 18–21 September
17 September 1927	'Two Blue Birds' in *Great Stories of All Nations* (New York)
ante 26 September 1927	Nancy Pearn and her friend Mrs Angell stay for two days at Villa Mirenda
27 September 1927	Visits Walburga Leitner (his landlady in Icking in 1912)
28 September 1927	Sends MS of Verga translations, with Introduction for the volume, to Nancy Pearn's secretary
29 September 1927	Max Mohr visits; perhaps on the same day Schoenberner and Hans Carossa visit
October 1927	'Flowery Tuscany I' in *New Criterion*; 'The Lovely Lady' in *The Black Cap*, ed. Cynthia Asquith
4 October 1927	Leaves Irschenhausen for Baden-Baden
4–18 October 1927	At Hotel Eden, Baden-Baden
ante 4 October 1927	*Forum* buys *The Escaped Cock*
ante 8 October 1927	Sends to Laurence Pollinger, at Curtis Brown's, the signed agreement for *The Woman Who Rode Away and Other Stories*
9 October 1927	Is examined by the doctor in the Landesbad and proposes to take 'the inhalation cure for ten days or so'; attends a performance in the Marionette Theatre in the spa hotel
16? October 1927	Else Jaffe and her children arrive in Baden-Baden
18 October 1927	Leaves Baden-Baden for Milan
19 October 1927	Lawrences travel by train from Milan to Florence; Wilkinsons drive them to Villa Mirenda
20 October 1927	Tea with the Wilkinsons at Villa Poggi
c. 28 October 1927	Writing 'a story' (perhaps 'Autobiographical Fragment') and 'dabbing at' his picture, *The Finding of Moses*
November 1927	'A New Theory of Neuroses', review of Burrow's *Social Basis of Consciousness*, in *Bookman*; 'Flowery Tuscany II' in *New Criterion*; 'In Love' in *Dial*; 'City of the Dead at Cerveteri' in *Travel* (in *World Today*, February 1928)

3 November 1927	'At present am not inclined to do anything'
6 November 1927	Painting *Jaguar Leaping at a Man*
7 November 1927	Frieda collects Lawrence's *Fauns and Nymphs* sent by Brewster
c. 8 November 1927	Wilkinsons take Lawrences by car to San Gemignano
ante 11 November 1927	Completes a water-colour, *Throwing Back the Apple*
ante 14 November 1927	Visited by Charles Scott-Moncrieff, Reggie Turner, Orioli and Harold Acton
17 November 1927	Sends *Rawdon's Roof* to Nancy Pearn; lunches at Turner's house in Florence; meets Michael Arlen on the Lungarno; sees Richard de la Condamine
19 November 1927	Arlen at Villa Mirenda for tea
December 1927	'Flowery Tuscany III' in *New Criterion*; 'Ancient Metropolis of the Etruscans' in *Travel* (in *World Today*, March 1928)
1 December 1927	Agrees that Alice Corbin Henderson should include 'Men in New Mexico', 'Autumn at Taos' and 'The Red Wolf' in *The Turquoise Trail* (1928)
c. 5 December 1927	Maria Huxley visits
8 December 1927	Writing *Lady Chatterley's Lover* 'all over again' (the third version)
18 December 1927	Rewriting of *Lady Chatterley's Lover* 'half' done; Wilkinson family have tea at Villa Mirenda before departing for Christmas in Rome
20 December 1927	Frieda in Florence; Lawrence has been 'a bit seedy' and stays at home
21 December 1927	Aldous and Maria Huxley visit
24 December 1927	Peasants at Villa Mirenda for party round the Christmas tree
25 December 1927	Huxleys drive Lawrences to spend the day at the Peterichs' house in Florence
27 December 1927	Huxleys at Villa Mirenda for lunch
ante 28 December 1927	Nellie Morrison begins typing *Lady Chatterley's Lover*
January 1928	'Painted Tombs of Tarquinia' in *Travel* (in *World Today*, April 1928)

5 January 1928	Introduction for Cape's edition of Grazia Deledda's *The Mother* (*La Madre*) sent to Nancy Pearn for typing
6 January 1928	Rewriting of *Lady Chatterley's Lover* 'done, all but the last chapter'; refuses invitation to translate Lorenzo Viani's *Parigi*
8 January 1928	After typing five chapters of *Lady Chatterley's Lover* Nellie Morrison refuses to proceed with the remainder (the rewriting of which Lawrence has just completed)
10 January 1928	Asks Catherine Carswell to arrange for typing of *Lady Chatterley's Lover*
11 January 1928	Has typed *Love Poems and Others* and nearly all *Amores* in preparation for *Collected Poems*; *Amores* completed by 16 January
13 January 1928	Suffering from influenza; departure for Switzerland (planned for 16 January) delayed
16 January 1928	Proofs of Secker's edition of *The Woman Who Rode Away* arrive lacking final pages of 'The Border Line'
20 January 1928	Travels by train to Les Diablerets, Switzerland, via Milan, Simplon Pass and Aigle
20 January–6 March 1928	At Chateau Beau Site, Les Diablerets
22 January 1928	Maria Huxley agrees to type 'the "worst" bits' of *Lady Chatterley's Lover*
25 January 1928	Sends over half the novel to Catherine Carswell who had arranged for its typing in London
27 January 1928	Has written a new ending for 'The Border Line' to replace missing pages
February 1928	*Cavalleria Rusticana and Other Stories* published in England by Cape (in USA by Dial Press, 1928); *The Escaped Cock* in *Forum*; 'The Wind-Swept Stronghold of Volterra' in *Travel* (in *World Today*, May 1928)
2 February 1928	Receives gift of cigarette case from Durham miners and arranges to send books in return
c. 3 February 1928	Returns proofs of *The Woman Who Rode Away* to Secker
4 February 1928	Preparing typescripts for expurgated edition of

	Lady Chatterley's Lover for possible publication in USA and UK
5 February 1928	Picnic on Pillon Pass
6 February 1928	Receiving typescript of opening three chapters of *Lady Chatterley's Lover* from Catherine Carswell; Maria Huxley 'typing the second half'
ante 10 February 1928	Copy for *Collected Poems* goes to Curtis Brown for Secker
10 February 1928	Has adopted *Lady Chatterley's Lover* as title of novel; sends three pages of chapter IX [i.e. XII] to Catherine Carswell
10–12 February 1928	Rolf Gardiner in Les Diablerets to meet Lawrence
13 February 1928	Two more chapters of novel typescript arrive from Catherine Carswell; sends her £5 towards typist's costs
14–16 February 1928	Max Mohr visits
16 February 1928	Returns revised proofs of *The Woman Who Rode Away* to Secker
17 February 1928	Selected poems in pamphlet series, *The Augustan Books of English Poetry* (Benn)
26 February 1928	Agrees to sell MS to Harry Crosby for a limited edition
27 February 1928	Frieda leaves for Baden-Baden
29 February 1928	More typescript arrives from Catherine Carswell but two chapters still lacking
March 1928	'John Galsworthy' in *Scrutinies by Various Writers*, ed. Edgell Rickword (Wishart); 'Giovanni Verga' in *Now & Then*
2 March 1928	Remainder of typescript of *Lady Chatterley's Lover* arrives
3 March 1928	Tells Giuseppe Orioli: 'All is ready! We can begin'
5 March 1928	Sends copies of the expurgated novel, called 'John Thomas and Lady Jane', to Secker and Knopf (via Curtis Brown)
6 March 1928	Leaves Les Diablerets, accompanied by Juliette Huxley as far as Aigle; by train to Milan where he meets Frieda
7 March 1928	Travels from Milan to Florence; Wilkinsons

	drive Lawrences to Villa Mirenda where peasants greet them with flowers
8 March 1928	Painting water-colour of 'torch-dance by daylight!'
9 March 1928	Takes typescript of *Lady Chatterley's Lover* to Orioli; together they take it to the printer, Tipografia Giuntina: 'great moment'. Proofs of *Collected Poems* arrive
10–11 March 1928	Else Jaffe and Alfred Weber at Villa Mirenda
c. 13 March 1928	Begins lengthy campaign by letter to persuade friends to subscribe for *Lady Chatterley's Lover*
14 March 1928	Secker declares he will not publish the novel even when 'expurgated'
15 March 1928	Correcting proofs of *Collected Poems*; returns them to Secker by 16 March
16 March 1928	Has 'done three more water-colours'; Barbara Weekley arrives from Alassio
18 March 1928	Robert Windeam and Deane Perceval lunch at the Mirenda
26 March 1928	Copies of *Scrutinies* arrive; meets and is reconciled with Norman Douglas, in Florence
ante 27 March 1928	Paints *Dandelions*
27 March 1928	Begins negotiations with Dorothy Warren which lead to exhibition of paintings in June/July 1929
28 March 1928	Barbara Weekley returns to Alassio; Wilkinson family leave Villa Poggi for England
April 1928	'Introduction' to *The Mother* (*La Madre*) by Grazzia Deledda (Cape)
1 April 1928	Receives gold pieces from Crosby for MS; Orioli delivers first proofs of *Lady Chatterley's Lover*, takes other MSS to be bound
2 April 1928	Has corrected forty-one pages of proofs; painting *The Rape of the Sabine Women*; Else Jaffe and Alfred Weber arrive in Florence from Capri
3 April 1928	Repays 'loan' of £10 to Montague Sherman
5 April 1928	Frieda, Else Jaffe and Weber lunch in Florence with Muriel Moller, Lawrence has 'a bit of a cold' and cannot go; Orioli returns bound MSS

9 April 1928	At Giogoli with Else Jaffe to visit peasant family, the Bandelli, formerly on Mirenda estate
11 April 1928	To Florence to see Frieda and Else Jaffe depart for Alassio; lunch with Muriel Moller
13 April 1928	'Doing up' his picture *Fauns and Nymphs*; Muriel Moller and Nellie Morrison at the Mirenda for tea; stays overnight in Orioli's flat in Florence
15? April 1928	Margaret Gardiner visits Mirenda
16 April 1928	Frieda returns from Alassio
17 April 1928	'In the middle of the proofs'; offers to write Introduction to Crosby's *Chariot of the Sun* (completed before 29 April)
19 April 1928	Lady Colefax comes to tea
23 April 1928	Lunches with Lady Colefax at Poggio Gherardo, near Florence
24 April 1928	Has 'done rather more than half the proofs'
25 April 1928	Finishing picture, *Family on a Verandah*
26 April 1928	Lady Colefax invited to tea
28 April 1928	*England, My England* published in Tauchnitz edition
1 May 1928	Posts bound MSS (including *Sun*) to Crosby
3 May 1928	In Florence; has lunch with Muriel Moller and tea with Mrs Otway
4 May 1928	Decides to rent Villa Mirenda for further six months; proofs of *Lady Chatterley's Lover* 'still only half done'; Mary Foote for tea
8 May 1928	'When She Asks Why?' in *Evening News*
9 May 1928	'Nothing doing here – just waiting for those proofs'
12 May 1928	Writes longer 'foreword' and shorter 'note' to *Collected Poems*
13 May 1928	Sends 'Laura Philippine' to Nancy Pearn
16 May 1928	First half of *Lady Chatterley's Lover* being printed
21 May 1928	Sends to Nancy Pearn article, 'That Women Know Best' for *Daily Chronicle*, and 'Chaos in Poetry' (published in *Echanges*, December 1929)

22 May 1928	Has 'a bit of flu and [is] in bed'; but is 'doing the last proofs'
24 May 1928	*The Woman Who Rode Away and Other Stories* published in England by Secker (on 25 May in USA by Knopf)
24 May 1928	Is 'just getting the last of the proofs'; has 'at least 450 orders from England', few from USA
25 May 1928	Receives more gold from Crosby
27 May 1928	Outing by car to see friends 'in a villa not far away'
31 May 1928	Receives 'the last of the proofs'; Laurence and Enid Hilton arrive in London with ten of Lawrence's paintings for later exhibition in the Warren Gallery
4 June 1928	Is satisfied with the title-page of *Lady Chatterley's Lover*; the printing of the novel approaching completion
6 June 1928	Brewsters, staying in Florence, visit Mirenda
7 June 1928	'Finished last of proofs & signed all sheets for Lady C.'
10 June 1928	Lawrences leave Villa Mirenda and travel via Pisa and Genoa, with the Brewsters, to Turin, where they spend the night: 'there was no definite notion of where [they] were going'
11–13 June 1928	At Chambéry, Aix-les-Bains and Grenoble
14–15 June 1928	At Hotel des Touristes, St Nizier-de-Pariset, near Grenoble; proprietor requires Lawrence to leave
17 June–6 July 1928	Lawrences and Brewsters at Grand Hotel, Chexbres-sur-Vevey, Switzerland; Frieda leaves for Baden-Baden on 19 June
21 June 1928	Working on second half of *The Escaped Cock*
22 June 1928	Informed that 'the first 200 copies of *Lady C.* are ready'
23 June 1928	Arranges for larger pictures in Villa Mirenda to be crated for despatch to England: Maria and Aldous Huxley arrive
25 June 1928	Frieda returns
27 June 1928	Sends article, 'Insouciance', to Nancy Pearn; Maria Huxley drives Lawrences to Castle of

	Chillon, then for tea in Montreux
28 June 1928	Huxleys leave for Forte dei Marmi; copy of *Lady Chatterley's Lover* arrives 'to our great excitement . . . a handsome and dignified volume'; sends 'Men Must Rule' to Nancy Pearn
July 1928	*Lady Chatterley's Lover* published
6 July 1928	Lawrences move to Hotel National, Gstaad; Brewsters remain at Chexbres
7 July 1928	'Laura Philippine' in *T. P.'s & Cassell's Weekly*
9 July–18 September 1928	Lawrences in chalet, Kesselmatte, near Gsteig
11 July 1928	Brewsters leave Chexbres for Hotel Viktoria, Gsteig
12 July 1928	'Over-Earnest Ladies' (MS title, 'Insouciance') in *Evening News*; sends articles, 'Matriarchy' and 'Ownership', to Nancy Pearn; is painting *Sun-men catching horses*
18 July 1928	Provides 'Autobiography' for Curtis Brown
ante 20 July 1928	Second half of *The Escaped Cock* completed
20 July 1928	Review in *Vogue* (sent to Nancy Pearn on 17 July) of Robert Byron's *The Station*, Clough Williams-Ellis' *England and the Octopus*, Maurice Baring's *Comfortless Memory* and Somerset Maugham's *Ashenden or the British Agent*
24 July 1928	Pays 4022 liras for binding of copies of *Lady Chatterley's Lover*; all copies ordered in England and paid for have been despatched
26 July 1928	Sends 'The Blue Moccasins' to Nancy Pearn (published in *Eve*, 22 November 1928)
28 July 1928	Asks Orioli to despatch all copies of *Lady Chatterley's Lover* ordered in USA; one London book exporter cancels order for 72 copies
30 July 1928	Two more book exporters cancel orders (42 copies); pays Florentine doctor's bill of 1345 liras
31 July 1928	Brewsters bring Indian author, Dhan Gopal Mukerji, to rea
August 1928	'Things' in *Bookman*

2 August 1928	'Master in His Own House' (MS title, 'Men Must Rule') in *Evening News* (in *Vanity Fair*, as 'Deserted Battlefields', November 1928)
6 August 1928	Signed and returned to Secker 102 sheets for special first edition of *Collected Poems*
9 August 1928	'I just dibble at tiny pictures, and potter about among the trees'
11 August 1928	Frieda has 'a grand birthday feast' at Hotel Viktoria
13 August 1928	Sends drawing of 'The Greater Sun' to Crosby who sought agreement to print 100 de luxe copies of *Sun*
14 August 1928	'I've been painting a bit, but not much else'
ante 15 August 1928	Has painted *Contadini*
20 August 1928	Instructs Nancy Pearn to send 'Why I Don't Like Living in London' to *Evening News*
c. 24 August 1928	Brewsters' friend, Boshi Sen, gives Lawrence massage
24 August 1928	Sends 'Cocksure Women and Hen-sure Men' to Nancy Pearn for *Evening News*
25 August 1928	His 'infernal cough . . . is for the time master of [his] movements'
26 August – 7 September 1928	Lawrence's sister, Emily King, and her daughter Margaret stay at Kesselmatte
28 August 1928	Farewell banquet for Brewsters and Boshi Sen
29 August 1928	Brewsters depart for Geneva and (on 11 September) Basle; writes 'Hymns in a Man's Life'
30 August 1928	Estimates total receipts for *Lady Chatterley's Lover* about £980, expenses about £300
ante 31 August 1928	Has painted *Close-Up* (*Kiss*)
September 1928	*Collected Poems*, 2 vols, published in England by Secker (July 1929 in USA by Cape and Smith); 'Kirchenleider im Leben Eines Mannes' ('Hymns in a Man's Life') in *Buch des Dankes Fur Hans Carossa* (Insel Verlag, Leipzig)
1 September 1928	'The U.S. mail is holding up *Lady Chatterley*'
2 September 1928	Sends MS of *The Escaped Cock*, two parts, to Enid Hilton for typing; has painted *North Sea*; sends Frieda's German translation of 'Hymns

	in a Man's Life' to Franz Schoenberner and the English version to Nancy Pearn
3 September 1928	'Dull London' (MS title, 'Why I Don't Like Living in London') in *Evening News*
4 September 1928	Estimates profit to date on *Lady Chatterley's Lover* as £713.11.9 on '*about* 560 copies'; visits Les Diablerets
5 September 1928	Receives, signs and returns to Secker the agreement for *Collected Poems*
7 September 1928	Emily King, returning via Paris, will post *Sun-men catching horses* to Crosby
8 September 1928	Receives contract from Elkin Mathews for *Rawdon's Roof*; returns it to Curtis Brown's office on 15 September
13 September 1928	Sends 'Red Trousers' to Nancy Pearn for *Evening News*
15–18 September 1928	Else Jaffe stays for the weekend
17? September 1928	Returns proofs of *Sun* to Crosby; revised proofs returned on 30 September
18 September 1928	Lawrences leave for Baden-Baden, Else Jaffe for Nice
18 September–1 October 1928	Lawrences, Frieda's mother and Brewsters at Hotel Löwen, Lichtental, Baden-Baden
22 September 1928	Receives typescript of *The Escaped Cock* from Enid Hilton; sends it to Curtis Brown's office on 24 September
27 September 1928	'Oh! For a New Crusade' (MS title, 'Red Trousers') in *Evening News*
October 1928	*Sun* published in Paris (limited edition) by Crosby
1 October 1928	Leaves Lichtental with the Brewsters for Toulon via Strasbourg and Lyon; arrives on 2 October; Brewsters continue to Nice and Italy
2 October 1928	Frieda leaves Lichtental for Florence; stays overnight in Orioli's flat, 3 October; goes to Villa Mirenda on 4th, to pack up their belongings and give up the Villa
2–15 October 1928	At Grand Hotel, Le Lavandou; Else Jaffe and Alfred Weber, Aldous and Maria Huxley there till 4 October
3 October 1928	Visits Ile de Port-Cros

5 October 1928	'If Women Were Supreme' (MS title, 'Matriarchy') in *Evening News*
7? October 1928	Richard Aldington and Dorothy Yorke arrive on Port-Cros
12 October 1928	Frieda arrives at Le Lavandou
13 October 1928	'Hymns in a Man's Life' in *Evening News*
15 October–17 November 1928	At La Vigie, Ile de Port-Cros, with Aldington, Dorothy Yorke and Brigit Patmore
20 October 1928	Signs sheets for copies of *Sun*
21 October 1928	Has begun to translate Lasca's *Story of Doctor Manente*; 'half done' by 27 October; 'nearly done' by 1 November
27 October 1928	'I have been in bed all week with that flu cold – and two days hemorrhage and feel rather rotten'; receives copy of *Collected Poems*
3 November 1928	Sends to Nancy Pearn corrected proofs of 'The Blue Moccasins' and article (for *Daily Express*), 'Is England Still a Man's Country?'
5 November 1928	Sends 'Sex Appeal' to Nancy Pearn
8 November 1928	Sends 'Do Women Change?' to Nancy Pearn
13 November 1928	Has received copies of Crosby's edition of *Sun* and Else Jaffe's German translation of *The Woman Who Rode Away and Other Stories*
17 November 1928	Leaves Ile de Port-Cros for Bandol

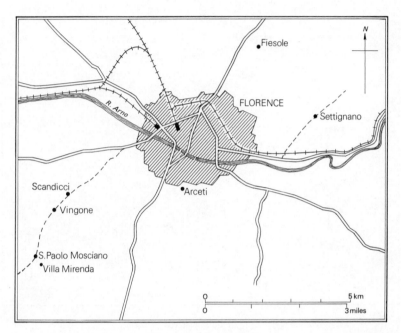

Florence and environs

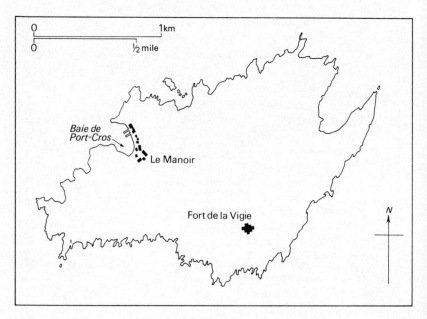

Ile de Port-Cros

INTRODUCTION

One obvious feature of the twenty-one months covered by this volume is the restricted range of Lawrence's movements when compared with earlier periods. More than half the time between March 1927 and mid-November 1928 he and Frieda lived at the Villa Mirenda in its isolation 1½ miles beyond the south-western fringes of Florence, 'away from Tourists and hotels and touts'.[1] True they spent a few weeks in Austria, a couple of months (August–October 1927) in Frieda's sister's house at Irschenhausen, two weeks with her mother in Baden-Baden and six weeks (January–March 1928) with the Huxleys at Les Diablerets in Switzerland; but the Mirenda was the centre from which they moved and to which they returned. This continued so until, after a brief visit to south-western France, they were in Gsteig, Switzerland, and Lawrence decided that he could not face another winter in the Mirenda. That was in August 1928; by mid-October Frieda had been back to the 'big old heavy villa, square, perched on a hill',[2] removed or disposed of their belongings, and the Lawrences were on the tiny island of Port-Cros off the coast near Toulon. There had been no intercontinental travel, no visit to England: both these remained true for the rest of Lawrence's life.

Characteristically he was often restive. As so frequently in the past he would toy with ideas of travel over great distances: to Taos (but Frieda was adamant in her refusal to go near their old friend Dorothy Brett and was dubious about Mabel Luhan as a neighbour); to New York, San Francisco and then perhaps to China and India – 'anything to shake off this stupor'; or with Richard Aldington to Egypt where they would call on Bonamy and Valentine Dobrée and 'perhaps get shot in Khartoum like General Gordon'.[3] In May 1927 Lawrence was sure his 'real inside doesn't turn towards America'; by November, sick of Europe, he must go to America which was 'somehow an antidote – so tonicky'.[4] Or, less ambitiously, he might spend a year in Ireland; he might even 'try Devonshire or somewhere nearer home. Time to go home, I feel.' In February 1928 he mused on the possibility of 'drifting around for a time – Germany, England, perhaps Ireland, for the the summer: and for the winter, heaven knows'; but perhaps Taos, perhaps Capri and the 'etruscans'. A sea-voyage round the world was another dream.[5] But, except in such moments of euphoria, honesty kept on breaking in. Travel had come to 'bore' him; the older he became the less he enjoyed 'the actual process of travelling'; and then the confession: 'I'm in despair, never able to

---

[1] Letter 3986.   [2] *Letters*, v. 448.   [3] Letters 4198, 4603.   [4] Letters 4021, 4208.
[5] Letters 4183, 4192, 4313, 4390.

say *I will come* or *I will go*, because of my wretched chest.'[6] He preferred visiting small towns in the country – 'big towns worry me'; country inns where 'there is a natural life' suited him better than boring hotels populated by 'thousands of elderly English virgins'; but the inescapable fact recurs: 'my broncs aren't good enough for the long travel'. There is a poignancy about the Shakespearean echo in his remark to Aldous Huxley: 'if you want to do a bit of a *giro*, so am I pining, pining to be amused, to forget and to escape the thousand natural snares'.[7]

Inevitably, then, Lawrence's health was one of his main preoccupations. Much of what limited travel was undertaken in the period of these letters resulted from his worsening physical condition. For example, when he was once more in bed 'with bronchials and haemorrhage' in July 1927 – the month when Frieda expressed her own alarm in a private letter to Lawrence's publisher Martin Secker[8] – the physician, Dr Giglioli (whom he regarded as the best in Florence) recommended him to go somewhere about 2000 feet above sea-level. Therefore, for three weeks in August the Lawrences stayed in Villach. As soon as they arrived Lawrence delighted in the cool freshness he found there – 'cool bed, . . . fresh mountain water, . . . fresh air, that isn't baked. . .'; after a week he told his childhood friend, Gertrude Cooper, herself tubercular, that he was better 'but the cough is a nuisance – I hope it will go away here in the mountains, in the cool'.[9] But it did not. In late September at Irschenhausen he used the same biblical allusion that is found in a letter twelve years before, early in the war, when he felt beneath 'a very black flood'; he told his old friend Koteliansky: 'I feel a bit like Noah's dove who has lost the ark and doesn't see any signs of an olive bough – and is getting a bit weary on the wing.'[10] In 1927, as in 1915, the despondency was profound. Though, a few days later, he declared himself 'a lot better', he admitted that he was not his 'real self. I seem to have lost something out of my vitality – I hope it will come back.'[11] Once again at Villa Mirenda, he could 'walk to the top of the hills, and feel like getting a grip on life again'; but one notices that his visit to Florence on 17 November was the first since the Lawrences returned from Baden on 19 October. Lawrence would not willingly have foregone the pleasure of meeting literary friends for so long; now, instead of encountering Reggie Turner, Giuseppe ('Pino') Orioli, Charles Scott-Moncrieff and Harold Acton on the Via Tornabuoni, they visited him at the Mirenda and he poured tea.[12] Then, early in 1928, 'everybody says the mountains, the

---

[6] Letters 3985, 4024, 4307.   [7] Letters 4125, 4425, 4325, 4408.
[8] Letters 4059, p. 105 n. 1.   [9] Letters 4094, 4105.   [10] *Letters*, ii. 9–10, Letter 4148.
[11] Letter 4157.
[12] Letters 4205, 4204. Cf. Harold Acton, *Memoirs of an Aesthete* (1948), p. 107, for a glimpse of the 'plethora of writers' and their life in Florence.

mountains. So we'll try'; hence the move to Les Diablerets. The second visit to Switzerland, four months later – this time 4000 feet up at Gsteig – was again on medical advice: 'let's hope I really can get better, I'm so sick of not being well.'[13] At St Nizier in France, en route for Gsteig, an hotelier had actually turned Lawrence out because of the severity of his cough and though his health improved slightly in the Swiss air, he had to admit that his 'infernal cough' was 'for the time master of [his] movements'. Thus, however jocular his remark to the Huxleys that he had designed his tombstone with the inscription, 'Departed this life etc., etc. – *He was fed up!*', despair was not far from the surface.[14]

The true source of Lawrence's ill health was not acknowledged. He did not conceal from his correspondents the ill health itself (that would have been impossible in any case); rather he assured them that it could be attributed to external agencies; an organic cause was never admitted. His condition was associated with his increasing age (he was then forty-one), or explained by the malaria he contracted in Mexico in 1925, by his (like Lady Ottoline Morrell's) not being 'vulgarly *physically* selfish, self-keeping and self-preserving . . . [wasting] one's common flesh too much', or – when he was on Port-Cros – by Frieda's having brought an influenza germ from Florence.[15] Outwardly Lawrence convinced himself that it was preferable to have diverse and liberating experiences, even at the cost of his own 'bad health', than to suffer the 'healthy and limited' life of a peasant. He could even suggest that, though 'these hemorrhages are rather shattering . . . perhaps they take some bad blood out of the system'. His sisters and Brett received assurances that his cough was simply a 'nuisance' and the cause of haemorrhages was bronchial and not pulmonary.[16]

That Lawrence's letters reveal frequent changes of mood is, in the light of this evidence, not surprising. He could vary between indifference to all creative activity, whether writing or painting: 'David sitting on his thumbs', as he put it on one occasion; or the feeling that he was undergoing a 'change of life, and a queer sort of recoil . . . drawing back from connection with everything'; to the conviction, at the end of 1927, that 'this is the low-water mark of existence. I never felt so near the brink of the abyss.'[17] Lawrence had experienced such despair before; his sensing that people regarded him as an 'animal in a cage – or should be in a cage – sort of wart-hog', reminds one of his self-comparison to a hunted animal when he felt 'pushed to the brink of existence' in 1916.[18] And yet, equally, his letters are also records of

[13] Letters 4262, 4529.   [14] Letters 4478, 4613, 4562.   [15] Letters 4251, 4025, 4437, 4723.
[16] Letters 4051, 4079, 4201, 4494, 4527.   [17] Letters 4184, 3995, 4238.
[18] Letter 4209; *Letters*, ii. 500.

astonishing resilience, of remarkable stores of mental and nervous energy. In August 1927, for example, though he was 'going round rather feebly' after serious haemorrhages and heat exhaustion, Lawrence read the distinguished psychoanalyst Trigant Burrow's *Social Basis of Consciousness* as soon as it arrived, wrote a long, fresh and searching response to it in a letter, and – within forty-eight hours, despite preparations to leave the Mirenda for Villach – wrote a review of the book running to nearly 3,000 words. After arriving in Villach and feeling invigorated by the mountain freshness, but weak nevertheless, he sent a translation of three stories from *Cavalleria Rusticana* to Nancy Pearn in his agent Curtis Brown's London office. There certainly were times, as in October–November 1927, when he was not inclined to work – 'I just don't really want to do anything'[19] – yet preparation for the publication of *Lady Chatterley's Lover*, the two-volume *Collected Poems*, the volume of stories entitled *The Woman Who Rode Away and Other Stories*, and what would (posthumously) be *Etruscan Places*, proceeded without serious interruption. He offered to write a prefatory essay for a volume of poems by the expatriate American Harry Crosby; he wrote a story for *Eve: The Lady's Pictorial*; he contributed a fine essay, 'Hymns in a Man's Life' to a volume in honour of the German novelist and physician, Hans Carossa; he translated Grazzini's *Story of Doctor Manente*, intended as Lawrence's contribution to a series of Italian Renaissance novelists to be published by Orioli. And there was much more.

The two major undertakings by Lawrence the professional writer, in the period of this volume – the publication of *Lady Chatterley's Lover* and the burst of highly successful journalism – should to a considerable extent be viewed in association with his determination to achieve financial security. Poverty, or at least insecurity, had been a recurring feature of his professional life. It was still so in April 1927; in June he conceded that he managed 'to scramble through, but no more'; in October his 'earnings aren't much, nowadays'; but in the following September he insisted that he was not hard up, had 'plenty of money to go on with' and had no need or desire to sell any of his pictures.[20] The change requires comment; several of Lawrence's important characteristics are revealed in the process.

In August 1927, for instance, he refused to accept an advance from his publisher, Secker: 'I don't need it, thank heaven – and I hate things in advance.' Though he was determined to be paid for whatever he did produce, Lawrence showed neither greed nor willingness to accept what he had not yet earned. Understandably he felt that he 'damn well ought to have enough to live on' and resentful that only 'by living like a road-sweeper' had he

---

[19] Letters 4083, 4086, 4118, 4198.   [20] Letters 3996, 4053, 4166, 4652.

sufficient.[21] Yet, even though one suspects a growing awareness that he must accumulate funds to meet inevitable demands should his health deteriorate further, and, perhaps, to secure Frieda's well-being in the event of his own death, Lawrence was innocent of mere self-regard. He never sought to avoid paying dues and debts; his personal generosity was never in question.

On several occasions Lawrence is found telling Brett that, if she will send him 'the bill for taxes and the winter feed for the horses' on the Kiowa Ranch in New Mexico, he will pay it; she is instructed to apply to him for a loan if she is in need; or, as he puts it in March 1928, '*do tell me* if there is anything I ought to pay'. Similarly he assures his sister Ada that, if Gertrude Cooper is in difficulty, he will assist her to the tune of £50 p.a.; and 'don't tell anybody', he insists.[22] He sends money to both his sisters and their children for holiday pocket-money; he arranges to buy German toys for Rachel Hawk's children in New Mexico, as well as for his nephew Bertram and niece Joan, at Christmas; and when he invites his sister Emily and niece Margaret to stay with him and Frieda in Switzerland, he offers money to cover their travelling expenses. When Montague Shearman reminds him about an outstanding 'loan', which Lawrence clearly believed was a gift, the £10 is paid immediately and without question. And his punctiliousness in paying his dues to Orioli for commission, and his debts to the Tipografia Giuntina for printing *Lady Chatterley's Lover*, is exemplary; nor does he forget a consideration for Carletto, Orioli's 'boy'.

As if to substantiate the claim just advanced, it is noticeable that in Lawrence's case generosity begot generosity. The letters frequently provide evidence of active concern on the part of his friends and acquaintances for his well-being. His neighbours at the Villa Mirenda, the Wilkinson family, were 'kindness itself'; when the Lawrences returned in March 1928 after a six-week absence in Les Diablerets, the Wilkinsons met them with a car at the railway station in Florence, drove them to the Mirenda where they found flowers and 'the peasants all there to greet and welcome us – very nice and friendly'. Other examples would include Orioli who was unfailingly kind; Frieda's family as a whole who showered affectionate regard on the man his 'Schwiegermutter' called 'my dear good Lorenzo';[23] and the Huxleys (including Juliette) who displayed particularly warm friendship towards him. Aldous and Maria Huxley invited the Lawrences to stay at Forte dei Marmi on the Ligurian coast, took them for Christmas to their friends Costanza Fasola and her husband 'Ekki' Peterich in Florence, and committed themselves to going *en quatre* to Taos in 1929. (That this last visit did not materialise cannot diminish the generosity of the offer.) It was also almost

---

[21] Letters 4083, 4209.   [22] Letters 4201, 4377, 4325, 4123.
[23] Letters 4085, 4326; letter from Baroness Richthofen to Emily King, 27 December 1927 (MS Needham).

certainly the Huxleys who ensured that the Lawrences met the celebrated society hostess Lady Colefax and thus brought about an exchange of visits between them.

Nevertheless, however generous Lawrence may have been, he could never escape the realisation that he had to stand on his own financial feet; he did not earn his living, as he told Trigant Burrow, 'it has to earn itself'. Though he responded to an inner and inexhaustible compulsion to write, he was increasingly aware of the core of truth in the Johnsonian axiom, 'No man but a blockhead ever wrote, except for money.'[24] Thus he agreed that the text of *Rawdon's Roof* should be altered by a magazine editor who would provide an immediate financial return; he contemplated the private publication of a volume of his paintings in order to avoid sharing the proceeds with his normal publishers; and in the case of *Lady Chatterley's Lover* he circumvented both publishers and literary agent through private publication. He came to recognise the value of his manuscripts and sold one to Harry Crosby. Lawrence was distinctly irritated by the prospect of signing 500 copies of *Rawdon's Roof* for a mere £25; when Secker proposed a limited and signed edition of *Collected Poems*, Lawrence insisted on a $33\frac{1}{3}\%$ royalty and instructed Laurence Pollinger (at Curtis Brown's) to arrange it: 'I'm tired of being always worsted.'[25] And there are several instances of his anger at what he considered publishers' indifference to their responsibility to promote the sale of his books.

One of the clearest proofs of his determination to exploit his earning capacity was his eager response to Nancy Pearn's challenge that he should write for the 'GBP' – the Great British Public – through the press. Arthur Olley, Literary Editor of the *Evening News*, invited Lawrence to write an article for the paper; Pearn (who transmitted the invitation) told him that if he could 'bear to tackle just those sorts of subjects which the Press adores', the resulting publicity might well be reflected in 'increasing book sales'.[26] He accepted her argument and acted on it at once. When he saw his first article in the paper on 8 May 1928, followed by a piece entitled 'I Could Not Have Married A Foreigner' by the novelist G. B. Stern, Lawrence 'had gooseflesh'; but it did not deter him from writing further articles. He published seven in the *Evening News* between 8 May and 13 October. (Noticeably he submitted without a single comment to editorial interference with the titles of his articles, and without annoyance when one piece was rejected. This is in sharp contrast to his anger when – out of deference to Compton Mackenzie's feelings – Secker refused to include 'The Man Who Loved Islands' in *The*

[24] Letter 4339; *Boswell's Life of Johnson*, ed. G. B. Hill and L. F. Powell (Oxford, 1934), iii. 19.
[25] Letters 4222, 4370, 4312, 4645, 4547.   [26] Pp. 403 n. 3, 401 n. 1.

Woman Who Rode Away volume. Though journalism paid better it did not warrant the same serious regard as imaginative literature.) 'I may as well earn this way', he remarked to Pearn; a week later he confessed to her, 'I find it really rather amusing to write these little articles.' Olley was delighted with his new journalist and proposed that Lawrence should write exclusively for his paper; Lawrence's response is instructive: he would agree on the presumption that 'we can make them go higher than their ten quid'.[27] Pearn duly extracted twelve guineas for each article thereafter. He wondered excitedly whether they could also be placed in USA; if they could 'That would be really hot dog!!' Lawrence subsequently wrote for the *Daily Chronicle*, the *Sunday Dispatch* and the *Daily Express*, but turned down an invitation from *Film Weekly* to contribute 'an article on the sort of film he would write or produce if there were no censor'. His journalism drew him to the attention of the BBC and he was invited to broadcast. However, despite Pearn's urging – 'We have found that broadcasting really is quite a useful and dignified bit of publicity' – Lawrence's blood ran cold at the thought and he refused.[28]

It is appropriate here to acknowledge Nancy Pearn's importance to Lawrence's financial security. Admittedly circumstances had chanced to make her his chief point of contact with the Curtis Brown agency in London. It is also true that a personal friendship had developed between them: he invited her and a friend to use the Mirenda when they were on an Italian holiday and the Lawrences were away; she felt able to address him as 'Dear darling Mr Lawrence' when she once needed to deflect his wrath. Nevertheless, he depended a great deal on her wholehearted commitment to his interests and on her professional shrewdness. It is easy to understand her anxiety at the supposed threat to his security and continued success posed by the notoriety she feared would follow the launch of *Lady Chatterley's Lover* in July 1928.[29]

The publication of that novel – comparable in its long-term significance to the appearance of *Ulysses* six years earlier – is the focus of the greatest attention in this volume. The letters, many now published for the first time, allow a more detailed account to be given than hitherto of the publishing process and consequences. It is best organised into three periods: before and after two crucial dates, 3 March and 28 June 1928. On 3 March Lawrence wrote from Les Diablerets to his friend and publisher, Orioli: 'All is ready! We can begin.' And the master-printer, L. Franceschini, began the typesetting. On 28 June, with Lawrence on the same mountain as in March (though this time staying at Chexbres-sur-Vevey), he wrote once more to Orioli:

[27] Letters 4428 and p. 401 n. 2, 4431 and n. 2.
[28] Letters 4492, 4725 and n. 4, 4644 and n. 1.   [29] Pp. 464 n. 2, 29 n. 5, Letter 4003.

Lady Chatterley came this morning, to our great excitement, and everybody thinks she looks most beautiful, outwardly. I do really think it is a handsome and dignified volume – a fine shape and proportion, and I like the terra cotta very much, and I think my phoenix is just the right bird for the cover.[30]

For Lawrence's mood and concerns before 3 March 1928, the first letter in the volume provides a useful guide. Addressing Nancy Pearn, on 22 March 1927, he wrote:

Tell Secker not to do anything about *Lady Chatterley's Lover*. I must go over it again – and am really not sure if I shall publish it – at least this year. And I think it is *utterly* unfit for serialising – they would call it indecent – though really, it's most decent.

Themes which were to become more and more prominent – uncertainty about his English publisher, anxiety about publishing the novel at all and the expectation that it would be classed by many as pornographic, co-existing with pride in his imaginative creation: all are here in little. They recur in his next letter to Pearn, three weeks later, on 12 April; his affectionate regard for the work is almost painfully manifest:

I'm in a quandary about my novel, *Lady Chatterley's Lover*. It's what the world would call very improper. But you know it's not really improper – I always labour at the same thing, to make the sex relation valid and precious, instead of shameful. And the novel is the furthest I've gone. To me it is beautiful and tender and frail as the naked self is – and I shrink very much even from having it typed. Probably the typist would want to interfere. – Anyhow Secker wants me to send it him at once . . . I am inclined to do just nothing.[31]

The same motifs are present; they were to appear and reappear on numerous occasions during the months which followed.

An epithet which is applied several times to the novel is 'tender': the book is 'tender and sensitive'; 'so tender and so daring'; 'very pure and tender'; indeed in January 1928 Lawrence decided that 'Tenderness' should be its title.[32] The word conveyed the nature of the creator's regard for his creation as much as the quality of the relationship presented in the novel. But he became increasingly aware that it would be widely seen as '"shocking" from the smut-hunting point of view', that possibly 'no publisher would even dare have the MS in his office' and that, even though it is 'an assertion of sound truth . . . pure . . . and warm-hearted', he could expect the book to face a largely hostile reception. The prospect was daunting. Gradually too he came to accept the inevitable: that, despite his offer to Secker and Alfred Knopf, his American publisher, to prepare an expurgated version for commercial publication – 'we can trim it up to pass' – neither of them would be ready to

---

[30] Letters 4321, 4495.   [31] Letters 3981, 3990.   [32] Letters 4210, 4211, 4229, 4263.

take the risk.[33] In any case he was 'tired of never getting anything from the publishers'; private publication became wellnigh irresistible. Particularly was this so after a fortuitous encounter in Florence with Michael Arlen in mid-November 1927. In letter after letter following this occasion Lawrence told his correspondents how Arlen had made nearly a million dollars from his novel *The Green Hat*, enough eventually to provide an income of 'perhaps £100,000 a year'. Lawrence was so impressed as to record at quite unusual length among his 'Memoranda' an account of Arlen's visit to the Mirenda two days later, on 19 November 1927. *The Green Hat* 'brought him 5,650 dollars one week', is part of the private record; another observation is – 'Definitely I hate the whole money-making world . . . But I won't be done by them either.' And the evidence to substantiate this determination is at hand: 'I'm thinking I shall publish my novel *Lady Chatterley's Lover* here in Florence, myself, privately – as [Norman] Douglas does – 700 copies at 2 guineas.' Two days after Arlen's visit he wrote to Orioli – who already acted as Douglas's publisher – alerting him to the probability that the novel would be privately published: 'you'd have to help me'.[34]

From here to the moment in early March 1928 when the typescript was ready for press, a new sense of urgency entered Lawrence's correspondence; he became both decisive and defiant: 'unless I publish it in some way *as it stands*, I'll never publish it at all.' He chivvied his typists, was contemptuous of one, his old friend Nellie Morrison, who abandoned the work in disgust, and was somewhat exasperated by the 'simple chicken-pox of mistakes' made by Maria Huxley (who did 'the "worst" bits of the novel!'). He was prepared to flout prudish publishers and '*hyprocrites lecteurs*': 'I do want to publish 1000 copies of the unexpurgated edition, and fling it in the face of the world . . . it's got to be done.' And he derided Curtis Brown's warning that *Lady Chatterley's Lover* would damage his reputation: 'Let it.'[35]

Between 3 March and 28 June 1928 Lawrence is known to have written over 200 letters. That is a measure of the sustained and energetic 'campaign' which he undertook once Orioli had received the complete typescript and presswork had begun. It was conducted simultaneously on several fronts. Lawrence continued to plead with Secker and Knopf to give patient consideration to the extent of expurgation required for public sale; the question of English and American copyright was also involved. But before the end of March he had concluded that Secker was 'himself an expurgated edition of a man' and was best ignored. For his part Knopf admired *Lady Chatterley's Lover*; he wanted to publish it and though he eventually decided

[33] Letters 4233, 4318.   [34] Letters 4233, 4213 and n. 2; MS NWU; Letters 4213, 4212.
[35] Letters 4248, 4255, 4303, 4277.

against doing so, at least he had not 'lifted shocked hands of virtuous indignation, like that London lot'. The Florentine printer was another source of stress – and amusement. There was comedy in the fact that in the printing shop 'nobody understands a word of English'; irritation was caused by the printer's slow progress, frustration when it emerged that he had sufficient type for only half the text at a time. But Lawrence's greatest challenge was to obtain subscribers, secure orders and payment (no copy was to be sent 'until it's paid for') and arrange for distribution in England and USA.[36]

For some time Lawrence's correspondents (except his sisters who were kept in total ignorance of the novel) had been informed about the possibility of private publication, but a letter to Mabel Luhan on 13 March 1928 can be regarded as the opening shot in his campaign to attract subscribers. She was the first to be given a general description of the novel which was, in effect, also a justification of it ('frankly and faithfully a phallic novel, but tender and delicate'), as well as order-forms (fifty in her case) for distribution among likely customers. About fifty (and perhaps more) people are known to have received a similar approach; the composition of the list repays study.[37] It includes old friends such as Lady Cynthia Asquith, Gordon Campbell, Earl Brewster and Catherine Carswell (who had arranged a considerable portion of the typing, in London); more recent friends and acquaintances like Bonamy Dobrée, Rolf Gardiner and Max Mohr; Lawrence's publishers Secker and Knopf, and members of Curtis Brown's offices in London and New York, not omitting the timorous Brown himself; editors of journals in which he had previously published – George Bond (*Southwest Review*), Edith Isaacs (*Theatre Arts Monthly*), Coburn Gilman (*Travel*), Harriet Monroe (*Poetry*); a man, J. Elder Walker, whom Lawrence encountered on shipboard while travelling from Ceylon to Australia in 1922; people whom he had met in Mexico like Idella Purnell, George Conway, Donald Miller and Genaro Estrada; and others whose relationship with Lawrence was fairly tenuous. One such was Elizabeth Hare of Long Island, known to be a wealthy patroness of writers and artists, and probably a friend of Brett's, who later showed herself keen to arrange an exhibition of Lawrence's paintings in New York. Another was Mary van Kleeck, a radical social reformer and, in 1928, Director of Industrial Studies for the Russell Sage Foundation in New York; she had chanced to meet the Lawrences, probably in Autumn 1924, when on holiday in Taos and, most likely, had no further contact with him.[38] That the net was spread wide is evident.

---

[36] Letters 4360, 4398, 4337, 4387, 4333.   [37] See Letter 4333 and p. 335 n. 2.

[38] See Mary Anderson and Mary N. Winslow, *Woman at Work* (Minneapolis, 1951), pp. 227–8; in the Sophia Smith Collection at Smith College, Massachusetts, is a letter to Van Kleeck, 18 July 1924, which refers to her proposed visit to New Mexico post 14 August 1924.

Lawrence had assigned 500 copies for sale in England (at £2), the same number in USA (at $10). Arrangements for distributing the novel in both countries caused him great anxiety; this was particularly true of America. He naturally turned for advice to people he knew in USA and whose judgement about books he trusted: to his bibliographer, Edward D. McDonald, and to Harold Mason who had published *Reflections on the Death of a Porcupine and Other Essays*. He asked McDonald whether there was 'much risk in the mail ... the book *isn't* improper: but it *is* phallic'; Mason did not hesitate to advise how to circumvent interference by the Post Office and Customs, telling Lawrence to address copies of the book to individuals – to send them in bulk to Mason's Centaur Press might make them more vulnerable. American booksellers were soon alarmed by the possibility of censorship at the point of entry to the country. When Lawrence became aware of this he arranged to consult an Italian export agency about the feasibility of sending one or two hundred copies via Galveston or New Orleans, thus avoiding the notoriously severe Customs authorities in New York.[39]

Subscriptions for the novel began to arrive steadily (including one for four copies of 'Mrs Clutterley's Lover'). In mid-April Lawrence informed Kot that 150 copies had been ordered from England, two from USA; a week later Secker, who (unlike Brett) was not given a complimentary copy, was told rather optimistically that the 500 allocated to England would soon have been applied for; however on 22 June Laurence Pollinger, a great enthusiast for the book, was assured that 'England has subscribed over six hundred'.[40] Lawrence would be gratified by the number of old friends and acquaintances who were among the first subscribers:[41] Catherine Carswell, Somerset Maugham, Kot (who ordered two copies which he asked should be numbers 1 and 17), Barbara Low, Lady Ottoline Morrell, Millicent Beveridge, Gertler, Compton Mackenzie, Desmond MacCarthy, H. G. Wells, Leonard Woolf, Harold Acton, and many others, ordered by early April. (On 25 April Lawrence noted that E. M. Forster and Clive Bell had not ordered, though Keynes had.) Subscriptions were received from individuals not personally known to Lawrence: a William Dibdin, of Bristol, who wanted to maintain his almost complete collection of Lawrence's publications; the economist Edward Beddington-Behrens (subsequently knighted for his services to the League of Nations); and, later, Lord Beaverbrook was added to this category when he ordered three copies, at the same time asking if Lawrence could help him find a first edition of *The Rainbow* to replace one which had disappeared from his library. American subscribers responded more slowly, but early ones

---

[39] Letter 4329; p. 363 n. 1; Letter 4436.   [40] Letters 4441, 4400, 4402, 4485.
[41] Subscribers' names are taken from DHL's 'Memoranda' (MS NWU).

included many well known to Lawrence. There was Ruth Wheelock whom he had known in Sicily and who had typed *Sea and Sardinia* and *Mr Noon*; Alfred Stieglitz; Mitchell Kennerley, the publisher responsible for American editions of *The Trespasser*, *Sons and Lovers*, etc. and whom Lawrence did not hold in high regard; his agent from whom he parted company five years before, Robert Mountsier; Mabel Luhan's psychiatrist, Dr Abraham A. Brill; Alfred Knopf; old friends such as Ted Gillete, Witter Bynner, Elizabeth Humes – and so on. There can be no doubt, then, that the 'campaign' to attract subscribers by enlisting the support of specific individuals who were virtually conscripted as agents, met with considerable success.

Some booksellers showed a keen interest in *Lady Chatterley's Lover* before it was released. On 24 April William Jackson, export booksellers in London, increased an initial order for 10 copies by a further 35; on 29 May the number was again increased, now to 70; but in this last letter an ominous note appeared: 'We want [an advance] copy badly, for we wish to see whether the book is of a questionable nature. Do you anticipate that there will be any difficulty concerning its entry into this country...?' Lawrence had heard that 'book-sellers are afraid of the mail'; his 'anxiety till *Lady C.* is safely delivered' is understandable.[42] However, on 28 June he was elated at the sight of the 'handsome and dignified volume'.

After that date schemes for distribution had to be implemented. 'Let's get started', he told Orioli on 5 July. Orioli was instructed in the same letter to send 'three or four copies every day to America, especially to the Philadelphia people [i.e. McDonald, Mason and their friends] – copies that are paid for, of course'. To England they were to be sent to 'people we know, who are not likely to talk – and to people like Dulau' (the distinguished London bookseller). By 12 July Orioli was despatching 20 copies a day.[43] Key recipients in USA, like Mason, McDonald and Stieglitz were asked to cable Orioli to confirm the arrival of their own copies; McDonald and Mabel Luhan in America, Kot, Barbara Low and, later, Enid Hilton (daughter of William and Sallie Hopkin whom Lawrence had known from his Eastwood days) and Richard Aldington in England, were to monitor the arrival of copies generally. Lawrence was apprehensive about possible repressive action not only in the USA but also by the English police. At the end of July he reported 'rumours that the police are going to raid the shops'; by the same date booksellers (William Jackson, Stevens & Brown, and Foyles) had returned 114 copies; and Lawrence's London group found themselves acting like secret agents to collect, store and distribute them. Aldington was asked 'to keep these copies

[42] Pp. 390 n. 2, 417–18 n. 4; Letters 4436, 4491.   [43] Letters 4511, 4529.

quite quietly, and tell nobody, and just let them lie till I have a use for them';
Enid Hilton was advised, when collecting returned copies from a bookseller,
to give a 'fake' address and that she was 'under *no* obligation to give Jackson's
[her] name'.[44] If any official action were taken against the book, members of
the London 'cell' were expected to warn one another. But despite the
rumours and fears, the police did nothing. In mid-August Lawrence could tell
Stieglitz that *Lady Chatterley's Lover* had 'exploded like a bomb among most
of my English friends, and they're still suffering from shell-shock. But they're
coming round already'. Aldington thought the novel 'a feather in the cap of
the 20th Century'; David Garnett wrote to congratulate Lawrence; but many
people were 'beastly' about it. (Edward Garnett who had told Lawrence years
before that he would 'welcome a description of the whole act', was sent a copy
from Gsteig.)[45]

Early reactions in the English press were not unfavourable. Perhaps the
first appeared in the *Star* on 1 August. Readers learned that 'there is a brisk
inquiry . . . for the latest D. H. Lawrence, which has just been printed
privately in Italy'; the writer of 'The "Star" Man's Diary' found 'the
treatment . . . frank in some ways and . . . obscure in others'; and though he did
not expect the work to 'enhance the reputation of this distinguished writer . . .
its literary quality is – need it be said? – of the highest.' At the end of
September John Rayner in *T. P.'s Weekly* told his readers that 'Mr Lawrence
has carried realism to a pitch seldom aspired to in the whole history of
literature. And the result is a fine novel, bold and stark.' Thus, though
Lawrence believed it cost him many friendships; though the *Sunday Chronicle*
attacked the book viciously on 14 October as 'one of the most filthy and
abominable ever written . . . an outrage on decency' and *John Bull* a week later
delivered its notorious attack on 'the most evil outpouring that has ever
besmirched the literature of our country': the reception accorded *Lady
Chatterley's Lover* in England was by no means unrelievedly hostile.

Lawrence received a clear warning of official reaction in USA when Mason
wrote on 31 July to say that his copy had been 'arrested'. He went on: 'You
have been too courageous for our timid and dove-like postal inspectors who
have been scared stiff by the naughty words you employed.' He suggested that
copies be passed from an English exporter to a friend on 'the American
Merchant' who would take them through Customs and subsequently mail
them from New York. However, the proposed exporter, William Jackson,
refused to handle a book of such a 'thoroughly obscene and disgusting
nature'. Many American subscribers, besides Mason, failed to receive their

---

[44] Letters 4562, 4556, 4572, 4573.   [45] Letters 4595, 4556, 4611, 4676.

copies; on 27 August Lawrence estimated that only 14 out of about 140 had been fortunate. He urged Maria Chambers, one of the unfortunates, not to 'go round talking to booksellers: they even may be police agents . . . the quieter one keeps, the better'.[46] Meanwhile his hopes were stirred by the prospect of an American edition of *Lady Chatterley's Lover* from the Vanguard Press; to enable Vanguard to assess the book, he suggested that Orioli should send three copies with a specially printed jacket and title-page to read: '*Joy Go With You – by Norman Kranzler (The Ponte Press)*'. (About a fortnight later he proposed for the false jacket the title of Butler's novel, *The Way of All Flesh*.) But the US mail and Customs authorities were too vigilant. An obscure Californian newspaper, the *Fresno Morning Republican*, may have been the first to announce, on 11 August: 'Postal Officers Confiscate Books . . . as unfit for the United States mails.' 'Damn the Americans – damn and damn them', was Lawrence's first reaction when the news reached him in late August; a week later America was described as suffering from a 'tyranny of imbeciles and canaille'; and soon afterwards he was 'tired of America and the knock-kneed fright in face of bullying hypocrisy'.[47] But this proved simplistic. The case of Herbert Seligmann (author, in 1924, of the first American book on Lawrence) establishes the point. He wrote a favourable review of *Lady Chatterley's Lover* and it was published in the *New York Sun* on 1 September, but the editors were so outraged by his 'pollution of their pages' that they took the unprecedented step of remaking the literary supplement to remove it in later editions'. Seligmann was never again invited to review for the *Sun*. So there were bullies but brave men were not in short supply. Indeed some of the most appreciative and laudatory comments on the novel came from American readers. Mason, for example, told Lawrence that it was 'really a magnificent book . . . I have yet to hear a dissenting voice . . . a work of great beauty and strength and there are pages of it that have never been excelled, in my opinion'; Stieglitz and Georgia O'Keefe wrote 'long effusions'; and Pascal Covici, a friend of Aldington's and New York publisher, considered it 'the most vital piece of fiction . . . in the last ten years'. Thus for Lawrence to be pleased with the 'intelligent appreciation . . . even enthusiastic' in England was appropriate; but to assert that 'all the Americans either squirm and look sickly, or become sordidly indignant', was wide of the mark.[48]

If evidence were required of Lawrence's skill as an entrepreneur, his letters of this period provide it. It is clear that he knew at any time where every unsold copy of *Lady Chatterley's Lover* was in London, no matter how confusing the situation created by booksellers returning their purchases and

[46] Pp. 449–50 n. 3, 518 n. 3; Letters 4623, 4613.   [47] Letters 4617, 4655, 4625, 4642, 4666.
[48] Pp. 607 n. 1, 548 n. 1; Letter 4643; p. 560 n. 1; Letter 4679.

his agents – Kot, Aldington and Enid Hilton – re-selling or moving them from one 'safe-house' to another. He recorded, in his 'Memoranda', the name of every purchaser, with the date and amount of each cheque; bills from the printer and binder were settled immediately and the amounts recorded; and those London friends who incurred expenses through distributing the novel received appropriate sums. At intervals Lawrence told Orioli what money he had made from the venture: on 4 September, for example, he estimated the profit on about 560 copies at £713. 11. 9 (on 26 March 1929 he entered in his 'Memoranda', 'gross profit £1239. 16. 3'). And, despite all the attendant stress, he told Pollinger in September: 'On the whole it's gone very well, and been exciting . . . I enjoyed putting it through, and dropping a little bomb in the world's crinoline of hypocrisy.' Frieda revelled in what she called the 'most exciting conspiracy-time over Lady Chatterley'. She told Orioli that 'the fighting does [Lawrence's] soul good! And I fairly flourish on it like a dandelion in the sun!'[49]

T. P.'s Weekly which came 'out so comparatively bravely' about *Lady Chatterley's Lover* had, two weeks earlier, praised Lawrence from another perspective: 'Some people are still unaware that this brilliant writer is also an artist of no mean merit.' The remark was prompted by an item in the gossip column which asserted that Lawrence '*must* be back in London by the middle of September . . . not to see another book launched – but to be present at the opening of an exhibition of his paintings to be held here in late September'.[50] In fact the exhibition was postponed, first till November, then till mid-1929; but the journalistic comment directs our attention to a further aspect of Lawrence's activities which has some prominence in his letters.

In this volume references to his paintings are scattered throughout. There is *Resurrection*, finished in May 1927; *The Finding of Moses*, begun in June 1927 and completed in April 1928; and in October 1927 he felt inclined to paint a picture of 'Adam and Eve driving the Lord God out of Paradise: Get out of here, you righteous old bird!' Before 11 November he had finished it. In November he was also painting *Jaguar Leaping at a Man*; the following March he painted *Fire Dance*; and in April 1928 he teased the Huxleys (particularly Maria whom he had invited to select any one of his paintings for herself) with the news: 'I painted a charming picture of a man pissing – I'm sure it is the one Maria will choose: called *Dandelions*, for short. Now I'm doing a small thing in oil, called *The Rape of the Sabine Women* or a Study in Arses.'[51] There is little wonder that when Lawrence made a note in his 'Memoranda' of the pictures

---

[49] Letter 4645; letter from Frieda Lawrence to Brett, 12 August 1928 (MS UCin); Letter 4566.
[50] Letter 4681; *T.P.'s Weekly*, 15 September 1928, p. 633. [51] Letters 4178, 4370.

sent from Villa Mirenda to London for the exhibition, it listed well over twenty large and small oils, and water-colours.

Readers of his letters know that it was not unusual for Lawrence to make a painter's judgement on a place where he happened to be. Thus 'the stark and shroudy whiteness' of Les Diablerets 'offends the painter in one – it is so uniform . . . against life'. No pictures are mentioned as having been painted during the six weeks there; but within twenty-four hours of returning to the Mirenda he was 'painting a water-colour: torch-dance by daylight!' which is vivid with powerful energy. His later remark that 'there's something very dramatic about paint' can appropriately be applied to it. Lawrence painted 'simply and solely for the fun of it, and damn the consequences'; thus when he had to consider detailed arrangements for the exhibition, including the possibility that some items might be sold, his reaction was characteristic: he proposed a 'high and prohibitive price on all the big pictures' so as not to sell them. He was 'pining' (he used the word on at least four occasions) to see the pictures framed and hung; but – 'I rather love them and want to keep them'.[52]

From April to November 1928 he was courted by directors of several galleries: Elizabeth Hare and Stieglitz in New York; in London Ena Mathias at the Claridge Gallery, Oliver Brown at the Leicester Galleries and Dorothy Warren at her own. Each was interested in mounting an exhibition of his paintings. Eventually he decided against New York: 'There is such a fracas and an alarm in America over my novel, such a panic, that I must postpone any thought of showing my pictures there. I'm sure the Customs in New York would destroy them! So that's off.' Initially he appeared to favour the Claridge Gallery but finally agreed to accept Dorothy Warren's invitation. (Lawrence had known her since 1916 though the renewal of their acquaintance came about through Frieda's daughter Barbara Weekley, herself a painter and a friend of Warren's.) Doing business with her was 'like riding to the moon on a soap-bubble' but Lawrence could not have been in any doubt about her enthusiasm. 'I am longing to have your show,' she told him. 'I really have been looking forward to it tremendously, and I should do everything in my power to make it a success.' By August 1928 he was alarmed lest any public hostility to *Lady Chatterley's Lover* might find a target in the exhibition. He was personally ready to defy 'such skunks' but he recognised that Dorothy Warren might suffer commercially and financially. But she was determined. She declared herself prepared for 'prudish objections and attacks on [herself] and [her] Gallery'. Her overriding motivation was unambiguous: 'I think your pictures fine and free and individual so that I want to show them.'[53]

---

[52] Letters 4285, 4328, 4636, 4629, 4652.
[53] Letters 4646, 4508; pp. 434–5 n. 3; Letter 4614 and p. 523 n. 2.

Dorothy Warren's significance in the Lawrence story continues beyond the end of the present volume. Certain other friends, however, deserve mention here. Some flit in and out of the letters: 'the deaf Miss Moller' and Mary Foote, an expatriate American painter, to both of whom Lawrence seems to have been unfailingly courteous; Adrian Stokes, later distinguished as art-historian and critic, references to whom suggest an easy intimacy; Rolf Gardiner's sister Margaret who discovered in Lawrence 'a quality of sincerity she had never met before'; or Osbert and Edith Sitwell with whom the Lawrences renewed their friendship, entertained them to tea and 'liked them much better than [they] had thought'. The letters to the servant Giulia Pini reveal a gentle and compassionate Lawrence, especially when she and her family were dispossessed from the Mirenda estate. He wrote again to Gordon and Beatrice Campbell and in exuberantly high spirits; he was obviously pleased to re-establish contact by letter with Lady Ottoline Morrell and to assure her that she had been 'an important influence in lots of lives';[54] but there was no letter to Middleton Murry. 'I can't stand *him*, at any price.' Murry wrote privately to Brett on 15 September 1928 and expressed his regret that 'Lawrence & I have never managed to keep together'; his remarkable capacity for self-deception revealed itself as he continued: 'I am nearer to [Lawrence] than any other man I have known, and I think that, had the stars been kind, we might have done together more than we shall ever do alone.' Then honesty broke in: 'I think the failure more my fault than his.'[55] With other old friends Lawrence's relationship continued firm. This was true, for example, of Earl and Achsah Brewster; they shared his interest, if not his style, in painting; he enjoyed Earl's company on a ten-day tour of Etruscan sites; and both Lawrence and Frieda were indebted to the Brewsters as companions for much of the last months covered by this volume. It was also true of Lawrence and Koteliansky. Friendship rather than good judgement led Lawrence to promote Kot's vain attempt to turn publisher for a series of 'intimate' self-revelations by major writers. He canvassed people such as Huxley and Douglas; he proposed others for consideration, from Forster and Edith Sitwell to Dos Passos and Robert Graves; and despite his own misgivings, Lawrence was prepared to make a personal contribution, distaste-ful to him though the effort evidently was.

There is a relatively small number of letters the writing of which compelled Lawrence to contemplate his origins and early life; they reveal a noteworthy ambivalence of response. For example, the two-week visit by his sister Emily and his niece Margaret to Kesselmatte, in August/September 1928, was not a

[54] Letter 4350; Margaret Gardiner, 'Meeting the Master'. *Horizon* ii (October 1940), 189; Letters 4026, 4437.
[55] Letter 4506; letter from Murry to Brett, 15 September 1928 (MS UCin).

great success. It forced him to acknowledge the gulf which separated him from them; 'the attitude of ordinary people to life' he found not merely distressing but hateful; and presumably some (in his view) rather clumsy attempts to repossess him for Eastwood and the family provoked the outburst: 'I'm not really "our Bert"'. Come to that, I never was.' There is a mixture of truth and untruth here but, from the perspective of 1928, the irritation is understandable. Yet, as the final letter in the volume shows, when circumstances prompted Lawrence to recall his youth and, in doing so, to remember the happiness he had experienced at the Haggs Farm with the Chambers family, he could be euphoric in his enthusiasm. 'Whatever I forget, I shall never forget the Haggs – I loved it so', he assured Jessie Chambers's brother David; 'whatever else I am, I am somewhere still the same Bert who rushed with such joy to the Haggs'.[56] And he responded as 'a miner's son' to an unknown adult-educationalist in the mining area of Durham, 'the Pitman Poet', Charles Wilson. But the miner's son was now a public figure, invited to send a New Year's message to 'the men'. Lawrence was clearly embarrassed by the request – the more so when Wilson sent not only a calendar but, a little later, a nickel cigarette case as well – and found it difficult to strike the right note. Nevertheless, though 'a bit shyly' and with due formality, he reacted in the character that had been thrust upon him. Durham miners may not fully have comprehended the message they received: that they could change the industrial system 'not by hating capitalism . . . but by just pulling the feathers out of the money bird'; and that 'men must develop their poetic intelligence if they are ever going to be men: the rest is a swindle'. Yet Lawrence's personal sympathy with the miners' economic hardships cannot be questioned – evidence to substantiate it is to be found elsewhere in the volume. Nor should one doubt his integrity when he assured Wilson that he valued the gifts because they came from 'the miners, to whom so much of me belongs'.[57]

In October/November 1928, at the end of this volume, Lawrence was on the island of Port-Cros. He and Frieda made a small group with Aldington, Arabella Yorke and Brigit Patmore, living in the 'vigie' and having to employ a Sicilian servant and his donkey to transport all goods from the port an hour away. The site was scenically splendid; in Aldington's words, the vigie, 600 feet above the sea,

looked over stupendous vistas of Mediterranean and mountainous coast. The island itself is broken into steep ridges and valleys, covered with magnificent Mediterranean pines, strawberry trees, wild lavender, rosemary, lentisk, cistus, and other aromatic plants and herbs; so that on a hot October afternoon the gentle sea air seemed scented with fresh incense.

[56] Letters 4638, 4636, 4628, 4749.   [57] Letters 4219, 4267, 4288.

But before long Lawrence was restive. He felt cut off, deliveries of mail were infrequent and irregular; 'I don't care for islands . . . I want to get on the mainland again.' His wish was soon granted. And when Aldington bade farewell to him in Toulon, he saw for the last time 'the most interesting human being [he had] known'.[58]

[58] Richard Aldington, *Life for Life's Sake* (1941), pp. 299, 304; Letter 4734.

THE LETTERS

3981. To Nancy Pearn, 22 March 1927

Text: MS UT; Huxley 682.

Palazzo Cimbrone, *Ravello* (Salerno)

22 March 1927

Dear Miss Pearn[1]

Tell Secker[2] not to do anything about *Lady Chatterley's Lover*.[3] I must go over it again – and am really not sure if I shall publish it – at least this year. And I think it is *utterly* unfit for serialising – they would call it indecent – though really, it's most decent. But one day I'll send it you to have typed.

Glad you have 'The Lovely Lady' – tell me what you think of her.[4]

I shall probably start on a little walking tour next week – on the 28th – walking north – so my address had better be Villa Mirenda again.[5]

Will you tell these people they can have 'Snake'.[6]

Yrs   D. H. Lawrence

3982. To Emily King, [24 March 1927]

Text: MS Needham; PC v. Ravello – Villa Cimbrone – Belvedere; Postmark, Ravello 25 3 27; Unpublished.

[Palazzo Cimbrone, Ravello, Salerno]

Thursday

I wonder how you all are[7] – especially Joan! – I've been here since Monday – was very hot and sunny, now it rains. The belvedere (outlook) is at the end of

---

[1] Annie ('Nancy') Ross Pearn (1892–1950), manager of the Magazine Department in the London office of Albert Curtis Brown (1866–1945), DHL's literary agent since 1921. See *Letters*, v. 57 n. 3.

[2] Martin Secker (1882–1978), DHL's London publisher. m. 1921, Caterina ('Rina') Maria Capellero (1896–1969). See *Letters*, i. 275 and n. 1.

[3] DHL began the first version of the novel in October 1926 and completed it c. 8 March 1927; see *Letters*, v. 563 n. 6, 651. Secker wanted to schedule the book for publication in the Autumn, Curtis Brown thought it should be serialised (letter from Nancy Pearn to DHL, 17 March 1927, TMSC UT).

[4] DHL had sent his story on 11 March 1927 (*Letters*, v. 654); it was published in Lady Cynthia Asquith's collection, *The Black Cap*, October 1927.

[5] The Villa Mirenda, near Scandicci on the outskirts of Florence, had been the Lawrences' home since May 1926.   [6] The 'people' are not identified; the poem was frequently reprinted.

[7] DHL's correspondent was his elder sister, Emily ('Pamela') Una King (1882–1962). She and her husband, Samuel Taylor King (1880–1965) had two daughters: Margaret ('Peg' or 'Peggy') Emily (b. 1909) and Joan Frieda (b. 1920).

the garden here – rather fine gardens.¹ I'm leaving on the 28th with Brewster, and we're doing a little walk along the coast towards Rome – I expect I shall be at the Mirenda by second week in April. I am looking for a letter from you.

Love   DHL

3983. To Hon. Dorothy Brett, [24 March 1927]

Text: MS UCin; Postmark, Ravello 26 3 27; Moore 970–2.

'Cimbrone', Ravello
24 March

[Achsah Brewster begins]

Dearest Brett:² –

Here we sit around the fire, Uncle David, Earl, Harwood and I. We have just been singing a Wagnerian opera.

[Lawrence begins]

What a pity you aren't here to do *Rheingold*! – The irises are out in the garden, and my blue Venus³ – you remember – is as blue as ever, poor dear!

[Earl Brewster begins]

Please send me that system of meditation which you write of having found of Buddhistic origin. I am much interested.

[Harwood Brewster begins]

Mynie, Pam, and Bal came last week for three days.⁴ We had a very exciting time – playing hide and seek, charades and Russian scandles.⁵ Do you know Russian scandles? We always got Dr. Monte and Miss Van Kerckoff into them.

[Achsah Brewster continues]

If you came riding up on Prince⁶ now we would give three cheers and pull up another chair and after tea go out on the belvedere to watch the storm clouds clear away.

---

¹ The Palazzo Cimbrone, with its extensive gardens, was owned by Ralph William Ernest Beckett, 3rd Baron Grimthorpe (1891–1963); it was temporarily occupied by DHL's friends, Earl Henry Brewster (1878–1957) and Achsah Barlow Brewster (1878–1945), American expatriate painters, with their daughter Harwood (1913–90) (cf. *Letters,* v. 75 nn. 1 and 3).

² Hon. Dorothy Eugenie Brett (1883–1977), artist, daughter of 2nd Viscount Esher; she studied at the Slade School of Art and first met DHL in 1915. She went to Taos with the Lawrences in March 1924, shared their life on Kiowa ranch and some of their travels; having been in Europe since October 1925 (meeting the Brewsters in March 1926), she returned alone to New Mexico in May 1926.

³ Achsah Brewster recalled DHL's walking 'past the Hermes statue and on past the blue-green bronze Venus' in the Cimbrone grounds (Brewster 277).

⁴ Hermione ('Mynie') and Pamela ('Pam') Reynolds lived with their father Richard W. Reynolds in Anacapri and were close friends of Harwood Brewster; Hilda Balfour ('Bal') was their English governess.   ⁵ 'Russian scandals' is a version of the juvenile game, 'Gossip'.

⁶ Brett's 'nice sorrel horse' (*Letters,* v. 236).

[Lawrence continues]

We might also get Prince to kick over a few statues. They seem to have had a few young ones since last year – this promiscuity of Mercurys and Niobes! – I daren't send you my novel to type, though I'd like to. But it's so improper, the American authorities would arrest you. – Well, well, man is a forked radish![1] – But my novel is done in the two best books you gave me, very neat and handsome – and now Achsah has just given me a red Hindu MS book as big as the hearthrug – I'm waiting for suggestions, what to write in it.

[Earl Brewster continues]

Uncle David and I are starting within a few days on a 'walking trip' (I never went on one yet where any *walking* was done – I mean on a *long* so called walking trip). But we think to explore the coast between Naples and Terracina. Then we may go to Africa, to Libya, or Dahomey.

[Harwood Brewster continues]

Mother and I will probably be going to Capri next week and then Uncle Davide and Daddy will go off on their walking tripe. I think it will be mostly trains and motor cars!

Uncle Davide has had two letters since he has been here from you.

We are all thinking of having an auction in the piazza of all the statues and old bits of furniture! How Lord Grimthorpe would like it!

[Achsah Brewster continues]

Uncle David and Earl are going for a little walking trip next week when Harwood and I go over to Capri. It is a lovely spring, with the flowers full blast and the sun agrees with us all. When Uncle David arrived he was rather low from influenza but is much better. If you were here it would be fun.

[Lawrence continues]

Don't go up to the ranch until it's really open. You'd better not isolate yourself too much. What's the point! I'm sorry Mabel was so seedy.[2] My whack of flu was much milder than last year, thank heaven, but it has a beastly way of sticking – however, the summer is due. Yesterday it poured with rain – today is mingled. – I haven't painted a stroke for a long time – felt a bit discouraged – perhaps I'll start again when I get back to the Mirenda. But I shan't do a crucifixion, even with Pan to put his fingers to his nose at the

---

[1] *2 Henry IV*, III. ii. 305. See also Brett's embarrassment at the Fiesta of the Rabanos (Radishes) in Oaxaca in her *Lawrence and Brett: A Friendship* (Philadelphia, 1933), pp. 195–7.

[2] Mabel Dodge Luhan (1879–1962), wealthy American patron of the arts who (in November 1921) invited DHL to join the art colony in Taos. In June 1923 she married the Indian, Tony Luhan, as her fourth husband. Author of *Lorenzo in Taos* (New York, 1932). See *Letters*, iv. 110 n. 4.

primrose Jesus.[1] Damn crosses! – I'm expecting the proofs of the Mexican essays[2] – will send them along to Mabel's for you. – Earl and I are going off on the q. t. for a bit – only everybody seems to have heard of it. I'll send you p-c's en route.

[Earl Brewster continues]

> 'There be many shapes of mystery,
> And many things god makes to be,
> Past hope or fear,
> And the end men looked for cometh not,
> And a path is there where no man thought
> So hath it fallen here.'[3]

[Harwood Brewster continues]

Thank you for your Valentine. I am waiting for my letter from you.

Daddy and Uncle David are going on a walking trip then when they come back we shall all go to Russia and from there to Thibet. In Thibet I shall start a book on My impressions of Uncle David! But not untill we get to Thibet.

Last night Uncle David told us about how he had to catch the cow.[4] He has also been telling us lovely stories.

Last week I received a book from Aunt Alpha[5] that a girl of nien wrote but as it was burnt she had to write it all over again when she was twelve. It has just been published and is all about little pink tiped white clouds and gold fishes and pink and blue and purple skys etc.

Best love and kisses,   Harwood
Much, much love,   Achsah
Much much mucher love   DHL
Ever ever so much love –   Earl

I write address.   DHL
I lick the envelp.   H.B.B.
I drop it in the box A. B.
I put the stamp on – EHB

---

[1] DHL had used the phrase 'your primrose Jesus' over a year earlier about Brett's painting of a crucifixion scene which includes the figure of Pan (*Letters*, v. 383). The heads of both Christ and Pan were modelled on DHL. For Brett's own description of the painting see *Letters*, v. 348 n. 3.

[2] To be published by Secker as *Mornings in Mexico*, in June 1927.

[3] A favourite 'tag' of Euripides; it forms a moralising coda from the Chorus in several of his plays (e.g. *Alcestis, Andromache, Helen, Medea*); this version accurately reproduces it from Gilbert Murray's translations of *The Bacchae* (1904).   [4] Susan, the cow, at Kiowa Ranch.

[5] Alpha Barlow, Achsah Brewster's sister. The book (published in London by Knopf, March 1927) was *The House Without Windows and Eepersip's Life There* by Barbara Newhall Follett (1914–   ). See *Barbara: The Unconscious Autobiography of a Child Genius*, ed. H. G. McCurdy (Chapel Hill, 1966).

3984. To Ada Clarke, [24 March 1927]
Text: MS Clarke; PC v. Ravello – Villa Cimbrone; Postmark, Ravello [. . .] 3 27;
Unpublished.

[Palazzo Cimbrone, Ravello, Salerno]
Thursday

I'm hoping for a letter from you, to know about Gertie.[1] I've been here since Monday – after very hot sun, today it rains. I'm leaving on the 28th with Brewster, and we are doing a little walking tour on the coast, towards Rome. I expect to be at the Mirenda by second week in April. – The picture shows a corner of the rose garden – and one of the garden houses where we have tea – the gardens are really fine. – My flu seems a good bit better.

love.   DHL

3985. To Emily King, [5 April 1927]
Text: MS Lazarus; Unpublished.

19 Corso d' Italia, Roma.
Tuesday 5 April

My dear Pamela

I'll just send a line to say I'm on my way back to the Mirenda. Frieda is due to arrive there today – I don't know if she's done it or not. I expected a letter from her here, but there is nothing.

I am not going straight back. Brewster is with me, and he and I are going to stop off at various places on the east coast, to look at Etruscan tombs and remains. Several people have asked me for travel articles, and I might do them on the Etruscan places. Anyhow I can try. So I suppose I shan't be home for another week at least.

I was glad to get your letter and know that Joan was better. You didn't say you had the cheque for your birthday, but since it was in the letter, I think you received it all right. – I'm sorry Peg is feeling nervy and upset. But very many people are like that this spring, here in Italy just the same. I don't know what's the matter with the world. Certainly we're an unsatisfactory lot of specimens nowadays.

If Sam thinks it is all right to go into that wholesale business, then probably it will be. Only it's best to be alert and on the spot.

The parks are lovely now with flowers, and the peach blossom is pink all in the country. It is real spring – but April, and uncertain. I do hope it won't rain

---

[1] Gertrude Cooper (1885–1942), a childhood friend of DHL's in Eastwood. She had lived with his younger sister Lettice Ada Clarke (1887–1948) and Ada's husband, William Edwin Clarke (1889–1964) in Ripley since 1919 (see *Letters*, i. 23 n. 1). Like DHL himself, Gertrude Cooper was tubercular; she had been admitted to Mundesley Hospital and had recently undergone major surgery (see Letter 4000).

on our little trip. One can't trudge off, or even drive off, into forlorn places, in the rain.

I shan't be sorry to be home again, and to be settled down for a spell. Travel no longer thrills me much – it begins to bore me. I think I shall buy an acre of forest and turn hermit. That's how I feel.

I hear that *David* is again postponed: till May.[1] I don't believe they'll ever do it. But I don't greatly care.

Write to me to the Mirenda and tell me the news.

Love to you all   DHL

3986. To Ada Clarke, [5 April 1927]
Text: MS Clarke; Unpublished.

Rome.
Tuesday 5 April

My dear Sister

Just a line to tell you I am on my way back to the Mirenda – where Frieda is due to arrive today. Brewster is with me, and we want to spend a few days seeing Etruscan remains, between here and Pisa – so I expect I shall be about a week before I actually arrive at Scandicci: that is, if the weather keeps fine. One can't look at Etruscan things in the rain.

I had a nice time at Ravello – and feel very much better for the change, the flu seems quite shaken off, thank heaven. We stayed the week-end at Sorrento, and walked to Termini at the end of the peninsula. It was nice – but everything is becoming quite spoiled by the tourist traffic. It brings the dreariness of endless money-grabbing with it, and ruins everything. I shan't be sorry to be back at the Mirenda, in the quiet, away from Tourists and hotels and touts.

Frieda hasn't said anything about her children.[2] Presumably they are not coming out. But her sister Johanna is due to come from Berlin with her husband, in May.[3] The worst of it is, we haven't much real accommodation.

[1] DHL had tried hard to have his play *David* (written Spring 1925) put into production, but had suffered repeated delays. Robert Atkins agreed to produce it for the 300 Club and Stage Society in October 1926 but postponed it till December; it was then postponed to March 1927, and finally produced by Ernest Milton (1890–1974) at the Regent Theatre, London, on 22–3 May 1927.

[2] Frieda's children by her marriage to Professor Ernest Weekley (1865–1954) were: Charles Montague (1900–82), since 1924 on the staff of the Victoria and Albert Museum; Elsa Agnes Frieda (1902–85), engaged (in 1926) to be married to Bernal Edward de Martelly Seaman (1900–90); and Barbara Joy (b. 1904).

[3] Johanna ('Nusch') von Krug (1882–1971). m. (1) Max von Schreibershofen (1864–1944), divorced 1923; (2) Emil von Krug (1870–1944), a Berlin banker; see Letters 4113 and 4123.

I wonder if you've seen Gertie, and how that is. What a God's mercy, when the business is over. Tell me if there is anything I can do – anything I could send.

The spring is here – cherry and peach blossom – and the uneasy days of April. We've had three bright days, so I expect it's going to rain again.

Did you get the books I sent, by the way?

Write to the Mirenda.

Love   DHL

3987. To Hon. Dorothy Brett, [6 April 1927]
Text: MS UCin; PC v. Necropoli etrusca di Caere (Cerveteri) Tomba dei rilievi; Postmark, Roma 7.4.27; Irvine, Brett 74.

Cerveteri
– 6 April

Came here from Rome with Earl today – a fascinating place of Etruscan tombs – the asphodels all out, and acres of narcissus on the campagna – very springlike. Hope all goes well with you.

DHL

3988. To Achsah Brewster, [8 April 1927]
Text: MS UT; PC v. Tarquinia – Barriera S. Oiusto; Postmark, Tarquinia 9 4 27; Unpublished.

Tarquinia
Friday evening

We had two very delightful days here, looking at painted tombs. Earl will bring you one day. And tomorrow we go to Vulci – expect to be in Volterra, the last place, by Monday. Hope you and Harwood are jolly.

DHL

3989. To Harold Mason, 12 April 1927
Text: MSS (Photocopy) UT and Mason; Postmark, Firenze 12. IV 1927; *Centaur* 29–30.

Villa Mirenda, Scandicci (Florence)
12 April 1927

Dear Mason[1]

I have been away for a few weeks, visiting friends near Amalfi and tombs of

---

[1] Harold Trump Mason (1893–1983), proprietor of the Centaur Book Shop in Philadelphia, and founder of the Centaur Press. m. (1) Anne Brakely (1892–1963); (2) Doris Duval. The Centaur Press published the Bibliographies Series in which Edward McDonald's *Bibliography* of DHL appeared (1925), and *Reflections on the Death of a Porcupine and Other Essays* (1925).

Etruscans in Maremma. I find your letter and *The Great American Ass*[1] – for both of which, many thanks. I read the letter and shall read the *Ass*, I am sure, with appreciation. It is very good of you to send me these books. – As for the porcupine not being a paying animal, I am more sorry for your sake than for mine. If he pricked a few people with his quills, it is all I ask for my part. But you have to feed the brute, and corporally produce him.

I'm glad you have good times and good drinks: home-brewed black beer sounds A. 1. to me. Here the art of adulteration has not improved, only the practice has extended. Water and powders from the chemist work wonders in a bottle, even right in the land of chianti. It is as if the age took *pleasure* in substitutes. – The grand advertisements for surrogato di caffè – which means chicory – would make you believe that the one discovery of the age was chicory instead of coffee – surrogate of coffee, caro mio!

But I was really happy looking at Etruscan tombs by the coast north of Rome – Cerveteri, Tarquinia etc. No rush there! Even the ass brays slowly and leisurely, and the tombs are far more twinkling and alive than the houses of men. If you want a slow tempo – adagio adagio – you can slow down to such a pitch that you're faintly moving backwards here in Italy. Just twenty miles from Rome. But it would bore you.

The play sounds terrifying.[2] I should think, if one went on boiling and hard-boiling the egg, ad infinitum, it would become a high explosive at last. But who knows! Myself, I can less and less stand hard-boiledness.

That's why I don't think we shall come to America this year. Sometimes, thinking of New Mexico, I am tempted. But when I remember that the great melting pot is always on the boil, and that the Easter eggs therein are boiling harder and harder and harder, till they'll have no mortal use whatsoever except to throw at people to kill them dead – then the temptation ceases to tempt, and I only want to retire away into the hills here, and be a hermit.

But still I hope that you and the Signora Anne have a pretty decent time – I believe you do, in spite of protests. And I hope Macdonald is feeling cheerful in his Drexel Institute.[3] The world isn't vastly different, anywhere, and I take sugar in my porridge.

My wife sends her greetings too – we'll meet again one day, this side or that, for sure.

Yours ever   D. H. Lawrence

There are such amusing centaurs in Etruscan tombs: centauresses too.

---

[1] Charles Leroy Edson's '*The Great American Ass*': *An Autobiography* (New York, 1926) was published anonymously.   [2] Not identified.

[3] Edward David McDonald (1883–1977) was Professor of English at the Drexel Institute in Philadelphia, 1919–54. m. Marguerite Bartelle. See *Letters*, v. 63 n. 3.

3990. To Nancy Pearn, 12 April 1927
Text: MS UT; Huxley 682–3.

Villa Mirenda, *Scandicci*, Florence

12 April 1927

Dear Miss Pearn

I got back here last night, so have an address once more. I had a very interesting time looking at Etruscan tombs in Tarquinia and in Maremma – and I want to do a few *Sketches of Etruscan Places*.

It was nice to hear of you and Mr Pollinger hauling on the ropes of my old barge[1] – though why you should have so much trouble, I dont know.

I enclose Cynthia Asquith's letter. I wish you would tell me your own opinion, candidly – about the story too.[2]

I'm in a quandary about my novel, *Lady Chatterley's Lover*. It's what the world would call very improper. But you know it's not really improper – I always labour at the same thing, to make the sex relation valid and precious, instead of shameful. And the novel is the furthest I've gone. To me it is beautiful and tender and frail as the naked self is – and I shrink very much even from having it typed. Probably the typist would want to interfere. – Anyhow Secker wants me to send it him at once. And Barmby writes that Knopf *cant possibly publish* till next spring,[3] so I must send the MS. to New York! à la bonne heure![4] I am inclined to do just nothing. What would you say? – you and Mr Pollinger, – whom I've never met, have I? I think perhaps it's a waste to write any more novels: I could probably live by little things. I mean in magazines.[5]

Anyhow I hope soon to send you some small things.

---

[1] In her letter to DHL, 6 April 1927 (TMSC UT), Nancy Pearn described her colleague Laurence Edward Pollinger (1898–1976) as 'one of our Book Managers [who] is taking over more and more of the detail of the book side of your work'. Later, as a director in the firm of Pearn, Pollinger and Higham, and, after 1958, in his own agency, he represented DHL's Estate. m. 1923, Katherine ('Kit') Winifred Norris (1899–1979).

[2] See Letter 3981 and n. 4. Lady Cynthia Asquith had requested cuts in 'The Lovely Lady'. In her reply (25 April 1927, TMSC UT) to this letter from DHL, Nancy Pearn supported Lady Cynthia to some extent: though the '"drainpip part", as she calls it, is [not] out of place ... The miaowing part I suppose could be omitted ... As a matter of fact I do not believe the story as a whole would be hurt by cutting slightly'. Cf. Letter 4017.

[3] Arthur William Barmby, b. 1880 in Sculcoates, Yorkshire, was in charge of DHL's affairs in Curtis Brown's New York office. Alfred Abraham Knopf (1892–1984), the well-known New York publisher and now DHL's American publisher, was subsequently responsible for publishing the first American impression of the authorised expurgated edn of *Lady Chatterley's Lover* (1932). See Roberts A42e.   [4] 'in good time!'

[5] In her letter of 25 April 1927, Nancy Pearn responded that DHL should be guided by his 'instinctive judgment' not to publish *Lady Chatterley's Lover*. Publication could be 'even dangerous financially speaking' to the magazine market.

What about your holiday? My wife's youngest daughter arrives today from London – so if you come out here you will see her.

                                    Saluti!   D. H. Lawrence

3991. To S. S. Koteliansky, 13 April 1927
Text: MS BL; Postmark, Scandicci 14.4.27; cited in Gransden 31.

                                    Villa Mirenda – *Scandicci* (Firenze)
                                    13 April 1927

My dear Kot[1]

I got back yesterday and found your book – had no idea that you were sending it, or even had written it. But it looks quite thrilling, and I shall read it as soon as I feel I'm here. – I was away at Ravello, above Amalfi, with friends, then walking and driving in Maremma, looking at Etruscan tombs in Cerveteri and Tarquinia and Vulci and those places. I was away about a month – liked it very much – Frieda went to Baden for a week or two, and got back a week before me. Now yesterday has arrived her younger daughter Barbara, so somehow it feels a bit of an upset. However, I suppose I shall soon settle down. At present I feel a bit abroad, somehow.

How have you been all this time? Is Sonia better, and Ghita getting on well at Oxford:[2] It is spring, and very lovely here, with all the trees in blossom and the birds singing, and the sun good and strong. I don't think I could live in a sunless country any more.

I heard from Mrs Whitworth that *David* is now due in May.[3] The man Monck, the producer, also shirked it: so I don't know whom they'll get, and dont care much. It feels forever so uncertain, I don't think I shall come over.

Is there any news? I have none. Brett is still in Taos, flourishing as a cow-boy figure, and urging us to come out. But not this year, I think.

If you see Barbara, tell her I'll write[4] – I'll really have to start in and do

---

[1] Samuel Solomonovich Koteliansky ('Kot') (1880–1955), Russian-born but naturalised British, was a close friend and regular correspondent of DHL's, 1914–30; see *Letters*, ii. 205 n. 4. He produced over thirty translations of Russian works; the most recent – to which DHL refers here – was *Solitaria* by V. V. Rozanov (April 1927); see Letter 4355 and n. 1.

[2] Kot lived at 5 Acacia Road, St John's Wood, initially with the Farbmans: Michael S. Farbman ('Grisha') (1880?–1933), a Russian journalist; his wife Sonia Issayevna ('Sophie'); and daughter Ghita. See *Letters*, ii. 570 n. 3.

[3] See Letter 3985 and p. 26 n. 1. DHL had been in correspondence with Phyllis Whitworth since September 1926 (*Letters*, v. 521 and n. 5) about producing the play. Another producer who, in November 1926, had been expected by DHL to stage *David* (*Letters*, v. 576), was Nugent Monck (1877–1958), associated with the Maddermarket Theatre, Norwich.

[4] Barbara Low (1877–1955), an old friend of DHL's. She was a pioneer in psychoanalysis in England. See *Letters*, ii. 279 n. 6.

some letters. What's happened to us? – I feel a stranger to myself. Is it a
'change of life'? Do you feel that way?

Write and tell me how things are.

DHL

3992. To Martin Secker, 13 April 1927
Text: MS UInd; Postmark, Scandicci 14. 4. 27.; Secker 86.

Villa Mirenda. Scandicci. (Firenze)
13 April 1927

Dear Secker

I got back here yesterday – stopped in Rome, and at Cerveteri, Tarquinia,
Vulci, Volterra, looking at Etruscan things. It was frightfully interesting, I
liked it immensely, and should like to go on and look at the other places.

Frieda has been here a week – with a bad cold, and a bit forlorn. And now
suddenly Barby has arrived, with their friend Mrs Seaman.[1] But we have put
Mrs Seaman down in the little Osteria at Vingone.

So altogether I feel a bit dazed and bewildered – am not here yet. I feel it'll
take me a day or two to collect myself and adjust myself to the new
circumstances. But the weather for the moment is lovely, and spring very
beautiful.

I found the proofs of *Mornings in Mexico* and managed to go through them
this morning. I think they'd missed a line out in one place: not my fault. – I
like these essays, especially the dance ones.[2] They give me a bit of a nostalgia
for New Mexico again – but I don't think of going back this year, at any rate. –
It makes a tiny book. I suppose you won't put pictures in. But I should like
you to put just that drawing of the corn dance figures which I made.[3] –
Barmby says Knopf is probably publishing without pictures, in America. I
don't care. – Barmby also says that Knopf couldn't possibly publish *Lady
Chatterley's Lover* till next spring, so I am to send the MS direct to New York,
not to London. I shan't. I shall just let it lie here. C'è tempo!

[1] Eileen Hilda Seaman (1873–1957), friend of the Weekley family and mother of Elsa Weekley's
future husband (cf. p. 26 n. 2). See *Letters*, v. 389. Vingone, where she stayed, was the terminus
of trams from central Florence and about 1½ miles from the Villa Mirenda.
[2] 'The Dance of the Sprouting Corn' and 'The Hopi Snake Dance', both first published in
Theatre Arts Monthly (viii, July 1924, 447–57 and viii, December 1924, 836–60; Roberts C122,
C127); the first had DHL's drawing (see next note).
[3] DHL's drawing, *The Corn Dance*, originally reproduced in the DHL number of the *Laughing
Horse* (April 1926), appeared on the dust-jacket of Secker's edn of *Mornings in Mexico*; a more
finished version had been printed in *Theatre Arts Monthly*, viii (July 1924): see *Letters*, v. 27 n.
7. Knopf's edn (August 1927) did not use it.

How are you all? – Barby had no news of you. She is here only for three weeks, then going to her school again. Elsa we may see later on in the summer – but I make no plans. – How is Adrian's Gemma getting on?[1] – does he still refuse to speak to her? – Thanks so much for sending always the *Lit. Sup.* and the *London Ill. News.*

Ever.   D. H. Lawrence

3993. To Baroness Anna von Richthofen, 14 April 1927
Text: MS UCB; Frieda Lawrence 238–9.

Villa Mirenda, Scandicci (Florenz)
14 April 1927

Meine liebe Schwiegermutter[2]

Ich bin wieder zuhaus – bin Montag-abend gekommen, von Volterra. Ich hatte eine sehr schöne Woche, mit dem Brewster. Wir waren in Cerveteri und Tarquinia und Vulci, Grosseto und Volterra – nimmer weit vom Meer, nord von Rom. Die Etrusker-Graben sind sehr interessant, und so nett und liebenswürdig. Sie waren ein lebendiges, frisches, lustiges Volk, lebten ihr eignes Leben, ohne das Leben von anderen herrschen zu wollen. Ich habe gern meine Etrusker. Sie hatten das Leben in sich selber, so brauchten sie nicht so viel herrschaften. Ich möchte ein Paar Skizzen von Etruskischen Orten schreiben – nichts wissenschaftlich, nur wie es jetzt ist, und die Eindruck man hat.

Ich fand die Frieda erkältet und ein wenig 'nieder.' Es geht ihr aber schon besser, sie ist wieder wohl und wieder sich selbst. Die Barby kam Dienstag – und natürlich, mit einer Mrs Seaman hinten, als dueña: sonst hatte der alte Weekley sie nicht kommen lassen. Die Mrs Seaman haben wir aber im Gasthaus in Vingone gestellt, die Barby ist hier. Sie ist nett, älter wie letztes Jahr – nicht so schön – hoch wie ein Telegrafstaub – und stiller – nicht viel Leben darin. Das ist aber London über sie. Sie bleibt nur drei Wochen, dann zurück zu ihrer Akademie-schule. – Man sieht so klar, sie ist nicht Fisch von unserm See. Sie versteht wirklich nicht unsere Art reden – sie fasst die Bedeuting der Wörter nur – in der Fluss der Meinung kann sie aber nicht schwimmen. Es ist mir, als ob ich eine andere Sprache sprechen sollte – Sprache von dem Kleinbürgertum, wo alles weiss oder schwarz ist, und mit Nägeln fest auf dem Mauer genagelt. Aber ich kann es[3] nicht. Du lieber Herrgott, gieb mir Leute die meine Sprache sprechen. – Das Kind ist aber

[1] The nanny of Adrian Secker (b. 1924) in Spotorno.
[2] Baroness Anna von Richthofen (1851–1930), Frieda's mother, was the widow of Baron Friedrich von Richthofen (1845–1915), a regular Army officer.   [3] es] est

nett, und nicht so frech wie letztes Jahr – oh, weit nicht so frech. Sie studiert gut in ihrer Schule, und will wirklich frei werden, von jenem alten Vater. Es dauert aber noch ein-und-halb Jahre, mindestens. Doch ist es besser dass sie arbeitet. Die Jungen können nicht lieben weder leben. Das beste ist, dass sie arbeiten. Es ist auch traurig, sie so Zwecklos, lebenslos zu sehen. Aber wenn sie Geld hätte, und ganz 'frei' wäre, wäre es noch schlimmer. Oh freiheit, was hast du für die arme Frauen gethan? Doch müssen sie immer noch ihr Lebensbrot mit diesem Gift schmieren – Gift der Freiheit.

Das Wetter, Gott sei dank, ist sehr schön. Es gibt noch Tulipanen im Korn, und Apfelblüte wo Pfirrsichblüthe waren. Die Bauern sind treu und nett, das Haus ist still. Man kann sehr gut hier sein. Die Frieda ist nach Scandicci gegangen, die Barby mit der Mrs Seaman nach Florenz. So bin ich allein.

Ich trage jetzt deine Strümpfe, die du mir gestickt hast. Sie sind schön, und grad die Farbe meiner Hosen, sehr elegant. Und die Schlips sind sehr schön: ich habe den 'speckled' gleich probiert.

Ich bin froh, dass es dir immer so gut geht, und deiner Stift immer schöner gemacht wird. Sicher geht die Welt vorwärts.

Später machen wir die Sommer-pläne, wann und wie wir kommen. Für den Moment, will man nicht an Reisen denken. Es ist genug.

Grüsse Else, wenn du sie siehst – die Frieda hat ihre Schwesterliebe wieder ganz neu und glänzend heimgebracht. Also gut! Grüsse auch die Damen meine Freundine.

Und wenn wir kommen, essen wir wieder Blaufelchen. Es gibt kein Fisch so gut, in Italien.

Also lebe wohl!　DHL

[Frieda Lawrence begins]
Ich wünsche Dir einen lustigen Osterhas! Es ist rührend Barby da zu haben! Sie ist *selig* und findet es zauberhaft, aber sie ist Londonblas, wird sich aber erholen! *Viel* ordentlicher und *elegant*! Nun bist Du wieder allein – Aber im Sommer komm' ich wirklich mit *beiden*, sie *möchten* kommen zu Dir, furchtbar gern!

In Liebe　F –

[My dear Schwiegermutter
　I am home again – came back Monday evening, from Volterra. I had a very lovely week, with Brewster. We were in Cerveteri and Tarquinia and Vulci, Grosseto and Volterra – not far from the sea, north of Rome. The Etruscan tombs are very interesting, and so nice and charming. They were a lively, fresh, jolly people, lived their own life, without wanting to dominate the life of others. I am fond of my Etruscans. They had life in themselves, so they didn't have so much need to dominate. I should like to write a couple of sketches of

Etruscan places – nothing scientific, but just as it is now, and the impression one has.

I found Frieda with a cold and a bit 'low.' But she is already better, she is well again and again herself. Barby came on Tuesday – and naturally, with a Mrs Seaman in tow, as dueña: otherwise old Weekley wouldn't have let her come. But we put Mrs Seaman in the inn in Vingone, Barby is here. She is nice, older than last year – not so pretty – tall as a telegraph pole – and quieter – not much life in her. But that is the effect of London on her. She is only staying three weeks, then back to her school. – One sees so clearly, she is no fish from our sea. She really does not understand our way of talking – she grasps the significance of the words only – but she cannot swim in the river of meaning. I feel as if I should speak another language – language of the petty bourgeoisie, where everything is white or black, and nailed fast to the wall. But I can't do it. Oh dear Lord, give me people who speak my language. – But the child is nice, and not so impertinent as last year – oh, not at all so impertinent. She studies well in her school, and really wants to get free from that old father. But it will take another year and a half, at least. Yet it is better that she works. The young can neither love nor live. The best is that they work. It is also sad to see her so aimless, lifeless. But if she had money, and was really 'free', it would be even worse. Oh freedom, what have you done for the poor women? Yet they still must spread their bread of life with this poison – poison of freedom.

The weather, thank God, is very beautiful. There are still tulips in the corn, and apple blossom where peach blossom was. The peasants are loyal and nice, the house is quiet. One can live here very well. Frieda has gone to Scandicci, Barby with Mrs Seaman to Florence. So I am alone.

I'm now wearing the socks which you knitted me. They are lovely, and just the colour of my trousers, very elegant. And the ties are very nice: I tried the 'speckled' one immediately.

I'm glad that you are always so well, and your Stift is always being made more and more beautiful. Surely the world advances.

Later on we shall make plans for the summer, when and how we come. For the moment, one doesn't want to think of travelling. It's enough.

Greet Else, when you see her[1] – Frieda has brought home her sister-love all new and shiny again. Well, good! Greet also my friends the ladies.

---

[1] Else Jaffe (1874–1973), Frieda's older sister, widow of Edgar Jaffe (1866–1921), Professor of Social Economics at the University of Heidelberg. They had three children: Friedrich ('Friedel') (b. 1903); Marianne (b. 1905); and Hans (b. 1909).

And when we come, we'll eat blue char again. There's no fish so good in Italy.

Goodbye then!   DHL

[Frieda Lawrence begins]

I wish you a jolly Easter bunny! It's touching to have Barby here! She is *blissful* and finds it magical, but she is London-pale, yet will recuperate. *Much* more orderly and *elegant*! Now you are alone again – But in the summer I'm really coming with *both*, they *would* like to come to you, terribly!

With love   F –]

3994. To Earl Brewster, 14 April 1927
Text: MS UT; Brewster 124–5.

Villa Mirenda, Scandicci (Firenze)
14 April 1927

Dear Earl

I got home all right on Monday night – pretty well shaken up, after five hours in that bus. But I caught the last train, by the skin of my teeth.

On Tuesday morning Frieda set off to meet her daughter Barbara – who arrived all right, with a woman, elderly, as dueña. But the woman we have put down in the inn at Vingone, and now we're all trying to settle down. I feel a bit awkward and strange, as if I hadn't all of me come back. But I suppose bit by bit one will gather oneself inside one's skin.

How did you get on? Hope you had a decent journey, and settled the bank business quickly, and found everything all right at Capri. It is funny how unsettled one does feel. I felt, when I got back here, as if I didn't want to stay – didn't want it. But if one sits still a bit, perhaps that passes away.

I liked our Etruscan trip so much. Pity it was so short. When I feel more myself, I am going to try doing some sketches. – The country between Volterra and San Gemignano is very queer and empty – very hilly in sharp little hills, and rather bare, and no villages. It would be nice to settle down one day in a district with few people. What people there were, seemed nice and fresh.

I found Frieda with a real bad cold – the tail end of which she handed on to me. She is better, but I am sneezing myself in two. No luck!

I found the Wilkinson's[1] with a little marmoset monkey, which *of course*

---

[1] The Wilkinson family were DHL's neighbours at the Villa Mirenda; they lived at the Villa Poggi. The family consisted of Arthur Gair Wilkinson (1882–1957), painter and puppeteer; his wife, Lilian ('Diddy'); and their children Frances ('Bim') and William ('Pino'). The Lawrences had known them for a year; their relations were generally very cordial. See *Letters*, v. 441 n. 1.

they'd let get cold, so it is surely dying – just lying giving up the ghost – a really disturbing sight. Makes one realise the calamity of getting into the wrong latitude.

Rose actually sent me my socks! – very nice of her: and I can't thank her, because I don't know her name. But I sent a line to Lucille.[1]

Well, let us know which spoke of the wheel of Destiny is coming round at you. One could wish the knees of the gods a little more comfortable, since one is left so long upon them. Tell Harwood I'm not forgetting her ribbons.

                                                                        DHL

3995. To Mabel Dodge Luhan, [14–15 April 1927]
Text: MS Brill; Luhan 325–7.

                                              Villa Mirenda, *Scandicci* (Florence)
                                                            14 April 1927

My dear Mabel

It seems long since I have written you – but you will hear through Brett all the news, or lack of it, from us. I have just got back from looking at Etruscan things – tombs – on the coast north of Rome – Tarquinia, Cerveteri, Vulci, Volterra. It was very interesting, very attractive. I should like to do a book of sketches of Etruscan places.

When I got back I corrected the proofs of the tiny book of essays, *Mornings in Mexico*. They are essays I like – and they have one basic theme. I liked particularly the 'Hopi Snake Dance'. I inscribed the book to you, as I said: since to you we really owe Taos and all that ensues from Taos.[2] – Reading the New Mexico essays gave me a desire to come back – made me feel that, as the wheel of destiny goes round, it will carry us back. I should love to see the dances at Santo Domingo, and the winter dances at Taos again – and go to Zuni, where I've never been.[3] One has gradually to let life carry one round.

As for a change of life – there's a very nice poem on it somewhere at the ranch – if somebody hasn't torn it out from the end of one of my books of MS.[4] When it comes to changes, there's nothing to be done but to accept 'em and go through with them and put up with the penalty of them, in the hopes of coming through into calmer water. Myself, I'm in just the same way – just

---

[1] Lucy ('Lucile') Katherine Beckett (1884–1979), daughter of the 2nd Baron Grimthorpe, had known the Brewsters since they all lived in Rome during the war years; see *Letters*, iii. 712 n. 1 and Letter 4201 and n. 5. When in Italy she lived in her brother's residence, the Palazzo Cimbrone (see p. 22 n. 1). Rose had been her lady's-maid for about twenty years; she became the virtual guardian of the Cimbrone.

[2] The book carried the simple dedication: 'To Mabel Lujan'.

[3] An Indian pueblo w. of Albuquerque, New Mexico.

[4] The MS of 'Change of Life' is now unlocated; it is described in Lawrence Clark Powell, *The Manuscripts of D. H. Lawrence: A Descriptive Catalogue* (Los Angeles, 1937), 63F.

simply suffering from a change of life, and a queer sort of recoil, as if one's whole soul were drawing back from connection with everything. This is the day they put Jesus in the tomb[1] – and really, those three days in the tomb begin to have a terrible significance and reality to me. And the Resurrection is an unsatisfactory business – just *noli me tangere*, and no more. Poveri noi![2] But pazienza, pazienza! The wheel will go round.

I haven't seen Orioli since I'm back, to ask about the final settlement of your books.[3] I'm sorry we didn't get the child picture – but we were only authorised to take the three. – As for the other things you mention in Curonia, I remember none of them. I didn't look at all carefully. But the place seemed to me almost stripped bare. – There was no sign of any *Arabian Nights* – nothing one wanted. I just got eight paper-back Balzac's and one or two Ouidas, the last for mere amusement. – But it seems to me you should have that silver. –

It is lovely spring here – the red tulips in the corn, and the last of the purple anemones. I have said we will keep this house another year – it doesn't cost much, so is no matter if one abandons it half-way. I feel for the time a sort of soreness, physical, mental, and spiritual, which is no doubt change of life, and I wish it would pass off. I think it is passing off. Meanwhile pazienza! But till it heals up, I don't feel like making much effort in any direction. It is *easiest* here.

My word, how you do but extend your boundaries, out there on the hill! You'll have a real Mabeltown before you've done. I believe that's your ambition – to have an earthly kingdom, and rule it. But my dear, it's an illusion like any other. But if houses are your passion, why, then have houses. We'll no doubt come and sit in one of them one day.

Frieda was back from Germany a week before I got home – I found her with a bad cold and feeling very low. The day after my arrival came her daughter Barbara – of course with an elderly woman, as dueña, in tow. But the elderly woman is put down in the inn, and we make the best of things.

I hope you're feeling really better from the flu. In my opinion, flu is one of the diseases of a changing constitution. It changes the very chemical composition of the blood – hence the bad effect on the heart – and the long time one takes to get round. And when one does get round, one has lost for good one's old self – some of it – though where the new self comes in, I don't quite see.

---

[1] Good Friday was 15 April 1927; DHL's letter was presumably written over two days.
[2] 'just *touch me not*, . . . Poor us!'
[3] Giuseppe ('Pino') M. Orioli (1884–1942), Italian antiquarian bookseller and publisher – he later published *Lady Chatterley's Lover* (1928) – had assisted DHL with the disposal of books and other objects from the Villa Curonia, at Mabel Luhan's request. (See also p. 564 n. 1.) The Villa, at Arcetri, near Florence, was the property of her second husband, Edwin Dodge.

When is Spud coming back to you?[1] – I stayed two nights in Christine Hughes' flat in Rome – she seemed rather calmer in herself, but Mary Christine would be *much* better home in Santa Fe.[2]

Best wishes, then   D. H. Lawrence

3996. To Ada Clarke, 20 April 1927
Text: MS Clarke; cited in Lawrence–Gelder 154.

Villa Mirenda, *Scandicci* (Firenze)
Wed. 20 April 1927

My dear Sister

I wrote to you from Rome a fortnight ago – and posted it myself – but have had no answer. I hope everything is all right, with Gertie and everybody – have been wondering why I have not heard.

I got home about a week ago, and Barby Weekley came the day after. She is much quieter this year. She arrived with a Mrs Seaman, but that woman we put down in the inn at Vingone, and we see hardly anything of her at all. As for Barby, she is much quieter this year – and is staying only another ten days. But I have made a permanent agreement with Frieda that she is to have *none* of her family again staying in the house – and I will ask none of mine: that is, unless either of us is here quite alone. This mix-up of relations is no good – we'll keep them apart. And that's final.

I had a very nice little trip with Brewster, walking and driving, looking at Etruscan tombs on the coast north of Rome. I liked it very much, and hope to do a few articles. – The Brewsters are still without a house, staying in an hotel on Capri, and feeling very unsettled indeed.

I haven't settled yet about staying on in this house. I must, before May 6th. But they asked me to pay more rent, which was impudence, considering how I have worked at the house. So I refused – now I'll hear what they say. I don't care terribly whether I stay or not – but expect we shall stay, as there is nowhere else definite where I want to go.

Frieda's sister Elsa asks us to go to Bavaria for the late summer – We might go, but I'm not sure. Brett and Mabel Lujan cabled today for us to go to Taos – but not this year. Besides, it is too expensive. I've not got any book this year, to come out, except the tiny vol. of *Mornings in Mexico* – so the earnings don't amount to a great deal. And now the Lira has fallen to 96 to £1., and will probably fall lower – which makes everything much dearer.

---

[1] Willard ('Spud', 'Spoodle') Johnson (1897–1968), American journalist, co-founder and editor of *Laughing Horse*, 1922–39. See *Letters*, iv. 316 n. 5.

[2] Christine Hughes and her daughter Mary Christine (1908?–   ) had known the Lawrences in New Mexico; their acquaintance was renewed in December 1926 when the Hughes were in Rome where Mary Christine studied music. See *Letters*, v. 158 n. 1.

I've not heard another word about *David*, who is doing it or what. So it's no use making any plans.

I wonder how you all are, and if you had a nice Easter. We just stayed still here – the days are lovely, though spring is rather late. One of the Miss Beveridges went back to Scotland today – Milly and Mabel Harrison stay on another three weeks.[1] – One feels rather unsettled, having broken up the routine – shouldn't mind if I went away somewhere.

Let me know how you all are –

love   DHL

3997. To Margaret King, [20 April 1927]

Text: MS Forster; PC v. Hiroshige. Mochizuki: Moonlight; Postmark, Scandicci 21. 4. 27; Unpublished.

[Villa Mirenda, Scandicci, Florence]
20 April

I wrote you from Rome two weeks ago, but have not heard from any of you. I hope all is well. I got back about a week ago – and Barby Weekley came the day after I arrived. She is staying about another twelve days. Elsa has not come this year. – How are you? Your mother said you weren't very well. I hope it's better: and that Joan is trippy. The weather is rather lovely – spring just turning into summer.

I had rather a nice time with Brewster, looking at Etruscan tombs at Tarquinia and Cerveteri, north of Rome, near the sea – quite lovely. Let me know how you are.

DHL

3998. To Christine Hughes, 25 April 1927

Text: MS UT; Postmark, Scandicci 27.4.27.; Lacy, *Escaped Cock* 65.

Villa Mirenda, *Scandicci* (Firenze)
Monday. 25 April 1927

Dear Christine

How are you by now? No news of your coming to Florence, so I expect you haven't yet let the flat. What a curse those things are.

We are going on as usual. Frieda's daughter Barbara stays until May 3rd – a week tomorrow – then goes back to London. She's supposed to paint, but hasn't done anything yet. I tell her, she's nearly as discontented and hard to

---

[1] Anne Millicent ('Milly') Beveridge (1871–1955), Scottish painter whom DHL met in Sicily in 1921 and who painted his portrait in that year (see *Letters*, iii. 671; v. 403 and n. 1). She and Mabel Harrison, a fellow artist, lived in Paris. In February 1927 the two women and Mary Beveridge had rented the Villa La Massa, near the Mirenda.

please as Mary Christine, who is a tough nut in that respect. What *does* ail the
young? I, who am hard boiled enough, am ten times as easy to amuse.

I've been doing a story of the Resurrection – what sort of a man 'rose up,'
after all that other pretty little experience.¹ Rather devastating!

The publisher is harrying me for that essay on Verga.² Either a publisher is
so dilatory, you think he's dead: or in such a hurry, you think he's taken salts. –
I am awfully disappointed not to have heard from you, or from de Bosis or
Santellana³ – where I can find material about Giovanni Verga – some sort of
personal facts – and some decent *Italian* critique. I scour Florence, but Verga
had better have been a Hottentot, the Italians would know more about him. I
suppose I'll have to invent it out of my own head – povero me!⁴ I wish I knew
someone who had *known* Verga – he only died five years ago.

Well, we are here, wherever you are. And it's nearly May! – Let me know
your plans and your achievements.

Yrs   D. H. Lawrence

3999. To Nancy Pearn, 26 April 1927
Text: MS YU; Unpublished.

Villa Mirenda. *Scandicci*. Florence.
26 April 1927

Cara Signorina –

I had your cable last night – guilty me! But just when I wanted to do the
article, I had such a whack of flu – then I went away to recuperate. However, I
send you a little thing post haste.⁵ If you dont like it, don't bother about it –
just give it to Barmby. Excuse scrap of MS. anyhow. – I also send two
photographs by Alinari of an Etruscan tomb at Tarquinia, on the coast north
of Rome.⁶ – I know Alinari lets people print his photographs – if he makes a

¹ *The Escaped Cock* was the story in question; it appeared in *Forum*, lxxix (February 1928), 286–
    96. (For Brewster's account of the origin of the title see Brewster 123–4.) Revised and expanded
    it was published separately by the Black Sun Press in 1929 (Roberts A50a and b). The first
    English edn, by Secker, was entitled *The Man Who Died* (Roberts A50c).
² Jonathan Cape (1879–1960), the London publisher, was 'harrying' him for the introductory
    essay to DHL's translation of *Mastro-don Gesualdo* by Giovanni Verga (1840–1922), to be
    published in Cape's *Travellers' Library*, March 1928 (see Letter 4016). The essay was longer
    than the biographical note DHL had written for the first publication of the story by Seltzer
    (1923), reissued by Cape in 1925 (Roberts A28).
³ Possibly Lanro de Bosis (1901–31), translator and playwright; Santellana is not known.
⁴ 'alas, poor me!'
⁵ The MS was of the essay 'Making Love to Music' (see Tedlock, *Lawrence MSS* 210), first
    published in *Phoenix* 160–6.
⁶ The firm of Fratelli Alinari had been photographing Italian works of art and architecture since
    1852; the collection is unrivalled.

charge, I'm not sure, but can pay him if you use a photograph. Dont you think they are rather nice?

I do hope this will be in time.

Sincerely   D. H. Lawrence

4000. To S. S. Koteliansky, 27 April 1927

Text: MS BL; Postmark, Firenze Ferrovia 28.4.27; cited in Gransden 31.

Villa Mirenda. Scandicci. Firenze
27 April 1927

My dear Kot

I read Rozanov as soon as he came: and wrote a criticism as soon as I'd read him: and send you the criticism so you will know what I think.[1] Do you agree at all?

As for my crit., will you send it on to Curtis Brown – Magazine Dept.[2] They may get someone to print it, though it's an off-chance. But they usually place anything I send. The *Calendar* would print it, but since it's their own publication, I'd rather it went somewhere else. If you know anybody, give it them. If not, no matter.

I was very pleased to have Rozanov – I'm really rather tired of Tchekov and Dostoevsky people: they're so Murryish.[3] By the way, any news of Our mutual friend?

It is full summer here – quite hot. I'm taking this house for another year, because nothing else occurs to me to do. I think we shall stay here later, this summer: till end of July: but I'm not sure. My old instinct, not to come to England, is still strong. And it is an instinct rather than anything else. Italy I like, when I'm in the country and there's nothing but peasants. But the towns are most irritable and tiresome, and Rome very antipatica nowadays. I've half a feeling I shall go to Spain before very long. Or Egypt! How do the Dobrées like it? If you'll send me their address, I'll write to them. I never read her book, because children-literature bores me, especially Proustian.[4] But I must get it, and actually try. Anyhow I'm glad it was a success.

I did a novel, too: English Midlands scene. The public would call it pornographic again, though it's the reverse: so I'm holding the MS. and

---

[1] Cf. Letter 3991 and n. 1. DHL's review of *Solitaria* appeared in *Calendar*, iv (July 1927), 164–8 (Roberts C156).   [2] I.e. to Nancy Pearn.

[3] John Middleton Murry (1889–1957), journalist and critic, once a close friend, now a distant acquaintance at whom DHL directed often scathing irony. m. (1) 1918, Katherine Mansfield (1888–1923); (2) 1924, Violet le Maistre (d. 1931).

[4] Bonamy Dobrée (1891–1974), Professor of English at the Egyptian University, Cairo; see *Letters*, v. 558 n. 1. m. 1913, Valentine Gladys Brooke-Pechell (d. 1974). Her book, *Your Cuckoo Sings By Kind*, was published in February 1927.

shan't even have it typed, yet awhile. Secker wants it this year, but wont get it.

Now I really want to do a series of 'Travel Sketches of Etruscan Places'. I liked my trip to Cerveteri and Tarquinia and Vulci so much, I'd like to jot them down while they are fresh. Then later go to Cortona and Chiusi and Orvieto etc. It's such good weather now, hot without exhausting. And so make a little book of Etruscan places. But I'm nearly like Rozanov, anything I *say* I'll do, I seem never to do: but something else. But there are so many little jobs on hand, that I've neglected and have piled up.

I'm sorry about Sonya not being well. I get to dread the thought of Sickness. Gertie has been a horrible business – in a hospital in London these last two months – left lung removed, six ribs removed, glands in the neck – too horrible – better die. Yet she's managed just to live through it. Good Lord, what next! Why aren't we better at dying, straight dying! What is left, after all those operations? Why not chloroform and the long sleep! How monstrous our humanity is! Why save life in this ghastly way?

They say the govt. is mobilising soldiers here. Lord knows what for. The exchange is down to 88, and everything dearer than England – no fun.

Frieda's daughter Barbara has been here the last two weeks – leaves next Tuesday. She's a bit hard to please. What ails the young, that they get nothing out of life? For certain, life doesn't get much out of them.

How is Gertler?[1] Did he go away? Does he keep pretty well? As for me, I've not done any painting lately. Feel I'd like to paint something red –

I still haven't written to Barbara. Ay di me! So many words exist already!

I'll read the Tchekov book next.[2] But Tchekov, being particularly a pet of Murry and Katharine, is rather potted shrimps to me.

                                                                            DHL

4001. To Richard Aldington and Dorothy Yorke, 28 April 1927

Text: MS ColU; Paul Delany, 'D. H. Lawrence: Twelve Letters', *DHL Review*, ii (Fall 1969), 203–5.

Villa Mirenda, *Scandicci*, Firenze

28 Aprile 1927

Dear Richard and Arabella[3]

Had both your letters yesterday – glad things are going a bit gaily, orange

---

[1] Mark Gertler (1892–1939), painter, a friend of DHL's since 1914; see *Letters*, ii. 214 n. 1. He had contracted tuberculosis. (When DHL wrote this letter Gertler was in Stratford-upon-Avon: *Mark Gertler: Selected Letters*, ed. Noel Carrington, 1965, p. 222.)

[2] Kot's translation of Chekhov's *Literary and Theatrical Reminiscences* had been published in March 1927.

[3] Richard Aldington (1892–1962), poet, novelist and, later, biographer of DHL, had separated from his wife Hilda Doolittle (1886–1961) (divorced 1938); from Autumn 1919 he lived with Dorothy ('Arabella') Yorke (1892–   ). She, an American, was the prototype for Josephine Ford in *Aaron's Rod*. They lived at Malthouse Cottage, Padworth, near Reading.

chairs getting orangier, doors vernal green, parrots in the window foliage! muy bonito![1] And cowslips! I love cowslips, almost enough to come back to England to see them. But they used to come *after* the bluebells, what are they doing before? I suppose the last shall be the first,[2] even there – revolutions! – And Flint![3] was ever a man more wrongly named! Why not Fluff!

We've done no spring-cleaning yet – have had F[rieda]'s youngest daughter Barbara here these three weeks – she leaves next week – so been sort of out of gear in housework. The young seem so out of gear themselves – and they throw one out a bit too. It's queer – they don't seem to care about a thing, and don't even dream – hopelessly hard-boiled about life. What life thinks of *them*, they never ask themselves. But I suppose they will go on till they get altogether stuck.

No, I didn't care for Ravello this year – and Ld. Grimthorpe's house was *so* full of junk and statuosities, one felt one might turn into an antique (pseudo) along with it all. But I did have a nice ten days with Brewster, looking at Etruscan tombs – I liked it very much – Cerveteri, Tarquinia (especially Tarquinia) Grosseto, Vulci, Volterra. I must go again one day – great charm in those dead places – And I want to go to Cortona and Chiusi and Orvieto and Bolseno – this side.

The summer is really here – the two horse-chestnuts by the front gate in flower – the pink peonies over – honeysuckle out – and[4] choruses of nightingales. You almost expect to see them tripping and kicking their legs along some bare bough, like a dancing chorus. How ever anybody managed to hear those birds *sad* beats me more than ever.

It's very nice of you to ask us to the Malthouse. But I don't know when we shall be in England. I am taking the Mirenda for another year – though as R[ichard] surmises, Italy is by no means cheap, with the Lira at 88 when Frieda changed on Monday – and prices not thinking of moving: butter 25, meat 20, a chilo, loaf 1.30 (small), oil 11.0 (chilo) jam $\frac{1}{2}$ chilo (poor) 7.50, honey ditto – nothing cheap – coffee 25. Sugar 7.50 tea 45. – I almost wish I had given up the Mirenda, and was trying somewhere else – perhaps Spain – or the ranch again – pero vedremo![5] I don't know about coming to England this summer – half think we may go to Bavaria – might see you there – what do you say?

I did a very nice novel – English Midlands – which they'll say is pornographic – and I feel tender about it – it's sort of tender – so I'm holding it back. Shan't give it anybody this year anyhow.

---

[1] 'very pretty!' [2] Luke xiii. 30.
[3] Frank Stewart Flint (1885–1960), Imagist poet. His poems, together with Aldington's and DHL's had appeared in *New Paths* (1918) (*Letters*, iii. 261 and n. 5).
[4] MS reads: 'and and'. [5] 'but we shall see!'

Oh Richard, if reading me makes you feel 'almost' envious, don't read me. It's no sort of a feeling to have. I shall be interested in your 7,000 words about me – though you bet, they'll be more about Richard than me.[1] I don't much care what people say about me – so long as it's pertinent – when it's impertinencies, it riles me a bit. Caro mio, I don't want bouquets. Think what my stage bow would be like.

Frieda still hasn't quite got over Baden. They fed her, and she ate too much, and sort of sank mercurially – and got a bad cold – and altogether the bosom of the family doesn't suit her, unless I'm there to stick thorns on all the roses. She sends her love.

au revoir!   DHL

4002. To Earl Brewster, 28 April 1927
Text: MS UT; Brewster 126.

Villa Mirenda, Scandicci (Firenze)
28 April 1927

Dear Earl

Why haven't I heard from you? It is near the end of April, you must be going somewhere – write and tell me where.

I bought Harwood 14 very nice hair-ribbons, and someone *stole* them from my pocket! But I'll buy them again.

Frieda's daughter departs Tuesday. Oh people!

I'm not painting – but wrote a story of the Resurrection – show it you one day.

send a line   DHL

4003. To Martin Secker, 29 April 1927
Text: MS UInd; Postmark, Scandicci 30 4 27.; cited in Huxley 683.

Villa Mirenda, Scandicci, Firenze
29 April 1927

Dear Secker

Many thanks for the *Women in Love* and *Sea and Sardinia* and *Plumed Serpent*. I do like the little red books.[2] Perhaps now the little dull people will manage to read them, in that cosy and familiar form.

---

[1] Aldington's pamphlet (34 pp.), *D. H. Lawrence: An Indiscretion*, formed No. 6 in the series of 'University of Washington Chapbooks', published by the University of Washington Book Store, Seattle, 1927 (Roberts F4a).
[2] Secker republished these volumes in a 3/6 pocket edn, March–May 1927.

I've been thinking about *Lady Chatterley's Lover* – and think I'll get him typed in London before long, and let you have a copy, so that you can see how possible or impossible he is. But there is much more latitude these days, and a man dare possibly possess a penis.

Barby Weekley goes home next Tuesday. We want her to bring Adrian his marionettes: hope she'll have room. Barby arrived rather off the hooks and hard to please, like a real modern young woman – sempre scontente e spiacinte[1] – but she has about settled down and become easy-going: only she doesn't paint any more: *that's* most decidedly off, for the time. – She arrived with a Mrs Seaman, whom I'd never seen, and who was poking her nose in to spy out the maleficent influences of the household. She's packed off to Lausanne, however, not having got much out of us.

I began my essays on the Etruscan things – I believe they'll be rather nice. Oh by the way, do send me Dennis' *Cities and Cemeteries of Etruria*. I should like to read it again, and my copy is in America. It's a good book. You can get in Everyman, 2 vols.[2] I'll send you the money.

We can put thrilling illustrations in an Etruscan book! – I'm very much interested to see the *Mornings* with pictures.

The last time Frieda changed she got 88 to £1. And since butter is still 25, meat 20 the chilo, coffee about 20, tea 50 – Italy is no longer cheap. Also there are 'rumours'. But I get bored by rumorisings.

It's sunny weather – full summer, and very lovely weather – not a cloudy day these last twenty days. We have come to the lying in the garden stage – and I go off into the woods to work – where the nightingales have a very gay time singing at me. They are very inquisitive, and come nearer to watch me turn a page. They seem to love to see the pages turned.

I've promised to be reconciled to Douglas, since I've been here a year and never spoken nor even nodded to him.[3] Hope I shan't run on the rocks again with him. Was reading some of his old *Siren Land* essays in old *English Reviews*. They are good, you know. They haven't gone thin.

---

[1] 'always discontented and dissatisfied'.

[2] George Dennis, *The Cities and Cemeteries of Etruria*, 2 vols (1848); published with introduction by W. M. Lindsay, in 'Everyman's Library', 1907.

[3] George Norman Douglas (1868–1952), expatriate novelist and essayist who lived in Italy and Capri. DHL had known him since 1913 (*Letters*, ii. 31 and n. 4), but the two men had become estranged over DHL's introduction to *Memoirs of the Foreign Legion* (1924) written by Maurice Magnus for whom Douglas was literary executor. Their quarrel became public through Douglas's *D. H. Lawrence and Maurice Magnus: A Plea for Better Manners* (1924) and DHL's riposte in the *New Statesman*, 20 February 1926, 'The Late Mr. Maurice Magnus' (*Letters*, v. 395–7). *Siren Land* was published in 1911.

What a Godsend that *Jud Süss*![1] Even here people think it *so* good. Only old Vernon Lee has no use for it – bottle-washings![2]

Again, they're 'supposed' to be doing *David* in May – I 'might' come over for it. – But we may not come to my native land at all this summer, go instead to Bavaria, to the Isartal.

Many greetings from all of us to all of you.

Yrs   D. H. Lawrence

I've just got a Letter from Mrs Whitworth saying *David* is due on May 22 and 23, and they want my help, and when can I go! So probably I'll have to come – though dont know precisely. – Also Curtis Brown's people lamenting over the news that *Lady Chatterley's Lover* is improper, as it will spoil my market!![3]

4004. To Marianne Moore, 29 April 1927

Text: MS YU; Nicholas Joost and Alvin Sullivan, *D. H. Lawrence and 'The Dial'* (Carbondale, 1970), p. 104.

Villa Mirenda, Scandicci (Firenze)
29 Aprile 1927

Dear Mrs Thayer[4]

I'm sending back the proofs of 'The Man Who Loved Islands' and 'More Modern Love' by this mail.[5] – I don't think one wants the comma always after the ejaculatory Well! It's spoken all in a breath.

As for the title, 'Modern Love' is so famous as Meredith's poem-suite, it seems unfair to take it:[6] besides, sounds too important. The story is too trivial for such a wholesale title. But keep the 'More': or perhaps call it just: 'In Love'. Perhaps with a query: 'In Love?'

But I leave the final choice to you, and thanks for the suggestions.

Yours Sincerely   D. H. Lawrence

---

[1] The translation by Willa and Edwin Muir of Lion Feuchtwanger's novel, *Jud Süss* (November 1926) had been a great success for Secker, though DHL regarded it as 'a vulgar affair' (*Letters*, v. 388, 655).

[2] Vernon Lee (pseud. for Violet Paget) (1856–1935), essayist and art critic who had lived in Italy since 1871.   [3] See p. 29 n. 5.

[4] Marianne Craig Moore (1887–1972), American poet. She never married; she was editor of *Dial*, 1925–9, and DHL assumed she was the wife of the previous editor, Scofield Thayer.

[5] 'The Man Who Loved Islands' appeared in *Dial*, lxxxiii (July 1927), 1–25 and in the *London Mercury* in August 1927; it was collected in *The Woman Who Rode Away and Other Stories* (Knopf, 1928); see p. 69 n. 1. 'In Love?' was published in *Dial*, lxxxiii (November 1927), 391–404, and in the English as well as the American edn of *The Woman Who Rode Away*. See Roberts C157 and C162.

[6] *Modern Love* (1862), a series of fifty connected poems, by George Meredith (1828–1909).

4005. To S. S. Koteliansky, 30 April 1927
Text: MS BL; Postmark, Scandicci 30.4.27.; Zytaruk 312.

Villa Mirenda, *Scandicci*, Firenze
30 Aprile 1927

My dear Kot

I hear *David* is on May 22 and 23 – and they urge me to come. I suppose they'll make a mess of it without me. So I shall pretty well have to come. Therefore I shall be in London by the end of next week, I suppose – Friday or Saturday. I'll let you know precisely. I'm not sure where I shall stay – perhaps in Rossetti Garden Mansions for a time, in Miss Beveridge's flat, while she is away. I'll see. – The Dobrées are still away.

I had the *Adelphi* – the penultimate: next to the last gasp. What are the 'domestic circumstances'? More little Murrys arriving?[1]

Well au revoir   DHL

4006. To Emily King, 30 April 1927
Text: MS Lazarus; Unpublished.

Villa Mirenda, *Scandicci*. Florence
30 April 1927

My dear Sister

I was glad to get your letter and know all is well. So the wholesale is off! I'm glad, because I felt it wasn't a straight thing. And I'm very glad if Sam leaves Carlton.[2] He would be so much better in some smaller place, some mining village like Eastwood or Kirkby, where you would know people.

The news about Gertie is rather awful. It's really better to die: if only one could die quickly.

I hear that they are producing *David* on May 22nd and 23rd. I ought to be there to help – they want me to come at once. I ought to go, as they'll make a mess of it if I'm not there. If I come, I suppose I shall be in London by end of next week – May 6th or 7th. I'll let you know. I'm not very keen on coming, it's lovely summer here now. But I suppose it must be done.

au revoir then   DHL

I expect Frieda will stay here – It's such a bother and expense, both coming.

---

[1] In January/February 1927 Murry's wife, Violet, had been diagnosed as tubercular; in May she was in hospital. Murry announced the closure of *Adelphi* as soon as the diagnosis was known. See Letter 4018 and F. A. Lea, *The Life of John Middleton Murry* (1959), pp. 145, 147, 177.

[2] The King family had lived in Carlton, Nottingham, since 1919 (*Letters*, iii. 434 n. 3); they moved into a new house in 1924 but retained the same grocery shop.

4007. To Mr Colman, 30 April 1927
Text: MS UTul; Unpublished.

Villa Mirenda, *Scandicci* (Florence)
30 April 1927

Dear Mr Colman[1]

The *Travels* seem to be coming through fairly regularly now: one still missing, I believe.

I began doing *Sketches of Etruscan Places*, which I was visiting earlier in the spring – Cerveteri, Tarquinia, Vulci, Volterra – places on the coast north of Rome. They'd be travel sketches, but with stuff about the Etruscan tombs. It interests me – But alas, I've got to get away to London to help at the rehearsals for my play *David*, by the Stage Society – and this interrupts me just as I had nicely begun. But I'll tell Barmby to let you see the essays, when I *do* get them done. I wanted to go to Chiusi and Cortona and Arezzo and Orvieto etc – *not* to London. I don't know if you like a bit of mild and very easy archaeological interest in your *Travel*. – And there are lovely Etruscan photographs by Alinari and Anderson and Brogi.[2]

However, we'll wait till something materialises. I expect I shall be a month in London.

Sincerely   D. H. Lawrence

4008. To Ada Clarke, 30 April 1927
Text: MS Clarke; cited in Lawrence–Gelder 155.

Villa Mirenda, Scandicci, Firenze
30 April 1927

My dear Sister

I had your letter and all about Gertie. If one let it work on one's imagination, one would get ill out of very horror. There's nothing to do but not think of it.

---

[1] It is virtually certain that DHL's correspondent had an editorial position on *Travel*. The editor of the journal in 1927 (Letter 4169) was Coburn Gilman (1893–   ); DHL probably conflated his names and produced 'Colman'.

DHL had already published two of the Mexican essays in *Travel*, April and November 1926 (Roberts C140 and C147); the magazine later printed four of the Etruscan essays: 'City of the Dead at Cerveteri', *Travel*, l (November 1927), 12–16, 50; 'Ancient Metropolis of the Etruscans', l (December 1927), 20–5, 55; 'Painted Tombs of Tarquinia', l (January 1928), 28–33, 40; 'The Wind-Swept Stronghold of Volterra', l (February 1928), 31–5, 44 (Roberts C163, C165, C166, C168).

[2] Anderson specialised in photographic reproductions of art objects; the firm was founded in Rome in 1854 by James Anderson (1813–77) and enlarged by his son Domenico. A comparable firm was established in Florence in 1860 by Giacomo Brogi (d. 1881); it specialised in Etruscan works of art.

I heard yesterday, they are doing *David* on May 22nd and 23rd – and they want me to go as soon as possible, to help. So I ought to come to England next week. I must decide. I don't really want to come. It's just lovely hot summer here. Yet I bet they'll make a mess of that play without me. I'll let you know. If I come, I shall be in London by the end of next week. Frieda will stay here.
And probably I'd return here in June – anyhow we can see about that.

au revoir   DHL

Barby Weekley leaves next Tuesday – I'd go a day or two later.

4009. To Earl Brewster, 3 May 1927
Text: MS UT; Brewster 126–8.

Villa Mirenda, *Scandicci*, Firenze
3 May 1927

Dear Earl

Your letter today. So the vacuities are still empty! – especially the material and domiciliary ones. Don't bother about the 'inside' ones: Kundalini:[1] believe me, that is *change of life*. It is just change of life. William Archer told a friend *how* he suffered, just the same way.[2] But you patiently put up with it, and you come through to something else, another, freer self. We have been too repressed and too 'spiritual' all our lives: and too much insisted on the sympathetic flow, without a balance of the combative. Now the hour-glass turns over.

I forgot to tell you that forwarded from Cimbrone came a cablegram from Mabel and Brett urging us all to go to Taos. There is a house for all of us, quite independent, and lots of room. You would have a studio – maybe even two. Mabel wouldn't want rent – or only a small sum, if you decided to stay on. There are horses to ride. And the country is *most* beautiful. I think, if you decided to go, you would like to stay at least a year. And I suppose we'd come too. But our difficulty is that Frieda wont go near Brett[3] again,[4] and is doubtful of Mabel. All very tiresome. – As for the Italian Countryside, God knows. I'm not sure that one couldn't live anywhere, if one just settled down to it. *Don't* take too much notice of your moods. Don't pay too much attention to your vacuities – they'll pass. It's a physiological state; grin and abide and wait till you're through. It doesn't much matter where you live – within reason.

[1] A Hindu term used in yoga meaning the libido; it is represented by a coiled serpent, the symbol of latent energy.
[2] William Archer (1856–1924), influential dramatic critic and advocate of the 'New Drama' of Ibsen *et al.*   [3] Brett] Mabel
[4] Her 'implacable intention' was declared in February 1926: see *Letters*, v. 390.

I'm supposed to be going to London at the end of this week, for at least a month. They are producing *David* on May 22 and 23. I've promised to go. But my Kundalini are behaving badly about it. I'm afraid they'll refuse to make the move. There is something very antipathetic to me about going to London, and especially in fuddling with theatrical people over that play. Even *David* itself is quite out of my mood at present – I feel I don't want to see it or hear it or even think about it. – We've got a revolt of the angels going on inside us: or of the devils. I don't care. If my Kundalini revolt, let 'em. I am prepared for anything. If the leopard can't change his spots, perhaps I can mine.

Frieda's daughter goes back this afternoon: so of course it's raining for the first time since she has been here. And we'll be going down with Pietro in the barrocino.[1]

You heard the catastrophe of Harwood's ribbons: just stolen from me. Really, it must be about the bottom of the wheel of fortune, with the Brewster family. Wheel is bound to make the upward turn now. – I'm ordering you the song-book with 'Widdicombe Fair' in it –

Tom Pearce, Tom Pearce, lend me your gray mare.[2]

I'll buy the ribbons over again.

I wrote a story of the Resurrection, where Jesus gets up and feels very sick about everything, and can't stand the old crowd any more – so cuts out – and as he heals up, he begins to find what an astonishing place the phenomenal world is, far more marvellous than any salvation or heaven – and thanks his stars he needn't have a 'mission' any more. It's called *The Escaped Cock*, from that toy in Volterra. Do you remember?

I'll see if I'm up to Mrs R[hys]-D[avids] and daughter.[3]

We've been lent Weege's book on the tombs – all the illustrations – very interesting indeed.[4] – I got photographs too from Alinari – and on the one from the Tomba dei Tori, the two little improper bits, 'un poco pornographico,' as brave as life. Amusing!

DHL

---

[1] Pietro Pini was the half-brother of the Lawrences' servant, Giulia (see p. 75 n. 3); a young farmer he modelled for DHL, probably for his picture *Contadini*. 'Barrocino' is a small cart.

[2] Achsah Brewster recalled DHL's delight in singing folk-songs including 'Widdicombe Fair' (Brewster 276) ['Tom Pearse, . . .'].

[3] Dr Caroline A. F. Rhys Davids, Lecturer at the London University School of Oriental Studies (*fl.* 1919–33). Her special subjects were Buddhist History and Literature; she had written an introductory note for Brewster's *Life of Gotama the Buddha* (1926).

[4] Fritz Weege, *Etruskische Malerei* (Halle, 1920).

4010. To Emily King, [4 May 1927]
Text: MS Needham; PC v. Corneto Tarquinia – Cattedrale; Postmark, Scandicci 5.5.27.;
Unpublished.

> [Villa Mirenda, Scandicci, Florence]
> *Wed.*

Now I've got a cold on my chest, as usual, after the broiling heat. I shant risk
travelling till it's better – too many people ill. – Barby left yesterday. How are
you all?

> DHL

4011. To S. S. Koteliansky, [5 May 1927]
Text: MS BL; PC v. Jewelled brooches from Kent, of Jutish type: Faversham; Postmark,
Scandicci 5.5.27.; cited in Gransden 31.

> [Villa Mirenda, Scandicci, Florence]
> 5 May

Have got a cold on my chest, as usual – shan't risk travelling till it feels better –
so heaven knows when I'll be in London. I'll write again.

> DHL

4012. To Martin Secker, [5 May 1927]
Text: MS UInd; PC v. Gold jewellery with garnets, 7th century; Postmark, Scandicci 5.5.27.;
Unpublished.

> [Villa Mirenda, Scandicci, Florence]
> *5 May*

I don't know when I shall get to London – chest gone groggy again, not bad,
but I shan't risk travelling. Will let you know. – Barby left Tuesday and took
the marionettes!

> DHL

4013. To Nancy Pearn, 5 May 1927
Text: MS UT; Unpublished.

> Villa Mirenda, *Scandicci*, Firenze.
> 5 May 1927

Dear Miss Pearn

I am sending you this mail a story: *The Escaped Cock.* You'll find it a tough
one to place. But there's no sea without storms.

Will you send me the 'Lovely Lady' story, and I'll do what I can to it.

I ought really to come to England now for that *David* play: but have got a

cold, bronchial as usual, and daren't travel. Must see next week. But doubt if
I'll risk it.

Yrs   D. H. Lawrence

I suppose you got the three little sketches: 'Flowery Tuscany'.[1]

4014. To Nancy Pearn, 6 May 1927
Text: MS UT; Unpublished.

Villa Mirenda, Scandicci, Firenze
6 May 1927

Dear Miss Pearn

I always forgot about the Ghost – I never did see one – and I couldn't
promise to pretend to one.[2] But if the feeling came over me, I would.

Could you possibly get a copy of 'The Nightingale' – that little article
which you sold to somebody[3] – and could you send it to

Frau Dr. Anton Kippenberg, Insel Verlag, Kurzestrasse, Leipsig,
Germany.

They want to print it in translation in the *Insel-Almanach*.[4]

Am still feeling meagre, and a bit worried because I *ought* to come to
England for *David*. But probably they're better without me.

Yrs   D. H. Lawrence

I corrected *Dial* proofs of 'The Man Who Loved Islands'. Did you plant it
on the *Mercury*?[5]

I did a review of Koteliansky's translation of the Russian *Rozanov*, which
Wishart is bringing out. I sent it to K. to see if he liked it – he's evidently
showing it to *The Nation*. But probably it will come on to you. Anyhow you'll
arrange for it: It might go to America. I don't mind if they leave any bit out,
that they want to.

---

[1] The three essays appeared in *New Criterion*, vi (October–December 1927), 305–10, 403–8,
516–22 (Roberts C159, C161, C164). Nancy Pearn was specially fond of these essays: 'my
treasured "Flowery Tuscany" sketches' (letter to DHL, 27 July 1927, TMSC UT). A fourth
'Flowery Tuscany' essay was first published in *Phoenix* as 'Germans and Latins'.
[2] On 8 April 1927 (TMSC UT) Nancy Pearn asked DHL whether he had ever seen a ghost; if he
had and was prepared to write c. 1,200 words about it, the *Weekly Dispatch* would welcome his
contribution to a series (which would include a piece by David Garnett).
[3] 'The Nightingale' was printed by *Forum* and by the *Spectator* in September 1927 (Roberts
C158).
[4] Dr Anton Kippenberg (1874–1950) was head of Insel-Verlag, Leipzig, the publishing house
which produced German translations of five works by DHL in his lifetime (see Roberts D73,
D75–8). 'Die Nachtigall', trans. Karl Lerbs, was published in *Insel-Almanach auf das Jahr
1928* (Leipzig, 1927), pp. 92–100.   [5] See p. 46 n. 5.

4015. To Baroness Anna von Richthofen, [7 May 1927]
Text: MS Jeffrey; PC v. [Anglo-Saxon Lancaster Cross in the British Museum, with inscription meaning 'Pray for Cunibald Cuthbert']; Postmark, Sca[ndicci] 7 5. 27; Unpublished.

[Villa Mirenda, Scandicci, Florence]
7 Mai Samstag

Heute kam der Schein zu sagen, die Noten liegen dort in Florenz – wir schicken den Pietro, um sie zu holen, Montag. Die Frieda glücklich – das Wetter sehr heiss, sehr schwül – es soll ein Gewitter kommen. Deinen Brief und die Karte haben wir heute auch
– Grüsse die Annie und leb wohl!

DHL

[*7 May* Saturday

Today the receipt came to say, the notes are lying there in Florence[1] – we're sending Pietro to collect them, Monday. Frieda happy – the weather very hot, very close – there should be a thunder-storm coming. Today we also had your letter and the card
– Greet Annie and farewell!

DHL]

4016. To Jonathan Cape, 9 May 1927
Text: MS ColU; Delany, *DHL Review*, ii. 205–6.

Villa Mirenda, *Scandicci* (Florence)
9 May 1927

Dear Jonathan Cape

I sent the Introduction to *Mastro-don Gesualdo* to Curtis Brown – let me know if there's anything you'd like altered.[2] If you think there should be a few more *facts*, you could get them from the old introduction, or from the introd. to *Little Novels of Sicily*. – If *Mastro-don* sells in the *Travellers' Library*, I might finish *Cavalleria Rusticana* for you.[3] I did half the translation a year or two ago.

---

[1] The reference is obscure.   [2] See Letter 3998 and p. 40 n. 2.
[3] DHL's translation of Verga's *Little Novels of Sicily* was published in New York by Seltzer, in England by Blackwell, in 1925. Cape published *Cavalleria Rusticana and Other Stories* in 1928 (in *Travellers' Library*, 1932). DHL's work on this volume went back, in some cases at least, to 1923 (see *Letters*, iv. 447).

Dorothy Richardson says I *must* read *The Time of Man* – by G. M. Roberts.[1] Will you please send me a copy.

> Yours Sincerely   D. H. Lawrence

4017. To Nancy Pearn, 12 May 1927
Text: MS UT; Unpublished.

> Villa Mirenda, *Scandicci*, Florence
> 12 May 1927

Dear Miss Pearn

I am sending by this mail the MS. of a shorter version of 'The Lovely Lady'. I think it is absurd to object to the rain pipe.[2]

There is also a review on *The Peep Show* for *The Calendar*, who asked me for something. Will you give it to Rickwood – he needn't use it if he doesn't want to.[3]

And will you please give the Cape agreement to Mr Pollinger.

I've not seen a ghost yet.

> D. H. Lawrence

4018. To Hon. Dorothy Brett, 13 May 1927
Text: MS UCin; Postmark, Scandicci 14 5 27; Moore 976–8.

> Villa Mirenda, *Scandicci*, Florence
> 13 May 1927

Dear Brett,

I'm sorry you mind so much our not coming this year to New Mex. But surely you have a very good time out there: probably much better than if you had us there – and more of the inevitable friction. And you must allow me to choose my own life, even to manage my own 'inertia.' Anyhow it's nonsense to talk of 'shaking anybody till their ears rattle', when you know you'll do no such thing. For many reasons I would really like to be at the ranch. But – there you are, there's always a but, and till it shifts, what's the good! There are things in life which neither you nor Mabel take into count, which yet are very

[1] DHL had known the novelist Dorothy Miller Richardson (1873–1957) – Mrs Alan Odle – since 1918 (*Letters*, iii. 244, 255). They met again in September 1926 (Nehls, iii. 103). The novel recommended to DHL was about rural life in Kentucky by Elizabeth Madox Roberts (1886–1941), published in England by Cape in February 1927.

[2] See p. 29 n. 2; see also Brian Finney, 'A Newly Discovered Text of D. H. Lawrence's "The Lovely Lady"', *Yale University Library Gazette*, xlix (1975), 245–52.

[3] DHL's review of Walter Wilkinson's *Peep Show* was printed in *Calendar*, iv (July 1927), 157–61. Edgell Rickwood (1898–1982) was the founder and editor of the journal; see *Letters*, v. 601 n. 2.

important to other people. Try to get that into your head, and *don't* want to live other people's lives for them.

Wouldn't you really rather stay down with Mabel this summer? It is much cheaper for you, and much easier, and much more comfortable. Why struggle with the ranch, anyway? – Unless you'd really like to buy it. Would you? I guess Frieda would sell it to you. You ask her.

It's a shame about the little racing mare – even about Poppy.[1] That *is* the drawback to Italian life – the lack of physical freedom. I'm getting a bit sick of that. But what's to be done? There are so many threads in the twist of one life, and some of them must run short.

To tell the truth, I'm not sure what I shall do. I've taken this house for another year – but it is cheap – and I'm sure we shan't stay put much longer, in this country. A move is coming – but I'm not quite sure where to. Anyhow I'm getting fed up with the certain unfreedom of Italy. Probably we shall go to Bavaria for the summer – and in the autumn decide on a longer remove.

I hear via Kot that Murry's wife has consumption, and the family is moving to Italy. The *Adelphi* finishes in June – at last.[2] But J[ohn] M[iddleton] plaintively asks subscribers for 10/- each, and then he'll issue a little mag., written *all* by himself, and published perhaps six times a year. He *can't* dry up.

David is being played on the 23rd – and I'm hesitating about going. I may set off tomorrow. But London repels rather than attracts me. I feel much more like moving away towards the far ends of the earth, than towards the world's metropolis.

I am trying to get snaps of the pictures – if they come out possible, I'll send them. I'm glad you are such a success: a real furore, I hear.

But whatever else you do, *don't* try to live my life for me. I'll do it myself. Surely you have your hands full, living your own.

I wrote Earl and Achsah again about their coming to Taos. But they wont face America.

Yrs   DHL

4019. To Earl Brewster, 13 May 1927
Text: MS UT; Brewster 129–30.

Villa Mirenda, *Scandicci* (Firenze)
13 May 1927

Dear Earl

Well how is it with you? I've been malarial and down in the mouth for about

---

[1] 'A big sorrel mare' (Brett, *Lawrence and Brett*, p. 46); DHL described it as 'his' (*Letters*, v. 59).
[2] See Letter 4005 and n. 1.

ten days, feeling as if I'd never rouse up again. O vita! O mors! I've put off going to London, in spite of a guilty Conscience and lamenting letters – but I really wasn't fit. And like you, I've had a spell of loathing the Italian countryside altogether, and feeling that Italy is no place for a *man* to live in. I nearly decided to go off to Bavaria. But it all costs so much – and I think the discontent is inside me, and I'd better abide and wait a bit. But O miserere! – I've taken the house at least for six months more. And one had better save up one's resources, for if one really wants to make a long move later. No use fidgetting. – I heard from a woman just passing from Egypt, she thought *Cyprus* such a good place – big, beautiful, and still cheap, and hardly touristed: and more or less under British guardianship, so one needn't be murdered or robbed. Il y a toujours le Chypre.[1]

I didn't see Mrs Rhys Davids. I feel I never want to see an unattached woman any more while I live: specially an elderly one. Christine Hughes now looms – with Mary C[hristine]. But I feel Florence won't hold 'em long. If only one felt tough and snorting like a war-horse. But I'm absolutely a fading lily: I can't hold up to the blast of their *will*.

We've had a week's rain, but now it's sunny. The country really is the most flowery I've ever known, and I get a certain consolation out of that. I found a very fine rare white orchid today, and a dark purple and yellow wild gladiolus, unknown to me.

What are you doing? Are you going to the fifty-a-month house on the Grande Marina? Lucky the price is fixed in dollars! How dear everything is! – And no word of Cimbrone? You are just as well out of it: if only you were in something else. – I'm going to try and sit still till July. I did paint a bit of my *Resurrection* picture[2] – un poco triste, ma mi pare forte. I got him as impersonal as a queer animal! But I can't finish it. Non ho la voglia – I've no will and no guts for anything: feel so unlike myself: lo spettro di me stesso! Time we all did a bit of resurrecting: siamo mezzo sepolti! Chissà, come va finire?[3] – If ever you open your trunks, send me some photographs for postures: I get stuck.

I've not been into Florence for ages – but I ordered you the songs. How is Achsah? Hope all's well.

                                                                           DHL

Brett in a fury that we won't go to Taos. Very tempting, that kind of female rage! The lure of it!

[1] 'There is always Cyprus.'   [2] See *The Paintings of D. H. Lawrence* (1929), plate [1].
[3] 'a bit sad, but it seems powerful to me . . . the ghost of myself . . . we are half buried! Who knows how it will turn out?'

4020. To Harwood Brewster, 15 May 1927
Text: MS Picard; Brewster 130–1.

Villa Mirenda, *Scandicci*, Firenze
15 May 1927

My dear Harwood

Here are a few ribbons – your Aunt Frieda got them yesterday in Florence – not the same as the bunch I bought myself for you – but who knows what villains or villainesses are bedizened up with them now, those others. If these aren't quite what you want for your hair, you can tie up charming bouquets with them to present to your mother's elderly-lady-guests. Otherwise there is always dear, dumb, smiling Rose to embellish, who never says a word, thank God.[1]

I am wondering what is happening to you. You've been a full month in that hotel: at least your parents have. Heavens, what waifs and strays! I suppose you'll land in another 'beautiful pretentious villa.' It's become a habit.

Have you begun bathing? It's rather cold here, after the thunder storms, that is, compared to the heat before. But I feel better when it's fresco. The garden is full of roses, and the poderi full of peas and beans and carciofi,[2] which is all to the good: really a happy vegetarian moment.

Well, I hope things are happening nicely for you all. Be an angel, and hold your chin up.

lo zio[3]   *David*

4021. To Mabel Dodge Luhan, 16 May 1927
Text: MS Brill; Luhan 327–9.

Villa Mirenda, *Scandicci*, Florence
16 May 1927

Dear Mabel

I have again shirked going to London, to *David* – I had a cold, and then I simply can't face mixing up with a lot of town people. – But I shall never go to Fontainebleau to see Gourdjieff – don't ask me.[4] He's not interesting to me, and a good deal of a charlatan. Make that little visit yourself – you'll never rest easy in your mind till you've done it.

I read the Jung things – many thanks – but I'm sort of tired of so many

---

[1] In Brewster 131, Rose is identified as a doll.   [2] 'artichokes'.   [3] 'uncle'.
[4] Georgei Ivanovitch Gurdjieff (1874?–1949) claimed to be the master of occult knowledge. Mabel Luhan had asked DHL on previous occasions whether she should visit the 'Institute for the Harmonious Development of Man' which Gurdjieff had founded at Fontainebleau (and where Katherine Mansfield died in 1923). DHL's contempt for it was vigorously expressed: see *Letters*, iv. 555.

words.[1] One changes – changes inside oneself – and then old interests die out. One has to change and accept it – and one's mentality becomes different along with the rest. I think men have perhaps a greater 'change of life' in the psyche, even than women. At least it seems happening so in myself. It's often unpleasant, but the only thing is to let it go on and accept the differences and let go the old.

That's really why it's no good coming to America at present. One is in a state of flux, and decided movements are no good. I wish I could have the space and openness of New Mexico, and a horse, and all that. But my real inside doesn't turn towards America, and so there it is.

I wonder if you have the books yet.[2] We haven't yet got the bill for the shipping as far as New Orleans. That is to be paid in Florence, and you have only to pay the railroad charge. Orioli has £10 – sterling – of your money, from sale of a few Henry James 1st edition American. He'll pay you the freightage with that, and if there's anything over, I'll send it you. And I burnt that little 5 dollar cheque of yours – the few books I had can stand over against that.

It's been a very lovely spring – the tulips were beautiful – now the pale mauve iris are just past their best, the rose gladiolus is in the wheat, and it is summer; sitting out all day under the trees on the grass. It is quite lovely really. Only I do wish there was a moor or a desert, and a horse. I think we shall stay on till mid-July, then probably go to Bavaria, the Isarthal, near Munich. I love that country. And in the late autumn we *may* go to Egypt. – I wrote to Brett telling her there was no need to go to the ranch, but to stay with you. She will do as she pleases, however. She writes furiously about my 'inertia' and the 'danger' of living 'in this hole.' But I wish she'd leave me to arrange my own life. She surely has enough to occupy her, with her own affairs! Anyhow it's useless for her to bother with mine.

We are expecting Christine Hughes in Florence, more or less on her way back to Santa Fe. I think she'll be glad to be back. Is Spud with you yet? He'll be glad of New Mexico too. But if one is a born American, it is different.

About starting a new vol. of your memoirs, God knows.[3] Perhaps you are too near to your American experiences, after Florence, to wish to put them down on paper. Probably you don't yet wish yourself to tell the truth about them. But when you have Spud back, you'll know better how you feel about it. I believe he is a good 'medium' for your work. Though summer is a bad time

---

[1] Carl Gustav Jung (1875–1961), the eminent psychologist. DHL had already indicated his lack of enthusiasm for Jung's theories: see *Letters*, v. 540.   [2] See Letter 3995 and p. 37 n. 3.
[3] DHL had frequently given advice about the writing of Mabel Luhan's *Intimate Memories*: see *Letters*, v. 423, 457, 510, etc.

to begin. Summer is for holidaying, in autumn one can begin to work. But don't try to do it if your inside holds back from it. It is far, far better to do nothing than to try to force an inspiration. That only messes up the whole impulse.

I'm glad you've got a snow-white palfrey, like the maid in the *Faerie Queene* – 'yet she much whiter'.[1] Dio buono, what a premium on whiteness.

The new vegetables, peas, asparagus, beans, potatoes, are in full swing – how good they are. And the garden is full of red roses.

I hope you're having a good time. It'll be June by the time you get this. Frieda sends 'tante cose.' Remember me to everybody.

D. H. Lawrence

Orioli sent you the *Portraits of M[abel] D[odge]* and the other book.[2]

4022. To Emily King, 19 May 1927
Text: MS Lazarus; Unpublished.

Villa Mirenda, Scandicci (Firenze).
19 May 1927

My dear Pamela,

I had your letter the other day. Really you have no luck with dogs. Never have another while you live in town. In the country it is possible: in town, impossible.

I hope Sam will leave the shop, nevertheless. I believe he could find something much better, and more congenial, in a smaller place, and among a real decent working class. If you have to leave your little house and garden, well, you'll find something else, and a change will do you good. I don't think that towny-suburban sort of life, with neighbours, is much use. It's too artificial.

I was disappointed not to get to the play. But on top of my cold came malaria, owing to the steaming hot damp weather that suddenly appeared – and I felt a wash-out. I wish to heaven I could really get to feel myself again. Since that whack in Mexico two years ago, I've never been right, and never felt nearly myself. Between malaria and continual bronchial trouble, I'm a misery to myself. I wish I could sort of get over it, and feel a bit solid again. – But one dreads long railway journeys, when one isn't feeling up to the mark.

It's already summer here – hot all the time. The garden is full of red roses –

---

[1] Edmund Spenser, *The Faerie Queene*, I. i. 4 (Una rode 'Upon a lowly Asse more white than snow,/Yet she much whiter').

[2] Gertrude Stein (1874–1946) wrote *Portrait of Mabel Dodge*; Mabel had copies bound for her friends. The 'other book' may have been by Robert de la Condamine (see p. 223 n. 3 and also *Letters*, v. 642 and n. 2).

so red – and the clumps of pale mauve irises are just passing, under the olives. They grow wild, in lovely sheaves. This is a most flowery country. The peasants are busy among the peas – it's one of their biggest crops, and now they're in full swing. They bring in them all the time to us, till I get stiff with peas. The broad-beans are good too; everything here has to be eaten very young. The new potatoes will stay new for about a fortnight more, then they'll begin to be hardish. We've been having them for about a fortnight – and asparagus and the real artichokes – big thistle-buds, they really are. The cherries are nearly ripe – we shall be eating them next week, I hope. They are splendid, big and juicy.

The Lira has risen in value lately. We always got 120 to £1. – now it's only 88 or 90. And with prices unchanged, it makes everything very dear: butter 2/6, meat 1/6 to 1/9 a lb – and so on – sugar about 8½d lb. The tourists, of course, have practically stopped coming. But I heard from Enid Hopkin, from Dieppe, that she and her husband might turn up.[1] They're having their holiday. But they'd better stay in France, where things are half the price of Italy.

However, I suppose we shall sit still, in the summer heat, and I'll try and get myself a bit in order.

It is amazing about Gertie. The very thought of it makes me ill – I know I should be dead several times over. But there, life is queer and tenacious, and she may live for years, now.

Our friends have all gone back to London, and it's much quieter. But of course we can always go and see people when we feel like it – The young Sitwells – that is, Edith and Osbert, not very young – are here, and want to come out to us.[2] But I haven't arranged it yet.

Tell me what Sam will do. – My love to you all.

DHL

4023. To Achsah Brewster, 19 May 1927
Text: MS UT; Brewster 131–3.

Villa Mirenda, *Scandicci*, Firenze
19 Maggio 1927

Dear Achsah

We went to Florence today – found your letter when we came home – pity I don't remember my own words of wisdom – I might extract a bit of comfort

---

[1] Enid Hilton, née Hopkin (b. 1896), daughter of DHL's Eastwood friends Willie and Sallie Hopkin (see *Letters*, i. 176). m. 1921?, Laurence Hilton.

[2] (Dame) Edith Sitwell (1887–1964), poet and critic, and (Sir) Osbert Sitwell (1892–1969), poet, essayist and critic. They would be staying at the family's Italian seat, Castello di Montegufoni, near Florence (see *Letters*, v. 468 n. 3) which the Lawrences visited in June 1926 (ibid., p. 474).

out of them, as one used as a child to extract out of those round little white pebbles we called 'milk stones', and sucked in the firm faith that one sucked milk out of them. Did you do that? To me they always tasted of rich lush milk! mere stones!

I remembered with a rush in Florence your request about a *large* amethyst set in pearls – so enquired at a good shop – very nice big one, in seed pearls L800.00 – and 10% discount – one would get it for 650 no doubt. A smaller, same style, L625 – one would get it 500 – both very nice. Another, very nice indeed, big, set in platinised-silver filigree with an odd pearl here and there – L500 – get it for L400. Is that what you wanted to know – or too late? Mi rincresci.[1]

So you're going back to Cimbrone! Beware of the glare of light. And tell Earl to buy a bottle of *Bitter Campari* – (*not* Cordial) – 19 Liras – and take it before meals, in water – very nice, and invaluable for liver in a livery place like Cimbrone.

No news here – rather hot – and Florence one of the most irritable towns on earth – as usual. Everything very expensive, with the exchange at 88 to a pound. We may go to Germany.

Saw – lunched today – Nellie Morrison and the Klapps – or Clapps[2] – Americans – they know you – but to tell you the truth – à la DHL – I can't stand high-browish spiritual upsoaring people any more – make me sick – and Nellie M. and Gino – Oh God – how much nicer the Prince of Wales – Edward – was when he served up a naked Cora Pearl on a huge silver platter, with a lemon in her mouth, as the pearl of fishes.[3] Gino ought to have been served up that way today. Give me coarseness!

I'm feeling better – as you may guess –

They'll do *David* without David H[erbert]. Damn them anyhow.

When do you go to Cimbrone? We may sort of dribble on here till mid July.

If I can do anything further for you in the pearl (not Cora) and amethyst line, let me know. Meanwhile remember me to everybody at Cimbrone, and be sure to thank Rose for my socks, and salute the two nice meek handmaidens from me.

I suppose Harwood got her ribbons at last – poor dear!

DHL

Went to the exhibition of modern Florentines in the Belle Arti. Magnelli

[1] 'I am sorry.'
[2] Nellie Morrison, whom DHL had known since 1921 (*Letters*, iii. 720 and n. 1); she lived in Florence and the Lawrences occupied her flat in August–September 1921. The identity of the Klapps and of Gino is not known.
[3] Cora Pearl (Emma Elizabeth Crouch) (1842–86), notorious courtesan. The Prince (later Edward VII) was not alone in having allegedly served up this dish: see Cyril Pearl, *The Girl with the Swansdown Seat* (1955), p. 149, and the *Dictionary of National Biography*.

looked very feeble. A rather good man – Colocicchi or something like that – such good painting of the banal – a bit like Rousseau le Douanier – and then a funny original Rosai, with a keen sense of ugliness – interesting – the rest piffle, oodles, slop.[1] How feeble the Italians are, in paint – at least those I saw! So old-fashioned and timid and gutsless. How is yours going? I'm stuck!

4024. To Ada Clarke, 19 May 1927
Text: MS Clarke; cited in Lawrence–Gelder 155–7.

Villa Mirenda, *Scandicci*, Firenze
19 May 1927

My dear Sister

I did really want to come to London for *David*. But I got a beastly cold, that everybody had, and then the weather suddenly went damp hot, and that gave me malaria again, and I felt rotten. I'm a good bit better now, but I hate the thought of that journey. The longer I live, the less I like the actual process of travelling – trains especially. So I shan't come to the play – and they can make what mess of it they like: though I believe they're doing their best.

It keeps pretty hot here – summer has come earlier this year. But there's a great feel of thunder and electricity all the time. The flowers are very fine, the garden is all red roses, the honeysuckle is in masses, and the broom all yellow in the woods. But it is summer, when one doesn't do much but lounge around and go for little walks in the evening or morning.

Milly Beveridge and Mabel Harrison left a week ago – I think they rather wish they hadn't. They liked it very much here. I heard from Enid Hopkin in Dieppe, that she and her rather nondescript husband may get as far as Florence – they are taking their holiday now. We can give them meals and picnics. But they're rather rash to come to Italy, with the exchange down to ninety and lower, and prices very high. Altogether Italy is much dearer now than England – butter 2/6, common jam 1/6 lb, and so on. – There are very few tourists, in consequence – and linen and fancy things coming down in price. – What would you like for your birthday – a bag – or linen – or what? You know the kind of things Florence has. Would you like two or three silver-top corks, with a lion on, or other figure? Tell me.

It is perfectly amazing about Gertie. Of course the thought of all those operations frightens me so much, I daren't think of her. I know I should die

---

[1] Alberto Magnelli (1888–1971) worked in Florence 1915–32; DHL had seen his paintings before: see *Letters*, v. 627 and n. 1. Giovanni Colacicchi (1900–   ), portrait and landscape artist who subsequently became director of the Accademia di Belle Arti in Florence. Rousseau le Douanier (1844–1910), French painter, the most celebrated among modern primitives. Ottone Rosai (1895–1957) best known for his presentation of working-class Florence.

six times over. – I wish really I felt more solid. When one turns forty, it seems
as if one's old ailments attack one with a double fury – I never seem to get
really free. And then one gets sort of disillusioned. I feel like turning hermit,
and hiding away the rest of my days, away from everybody. But I suppose it is
a phase, a sort of psychic change of life many men go through after forty. I
wish it would hurry up and get over, and leave me feeling more or less myself.

Is there anything I can do for Gertie – anything to send her?

I'm glad you're busy in the shop – there's nothing like being occupied in
this disintegrating world.

Pamela apparently doesn't want to leave her little house. Well, people must
do as they wish – it's no use talking.

I hope you're all all right. Love to you all.

DHL

4025. To Gertrude Cooper, 19 May 1927
Text: MS Clarke; cited in Lawrence–Gelder 157–9.

Villa Mirenda, Scandicci, Florence
19 May 1927

My dear Gertie

I haven't written you for so long because I was afraid of all those operations,
and didn't know if you could be bothered with letters. But now Ada says you
are walking about a bit, and going back to Mundesley. How marvellous that is!
At last you are really on the way home, to Ripley and a decent life. It seems a
miracle: and is a miracle: almost a resurrection. You'll be in time for the end of
the spring, and the coming summer – how splendid it will be, to be in the
world again, and able to appreciate it all. Men and Nature work wonders
between them – and the will-to-live is a miracle in itself. I shall be so glad to
know you are back in Mundesley – the first stage of home – strolling in the
grounds and seeing the flowers come out. We have thought so much about you
– and felt pretty bad about it all. I dream so often of Frances.[1] I dreamed even
last night she was setting off for school with her hair done on top of her head,
as jaunty as could be. And today I heard from Ada you were walking about a
bit.

Has she told you that Jackie has got mumps, and Bertie a cold on his chest?[2]
That's a bother. But it's a bad time for sickness, here too. The old people are
popping off, and those who are well are having chest colds and abdominal

---

[1] Frances ('Frankie') Amelia Cooper (1884–1918), Gertrude's sister, died of tuberculosis in
1918 (see *Letters*, i. 34; iii. 307 and n. 4).

[2] John ('Jack', 'Jackie') Lawrence Clarke (1915–42) and William Herbert ('Bertie') Clarke (b.
1923), Ada's sons.

colds. It's the queer, hot, fierce weather come too suddenly. – I expect the children at Ripley will be all right in a week or so. How nice when you're there again to look after them a bit – when you're better!

I wanted to come to London for my play – then I got a bad cold and a whack of malaria, and felt as miserable as a wet hen. But now, thank goodness, I'm feeling better. We went to Florence today, and it was so hot! amazing! It's full blazing summer here – some of the hay is already cut and cocked up – the garden fairly blazes with red roses – they smell so sweet – and the fireflies go winking round under the olives and among the flowers, at night, like lost souls – and by the pools, the toads croak and bark like dogs, really big dogs. It's really summer – peas and beans and asparagus in full swing, strawberries ripe, and the very first cherries. It's hard to believe it's only the middle of May. – There are no gooseberries in Italy – and I like them so much.

I heard from Enid Hopkin. She was in Dieppe, with her rather ineffectual husband, and she said they might come to Florence and look us up. I'm surprised if they do, Italy is now so expensive, with the exchange gone up. It will cost them more than England – and *far* more than France. – Enid said the 'baby' rumour was because Betty – Willy's new wife – made herself a *cloak*.[1] Anyhow thank God it's not true. No more little Willies, little Enids either!

Write to me when you are well enough, and tell me your news. I hope I shall see you some time this summer. Heavens, what a year it's been! Never mind, so long as it comes out well.

Frieda sends her love, and will write soon.

Love from me!   DHL

4026. To Richard Aldington, 24 May 1927
Text: MS SIU; Moore 978–9.

Villa Mirenda, Scandicci, Firenze
24 Maggio 1927

My dear Richard

Many thanks for your *Indiscretion*.[2] No need to be in any trepidation on my account – you hand me out plenty of bouquets, as you say: I shall save up the ribbons. But caro, you are so funny. Why do you write on the one hand as if you were my grandmother – about sixty years older than me, and forced rather to apologise for the *enfant terrible* in the family? Why will you be so old and responsible. Sei un giovanotto un po' crudo, sai![3] – And on the other

---

[1] After the death of his wife Sallie (in 1923), Willie Hopkin had married Olive Lizzie Slack (in 1925). The rumour that she was pregnant may have originated with Ada (*Letters*, v. 643).
[2] See Letter 4001 and p. 44 n. 1.   [3] 'You are rather a rough young man, you know!'

hand, why do you write as if you were on hot bricks? Is the game worth the candle, or isn't it? Make up your mind. I mean the whole game of life and literature – not merely my worthy self. You don't believe it's worth it, anyhow. Well then, don't worry any more, be good and commercial. But don't, don't feel yourself one of the pillars of society. My dear chap, *where* did you get all this conscience of yours? You haven't got it, really. Et iteratum est ab omnibus: ubi est ille Ricardus?[1] – I never knew a man who seemed more to me to be living from a character not his own, than you. What *is* it that you are afraid of? – *ultimately?* – is it death? or pain? or just fear of the negative infinite of all things? What ails thee, lad?

We had Osbert and Edith Sitwell to tea yesterday. They were very nice, and we liked them much better than we had thought.[2] But he the same makes me feel sort of upset and worried. Of him the same I want to ask: But what ails thee, then? Tha's got nowt amiss as much as a' that! –

It's summer here, and all the cistus, white ones and pink, wide out in the wood – and fireflies at night, the uncertain sparky sort. It's been a marvellous year for flowers, and promises well for everything. We are in the thick of good fat asparagus, and peas, and beans, and carciofi: and the peasants brought us a basket of the first cherries on Saturday. So quickly the time goes by! – But I'm sorry if you wont reap the fruits of Arabella's garden, nice and sevenfold.

There's not much sign of reduction of prices yet – except bread. And on Saturday the controller said butter must go down from 25 to 15 Liras. So the shop people wouldn't sell any – only *sub rosa*, to our peasant, for 20. O Italia! Pour moi, je m'en fiche![3]

It is very nice and peaceful – one can be out of doors – and take a siesta in the afternoon. La vita non si ferma mai.[4] – The peasants are making hay. – They are doing a translation of *Sons and Lovers* in Spanish – I mean a Barcelona firm.[5] – I shan't publish my novel this year, anyhow. – Qui non si frega! – I saw that written on a gate. 'Here we don't give a damn!' I suppose we shan't come to England – go to Bavaria perhaps, end of July. And you, what will you do? – Don't read my books – really! It only interrupts the peculiar rhythm you make for yourself.

Love from both to both   DHL

[1] 'And everyone repeated: where is that Richard?'
[2] For Sir Osbert Sitwell's account of the 'two extremely delightful hours' they spent with the Lawrences, see Nehls, iii. 142–3.   [3] 'As far as I'm concerned, I don't care a rap!'
[4] 'Life never stops.'
[5] Presumably it was never published; the first known Spanish translation appeared in 1933 (Roberts D217).

4027. To S. S. Koteliansky, 27 May 1927
Text: MS BL; Postmark, Firenze 27.V 1927; Moore 979–80.

Villa Mirenda, *Scandicci*, Florence

27 May 1927

My dear Kot

    Your letter today – I was very glad to hear about *David* from you.[1] It seems to me just as well I wasn't there – you can't make a silk purse out of a sow's ear. But if ever the thing is regularly produced, I'll come and see what I can do: though I doubt if it would be much. Actors haven't enough *inside* to them. Anyhow I have a fairly good idea, from what you say, of what it was like.

    I too am sick of these bronchial colds, mixed with malaria. I've never been

---

[1] *David* was presented at the Regent Theatre, London, 22–3 May 1927. Kot's letter, 23 May, (MS BL) is in an envelope marked: 'Given by Lawrence to Miss Millicent Beveridge'. The (incomplete) MS reads as follows:

My Dear Lawrence,

    The Dobrées having sent us (Gertler and myself) their tickets, we went to see 'David' produced last night. My impression is that the play was a success. The producer at the end of the performance thanked the public for the enthusiastic reception of the play, and expressed regret that through indisposition you had been prevented from being present at the performance.

    I believe that with a few alterations the play could be a very great success. The production is not bad, nor is the setting; but a bit more study and care could have made it extremely good. It was done on the rather too familiar and common notions of Jewish types, than on a proper study of the ancient Jewish type. A stricter historical treatment would have helped considerably to the understanding of the whole play and of the chief characters. The chief fault was in the fact that Saul (by Peter Creswell – I don't know who that actor is) acted very badly; that he misunderstood your Saul completely, and made of him a rather stagey, very common thing. It is a wonder that his acting did not kill the play. David was not bad, but neither was he good. (Robert Haries) I don't know who the actor is; but I don't think he is English. Judging by his voice, which was not pleasant, and its poor modulations, he is either a Jew or a Welshman. Yet he tried to act 'David' according to your text, but without a real intimate understanding of the character. The best, I think, was Jonathan (Frank Vosper). He not only acted quite well, but he seemed to me to understand and interpret your Jonathan correctly. Michal (Angela Baddeley) acted very, very well. She was your Michal, remarkably well realised. She and Vosper, I believe, saved the play from Saul's bad and cheap acting. Samuel (Harcourt Williams) was not bad; if he acted less the stage Jew prophet, but realised your character, he could have created a splendid part. Yet he did not spoil the play (which Saul definitely did). Then the scene of Samuel and the prophets, which in the hands of a good producer might have been one of the most remarkable scenes of the play, was done badly, – rather like a cheap cinema, than a simple grand scene.

    Of one thing I am perfectly certain that in the hands of a first rate producer, with real good actors of Saul and David, the play could be extremely good. What I say seems to me so obvious that, – if there were present at the performance one or two producers, some good actors and actresses, – someone is bound to produce the play not only for the sake of its artistic value, but because it can be made a great financial success. –

    I think also that the producer ought not to have brought on the stage Goliath's head. It was a bit ridiculous, – this realism of a stuffed thing-head, robbed the poetry of the event; and the head might have lain behind the scenes, just as the fight between Goliath and David was done behind the scenes.

right since I was ill in Mexico two years ago – beastly bronchial trouble, and the germs get it in an instant. But *really*, I am stronger. I think this climate here is a bit sudden and trying, too. In July we'll go to Bavaria, and see what a bit of an altitude will do. I loved Bavaria, before the war.

Osbert and Edith Sitwell came to tea the other day. They were really very nice, not a bit affected or bouncing: only absorbed in themselves and their parents. I never in my life saw such a strong, strange *family* complex: as if they were marooned on a desert island, and nobody in the world but their lost selves. Queer! They've gone back to England now.

It is summer, so I'm not doing much – finishing a *Resurrection* picture – and doing bits of things. Oh, I wish you'd ask Edgell Rickword to ask Dobrée to do a 'Scrutiny' of Bernard Shaw.[1] I've done Galsworthy already – I don't really want to do Shaw: slaying my elders only interests me in spasms. Do ring up Rickword, and say I suggest *Dobrée* for the 'Scrutiny' on Bernard Shaw.

You say they – the Dobrées – will be back in London in June. I'll write to them then. I have lost their Egyptian address.

Is there any further news of Jesus' biographer and better?[2]

I ordered you, and Gertler, a copy of *Mornings in Mexico* – a little book Secker is just bringing out. I am holding back the novel till next year, anyhow.

How is Sonia?

Remember me to everybody.

DHL

4028. To Emily King, [27 May 1927]
Text: MS Needham; PC v. Louis Carmontelle, Le Coureur de St. Cloud; Postmark, Firenze 27. V 1927; Unpublished.

[Villa Mirenda, Scandicci, Florence]
27 May

I had your letter today – am feeling a good deal better – I suppose it is the changeable spring. I heard from London, *David* was pretty well received – haven't seen any notices from the papers yet. I'm sorry I wasn't there. – It will be good for you all to go to Yarmouth. Have you any other plans? – Osbert and Edith Sitwell came to tea on Monday – They were very nice. I suppose you'll be getting my new little book of essays shortly.[3]

Love. DHL

---

[1] DHL had written his 'Scrutiny' on Galsworthy in February 1927 (see *Letters*, v. 649) for a collection, *Scrutinies*, which Rickword published (and Wishart & Co. printed) in March 1928 (Roberts B24). The essay on Shaw was written by the poet Walter James Turner (1889–1946) who had been dramatic critic of the *London Mercury*, 1919–23. Dobrée made no contribution to the book.   [2] I.e. Middleton Murry, author of a *Life of Jesus* (1926).
[3] *Mornings in Mexico.*

4029. To Martin Secker, 27 May 1927
Text: MS UInd; Postmark, Firenze 27 5 27; Secker 88–9.

Villa Mirenda, *Scandicci*, Florence
27 May 1927

Dear Secker

I'm sorry there won't be illustrations in *Mornings* after all. What made you change, at the last moment.[1] – I enclose a list of the people I should like you to send copies to. Send one to M. P. Willcocks for her essay on me – for trade purposes – will you? – You have the address? – Little Down, Sticklepath, *Okehampton*, Devon. Am I right, thinking she is *Miss* – or is she Mr.?[2]

I heard today about *David*. It seems to have been decently well received.

No, I won't publish *Lady Chatterley's Lover* this year – I've decided not to. But perhaps in the spring next year. – When I rouse myself I'll be sending along the MS to be typed.

Osbert Sitwell and Edith came to tea the other day. We liked them both, really – they weren't a bit affected or sidey with us. He says you're swopping one of his books for one of mine, with Duckworth – I suppose, *Sons and Lovers*.[3] – I shall probably be translating *Cavalleria Rusticana* for Jonathan Cape – to go with his *Mastro don Gesualdo* – which he's putting in the Travellers Library.[4] He says he's sold so far 2100 of *Twilight in Italy* – not bad. – I hear from Cape he's going to publish a book about me by some young man – but says he'll send me the MS first.[5]

I've once more had a bronchial cold plus malaria – but am feeling better. It is summer, and lazy weather. I'm finishing a picture of the *Resurrection*, and doing a few trifles: but nothing much. This is not a working season.

Did Faith Mackenzie object to her portrait-sketch in 'Two Blue Birds'? Surely not. Nor he! – I hope he won't mind either 'The Man Who Loved

---

[1] Secker wrote to Pollinger (at Curtis Brown's) on 16 May 1927 (Secker Letter-Book, UIll): 'We have come to the same no-illustration decision regarding [*Mornings in Mexico*] as that already arrived at by Mr Knopf'. As late as March Secker was intending to include 'a few half-tone illustrations'; the change of policy is unexplained.

[2] Mary Patricia Willcocks (1869–), novelist, biographer and translator. Author of *Between the Old World and the New: being Studies in the Literary Personality from Goethe and Balzac to Anatole France and Thomas Hardy* (1925). No essay on DHL by her is known.

[3] For some months Secker had tried to persuade Duckworth to release the four fiction titles Duckworth controlled: *The White Peacock, The Trespasser, Sons and Lovers* and *The Prussian Officer*. Secker wanted to include the first three in his 3/6 edn of DHL's novels. In return he offered to cede to Duckworth his rights in Osbert Sitwell's *Triple Fugue* (1924) and *Discursions on Travel, Art and Life* (1925). On 25 May 1927 (Secker Letter-Book, UIll) Secker chose '"The White Peacock" and "Sons and Lovers" to take the place immediately of the two Sitwell books'; the other two DHL titles would come to Secker 'later in the year'.

[4] See Letter 4016 and n. 3.

[5] The first book published by Cape on DHL was Stephen Potter's *D. H. Lawrence* (1930).

Islands' when it comes in the *London Mercury*.[1] He only *suggests* the idea – it's no portrait.

We shall probably stay on here till mid. or end July – then, I think, to Germany. I doubt if we shall come to England. Ma chi lo sa? –[2]

Italy is very expensive, with the exchange at 89, and most prices just the same. The good meat is still 20 al chilo – butter is supposed to be down to 15, but is really 20, and then a fearful howl. Italy is a tiresome country, really. With the exchange at 89, why don't they put down the letter rate? L1.25 is about 4d a letter.

Many thanks for sending the *Times Lit.* and the *London News* so regularly. I'll put the list of *Mornings* here. Do you know if Knopf is simultaneous?[3]

from both, *tante cose*!   D. H. Lawrence

1.   Mrs L A Clarke.   Gee St.   *Ripley nr. Derby*.
1.   Mrs S. King.   16 Brooklands Rd.   Sneinton Hill, *Nottingham*
1.   Hon Dorothy Brett.   c/o Del Monte Ranch.   *Questa*.   New Mexico, USA.
1.   Mrs Mabel Lujan.   *Taos*.   New Mexico, USA.
1.   E.H.Brewster.   Hotel Capri.   *Capri*   (Napoli)
1.   S. Koteliansky.   5 Acacia Rd.   *St Johns Wood, N.W.8*.
1.   Miss Barbara Low.   13 Guilford St.   *W. C. 1*.
1.   Mark Gertler.   Penn Studio.   Rudall Crescent.   *Hampstead, N.W.3*.
1.   Miss Millicent Beveridge.   20 Rossetti Garden Mansions, *Chelsea*, S.W.3.
1.   Miss Mabel Harrison.   49 Bvd. Montparnasse.   *Paris*

Send me a couple of *Mornings* here, won't you?

4030. To Ada Clarke, [27 May 1927]

Text: MS Clarke; PC v. François Lemoine, Head of a Girl; Postmark, Firenze 27. V 1927; Unpublished.

[Villa Mirenda, Scandicci, Florence]
May 27

I suppose our letters crossed. – So sorry the children aren't well – but hear today from Emily, you are going to Yarmouth – so guess Jack is better, and Bertie. – I'm a good deal better. – I wrote to Gertie to Mundesley. I wasn't

---

[1] 'Two Blue Birds' had been published in April 1927 (*Dial*, lxxxii. 287–301); 'The Man Who Loved Islands' would appear in the *London Mercury* in August 1927 (see p. 46 n. 5). Faith Compton Mackenzie (1888–1960) was not pleased by her 'portrait-sketch'; her husband, the novelist Edward Montague Compton Mackenzie (1883–1972) was highly displeased by what he regarded as a caricature of himself (see Letters 4196 and 4207 and *Letters*, iii. 594 and n. 2). Because of Mackenzie's anger the story was excluded from Secker's edn of *The Woman Who Rode Away* (Roberts A41a).   [2] 'But who knows? –'
[3] Secker's edn appeared in June 1927, Knopf's on 5 August.

sure if she was well enough to be bothered with letters before. They wrote me
from London that *David* was very well received – seems to have been a
success. Now we'll see if anyone will produce it publicly.

Love!   DHL

4031. To Nancy Pearn, 27 May 1927
Text: MS UT; Unpublished.

Villa Mirenda, *Scandicci*, Florence
27 May 1927

Dear Miss Pearn

Here is your programme – glad you liked the play – and wish I'd been
there.[1] Perhaps one day they'll do it on the public stage – then we'll all go!

I am a bit vexed with Secker about those illustrations to *Mornings in
Mexico*. Right up to three weeks ago he said he was putting them in. Not that I
insisted at all, but he seemed to want to. Then suddenly he's off. Bella gente![2]

I'm sending you another story – 'founded on fact' as they say – alas, too
true. But more impossible than the last, to print. So don't bother about it
much, till a chance may turn up. 'Enough of That!' – 'None of That!'[3]

Do you know if Knopf is bringing out *Mornings in Mexico* simultaneously
with Secker, on June 9th?

I'm thinking of translating Giovanni Verga's *Cavalleria Rusticana*, for
Cape. They are stories and sketches. Shall I send them in, one by one, as I
finish? They might go somewhere.

We think of going to Bavaria in July. When do you get your holiday?

Yrs   D. H. Lawrence

4032. To Mary Willcocks, [27 May 1927]
Text: Sotheby & Co. Catalogue, 7–8 December 1959, Item 415, p. 85; Unpublished.

[Villa Mirenda, Scandicci, Florence]
[27 May 1927]

[Lawrence explains his reasons for writing *The Plumed Serpent* and discusses
Mexican Indians (comparing them with the negroes).]

---

[1] Nancy Pearn wrote on 23 May 1927 (TMSC UT) about the performance of *David*: 'I thought,
especially in view of the limited opportunities for rehearsals, that it was tremendously well
done, both from the production and the acting point of view . . . Altogether I think you would
not have been much disappointed.'   [2] 'Fine folk!'
[3] The claim that 'None of That' is 'founded on fact' can be partly sustained. Ethel Cane was
modelled on both Mabel Luhan and Dora Carrington (1893–1932), a painter and friend of
Brett and Gertler, whom DHL had known since 1916 (*Letters*, ii. 508 n. 2). The matador,
Cuesta, is strongly reminiscent of Rodolfo Gaona (1888–1975), a famous Mexican bullfighter.
See Ross Parmenter, *Lawrence in Oaxaca* (Salt Lake City, 1984), pp. 223, 226–7. Nancy Pearn
failed to place the story with a magazine; it was first published in *The Woman Who Rode Away*.

4033. To Lady Cynthia Asquith, 28 May 1927
Text: MS UT; Finney, *Yale University Library Gazette*, xlix. 246–7.

Villa Mirenda, *Scandicci*, Firenze
28 May 1927

Have your note about 'The Lovely Lady'.[1] Unfortunately I haven't a copy of the briefer version – which you now hold; – only of the longer version. And I can't in the least remember the differences between the two. If there's time, ask Miss Pearn if she has a copy of the first version – and then mark any bit you'd like me to put into your final version – and send both along – and I'll run 'em together. If there's not time, I'll try and put the bit in, if you send me your short copy by return. – When must you go to press? – As for proofs, I'm very glad if you correct them.

I wanted to come to England for the 300's *David*, but wasn't well. Now I don't know if I shall come this summer. – I just had three reviews of the play – the production.[2]

Really, those reviewers should be made waitresses in Lyons' Cafés. It's about all they've got the spunk for.

I think we shall go to Bavaria in July – or to America – somewhere.

Hope you're all all right – we're pretty well. Frieda sends love –

tante cose!   D. H. Lawrence

4034. To Earl Brewster, 28 May 1927
Text: MS UT; Brewster 133–5.

Villa Mirenda, *Scandicci* (Firenze)
28 May 1927

Dear Earl

So you lie and muse of Cyprus – with a 'u' in English, unlike Harwoods hunymoon – and of bho-trees and winding lanes, silence and the sea, long conversations, disciples, and success. Caro, it's no good. We shall never go to Cyprus, nor to any other happy isle. You will hover round Capri, and I shall

---

[1] DHL's correspondent was Lady Cynthia Asquith, née Charteris (1887–1960) with whom he had exchanged letters since they met in July 1913 (*Letters*, ii. 41 and n. 4). m. 1910, Herbert Asquith (1881–1947), barrister, poet and novelist. On 'The Lovely Lady' see p. 29 n. 2 and Letter 4017.

  Nancy Pearn (acting for Curtis Brown) was Lady Cynthia's agent as well as DHL's (Nicola Beauman, *Cynthia Asquith*, 1987, p. 289). It appears that she was more sympathetic to DHL whenever 'her' two authors' interests were in conflict: cf. *Letters*, v. 341 n. 2.

[2] He would almost certainly have received *The Times* review, 24 May 1927, which judged the play 'neither drama nor poetry' (for the text see Keith Sagar, *A D. H. Lawrence Handbook*, Manchester, 1982, pp. 296–7). The other two may have been Richard Jennings in *Spectator*, cxxxviii (28 May 1927), 939–40 – 'not necessarily anything dramatic at all' – and by 'Omicron' in *Nation and Athenæum*, xli (28 May 1927), 261–2 – the play is marred by 'tedious Wardour Street diction' and is 'merely pastiche on pastiche'.

go out into the world again, to kick it and stub my toes. It's no good my thinking of retreat: I rouse up, and feel I don't want to. My business is a fight, and I've got to keep it up. I'm reminded of the fact by the impudent reviews of the production of *David*. They say it was just dull. I say they are eunuchs, and have no balls. It is a fight. The same old one. Caro, don't ask me to pray for peace. I don't want it. I want subtly, but tremendously, to kick the backsides of the ball-less. There are so many of them. '*S got no ballocks*! we used to say of the mealy-mouthed, when I was a boy. They must be kicked for it – kicked.

I think, later on, I shall go back to America for a time. That rouses the fight in me. America is a good fighting country – There's no spunk in Europe. Probably even I'll take my pictures to America and show them there. Doesn't that rile you, to think of? Why don't you do the same? – How's your Jew, by the way?[1] Doing anything for you? Heaven helps him who helps himself. Spunk, my boy! and a fight. Probably we'll go to New Mexico next year – one knows the pit-falls and the snares – but one must keep one's pecker up. You've never fought enough. I, perhaps, too much. But avanti uomini! Siamo sempre uomini liberi![2]

I still propose Bavaria in July. I would like mountain air for a time, and to be among a fighting race. One goes a bit soddened in Italy. I believe I could never stay in this country longer than two years on end. Perhaps not in any country. What's the odds! You'd better prepare to come along to America too, later on.

I finished my *Resurrection* picture, and like it. It's Jesus stepping up, rather grey in the face, from the tomb, with his old ma helping him from behind, and Mary Magdalen easing him up towards her bosom in front. Now I must think of a really thrilling subject for a new [picture][3] – have you got any idea?

Achsah didn't mention those Clapps – or Klapps – He looked like a rat, exactly – a large, beady, foraging sharp rat – and she like a weevil. – I've ordered a book with the pictures of the other Indian Cave – forget its name – not Ajanta. The Indian Society is just bringing it out – 2 guineas: but it looked very attractive.[4]

Would you hate to send me a pair of those rope-soled Capri shoes – as strong as possible. If they're easy on you, they fit me. And a pair for Frieda – she takes one size smaller. We can't buy them in Florence, and I like them in summer so much. Let the tradesman post them and send the bill, and I'll send you the money.

au revoir   DHL

---

[1] Unidentified.   [2] 'But forward men! We are always free men!'
[3] MS reads: 'new – have'.
[4] DHL was referring to *The Bagh Caves in the Gwalior State*, text by Sir John Marshall *et al.*, published by the India Society in October 1927. Cf. Letters 4067, 4198.

Neither Anna di Chiara[1] nor Christine Hughes has yet turned up. Tell Mrs di C. to send us a line when she's here!

4035. To Mabel Dodge Luhan, 28 May 1927
Text: MS Brill; Luhan 329–31.

Villa Mirenda, *Scandicci*, Florence
28 May 1927

Dear Mabel

You are about right about that 'change of life' business. It's what ails me, as I said in my other letter. And partly the reason why I lie low here, is to let it happen, and not interfere with it, so it gets through as soon as possible. It's hell while it lasts – but I think I sort of see a glimpse of daylight through the other side. One emerges with a body all right – but a different one, perhaps – not so mentalised.

Anyhow I begin to feel like bursting out again. I doubt if Europe will hold me many more months. And the obvious thing is to come back to New Mexico. But I'd better wait still, to see how many more set-backs I get. It's no good moving till I am sort of sure on my pins. But I'm getting to feel very stuffy and shut in, here in Italy.

Tell Brett not to preach at me about faith and so on. What the hell does she know about anybody else's faith. Let her mind her p's and q's, and not fall off her horse, because that's dangerous. And leave me to manage my own faith – quite another chiquita.[2]

I hear Secker is publishing his *Mornings in Mexico* on July 9th – don't know if Knopf comes out simultaneous. He ought to. But I ordered you both an English copy – and I'll order you another American.

They produced *David* last week. I heard the audience was really rather enthusiastic, but the press notices are very unfavorable. It's those mangy feeble reviewers; they haven't enough spunk to hear a cow bellow. The worst of the youngish Englishman is, he's such a *baby*; one can't imagine his backside isn't swaddled in a napkin: and such a prig, one imagines he must either be a lady in disguise, or a hermaphrodite. – We had Osbert and Edith Sitwell here to tea the other day. They were very nice. He loathed America. But my God, it makes me want to come back there, to get away from these European pap-drivelling little boys. They see *nothing* in America at all: not even the *real* menace: and none of the grim Yankee dauntlessness, which has *not* got its bottom swathed in a napkin. Anything, Anything, anything for a bit of dauntless courage.

---

[1] An American (married to Ferdinando di Chiara) whom DHL met in Capri early in 1920.
[2] '(small) matter'.

Italy is rather down in the mouth and pippy – over the rise of the Lira, the flight of the tourist, the necessity to put down prices and wages. Altogether nobody shows any sign of real spunk, anywhere. It's tiring.

I haven't been able to get my pictures snapped yet. But I've finished the *Resurrection*: also a story on the same theme.[1] I think I'll bring my pictures to New York, and show them. Shall I? Never show them in Europe at all. I've got six big ones and some small. Shall we show them in New York – in autumn or early spring? And then move out to Taos and paint some more? It would be rather fun. I'm just getting into my own style.

You don't owe anything over the books[2] – we'll probably owe you some few dollars, as I said. But the bill for freightage to New Orleans hasn't come yet.

I'm glad Spud is back. After all, what's the world worth! – one can only kick it, when one gets a chance. I'm afraid change of life doesn't change one's feelings much in that respect. One can never make success *in* the world – only against it.

I'm holding my novel back – not even having it typed. Much better if I print only periodical stuff.

Do you ever hear anything of Nina?[3] It will soon be two years since we stayed with her. Wonder what she's like by now.

We expected Christine Hughes through from Rome. But no sign of her so far – dead silence.

We may go to Bavaria in July, for a bit – but I feel I'm coming unstuck from Europe.

Hope all goes well. Remember me to everybody.

DHL

4036. To Else Jaffe, 1 June 1927
Text: MS Jeffrey; Frieda Lawrence 240–2.

Villa Mirenda, *Scandicci* (Florence)
1 June 1927

My dear Else

Could you get me a copy of F. Weege's *Etruskische Malerei* – costs about 20 Mark – at least, in England 20/-. If the bookseller can get me a copy, and send it me here by *registered* post – else they'll steal it – Drucksache,[4] – I shall be very glad, and will send you the money at once, when you let me know how much it was. It is a nice book – very – I saw it at a friend's house – and I should

---

[1] See Letter 3998 and n. 1.   [2] See Letter 3995 and p. 37 n. 3.
[3] Cornelia ('Nina') Rumsey Wilcox (1880–1968), the divorced wife of Lee Witt, was a childhood friend of Mabel Luhan's and known to DHL since 1922 (see *Letters*, iv. 332 and n. 4).
[4] 'Printed matter'.

like to have it. I heard when I was in Tarquinia that Weege was in Florence – but not doing any more etruscan books.

It is very hot here – too hot to sit in the sun for breakfast, even before seven in the morning. One gets up early, then has a siesta in the afternoon. Frieda is still peacefully slumbering – I wakened up early from mine – and not a soul is alive on all the poderi[1] – peasants sleeping too. The Arno valley lies hot and still, in the sun, but there is a little breeze, so I shall go down and sit on the grass in a deckchair under the nespole[2] trees. The nespoli are just ripe – I shall climb up and get the first today – warm – they're good like that. The big cherries also are ripe – Giulia brings them in[3] – very good. It seems to me always very pleasant when it is full summer, and one ceases to bother about anything, goes drowsy like an insect.

We heard from friends that the performance of *David* went off very well, and the play was well received. But the notices in the newspapers are very contrary. They say the play was very dull, that it was like a cinema with too much talking, that it was boring and no drama in it, and that it was a very great mistake for a clever man like me to offer such a thing for the actual stage. – A clever man like me doesn't fret over what they say. If the producers made a bad film of it, that's the producers' fault. And if the dramatic critics can only listen to snappy talk about divorces and money, that's their fault too. They should pray to the Lord – Lend thou the listening ear! – and not blame me. – Anyhow, io non mi frego![4] – Frieda, however, was very disappointed and downcast about it, and almost refused to be comforted.[5] – We shall hear more later.

Unless it gets sizzling hot, I suppose we shall stay here till towards the end of July. We may do a little 'giro' to Cortona and Arezzo and Chiusi and Orvieto, coming back by Assisi and Perugia: if it's not too hot. Then for[6] August we can go to Baden to the Schwiegermutter – that hot and tiresome month, when everybody in the whole world is somewhere where they shouldn't be. Did you say you were going to la haute Savoie? That'll be very nice – I've got some friends gone there just now. If it weren't the wrong time of year – a bit too warm for you – I should suggest you bring the children here and make use of this flat while we're away, and the young ones could explore Florence and all this countryside, which is very nice. They'd like it – but you would probably rather be cooler, and quite free from housekeeping.

The Brett has gone back to the ranch, and is frantic because we don't go too.

---

[1] 'farms'.   [2] 'medlars'.
[3] Giulia Pini, daughter of a nearby peasant family, was employed as a servant by the Lawrences who treated her with great affection.   [4] 'for myself, I don't care!'
[5] Cf. Jeremiah xxxi. 15 ('Rachel . . . refuseth to be comforted').   [6] for] in

Mabel also writes urgingly. She has built two or three more houses, and keeps one for us. But this summer anyhow we shan't go. I should like to see Bavaria again: and September would be lovely. If we went there any earlier, we would stay in that inn in Beuerberg, where we began our career, at the end of May fifteen years ago.[1] I liked Beuerberg so much. But now in summer I suppose the inn is crammed full.

I had notice from Curtis Brown today they had received £10 for 'The Woman Who Rode Away'.[2] – As soon as it appears, in the *Dial* or the *London Mercury* – either in the June number or the July, I forget – I'll send you 'The Man Who Loved Islands'. I believe you'd like that, and it might amuse you to translate.

Well – it's not often I write such a long letter nowadays. The days go by, and we hardly see anybody – which is what I prefer. Frieda grumbles sometimes, but when people come, she doesn't want them. She has an idea she is a social soul who loves her fellow-men to distraction. I don't see it quite – But I suppose one idea of oneself is as good as another.

Remember me to the children, and to Alfred[3] – and tante belle cose!

DHL

4037. To Cyril Beaumont, 4 June 1927
Text: MS SIU; Unpublished.

Villa Mirenda, *Scandicci* (Firenze)
4 June 1927

Dear Beaumont[4]

Do print whatever bits you like from my letters, – if they seem to you worth it, which they don't to me.

Heaven knows whether I'll ever rake together a little vol. of verse again – if I do I'll let you know.

Regards   D. H. Lawrence

---

[1] DHL and Frieda spent their 'honeymoon' at the Gasthaus zur Post in Beuerberg, 25 May–1 June 1912; see *Letters*, i. 411–15.

[2] It had been published in *Dial*, lxxix (July–August 1925), 1–20, 121–36 (Roberts C131–2), and *Criterion* (July 1925 and January 1926); why Curtis Brown was getting £10 for it now is not known.

[3] Alfred Weber (1868–1958), Professor of Sociology and Political Science in the University of Heidelberg; Else's 'lover . . . such a jolly fellow' (*Letters*, i. 413).

[4] Cyril William Beaumont (1891–1976), bookseller and publisher. DHL's association with him began in 1918 (*Letters*, iii. 212 and n. 1); he published DHL's *Bay* in 1919 (the 'little vol. of verse' referred to in this letter). Beaumont was now obtaining permission to include DHL's letters written to him, in *The First Score* (September 1927), an account of the Beaumont Press.

4038. To Martin Secker, 6 June 1927

Text: MS UInd; Postmark, Scandicci 7. 6.27.; Secker 89–90.

Villa Mirenda, *Scandicci*, Florence
6 June 1927

Dear Secker

The two copies of *Mornings in Mexico* came this morning – look very fine – almost a respectable book. I expected it tiny. I don't mind its not having pictures, really. – I like the 'Dance' essays very much, myself – but Frieda likes the first four best.

I heard from Pollinger of Curtis Brown's wanting to make a contract for *Lady Chatterley* and two other books. But I don't want to make contracts for *Lady Chatterley* – that young woman may still go in the fire – and I don't want to make contracts for anything – I don't like it – I feel I've got a string round my wrist, and it puts me off. – And don't you bother me about it, I'm much nicer when I'm *not* contracted.

I began doing the Etruscan book – have done about 80 pp. MSS. Of course it fascinates *me* – but the public is an ass I don't understand. I've got some lovely photographs, too, from Alinari. I might possibly, if the gods wish it, get these *Sketches of Etruscan Places* done by early autumn – and you might, if you liked, in that case get it out for Christmas.[1] But God knows how it'll go. – It would have to be a book with many full illustrations – a hundred even – and as such it could be a standard popularish – not scientific – book on the Etruscan things and places, and might really sell, for the photographs at least are striking and beautiful. When I've finished 'Tarquinia', I'll let you see the essays on Cerveteri and Tarquinia, with some of the photographs, and you can let me know what you think, for the rest of the book. Perhaps in about two weeks I can send you so much.

The weather made a break – rained and was even coldish – is clear again. We've both got bits of colds, Frieda in her tummy. Huxley and Maria are spending the summer at Forte dei Marmi – near Viareggio.[2] They invite us there. We may go for a couple of days. – I think we shall stay here till end of July, but Italy is *very* expensive, prices have barely changed at all. We really ought to go away.

I'm glad all goes well, also at Bridgefoot.[3] *David* I hear was a bit of a dud,

[1] Christmas.] autumn.
[2] Aldous Huxley (1894–1963), novelist, essayist and later, editor of DHL's letters. m. 1919, Maria Nys (1898–1955). See *Letters*, ii. 325 n. 1. DHL knew them both from Garsington in 1915; they became particularly close friends of the Lawrences in the 1920s.
[3] The Seckers' home at Iver, Bucks.

but that's not the play's fault. I really expected it. – How does the 3/6 edition go?[1] it *ought* to prosper!

Yrs   D. H. Lawrence

4039. To Jocelyn Olway, 7 June 1927
Text: MS DeGruson; Unpublished.

Villa Mirenda, Scandicci (Firenze)
7 June 1927

Dear Mrs Olway[2]

You didn't then find anything in Vallombrosa? – Many thanks for the invitation on Friday: but this week we're having to look after our two American friends from New Mexico.[3]

I'll ask about other villas here. The villino La Massa would be too poky for you, I'm afraid: poky little rooms: a little 7-roomed cottage, tiny: but just near here.[4] If I go on with my work I'm doing, we shall be here till end of July – then go away August and September. You're perfectly welcome to the place, but all your complaints hold good here: no light, rainwater to be pumped up, sanitary arrangements primitive, the whole thing very rough – linen just calico, beds hard, etc. Such as it is, however, you are welcome to it for August and September. Meanwhile I'll ask about something else, and let you know: but it won't be till beginning of next week. – I suppose the half of the Evans' house is unfurnished? I believe that's nice.

Many thanks for the jolly luncheon the other day – and regards from my wife and me – also to Mlle. Valerie.[5]

Sincerely   D. H. Lawrence

4040. To Earl Brewster, [9 June 1927]
Text: MS UT; Brewster 135–7.

Villa Mirenda, Scandicci (Firenze)
Thursday 9 June

Dear Earl

Many thanks for the shoes, which came yesterday. They are a great success, and Frieda is very pleased with hers: says they're gothic – nearly as good as that Mrs Clapp – or Klapp – who said 'To me it's Châtres! Châtres!' – over

---

[1] See Letter 4003 and p. 44 n. 2.

[2] Nothing is known of DHL's correspondent beyond her friendship with Orioli and her address (from DHL's address book UT): Palazzo Ristori, via Melegnano, Florence 5.

[3] Christine and Mary Christine Hughes.

[4] The Villa La Massa, recently vacated by Millicent Beveridge and Mabel Harrison (Letter 4024). Cf. *Letters*, v. 643.   [5] The Evans and Mlle Valerie are unidentified.

the little old knitted silk tobacco pouch. I enclose cheque for ten bob – hope it's enough.

Christine Hughes and Mary Christine are in Florence – Did I tell you they had a bad motor accident – one of Mary Christine's Roman 'boys' driving them 'like hell' to pass another car: overturned them, car rolled over twice, hit Christine etc – this is a month ago – they were in hospital a bit – no serious damage – but voices bluer than ever. Really, *nothing* is worse than these Americans. They've cut out *everything* except personal conceit and clothes. I was in the Uffizi – Ufizzi – Uffizzi?? – with them yesterday – 'my – look what awful hands she's got!' is all that comes out of Mary Christine for Lippo Lippi – they've never even *heard* of Botticelli – call him Bo'acelli with the stopped breath instead of the 't' – they don't know what the Renaissance was –. Standing in the Piazza Signoria I say – There's that Michelangelo *David* – and they reply: Which one is it then? – that one at the end? – meaning the Bandinelli.[1] Then Mary C. discovers that – 'that guy's got a stone in his hand, so I guess he's the nut.' – It's partly affectation, but it's such a complete one that it's effectual. They simply *can't see* anything: you might as well ask a dog to look at a picture or a statue. They're stone blind, culturally. All they can do is to call a man 'that guy' or a woman 'that skirt.' Christine would *like* to be able to see: but it's too late: the American cataract has closed over her vision, she's blind. Mary C. frankly loathes anything that wants to be looked at – except herself, other girls, clothes and shops. – But it's a process of atavism so rapid and so appalling, I could kill them dead. It's pure atavism. They've negated and negated and negated till there's *nothing* – and they themselves are empty vessels with a squirming mass of nerves. God, how loathsome! They're coming this evening to us – then leaving for Venice tomorrow – and sailing for New York end of the month. It's horrible. And it's largely the result of an affectation of 'freedom' from old standards, become a fixed habit and a loathsome disease. – Because there's the elements of a nice woman in each of them. But oh, how glad I shall be to see the last of them. – And I feel I'd rather go and live in a hyaena house than go to live in America.

So much for me!

Nevertheless, I think the world must be fought, not retreated from.

Did you get *Mornings in Mexico*? I had my copy.

I began the Etruscan essays: have done 'Cerveteri' and 'Tarquinia' so far. They interest me very much. One can get lovely photographs from Alinari's, so one could make a fine book. Perhaps Frieda and I will do a trip to Cortona, Arezzo, Chiusi, Orvieto, Perugia next week or the week after – before we go to

---

[1] The *Hercules and Cacus* (1534) by Bartolommeo Bandinelli (1488–1559) stands in the Piazza della Signoria.

Germany – so I could do enough essays – or Sketches – *Sketches of Etruscan Places* – for a book. That would keep us here till end of July – then we'd go to Germany. I think I shall cut out England this time. – The worst of travelling now in Italy, it costs so much, with the exchange where it is. Any country is cheaper.

The time goes by quickly, now the hot weather is here. But I like it like this.

Thank Achsah for her letter. You'll be glad to settle down in Cimbrone again – not long now.

I believe it's going to rain!

DHL

4041. To Mary Willcocks, [10 June 1927]

Text: Sotheby Parke Bernet Catalogue, 21 May 1974, Item 28; Unpublished.

[Villa Mirenda, Scandicci, Florence]

[10 June 1927]

What the dark God is can never be said – Nor, in the knowledge sense, known . . . I think the earth is alive – I think all the universe is alive . . . the body is the man – all the rest emanates from the body . . . the Indian religious dances are the most beautiful and purely religious things I have ever seen – and the so called devil dance in Ceylon is mysterious and lovely, compared to jazz . . . One must accept change, a great slow change and a slow bitter revocation of what one most dearly is. But one must accept it – or go utterly stale.[1]

4042. To Ada Clarke, 11 June 1927

Text: MS Clarke; cited in Lawrence–Gelder 159–60.

Villa Mirenda, *Scandicci*, Florence.

11 June 1927

My dear Sister

I suppose you are back again now from Yarmouth. Did you have a good time? You didn't send me a post-card. Did you see Gertie? – poor Gertie! She hasn't answered my letter, and my heart always goes down to my boots when I don't hear from her – or of her. Let me know how she is. – You had a good week, no doubt. Here it was hot: with just one thunder-rainy evening. And how was Emily? – and has Sam anything in view?

I keep hearing about *David*. Apparently the show was really quite a success – people talk a good deal about it. The critics don't matter – they are too stale and false.

---

[1] The Sotheby & Co. Catalogue for 7–8 December 1959, Item 415 quotes the additional phrase: 'We are too clever to live . . .'

I am feeling better since the summer is here and one lounges about all day. We get up at six, and sleep a bit in the afternoon. It's very quiet and nice. – I think next week we shall go with Maria Huxley in the motor to Forte dei Marmi – not very far – on the sea – for a day or two. They've taken a house there for the summer, and Aldous wants to *work*. He works so much. But I think we shall stay here till end of July, though Italy is ruinously expensive.

I didn't buy you anything for your birthday – just a light woolen scarf from here, as a memento. And I enclose two pounds, so you can get yourself some little thing. No good trying to buy anything in Italy now: prices are double of England.

I can imagine the children enjoyed themselves at the sea – Eddie too. I look forward to a bathe myself, next week – if Maria turns up. Does the business still go well? And at Mansfield, how is that?[1] – I am writing my essays about the Etruscans, that I've talked about so much, and never got done. Let's hope I have luck with them this time. – And painting a smallish picture *Finding of Moses* – all negresses![2] It's amusing, because I don't quite know how to do it.

Well, I hope everything is all right. One is never *quite* easy in one's mind nowadays. And I hope you'll have a jolly birthday. Isn't it 40? I'm nearly 42. Talk about making old bones, we're getting on!

Love. DHL

4043. To S. S. Koteliansky, 13 June 1927

Text: MS BL; Postmark, Firenze 14.VI 1927; [Stephen Spender], 'Letters to S. S. Koteliansky', *Encounter*, i (December 1953), 33–4.

Villa Mirenda, Scandicci, Florence.

13 June 1927.

My dear Kot

Your letter today! No luck with Rozanov![3] I'm sorry! But not surprised. What dirty rag of a paper would dare print the review! The world goes from bad to worse. But cheer up, we're not dead yet!

Maria Huxley came yesterday, with the Franchettis.[4] He is a Jew, Barone Luigi – and as rich as Crœsus. He plays the piano very well, and is quite nice – but I agree entirely – I have absolutely no basic sympathy with people of 'assured incomes.' All words become a lie, in their mouth, in their ears also. I *loathe* rich people.

---

[1] Edwin Clarke had opened a shop in Mansfield (in addition to the one in Ripley); it did not flourish (cf. *Letters*, v. 631 and n. 4).

[2] It was collected in *The Paintings of D. H. Lawrence*, plate [4], and reproduced in *Creative Art*, July 1929 (Roberts C188).   [3] Cf. Letter 4000 and n. 1.

[4] Baron Luigi Franchetti, the pianist, and his wife Yvonne, née Palavacino (who became Hamish Hamilton's wife in 1940) were very close friends of the Huxleys.

We are going on Wed. for a couple of days with Maria to Forte dei Marmi – north of Pisa, not very far from here. Aldous did not come in to Florence with Maria, as he is working very hard, to finish a book by July.[1] God help him – Sullivan arrives there – at the Huxleys – on Monday – 20th – but we shall be back here by then.[2] Two days is enough. – Perhaps Maria will bring him over – Sullivan – to see us. I should like to see him, because of associations, but I no longer expect to care about people, one way or another.

I am working at my Etruscan book – a piece of hopeless unpopularity, as far as I can see. But the pictures may help it. We shall probably do a bit of a tour to Etruscan places when we get back from the Huxleys. – I think we shall be here till end of July – though the weather is queer and uncertain.

I feel a bit like you: nothing nice ever happens, or ever will happen. I dreamed I was made head of a school somewhere, I think, in Canada. I felt so queer about it: such a vivid dream – that I half wonder if it is *my* destiny! A job! – But I manage to make a living still.

I feel sometimes tempted to go back to America – Europe is like a dying pig uttering a long, infinitely-conceited squeak. At least America isn't so depressing. I feel tempted to go, in the autumn.

I wish you would go and see Milly Beveridge – she too was at *David* and the discussion – and she had a little house here this spring. The address is 20 Rossetti Garden Mansions. S.W.3. – you remember we had 25 last summer. She is nice and intelligent – not young – has an assured income but not a very big one – paints – and I like her, and I think you would. Ring her up one morning about 10.0, and go to tea with her. I told her I'd[3] tell you.

Suddenly pouring with rain. It'll be no fun motoring to Forte if it continues. I'll let you know what the visit was like.

Poor Ottoline![4] I really begin to sympathise with her. I shall write a book from *her* point of view – all the little artists coming – etc – etc. That Turner is small beer:[5] may even be successful small beer, as he has a cadging sort of nature.

Brett flourishes in Taos – has a fine motor-car of her own, which she drives herself – two horses, which she rides – and fell off lately – and exhibits pictures

[1] He was completing a book of essays, *Proper Studies*, published in November 1927. (For DHL's reaction to it see Letter 4204.)
[2] John William Navin Sullivan (1886–1937), philosophical and scientific writer, friend of Murry, Huxley and Kot; contributed to *Athenæum* and *Adelphi*; author of *Aspects of Science* (1923, 1926), *The History of Mathematics* (1925), *Beethoven* (October 1927), etc.
[3] I'd] I'd I'd
[4] Lady Ottoline Violet Anne Morrell (1873–1938), patroness of the arts and society hostess; her friendship with DHL had not recovered from her discovery that she was the prototype for Hermione Roddice in *Women in Love*. See *Letters*, ii. 253 n. 3.   [5] See p. 67 n. 1.

in the 'hotel' which cause a 'furore.' – She is furious because we don't go out there – but really; these wonderful women begin to scare my soul.

I'll tell you any news if any crops up. Meanwhile it's a desert.

Greet everybody from me.

DHL

Where did Murry get the *Adelphi* money, do you know?[1] And is he yet come to Italy?

The *Calendar* is in all probability dying next month.[2]

4044. To John Clarke, [13 June? 1927]
Text: Lawrence–Gelder 182–3.

[Villa Mirenda, Scandicci, Florence]

[13 June? 1927]

I had your mother's letter just now, and your 'Riddings' snapshot. What a little ruffian you are getting. I know we shall have another scamp in the family. Great news about the house – I must look round for things for it. Ask your mother to tell me what kind of things she wants for it. With my love – so hot here still, and never any rain.

4045. To Edward Bierstadt, 14 June 1927
Text: MS UTul; Unpublished.

Villa Mirenda, Scandicci – (Florence)

14 June 1927

Dear Mr Bierstadt[3]

I am sending today to Curtis Brown the first of the *Sketches of Etruscan Places* I spoke about – 'Cerveteri':[4] and eight photographs. These sketches are written for a book, so are too long for you. But you can cut them as much as you like: just leave out what you like and take of the photographs what you please.

But *please* let Curtis Brown's have the photographs safely back, will you! – for the book.

I shall send four more of these Sketches in about a fortnight – but dont bother with them if you dont care for them.

Sincerely   D. H. Lawrence

The June[5] *Travel* was good: Medina and Mecca, and Fiji.

---

[1] Murry's friend, Vivian Locke-Ellis provided £400 to launch the *Adelphi*; see *Letters,* iv. 565 n. 2. Sullivan suggested the title.

[2] DHL was correct: the *Calendar* (formerly *Calendar of Modern Letters*) ran April 1926–July 1927.   [3] Edward Hale Bierstadt was editor of *Travel* in 1926 (cf. p. 48 n. 1).

[4] Published as 'City of the Dead at Cerveteri'; see p. 48 n. 1.   [5] June] April

4046. To Martin Secker, 14 June 1927
Text: MS UInd; Postmark, Pisa Ferrovia, 15. VI. 1927; Secker 90.

Villa Mirenda, *Scandicci* (Firenze)
14 June 1927
Dear Secker

I am sending to Curtis Brown today the first of the *Sketches of Etruscan Places*: 'Cerveteri'. It is about 6000 words. I contemplate doing a dozen essays of that length – or perhaps 14. This one has eight photographs: and that might be the average. I have done four more essays, but am waiting to get them typed, and for photographs. I'll send them along in about a week. – Will you let me know at once what you think about a book of this sort. If you are doubtful of it, I won't press ahead with it. It would have to have about a hundred illustrations.

We are going tomorrow to Huxley's at Forte dei Marmi for a day or two.
Write at once about *Sketches of Etruscan Places*, won't you.

Yrs   D. H. Lawrence

4047. To Nancy Pearn, 14 June 1927
Text: MS UT; Unpublished.

Villa Mirenda, Scandicci (Firenze)
14 June 1927
Dear Miss Pearn

Will you please give this lady the permission to include the poem 'Bei Hennef' in her anthology.[1]

I'm sorry for Koteliansky's sake about the *Solitaria* review: for my own, I don't care what you do with it: but *The Calendar* dies, I believe, with the next number. Only I'm sorry you had so much trouble with such a trifle.

I'm sending you the first essay of a set of *Sketches of Etruscan Places*. These I intend for a book, with photographs. I want you to show Secker the essay and the photographs, because I want to know if he likes them. And then please will you send one MS. and all the photographs on to America, as I have definitely promised the editor of *Travel* to send him these sketches, with photographs. – He can cut the essay up as much as he likes, for periodical use: the same in England – they can leave out of it whatever they like, for periodical purposes. But I want the MS. kept whole for the book later on. – *And Travel must return the photographs.*

In about a week I'll send four more of these essays – when I have collected photographs.

---

[1] A letter from Nancy Pearn, 26 July 1927, reveals that the anthology was American; its title is not known.

We are going off[1] for a day or two to Aldous Huxleys by the sea. Where did you go?

You are wise not to come to Italy till prices really do come down.

                                                                        D. H. Lawrence

4048. To Earl Brewster, 14 June 1927
Text: MS UT; Unpublished.

                                                Villa Mirenda, *Scandicci* (Firenze)
                                                                        14 June 1927

Dear Earl

I am in rather a fix for some photographs for my Etruscan essays. I can get some, very good, from Alinari and Brogi here: but some they haven't done. And I don't know a soul in Rome now. Is Miss Mather there?[2] Could you ask her to get me one or two things? I could write to Anderson direct, but I don't know if *he* has done the things I want. I know Moscioni has done two[3] *Tomba della Caccia e Pesca* at Tarquinia, and I want that very much. But who and where is Moscioni?[4] Anderson *may* have done it.

Do you think Miss Mather would ask for me: or anybody else you know?

                Tarquinia: Tomba della Caccia e Pesca
                two pictures (or more if more are reproduced)

We are going tomorrow to the Huxleys at Forte dei Marmi for a day or two. Hope you got my other letter – and forgive my bothering you.

                                                                        DHL

Of course I'll pay for the things –

Also I want *very much* a photograph of Vulci (Volci): *The Ponte dell' Abbadia*, and any tomb that has been photographed. I can get nothing in Florence – you remember Volci – near Montalto di Castro, in Maremma. Anderson might have something, or Gabli.

4049. To Hon. Dorothy Brett, [15? June 1927]
Text: MS UCin; Postmark, Forte dei Marmi, Lucca 15 6.27.; Irvine, Brett 74–5.

                                                Villa Mirenda, *Scandicci* (Firenze)
                                                                        14 June 1927[5]

Dear Brett

So you are back at the ranch – and it is mid-June, and real hot weather. I am

---

[1] MS reads 'of'.
[2] Margaret G. Mather, American expatriate, lived on the Trinita dei Monti in Rome; she was the sister of Frank Jewett Mather (1868–1953), Professor of Art and Archaeology at Princeton, 1910–33.   [3] MS reads 'to'.
[4] Romualdo Moscioni was a photographer in Rome (cf. Letter 4053).
[5] It is possible – in view of remarks about their departure for Forte dei Marmi in Letters 4046 and 4048 – that this letter should have been dated 15 June.

so glad to hear the ditch is running well – that is one of the achievements. – And so the chicken-house is to be another cabin! – and no chickens! Anyhow Trinidad and Ruffina will make as much cackle.[1] – It really will be a place for a colony, when we get back. Imagine the internal combustion of the colony, though. – But I do often wish I were there – the fine pure high air, the big view. Italy gets stuffy – more and more stuffy each month. I think we shall quit in the autumn – perhaps come to America the other way round, as we did the first time – and land in San Francisco in spring – if the cash, not very plentiful, would carry us so far.

Christine Hughes and Mary Christine were here a couple of times last week, before they passed on to Venice. I expect by now they are in Switzerland, but they haven't written. I believe they'll be glad to be back in New Mex. They want to come and see you at the ranch when they are back – July or August.

We are waiting for Maria Huxley – she is supposed to be here at nine this morning to pick us up and take us to Forte dei Marmi, on the sea north of Pisa, where they have a little house for the summer. We shall stay perhaps two days – then back here. Sullivan is going to them – arrives next Monday, I believe. I expect they'll bring him here to see us.

I am busy doing my etruscan essays: I think we shall go to Cortona and Chiusi and Orvieto next week or the week after. When that etruscan book is done, then, for the time being I've done with Italy. – I expect we'll go to Bavaria till end of Sept. – leave here end of July.

There's Maria tooting! I'll write again soon.

                                                                          DHL

4050. To Margaret King, [16 June 1927]
Text: MS Sagar; PC v. Spiaggia Forte dei Marmi e Ponte caricatore; Postmark, Fo[rte dei Marmi] [. . .]; Unpublished.

                                                          [Forte dei Marmi, Lucca]
                                                                      Thursday

Hot here on the sea – a little villa among the pines on the sand. I am bathing, too – the sea is already so warm – almost too warm. It's not far from Carrara, and they bring down the marble to load on the ships. Did you have a good holiday.

                                                                          DHL

---

[1] Trinidad Archuleta, nephew of Tony Luhan. m. 1922, Rufina ('the Ruffian') Romero. See *Letters*, v. 42 and n. 6, 49 and n. 3. They were Indians employed by the Lawrences at Kiowa Ranch.

4051. To Gertrude Cooper, 21 June 1927
Text: MS Clarke; Lawrence–Gelder 160–2.

Villa Mirenda, *Scandicci* (Florence)
21 June 1927

My dear Gertie

I was glad to hear from you, but sad to know you are still in bed. It's an awful long time! I do hope the temperature will soon stay down, and you can be about again.

I heard from Emily, from Yarmouth, but Ada didn't write. I think they all had a good time. It's a pity they didn't have some of the hot weather from here. We've got it really fierce, except that there is a little cool wind from the mountains. I've never known the sun so strong, for the time of the year.

We too were away at the seaside, about a hundred miles from here, not far, a place called Forte dei Marmi. Maria Huxley motored us down. They have a little villa on the beach among the pine trees – quite pleasant – but the air heavier and hotter than it is here, on our hill. We bathed in the sea: but it wasn't *very* good; so warm, and a bit sticky. Maria got stung by a great jelly fish, as she was swimming; a place on her arm like a big burn, or a scald. – Coming back, they motored us to Lucca, and there we took the train. – But I am not fond of the flat sandy shores in Italy. The sea is so dead and lifeless and enervating. The rocky shore is the best, on the Mediterranean.

It isn't eight oclock in the morning, but the sun is already fierce, and the cicalas – big grasshoppers – are singing away in the trees, till you'd think a dozen little people were working little sewing-machines outside. The flowers are over – cherries and strawberries finished – the apricots just coming. Everywhere the peasants are cutting the wheat. It's a fine crop this year, tall and handsome, and a lovely purply-brown colour. All the family set out at about four in the morning, and they work one behind the other, women and men and girls, cutting away with the sickles, and laying the armfuls by: just as Ruth did in the Bible.[1] – Then they leave off about eleven, and eat, then sleep till four or five in the afternoon, then work again till eight or half-past, when the fireflies are drifting about. But when the corn is cut, the fireflies go.

Sometimes I think it would be good to be healthy and limited like the peasants. But then it seems to me they have so little in their lives, one had better put up with one's own bad health, and have one's own experiences. At least they are more vivid than anything these peasants know.

We expect to stay here about another month, then go to Germany, for a little mountain air to freshen us up. I might come to England, by myself. Then

[1] Ruth ii.

88   *[25 June 1927]*

I hope I shall find you in Ripley, safe and sound and enjoying life a bit. It's been a long, long spell.

Do you have any news of Wilson and of Edna?[1] I often wonder how that young hussy is. It's a pity she can't marry some steady man who would keep her in order.

Well, I do hope this letter will find you up and walking around a bit. Really, so much bed is hard work.

With love from us both.   DHL

4052. To Giuseppe Orioli, [25 June 1927]
Text: MS UCLA; Unpublished.

[Villa Mirenda, Scandicci, Florence]
[25 June 1927]
Dear Pino

Glad you're feeling better. Why don't you come out and see us, and bring your boy?[2]

I suppose nobody had Luigi Rossi's book on Verga?[3]

If you happen to go in the bookshops, would you ask if they have a book that is out of print in Germany, and I want to get it – a friend found a copy in London; I don't think it's difficult:

Etruskische Malerei by F. Weege (Leipzig)

It's a book of reproductions of the tombs of Tarquinia, and costs about a pound in London.

I think next week we'll do a little giro to Cortona and Arezzo and Chiusi and Orvieto – to see etruscan things there. Otherwise no news.

DHL

[J. I. DAVIS & G. M. ORIOLI, LIBRERIA ANTIQUARIA]
Turiddu (name)[4]
facemu cuntu ca chioppi e scampau, e la nostra amicizia finiu

---

[1] Wilson may have been the husband of Gertrude Cooper's deceased sister Florence; Edna was her niece. They are referred to in a similar way in *Letters*, v. 583.
[2] Carlo ('Carletto') Zanotti.   [3] Luigi Russo, *Giovanni Verga* (Naples, 1920).
[4] The purpose of this list on the verso of the letter, written in DHL's hand on Orioli's headed notepaper is not known, but its relation to the Sicilian language of Verga's *Cavalleria Rusticana* stories is certain. 'Turiddu', for example, is a character in 'Cavalleria Rusticana'. Roughly translated the other words mean: 'let us assume that it rained and the good weather returned, and our friendship came to an end'; 'grapes of poor quality'; 'Evening and the ninth hour' [i.e. 3 p.m.]; 'ounces – wheat (of money)'; 'saddle-bag (name of a horse)'; 'Hen (name)'; 'mound (of wheat)'; 'the three kings (stars)'; 'the chicken-run'.

racinedda
Vespero e nona
onze – grano (di denaro)
zaino (nome di cavallo)
Pudda (nome)
tumulo (di grano)
i tre re (stelle)
la puddara

4053. To Earl Brewster, [25 June 1927]
Text: MS UT; Brewster 138–9.

Villa Mirenda, Scandicci – (Firenze.)
[25 June 1927]

My dear Earl

Many thanks for your letter just come – and card from Anderson. I am sad about the photographs. But I have written to Moscioni – Fotografista – Roma – and it may get him. Anna di Chiara came Sunday – and she will *try* to get hold of a man she knows – else no luck. I *must* get those photographs. – Also the Tarquinia book I want is out of print – oh Lord!

Forte dei Marmi was beastly, as a place: flat, dead sea, jelly fishy, and millions of villas. But the Huxleys were very nice with us, and they have such a nice little lad[1] – we motored home via Lucca. – It is much the best here, where we have space and cool and the woods to go in. We took supper out last night, and from the top of the hill watched the fireworks of San Giovanni day in Florence[2] – it was amusing – and man with his fireworks seems curiously silly, in the distance. But up there was almost cold – too cool, anyhow.

I had imagined you transferred to Cimbrone. God! the place will be thick with 'huney' by the time you get there. How beastly it all is! I do think you should find yourselves any bit of a house, rather than be left at other people's mercies and honied delays. Do look in Anacapri for something.

I wrote my essay on Volterra – made me think of you. One day we will really go after more Etruscans together. Meanwhile I think I shall go to Arezzo and Cortona, Chiusi, Orvieto, Perugia with Frieda, towards end of next week. I'd like to do those places before we leave. With Cerveteri and Tarquinia, Vulci and Volterra, that makes nine of the great cities – the twelve. – But it leaves a whole bookful of little places – Veii, Civita Castellana, Norchia, Vetulonia, Cosa, Populonia, Bieda – we might do those, and make a second vol. – after.

---

[1] Matthew Huxley, b. 1920.   [2] 24 June, hence the proposed date for this letter.

Don't dream of paying Routledge anything – He'll make good for his side.[1]
As for yours, it's God help us, when it comes to earning money by sincere
work. I manage still to scramble through, but no more. The world is beastly,
and gets beastlier; and what are we going to do! The only solution is to need
little.

We stay on here – thinking of going to those Etruscan places. I had a sore
chest again this week, and felt 'low.' It's not really better yet. What have the
gods got against us. I feel really sfortunato,[2] sometimes.

Tell Harwood I'll write her a letter.

My dear chap, don't expect heaven – in the shape of other people – ever to
do anything for you. You'll be let down. And remember, one of your most
dangerous troubles is certain *idleness* – forgive me, I don't mean 'do-nothing'
– what Rochefoucauld calls the passion de la paresse – 'le repos de la paresse
est un charme secret de l'âme – la paresse est comme une béatitude de l'âme,
qui la console de toutes ses pertes, et qui lui tient lieu de tous les biens.'[3] – And
I'm afraid the danger of Buddha to us, is that he tends to foster in us a peculiar
paresse de l'âme. – You ought *really* to solve at least a bit of your present
difficulty – the homeless houseless bit. These hotels and Cimbrones are no
good. Decide something, really. This indecision for you is like a sickness.
You've drifted now long enough to realise that you aren't moving anywhere,
you're only becoming water-logged and really derelict. *Decide something*,
before the first 'days' of July!

DHL

4054. To Earl Brewster, [27 June 1927]
Text: MS UT; Brewster 140–2.

Villa Mirenda, *Scandicci* (Firenze)
Monday

Dear Earl

I got photographs from Anderson of the Tomba della Caccia e Pesca today
– good – they are Moscioni publications: but nothing, alas, of Vulci – Perhaps
even Moscioni don't do that. Que faire?[4] – But many thanks, really! They sent
no bill: so do you either send it on to me, or tell me what it is, and I'll forward
the money.

---

[1] The reference is obscure (Brewster omitted this passage from his published text of the letter).
Brewster's *Life of Gotama the Buddha* was published by Kegan Paul who had amalgamated
with Routledge in 1911.   [2] 'unlucky'.
[3] From 'Maximes Supprimées', DCXXX, in *Oeuvres de La Rochefoucauld*, ed. M. D. L. Gilbert
(Paris, 1868), i. 264: 'the tranquillity of laziness is a secret charm of the soul . . . laziness is a kind
of supreme happiness of the soul, which offers consolation for all its losses and takes the place of
all that is most precious.'   [4] 'What is to be done?'

Your letter and Achsah's also came. Glad you like *Mornings*. I like 'Indians and Entertainment' and 'Hopi Snake Dance' best: but all women seem to like 'Corasmin' best.

About Cyprus: really, would it, even if it were nice, be very different from here? Here we have space and quiet, and can be left absolutely alone if we like – and there's the woods to go in – Cyprus might add the sea – but then also it would add a thousand difficulties of distance and language. – I don't a bit agree with Achsah and Milton – I usually disagree with John – that the mind to me a kingdom is.[1] At least it is a kingdom, but so is England a kingdom, a tight and unsatisfactory one in which I should die outright if pinned to it. So with the mind. One's *ambiente*[2] matters awfully. At the same time, you *like* Capri – you always want to go back to it when you've been away – and you stay a good deal within your own gates when you've got any. So that the odds, even for you, between Capri and Cyprus are not enormous. – As for building, it seems to me a terribly expensive moment: the same for buying. Yet if Achsah has the money, and the real will to do it – well, then it's her affair. She doesn't want to be dragged off to distant and difficult places: that's flat. If she'll be happy all her life on Capri – then you'll be as happy there as anywhere else. Remember how you can't rest on your feet, when you are away, until you get back there again. *Don't have* ideas about places, just because you're not in them. All places are tough and terrestial. If Achsah wants to fix up a place on Capri, *really*: then don't prevent her. You'll live there peacefully enough, most of the year, tourists or no tourists: and once you've got a place of your own, you'll be able to leave it for some weeks at a time, and try other spots. – There was a good villa and garden – twenty bedrooms, lovely great drawing-rooms – sold for £2000 the other day – near here. That is nearly ten thousand dollars. But didn't seem to me dear – though myself, I'd never want a huge place.

Seems to me the best thing for you to do is to let Achsah fix herself up in the way she wants to – if she *really* wants to – and you accommodate yourself as far as is necessary. *You* have nothing to propose: except places in the air. So let Achsah go ahead.

As for Cyprus, we'll go there one day – why not. But an island known is better than twenty isles unknown. You stick to Capri. It's easy to leave, any fine morning – for twenty Liras. Cyprus would cost twenty pounds sterling to get out of.

I enclose Brett's letter. That's the way she writes now! Seems to me cheek. 'You come over here and keep me amused –' – then wraps it up in 'acts of faith.'

---

[1] The allusion is to the poem by Sir Edward Dyer (1540–1607), 'My Mind to Me a Kingdom Is'. See also *Paradise Lost*, i. 254–5; *Paradise Regained*, iv. 222–3.   [2] 'environment'.

I want to go etruscanising at the end of this week – weather being decent. It's wild windy and weird today.

I don't know of any decent American book on the yoga – the one I read, the very first I ever read, was called *The Apocalypse Unveiled* – I forget the author.[1] It's not important. But it gave me the first clue. It is quoted by writers – western – on yoga matters – usually rather scornfully.

Well, I do hope you'll fix up something about an abode. It's no good going on as you are. – I suppose you got the letter I addressed to you at Hotel Belvedere: Anacapri: instead of Bella Vista.

It's a pity one needs houses and homes. But one *does*: no matter how much the mind is its own country.

DHL

Hope you're feeling better. – I am, more or less.[2]

4055. To Eileen Seaman, 2 July 1927
Text: MS Teale; Unpublished.

Villa Mirenda, Scandicci. (Florence)
2 July 1927

Dear Mrs Seaman

It was a blow to hear about Henry: I only saw him once, but remember him very well.[3] But now, poor chap, he's safe. Only it is a very cruel shock for you and Mr Seaman and the children, and I'm awfully sorry. There's nothing one can say, beyond sending a word of sympathy.

Sincerely   D. H. Lawrence

4056. To Barbara Weekley, [2? July 1927]
Text: Vivian de Sola Pinto, *D. H. Lawrence After Thirty Years 1930–1960: Catalogue of an Exhibition held in the Art Gallery of the University of Nottingham 17 June–30 July 1960* (Nottingham, 1960), p. 44.

[Villa Mirenda, Scandicci, Florence]
[2? July 1927]

It was really what he wanted, poor chap.[4] It is all wrong: he had that kind of life and sweetness the world doesn't want any more.

---

[1] The author was James Morgan Pryse, whose book *The Apocalypse Unsealed* (1910), DHL knew in 1917 (*Letters*, iii. 150 and n. 3).

[2] Alongside DHL's last paragraph and postscript someone unknown added: "Why Religion" by Horace M. Kallen $3   Boni and Liveright NY.' The book by Horace Meyer Kallen (1882–   ) appeared in 1927.

[3] Henry Chepmell Seaman (1905–27), second son of Arthur George Seaman (1871–1944) and his wife Eileen (Letter 3992 and n. 1). He was killed in a motor-cycling accident in North Wales.

[4] Henry Seaman; see note above. (For a variant text of this letter see Nehls, iii. 163.)

4057. To Martin Secker, 2 July 1927
Text: MS UInd; Postmark, Scandicci 2.7.27; Secker 90–1.

Villa Mirenda, *Scandicci* (Florence)
2 July 1927

Dear Secker

I have done so far six essays of my Etruscans: I. 'Cerveteri.' II. III. IV. 'Tarquinia.' V. 'Vulci.' VI 'Volterra.' – I want to do Florence and Fiesole. – Cortona – Arezzo – Chiusi – Orvieto – Perugia. – These are all the big places, easy to get at. There are little ones, but they'll have to go in another book. I struggle and get what photographs I can. But some I *can't* get: to my despair: especially of Vulci.

I am sending these essays already done to a friend, Millicent Beveridge. 20 Rossetti Garden Mansions, S.W.3. She and sister had a little villa here this spring – and I stayed with them in Scotland last year. She is seeing about photographs for me from the British Museum. I asked her to call and talk it over with you, to see if you know which photographer to get, etc. The things in the B. M. are not photographed. – So if she calls, you will understand. She is on the telephone too. And when she has read the MS. I want her to bring it to you – and *give me your candid opinion*. I want this book – which will be a bit expensive to you, owing to illustrations – to be as popular as I can make it. And I am open to any suggestions you can make me.

We want to go next week to Cortona and the other places south. I should like to collect the material before we leave at the end of the month for the north.

It's cooler here, but very dry, and rather nice.

You'll like Milly Beveridge – she is Scotch – painted that portrait of me – and is rather old-fashioned. I think Rina might like her, really. But she'll be leaving for Inverness-shire in about ten days.

This etruscan book will be a load off my mind if I can get it done.

Hope all goes well.

D. H. Lawrence

4058. To Arthur Wilkinson, [2 July 1927]
Text: MS Schlaefle; PC v. Dancing Girls. Mughal School; Postmark, Scandicci 2 7 27; Unpublished.

[Villa Mirenda, Scandicci, Florence]
2 July

Should have sent a line before, but nothing happened – the boy has not been yet with more Rovita water – we have not gone away – haven't even set off to

Chiusi and Orvieto, though we may do so next week: in short, it's a status quo, and a semper idem. I feel I don't care very much what I do – though we shall leave at the end of the month, probably now for Austria. – We've had no rain, everything is very dry: corn is all in: Z[aira] and the dog are in Florence.[1] – I'm glad you like your place – it looks awfully nice from the card. I suppose you'll be turning home in about a week.[2]

Saluti a tutti.   D. H. Lawrence

4059. To Baroness Anna von Richthofen, 11 July 1927
Text: MS UCB; Frieda Lawrence 243–4.

Villa Mirenda, Scandicci (Florence)
11 July 1927

Meine liebe Schwiegermutter

Dein Schwiegersohn ist ein armer Tropf, und wieder im Bett liegt – wieder mit Bronchien und Hemorrhags. Wir haben den besten Artz von Florenz – gibt Coagulin – aber ich bin noch in der Ecke – Es ist nichts gefährliches – gar nicht – aber – aber –

Und du, wie geht's dir? Du nimmst natürlich nicht Seebade? Der Artzt sagt, meine Hemorrhage kommt von Meerbaden, die ich in Forte genommen habe.

Und freut es dir, dein Konstanz? Wir waren einmal im Walthaus Jakob zum Abentessen – als der Mountsier mitgereist hat – errinnerst du? Es war schön. Aber bist du nicht ein wenig scheu und heimatlos? oder wirst du immer jünger, und machst dir einen Bubikopf, und abkürzest du deinen Rock? Man kann nimmer wissen, was eine Frau machen will, in ihrem grünen sechs-und-siebzigsten Jahr.

Die Freunde sind sehr gut – kommt jemand aus von Florenz beinah jeden Tag – ich bin nur 5 Tage im Bett – und der Doctor sagt ich kann in 15 abreisen – nach jenen Wortersee[3] – aber wir wissen noch nicht wo es ist, der Emil soll schreiben. Der Artzt sagt ich soll 800 meter hoch gehen, in Tannen – nicht höher.

Wenn es ging mir nur einmal wieder ganz wohl!

Ich schicke dir nur zwei Pfund für deine Feste[4] – die Frieda sagt ich soll die Reste mit-bringen, dass wir können es dir geben wann wir da sind, und noch Feier machen.

---

[1] See Letter 4425 and p. 398 n. 2.
[2] The Wilkinsons were at Portovenere on the Gulf of Spezia.   [3] I.e. 'Worther See'.
[4] Above 'Feste' 'Feier' is written in an unknown hand.

Die Else soll uns noch ein Wort schreiben – und vielen Dank an ihr für ihre Briefe. – Das Buch habe ich von London – geleiht.

Aber die Etrusker und alles Arbeit kann mit dem Teufel schlafen – wenn ich nur wohl bin, will ich mir nur amusieren und alles vergessen.

Sei du nur zufrieden, und nimm dich die Erdesfreuden ganz ruhig an. Wir kommen gleich und schmecken die Badener Würstle zusammen.

DHL

[My dear Schwiegermutter

Your son-in-law is a poor wretch, and is in bed once more – again with bronchials and haemorrhage. We have the best doctor from Florence – gives coagulin – but I've not yet turned the corner – It's nothing dangerous – not at all – but – but –

And do you like it, your Constance? We were once at the Walthaus Jakob for dinner – when Mountsier was travelling with us – do you remember?[1] It was lovely. But aren't you a little shy and homeless? or are you going on getting younger, shingling your hair and shortening your skirt? One can never tell what a woman in her green seventy-sixth year will want to do.

Friends are very good – somebody comes out from Florence almost every day – I've only been in bed 5 days – and the doctor says I can go away in a fortnight – to that Wortersee – but we don't know yet where it is, Emil should write. The doctor says I should go up to 800 metres, into the pines – no higher.
fortnight – to that Wortersee – but we don't know where it is, Emil should write. The doctor says I should go up to 800 metres, into the pines – no higher.

If only I were quite well once again!

I send you only two pounds for your celebration – Frieda says I should bring the remainder with me, so we can give it you when we're there, and have another celebration.

Else should write to us – and many thanks to her for her letters. – I have the book from London – borrowed.

But the Etruscans and all work can sleep with the devil – once I'm well, I shall only want to enjoy myself and forget everything.

You just be content, and quietly accept the joys of this earth. We're coming soon and will taste Baden sausages together.

DHL]

---

[1] The Lawrences, having left Baden-Baden, were in Constance 14–18 July 1921 (*Letters*, iv. 52). With them was Robert Mountsier (1888–1972) who was then DHL's literary agent in USA (see *Letters*, iii. 24 n. 4).

4060. To Rolf Gardiner, 11 July 1927
Text: MS Lazarus; Huxley 684.

Villa Mirenda, *Scandicci* (Florence)
11 July 1927

Dear Gardiner[1]

Thanks for the Camp report. It's amusing – to a novelist, the thing interesting. – I don't believe you'll ever get modern Germans free from an acute sense of their nationality – and in contact with foreigners they'll *feel* political for years to come. They have no self-possession – and they have that naïve feeling that it's somebody else's fault. – Apart from that, they *are* lustig,[2] which the English never are. And I think they are capable of mass-movement – which the English aren't, again, not the intelligent ones.

But don't forget you yourself want to be too suddenly and completely a leader – spring ready-armed from the head of Jove.[3] The English will never follow – not even a handful – you see if they do. They'll come for fun, and if it's no fun – basta!

But go ahead – there's nothing without trying.

fra noi e il paradiso c'è l'inferno e poi il purgatorio.[4]

I shall be interested to know what you make of your 'centre', when you've got it. It seems to me the most important – the world sails on towards a débâcle – camps and wanderings won't help that – but a little ark somewhere in a quiet place will be valuable. So make it if you can.

I dont think we shall come to England this summer. We want to leave in a fortnight for a place in Carinthia – then Sept. in the Isartal near München – then a bit in Baden – then back here. So I cant come to the Cheviots. But one day I really should like to come to one of your meetings, somewhere, if I can come as an outsider, not too strenuous. My health is very tiresome lately.

Good luck, then – and au revoir.   D. H. Lawrence

By the way, is Götsch a German or a Jew or a Scandinavian or what, by blood?[5]

Your camp sounded just a wee bit like going to prison for two weeks 'hard.'

---

[1] Rolf Gardiner (1902–71), one of DHL's correspondents since July 1924, had pioneered Land Service Camps for Youth in northern Europe (see *Letters*, v. 66 n. 5). The 'report' to which DHL refers would be about an Anglo-German camp and expedition at Danzig and along the Vistula (Nehls, iii. 124).   [2] 'merry, lively'.

[3] The allusion is to the birth of Athena.

[4] 'between us and paradise there is hell and then purgatory.'

[5] Gardiner's friend, Georg Götsch, subsequently director of the Musikheim at Frankfort-on-Oder (Nehls, iii. 124).

4061. To Emily King, 11 July 1927
Text: MS Lazarus; Unpublished.

Villa Mirenda, Scandicci. Florence
11 July 1927

My dear Pamela

I'm glad you've got a car and a new business. Sam started today! And it's just as well if you needn't live in Bulwell, it's another hole. But I do hope its a good business.[1]

And that reminds me this letter ought really to be to Peg – I owe it her.

I'm in the dumps having a bronchial attack again. I was so much better. The Dr. says I brought it

(the eclipse!)[2]

on bathing in the sea at Forte. But it's not much, and in about a fortnight we hope to leave for Austria – place I know nothing about – on the Worthersee – the lake of Worth – in Austria – in Carinthia – somewhere north of Trieste. Frieda's sister Johanna and husband are going there – and the doctor says it's just right – about 2000 ft up, and pine forest. He says that's the thing. I should really like to get this bronchial trouble cleared up a bit, for it's been a curse lately. But the doctor gives me stuff, and says I ought to get it better all right, if I take a bit of trouble about it – but to stay awhile in the mountains, not the sea.

We've at last had a bit of rain, but not much – It's been so hot and dry – and still is pretty hot. A change will be good.

But we're very well situated here – in the open – and friends come out to see us every day.

I do hope the business will be a good one, and that Sam will be careful, driving that car.

Love   DHL

Will write again soon.

4062. To Ada Clarke, 11 July 1927
Text: MS Clarke; Postmark, Firenze 12.VII.1927; Unpublished.

Villa Mirenda, Scandicci, Florence
11 July 1927

My dear Sister

I suppose your busy time will be slackening off a bit now, so you'll be able to

---

[1] Samuel King had bought a grocery (and to some extent a hardware) shop in Bulwell, a suburb of Nottingham. He ran it until 1932 though not without difficulty (see Letter 4389).
[2] An accidental ink blot was given a comet's tail thus alluding to the remarkable eclipse of the sun on 30 June 1927.

enjoy your garden. We've actually had a bit of rain – after the long dry spell – but it's pretty hot again.

We want to go away in about a fortnight to a place in Austria where I've never been. But Frieda's younger sister and her husband are going there, and it sounds all right. The doctor says its what I want.

I've got another bronchial attack – and I was so much better. The doctor says I brought it on sea-bathing at Forte. He's giving me treatment – he's the best doctor in Florence – Italian – they are very good – and he says I must go up about 2000 feet, among pine woods, and I ought to get this chronic bronchial congestion cleared up a lot. I hope so, for I'm tired of it.

Did you get your copy of *Mornings in Mexico*? I suppose you did. I was busy working on a book of *Sketches of Etruscan Places*, which will have lots of illustrations. But I shall leave it now, and go away as soon as I'm fixed – and finish it – D. V. – in the autumn.

Friends are very good – they come out somebody every day from Florence if I'm seedy.

I shall write again directly – let me know you are all all right.

Love   DHL

4063. To S. S. Koteliansky, 12 July 1927
Text: MS BL; Postmark, Firenze 13. VII 1927; Moore 989.

Villa Mirenda, Scandicci, Florence
12 July 1927

My dear Kot

Poor me! I'm in bed again with bronchials and bronchial hemorrhage – for the last week – so sick of it. I have the best doctor from Florence – but he can only give Coagulin – says not to bother – but I really get depressed. The doctor says best go to the mountains, about 2000 ft, to pine woods. If I'm well enough, I think we shall go to Austria, to the Worthersee, near Villach, in a fortnight. I hope I can go, I am sick of this business. – Frieda's sister and husband from Berlin will be there – at the Worthersee – for August.

There isn't any other news, except that I am sick.

How are you all? Don't be black-moodish, think, you might have bronchial hemorrhage and many other ills.

DHL

4064. To Dr Trigant Burrow, 13 July 1927
Text: MS (Photocopy) HU; Huxley 685–6.

Villa Mirenda, *Scandicci*, Florence
13 July 1927

Dear Trigant Burrow[1]

You are the most amusing person that writes to me. It is really funny – resistances[2] – that we are all of us all the while existing by resisting – and that the p[sycho]-a[nalytic] doctor and his patient only come to hugs in order to offer a perfect resistance to mother or father or Mrs Grundy – sublimating one resistance into another resistance – each man his own nonpareil, and spending his life secretly or openly resisting the nonpareil pretensions of all other men – a very true picture of us all, poor dears.[3] All bullies, all being bullied.

What ails me is the absolute frustration of my primeval societal instinct. The hero illusion starts with the individualist illusion, and all resistances ensue. I think societal instinct much deeper than sex instinct – and societal repression much more devastating. There is no repression of the sexual individual comparable to the repression of the societal man in me, by the individual ego, my own and everybody elses. I am weary even of my own individuality, and simply nauseated by other people's. I should very much like to meet somebody who has been through your laboratory, and come societally unrepressed. Is there anybody? If it werent for money, the peasants here wouldn't be bad. But money is the stake through the bowels of the societal suicide. – What a beastly word, *societal*!

This is to say, if you come to Europe, do let me know. I should like to meet you. I love the way you pull the loose legs out of the tripods of the p-a-ytical pythonesses.

Of course, men will *never* agree – Can't – in their '*subjective sense perceptions*'. Subjective sense perceptions are individualistic, *ab ovo*. But do tell them to try! What a scrimmage among the mental scientists, and a tearing of mental hair!

Mental science anyhow can't exist – any more than the goose can lay the golden egg. But keep 'em at it, pretending.

[1] Dr Trigant Burrow (1875–1950), American psychoanalyst and writer; recently president of the American Psychoanalytic Association. Director of the Lifwynn Foundation for Laboratory Research in Analytic and Social Psychiatry (to which DHL refers in his letter). See *Letters*, v. 261 n. 1.

[2] A topic on which Burrow had published an article, 'Speaking of Resistances', in *Psyche*, vii (January 1927), 20–7, and had presumably sent DHL an offprint.

[3] Burrow asserted that 'our problem is a social one in which we are all participants in a social *system* of resistances' (*Psyche*, vii. 26).

I think we shall be in Austria – near Villach – for August – and in Bavaria – near Munich – for Sept. Are you coming to Europe? – to the p.-a-thing in Innsbruck?

Every Jew is a Jehovah, and every Christian is a Jesus, and every scientist is the Logos, and there's never a man about.

I've got bronchials and am in bed for a bit, and furious.

You can convince a man that he lusts after his grandmother – he doesn't mind! – but how are you going to bring him to see that as an individual he's a blown egg!

I'll try and find your paper on the 'Genesis and Meaning of Homosexuality'[1] – you should have said 'Genesis and Exodus.' – But I've long wanted to know the meaning – and there you told it in 1917!

D. H. Lawrence

Letters to here will follow on, when we move.

4065. To Aldous and Maria Huxley, [15 July 1927]
Text: Huxley 686.

Villa Mirenda, Scandicci, Firenze
Friday, July 1927.

Dear Aldous and Maria, –

No luck! I've been in bed last eight days with bronchial hemorrhage – and Dr. Giglioli![2] Getting up a bit now – but not *terra firma*. – We shall go away if we can in about ten days – to Austria, near Villach – other side of your Dolomites – must go *up* a bit – am so weary of myself.

We'll send the books back. *Proust* too much water-jelly – I can't read him. *Faux Monnayeurs* was interesting as a revelation of the modern state of mind[3] – but it's done to shock and surprise, *pour épater* – and *fanfarons de vice*![4] – not real.

Did Sullivan come? I'm sorry we shan't see him. But in the autumn, when we come back, we'll have a meeting, and plan for a forgathering in the snows of the New Year.

Meanwhile many *belle cose* to you all.   D. H. Lawrence

---

[1] Published in the *Psychoanalytic Review*, iv (1917), 272–84.
[2] The 'best doctor in Florence' (Letter 4062); 'head of the Medical Profession for Tuscany' (Letter 4079).
[3] André Gide's *Les Faux-Monnayeurs* (Paris, 1925), trans. Dorothy Bussy as *The Counterfeiters* (1928).   [4] '*in order to startle* – and *a flaunter of vices!*'

4066. To Mabel Dodge Luhan, 15 July 1927
Text: MS Brill; Luhan 331–2.

Villa Mirenda, *Scandicci*, Florence
15 July 1927

My dear Mabel

I'm glad you've got the books and pictures. Were they more or less what you wanted? Let me know how much you pay transport; we have tried two or three times to pay the shipping, but the Egidi people haven't got the returns yet.[1] You remember there is £10. sterling of yours in Orioli's hands.

I've had another whack of bronchials – due to sea-bathing when I shouldn't. But the doctor says it should clear up all right.

We want to go away to the mountains near Villach in Austria, about 2000 feet up, as soon as I'm up to the journey – in about ten days. I'm not sure of the address – but letters will come on safely from here.

I had a letter from Bessie Freeman today – in Paris – so queer![2] Her beloved brother died: and she seems to have gone off some edge or other – been in India: and spending months alone in the desert with eight Arabs. 'Why am I the only woman in the world who could do it safely?' – She wanted to be remembered to you and says she always liked you so much.

I can't say definitely about the autumn. I must see how my damned bronchials react. The doctors all say Taos is too high: good for lungs, bad for bronchitis. I'd like to see the open spaces again, though – and the cottonwood trees in October.

The man is supposed to come and snap my pictures tomorrow – if he does!

Tell Brett Mrs Ashly[3] wrote from Rome for news of her.

I dreamed so plainly of Tony.

DHL

I suppose you and Brett got your copies of *Mornings in Mexico*. Knopf isn't getting his American edition out till Septem. – Remember me to Spud.

DHL

[1] G. Egidi was a general shipping agent (see *Letters*, v. 618–19).
[2] Elizabeth ('Bessie') Wilkeson Freeman (1876–1951), a childhood friend of Mabel Luhan through whom DHL met her in 1922 (see *Letters*, iv. 331 and n. 3). He visited her in Buffalo in August 1923 (ibid., p. 493). DHL had met her (unnamed) brother: see ibid., pp. 484, 490.
[3] Unidentified.

4067. To Edward Goldston, 16 July 1927
Text: MS Eton; Unpublished.

Villa Mirenda, *Scandicci*, Florence. Italy
16[1] July 1927

Dear Sir[2]

When will the *Bagh Caves* be ready?[3] I ask because I hoped to get the[4] book before leaving – in about ten days.

Will you please tell me how much a copy of Fritz Weege's:
       Etruskische Malerei. Halle. 1921 *Max Niemayer Verlag.*
now costs. If the price isn't high, I want a copy – and I think you told my friend Miss Beveridge you could get one. – Could you let me know by return?
Yrs   D. H. Lawrence

4068. To Upton Sinclair, 16 July 1927
Text: MS UInd; Moore 991.

Villa Mirenda, *Scandicci*. Florence, Italy
16 July 1927

Dear Upton Sinclair[5]

Many thanks for the copy of *Oil.* I read it with keen interest, and consider it a splendid novel of fact. It is absurd for anyone to call it indecent: it is never indecent, neither in word nor suggestion, but very honest and very decent. If they put a ban on it, it will not be for its indecency.

And why should they put a ban on it? The real hero is 'Dad' – J. Arnold Ross – and the thrill of the book is the way he becomes an oil magnate: the old American thrill of a lone hand and a huge success. The book won't make Bolshevists: whoever reads it will want to be like 'Dad,' not like Paul or Bunny. And so long as people want to be like J. Arnold Ross, what danger is there? Anyhow he's more of a man than any of the other characters.

But the novel seems to me a splendid big picture of actual life: what more do they want?

Anyhow, here's success to you and the book!
Yours Sincerely   D. H. Lawrence

[1] 16] 12
[2] Edward Goldston, bookseller; with his wife, Fay, published and dealt in books on oriental art and archaeology from 25 Museum Street, London. See Andrew Bloch, *The Book Collector's Vade Mecum* (1932), pp. 289–90.   [3] See p. 72 n. 4.   [4] the] them
[5] Upton Beall Sinclair (1878–1968), American novelist. Though he was not an orthodox Marxist, his socialist views involved him in countless disputes and attacks. *Oil!* was published in 1927 (New York) and reached a 4th printing by June 1927.

4069. To Else Jaffe, [18 July 1927]
Text: MS Jeffrey; Frieda Lawrence 276–7.

Villa Mirenda, *Scandicci*, Firenze
Montag

Liebe Else

You wrote me so nicely from Constance. – I'd glad you had a good time with the Schwiegermutter. I can so well understand she didn't want to see her old home. It's too upsetting: the past is so far off.

I am better – getting up again, and going about the house – but feeling feeble. I went downstairs and out of doors a few yards yesterday – but it's too hot to go out till sundown. However, this day week – or tomorrow week – I hope we can leave for Villach. I shall feel better a little higher. It's lovely weather here, sunny, and not too hot at all if one keeps quiet. But it's much too hot to walk in the sun. If I was well, I should enjoy it. Frieda for the first time really likes the heat. But now I feel I should like to see the world green, and hear the waters running: and to taste good northern food.

I almost wish we'd arranged with you to rent Irschenhausen for August too, and gone straight there. But it will be nice to see Nusch too – and as you say, if one can be really amused, that is the chief thing. My illnesses I know come from chagrin – chagrin that goes deep in and comes out afterwards *in hemorrhage* or what not. When one learns, also, not to be chagrined, then one can become like your Burgermeister – was he a Burgermeister? – fat and lustig to the age of eighty. Anyhow I'd be glad to be fat and lustig once before I die: even a bit versoffen,[1] if that's a way of not having a sore chest.

I wonder if the 'revolution' in Vienna, which the papers report, amounts to anything?[2] Probably not. I think if we didn't go to Austria we'd go either to Bavaria, or somewhere high in Baden.

We shall see you then in September. It is good of you to let us have the Irschenhausen house – but I must pay you a rent.

Wiedersehen.   DHL

I sent you a *Dial* with a story in it – don't know if you'll like it.[3]

[1] 'boozy'.
[2] According to *The Times*, 16 July 1927, there was a riot 'with the fierceness of revolution' at the verdict to acquit members of the 'Nationalist Front Fighters' of the murder of two socialists. Over 80 people were killed. Strikes followed; they collapsed and normality was restored by 20 July.   [3] 'The Man Who Loved Islands': see Letter 4036.

4070. To Giuseppe Orioli, [19 July 1927]
Text: MS UCLA; Unpublished.

Villa Mirenda
Tuesday

Dear Pino

I was better and walked to the wood yesterday – and early this morning the hemorrhage came again. Frieda wept, and I felt like all the martyrs in one. But it doesn't seem bad, and I shall get up again tomorrow – deo volenti.

Will you get me some money – there isn't any? I think one of the Wilkinsons will come in again tomorrow – or perhaps Frieda, in the evening – she'd get in about 5.0, I expect – or 5.30. – then it will be cool. – You could leave the money with your boy, for her. We shall never stop bothering you. It's too bad. When you can, and when I can, you must let me do things for you too.

If I knew when you would like to come out I would send Pietro down to Vingone.[1]

suo aff[ettuosissi]mo[2]   D. H. Lawrence

4071. To Bessie Freeman, 19 July 1927
Text: MS UNYB; Unpublished.

Villa Mirenda, *Scandicci*, Florence. Italy.
19 July 1927

Dear Bessie Freeman

Your letter turned up here – we've had this place a year. – I'm in bed again with bronchial trouble, and sick of it. But I *hope* we can leave in about eight days for the mountains in Austria – near Villach. That ought to put me right.

Your news in your letter was sad – your brother. Nice people die. It's what scares me more and more. And you become such a traveller and a stranger to yourself! I can't believe it.

I think we shall be in Austria for August, and probably in Bavaria near Munich for September – then I expect BadenBaden, where my mother-in-law lives – then, I presume, back here. – All this, of course, is on the knees of the gods. At the moment I'm in bed.

Frieda is well, and sends her love. You will be able to reply here, before we leave.

affectionately   D. H. Lawrence

[1] Cf. Letter 4009 and p. 50 n. 1, and p. 31 n. 1.   [2] 'yours very affectionately'.

4072. To Martin Secker, [22 July 1927]
Text: MS UInd; Secker 91.

Villa Mirenda, *Scandicci*, Florence
Friday

Dear Secker

I am still in bed, as the bronchial hemorrhage keeps coming back. I am tired of it, it is so long.[1] If it would stop I should soon be up, and we could go away. It is so hot. I feel I should be better once I got away. No luck at all!

I want Frieda to post the rest of the Etruscan Sketches to Curtis Brown tomorrow – the first six. It is all I have done – but half the book: and all the photographs. But I could not get any of Vulci. The best thing is to get from the Brit Museum Print Room Plate 35 – of *Forty Drawings by British Artists* – a view of the Ponte and Castello at Vulci – very nice – and very necessary. It is a sketch from S. J. Ainsleys: 'Views of Etruria' (Vol. 1.) – pub. about 1850.[2] Would you make a note of it? – I shant be able to do any more of my Etruscans this summer.

When are you going to Jetho?[3]

Hope you are all well and cheerful.

DHL

4073. To Emily King, [25 July 1927]
Text: MS Lazarus; Postmark, [Sca]nd[icci] 27. 7. 27.; Unpublished.

Villa Mirenda, *Scandicci*, Florence
Monday

My dear Pamela

I thought I was better of my bronchials last week – but then the hemorrhage came back – it's so awfully hot – so the doctor made me go to bed for another week. I'm better really – if only the thing won't recur. It's nothing

---

[1] Frieda wrote privately to Secker c. 24 July 1927 (as he reported to Pollinger on 27 July), expressing alarm at DHL's condition (Secker Letter-Book, UIll).

[2] DHL was referring to *Forty Drawings of Roman Scenes by British Artists (1715–1850) from Originals in the British Museum* (1911). Plate xxxv in this work is *Ponte della Bardia, Vulci* (dated 1842) by Samuel James Ainsley (fl. 1820–74), etcher and lithographer who travelled in Etruria, 1842–3, with George Dennis (cf. Letter 4003 and p. 45 n. 2). Ainsley's drawing is described (p. 20): '[it] represents the Ponte della Bardia at Vulci from the south, with a mediaeval castle to the right, on the east bank of the river Fiora'. It would have been a perfect accompaniment to DHL's text but for some reason his advice was not taken; the chapter on Vulci is alone in *Sketches of Etruscan Places* in having no illustrations. (Ainsley sketched many 'Views of Etruria', but no independent publication of them has been traced.)

[3] Secker was the friend as well as the publisher of Compton Mackenzie who, in 1920, had bought the islands of Jethou and Herm in the English Channel (*Letters*, iii. 594 and n. 1).

very serious, but one has to lie up with it. In myself I'm not very ill. – And don't think we're abandoned. English friends come over from Florence all the time, and the Huxleys came from Forte, and our neighbours the Wilkinsons are very good. – But I shall be awfully glad when the thing has cleared up and I'm up and about again, and independent. I should be glad to go away now – it's very hot. – But as soon as I have been up for a week, we shall leave for the mountains in Austria.

I wonder if it's hotter and drier in England. Here the mornings and evenings are lovely, but midday and afternoon is fierce, and the earth is so dry, it is splitting in huge cracks.

I'm sending a pound each for Peg and Joan for the holiday, for a bit of pocket money, I hope they'll have a good time.

I wonder so much how the Bulwell business goes, and if Sam likes it. I suppose trade isn't very brisk. Here everything is at a standstill – nothing doing at all.

This is just a note – there doesn't seem much to say when one is in bed. But I really hope to get up on Wednesday.

Love to you all   DHL

4074. To Ada Clarke, [25 July 1927]
Text: MS Clarke; Unpublished.

Villa Mirenda, Scandicci, Florence
Monday

My dear Sister

We shant get away as soon as I thought – my bit of bronchial hemorrhage doesn't clear up so fast – at least it has cleared up twice and come back – so the doctor has kept me in bed. But now I really do hope it's gone for good. The doctor made me go back to bed – he says it's nothing serious, but I *must* keep still. However I hope to get up Wednesday – and then in a week we'll leave for the mountains. It's very hot, and that makes it harder for the chest to heal up. – The Huxleys came over, and English friends come from Florence – and our neighbours the Wilkinsons are really very good. But it's hard work for everybody, it's so hot. – In myself I am pretty well – it's just this bronchial business. But the doctor is very good – and says when we get away to the mountains I shall be all the better for this rest. Frieda will be glad of a change too.

The earth is opening in great cracks here, it is so dry – and the maize hasn't formed ears at all.

You will will be off to the seaside with the children. I wish we could send you a bit of this heat – it would just suit Mablethorpe.[1]

I'm sorry about the Mansfield business. Here in Italy everything is at a standstill – nothing doing at all.

I'll write again soon. This is to send the children a pound each for the holiday. Give it to them. And I do hope you'll have a good time.

Love   DHL

4075. To Edward Goldston, 26 July 1927
Text: MS Eton; Unpublished.

Villa Mirenda, *Scandicci*, Florence
26 July 1927

Dear Mr Goldston

Thanks for your letter. Do send me Weege's *Etruskische Malerei* if you can get it for about a guinea – and I'll send a cheque. I shan't be able to leave here so soon, as I am in bed with bronchial trouble.

Yours Sincerely   D. H. Lawrence

4076. To Earl Brewster, [29 July 1927]
Text: MS UT; cited in Brewster 142.

Villa Mirenda, *Scandicci*, Firenze
Friday

Dear Earl

I've been in bed three weeks with bronchial hemorrhage – brought on by sea-bathing – doctor said. Am up and creeping round a bit now – and we hope to leave for the mountains in Austria on August 4th. There's my joyful news – it's been beastly.

Anna di Chiara said you'd gone to Cimbrone and like it better. I'm glad it suits you now. It's pretty hot here.

Do send me my picture some time, if it's no trouble to you.[2] If we've gone away, the Wilkinsons will take it in.

I'll send that cheque again if it doesn't turn up. Let me know.

Greet everybody from me.

D. H. Lawrence

---

[1] DHL remembered Mablethorpe, on the Lincolnshire coast, from childhood holidays and from a holiday in 1926 (see *Letters*, v. 514).   [2] Cf. Letters 4114 and p. 133 n. 2 and 4184.

4077. To Bessie Freeman, [30 July 1927]

Text: MS UNYB; Postmark, Scan[dicci] 31.7.27; Unpublished.

Villa Mirenda, *Scandicci* (Florence)

Saturday

Dear Bessie Freeman

Your letter just come. I am up and creeping feebly about – but I think I'm better. The doctor says we should go to the mountains at once – so we want to leave on Wed. night or Thursday night – depends on the *wagon-lit* – for Villach, in Austria – north of Venice. I don't know if you'd like to come there: it's rather a long way for you. I suppose your way would be Basle, Zürich, Innsbruck, Villach: through Switzerland. – I don't even know where we shall stay in Villach – we want to go to the Wörthersee – Lake of Wörth – or to the Ossiachersee – Lake of Ossiach – just near Villach – for a week or two. But I could ask for a letter from you at Villach poste restante. Let me know, and we'll look out for you. – On the 8th August my sister-in-law, Frau Emil Krug, arrives with her husband at the Grand Hotel, *Annenheim*, near/bei Villach – so that is a sure address. We ought to stay there too – having promised – but Frieda so hates those Grand Hotel places, and I don't like them – so we shall look round for something congenial and near – I only hope I shall feel tougher than I feel at present.

It's just as well you don't go to Venice – it's *so* hot. One needs the mountains.

We shan't leave here before Wednesday night – it may be Thursday, or even Friday night. So if you think of going to Villach, you might send me a telegram.

Then when we meet we can talk about everything.

Love from F. and me   D. H. Lawrence

4078. To Reginald Turner, 31 July 1927

Text: MS UCLA; Postmark, Firenze 1.8 1927; Moore 992.

Villa Mirenda, Scandicci (Firenze)

31 July 1927

Dear Reggie[1] (du côté de chez Schwann)

Pino is here and says you're going to Lucerne, so write there. It's very hot – but I'm up again – went downstairs yesterday and sat in the garden – but felt like a girarrosto,[2] with the hot wind going over me. We hope to get away Thursday night to Villach in Austria – pray to the gods for us, for I want to go.

---

[1] Reginald ('Reggie') Turner (1869–1938), journalist and novelist, and a permanent member of the expatriate community in Florence. DHL first met him in 1920 (see *Letters*, iii. 594 n. 4). (The letter was addressed to Hotel Swan, Lucerne.)   [2] 'spit'.

Pino is here today – has had mal di pancia – but is better and chirpy. We drank Gancia, and he was quite 'spumante'. He's going to Vallombrosa tomorrow. We and the Wilk[inson]s are the last remains in the tierra caliente.[1]

The peasants report that those Robertsons near here (is it?)[2] – those Chileños or Peruvians – have decamped and left many debts – even to the Scandicci barber! Questi inglesi!

Giglioli still rushes up at dusk and tells me all the news in three minutes. I never knew a man who did Frieda such a lot of good. Stormy as he is, he calms her like Jesus on the waters.[3] He's really very kind – and I still swallow his abominable Coagulena.

I hope you're being well treated by the world, and *moderately* happy. You'll never be more.

tante cose!   D. H. Lawrence

4079. To Mark Gertler, 31 July 1927
Text: MS SIU; Postmark, Firenze 2. 8 1927; Moore, *Intelligent Heart* 366–7.

Villa Mirenda, *Scandicci*, Florence
31 July 1927

Dear Gertler

I am up and creeping round – feeling limp – but better. I had the best doctor in Florence – Prof. Giglioli – head of the Medical Profession for Tuscany. It's chronic bronchial congestion – and it brought me on a series of bronchial hemorrhages this time. I've had little ones before. It would be serious if they didn't stop, he says: but they do stop: so it's nothing to worry about – only one must lie in bed when they come on – and always be a bit careful – not take sea-baths, as I did at Forte. I think he's about right. He says now we're to go to the mountains so we're leaving for Austria – D. V. – on Thursday night. I can get into a sleeper in Florence, and stay in till Villach, so I should be all right. I'll send the address there, as I'm not sure. These hemorrhages are rather shattering – but perhaps they take some bad blood out of the system. The doctor says no good going in a Sanatorium, if I will only lie down when I don't feel well – and not work. Which I shall really try to do. – I don't really feel bad.

So tell Kot. to get a doctor himself, and not bother about me.

We saw Sullivan – he came with the Huxleys – and he was nice, but sad – I thought he would be rather bouncing – not a bit. He's coming back to England directly.

[1] 'stomach ache . . . the hot land'.   [2] Unidentified.   [3] Cf. Mark iv. 39.

Ask Kot. to tell Barbara I'll write from Villach.

I do hope you're well – cheerful. Frieda sends her love, with mine.

DHL

Did we ever thank you for your booklet of pictures – everybody looks at them. They nearly all like the child best.[1]

4080. To Emily King, [31 July 1927]

Text: MS Needham; PC v. Leonardo da Vinci, L'Annunziazione; Postmark, Firenze 2 8 1927; Unpublished.

[Villa Mirenda, Scandicci, Florence]
Sunday

I'm feeling a good deal better – am up – and we've taken berths in the sleeping-car for Thursday night – and we have no change, to Villach. I'll send the address from there. Will you tell Ada, as she will be away now. Now I do hope everything will go right. It's still very hot, and no rain.

love. DHL

Just had Peg's letter – I wrote you last week – didn't you get it?

4081. To Nancy Pearn, 31 July 1927

Text: MS UT; Unpublished.

Villa Mirenda, *Scandicci*, Firenze
31 July 1927

Dear Miss Pearn

The 'Nightingale' seems all right, without any more corrections.

I will send you also the first two stories from Giovanni Verga's *Cavalleria Rusticana*, which I am translating for Jonathan Cape.[2]

We have taken berths on the train for Austria for Thursday night – I think I shall be all right with a sleeper – am not sure of the address in Villach, but will send it at once. Dont write to me any more here after this – and would you please tell the other depts.

I am feeling better, but almost afraid to say so. – It's pretty hot.

Hope all goes well with you.

Yrs   D. H. Lawrence

The notes to the Verga stories, I don't care if editors put them in or leave them out.[3]

[1] In January 1927 DHL told Kot that he had not thanked Gertler 'for the little book of pictures'; there is no evidence that he had done so till now. The 'booklet' was probably *Mark Gertler*, intro. Hubert Wellington, the first in a series (published by Fleuron, October 1925) on 'British Artists of Today'. See *Letters*, v. 628 and n. 1. Picture no. 10, *Young Girlhood* is probably 'the child' referred to.   [2] See Letters 4016 and n. 3, and 4031.
[3] Despite Nancy Pearn's attempts to place the stories in magazines, none was accepted.

4082. To Norman Douglas, [31 July 1927]

Text: MS YU; Unpublished.

Villa Mirenda, *Scandicci*, Firenze
Sunday 31 July

Dear Douglas

I was glad to have a note from you, and to know you are in the cool. It's awful hot here – and a frictional, irritant kind of heat. But we're getting out Thursday night – D. V. – going to Villach – to the Wörthersee or Ossiachersee – meet F[rieda]'s younger sister there – *und Mann*. I hope it'll be nice, and we'll soon forget tutti questi guai![1] – Pino goes to Vallombrosa tomorrow – the Valley of the Shadow! Hope you're feeling chirpy. I long to be feeling chirpy again.

Herzliche Grüsse[2] from F.   D. H. Lawrence

4083. To Martin Secker, 1 August 1927

Text: MS UInd; Postmark, Firenze 2. 8. 1927; Secker 92.

Villa Mirenda, *Scandicci*, Firenze
1 August 1927

Dear Secker

I am up and going round rather feebly – but we've booked berths on the train for Thursday night, to Villach in Austria – and we're praying that nothing else will go wrong. We get to Villach Friday afternoon without change so that should be all right. I'll send you the address from there.

Were you happy on Jethu? – I saw Brett Young a year ago[3] – gone awfully soft – everybody seems to go soft and squashy – only caring about money. Anyhow Mackenzie isn't that way.

I sent the other Etruscan essays to Curtis Browns. Did they send them over to you?

It's very hot – very – the bed is quite burning at evening – and it seems as if it will never rain again – the Arno almost dry, the earth cracked open. One will be thankful to get out.

It is good of you to offer money in advance – but I don't need it, thank heaven – and I hate things in advance.

Douglas wrote me quite nicely – he's in the Pistoiese, not far away – in the mountains.[4]

I expect its nice at Bridgefoot now –

tante cose!   D. H. Lawrence

[1] 'all these troubles!'   [2] 'Cordial greetings'.

[3] The Lawrences first met Francis Brett Young (1884–1954), novelist, and his wife Jessica, in Anacapri in December 1919 (see *Letters*, iii. 438 and nn. 1 and 2).

[4] About 20 miles n.w. of Florence.

4084. To Nellie Morrison, 1 August 1927
Text: TMSC NWU; Unpublished.

Villa Mirenda, Scandicci, Firenze.
1st. August 1927.

Dear Nelly Morrison,

At last I am up and padding rather feebly around. We have taken berths on the train for Thursday night, to go to Villach in Austria. I pray the gods everything may go smoothly. We are both tired of this heat, which is burning and irritating, especially towards evening. Everybody has gone away, save the Wilkinsons, who are really very kind to us. Orioli has gone to Vallombrosa, Reggie is in Lucerne. They'll both be in Paris by 1st. September.

Doctor Giglioli still rushes up at evening, to tell me boisterously that I am all right, and that I have a 'good healing power'!

I hope you're having a nice time. Remember us both to Gino.

Love from us both,   D. H. Lawrence

4085. To Giuseppe Orioli, [3 August 1927]
Text: MS UCLA; Unpublished.

Villa Mirenda, Scandicci – Firenze
Wednesday evening

Dear Pino

Well things have gone all right so far. If Cooks have the passports and tickets tomorrow, we shall get off, surely. I will try to remember to leave you the 29 Liras at your flat, that I owe you – if not, *do* please remind me of it one day.

No, I enjoyed Sunday, and wasn't a bit tired. The Wilk[inson]s came in, in the evening, and they love the bits of scandal, especially about Ruby,[1] because a friend of theirs was at the wedding, and crowed over them very much.

Giglioli came again yesterday, and says he may see us in Munich!

You've been awfully kind, and we're both very grateful. The Wilks too have been kindness itself, so you see one mustn't judge too hastily.

I hope you're having a decent time up there at Vallombrosa. We imagine we can see the lights of it at night. – More stacks have burnt down: but not here, fortunately.[2]

Au revoir, then – we *might* meet in Paris. I'll write from Villach.

DHL

---

[1] Unidentified.

[2] Serious economic and industrial depression in Italy provoked social unrest (see *The Times*, 9 July 1927).

4086. To Dr Trigant Burrow, 3 August 1927

Text: MS (Photocopy) HU; Huxley 687–9.

Villa Mirenda, *Scandicci* (Florence)

3 August 1927

Dear Trigant Burrow

Your book came three days ago, and I have now read it.[1] I find it extremely good. Your findings about sex and sexuality seem to me exactly it: that's how it is: and your criticism of psychoanalysis as practised is to the quick. I believe as you do – one must use words like believe – that it is[2] our being cut off that is our ailment, and out of this ailment everything bad arises. I wish I saw a little clearer how you get over the cut-offness. I must come and be present at your group-analysis work one day, if I may. Myself, I suffer badly from being so cut-off. But what is one to do? One can't link up with the social unconscious. At times, one is *forced* to be essentially a hermit. I don't want to be. But anything else is either a personal tussle, or a money tussle: sickening: except, of course, just for ordinary acquaintance, which remains acquaintance. One has no real human relations – that is so devastating.

I didn't like your last chapter.[3] One should never bow to ones audience. As for 'forgiving', I never know what it means. *To forgive all is to understand all.*[4] Whatever do you mean? There is no such *animal.* – Can one 'forgive' the social unconscious? – in oneself or outside? What's the point? – But you have some special meaning for forgive. – Only that last chapter has a bit of a humble christian apology sound – and the rest was so brave.

And then there will *never* be a millennium. There will *never* be a 'true societal flow' – all things are relative. Men were never, in the past, fully societal – and they never will be in the future. But more so, more than now. Now is the time between Good Friday and Easter. We're absolutely in the tomb. If only one saw a chink of light in the tomb door. – But your book too is a chink.

But do you know, I think you are really more a philosopher, or artist, than a scientist – and that you have a deep *natural* resistance to this scientific

---

[1] On 12 July 1927 Burrow wrote DHL that he had asked his English publisher, Kegan Paul, to send him a copy of *The Social Basis of Consciousness: A Study in Organic Psychology* (June 1927). Burrow remarked in his letter: 'I wanted to send you just this line and have you know of my pleasure in placing your name among the first to whom my book should go. I have always appreciated your sympathetic understanding of my endeavors' (Nehls, iii. 682).

[2] MS reads 'is is'.

[3] The chapter is entitled: 'Ultimate Resolution of the Societal Neurosis in its Personal Implication'.

[4] Burrow preferred this formulation to the 'familiar French saying, "Tout comprendre est tout pardonner" [which] . . . has assembled the right elements but in the wrong order' (*Social Basis of Consciousness*, p. 242).

jargonising – which makes your style sometimes so excruciating – whereas the moment you let go, it is perfect to your matter.

And I do think, that man is related to the universe in some 'religious' way, even prior to his relation to his fellow man. And I do think that the only way of true relationship between men is to meet in some common 'belief' – if the belief is but physical and not merely mental. I hate religion in its religiosity as much as you do. But you who like etymologies, look at religio. – Monism is the religion of the cut-off, father-worship is the cult of the cut-off: but it's the cut-offness that's to fault. – There is a *principle* in the universe, towards which man turns religiously – a *life* of the universe itself. And the hero is he who touches and transmits the life of the universe. The hero is good – your own effort is heroic – how else understand it. It's only this image business which is so hateful. Napoleon was all right: it was the Emperor that was out of gear.

Do you know somebody who said: *On connait les femmes, ou on les aime; il n'y a pas de milieu.*[1] It's Frenchy, but I'm not sure it isn't true. I'm not sure if a mental relation with a woman doesn't make it impossible to love her. To know the *mind* of a woman is to end in hating her. – Love means the pre-cognitive flow – neither strictly has a mind – it is the honest state before the apple. Bite the apple, and the love is killed. Between man and woman it's a question of understanding *or* love. I am almost convinced.

> 'Where the apple reddens
>   never pry
> Lest we Lose our Edens
>   you and I –'[2]

The Edens are so badly lost anyhow. But it was the apple, not the Lord, did it. There is a fundamental antagonism between the mental cognitive mode and the naïve or physical or sexual mode of consciousness. As long as time lasts, it will be a battle or a truce between the two. – How to prevent suburbia spreading over Eden (too late! it's done) – how to prevent Eden running to a great wild wilderness – there you are. – But you're wrong, I *think*, about marriage. – Are you married?

How to regain the naïve or innocent soul – how to make it the man within man – your 'societal': and at the same time keep the cognitive mode for defences and adjustments and 'work' – voilà!

As for myself, I'm in despair. I've been in bed this last month with bronchial hemorrhages – due, radically to chagrin – though I was born

---

[1] '*One is acquainted with women, or one loves them; there is no middle state.*' (Source not identified.)
[2] Robert Browning, 'A Woman's Last Word', ll. 17–20 ['. . . Edens,/Eve and . . .'].

bronchial – born in chagrin too. But I'm better – shaky – shaky – and we're going to Austria tomorrow D.V. – whoever D. may be – to the mountains.

I shall write a review of your book if I can.[1] Probably even then nobody will print it. But it is most in sympathy with me of any book I've read for a long time. Pardon the egoism – What is one to say! – I hope we may meet, really.

D. H. Lawrence[2]

---

[1] DHL's review appeared in *Bookman* (New York), lxvi (November 1927), 314–17 (reprinted in *Phoenix* 377–82). He praised the book as one 'for every man interested in the human consciousness', Burrow's conclusions being 'much deeper and more vital' than Freud's. Burrow thanked him for the review by letter on 21 December 1927 (Burrow, *A Search for Man's Sanity*, New York, 1958, pp. 195–6).

[2] Burrow replied to this letter at length on 9 September 1927 (Burrow, *Search for Man's Sanity*, pp. 184–8):

. . . I do know what you mean, and I am heartily with you, I think, in your feeling about religion. But isn't it with religion as it is with love – love that cannot endure to hear its own name so much as whispered? . . .

Yes I am married, very much so. I also have a son, 22, . . . and a daughter, 18. Mrs Burrow and Emily . . . were in Italy for a while on their tour of Europe this summer.

But about marriage. What I said of marriage, I said of marriage as ownership. And marriage *is* ownership – let's face it. I think no two people were ever more stupid and reluctant to face this unsavory actuality in their lives than my wife and myself, but we have kept at it, and the deeper understanding and sympathy and confidence that have come of it, I count among the richest meanings of the many rich meanings that life has brought to me.

About the 'cut-offness' – I do not want to be tedious and seem to talk to you, as people so often feel that I do, with teasing paradox – but really it is not you who are cut off, but the image *you* have of 'you'. So that your question as to what one is to do about the cut-offness, I can only answer, as far as my experience goes, by saying that this image that is socially reciprocated everywhere must, it seems to me, be dissolved in the common pool of social images that now make for those differentiae among us that are really the projected image of each. If it is not your organism that is cut-off – your organism with its feelings and instincts and its unending joy of life – but some purely artificial image, superstitiously sponsored under the traditional mood-protectorate of a primitive fear-ridden society, what avails it to look to the organism for one's mending? . . .

You are right – one cannot forgive. All our forgivingness is spiritual snobbery. But then for us to say with our minds that forgivingness is stupid leads us from the actuality of a mood that does in fact cherish (as a mood based upon the parent-image must) a deep-seated sense of guilt, or self-blame. If I am stupid enough to blame myself, it is up to me to be stupid enough to forgive myself. A stupid equation, but not so stupid as an equation left unresolved.

I love what you say about my excruciating style. It *is* awful, and you have diagnosed me in no imprecise manner. The as yet unresolved conflict within me between science and art is the thunderous noise one hears on every page as I come laboring along. It seemed to me that in some of my later things my breathing was less stertorous. I hope so. . . .

P.S. Won't you reserve your verdict and not say quite yet that 'men were never fully societal'? Do you know Kropotkin's *Mutual Aid*, and do you know the passages in *The Origin of Species* from which Kropotkin really fashioned his thesis? It is the subjective sense of this societal and organic interconnection or continuum among us as a species that is really the whole meaning of my position, and group-analysis but the clearing away of the manifold image differentiae that have so separated man from himself.

4087. To Giuseppe Orioli, [4 August 1927]
Text: MS UCLA; cited in Moore, *Poste Restante* 92.

[6 Lungarno Corsini, Florence]
Thursday night

Dear Pino

Well here we are at your flat – such a nice motor driver. Rosa is here,[1] and has gone out for a scrap of food – so we are well off. Many thanks, really. – I enclose thirty Lire, which I owe you: can't find an envelope, but no matter. I'll write from Austria.

Love   DHL

4088. To Baroness Anna von Richthofen, [5 August 1927]
Text: MS Jeffrey; PC v. Villach mit Dobratsch; Postmark, Villach [. . .] 27; Frieda Lawrence, *Nur Der Wind* (Berlin, 1936), p. 291.

Villach
– Freitag

Wir hatten eine sehr gute Reise, ich war nicht sehr müde. Hier ist sehr schön – und kühl, und es regnet ein wenig – es is wie Himmel, kühl wieder sein, und Regen riechen. Wir gehen morgen zum Ossiachersee, und ich schicke dir die Adresse.

DHL

[–Friday
We had a very good journey, I wasn't very tired. It's very lovely here – and cool, and it rains a bit – it's like heaven, to be cool again, and to smell rain. Tomorrow we're going to the Ossiacher lake, and I'll send you the address.
DHL]

4089. To Giuseppe Orioli, [5 August 1927]
Text: MS NWU; PC v. Villach von Osten; Postmark, Villach [. . .]; Unpublished.

Villach
– Friday

We had a very easy journey, not very tired. It is heaven to be cool again, really cool, and a deep green river from the ice, and a bit of rain. – I left your money on your table at your flat. – Will send address. again many thanks.

DHL

[1] Orioli's servant.

4090. To Emily King, [5 August 1927]

Text: MS Needham; PC v. Villach mit Mittagskogel; Postmark [. . .]7; Unpublished.

Villach
– Friday

– Had a very easy journey, got here nicely – It's so good to be *cool*, really cool: and to see a bit of rain – We shall go out to the lake tomorrow, and get a place there to stay – will send address.

love. DHL

4091. To Ada Clarke, [5 August 1927]

Text: MS Clarke; PC v. Villach. Draupartie; Postmark, [. . .]; Unpublished.

Villach
– Friday

Had a good journey not very tired – wonderful to be really cool again, like a new life – and to see a green icy river, and feel a bit of rain – I'll send an address tomorrow. Hope you're having a good time.

DHL

4092. To Arthur Wilkinson, [5 August 1927]

Text: MS Schlaefle; PC v. Villach mit Dobratsch; Postmark, Villach [. . .]; Unpublished.

Villach.
Friday

Got here very nicely – easy journey – so queer to be quite cool – raining a bit – like another life. It's rather lovely here, a green ice-river – I mean from the ice – and the people all sort of wanderers – *so* different. Wish you were all here. Will send address tomorrow.

DHL

4093. To Baroness Anna von Richthofen, [7 August 1927]

Text: MS Jeffrey; PC v. Villach; Postmark, Villach 7. VIII 27; Unpublished.

Hotel Fischer. *Villach*, Kärnten
Sonntag

wir bleiben hier in diesem netten Gasthaus in der Stadt – es ist so interessant. Es geht mir schon besser – wir waren gestern am Ossiachersee – schön – Die Nusch kommt morgen. Wie geht's dir?

DHL

[Sunday
we're staying here in this nice inn in the town – it is so interesting. I'm already

better – yesterday we were at the Ossiacher lake – lovely – Nusch arrives tomorrow. How are you?

DHL]

4094. To Emily King, [7 August 1927]
Text: MS Lazarus; Unpublished.

Hotel Fischer, *Villach*, Kärnten. Austria
Sunday

My dear Sister

We are staying on in this simple hotel – an inn really – in the little town, because it's amusing seeing the people and the bit of life, after the very quiet Mirenda.

I am already much better – yesterday we went to the Lake, and in a motor boat to the end, and I was not so very tired. I don't walk far yet, but getting out of that dry heat of Tuscany, one feels another creature. To go to bed in a cool bed, and to drink fresh mountain water, and to breathe fresh air, that isn't baked – I can't tell you how nice it feels. I shan't stay south for the hot weather any more. – Then to be without flies and mosquitoes! – one had no peace, night or day.

Villach lies in a bit of a plain, the mountains around. But there are small motor-charabancs everywhere – and quite a lot of summer visitors, nearly all from Vienna. It's so different from Italy – people wear old clothes, and carry knapsacks, and don't mind looking like tramps – And they are so big and healthy. But the nation as a nation is very poor – almost non-existent. Italy has shoved her frontier right up into the mountains, almost to here – many many miles. – There seems to be no real government – the thing just drifts on by itself – the people all very nice and considerate – they never give you your change if you don't ask for it – yet they don't seem to care, not about anything in the world. But they are clean and healthy and perfectly aimiable, and it's a great rest after the nervousness and tension and bullying of Italy.

Write to me here. Did you get my letter with the £2. for the children? Frieda's sister comes tomorrow.

Love. DHL

4095. To Arthur Wilkinson, [7 August 1927]
Text: MS Schlaefle; cited in Pinto, *D. H. Lawrence After Thirty Years*, p. 48.

Hotel Fischer, Villach, Kärnten. Austria
Sunday.

Dear W[ilkinson]

We think after all we'll stay in this hotel – really a Gasthaus, an inn – in the little town. We went out to the Lake yesterday – but the Grand Hotel is so Grand Hotelish, and the other places just water and land: and here it's rather amusing, one can go out to so many places. – The expenses are just ordinary – exchange 34 to £1. – and room 8.50 – dinner about 3.50 – so on.

It's queer to be in a country with practically no government – a queer shabby kind of populace – quite nice – and no bosses or bossing at all – a queer empty sort of feeling, all the *forza* of Italy suddenly removed, and the *sforza* too.[1] It is much more restful to the nerves. I am much better already – went out to the lake yesterday – then down to the end of the lake on a motor-boat – all the Viennese sunning their large and naked bodies like whitish seals on the shore – save for little bathing drawers – it is *de rigeur* to be naked all day long – and nobody making the slightest effort for anything – the slackest world you ever knew. In the evening was a Firework festa by the river – very funny – home-made fireworks, in this destitute country – pans of fire blazing and floating swiftly, very swiftly, away on the full icy river, one after another – squibby fountains of fire from damp powder, on moored rafts – and a few rockets that let out six red sparks – and crowds and crowds of queer aimiable people in odd dress, and nobody to boss: dancing, beer-drinking, skittles etc. A queer world.

Frieda's sister comes tomorrow. Today I think we'll go to the Wörthersee – the Lake of Wörth – I'm quite a traveller, and all right so long as I needn't walk far. I feel a different creature here in the cool – and am eternally grateful to you all for getting me out.

There are such amusing men's jackets, that the people wear – all colours, in checks – am so tempted to buy you one – and myself – we'd look such shoots – I'd buy you a green and purple check – myself, I think, yellow and pea-green – shall I?

grüsse   DHL

4096. To Nancy Pearn, [7 August 1927]
Text: MS UT; Unpublished.

Hotel Fischer, *Villach*, Kärnten. Austria.
Sunday 8 Aug 1927

Dear Miss Pearn

Here we are, and I feel already much better, in the cool. It is heaven to go to bed in a cool bed – and to have really fresh mountain water to drink – and to be able to walk out a bit.

---

[1] *'strength . . . effort'*.

I think we shall stay here at least a fortnight – till I'm a bit more solid. So if there is anything to send, write to me here.

I left a review of Trigant Burrow's *Social basis of Consciousness* to be sent to you. I should be glad if someone printed it – even in America too – because I should like to help the book for him, if I could. But if it's a lot of trouble, don't you bother.

My wife is feeling very chirpy among the mountains again, and sends many greetings, with mine.

D. H. Lawrence

4097. To Aldous and Maria Huxley, 8 August 1927
Text: Huxley 689–90.

Hotel Fischer, Villach, Kärnten, Austria.
8 Aug., 1927.

Dear Aldous and Maria, –

Well here we are – got through on Thursday night in the *wagon-lit* – not too tired and no bad consequences. I feel already much better. What with cool air, a *cool bed*, cool mountain water – it's like a new life. I never *would* have got well, down there in that heat in Tuscany. I hope to heaven you are feeling all right. But if one is well to start with, one doesn't mind.

It is such a mercy to be able to breathe and move. I take little walks to the country – and we sit by the river – the Drave – in the little town, under the clipped trees, very 18th-century German–Werther period.[1] The river comes from the ice, and is very full and swift and pale and silent. It rather fascinates me. – And the people are so queer – those big bare Germanic legs, in *Tyroler Lederhosen* – the big bare bodies lying in the sun along the lakeside – a queer impression as if the clock was going rapidly backwards – the reversal of time – everything quiet, sort of vague – yet not dead – and everything going like the river, by itself – no apparent government, no apparent control at all. There is something restful about it – makes one wonder. I think it really is a *Schöpferische Pause.*[2] But one has to get into the backwater of the pause, to realise it a bit.

I hope you are all gay. Is Sullivan still there? Is Rose mahogany by now?[3] –

[1] I.e. the period immediately following the publication of Goethe's immensely popular novel, *Werther* (1774).
[2] Punning on the title ('Creative Pause') of a work of educational theory (1922) by Fritz Klatt (1888–1945) which DHL encountered in 1926 (*Letters*, v. 509).
[3] Rose Nys, Maria Huxley's youngest sister.

Two kisses to the boy, to thank him for his nice letter.
    Send us a line.

                                        Love,   D. H. Lawrence
    I think so often of the lotus flowers – I *must* paint them one day.

4098. To Ada Clarke, 8 August 1927
Text: MS Clarke; Lawrence–Gelder 164–6.

                        Hotel Fischer, *Villach*, Kärnten. Austria.
                                                8 Aug. 1927

My dear Sister
    It is so nice to be out of that hot Italy, and in the mountains where the air is
cool. I can imagine nothing better than a really cool bed, after one that burned
when you lay on it; and really fresh mountain water, after the tepid Italian
stuff. Of course it was a specially hot summer, even for Tuscany – and quite
exceptionally dry, no rain for three months. I wouldn't have minded if I'd
been well, but being seedy, how I hated it.
    I feel much better already, here – and can take little walks into the country.
This is a small old-fashioned town – with a nice full swift river, the Drave –
and trees along the river, and seats, where one can sit and watch the people and
the swallows, and feel like an old veteran. There are lots of summer visitors
passing all the time to the lakes and mountains – practically all Viennese.
They wear[1] any kind of clothes – the men the short Tyrolese leather trousers
and bare legs. They are big strapping people – rather vague now – gone
indifferent to all the woes. The country itself is dirt poor – the shops are
pathetic – all the rubbishy stuff nobody else will buy. Nearly all the banks
closed for good – and the ordinary people having very little money. But they
don't seem to care. They aren't very honest – they don't give you your change,
that kind of thing: but even that they do so vaguely, they don't really care.
There is no sense of control at all – most queer, after the bossiness of Fascist
Italy. And the whole thing drifts along with no trouble, everybody really very
nice, very good-mannered – pleasant. It's a great rest after Italy, and I hope I
shall soon feel fit for long walks – I can only go small ways yet. – We shall stay
on in this inn in town, I think, it is so amusing, and one can go excursions.
    I hope you are having a real good time at the sea. I have thought of you. Did
you get the money for the children?

                                                Love.   DHL

[1] MS reads 'were'.

4099. To Giulia Pini, [8 August 1927]

Text: MS NL; PC v. Villach von Osten; Postmark, [. . .]; Unpublished.

Hotel Fischer. Villach. Austria

lunedì

Abbiamo fatto molto bene il viaggio, io mi trovo molto meglio qui nelle montagne, dove l'aria è fresca. C'è un lago qui vicino, molto bello – la signora fa i bagni, io no.

Saluti a tutti   D. H. Lawrence

[*Monday*

We have enjoyed the journey very much, I feel much better here in the mountains, where the air is fresh. There is a lake nearby, very beautiful – my wife goes swimming, not I.

Best wishes to everybody   D. H. Lawrence]

4100. To S. S. Koteliansky, 10 August 1927

Text: MS BL; Postmark, V[illa]ch 10 VIII 27; Zytaruk 319.

Hotel Fischer, *Villach*. Kärnten. Austria

10 August 1927

My dear Kot

We got here on Friday – had a bed on the train all the way, so stood the journey all right. I am feeling much better, here in the cool. That heat and dryness of Tuscany was just too much for me, when I wasn't well. It seems still heavenly to go to bed in a cool bed, and not to have to sweat all the time. My chest is still a bit sore – I have to go carefully – but I can go little walks, and go in the motor to the lake – so feel myself in the land of the living once more.

Frieda's sister is staying on the lake – about six miles away. F. has gone swimming. We remained in this gasthaus in town – amusing, with all the Tyroler people coming through – no English nor American.

Austria is the same as ever – the land itself poor, very poor – the people healthy and easy-going – they don't really bother themselves – never try to get a grip on anything, not even the cash. They aren't very honest, swindle you when they can, but even then in a vague, happy-go-lucky way, very different from the Italian intensity. There seems to be no government at all – the whole show just drifts on – to another collapse, everybody says. I hope not. I can't help sympathising with them for not caring – why should one care?

I suppose we shall be here another fortnight, then move towards Bavaria, where we are to spend September. I hope my chest stays good: it is an affliction. – How are you feeling. Better, I hope. If only you went out more! Remember me to everybody.

DHL

4101. To Giuseppe Orioli, [10 August 1927]
Text: MS NWU; PC v. Maria Wörth am Wörthersee; Postmark, Villach 10 [. . .] 27; Unpublished.

Hotel Fischer. *Villach*. Austria.
10. Aug.

– We are staying on at this inn in the little town – it is very amusing, all the Tyrol and mountain-tramping people passing through – lots of Viennese, but not one English or American. I'm feeling much fresher. Frieda's sister is staying on the lake just near – F. gone swimming. How are you? Send me a line. I expect we shall be here another fortnight.

DHL

4102. To Earl Brewster, 10 August 1927
Text: MS UT; Brewster 143–4.

Hotel Fischer, *Villach*, Kärnten, Austria
10 August 1927

Dear Earl

We got here on Friday, and very much relieved to be in the cool once more, to have a cool bed and drink fresh mountain water. One can stand heat while one is well, but as soon as one goes off colour, it is very trying.

I am a good deal better already, for these few days higher up. Villach is a little old German town, with a quick, full, silent river flowing through, from the ice – the Drave – and at present, lots of visitors in Tyrolese short leather trousers and women with bare arms and little coloured aprons – you know the style of thing – all on the move, to the mountains, from the mountains, tramp, tramp, tramp. It is very different from Italy, and for the time, very refreshing.

I suppose we shall stay here another fortnight – Frieda's younger sister and husband are here – then move on to Bavaria, where we are due to spend September. I expect we shall be back at the Mirenda by the middle of October. – I do hope to heaven my chest will stay right.

I am so glad you enjoy Cimbrone in the summer, and are all busy working. One must either work or travel, it seems to me. I am no good as a meditator.

Did you find the cheque? Tell me, and I'll send it again if it's gone. But you must have it somewhere.

Be sure and thank Rose for sending me my socks – I don't know her name.

Are there any visitors still? – any flowers in the garden? Anyhow it's very nice to have *space*. When did you say Lucille was coming? – You *must* find yourselves a place of your own, it seems to me.

Remember me to Alpha – tell Achsah we had her letter –

affmo D. H. Lawrence

4103. To Martin Secker, [10 August 1927]
Text: MS UInd; PC v. Pörtschach a. Wörthersee; Postmark, Villach 10 [. . .] 27; Secker 92.

Hotel Fischer. *Villach*. Kärnten. Austria

10 Aug

We got here friday – managed very well. I feel a good deal better, up in the cool air, with a cool bed at night, and fresh mountain water. Tuscany was hell, so hot, when one was sick. Now I walk out little walks, and begin to feel a man again. Frieda's sister is staying on the lake just near. F. gone swimming, we prefer this big Gasthaus in the little old town – all the.people passing through in Tyroler get-up – very amusing – no English or American. Send a line.

DHL

4104. To Dorothy Yorke, 11 August 1927
Text: MS SIU; Moore, *Intelligent Heart* 367–8.

Hotel[1] Fischer, *Villach*, Kärnten. Austria

11 Aug. 1927

Dear Arabella

Your man Slonimsky sent his letter from Florence the day we left[2] – and it has just come on here. If you write him, tell him I'm sorry we missed him.

We usually get out of the heat earlier, but this year I was in bed with bronchials and bronchial hemorrhage all July, and felt a poor specimen. Also it was terribly hot – no rain for three months. But I crawled into a wagon-lit, and we got here Friday. It is cool, among the mountains, and I feel a good deal better. But I am afflicted with these bronchials of mine.

Frieda's younger sister is here, with her husband, staying on the Ossiachersee about six miles away. F. has just gone there swimming – it's her birthday – I shall go out to lunch. I cant swim, or bathe – or even walk very far. Makes me so cross. But it is pleasant here, in this big Gasthaus in the little town – all the Tyroler mountainy people going through – and the food is really good. Also I like Villach – little old German place – and the nice full river – the Drau – that goes so quick and silent.

[1] Hotel] Villa
[2] Henry Slominsky, American, friend of John Cournos when he lived in Philadelphia (cf. *Letters*, iv. 296 n. 1).

I think we shall stay till about 24th – then move north – we're supposed to spend September in Bavaria.

Be sure and tell Slonimsky. – and I hope you're having a nice summer.

DHL

4105. To Gertrude Cooper, [11 August 1927]

Text: MS Clarke; PC v. St. Rupprecht u. Ossiacher See; Postmark, Villach 11.VIII.27; Unpublished.

Hotel Fischer. *Villach*. Kärnten. Austria

[11 August 1927]

Had your letter today – I do wish you were a bit further ahead, it is so terribly long.[1] We got out of Italy a week ago, myself rather feeble after a month in bed. What a curse a chest can be. I am better, but the cough is a nuisance – I hope it will go away here in the mountains, in the cool. The heat of Italy was fearful, the last month, no rain, everything burnt up. It is much fresher here, but lovely weather. This lake is just near, and we go out for Frieda to swim. Her sister is there too, staying on the lake. I expect we shall be here another fortnight, then go to Germany for September. I do so wish you could walk and get about – it is wearying!

DHL

4106. To Arthur Wilkinson, [11 August 1927]

Text: MS Schlaefle; PC v. Annenheim am Ossiacher See; Postmark, Villach 11.VIII.27; Unpublished.

[Hotel Fischer, *Villach*, Kärnten, Austria]

11 Aug

The ten letters and yours arrived today – many thanks. No, don't send any papers or books. – This is the terrace of the hotel where F[rieda]'s sister is – we go out every day, for F. to bathe. It is her birthday today, so we are celebrating out there with a Bohle.[2] I am better, but the cough is a nuisance. – Yes, the meadows are green green, by the lake – the pine woods very dark – there are harebells and bilberries. – I bought my jacket, green, red, purple, rather dark – wool – and green collar – they are really to go with Tyroler costume – bare knees. If I decide to get you one, I shall post it. But they'll look mighty queer in Italy[3] and England.

DHL

Do I put right stamps on? It is different for England, Germany, and Italy.

---

[1] The card was addressed to Mundesley Hospital (cf. Letter 4025).   [2] 'hot punch'.

[3] in Italy] in Austria and Italy

4107. To Harwood Brewster, 12 August 1927
Text: MS Picard; Brewster 144–5.

Hotel Fischer. *Villach.* Kärnten. Austria

12 August 1927

My dear Harwood

I have owed you a letter a long time – but have been such a sad bird with my precious chest, so you must accept my excuses.

I couldn't help buying you a shiny hair-ribbon of this peasant ribbon – I've got another also; if this one comes safely, I'll send it: a green one. I think they're rather smart, but Frieda thinks they're 'loud.' They can be deafening, for what I care: they are gay.

We stayed on here in the little town, instead of going out – about 6 miles – to the lake, because the hotel there is so hotelly. But F's sister and husband insist we ought to join them there. It's very nice, a clear little green lake with steep pine-covered sides and little peasant clearings – everything very green and fresh, still forget-me-nots and harebells – and blueberries. I find it *very* refreshing to come north, after a year in Italy. And the Austrians are amusing, so big and healthy and happy-go-lucky – they lie about with very small bathing-drawers, by the lake, and it's perfectly amazing, what huge great limbs they've got. They're like sea-lions, so inert and prostrate. Nobody has much money, and the poor people want to make a revolution every five minutes – but I can't see what there is to revolute against. It's all somehow beside the point – and like being asleep. – Your Aunt Frieda goes swimming like the rest, and is so frightened at the size of the others, she eats no tea. I have a bit of cake all alone.

I am better, but not bouncing, and the cough is a nuisance, and I wish I could get a new breathing apparatus. But it's no good grumbling.

I suppose you *are* bouncing as ever: holding up your chin and being a Schwannhild and a Mélisande[1] and a willow-wand and all that: I hope you are having a gay time at Cimbrone: give the blue Venus a kiss from me, and wipe young Mercury's nose.[2] As for the rest of the statues, I refuse to have any communication with them.

Herzliche Grüsse   David

---

[1] Schwannhild – DHL's name for Harwood Brewster (Brewster 271) – Old Norse heroine, daughter of Sigurd and Gudrun; Melisande (Melusina) the most famous enchantress in French romance.
[2] Statues in the Cimbrone grounds (see Letter 3983 and p. 22 n. 3).

4108. To Hon. Dorothy Brett, [13 August 1927]

Text: MS UCin; Postmark, Villach 13.VIII.27; Moore 997.

Hotel Fischer, *Villach*, Austria
14 Aug 1927

Dear Brett

We came here a week ago – It was fearfully hot and dry at the Mirenda, and I had rather a bad whack of bronchials. However, it is passing off here in the mountains.

This is a little German old-fashioned place N.E. of Venice. There's a full, quick river flowing through – and Tyrol mountain-tourists with bare knees, you know the sort – and lots of beer – Austria feels very happy-go-lucky, poor as ever, but nobody bothers about anything. I think we shall stay here till end of August, then go to Bavaria for September. I don't feel in any hurry to get back to Italy, prefer to be in the mountains for a time.

I enclose snaps of five[1] of my pictures – there's a *Fight with an Amazon*[2] – not here – and two little ones. I don't think the photographs give one much idea – We heard from F[rieda]'s daughter Barby that Dorothy Warren has got the smartest private art-gallery place in London[3] – asked Barby to show her pictures – and she, B., sold one to Lord Something Churchill, she didn't say for how much.[4] Dorothy Warren wants me to send my pictures to her – but I'm diffident – don't feel very showy.

I had your letter about Clarence – I'm sorry he is so stuck in those movies.[5] How is Spud, by the way? Nobody tells me.

I think if my bronchials remain stuck, we'll have to bust all our money sailing round the world to San Francisco – the sea-voyage does one good. But I'm hoping they'll clear up.

Tell Mabel I'll send her snaps if she wants them. Did you ever get your

[1] five] six
[2] DHL told Brett on 19 December 1926 that he had done this painting, 'a quick one' (*Letters*, v. 606).
[3] Dorothy Cecil Wynter Warren (1896–1954) met DHL at Garsington, 1915–16 (Lady Ottoline Morrell was her aunt); he thought her 'beautiful' (*Letters*, ii. 504 n. 2, 516). She was a friend of Catherine Carswell, Gertler and Barbara Weekley. The Warren Gallery, at 39A Maddox Street, London W. 1, later housed the exhibition of DHL's paintings, June–September 1929, which was raided by the police.
[4] Lord Ivor Charles Spencer-Churchill (1898–1956), one of the most discerning patrons of contemporary French and British artists. See the article on his collection, *The Times*, 27 June 1928, pp. 17–18. Cf. Letter 4144.
[5] Clarence E. Thompson, intimate friend of Mabel Luhan; DHL first met him in Taos in 1924. He had become a screen-writer. See *Letters*, v. 42 n. 2.

copy of *Mornings in Mexico*? How is the weather at the ranch. Sudden deluge
here, but nice after the dryness of Italy.

Grüsse   DHL

Do send snaps of yours.

4109. To Nancy Pearn, 13 August 1927
Text: MS Lazarus; Unpublished.

Hotel Fischer, Villach, Kärnten, Austria.

13 Aug. 1927

Dear Miss Pearn

Your letter today.

I am getting better – slowly – but I hope surely – a bit tired of my state.

This is to say, I'm afraid we shan't be back in Italy till mid-October – I'm
afraid I must stay about 2000 ft. above sea-level a bit – so we shall have my
sister-in-law's summer house in Bavaria for Sept., I think.[1] But you *must* go
out to the Villa Mirenda. I enclose a letter to our neighbours, the Wilkinsons[2]
– our only neighbours – five minutes away. They are vegetarians and a bit
Bernard Shawey (they don't like him though) – and they have a puppet show
(the Gair-Wilkinsons – that *Peep-Show* book is by his brother)[3] when they're
in London – live on a raw carrot sort of thing – but they are nice, and were very
kind to me, and are sure to be nice to you. I'll write them. And if you'd like to
camp in our flat in the Villa Mirenda – there it is – and the peasant girl Giulia
will look after you. The Wilkinsons would see you were all right. The beds are
hard, and my pictures might scare you – but for the rest it's all right. –
Remember you go out from behind the *Cathedral Baptistry* in Florence – Via
dei Pecori – by tram *no. 16*, to *Vingone* terminus: and there the Wilkinsons
would meet you or send the pony cart down for you. And as I say, if you have a
friend and would like to camp in the Villa Mirenda, *do* do so.

Duomo (cathedral) – tram 16. – to Vingone terminus – from there it is
nearly two miles.

I'm so sorry we shall be away.

Yrs   D. H. Lawrence

---

[1] Else Jaffe's house at Irschenhausen.
[2] DHL's enclosure is missing.
[3] See Letter 4017 and n. 3. Walter Wilkinson, author of *The Peep Show*, was a professional
puppeteer; he published several accounts of his travels with puppet-shows: *Puppets in
Yorkshire* (1931), *Puppets into Scotland* (1935), *Puppets through America* (1938), etc.

4110. To Baroness Anna von Richthofen, [17 August 1927]

Text: MS Jeffrey; PC v. Ossiach am Ossiacher See; Postmark, [. . .] 17 VIII. 27; Frieda
Lawrence, *Nur Der Wind*, p. 291.

[Hotel Fischer, *Villach*, Kärnten, Austria]
Mitwoch

Die Adresse Krug's ist Grand Hotel. Annenheim bei Villach – sie sind heute
nach Millstatt gefahren – 2¼ Stunde in Auto, zu weit für mich. Es hat
furchtbar geregnet, ist wieder schön, Sonne und kühle Luft. Es geht mir
immer besser – langsam, aber sicher. Wann kommt die Else dir zurück? – In
Italien hat's noch nicht geregnet, und Hitze nicht zu ertragen. Gott sei dank,
ich bin fort. Wir haben Aquarellenfarben gekauft, und wollen malen: so will
ich dir ein Bildle machen. Ich suche ein Leihbibliotek für die Bücher – wir
lesen jetzt Theodor Storm, in 18 Bänden – von der Wirtin. Ich bin froh, es
geht dir gut. War's zu heiss in Baden. Wir futtern sehr gut hier – Reh!

DHL

[Wednesday
The Krugs' address is Grand Hotel. Annenheim near Villach – today they've
gone to Millstatt – 2¼ hours in the car, too far for me. It's rained terribly, is
now fine again, sun and cool air. I'm getting better and better – slowly but
surely. When does Else come back to you? – There's been no rain in Italy yet,
and unbearable heat. Thank God I've got away. We've bought water-colours,
and intend to paint: so I will do you a little picture. I'm looking for a lending
library for books – at the moment we're reading Theodor Storm, in 18
volumes[1] – from the landlady. I'm happy that you're well. It was too hot in
Baden. Grub is very good here – venison!

DHL]

4111. To Martin Secker, 17 August 1927

Text: MS UInd; Postmark, Villach 18.VIII.1927; Secker 93.

Hotel Fischer, *Villach*, Kärnten. Austria.
17 Aug 1927

Dear Secker

Glad to get your letter today, and very kind of you to send the papers. They
are quite welcome, as I am tired of Theodor Storm.

I am getting on pretty well – hope I shall *really* get my bronchials better
fixed up this time. Today we have been all day at a lovely little lake, the

[1] Theodor Woldsen Storm (1817–88), prolific writer of novels, poetry and letters.

Faakersee – turquoise blue, with the bare rock of the Karawanken mountains
behind. It is still lovely to see the meadows lush green, instead of that parched
Tuscany – it hasn't rained there *yet* – and the big patches of pinky buckwheat
are pretty – I didn't know buckwheat in flower before. – The Austrians are
really very nice – so happy-go-lucky and easy – and on the whole, healthy and
handsome. It is a relief to be here, after the friction and bossiness of Italy. And
people really don't struggle very hard to make money – they don't seem to
care.

Didn't Curtis Brown's show you the Etruscan Essays? They had them, and
photographs, and I particularly want to know what you think of them. If you
haven't seen them yet – I specially told Miss Pearn to send them over to you –
just get them, and then tell me really what you think. Half the book is there.
But if you don't like it, I shan't be in any hurry to finish it: though it interests
me very much, and I think it's good. – If you'd like to do a vol. of short stories
in early spring, then do so – I'm sure there are plenty, with 'Woman Who
Rode Away', which is long. Did you read 'The Man Who Loved Islands'? in
the *London Mercury*? I do hope Mackenzie wouldn't mind – the thing isn't
personal at all.

I should love to do the west coast of Ireland one[1] day. Shall we do it perhaps
together? It should be a jolly trip, next year.

I am doing translations of the *Cavalleria Rusticana* stories, for Cape – to go
with his *Mastro-don Gesualdo*. You won't mind that.

I left the MS. of *Lady Chatterley* at the Mirenda – one day I'll show it you
privately. I want to write a continuation of it, later.

I think we shall stay here till about the 28th. We are due to spend Sept. in
the Isartal, near München – in a house of F[rieda]'s sister. – The younger
sister is here from Berlin – viel Quatsch![2] – Remember us nicely to Rina and
the boy, and to Mrs Lamont.[3]

                                                                          DHL

4112. To Emily King, [17 August 1927]
Text: MS Needham; PC v. Grossglocknergipfel 3798 m; Postmark, [. . .]; Unpublished.

                                   [Hotel Fischer, *Villach*, Kärnten, Austria]
                                                                          Wed

Had your letter yesterday – and the other one came on from Florence – was
glad to hear about the business, and hope it will flourish. When are the

---

[1] one] together one   [2] 'much rubbish!'
[3] The 'boy' was Adrian Secker; Lucy Lamont (1859–1953), widow of the Scottish painter
    Reynolds Lamont (1826–98), lived with the Seckers at Bridgefoot (see *Letters*, v. 315 n. 2).

children coming back from the sea? We had a night of fierce rain – snow on the mountains – but now the sun is strong again, though the air is deliciously cool. I prefer it cool. The Wilkinsons write, still no rain at the Mirenda: awful. I am getting a bit better all the time, thank heaven. We shall be here another week. The view is the top of the mountain near here.

Love. DHL

4113. To Giuseppe Orioli, [20 August 1927]
Text: MS UCLA; cited in Moore, *Intelligent Heart* 368.

Hotel Fischer, Villach. Austria.
Saturday.

Dear Pino

I wonder if you are still at Vallombrosa – and if it has rained. Here there have been great thunderstorms and torrents of rain, and it is almost cold, I am thinking of woolen underwear: nippy!

What is your news? how is Reggie? and is he still at Lucerne? is your boy back again, and how did he like being up there in Piedmont? We hear only from the Wilk[inson]s, who faithfully send me on my letters; they are almost roasted alive in San Polo, and I think a bit bored. But they too go to the hills next week.

Is everywhere crowded? here there are endless numbers of tourists, everywhere full up: but they are all Austrians, no Inglesi nor Americani. I am the only phoenix! I like it all right – we make little excursions in the motor-buses to the various lakes, which are quite beautiful. Frieda's sister is on the Ossiachersee, just near – we see them a good deal – but she, my cognata, is not very contented, having got a newish bourgeois banker husband, ten years older than herself, instead of a neer-do-well ex-army officer – she changed them four years ago – the husbands, I mean[1] – and the good bourgeois bores her and oppresses her, and she is in a bad humour, having always lived a gay life; and altogether I think the female of the species is a trial nowadays.

Please tell me what part of the anatomy are the froge? when the cavalla – gonfiara le froge al pari di un mastino ringhioso[2] – which part of her precious self did she swell out? – and what do you imagine is a *campiere*? – a *campaio*[3] I take it is a man in charge of certain[4] fields – but what is a campiere? – and if you see a good fat dictionary with no *crusca*,[5] do peep in and see how much an *onza* was worth – about 15 Lire, I believe. – But about the last, don't bother. – As

---

[1] See p. 26 n. 3.   [2] 'mare swells out her nostrils like a snarling hound'.
[3] 'campiere' is the Sicilian version of 'campaio'.   [4] certain] the certain
[5] 'bran' (DHL was punning on the dictionary published by the Accademia della Crusca).

you may guess, I translate my Verga on rainy days, and I still like him, and still worry you about him.

I think we shall be here till the 28th – so write to me.

DHL

4114. To Earl Brewster, 22 August 1927
Text: MS UT; Brewster 146–7.

Hotel Fischer, *Villach*, Kärnten, Austria
Monday 22 August 1927

Dear Earl

I had your letter – glad all goes well at Cimbrone – but don't envy you that heat. It's almost cold here – and I like it – but sunny. I'm much better, though now sneezing violently, for a variation.

I think one can summon up energy – in fact am sure. But it is much easier to summon it up if one has an object in view – that is, for some definite purpose – than just for the sake of having the energy. And curiously, it seems much easier to summon up energy for some egoistic or mercenary purpose, particularly for the enforcing of the egoistic *will*, than for a good purpose. For a good purpose, or a good flow, it seems much easier to summon up energy collectively – if two or three are gathered together.[1] But the charlatan and the witch and the fakir can summon up a lot of energy just for their own ends. I'm surprised what a lot of that there is in the world – especially in the business world – a fakir-like energised charlatanry, consciously self-energised. I believe Henry Ford and President Wilson were that way, and very many others.[2] Que veux-tu?[3]

We are still here – shall stay presumably another week, till the 29th. Then from the 1st Sept. the address will be

per Adr. Frau Dr. Jaffe-Richthofen –

Irschenhausen, Post Ebenhausen. *presso Monaco di Baviera*

We shall have a wooden chalet-house there – belonging to F[rieda]'s sister – and shall stay the month, I expect.

I enclose this little cheque which I found in my bag. If the other one has[4] already turned up, give this to Harwood, and she can buy herself a powder-puff and a pot of rouge.

Today is Jahrmarkt[5] here, and I hear the lowing of cattle and the neighing

[1] Cf. Mark xviii. 20.
[2] Henry Ford (1863–1947), American industrialist; Thomas Woodrow Wilson (1856–1942), twenty-eighth President of USA.   [3] 'What would you expect?'   [4] has] had
[5] The annual fair.

of horses in my ear, so will get up and look at the spoil of the Amalekite.[1] It is a sunny day with an almost chill air, a bit of snow on the mountains.

I'm glad you are all busy painting. Do my orange-coloured nymphs and fauns look a sight?[2] I bought water-colours here, but so far, have not wet a brush.

I don't think we shall stay long in the Mirenda. Probably in the New Year we shall go up into the mountains, perhaps Cortina, to the snow. The mountains seem better for me. Alas, the lotus is not my blossom, though it's a lovely flower. –

What are your plans too? – indefinite Cimbrone? I should think lotus flowers would grow well in a pool there – if there is ever a pool: instead of the roses of the late lord's ladies.

Herzliche Grüsse   DHL

4115. To Giulia Pini, [23 August, 1927]
Text: MS UT; PC v. Villach; Postmark, [. . .]; Unpublished.

Villach, Austria –
23 agosto.

Cara Giulia

– Partiamo di qui lunedì, il 29, e andiamo in Germania, alla sorella della Signora. Di là, ti scriverò. – Stiamo bene tutti due – io sono guarito. I signori della Villa Poggi scrivano sempre – se vuoi mandarci una parola, puoi dirla a loro. Vanno tutti bene a San Polo? ha piovuto ancora? – e l'uva, come è?

– tanti saluti a tutti.   D. H. Lawrence

[23 August

Dear Giulia

– We are leaving here on Monday, the 29th, and we are going to Germany, to my wife's sister. I will write to you from there. – We are well both of us – I have recovered. The people at the Villa Poggi are always writing – if you want to send us a word, you can tell them. Is everybody all right in San Polo? has it rained again? – and the grapes, how are they?

– best wishes to everybody.   D. H. Lawrence]

---

[1] Cf. 1 Samuel xv. 14–15, 18–19.
[2] When at Ravello, 22–8 March 1927, DHL painted *Fauns and Nymphs*, one of his largest pictures (38″ × 32″), *The Paintings of D. H. Lawrence*, plate [12]. Achsah Brewster describes the 'excitement' in which the painting was done (Brewster 275).

4116. To Ada Clarke, [23 August 1927]

Text: MS Clarke; PC v. Tauernbahn. Rottauer-Viadukt mit Station Kolbnitz; Postmark, [. . .]; Unpublished.

[Hotel Fischer, *Villach*, Kärnten, Austria]
23. Aug

Glad to have your letter and to know you feel good and brisk. I am getting on all right. We shall leave here next Monday – 29th – and on the 1st September we shall be at:

c/o Frau Dr. Jaffé-Richthofen, Irschenhausen,
Post Ebenhausen, near Munich.

Emily sent very jolly snaps of the children too. Weather almost hot again here.

Love.   DHL

4117. To Emily King, [23 August 1927]

Text: MS Needham; PC v. Villach, Draupartie mit Blick auf die Karawanken; Postmark, Villach 23.VIII.27; Unpublished.

[Hotel Fischer, *Villach*, Kärnten, Austria]
23 Aug

Had your letter yesterday – the snaps of the children are very amusing, – they look awfully jolly. We leave here next Monday – 29th – and on the 1st Sept. shall be

c/o Frau Dr Else Jaffe-Richthofen, Irschenhausen,
Post Ebenhausen, near Munich.

I will write directly – or F[rieda] will.

love.   DHL

4118. To Nancy Pearn, 23 August 1927

Text: MS UT; Unpublished.

Hotel Fischer, *Villach*. Kärnten. Austria
23 Aug 1927

Dear Miss Pearn

I wonder if you have started yet on your holiday.

We leave here next Monday, 29th – and on Sept. 1st shall be at

c/o Frau Dr. Jaffe-Richthofen, Irschenhausen,
Post Ebenhausen, near *Munich*

Would you please give the address to the other depts? I suppose we shall stay a month in Bavaria.

You had my letter enclosing the introduction to Mrs Wilkinson, our neighbour? – she said she had written to you. I do hope you'll have a real good holiday.

I sent three of the stories from the *Cavalleria Rusticana* volume – hope they came safely.

Again best wishes for the holiday, from us both.

D. H. Lawrence

4119. To S. S. Koteliansky, [24 August 1927]

Text: MS BL; PC v. Villach. Partie am Drau-Ufer; Postmark, [Vill]ach 2[. . .]; Zytaruk 320.

[Hotel Fischer, *Villach*, Kärnten, Austria]

24 Aug

I had your letter – cross as ever – as for Frieda, it is mere heedlessness, nothing worse. – Still quite sunny and hot here, but not too much. We leave next Monday, 29th – for Salzburg – and on 1st Sept. are at

c/o Frau Dr Jaffe-Richthofen, Irschenhausen,

Post *Ebenhausen*, nr Munich

are you alone in the cave?[1] – like that hot summer when we came too? It's a pity you can't go really away somewhere for a while. I'll write a letter properly, just now.

DHL

4120. To Giuseppe Orioli, [24 August 1927]

Text: MS NWU; PC v. Dobratsch (2167m) Deutsche Kirche mit Julische Alpen; Postmark Vill[ach] [. . .]; cited in Moore, *Poste Restante* 93.

Villach

24 aug.

I sent you a letter the other day to Hotel Panorama – will they forward it, if you're not there? We leave here next Monday – 29th for Salzburg – and on 1st Sept. the address is

c/o Frau Dr. Jaffe-Richthofen, Irschenhausen,

Post *Ebenhausen*, nr Munich

When do you go to Paris? I think we shall stay in Bavaria all Sept. Is Douglas back, and has it rained?

DHL

4121. To Mabel Dodge Luhan, 25 August 1927

Text: MS Brill; Luhan 333–4.

Hotel Fischer. Villach. Austria

25 Aug 1927

Dear Mabel

Heard from Brett today – she says you are learning to drive the Buick and

---

[1] Kot's home had been known as 'the cave' or 'cavern' since at least 1918 (see *Letters*, iii. 250).

stepping on the gas like ten heroines. Don't do it. Camminando si arriva.[1]
Stepping on the gas one goes over the edge, which is not an arrival.

We've been here three weeks – me convalescing, and not very pleased with
myself. I had a miserable month at the Mirenda with my bronchials and
hemorrhages – seems to get me in July – and I'm still only about a third there.
I do hate it. We're going next week to a house of my sister-in-laws in Bavaria,
to stay a month, as arranged: but send me a line

c/o Frau Baronin von Richthofen,

Ludwig-Wilhelmstift, *BadenBaden.*

I still think with hankering of the ranch in the early spring – if I can, we
shall come. A change of continent would do me good. Except that the altitude,
for bronchials, is what the doctor calls a bleeding altitude. But who knows – I
was so well again there that last summer.

What about the Memoirs?[2] are you waiting a while?

And were those books all right? I'll bet, when you saw them you only cursed
them. But we did our best.

Austria is queer – seems to have gone quite void. It's like being at the centre
of a vital vacuum. The people are healthy, rather handsome, and don't seem to
care about a thing – a void, where caring is concerned. Most queer! But the
peasants look unpleasant and stink of greed. – This queer vacuum is the centre
of Europe. I wonder what wind will whirl in to fill it up. Anyhow the world is
far past my understanding. – A German wrote a book called *Schöpferische
Pause* – Creative Pause. I don't know whether this is one. It seems to me more
than pause, even more than a blank full stop. Yet with such healthy bodies
bathing and lying by the lake, you never saw. California on a small scale.
L'ideale del vuoto.[3]

Taos sounds nothing but a mad Valkyrie of motor cars in Brett's last. Send
in a line to say you are all soothed down to ten miles an hour.

DHL

4122. To Rowena Killick, 26 August 1927
Text: MS UT; Unpublished.

Hotel Fischer. Villach. Austria

26 August 1927

Dear Miss Kilnich[4]

Herewith the corrected proofs of the Galsworthy 'Scrutiny'.[5]

[1] 'You arrive by taking it easy.'   [2] See Letter 4021 and p. 58 n. 3.
[3] 'The ideal of the void.'
[4] Rowena Killick was Nancy Pearn's secretary and acted on her behalf when Pearn was on
holiday.   [5] See Letter 4027 and p. 67 n. 1.

Have you received the MS. of the three stories of *Cavalleria Rusticana*?
They are for Jonathan Cape ultimately, but someone might print them
periodically.

I don't know if Miss Pearn had my last letters. Will you please note that the
address after next Monday is:

c/o Frau Dr Jaffe-Richthofen,

Irschenhausen, *Post Ebenhausen*, near Munich.

and would you mind giving it to the other departments.

Yours Sincerely   D. H. Lawrence

4123. To Ada Clarke, 27 August 1927
Text: MS Clarke; cited in Lawrence–Gelder 166–7.

Hotel Fischer, Villach, Austria
27 Aug 1927

My dear Sister

I was thinking about your letter, and Gertie. Poor thing, one can
understand she wants to get away from that place. Yet while she needs special
care and attention, how can you have her in Ripley! It is much better to wait
the while, till she is more independent. But it must be most, most wearying for
her. And her money dwindling away. But she needn't worry about that. If she
even gets stony, we can manage her between us. I could tell the bank to pay her
£50 a year – and I'd never know, when it goes out that way. Somehow I don't
like sending bits of money and presents and things. But if I told the bank to
pay her a pound a week – as I say, I should never know. So don't let her bother
about money, but let me know if she still has enough, or if I should begin to
help her now. I could pay it to you, so she needn't worry. And don't tell
anybody, I hate these money things talked about.

I am a good bit better – cough still a nuisance, but less than it was.
Yesterday it poured with rain, and at evening the mountains came out white
with snow, almost to the foot – and the air almost freezing. It is still icy cold
this morning, but the sun is out, so it wont last. F[rieda] has got a cold, all the
same. I do hope to heaven I wont get it. Irschenhausen is higher than here –
over 2000 ft – so it'll be chilly there, if this spell lasts. – We leave on Tuesday,
and go straight to Munich, and Else will meet us there. I gave you the address:

c/o Frau Dr Else Jaffe-Richthofen,

Irschenhausen, *Post Ebenhausen*, nr Munich.

Johanna and her husband Emil are stopping on here till the 3rd. He is quite
nice – a man of 52, manager in a bank in Berlin – but she can't stand him, and
pines for nothing but to be away from him. She says it's not him she hates, but
marriage itself. Certainly there's a certain heavy sort of bourgeois dulness in

him, that must be a bit stifling. But if she'd make the best of it, instead of the worst, it would be so much better. I do get sick of these discontented women, who'd be discontented if you gave them Paradise in their hand.

It's been nice staying here – going out on the autos to all the lakes among the hills round about – and everybody quite friendly and nice. But one does get tired of an hotel, even when the food is really good and the servants as nice as they are here. I think we shall enjoy that cosy wooden house in the Isartal – I've not seen it since 1913, when Edgar was there.

What are things like among the miners? – are they rather depressed? The foreign papers give a bad account of the condition of England – trade and so on – But one never knows.

Love to all!   DHL

4124. To Miss Wells, 29 August 1927
Text: MS UT; Unpublished.

per Adr Frau Dr Jaffe-Richthofen, Irschenhausen, Post Ebenhausen, near
Munich
29 Aug 1927

Dear Miss Wells[1]

Thanks for your letter. I didn't know about that law.[2] Rather a blow to lose $\frac{1}{5}$ of one's meagre earnings!

Will you tell me please if the publisher will always deduct the tax? – so that I have no responsibility. – And does the law apply to stories sold to magazines, or only strictly to *royalties*?

Yours Sincerely   D. H. Lawrence

I expect to be at the above address for the month of September.

4125. To Lilian Wilkinson, 3 September 1927
Text: MS Schlaefle; cited in Sagar, Wilkinsons 70.

Irschenhausen, Post Ebenhausen, bei München
3 Sept. 1927

Dear Mrs Wilkinson

Are you back from your walk? – I found the two cards from Poppy – i[3] – and thankful you weren't snowed in. We got here on Wednesday evening – lovely weather – found my sister-in-law in Munich. It's so queer being here, where I've not been since 1913 – Nothing is altered, except trees grown tall. The

---

[1] She was on the staff of Curtis Brown's London office (cf. *Letters*, v. 449 n. 2).
[2] It came into force in July 1927; see Letter 4131.
[3] Poppi, a small town 25 miles e. of Florence.

little house sits – brown wood and red roof – in its corner of meadow on the shoulder in the forest – and looks wide away over the Isar Valley, and the big mountains shadowy. It is so still, so motionless, and nobody – as if there were nobody in the world. The woods are beech and fir – lovely, quite lovely really – the squirrels so tame they don't run away. In the spring and early summer the deer come round the fence – but now they are deep in the forest. – It is surprising how little this country has changed – a big open landscape striped with forest and strips of field. I like it very much – there is no time, and no event – only the sun shines with that pleasant hotness of autumn, and in the shadow it is chill. If ever you come to Bavaria we must try to get you this house.

We had a letter from Giulia today, so nice, and so amusing, with its quaint spelling. If you see her, tell her we have it.

Miss Pearn said she would love to come out and see you, and she might even like to camp in our flat. I told[1] Giulia about it – and she asks which beds she is to prepare. Perhaps you will tell her, when you know a little more definitely what Miss Pearn intends. I hate bothering you – but perhaps you won't mind. I only hope Miss Pearn would be comfortable enough.

I feel it *must* be cool in San Paolo by now. Here the nights are really cold – and we shut the double doors – the doors and windows are all double. The autumn crocuses are out in the lush green meadows – in the stillness of autumn, only ducks quacking. I am just going to take my little afternoon doze on the balcony – Frieda and Else are going by train one station to Wolfratshausen, the old little town of the Isar Valley – and you never knew such stillness, as there is. – But we've got the good servant Anna who was here years ago[2] – can all be completely lazy. – I do hope you're feeling fresh and chirpy after your walking tour – I'm sure it was fun. Tell Bims I had her card.[3]

I hated Munich – *such* a big town, though beautiful in its way. But big towns worry me. Write and tell us the news; very many greetings.

D. H. Lawrence

4126. To Rowena Killick, 3 September 1927
Text: MS UT; Unpublished.

Irschenhausen, *Post Ebenhausen*, bei München
3 Sept. 1927

Dear Miss Killnich
    Do keep the third copy of the *Cavalleria Rusticana* stories for me till all are

---

[1] told] asked
[2] In Letter 4129 she is described having been the servant of Edgar Jaffe (who died in 1921).
[3] 'Bim(s)' was the nickname of Frances Gair Wilkinson.

typed, then I'll go over them.[1] The book was first published in 1880 – and I believe was never copyrighted at all. –

Have you got a copy[2] of that story 'The Rocking-Horse Winner'? Or else could you please send me a copy of Cynthia Asquith's *Ghost Book*, in which the story appeared. My sister-in-law wants to translate it for *Jugend*, and I think it would do very well.[3]

Has Miss Pearn actually gone off?

Sincerely   D. H. Lawrence

4127. To Emily King, [4 September 1927]

Text: MS Needham; PC v. Wolfratshausen; Postmark, München 4 9 27; Unpublished.

[Irschenhausen, *Post Ebenhausen*, bei München]
Sunday

– We met Else in Munich on Wednesday, and came straight here – it's just the same, though I've not been here since 1913 – so still and lovely, with the forest behind and the space of the valley in front. I like it very much, and am feeling much better – I think the air suits me here – just over 2000 ft. – will write a letter.

love   DHL

4128. To Ada Clarke, [4 September 1927]

Text: MS Clarke; PC v. Wolfratshausen; Postmark, München 4 9 27; Lawrence–Gelder 167–8.

[Irschenhausen, *Post Ebenhausen*, bei München]
Sunday

We came here on Wed. evening – met Else in Munich – it is just the same, the little wooden house in a corner of the forest, so still and pleasant. I like it here, and really feel much better. I had your letter, and so glad G[ertie] is so well – what a relief to think of her really going about comfortably. Autumn here, but lovely.

DHL

---

[1] Nancy Pearn told DHL on 30 August 1927 (TMSC UT) that three typed copies had been made; she offered to send one to him.

[2] copy] story (Nancy Pearn sent a copy of the story to DHL on 16 September 1927, TMSC UT.)

[3] The story (written in February 1926) appeared in the volume compiled by Lady Cynthia in September 1926 (see *Letters*, v. 400 n. 1). Else Jaffe did not publish a translation of it in *Jugend*.

4129. To Emil Krug, 7 September 1927
Text: MS UT; Unpublished.

Irschenhausen, *Post Ebenhausen*, bei München
7 Sept 1927

Dear Emil

I should have written to you to Annenheim, if I had known you were staying on so long. We had a good journey to München – got there an hour late, though – and on the Wednesday we came here with Else. It is awfully nice, a little wooden house in the corner of the forest: and I think, just the right thing for me. I drink goat's milk, and Anna, Edgar's servant, looks after us well.

Nusch came on Monday – had to carry her bag two kilometers from Ebenhausen, because no-one expected her yet. She is looking very brown, and much better, even for the last week in Annenheim. She leaves tomorrow for Stuttgart.

You can imagine the three sisters here together, how they talk! They sit in the sun or in the shade, and schwätzen schwätzen[1] all day long. Impossible that any three people should have so much to say to one another. But of course, they are perfectly happy, just talking.

It is lovely weather, warm, lovely sunshine, Nusch living in her pyjamas. We thought of you yesterday, having to go back into that office. Bitter! Life should be arranged differently.

My little Kittele – Kitterle[2] – how do you spell it? – is very much admired here, I feel a great swell in it, almost a Lord Byron.

Germany is really much more cheerful than Austria – poor Austria. I was amazed at the busy prosperity of Munich: such energy too. And these little villages are so clean and so newly painted and so spick-and-span, quite a pleasure.

I do hope you're not finding work *too* repulsive, after the free time. It was a good time we had together in Kärnten, and we'll have more good times in the future.

Ever   DHL

4130. To Emily King, 7 September 1927
Text: MS Lazarus; Moore 1000–1.

Irschenhausen, *Post Ebenhausen*, nr Munich
7[3] Sept 1927

My dear Sister

It is such lovely weather here the days slip by like nothing – then Johanna

---

[1] 'gossip gossip'.   [2] 'blouse or smock' ('kittel').   [3] 7] 6

came on Monday, on her way from Austria to Baden – Else met us in Munich when we arrived – so you may guess there is a chatter all day long, with the three sisters.

I like this place very much – It is fourteen years since I was here last – 1913 – one can hardly believe it – and the place is just the same, only the trees grown taller and the paint got shabby. One feels my brother-in-law Edgar so strongly – he died in 1918[1] – almost as if he were somewhere about the place. He loved his little Bow-wow! as he called it – meaning a dog-kennel. It's a nice little wooden house – a little châlet – in a meadow of its own on the hill shoulder in a corner of the forest. The forest goes on for miles behind – with open places – and in winter and spring the deer all come out – but now they're retired away. One wanders about where one will – nothing is shut off, all the country is open. I really like it very much, one feels free, on the open earth. Italy is so very much more occupied. There are very few people here. We've got a good servant – Edgar's Anna of 14 years ago – and I drink goat's milk, and really feel better. I hope the lovely autumn sunshine will last: and the moon in the fresh nights.

Johanna leaves tomorrow for Baden – and Else next Monday for Heidelberg – then we shall be alone a few days, and Barby Weekley will come – she is visiting a professor's family in Cologne. The old Grandmother Weekley died last week, at the age of 86:[2] she whom Frieda was supposed to be hurrying to the grave with grief fifteen years ago!

My agents just told me I lose 20% of all the money I make on my books: the govt. takes so much tax on royalties due to all persons living abroad. But if I lived in England I suppose the income tax would be about as much. Anyhow one can't help it.

One feels much more cheerful not being in Austria. That poor country is absolutely broken – and endless poverty, and no hope: because the Versailles treaty took away all the industrial regions. It's a scandal. Germany is busy and flourishing – everywhere so spick and span and cared-for, everybody working so hard, and life fairly cheap: much cheaper than Italy.

I suppose Joan's back at school, and Peg at work. I hope Sam's shop does well.

Love!   DHL

---

[1] Cf. p. 139 n. 2.
[2] Agnes Weekley (1840–1927), d. 29 August 1927.

4131. To Ada Clarke, 7 September 1927
Text: MS Clarke; cited in Lawrence–Gelder 168–9.

Irschenhausen, *Post Ebenhausen*, nr Munich

7 Sept 1927

My dear Sister

I've been here a week now – it's awfully nice, the little wooden house and forest behind, the big open country in front with the mountains. The weather is lovely, sunny all day, and the moon at night. I feel it suits me here. I drink goat's milk, and we walk through the woods – all beech and fir-trees. There are lots of deer in winter and spring, but at this season they draw away to the more remote places. We've got a good servant – the one we knew in the past. Altogether the place is so little changed, it is hard to believe thirteen years have gone by. One feels the ghost of my brother-in-law everywhere – he loved this little place, and I'm sure, if he haunts anywhere, it is here. One must always think of him. – Johanna goes on tomorrow to BadenBaden: she's so happy to be away from poor Emil for a bit, she's another woman. Else stays till next Monday, then goes on to Heidelberg to her children. Then we shall be alone awhile – and Barby Weekley is coming for a few days. She is at present in Cologne visiting a professor, her father's friend – and wants to come here –. Meanwhile their old grandmother has at last died – Weekley's mother – at the age of 86. Wonderful how some people live on.

If you send me anything for my birthday, send me two cotton shirts – not wool, I don't wear woolen shirts, nor silk, because I don't like it – but just two ordinary cotton shirts with collar attached, not loose – I take $15\frac{1}{2}$ collar – and the short measure in sleeves. My shirts are all beginning to go – it's four years since I bought any. But don't send anything else, there's only the customs.

Germany is much more cheerful than Austria, much more flourishing. In fact it seems tremendously alive and busy. Austria was too poor, too helpless, one couldn't stand it long.

I suppose you'll be having Gertie home in about three weeks. Wonderful if she's so strong as you say. And I'm glad she's not penniless. – There's a new law that takes 20% tax on all royalties of persons living abroad – it came into force in July last – so there's a slice off one's not very grand earnings. But we're lucky to have got off taxes so long.

Love to the children – I suppose Jack is home again now.

DHL

4132. To S. S. Koteliansky, [9 September 1927]
Text: MS BL; PC v. Isartal, Blick auf Mühltal; Postmark, Ickin[g] [. . .]; Zytaruk 320.

Irschenhausen, *Post Ebenhausen*, bei München
9 Sept

It is so quiet here, one forgets how the days go by. Bavaria is just the same, at least the Isartal – and one looks for one's old self – I am a good deal better – but the cough still a nuisance – still, *really* better. We'll be here till end of month, then Baden. Are you alone still? – Barby Weekley comes next week!

Grüsse.   DHL

4133. To Arthur Wilkinson, [10 September 1927]
Text: MS Schlaefle; PC v. Isar & Loisach Zusammenfluss bei Wolfratshausen; Postmark, Ebenhausen 10.9.27; Unpublished.

Irschenhausen.
Sat.

Thanks for sending on the letters – I think they've all come. I can't believe you never got a drenching on that trip – here it's mixed, sun and rain – today is bright clouds and blue mountains. We've got a William Busch book for you – *Plisch und Plum*[1] – very nice, but we must translate the verses. You'd better be learning some German, to get going. We expect F[rieda]'s daughter Barby next week – the ancient grandmother died. – Have your visitors come? and any news of Miss Pearn? Actually I painted a little water-color of flowers – but feel strange with the wetness of the medium. Send a line.

DHL

4134. To Martin Secker, [12 September 1927]
Text: MS UInd; PC v. Schäftlarn, Werkkanal mit Blick auf das Kloster; Postmark, Augsb[urg] 12.9.27; Secker 94.

Irschenhausen. *Post Ebenhausen*, bei München
[12 September 1927][2]

I was expecting a word from you – didn't I send you the address? We've been here nearly two weeks, and I feel much better. The weather is mixed, pouring one day, then perfect for two or three days. I like it here very much. We expect Barby Weekley next week – or this week – did you know the old grandmother died? Let me know how you all are, and if there is any news.

DHL

[1] *Plisch und Plum* (Munich, 1882) was one of the volumes of versified, pungent satire (illustrated by vigorous line drawings) by the German caricaturist, Wilhelm Busch (1832–1908).
[2] The postmark suggests that Else Jaffe took this card with her from Irschenhausen and posted it in Augsburg.

4135. To Baroness Anna von Richthofen, 12 September 1927
Text: MS UCB; Frieda Lawrence 245–6.

Irschenhausen. *Post. Ebenhausen*, München
12 Sept 1927

Meine liebe Schwiegermutter

Das Paketle hatten wir heut Morgen, und so nett von dir. Aber warum hast du so viel Geld ausgegeben? das solltest du wirklich nicht. Die Taschentücher sind echt schön, ich mag sie sehr, und die Pralinen sind für Prinzen: nur zwei Reihen noch – gegessen. Dass ein Bisschen Wurst dabei war, das ist recht; Brot ist der Stab vom Leben, aber mit Wurst dazu wird es auch Regenschirm.

Du warst einsam, Ich weiss es, und ganz 'forlorn', die drei Töchter weit in der Welt herausgelaufen. Aber jetzt wirst du wieder zufrieden sein: die Nusch hast du da, die Else ist heut morgen gereist, und kommt morgen Abend an Heidelberg: sie schläft heut' Nacht in Augsburg: warum, Gott weiss. Aber wir waren ganz glücklich zusammen, mit Patience und Taschenstichen und spazieren, es ist Schade sie ist fort.

Das Wetter ist kalt geworden, und regnet – die Nusch ihre Barometer ist immer noch ein böses grinzendes schlechtsprechendes Gesicht im Kammer. Aber im Isartal hangt ein bunter Regenbogenzipfel, der Herrgott haltet immer noch sein Versprechen.

Von der Barby haben wir nicht gehört – ich glaube aber sie kommt direkt hier, vielleicht Samstag. – Der Emil schrieb mir ein so netten Brief, und schickt *30 Flaschen* Malzbier. Denk dir, wie wir versoffen werden, und zu dir kommen werden mit roten Nasen und Wasserigen Augen.

Es ist wirklich Schade dass wir nicht länger zusammen bleiben können, mit Nusch oder mit Else und dir. Immer dieser dumme Wegreisen.

Aber bald sehen wir dich, so leb' wohl!

DHL

Es ist Abend, die Wolken Gold, die Berge stehen wieder da, mit langen weissen Dampfkissen.

[My dear Schwiegermutter

We had the little parcel this morning, and so nice of you. But why did you spend so much money? you really shouldn't. The handkerchiefs are very nice, I like them a lot, and the chocolates are fit for a king: only two rows left – eaten up. Good that there was a bit of sausage too; bread is the staff of life, but with sausage it becomes an umbrella too.

You were lonely, I know, and quite 'forlorn', with the three daughters ranging over the wide world. But now you'll be contented again: Nusch you have there, Else set off this morning and arrives in Heidelberg tomorrow night: she stays overnight in Augsburg: God knows why. But we were very happy together, with Patience and bag-embroidery and walks, it's a shame she's gone.

The weather has turned cold, and it's raining – Nusch's barometer is still a malicious grinning face in the room, announcing dreadful news. But there's a gay-coloured tip of a rainbow over the Isar valley, the Lord God still keeps his word.

From Barby we've not heard – but I think she is coming straight here, perhaps on Saturday. – Emil wrote me such a nice letter, and sends *30 bottles* of malt beer. Think how drunk we shall get, and how we'll come to you with red noses and watery eyes.

It's a real shame that we can't stay together longer, with Nusch or with Else and you. Always this stupid travelling away.

But we'll see you soon, so good bye!

DHL

It's evening, the clouds gold, the mountains standing there again, with long white vapour pillows.]

4136. To Margaret King, 13 September 1927

Text: MS Needham; cited in V. de S. Pinto, 'D. H. Lawrence: Letter-Writer and Craftsman in Verse', *Renaissance and Modern Studies*, i (1957), 6, 7.

Irschenhausen. Post Ebenhausen, bei München.

13 Sept 1927

My dear Peg

Your mother says I owe you a letter, I'm afraid you're not the only one. I really hardly write any nowadays, except just business notes.

It's sharp and nippy here, the autumn crocuses looking very pink in the grass: it means winter before long. And you're thinking of night-school again! Spanish or German, you say? Spanish is much easier – but what are you going to do with it? – unless you get with a firm that has Spanish-American correspondence. It's not worth while learning Spanish to read *Don Quixote*. You'll have to choose for yourself. Which of the two countries do you think you'll travel in?

You might one day come here, it's very nice, with the forest behind the house, and the wide open valley in front, with the big mountains beyond. This morning we saw a few deer in the clearing about five minutes from the house: a red stag hiding behind a clump of trees to watch us, and just leaving his inquisitive rump in sight, for a hunter to shoot at. They are very curious creatures – full of curiosity.

Your mother asked me what I wanted for my birthday, but I don't think there is anything. Frieda's mother sent me six hankies – and socks. But perhaps you might send some tea to my two sister-in-laws. It cost 10/- a pound here, and bad at that. Your mother might send them each two pounds of good light India tea – not Ceylon; then I've kept my promise. I know the big tea-firms send tea abroad and pay the duty: and they do it very nicely, I have seen advertisements in the paper.

I'm feeling better – have just come in from a walk, about three miles, and not tired. Only this bronchial cough is still a nuisance: but I must say, much better. It suits me here, the stillness, and the good food and milk. We have a servant who is an excellent cook – and Emil has sent me 30 bottles of special malt beer – I am looked after hard, I can tell you. Else went away yesterday, so we are alone for a bit: but probably Barby Weekley will turn up, just for a day or two, at the week-end. The old Weekley grandmother died, aged 86, and the Weekleys are making as much tragedy over it as if she'd been a young Ophelia. Sentimentalising lot!

We've had some rainy days – bright again now, but sharp cold. I hope it's decent in England. It's a good thing I didn't come this year – wasn't well enough, anyhow. But next year it will be fine, and we'll come for a longer time.

I'll put the two addresses for the tea. I hope the shop flourishes, and you all are well.

Love to you all.   DHL

Frau Dr Else Jaffe-Richthofen,
Bismarkstr. 17, Heidelberg
Frau Johanna Krug, Nymphenburgerstr. 9II,
Berlin/ Schöneberg

Johanna gave me a travelling barometer – it's just moving up to 'fine.'

4137. To Emil Krug, 15 September 1927
Text: TMSC Deasey; Unpublished.

Irschenhausen, Post Ebenhausen, bei München
15 Sept 1927

My dear Emil

The beer came yesterday – at least the maid fetched it in the Handwägele from Ebenhausen station, and I couldn't help laughing when I saw the thirty bottles nodding in the perambulator. But I started in at once to drink it, and I'm sure it is good stuff; I'm sure it is good for the digestion, as well as nourishing. I can see myself getting fat on it: a thousand thanks to you. Nusch bought me a little barometer, very pretty, which still points to the 'n' in *veränderlich*,[1] though it is a lovely sunny day, and though Frieda, in spite of my protests, knocks on its face as if she expected it to say 'come in!'. I feel I have come in for more presents this time than is my due; but I decide it must be because, if one becomes a man at twenty-one, then one must become twice a man at forty-two.

We are all alone here. Else left on Monday, and now even the maid, Anna, has gone to München till Saturday: so there is peace perfect peace.[2] It was great fun when Nusch and Else were here, because they were both in a good humour: and a woman in a good humour is absolutely a different animal from a woman in a bad humour. But it is also very nice to be quite still: and this is one of the stillest places I know. The trees seem to make a silence. I really like it very much here, and I am honestly much better. We saw three deer in the clearing behind the house, day before yesterday. They looked so alert and clean and alive, so much nicer than people.

On Saturday Frieda's daughter Barbara is coming for a few days – she is visiting 'Fabrik-besitzer Becker' in Köln. I shall buy a dog, and call myself 'Hundbesitzer Lawrence'[3] on my letters. So we shall once more hear all the news of *erste Else Familie*.

So many thanks for the beer, and your kindness in thinking of it. I hope you are enjoying peaceful evenings with your books. It is so good when one can be happy by oneself.

Wiedersehen!   DHL

4138. To Else Jaffe, [16–17 September 1927]
Text: MS Jeffrey; Frieda Lawrence 247.

[Irschenhausen, *Post Ebenhausen*, bei München]
[Frieda Lawrence begins]

Freitag

Liebe Else!

Geld ist da, Lorenzo *hackte Holz* als ich von der Häuslmeyer kam – grad 3 schöne Tage, zweimal haben wir *noch* Rehe gesehen, sie kuckten uns neugierig an – Schönberner, er gefiel uns und Kahlers kamen – *sehr* nett beide aber müde und nervös, sie reizend, wir gehen am Sonntag mit Barby hin! Den Kuhstall am Fenster, der sich einbildete ein Vogelkäfig zu sein, hab ich fort gerissen – Blumen hab ich gepflanzt; Lorenzo besuchte auch die Nachbarin, sie will 500 für die Lilien, 400 für die andern – hetz Dich nicht ab, wir sind ja

[1] '*changeable*'.
[2] Cf. 'Peace, perfect peace', a famous hymn by Edward Henry Bickersteth (1825–1906).
[3] 'Factory-owner Becker . . . Dog-owner Lawrence'.

auch keine heurigen Hasen mehr – Anna kommt morgen wieder, so ist's angenehm, ihr bayrisch beglückt mich: – I glaub an gar nix, als daß 3 lb Fleisch a guta Suppen is! Und die Baronin Gorug war eine 'Bafaria' wie ich! Die Leitner kam auch! Lawr hat noch einen Schritt zur Besserung gemacht! Anni kommt auch vorbei! [DHL interjects:] von Zell.

Deine   F.

[Friday

Dear Else,

The money has come, Lorenzo *was cutting wood* when I came back from Frau Häuslmeyer[1] – just three nice days, twice *more* we've seen deer, they looked at us curiously – Schönberner (we liked him) and Kahlers came[2] – both *very* nice but tired and on edge, she charming, we're going there on Sunday with Barby! I've torn down the cowshed by the window – the shed which thought it was a birdcage – I've planted flowers; Lorenzo visited the lady next door too, she wants 500 for the lilies, 400 for the others – don't be in too much of a hurry, we aren't that young any more either – Anna comes again tomorrow, that's nice, I do enjoy her Bavarian dialect: – I believe in nothing at all, except that 3 lb. of meat makes a good soup![3] And Baroness Gorug was a 'Bafarian' like me! Frau Leitner came too![4] Lawr has taken another step towards getting better! Anni comes in too! from Zell.

Your   F.]

[Lawrence begins]

Sat morning

Dear Else

So nice of you to send all those toilet things, and the money – but why didn't you keep the money to pay for them. Let me know how much they cost.

The *Jugend* man came – a nice little soul after all – but they'll do him in – he'll never stand the modern mill. And the Kahlers came – both very nice – but like all the people of that class nowadays, they've lost their *raison d'être*,

---

[1] Therese Häuslmair (1880–1965). m. Johann Häuslmair (1873–1966).

[2] Franz Schoenberner (the '*Jugend* man'): see Letter 4142 and n. 1; the Kahlers have not been identified, though an Eric S. Kahler is listed as having ordered a copy of *Lady Chatterley's Lover* ('Memoranda', MS NWU).

[3] Frieda attempts a transcription of the Bavarian dialect spoken by the servant Anna. A literal translation is given above; a more idiomatic rendering might be: 'Ah believes in nowt at 'a, 'cept that 3 pounds o' meat makes a great soup!'

[4] The Baroness is unidentified; Walburga Leitner (1859–1928) and her husband Josef (1850–1924) had been DHL's landlords in Icking in 1912.

and there seems no reason whatever why they should exist – they haven't even, like the Nachbarin,[1] the poignancy of woes.

A rainy morning and a cold wind.

Barby arrives in München at 10.40 tonight – so Frieda will go in by a late train, and they'll come out tomorrow morning. We've promised to go to the Kahlers tomorrow to tea.

Did you get the book I sent? – The *Jugend* man wants only a short-short story – 4 schreibmaschine-seiten:[2] that's about 2000 words. No stories are as short as that – usually 5000. I must try and hunt him something up.

Hope all is well in Heidelberg. Greet everybody!

DHL

This swanky paper comes from Fr. Häuselmaier – or however she is called.

4139. To Earl and Achsah Brewster, 17 September 1927
Text: MS UT; Brewster 148–50.

Irschenhausen. *Post Ebenhausen*, bei München
17 Sept. 1927

Dear Earl and Achsah,

Your letters today! *Now* what's amiss? and what has Achsah been 'learning'. I know that always means the sadder and wiser sort of thing.[3]

And so you're once more flotsam! For goodness sake, cari miei, take a direction and swim for it. I do think this being washed about by wayward currents is too enervating. While you're in Rome, *really* look if there isn't a house in the hills north of Rome: but look *determinedly*. I begin to think Capri perhaps does you harm. I'm sure you'd be able to rent a decent house, if only till next summer – ask the agents – and really try somewhere else. But do, do spit on your hands and get a grip on the Roman country, and try something there, before going back to Capri. Then if it *must* be Capri, let it be Capri, and beat no more about the thorny bush. But *do* do look in the etruscan villages on the old road to Florence, about thirty miles out of Rome. I feel they'd be nice. – Something has collapsed in your old order of life. Now accept it as collapsed, and prepare another thing. Several of the archangels have broken their wings lately, and will fly no more. So we have to adapt ourselves to a world without archangels, and accept a lesser brightness, but perhaps a shadow that is eventually more satisfying. Make friends with the new shadow of destiny, and then look for a place to live in. But it is time to know earnestly that there has been a change, that the wings of the archangels have snapped at last, that there

---

[1] 'neighbour'.   [2] '4 typed pages'.
[3] Cf. Coleridge, 'The Ancient Mariner', l. 624. See also Letter 4208.

are no sheltering wings, only a strange new shadow which after all will have many mansions.[1]

Myself, I am glad to be here, in this little wooden house with the forest round the back, and in front the wide open valley going to the blue mountains. I like the dark fir trees, and the clearings where we see the red deer. I like the deep, matted wet grass when the harebells are now so dark blue, and the chicory heavenly. I love above all the stillness of innumerable trees that are none the less silently growing, and pressing themselves on the air so softly yet so indomitably. I am glad not to be in Italy for a while. I don't [mind] if[2] it rains some days, and is dark. I like it. I don't mind that it is rather cold. I like it. I find Italy has almost withered me. Here something softens out again.

I don't do much except take walks in the forest, and translate Verga's *Cavalleria Rusticana*, and play patience. I am glad when I don't work – I have worked too much.

Tonight Frieda's daughter Barbara is coming, but only for a few days. We shall stay here, I think at least till 1st Oct., perhaps longer, if it doesn't turn too cold. Then we must go to BadenBaden for two weeks, so we shan't be home at the earliest till middle October, probably later. I suppose you wouldn't like to camp in the Mirenda for a month? if so, there it is, for what it is: you've only to write to Arthur G. Wilkinson, Villa Poggi – they'd arrange for you.

Thank Harwood for her letter, which I got the first days here. And all good wishes from us both to you all.

DHL

4140. To Martin Secker, 17 September 1927

Text: MS UInd; Postmark, Icking 17 [. . .]; Secker 94–5.

Irschenhausen, *Post Ebenhausen*, bei München
17 Sept 1927

Dear Secker

Thanks for yours and the enclosures today. Stupid of Curtis Browns not to give you that Etruscan MS. and photographs, as I *insisted* they should at the time: I want your opinion.

Edward O Brien writes today, can he include 'The Woman Who Rode Away' in his – *Best Short Stories for 1926*.[3] – I leave it to you. He only gives £2. anyhow, and if you'd rather he didn't have the thing, I don't care. Will you speak to Curtis Browns about it – they handle it.

---

[1] Cf. John xiv. 2.   [2] MS reads 'don't if'.

[3] Edward Joseph Harrington O'Brien (1890–1941), American author and editor, had published stories by DHL in *The Best British Short Stories* of 1923 and 1925; the volume for 1926 included 'The Woman Who Rode Away'.

I was surprised to hear from Pollinger that you were getting *Little Novels of Sicily* from Blackwell.[1] Why don't you tell me those things – then of course I would have offered you the *Cavalleria Rusticana* translation, which is a companion vol. to *Little Novels*. Then I went and offered it to Cape, thinking you'd have no interest in it. The translation is nearly done: it's a little book: then I shall do a longish foreword. I wrote Pollinger to sound Cape, and if Cape doesn't want the translation particularly, to offer it to you. It might go moderately well, but not à la Juif doux.[2]

I think *The Woman Who Rode Away* is rather a good title. The other stories I have in mind are *Glad Ghosts*, 'The Man Who Loved Islands', 'Two Blue Birds', 'In-Love', *Sun*, 'The Last Laugh', 'Jimmy and the Desperate Woman', 'Smile', 'The Rocking-horse Winner', and 'The Lovely Lady'.[3] See if Pollinger's list is the same. There are also somewhere in existence two animal sketches, 'Adolf' and 'Rex'.[4]

I'm getting on nicely – the weather is mixed – but I like it here very much – forest where one can go anywhere, and the deer are – just behind the house. – Barby arrives in München tonight – F[rieda] goes in to meet her. She stays only a day or two. We shall stay whilever it is not too cold – I'm not eager to go back to Italy – I like it here. – Did Rina just go to Spotorno? Didn't you go away?

Leb wohl![5]   DHL

4141. To Arthur Wilkinson, [19 September 1927]

Text: MS Schlaefle; PC v. Georgenstein; Postmark, München 19 9. 27; Unpublished.

[Irschenhausen, *Post Ebenhausen*, bei München]

19 Sept

I never thanked you for the birthday letters, which were so jolly: quite a festa in themselves. Glad to hear it's fresher at S. Paolo – though the scandals and the figure on the stone bench under the windows make my blood run cold. What next! – What about your visitors? – and Miss Pearn? – any signs? Barby Weekley is here till Wednesday: it's been pouring with rain: and the mts have come out very blue and Scotchy under wooly whitey clouds. Did you get

[1] See p. 53 n. 3. Secker published the volume in his *New Adelphi Library* in March 1928 (Roberts A30).
[2] I.e. not with the great success associated with *Jud Süss* (see *Letters*, v. 388 n. 3). Cf. p. 173.
[3] With three exceptions – 'The Man Who Loved Islands', 'The Rocking-Horse Winner' and 'The Lovely Lady' – all these stories were collected in *The Woman Who Rode Away* (Secker, 24 May 1928). Knopf's edn (25 May 1928) included 'The Man Who Loved Islands'; both edns added 'The Border-Line' and 'None of That' to DHL's list here.
[4] They first appeared in *Dial*, lxix (September 1920), 269–76 and lxx (February 1921), 169–76 and were first collected in *Phoenix* (Roberts C73 and C77).   [5] 'Farewell!'

Plisch und Plum? – You must turn it in to proper verse – mine is just literal. A new job for the family.

leb wohl! DHL

4142. To Franz Schoenberner, 20 September 1927
Text: MS UT; Moore 1002.

Irschenhausen, Post Ebenhausen, Isartal.
20 Sept 1927

Dear Mr. Schoenberner[1]

Many thanks for your letter and for the criticisms: the latter are at least very much more intelligent than some I received this morning from America. – The bundle of *Jugends* has not turned up – no doubt it has been stolen in the post. It is a nuisance, the way one loses *Drucksache*. Is it true, as the postman here said, that one cannot *einschreiben*[2] the Drucksache in this country? Is it possible? Because I gave him some MS. to send to England as Drucksache eingeschrieben, and he sent it without registering – a great nuisance if it gets lost.

I haven't been able to find a story of my own short enough for you yet. Perhaps the one I am sending to Frau Jaffe would do if you used it in two parts. But I'll try to get hold of a little 'dog' story.[3]

If we come in to Munich it will be next week, so I shall let you know. The weather is so bad, it is no use setting out anywhere.

We got a copy of *Jugend* – the one with 'Mord in Neapel'[4] – so I think I see the kind of story you want.

My wife sends greetings, with mine, and we'll see if we can't meet next week.

Yours Sincerely   D. H. Lawrence

4143. To Rowena Killick, 20 September 1927
Text: MS UT; Unpublished.

Irschenhausen, Post Ebenhausen, nr Munich.
20 Sept 1927

Dear Miss Kitnich

Do let me know if you get the little book of *Cavalleria Rusticana*

---

[1] Franz Schoenberner (1892–   ), b. Berlin, had visited DHL a few days before (Letter 4138). He was editor of *Jugend* (1926–9) and later of *Simplicissimus* (1929–33), both in Munich; he left Germany in 1933 and from 1941 lived in USA. His memoir of DHL is contained in *Confessions of a European Intellectual* (New York, 1946). See also Nehls, iii. 155–61.   [2] 'register'.

[3] Else Jaffe's German translation of DHL's dog story, 'Rex', appeared in *Jugend*, October 1928 (Roberts C77).   [4] 'Murder in Naples'.

translations which I sent on the 16th.[1] I find the postman posted it *without* registering – and the unregistered printed matter gets lost half the time in this country. A great bore if that MS. were lost.

Do you know if Miss Pearn has anywhere a little animal story of mine, written long ago, about a dog, called 'Rex.' I have no copy – and I don't suppose Miss Pearn has: but if she did happen to have one, would you send me a copy please. It's quite a short little thing.

Thanks for the copy of 'The Rocking-horse Winner'.

Yours Sincerely   D. H. Lawrence

4144. To Hon. Dorothy Brett, 22 September 1927
Text: MS UCin; Postmark, [. . .]; Irvine, Brett 75–7.

Irschenhausen. Post Ebenhausen. nr. Munich.
22 Sept 1927

Dear Brett

We've been here three weeks – in its way, it's rather like the ranch – a little wooden house with forest behind, looking across a wide valley at the blue mountains. It's awfully nice, really – so silent and alone. We have a very good cook, and I am fed on trout and partridge and venison. I think of you when she brings the trout, fine ones, about a foot or 16 inches long, and perfectly fresh. There are deer in the woods behind us; we see them darting past the tree-trunks almost every day, like a little Persian painting. Else, Friedel's mother,[2] was with us the first fortnight – very nice, I liked her very much – then F[rieda]'s daughter Barby was here a few days – a bit wistful, poor thing, a bit sick of the London existence. – I keep on swallowing malt and beer and milk and chalk, for my fatal tubes. But it was a bad whack, that last go in the Mirenda, not easily shaken off. But it's much better, this place suits me: about 2500 ft. – I mustn't go above 3000 till those weak places are hardened up. And I'm determined to get them hardened, if I can. They've nagged me all my life, off and on in bad bouts and mild. I'm going to try all the things to see what can be done. Next week I'll have a talk with a Munich specialist.[3] But it is a thing Englishmen are liable to, and especially at my age, and it usually lasts a year or two. But I count it $2\frac{1}{2}$ years since that go in Mexico – I've never been really right since. So now the thing *must* heal up. It's no good thinking of the ranch, that altitude, till the damned place is hardened over. But once I can really start getting it solid, it wont take long. Anyhow I do feel much better. And I'm not working at all. It's much better when I *don't* work. And here I can loafe.

But if I were you, I wouldn't come to Europe. What's the point? There's

---

[1] Rowena Killick acknowledged its safe arrival, on 24 September 1927 (TMSC UT).
[2] Brett had met Friedel Jaffe when he visited the Lawrences at Kiowa Ranch, 19 May–18 July 1925.   [3] Dr Hans Carossa: see next letter and p. 156 n. 1.

nothing to do over here, for you. As for me, I am simply concentrating now on getting my bronchials hardened up. We shall stay here till it gets too damp, then go to Baden and do an inhalation cure for 15 days – if the Munich doctor thinks it would help. Then we'll go to the Mirenda for a bit, and perhaps in January go to Cortina, just over 3000, to the snow, because the Huxleys said it did wonders for them last winter – so they're going again – and we'll go with them, most likely. There's nothing to be done but set one's teeth and get oneself really well – then one can make a new start.

I never hear of Murry now. Kot, in abysses of gloom, writes occasionally. Gertler writes – swallowing milk upon milk, and feeling he's triumphed in merely being alive. Everything is at a low-water mark. The Brewsters are again turned out of Cimbrone, fluttering in Rome like poor white pigeons that have nowhere to settle and must keep on fluttering. They really are distressing – having spent pretty well all their money, and nobody wants them, and altogether it's a Noah's flood for them. For heavens sake, don't leave the ranch and New Mexico for here. Nothing new turns up – not a thing: and there's never a pony to ride. But don't try living at the ranch in the winter – hire one of Mabel's houses.

Did you by the way get the very bad snaps of my pictures I sent you from Villach? – and the second copy of *Mornings in Mexico*? We were thinking of you all at San Geronimo time.

Did I tell you, Dorothy Warren has one of the smart galleries in Bond St. – and she showed a few of Barby's pictures – and sold one to Lord Ivor Churchill for 7 guineas – a little sketch. So Dorothy W. will show us all when we're ready for showing. At the moment I feel paint is terribly remote.

If only a storm would come and sweep away all the old nuisances over 65, I think – we might really see a new start somewhere. But they hang on! Remember us both to Bill and Rachel – also to Bobby and Betty.[1] I feel there ought to be a sort of all-round clearance and freshening up of everything and everybody. I suppose I must try on myself first.

Leb' wohl!   DHL

4145. To Franz Schoenberner, [24 September 1927]
Text: MS UT; Schoenberner, *Confessions*, p. 287.

Haus Jaffe. Irschenhausen, Post Ebenhausen
Saturday

Dear Mr Schoenberner
    Many thanks for the *Jugends*, which came safely yesterday. We looked at

---

[1] William ('Bill') Hawk (1891–1975) and his wife Rachel (b. 1898) ran a small dairy farm on the Del Monte Ranch (which was owned by his parents) near Taos. Barbara ('Bobbie') Gillete and Betty Cottam were William's sisters.

them all the evening – but I haven't read the stories yet, only the jokes! Some of them are very good – and the whole thing is alive – but the curious sexual cynicism is a bit alarming, because it's just how the world is. But whatever will be the end of it, if there is nothing to counterbalance it? I tell you, when I've looked through ten *Jugends*, I feel thoroughly frightened.

I think we shall come to Munich next Thursday, or if it rains, Friday – and perhaps we might meet somewhere for coffee, at about 2.o'clock, if that is convenient. We'll have lunch in town first – meals are a bore anyhow.

I forgot to say I should be very pleased to meet Hans Carossa – and if a poet who is a doctor can't tell me what to do with myself, then who can?[1]

Do you know anything of Max Möhr the dramatist?[2] I hear he might possibly come and see me.

Let me know if Thursday or Friday will do for you and Frau Schoenberner, and for Carossa.

All good wishes!   D. H. Lawrence

4146. To Else Jaffe, [25 September 1927]
Text: MS Jeffrey; Frieda Lawrence 248–9.

Irschenhausen.
Sunday

My dear Else[3]

Many thanks for the pen, which I am so glad to have in my fingers again – it's an old friend: it wrote *Boy in the Bush* and *St Mawr* and 'Princess' and 'Woman Who Rode Away' and *Plumed Serpent* and all the stories in between: not bad, even if it is a nasty orangy brown colour. But I've got even to like the colour. – They seem to have mended it all right, it goes well.

– This is the horridest day of all, after tea, and still pouring with rain: and I would like to go out! If only I had strong boots and a rain-proof. I would of course if we were staying. – Yesterday was lovely and sunny till tea-time.

This week-end we are alone – Anna is coming tomorrow. Then I suppose the Mayers will come[4] – and the Kahlers – and I've promised to go to

[1] Hans Carossa (1878–1956), German novelist, poet, autobiographer and physician; he special-ised in the treatment of tuberculosis. See Nehls, iii. 159–60; Clair Baier in *German Life and Letters*, xxxii (July 1979), 327–30.
[2] Max Mohr (1891–1944), German playwright, novelist and physician. He left Germany in 1933 to live in Shanghai.
[3] The following is written in an unknown hand (perhaps Else Jaffe's) between the address and DHL's salutation: 'Bitte zurück! – Der Zahn ist schon schmerzlos raus. Grüsse E.' ['Please send back! – The tooth is out already, painlessly. Greetings E.']
[4] Elizabeth Mayer, German translator, and her psychiatrist husband, were close friends of Else Jaffe. See Elizabeth Mayer's account of their visit to DHL in September 1927: *A D. H. Lawrence Miscellany*, ed. Harry T. Moore (Carbondale, 1959), pp. 141–3.

Schoenberners, and to meet Hans Carossa there. – I heard from England that
a man who writes plays and thinks I'm the greatest living novelist (quot.) and
who lives on Tegernsee, may come and see me: Max Möhr: do you know
anything about him? I dont.

I began the little bag – with green grass in waves, and dandelion seed-stems
– you know, the fluffy balls – and it's going to have bees. But today is so dark
and the stuff is so black! But it will be rather a small bag.

I suppose we shall stay here till Monday week – is that Oct 2nd. I don't feel
a bit anxious to return to Italy – but I think Frieda does. I don't mind, for the
time being, if it rains and is dark. – By the way, you should see how pretty your
garden looks, with the gold, and the mauve of the michaelmas daisies, and the
big autumn daisy, and the pink phlox: it looks really gay, on a sunny day. – We
have gathered the apples – so bright and red – and the last two hazel-nuts. I'm
afraid either squirrels or children had fetched the others. The woods are
simply populated with mushrooms, all sorts, in weird camps everywhere –
really like strange inhabitants come in. We eat the little yellow ones, and keep
picking Steinpilze[1] and throwing them away again. The cows come every
afternoon on to our grass, with a terrific tintinnabulation, like a host of
tinkling Sundays. There is a Jersey who is pining to come to tea in the porch –
and a white calf that suddenly goes round the moon. Frieda reads Goethe, and
I play patience – today I have finished my *Cavalleria Rusticana* translation:
now I've only to do the introduction: if that fool of a young postman hasn't lost
my bookful of MS. that I sent to England – Frieda told him loudly *registered* –
he says he sent it unregistered – and Drucksache. I shall curse him if I have to
do it all over again.

It's nightfall – I think I shall go out, spite of rain, for a few minutes.

wiedersehen!   DHL

4147. To Arthur and Lilian Wilkinson, [26 September 1927]
Text: MS Schlaefle; Sagar, Wilkinsons 70–1.

Irschenhausen, *Post Ebenhausen*, München
Monday

Dear Wilkeses

Awfully nice of you to look after Miss Pearn and friend[2] so kindly. Dont
forget I owe you various items like barrocino and so on, and hang a bill on my
nose when I come back, for *I'm* very likely to forget.

I'm glad the Wilhelm Busch arrived – the postman forgot to register it, so I
was afraid it would go lost. By Jove, you'll be speaking fluent Buschian

[1] Edible mushrooms.   [2] Mrs Angell.

German when we meet – 'Also Lorenzo, schön dass Sie wieder da sind, nicht?
– und wie war's –!'¹ I can just hear you.

What's your weather? Oh, I've got a little barometer too – my sister in law
gave it me for my 42nd. It fell on Saturday – a lovely day – to Viel Regen² –
and sure enough Sunday poured a black and ceaseless rain all the hours God
sent, and I began to feel like a plinosaur or an ichthyosaur or something sour.
But today it's finished³ – and turning colder. – The peasants have decided that
this is the hour to let their cows eat off our grass – so up they trail every
afternoon, with such a ringing of bells all round the house till nightfall that
you'd think you were going into a hundred village shops all the time – or that
you kept a shop with a hundred doors and a roaring trade – they're just like
village shop-bells.

We lead an uneventful life – the mountains come and go and lovely is the
show⁴ – sort of thing – I play patience!! oh Lilian Gair, I've come down a peg
or two, lower than bezique, lower than piquet – patience, on a stool instead of
a monument!⁵ But you can teach me some other sorts when I'm back: you're
bound to know my one and only sort. – The woods are simply uncanny with
mushrooms, all sorts and sizes and shapes and smells, in camps and circles and
odd ones – the brightest red, the whitest white, the blackest black, the
seaweediest green – and we pick the little orange-yellow ones and eat them
fried in butter. – The dark-blue autumn gentian is out – and the deer are
about – little roe-buck – they fly across the paths just like a Persian picture –
and then they stop fascinated by my famous little white jacket. The jays are so
cheeky they almost steal the tears out of your eyes. I really like it here – but
when it's dark and rainy then you sing: 'A little ship was on the sea'⁶ – for the
oceans of old Time seem to sweep over you.

I expect we shall go to Baden next week – Frieda wants to. We have a good
cook – and she goes in to München and brings out FOOD: today for lunch,
fine trout, for supper – partridges. Der Mister muss futtern⁷ – she says. We
spend more than we earn – and, as Richard Aldington says – you can't even
have poor relief if you've been two years out of England!! So you see, *you'll* get
no poor relief either!! when you go back.

¹ 'So Lorenzo, good that you're back, isn't it? – and how was it –!'   ² 'Much rain'.
³ MS reads 'finish'.
⁴ Cf. Wordsworth, *Ode: Intimations of Immortality* (1807), ll. 10–11 ['The Rainbow comes and
goes,/And lovely is the Rose'].
⁵ Cf. Shakespeare, *Twelfth Night*, II. iv. 16 ['She sat like patience on a monument'].
⁶ 'A Little Ship was on the sea. Sacred song', by Arthur J. Barth (1871).
⁷ 'Sir has to pitch in'.

Well, be warned, and don't eat your chickens before they're hatched.
Au revoir, then! Ist der Walther immer noch da?

Tausendmal Grüsse[1]   DHL

4148. To S. S. Koteliansky, 26 September 1927
Text: MS BL; Postmark, München 26.9.27; Moore 1004–5.

Irschenhausen, Post Ebenhausen, bei München
26 Sept 1927

My dear Kot

I had your last little De Profundis: the worst of you is, there's never any *oro te* follows.[2] Now what's the matter? anything new, or just the continual accumulation of the same old badness? It seems to be a fight between you and time: whether Time will wear out your inertia, or your inertia will wear Time out. Caro, there's nothing to be said to you: one has long realised the futility. But if I can do anything for you, let me know. And meanwhile, omnium desperandum.

We are still here: shall be here I suppose another week. The weather alternates between marvellous black steady days of rain, and marvellous warm bright days of sun. I likewise alternate between feeling much better, and almost sprinting along the road in my old self, and then feeling still a bit of a wreck. The Lord knows what's in it. I feel a bit like Noah's dove who has lost the ark and doesn't see any signs of an olive bough[3] – and is getting a bit weary on the wing. An olive tree is a low little tree, and doesn't grow on mountain tops. How is it that dove didn't come home with a sprig of fir or birch or beech? I think I'll take a pine-needle in my beak, not wait for olives.

There's no news – except the govt. now takes 20% of the royalties of persons living abroad. I begrudge it. I don't feel very keen on going back to Italy – don't know why. But the climate will drive us back. We're due to stay in BadenBaden a fortnight, anyhow. I like it here, the stillness and the forest and the still-unbroken quality of the silence. The deer go rushing past in front of one. – Let me know when I can be of any avail.

DHL

---

[1] 'Is Walter still there? Many many greetings'.
[2] Allusion to Psalm cxxx: 'Out of the deep . . . have I cried [I pray] unto thee'.
[3] Cf. Genesis viii. 11 ('the dove came in to him . . . and, lo, in her mouth was an olive leaf pluckt off'). Cf. *Letters*, ii. 330.

4149. To Max Mohr, 26 September 1927
Text: MS HMohr; Unpublished.

p/A. Frau Dr Jaffé, Irschenhausen, *Post Ebenhausen*, Isartal.

26 Sept 1927

Ge-ehrte Herr Mohr

Vielen Dank für Brief und Buch – schreiben Sie nur nicht mit Gotischer Handschrift, es ist so schwer. Den *Ramper* habe ich gelesen: es ist sehr interessant; aber warum haben Sie den Tiermensch so bloss leer und blank und *nichts* gemacht: nur Üi schreien können, und schlafen? Das hat gar kein Zweck! Auch der Eisbär schreit aus Wollust und aus Hunger – das ist doch zwei Schreien! – eins mehr wie den Tiermensch. Nein, der Ramper selber ist zu absolut negativ. Wissen Sie, sie wissen's wohl, jedes Tier hat seine eigne Intelligenz, seinen eignen klugen Verstand. So soll das Menschtier auch seinen eignen haben: er ist ein Eistier, so muss er scharf und still und schlau und grausam und widerlich und gefährlich wie ein Eisbär sein: und lustig wie ein Walfisch oder ein Walruss oder ein *Seal* (was ist *Seal* auf deutsch?): er lässt sich nicht so in einem Palastvarieté behandeln. Ja, wenn ein Mensch wirklich eine Tiernatur kriegt, dann ist es mehr wie die alten Geschichten, wo die Frau eine weisse Wölfin wird, oder der Soldat ein Nachtwolf, oder die Frau eine 'Seal', wie in Schottischen Liedern. Und denken Sie, das Tier ist auch *Menschtier*, soll Menschenschlauheit und gefährliches Misstrauen auch haben. Nein, lieber Herr Mohr, Sie haben zu wenig Respekt vor den Tieren. Doch ist das Idee sehr interessant. Schreiben Sie einmal wieder noch ein Tierstück, wo das Tier lebt und spielt und hat feinere, andere Qualitäten wie die einfachen Menchen: und kämpft wirklich gegen guten Worten und gegen die Maschine. Mit unserer echter Tiernatur, die wir in uns immer noch haben, müssen wir gegen die Welt des 'reines Idees' – besonders rein – und der Maschine kampfen und fechten. Das meinen Sie auch, in *Ramper*.

Wollen Sie nicht hier kommen, zu uns? Wir hätten sehr gern nach Wolfsgrube gekommen, ich war aber krank in Italien, wo wir wohnen, und bin immer noch nicht sehr wohl, so wäre die Reise vielleicht zu ermüdend. Wenn Sie von Bad Tölz nach Bad Heilbronn oder Bichl kommen können, dann ist es gar nicht weit von Bichl nach Icking, unsere nächste Station auf der Isartalbahn. Wir sind ungefähr 25 Minuten oben von Icking – das Haus der Frau Dr Jaffé, oben vom Ententeich. Aber wann wir wissen dass Sie kommen, werden wir am Bahnhof stehen, und Sie werden uns gleich erkennen – Ich habe rote Bart.

Ich weiss nicht warum ich auf Deutsch schreibe – so schlecht ist auch mein deutsch. Vielleicht weil ich eben jetzt *Ramper* gelesen habe, und es klingt noch im Ohren.

Meine Frau sagt, warum sind die Leute alle so gut und liebenswürdig in dem Schauspiel, so sind sie nicht für uns andere, auf der Erde. Und ein Tiermensch der nur mit Frauenperlenketten und Wurstfabrikantingeld gerettet werden kann, nein, das ist ein hilfloses Tier, und braucht noch eine Mutter mehr. Wir andere arme Tiere müssen schwimmen oder sinken ohne Perlen oder Wurstgeld, wie wir können.

Nein, aber entschuldige wenn ich ein wenig spotten: ich möchte selber ein so vollgiftliches Tier sein.

Kommen Sie doch, und bald, weil wir wollen nächste Woche nach BadenBaden gehen, dann wieder nach Italien.

D. H. Lawrence

Wenn Sie zum Gasthaus hier telefoniern wollen, den Herrn Friedinger (Wirt), er wird uns immer wissen lassen. die Nummer ist 137 Ebenhausen.

[Dear Sir

Many thanks for letter and book – only don't write in gothic script, it is so difficult. I've read *Ramper*:[1] it is very interesting; but why have you made the animal-man so utterly empty and blank and null: only able to cry Üi, and sleep? That really is pointless! Even the polar bear cries from lust and from hunger – that's already two kinds of cry – one more than the animal-man. No, Ramper himself is too completely negative. You know, of course you know, every animal has its own intelligence, its own clever mind. Likewise the man-animal must have his own; he's an ice-creature, so he has to be sharp and quiet and sly and cruel and horrible and dangerous as a polar bear: and jolly as a whale or a walrus or a *seal* (what is *seal* in German?): he wouldn't let himself be exhibited in a Palace of Varieties. Yes, when a human being really takes on an animal nature, then it's more like the old stories, where the woman turns into a white wolf, or the soldier into a werewolf, or the woman into a seal, as in the Scottish songs. And just think, the animal is also *man-animal*, must have human cunning and dangerous distrustfulness as well. No, dear Herr Mohr, you have too little respect for animals. But the idea is very interesting. Sometime do write another animal piece, in which the animal lives and plays and has finer, different qualities from those of simple human beings: and really fights against good words and against the machine. With our real animal nature, which we still bear within us, we must battle and fight against the world of the 'pure idea' – particularly pure – and of the machine. That is what you mean, too, in *Ramper*.

---

[1] Mohr's play (1925).

Wouldn't you like to come here, to us? We would have loved to come to Wolfsgrube, but I was ill in Italy, where we live, and am still not very well, so the journey would perhaps be too tiring. If you could come from Bad Tölz to Bad Heilbrunn or Bichl, then it's not far from Bichl to Icking, our nearest station on the Isar valley railway. We are about 25 minutes up from Icking – the house of Frau Dr Jaffe, up from the duck-pond. But if we know you are coming, we'll be at the station, and you'll recognise us at once – I have a red beard.

I don't know why I'm writing in German – my German is so bad too. Perhaps because I've just this moment been reading *Ramper*, and it's still ringing in my ears.

My wife says, why are the people all so good and kind in the play, they're not like that for the rest of us, on the earth. And an animal-man who can only be saved by ladies' pearl necklaces and the money of the sausage-maker's wife, no, that is a helpless animal, and more in need of another mother. The rest of us poor creatures have to swim or sink without pearls or sausage money, as best we can.

No, but apologies if I'm a bit satirical: I should myself like to be a thoroughly poisonous animal.

Do come, and soon, because next week we want to go to BadenBaden, then back to Italy.

D. H. Lawrence

If you want to telephone the Inn here, Herr Friedinger (landlord), will always let us know. the number is 137 Ebenhausen.]

4150. To Franz Schoenberner, [27 September 1927]
Text: MS UT; Schoenberner, *Confessions*, pp. 287–8.

Haus Jaffe. Irschenhausen, *bei Ebenhausen*
Dienstag

Lieber Herr Schoenberner

Jetzt bin ich natürlich erkältet – nicht schlecht, aber es soll nicht schlechter werden – und meine Frau sagt ich muss nicht diese Woche nach München kommen. Können Sie denn nicht mit Ihrer Frau Gemahlin und Hans Carossa hier wieder kommen – vielleicht Sonntag, wenn Sie alle frei sind? Für uns beide wäre es eine Freude: aber vielleicht für Ihnen ist es zu weit und ermüdend. Doch ist es schön, wenn es nicht giesst. Wir wollen nächste Woche nach BadenBaden gehen.

Ich lese die *Jugend* – es amusiert mich, und ich finde es ein Bisschen 'schocking.' Die Hauptsache ist dass es lebt. Ich bin selber etwas alt-modisch, und kann nie Bubiköpfe lieb haben. Meine Erziehung hat sicher noch ein Paar Schritten zu machen.

Kommen Sie denn hier mit Frau Schoenberner und Carossa, wenn es nicht zu langweiliegend ist. Es tut mir Leid dass ich nicht nach München kommen kann: meine Gesundheit ist eine wirkliche Last.

Auf Wiedersehen   D. H. Lawrence

[Tuesday

Dear Mr Schoenberner

Now of course I have a cold – not a bad one, but it shouldn't get any worse – and my wife says I mustn't come to Munich this week. So can't you come here again with your wife and Hans Carossa – perhaps on Sunday, when you are all free? It would be a pleasure for us both: but perhaps it is too far and tiring for you. But it is lovely, when it's not pouring. We want to go to BadenBaden next week.

I am reading the *Jugend* – it amuses me, and I find it a bit 'shocking.' The chief thing is that it's alive. Myself, I'm a bit old fashioned, and can never feel fond of bobbed hair. My education certainly needs to take a couple more steps.

So come here with Frau Schoenberner and Carossa, if it's not too dull. I'm sorry I can't come to Munich: my health is a real nuisance.

Auf Wiedersehen   D. H. Lawrence]

4151. To Giuseppe Orioli, 28 September 1927
Text: MS UCLA; cited in Moore, *Intelligent Heart* 370.

Irschenhausen, Post Ebenhausen, bei München
28 Sept 1927

Dear Pino

I went and lost your Paris address: rue Cambon??? but by now you'll be back in the city of the lily: hope it's blossoming rosily, and isn't 'cambiata in un cavol'fiore di Rovvezzano.'[1] We are here in the Bavarian highlands, in a little wooden house with the forest behind and the blue mountains away across in front – very nice and usually very still – but the contadino has sent his girl with the cows to eat off the grass of our little meadow, so there's such a tinkling of bells you'd think all the angels of heaven were having a wedding. I've liked it here very much, the stillness and loneliness, but now it's getting a bit wintry and damp. Sometimes it pours with rain, and then we feel like two

[1] Florence is 'the City of Lilies'; DHL hopes it is not 'changed into a cauliflower.'

lonely pale fishes at the bottom of a dark sea. I believe Frieda rather hates it, and is pining for San Polo: but I, for some reason, rather like it: it makes me sleep a lot, and I think that's about the best thing one can do in this world. I am a good deal better, but still no Hercules. – How are you? and how did you enjoy Paris and Reggie? – I hope you had a really good time. Give the family love to Reggie, and all the auf Wiedersehen greetings. We leave here next week Tuesday for *BadenBaden*:

c/o Frau Baronin von Richthofen, Ludwig-Wilhelmstift.

Write us a line there to say all goes well. I expect we shall stay in Baden two weeks: so we'll get back to the Mirenda at that rate just about Oct. 20th. Is there anything I can bring you from Germany? – We have such a good cook here, and trout and partridges and venison, like real signori for dinner. But soon we shall be back to a Scandicci loaf of hard bread. – Giulia wrote quite a nice letter – quite a proud massaia,[1] left in charge of the flat. How is Carlino? growing a signorino too by now.

Au revoir – leb wohl!   DHL

If you see Giglioli remember me to him and tell him we'll be back.

4152. To Margaret King, [28 September 1927]
Text: MS Needham; PC v. Skisport bei Icking – 'Cafe weisse Wand' – Isartal; Postmark, Ebenhausen [. . .]; Unpublished.

[Irschenhausen, Post Ebenhausen, bei München]
Wed

Many thanks for sending off the tea – We leave here next Tuesday – Oct. 4th – for BadenBaden. You know the address

c/o Frau Baronin v. Richthofen, Ludwig-Wilhelmstift

It is turning cold here, but we found a few violets under the porch today, smelling so sweet. But I believe tonight it will freeze. In winter there is much snow, and skiing – but that begins in December. First comes the rain. I hope you'll get on with the German – and come and stay with us here one day – perhaps even next year.

love to you all.   DHL

4153. To Giulia Pini, [28 September 1927]
Text: MS UT; PC v. Isartal m. Kloster-Schäftlarn; Postmark, Ebenhausen 29.9.27; Unpublished.

Irschenhausen. Baviera.
28 Settembre.

Mi scrisse la signorina amica che passò due giorni alla Villa, e che molto lo

[1] 'housewife'.

godeva; e che tu hai fatto tutto molto bene. Benissimo! – Siamo qui per cinque giorni ancora, poi andiamo a BadenBaden, alla Signora Baronessa – mia suocera. Ci restiamo forse quindici giorni, poi ritorniamo a San Polo, dove giungiamo verso il 20 Ottobre. La signora vuole molto tornare – ma deve vedere prima la mamma. Noi stiamo bene – come vanno tutti a San Polo? Qui fa già freddo.

Tanti salutti a tutti anche ai Salvestrini!   D. H. Lawrence

[28 September.
My young lady friend wrote me that she spent two days at the Villa, and that she enjoyed it very much; and that you did everything very well. Excellent! – We are here for five more days, then we are going to BadenBaden, to the Baroness – my mother-in-law. We will stay there for perhaps fifteen days, then we shall return to San Polo, where we should arrive around the 20th October. My wife would very much like to come back – but she must see her mother first. We are well – how is everybody in San Polo? It has gone cold here already.

Best wishes to everybody, to the Salvestrini[1] as well!   D. H. Lawrence]

4154. To William Wilkinson, [28 September 1927]

Text: MS Schlaefle; PC v. Isartal m. Kloster-Schäftlarn; Postmark, Ebenhausen 29.9.27; Unpublished.

[Irschenhausen, Post Ebenhausen, bei München]
Wed.

I hear you had great doings at San Polo, what with Miss Pearn and the Quachers.[2] Walter wrote today from Watford – a bit forlorn! We are leaving next Tuesday for BadenBaden – 4th, that is – you know the address

c/o Frau Baronin von Richthofen. Ludwig-Wilhelmstift

It's turning cold here, the beeches going yellow – I think it will freeze tonight. But we got a few violets under the porch this afternoon, sweet as any spring ones. Now one feels winter coming on, one's thoughts turn south again – the swallows have only just gone from here. You must come one day and have this little house – in January and Feb. there is ski-ing every year. Your mother's letter not here yet.

au revoir.   DHL

---

[1] Another peasant family who, with the Pinis, lived near the Villa Mirenda. (DHL's concern for them is evident as late as August 1929.)   [2] Unidentified.

166 [28 September 1927]

4155. To Baroness Anna von Richthofen, [28 September 1927]
Text: MS UCB; PC; Postmark, Ebenhausen 29. 9 27; Frieda Lawrence 250.

Irschenhausen.

Mittwoch

Die Else schrieb, die Nusch ist noch da. Na Johanna, du Osterlamm, opferts du dich noch nicht auf dem Altar der Ehe! Warte denn nur bis Dienstag, wenn wir kommen. Wir nehmen den Zug von 12.0, und sind in Baden um 7 uhr abends – ist das richtig, Schwiegermutter? Und du häuschst uns im Augustabad, wo Blaufelchen so gut schmeckt, nicht wahr? – Es ist heute Abent kälter geworden – wir waren beide etwas erkältet. Sonntag war ein Schauer und ein Finsternis von Regen – doch sind wir herausgegangen, am Abend, und nass geworden – Aber es geht schon besser. Die Anna ist hier, und sorgt so gut für uns. – Die Barby ist schon wieder in London, man kann kaum glauben dass sie hier war. – Ich habe beinah alles Bier – das von Emil – schon getrunken: es bleiben noch nur fünf Flaschen. Münchener Rekord, nicht? Gestern waren wir bei der Frau Leitner – so nett und klein – aber so eine Geschwätz! Sie schickt alle Grüsse an dir. – Die Buchen fangen nun an, gelb zu werden – und heute nachmittag haben wir ein Paar Violetten unterm Balkon gepflückt – düften süss wie Frühling – und die Blumen immer noch wunderschön. Die Kahlers kommen Morgen – und es soll einen Naturbursch – Max Mohr – Dramatiker – vom Tegernsee kommen. – Also Schwiegermutter – und ich hoffe, du auch, Nusch – wir sehen uns Dienstag wieder, und alles kann dann gesagt werden.

Wiedersehen DHL

[Wednesday
Else wrote, Nusch is still there. Now Johanna, you Easter lamb, don't you sacrifice yourself yet on the altar of marriage! Just hang on till Tuesday, when we come. We are taking the 12.00 train, and arrive in Baden at 7 in the evening – is that right, Schwiegermutter? And you're putting us up in the Augustabad, where the blue char are so good, right? – This evening it has turned colder – we both had a bit of a cold. Sunday was a horror of darkness and rain – still, we went out in the evening, and got wet – But things are already getting better. Anna is here, and takes such good care of us. – Barby is already back in London, it's hard to believe that she was here. – I've already drunk nearly all the beer – that from Emil – there are only five bottles left. A record for Munich,[1] don't you think? We went to see Mrs Leitner yesterday – so nice and small – but what chatter! She sends you many greetings. – The beeches are starting to turn yellow – and this afternoon we picked a few violets

[1] Probably a pun on the name of a Munich beer, 'Rekord'.

under the balcony – smell sweet as spring – and the flowers still really lovely.
The Kahlers come tomorrow – and a child of nature, Max Mohr – playwright
– should come from Tegernsee. – So, Schwiegermutter – and you too, I hope,
Nusch – we'll be meeting up on Tuesday, and everything can then be talked
over.

Wiedersehen   DHL]

4156. To Rowena Killick, 28 September 1927
Text: MS UT; Unpublished.

Irschenhausen. Post Ebenhausen, nr Munich
28 Sept 1927

Dear Miss Kitnich

I send you today the final MS. of the Verga translations, together with my
Introduction. Will you have them typed out for me.

We are leaving here next Tuesday, 4th. October – and the address for about
a fortnight will be

p/A. Frau von Richthofen,
Ludwig-Wilhelmstift, *Baden-Baden*, Germany.

Then we shall go back to Italy. –

I heard, by the way, from Miss Pearn. She seems to be having a good time.

I will let you know when I would like you to send me the complete MS. of
Cavalleria Rusticana – for me to go through it.

Yours sincerely   D. H. Lawrence

4157. To Martin Secker, 30 September 1927
Text: MS UInd; Postmark, München 1.10.27.; Secker 95–6.

Irschenhausen. *Post Ebenhausen*. bei München
30 Sept 1927

Dear Secker

Thanks for yours: I'm glad you don't care about *Cavalleria Rusticana*:
though it's a pity it couldn't have gone together with *Little Novels of Sicily*,
they are companion vols. – And thanks for the three vols of the 3/6[1] – of course
I've already given two of them away. A dramatist Max Mohr came to see me:
queer chap, writes queer plays, nearly good. Then[2] the *Jugend* man from
Munich – and Hans Carossa, another author. I'm surprised how well they
know me: or my books.

I dont think it would be bad to do the poems in one vol: or a selection, for
I'd like to leave some out, and put some in. Beaumont only had *Bay* rights for

---

[1] Secker had issued *Aaron's Rod, Sons and Lovers* and *The White Peacock* in his 3/6 edn, in
September (cf. Letter 4003 and p. 44 n. 2).   [2] MS reads 'The'.

two years, so that is free: and *Chatto* and Windus let *Look! We have Come Through* go out of print, and stay out – and I wrote them about it and asked them if they were willing for the rights to lapse to you – and they said, rather ruefully, yes![1] So that is free. There remains only Duckworth, with *Love Poems* and *Amores*: and since he's let the novels go, I suppose he'd let these. – We might make rather a nice vol.[2] I could work at it when I got back to the Mirenda. I found my own first copy of *Love Poems* in the cupboard here: we were here in 1913.

We leave on Tuesday for BadenBaden – c/o Frau v. Richthofen. Ludwig-Wilhelmstift. It is beginning to feel a bit wintry: then one wants to go south. I hope you'll get those Etruscan essays soon. I hear *Travel* is publishing four of the first six, with pictures – beginning in November. So it's not work in vain.

You'd be surprised how busy and efficient the German towns seem to be: going ahead full speed. But after one has been in the country a month, one feels the underneath sadness and hopelessness still – that fiendish war.

I expect we shall be in Baden a fortnight, then back to the Mirenda. Did Rina have a nice time in Spot[orno]? Barby was only here three days, but I think she liked it. She's back in Chiswick now.

If ever you want an odd sort of clerk, do try Walter Wilkinson – brother of our neighbour at the Mirenda. – He's a puppet-show man really – but a nice gentle soul with a bad cockney accent: but you'd surely like him, and you could trust him perfectly.

I am a lot better, but not my real self. I seem to have lost something out of my vitality – I hope it will come back.

I finished the *Cavalleria Rusticana* translation for Cape – you might like to bring out the *Little Novels* about the same time as he does the other book.

Send me the list of short stories to Baden.

All schöne Grüsse from us both to you all.   DHL

4158. To S. S. Koteliansky, [6 October 1927]
Text: MS BL; Postmark, Baden-Baden 6.10.27; cited in Gransden 31.

Hotel Eden, BadenBaden
Thursday

My dear Kot
Had your letter and MS. in Irschenhausen. I'll try and work the stories up,

[1] Chatto & Windus informed DHL on 19 January 1922 that they did not intend to reprint the volume and therefore their rights in it reverted to him (see *Letters*, iv. 176 n. 2).
[2] This proposal led, a year later, to the publication of DHL's *Collected Poems* by Secker, in two volumes (Roberts A43).

when I have an inspired moment, and let you see what I can make of them.[1] As they stand they wouldn't sell, of course, though the kernel is interesting.

We are very grand in an hotel here, with rooms and bathroom and all very fine for 10/- a day each. It would cost full double in Italy. But I suppose we are living off past splendours. Germany is very much revived and more prosperous, yet curiously for me has gone suddenly dead. It is as if the angel of death[2] again were waving his wings over the middle of Europe. I don't know where I get the feeling from. My mother-in-law at seventy-six is younger than ever. Perhaps now only she has reached her real spontaneous youth: probably her teens were self-conscious and old, so her seventies are spontaneous and young, and she doesn't care a fig about anything.

The Dobrées ask us to Egypt. Shall we go, if we can scrape together the money? I doubt if I can manage it financially – but I might – the passage is so dear. It's the English govt. takes 20% tax on royalties of persons abroad – and Curtis Brown 10% – on every small penny of royalty.

I wish you had a job, I do really. I even wish we started a non-yellow magazine[3] – I'd make mine pink. But the way is long the wind is cold etc.[4] We *never* get round a certain corner.

I suppose we'll be here till Monday week.

                                                            Grüsse   DHL

4159. To Arthur Wilkinson, [6 October 1927]
Text: MS Schlaefle; PC; Postmark, Baden-Baden 6.10.27; cited in Sagar, Wilkinsons 71.

                                                    Hotel Eden. BadenBaden
                                                                    Thursday

Your letter and L[ilian] G[air]'s and Pino's card all come today – give us a Heimweh[5] for San Polo. Here it is a frosty morning, yellow sun earlier, now rather clouded over – beech trees going yellow[6] – that funny sort of stillness of a threatening winter. Now we shall be glad to see a bright day again: *really* bright. I expect we shall leave here on Monday week – is that the 17th? – and stay a night in Milan – so it's not long. – Look and see what that MS is, will you? – I don't suppose I *ever* want to see it. – We've got an invitation to Egypt – shall we go? – I feel I don't care much what I do or where I go. – Wonder

---

[1] Probably two stories recorded by Kot's mother, Beila Koteliansky (1852–1929); trans. by Kot, they appeared as 'Two Jewish Stories' in the *London Mercury*, February 1937, pp. 362–70. For Kot's prefatory note in which he recalls seeking DHL's assistance with the translation, see Zytaruk xxviii. DHL made an attempt to rewrite one story, 'Maimonides and Aristotle', but left it unfinished; the fragment was included in *Phoenix* 808–10.   [2] Azrael.
[3] Cf. *The Yellow Book*, the famous quarterly 1894–7, ed. Aubrey Beardsley and Henry Harland.
[4] Sir Walter Scott, *The Lay of the Last Minstrel* (1805), l. 1 ['The way was long, the wind was cold'].   [5] 'homesickness'.   [6] yellow] green

why Miss Pearn didn't like Firenze? What's the exchange nowadays? Is there peace at the Mirenda, or doth Tito bark? We've got more Wm. Busch – *Fromme Helene*[1] – a bit thick. – I really feel like coming back now – wouldn't mind starting tomorrow.

au revoir.   DHL[2]

4160. To Bonamy Dobrée, 6 October 1927
Text: MS Brotherton; Unpublished.

Hotel Eden, BadenBaden
6 Oct 1927

Dear Dobrée

I had your letter just as we left Irschenhausen. It would be fun to come to Egypt: only I'm afraid, too expensive. Isn't the journey very dear? and my finances are low, I'm not much of an earner. When I get back to Florence I'll ask Cooks, and see if we can do it. It's awfully nice of you to offer us hospitality – Without that, Egypt would have to remain off my map. But we'd have to share in the household expenses, must.

Then again there's my wretched bronchials – gave me an awful time this summer. Is Egypt all right in winter, for bronchials? I'm much better now, but must go gingerly.

I'll write to Mrs Dobrée and ask her anyhow if she'd like to stay a bit with us in the Villa Mirenda on her way out. We shall be back there by the 20th – in two weeks' time –

But I sort of sniff a whiff of possibility in the Egyptian idea. It would be awfully nice to spend some time with you and Mrs Dobrée too, because I'm sure we should get on.

Germany is beginning to depress me thoroughly: a sort of disillusioned stark materialism, with no hope in it and no glamour of 'rising higher,' only mere having: very grim and horrid, with a surface aimiability. I want to tuck my tail between my legs and run.

I'm glad you don't mind your job. Anything that's got the least little bit of adventure in it is worth while. I'm sure you don't care whether you improve the unimprovable Egypt or not.

Well, perhaps we'll meet beneath the chin of the Sphinx. Let's hope she'll put us a less puerile riddle.

Yrs   D. H. Lawrence

---

[1] *Die Fromme Helene* (Heidelberg, 1872), another of Busch's verse tales (cf. Letter 4133 and n. 1).
[2] DHL signed his full name, as sender, on the front of this PC and of Letter 4175.

4161. To Valentine Dobrée, 6 October 1927
Text: MS Brotherton; Unpublished.

Hotel Eden, BadenBaden
6 Oct 1927

Dear Mrs Dobrée

We had Dobrées letter just as we were leaving Bavaria. Awfully nice of you to ask us to Egypt. We should like to come, but finances pretty low. It costs an awful lot to get there, doesn't it? I'll ask about it all at Cooks when we get back to Florence.

We shall be back at the Villa Mirenda, Scandicci, on or before the 20th – pray God, for I've had enough now of Germany. When will you be sailing? Won't you come and stay a bit with us on the way? It's not very comfortable, our flat, but perhaps you're not *awfully* particular. We're on the rough and ready side, I'm afraid. But anyhow it's quite nice country, and perhaps you like Florence. – My wife will write too – though she's a bad hand at letters.

What do you think too of Egypt in winter, for my beastly bronchials? They gave me the hell of a time this summer, but are a lot better, though I still feel a bit sorry for myself.

It's suddenly so cold here. How is Hampstead? Remember me to Gertler, and come anyhow to the Mirenda.

Yrs sincerely   D. H. Lawrence

4162. To Else Jaffe, [7 October 1927]
Text: MS Jeffrey; Frieda Lawrence 251–2.

Hotel Eden, BadenBaden
Freitag

Meine liebe Else

Du auch hast einen Geburtstag – aber ich finde man muss vier oder achtzig sein, um wichtige Geburtstage zu haben. Über Jahreszahl reden wir nicht.

Ich hatte deinen Brief. Ja, wir sahen den Hans Carossa – ein netter man, mild wie Kartoffelbrei. Er hörte mir an – ich meine, meine Atmenswegen – könnte von Lungen nichts hören, sagt das muss geheilt sein – nur die Bronchien – und die Ärtzte interessieren sich gar nicht an den Bronchien. – Er sagt aber ich soll keine Einhalieren machen, mit heisser Luft: das bringt wieder verblutung. – Die Reise war hässlich, eine Menge Leute, viel Staub, und ich war etwas erkältet – es geht aber wieder besser. Wir sind sehr fein im Eden – zwei Zimmer mit Bad – und das Essen sehr gut – gestern war es Gans, Michaelmas Goose, ausgezeichnet. Ich kann besser essen – aber sie bringen man so furchtbar viel, wagenvolle Kartoffeln und Schnitzel gross wie ein

Fussteppich – und wie die Leute futtern! – das nimmt mir ein wenig meine
scheue Appetit weg. – Die Schwiegermutter wird immer jünger – wir mussen
ihre Geburtstage von oben ab rechnen: nächtes mal wird sie 66, dann 55. So
ist es mit der Älter, die einzige richtige kummerslose Zeit der Jugend, wenn
man mehr wie 70 hat.

Der Max Mohr kam gelaufen in einem Auto vom Tegernsee, wo er ein
Bauernhaus hat – mit Frau und Kind – ein Mann von 36 oder so. Er sollte ein
Naturbursch sein, wir waren aber über die Natur sehr entäuscht. Doch ist er
interessant und gut, aber ein letzter Mann, der ganz und gar am Ende des
Weges gekommen ist, und kann nicht weder in der Wildnis fortwandern, oder
einen Schritt in das Unbewussten nehmen. So ist er sehr unglücklich – war
Artzt – in England Kriegsgefangener – und etwas wie der Hadu seine
Psychologie. Wir haben seine Theaterstücke, schenken sie dir: sie sind nicht
sehr wichtig. – Der Kahler kam zum letzten Abend – sehr nervös war er – wir
sehen die beide vielleicht wieder in Italien.

Wann kommst du hier? Komm denn diesen Wochenende. Wir bleiben bis
17n – haben's sehr gut, aber die Welt kommt mir schon wieder so *finster* vor.
Das erschreckt mir, und ich muss nach Süden. –

Ich schicke dir das Novelle – zu lang für *Jugend*, aber du könntest es
vielleicht anderswo verkaufen. Wäre nicht 'Tickets Please!' aus *England my
England!* eben richtig für die *Jugend*. Hast du es? Das Stück vom Hund kann
ich nicht finden. Aber komm, und wir werden über alles mitreden. Sind
Friedel und Marianne da?

                                    Grüsse an sie, auch an Alfred.   DHL

                                                                    [Friday
My dear Else,

You too have a birthday – but I think that, to have important birthdays, one
must be either four or eighty. We won't speak about the number of years.[1]

I had your letter. Yes, we saw Hans Carossa – a nice man, mild as mashed
potatoes. He listened to me – I mean, to my breathing-passages – could hear
nothing in the lungs, says that must be healed – only the bronchials – and
doctors aren't a bit interested in bronchials. – But he says I shouldn't do any
hot-air inhalations: that will start the bleeding again. – The journey was
horrible, crowds of people, lots of dust, and I had a bit of a cold – but things
are getting better again. We are very grand in the Eden – two rooms, with
bathroom – and the food is very good – yesterday it was goose, Michaelmas
goose, superb. I can eat better – but they bring one such a frightful lot, trolley

[1] Else was forty-five.

loads of potatoes and cutlets big as carpets – and how the people pitch in! – that takes my shy appetite away a bit. – The Schwiegermutter grows younger all the time – we should start counting her birthdays backwards: next time she'll be 66, then 55. That's how it is with old age, the only real affliction-free time of youth, when one is over 70.

Max Mohr ran up in his car from Tegernsee, where he has a house in the country – with wife and child – a man of 36 or so. He was meant to be a child of nature, but we were very disappointed in the nature. Yet he is good and interesting, but a last man, who has arrived at the very end of the road, and who can neither go on travelling in the wilderness, nor take a step into the unconscious. So he is very unhappy – was a doctor – prisoner of war in England – and psychologically a bit like Hadu.[1] We have his plays, we'll give them you: they are not very significant. – Kahler came over on our last evening – he was very on edge – we'll perhaps see them both again in Italy.

When are you coming here? Do come this weekend. We stay till the 17th – have a fine time here, but once again the world seems so *dark* to me. That scares me, and I have to go south. –

I send you the story – too long for the *Jugend*, but you could perhaps sell it somewhere else. Wouldn't 'Tickets Please!' from *England my England!* be just right for the *Jugend*. Do you have it? I can't find the piece about the dog.[2] But come, and we'll discuss it all. Are Friedel and Marianne there?

Greetings to them, to Alfred too.   DHL]

4163. To S. S. Koteliansky, 8 October 1927

Text: MS BL; Postmark, Frankfurt–Basel 9.10.27; Moore 1006–7.

Villa Mirenda, Hotel Eden. BadenBaden
8 Oct 1927

My dear Kot

Your letter about your scheme came on today.[3] I am a useless person to consult commercially. You know Secker asked me if *Jud Süss* was worth publishing in translation – and I said no![4] Luckily he did it, and saved his life and almost made his fortune. So there am I, as a business adviser!

Do you think you could sell such little books as 8000 words at 15/- each? I doubt it: unless you had something very special, and a bit risky, inside. But

---

[1] Hadubrand von Schreibershofen (b. 1905), Johanna von Krug's son by her first husband.
[2] See Letter 4142 and n. 2.
[3] Kot's 'scheme' to become a publisher occupies some part of each of DHL's letters to him until the end of 1927.
[4] See Letter 4003 and p. 46 n. 1, and *Letters*, v. 655 for DHL's acknowledgment of his lack of commercial sense.

where will you get anything very special and risky? It's as good as impossible.
Unless you think of something clever. You see no man today will risk himself
in print, at least under his own name. Everybody turns out the expected stuff.
Unless you could persuade a few people to do you an *anonymous* declaration: a
confessio or an apologia in which he really said all he wanted to say – really let
go. If you could get Wells to do a black prophecy and somebody else to reveal
other intimate things that can't get into print – that Mayo woman say the *worst*
about India[1] – that kind of thing – all say the worst they all feel – you might get
something even worth 15/- – But they'd have to be anonymous. And you'd
have to have at least half a dozen MS before you made any announcement. –
Otherwise, I doubt if you'll possibly get anything worth printing. You won't
be able to pay enough. – What you might do, you might write to a few people
who have strong feelings, and ask them if they have anything that no paper
would print, which they would like to have printed – anonymously or
otherwise. Then see. Otherwise nobody will give you anything really worth
having. And you can't offer the world tripe at 15/- for 10,000 words. – Then if
you want to do Nonsuch Press stuff,[2] you must leave out Kuprin and me.[3]
That Nonsuch sort of stuff is for the pretty-pretty public. If you can really
catch the pretty-pretty public, all right – but not with corn like mine. My dear
Kot, *do* do something. But it must be feasible. Publish books at 15/- for 10,000
words if you like. But first find the things to publish, worth publishing. I
should be a bit ashamed to see a story like 'The Man Who Loved Islands'
done up at 15/-, when the *London Mercury* will print it in the ordinary course.
What is your point? very exquisite production? Then do the classics, that
people feel safe about.

I believe you could do something. But you've got to hit a special line. I'll try

---

[1] H. G. Wells published several prophecies, e.g. *A Forecast of the World's Affairs* (1925), *The
Way the World is Going: Guesses and Forecasts of the Years Ahead* (1928). Katharine Mayo
(1868–1940), American journalist, published her study of child marriage in India, *Mother India*
(July 1927); it was the subject of a protest meeting in Calcutta in September (at which the book
was burned), heated discussion by the Calcutta Corporation in October and a *Times* leading
article on 27 March 1928.
[2] The Nonesuch Press was founded in 1923 by (Sir) Francis Meynell (1891–1975) and David
Garnett (1892–1981); DHL had been closely associated with both families in earlier years but
now was disenchanted (see his dismissive remark about Garnett's *The Lady into Fox*, *Letters*,
iv. 500). Though the Nonesuch did publish some 'pretty-pretty' books, it exerted a major
influence on literary taste through important edns of Donne, Congreve, Wycherley, etc.;
Geoffrey Keynes's Nonesuch edn of Blake's *Poetry and Prose* had recently appeared (August
1927).
[3] Kot and Middleton Murry had translated *The River of Life and Other Stories* by Aleksandr
Ivanovich Kuprin (1870–1938) in 1916 (see *Letters*, ii. 562 n. 3); no other trans. of Kuprin by
Kot is known.

and think of something. But I of course incline to something cheap – a tiny little magazine at 6d that honestly says something.

But I'll try to think of something. Did Leonard Wolffs stuff – his little books – sell?[1] – But they didn't cost 15/-. Why 15/-? What justification?

DHL

4164. To Hon. Dorothy Brett, 8 October 1927
Text: MS UCin; Postmark, Frankfurt–Basel 9.10.27; Irvine, Brett 77–8.

BadenBaden.
8 October 1927

Dear Brett

I'm sorry you went and rode other people's pintos, and got bucked off. Keep now to your resolution, and *never* ride other people's horses: especially when you've got good ones of your own.

We came here the other day – the same old unreal Baden, living off its past. It bores me a bit, but we'll put up with it till the 17th, for my mother-in-law's sake, and for my bit of an inhalation cure. They have all sorts of cures here: I'm just going to do the breathing the cold radium air ones. I believe I really am going to get myself solid, with patience – but always it takes time.

Today is a lovely October day, with the first leaves falling in the little wind. I hope it'll stay like that. I wish really we were at the ranch. I feel a bit shut in in Europe lately. But I wonder if I'd be able to risk that altitude yet! I wouldn't hardly dare gallop a horse. Those accursed hemorrhages! But they haven't come back again.

The Dobrées asked us to Egypt this winter. They have a house outside Cairo. I would rather like to go, just for a couple of months, but am afraid it is impossible, funds pretty low, and it costs as much to get to Cairo as to New York. Troppo![2]

I'll bet Mabel suffered from her mother[3] – Let's hope it's over now, and all serene.

When you're at the ranch, would you look in my papers and see if you can find the story called 'The Last Laugh' – it came in a rather silly book *The New Decameron*, about three years ago:[4] also there should be a rabbit sketch

---

[1] Leonard Sidney Woolf (1880–1969), with his wife, the novelist, Virginia Woolf (1882–1941), ran the Hogarth Press; he was a close friend of Kot's. Among many other books, Woolf had published seven books of Kot's translations from Russian.

[2] 'Too much!'

[3] Sarah Cook Ganson 'was strong and decisive but also cold, unfeeling, and entirely self-centered . . . She seemed indifferent toward her husband as well as toward her child' (Lois P. Rudnick, *Mabel Dodge Luhan*, Albuquerque, 1984, p. 6).

[4] *The New Decameron* IV (1925), pp. 235–61 (Roberts B15).

'Adolf', and a dog sketch 'Rex' – I think both came in the *Dial*.[1] Secker is bringing out a book of collected short stories in the early spring, and I would like these. – Also please send me a copy of my bibliography – there must be several there.

We shall be back at the Villa Mirenda by the 20th of this month, I suppose. I want to paint another picture. I've got no tools for wood-cuts. – And I dont want to bother writing books. The Brit govt. now takes 20% of the royalties of persons living abroad – and Curtis Brown gets 10% – so of the bit I make I only get 70% – I shall try and write little stories.

Four of my Etruscan essays are to appear in *Travel* – beginning in November, I believe[2] – and the *Forum* has bought my Resurrection story *The Escaped Cock*.[3] I think it's a good one. But I don't know when they'll publish. But of course I can't sell to the *Sat. Evening Post* or *Good Housekeeping* – which really pay.

I'll do something for Spud if I can – but here in Germany I don't do anything at all. Dont have accidents, they're unnecessary. Remember me to Rachel and William.

DHL

4165. To Martin Secker, 8 October 1927
Text: MS UInd; Postmark, Baden-Baden 8.10.27; Secker 96.

Hotel Eden, BadenBaden
8 Okt. 1927

Dear Secker

I sent the signed agreement for the Stories to Pollinger.[4] Have you counted the words? Are there plenty? Because the story 'In Love' won't appear in the *Dial* and in *Hutchinson's* apparently till January – and Curtis Browns have no MS of 'The Last Laugh' and the two animal sketches, they say – nor have I, here, but I have them at the ranch. Also, since 'The Last Laugh' appeared in Basil Blackwells *New Decameron* about three years ago, you could no doubt get a copy of that at once. – I see however that Curtis Browns have included 'None of That' – which is rather long, and which they have never offered for periodical publication. What do you think of that story, by the way – I know Miss Pearn didn't like it – but it's good – in itself – and 'founded on fact', as they say.[5]

---

[1] See Letter 4140 and p. 152 n. 4. (Neither was included in *The Woman Who Rode Away*.)
[2] See p. 48 n. 1.
[3] Nancy Pearn had written on 4 October 1927 (TMSC UT) to tell DHL that *Forum* had taken the story for $150.
[4] For the contents of *The Woman Who Rode Away* see Letter 4140 and p. 152 n. 3.
[5] See Letter 4031 and n. 3.

I was thinking, did you get rid of that Shestov translation *All Things are Possible?* Because now, with an introd. by Prince Mirsky, you could probably sell three thousand of it.[1] I hope you held the copies.

We shall be here till the 17th, I suppose, then back to the Mirenda. Baden is much the same, but more visitors – quite a lot, even now – and the Kurhaus going fairly strong, even *very mild* gambling allowed. But the place still belongs to the past – hopelessly past.

The Dobrées invited us to Egypt this winter. I would rather like to go – but I doubt if I have enough money – getting rather low.

Let me know about the stories.

D. H. Lawrence

4166. To Emily King, [9 October 1927]
Text: MS Lazarus; cited in Moore 1007–8.

Hotel Eden. BadenBaden.
Sunday

My dear Pamela

We had your letter and Peg's note. So now it's Joan's turn! I hope to heaven she was able to pop into the hospital and get that job done. It's not much in itself, but one is relieved when it's all well over.

I was examined again by the Doctor in charge of the Bath here: he looked me over last year – says I'm really rather better than I was last year – catarrh clearer on the lower lungs, but still not clear at the top, and bronchial passages inflamed. And I don't weigh enough – but I never did. He wants me to go into a sanatorium for two months, just to build up. But my Florence doctor, one of the best in Italy, said there was no need to go into a sanatorium, especially if I could eat with appetite. And I'm just getting my appetite back, and beginning to feel really really more myself. And doctors and sanatoriums only lower my spirits. I shall take the inhalation cure for ten days or so here – sort of air from the radium springs – and if I keep on as well as I am, I shan't go into any sanatorium. Why should I? The only thing is to get better – and I'll really try to do that and nothing else.

It was a lovely day – clear sun all day, and the woods just yellowing. I've got a fine big room in this hotel – and Frieda a smaller room – with our bathroom between us – food very good – what more can one have? Look at poor G[ertie] and sanatoriums. I'm sure the thought of her simply breaks my heart: a year now. And it's no joke for Ada having her home, with all the responsibility. My

---

[1] Secker published DHL's and Kot's trans. of Leo Shestov's *All Things are Possible* in 1920. The volume was not reissued so the possibility of an introduction by the critic, historian and translator of Russian Literature, Prince Dmitry Petrovich Svyatopolk-Mirsky (1890–1939), Lecturer in Russian in the University of London, 1922–32, did not arise.

word, as we come into the middle of our lives, which is supposed to be our prime and our best period, we seem to come into a rare old peck of troubles.

It seems to me the best time is when one is over seventy. Frieda's mother is seventy-six, and seems to get younger instead of older. Now she bothers no more about anything, and just enjoys her days as they slip by, as one is supposed to do when one is a child. She really is very nice, and thinks of everything she possibly can for me, buys anything she thinks I might like – really very nice. Frieda's sisters the same. Emil sent me 3 doz. special malt beer from Berlin, Else got me still another doctor, they really do all they can. And as for me, with this beastly catarrh of the lungs which I've always had, and which is largely a thing of the general condition of body and spirits, I must build myself up slowly, and so I will. I do feel myself better every week. But I have to be so careful.

I shall be rather glad to go back to the Mirenda now. The autumn there is so lovely, and it's so still. And I can paint again – I feel like painting, not like writing. And then if we can get back, we won't have to spend so much. All this is very expensive, and my earnings aren't much, nowadays.

Well I do hope that business of Joan's is through. If only we have the energy, I want to send her some of these little Black Forest toys. But Frieda is having a course of the dentist, and isn't in the pink. She is pining too, to get back to Italy. She likes it much better there.

Tell Peg I don't envy her her struggles with the German language. It's pretty trying. I nearly cracked my brains listening to the patter at the Marionette Theatre in the Kurhaus this afternoon. Tell Peg not to study too hard at anything – *nothing on earth* is worth wasting one's reserve of strength for. You know that when you've wasted it. – I'm sorry about the colliers.[1] God knows what'll be the end of *that* business. Thank heaven we've only got to live once. Hope Sam is all right.

Love. DHL

4167. To Ada Clarke, [9 October 1927]
Text: MS Clarke; cited in Lawrence–Gelder 197–8.

Hotel Eden. BadenBaden.
Sunday

My dear Sister

I put off writing hoping the shirts would come, but they are not here yet.

[1] Nottinghamshire miners were enduring a severe economic depression resulting in part from the major strike of 1926. Colliers' wages were reduced in consequence of lower profits; at Kimberley, in December 1927, 30% of the miners were suspended indefinitely. See *The Times*, 9 August and 6 December 1927.

However, they are sure to send them on from Ebenhausen, the letters come on all right.

A mercy Bertie has got over the measles so well. I do hope you've taken care to see there were no after-effects. I believe all three of us, Emily and you and I, got a lot of catarrh trouble as the effect of measles. I know my deafness came then.

I was in the Landesbad this morning and examined by the doctor in charge. He says I am really rather better than last year – only the catarrh of the lungs at the top now, the lower lungs much better – but the bronchial passages still bad. I am starting an inhalation cure tomorrow, for ten days. He says I am much under weight, and wants to put me in a sanatorium to build that up. But since I've always been under weight, and am much lighter *built* than doctors will allow; and since, with me, it's nearly all a question of spirits; and since doctors and sanatoriums only depress me; and I'm just beginning to get back a bit of my *real* self, and my appetite, why should I stick myself in a German sanatorium? I won't! I really feel I'm on the mend, to get better than I've been for the last three years. So I'll go gently by myself. I'll do the inhalation cure for ten days, if it suits me. Then we'll go back to the Mirenda. It's all pretty expensive. We've got fine rooms with bath in this hotel – and food good – but one just *has* to look after oneself now. I want to get that catarrh of the lungs down.

The Dobrées – friends – want us to go to Egypt for the bad months of the winter. I should rather like to go. They have a house at Gizeh, outside Cairo. But the journey and all is very expensive, as much as to America. I'm afraid we shan't be able to do it. Then the doctor seems to prefer the idea of the mountains in January, up to the snow. They say its a marvellous tonic. So we shall see. I'm determined to get myself more sound than I've been lately – and not to think of anything else but that, really.

Poor Gertie, I've been wondering so much about her. It's truly a rather bitter responsibility for you, having her home. But poor thing, what can one do! There certainly is no Providence to shield us from heredity: or at least, poor G. and her family. If ever I can do anything, let me know. And if I can help with money, only tell me. I wish to God she might get reasonably well, to be able to enjoy her days a bit. We get our own sins visited on our heads, and our father's and grandfather's as well.[1]

My mother-in-law is wonderful – seems to get younger. She was out with us to tea at the Kurhaus, and after to the Marionette Theatre – very pretty and elegant. She is really very nice – and whatever she can do for me, she does it –

---

[1] Cf. Book of Common Prayer: 'visit the sins of the fathers upon the children unto the third and fourth generations'.

thinks of everything possible. Frieda's sisters the same – they really cudgel their brains to think of any way to help. I must say people are kind – so were our neighbours the Wilkinsons, at the Mirenda.

It was a lovely day – the beech trees just going yellow, and a soft blue sky and clear sun, the rather elegant park, and the woods beyond, on the steep hills – but it all belongs to sixty years ago, to the days of Turgenev and King Edward and heaps of money flowing.[1] The Kurhaus – where the concerts and gambling and all that took place, is much more elegant and lovely than Monte Carlo. But the modern public is a dreary thing.

Well, I hope things are shaping all right now. Coal in England is done, and the colliers are done in, poor devils! It makes one sick. But it's the end of an epoch. God knows what comes next.

Love to the children and to Eddie. Tell him not to lock himself inside his new car, he might never get out. I hope Bertram is rosy again – As for poor Gertie, let me know.

Love.   DHL

4168. To S. S. Koteliansky, [10 October 1927]
Text: MS BL; Postmark, Baden-Baden 11.10.27; Moore 1009–10.

Kurhaus Eden. BadenBaden
Monday

My dear Kot

I can more or less see the possibility of your 'intimate series', if you can get hold of any MSS. that are in any way really intimate. But as far as I know authors, it's next door to impossible. Myself, I find it terribly difficult to write intimately – one feels colder and colder about unbosoming oneself. And you'd need at least six genuine good MSS. before you start. I shall see Douglas and Huxley in Florence – and I'll put the matter to them, privately. Then there's E. M. Forster – perhaps A. E. Coppard – Osbert Sitwell – Edith Sitwell – Gerhardi – Dos Passos – Sherwood Anderson – Gertrude Stein – Robert Graves – all *might* do an interesting thing, *if they will*.[2] And one could think of

---

[1] Ivan Sergeevich Turgenev (1818–93) lived in Baden-Baden, c. 1856–70; Edward VII (1841–1910) visited the spa and casino periodically 1867–83.

[2] DHL was drawing on some personal acquaintance: he had known Edward Morgan Forster (1879–1970) since 1915; Edith and Osbert Sitwell visited Villa Mirenda on 23 May (Letter 4026); and he met William Alexander Gerhardie (1895–1977), novelist and critic, in London in October 1925 (*Letters*, v. 322). He did not know the poet Alfred Edgar Coppard (1878–1957) though he knew of him (see *Letters*, v. 284 n. 1, 641); he had not met the American novelist John Dos Passos (1896–1970), nor the American writer Gertrude Stein (1874–1946), though he knew her brother (*Letters*, iii. 463); and he was not acquainted with the American novelist, Sherwood Anderson (1876–1941) or with the poet and novelist Robert Graves (1895–1985).

others. But I doubt so terribly if anybody will write and *sign* anything truly intimate or particularly worth having. And there must be some point to the series: you don't want just to start out cadging 15/- or 21/- for limited edition stuff which is only like all other stuff. Myself, I'll give you anything I can give: but what in God's name am I to write *intimately*? If there were some clue – some point upon which we're to be intimate, so that the things hung together a bit: if even only a suggestion from everybody of what they think the most important thing in life – something of that sort – But you *must* have a point.

And I'm a bit doubtful of the sixpenny stories. Better perhaps a little fortnightly or monthly of ten or twelve thousand words: a little magazine something like that *Laughing Horse* from Santa Fe – did you see the number Spud Johnson did on me?[1] – it wasn't good, but a little private sort of magazine like that can be made to pay, just to pay, especially if you canvass personally for material, and appeal only to a decently educated public – not like the *Adelphi*, which wanted all the chapel and church imbeciles, and fell through the holes in its own socks. The point is, you've got to offer something genuine: there's plenty of hotch-potch already. You'll never make much money with genuine stuff, but you'll be sound.

There goes the dinner bell.

But you've got to get down to some bed rock somewhere – there have been too many piffling little 'enterprises.'

DHL

4169. To Coburn Gilman, 10 October 1927
Text: MS UT; Postmark, Baden-Baden 11.10.27; Unpublished.

Hotel Eden. BadenBaden
10 Oct 1927

Dear Mr Gilman

I'm glad you liked the Etruscan Sketches. – Would you mind letting Mrs McCord have the MS. and the pictures for a day or two, just to show to Alfred Knopf.[2] I should be much obliged. And if you get any extra photographs, do please let me have them when you've done with them.

I'm doing a brief cure here, for my wretched breathing passages, then we go back to Italy. I want to do sketches on 'The Olive Tree' and 'Cypresses' – if I do them, I'll let you know.[3] We might just possibly go to Egypt this winter – perhaps do a travel sketch or two there. Knees of the Gods!

I hope you're having a good time with *Travel*. –

Yours Sincerely   D. H. Lawrence

[1] See p. 38 n. 1. The DHL issue was No. 13, April 1926.
[2] Lina McCord was a member of Curtis Brown's office staff in New York.
[3] They were not written.

4170. To Alfred Knopf, 10 October 1927
Text: Moore 1008–9.

Hotel Eden, Baden-Baden
10 October 1927

Dear Knopf

We aren't back in Italy yet – but hope to depart next week. I'm doing a bit of an inhalation cure here for my miserable tubes. I think Europe *is* a bit depressing – but especially northern and central Europe. Austria was awful, and Germany, just underneath her new-assumed sprightliness, is awful too. What the devil's the matter with the world?

About a new MS. – you know Secker is doing a vol. of short stories in the spring – though I suppose you don't call that a new MS., since they've all appeared somewhere or other. But I wish you'd ask Curtis Brown to let you see the six Etruscan sketches: *Sketches of Etruscan Places*: with the photographs. I believe *Travel* is publishing four of them, with pictures: beginning next month.

I intended to do twelve sketches, on different places – but when I was ill, I left off at Volterra. I wanted to do a book about 80,000 words, to be illustrated with some 80 or 100 photographs. You'll see the idea from the first six sketches. – Now I don't care very much whether I finish the thing or not. In my present state, I feel I never want to write another book. What's the good! I can eke out a living on stories and little articles, that don't cost a tithe of the output a book costs. Why write novels any more! Then the Brit. govt. takes 20% of the royalties – and there's the agent – what do I get out of it, after sweating myself to nothing! Not good enough. – The novel I wrote last winter is good, but they'd call it pornographic, so I shan't publish it.

But that's not the point. The point is, if you felt at all keen about the Etruscan book, I'd sweat round Arezzo and Chiusi and Orvieto and those places, and do the other six sketches this autumn. But if you feel cool about it, then none of us need bother. I'm glad when I needn't make any effort whatsoever – don't feel up to much.

Let me know just how you feel – you didn't like the *idea* of the Etruscan book – and I don't really care.

Remember us both to Mrs Knopf.[1] It's lovely autumn now, and I almost wish I was in America. Europe really *is* a dud. I wish I was at the ranch – anyhow there's *room* there.

Write to the Villa Mirenda.

---

[1] Blanche Knopf, née Wolf (1894–1966). m. Alfred Knopf, 1916. She was Vice-President of her husband's company, 1921–57.

4171. To Max Mohr, 10 October 1927
Text: MS HMohr; Mohr, Briefe 527–8.

Kurhaus Eden. BadenBaden.

10 Oct 1927

Dear Max Mohr

Awfully nice of you to send the Rousseau lion and *Jean Paul* book.[1] The
first is very naïve and touching – as for the second, I shall read it this winter
when I feel kräftig.[2] – I have already read the Tulpin play.[3] It has a queer
flavour of its own, you shouldn't abuse it. But you are bad at heroes. Your
Columbuses always seem to be weeping into a wet pockethandkerchief. Your
villainous Christys are much more alive and frisky. My Schwiegermutter was
very amusing about it: – 'Aber *das* ist kein Kunstwerk! – und die Sprache die
sie sprechen! aber nein, der, der Mohr, der ist kein gebildeter Mann.' – All the
same, she is really interested, and goes on reading. As she says: 'Einmal haben
sie uns Iphigenia vorgestellt, und jetzt –! Aber wie die Welt herunter
gekommen ist, nein, ein Schauer! –'[4] But whatever your plays are, you have a
queer power of putting one right into the scene, whether one wants to go or
not. I am reading the *Improvisationen* now.[5]

As for one's old works – I feel just the same as you about it. I read five pages
of one of my own books, and shudder, and put the thing away.

Here my manhood, as you call it, patiently listens to Konzerten in
Kurgarten, goes to tea in the Waldkaffee with the beloved women, and in the
morning, sits in a white coat and hood, in a vaporous room with other figures
vaguely seen through the mists in more white mantles and hoods, like a
Fehmgericht,[6] doing an Inhalationkur. It is my one desire, to get well as soon
as possible – but really well. I am sick of books and all things literary,
especially Quatsch.[7] I should love to set out with the Zieharmonika,[8] and turn
my back on the world. As soon as this beastly cough goes down, we'll do it,
shall we? – go to Greenland with a Zieharmonika! But I'm afraid, if there's a

---

[1] *La Bohémienne Endormie* (1897), the masterpiece by Henri (the Douanier) Rousseau (1844–
1910) which had been returned to Paris in 1926 (from USA); perhaps *Jean Paul* [Richter]
(Leipzig, 1925), by Walther Harich (1888–1931).   [2] 'strong'.
[3] *Platingruben in Tulpin* (Munich, 1927), a comedy in three acts.
[4] 'But *that* isn't a work of art! – and the language that they use! no, really, that man, that Mohr,
that's not a cultivated man –' . . . 'Once they put on Iphigenia for us, and now –! Yet how the
world has gone downhill, no, what a horror! –'
[5] *Improvisationem im Juni* (Munich, 1923), a comedy in two acts.
[6] More usually 'vehmgericht': a mediaeval German court where certain individuals – hooded to
protect their identities – held trials outside the normal processes of law.
[7] 'rubbish'.   [8] 'accordion'.

sound of Zieharmonikas anywhere, one at least of the beloved women will not be left behind. We shall have to pretend we're going to a literary gathering of the international P. E. N. club. Ugh! how awful! But if we set out with music and light heels, how can you expect the women to let us go alone? Aspettiamo pure!

Really, in Baden one ought to be at least 75 years old, and at least an Excellenz, at the very least, a Generälchen. This place is such a back number, such a chapter in faded history, one hardly dares exist at all. I efface every possible bit of my manhood, and go around as much as possible like a paper silhouette of myself. – The chief monument at the moment is a white Hindenburg bust,[1] marvellous, standing among all the Wurst and Ripple in the sausage shop, and made 'aus feinster Rindfett.' Das es nicht blosse Schweineschmalz ist, Gott sei dank![2]

We hope to leave next Monday, 17th, for Italy. The address there is

Villa Mirenda, *Scandicci*, (Florenz)

Greetings from us both – also to the Frau Gemahlin[3] – and I'll tell you when to tune up the Zieharmonika.

Yours Sincerely   D. H. Lawrence

4172. To Franz Schoenberner, [11 October 1927]
Text: MS UT; Unpublished.

Kurhaus Eden. BadenBaden.

11 Okt

Lieber Schoenberner

So, wir sind acht Tage hier, und wie immer, weit in der Vergangenheit hinein. Wir spielen Whist mit uralten Excellenzen-weiber und Generalen, und ich meine, ich bin mein eigner Grossvater. Nein, Baden ist absolut unmöglich, unmöglich wie Versailles oder Paradies. – Ich thue auch eine Inhalationkur, sitze da im weissen Mantel mitten im Dampf, und sehe andere dummen Gespenster durch den Nebel, und kenne mich nicht mehr. Was man erfahren soll – und durchleben kann! – Wir reisen nächste Dienstag – 18n – nach Mailand, und hoffentlich kommen am 19n an die Villa Mirenda – *Scandicci*. Florenz.

Wie geht es Ihnen? und die *Jugend*? das ist aber ein Arbeit, sie immer jung zu halten. Sagen Sie an Hans Carossa, ich nehme ordentlich den Junicosan, ich glaube es tut mir gut, ich fühle mich wirklich besser. Die Reise war aber

---

[1] Field Marshall Paul von Hindenburg (1847–1934), President of the second Weimar Republic, 1925–34.
[2] 'sausage and chops . . . "made of the finest beef-fat." Thank God it isn't mere pork-dripping!'
[3] Kathe Mohr.

ermüdend, und ich merke, wie die Leute sich auf einander springen und sich hassen, wenn sie nur ein wenig gekratzt sind. Oberflächlich sehen sie ganz gutmütig aus – Aber hier ist man in der Vergangenheit verloren, wie ein Straussvogel mit dem Kopf im Sand.

Haben Sie die Fotografien machen gelassen? Wenn die Platten zu schlecht waren, lassen Sie sie bleiben.

Viele Grüsse von uns beide an Ihnen und an die Frau Gemahlin: ich hoffe es geht ihr auch gut, sie ist wie mich, nimmer zu kräftig.

D. H. Lawrence

[11 Oct

Dear Schoenberner

So, we've been here a week and, as always, far back into the past. We play whist with the ancient wives of Excellencies and with generals, and I believe I'm my own grandfather. No, Baden is quite impossible, impossible as Versailles or Paradise. – I'm also doing a course of inhalations, sit there in a white coat amidst the steam, and watch other stupid ghosts through the mist, and don't know myself any more. What one has to experience – and live through! – We set off next Tuesday – 18th – to Milan, and on the 19th hope to get to the Villa Mirenda – *Scandicci*, Florence.

How are you? and the *Jugend*? that really is work, keeping it always young. Tell Hans Carossa, I'm taking the Junicosan regularly, I think it does me good, I really feel better. The journey was tiring, though, and I notice how people jump at each other and hate each other when they're only a little angered. Superficially they appear good-natured enough – But here one is lost in the past, like an ostrich with its head in the sand.

Have you had the photographs done? If the plates were too bad, don't bother about them.

Many greetings from us both to you and to your wife: I hope she's well too, she's like me, never too strong.

D. H. Lawrence]

4173. To Giulia Pini, [12 October 1927]
Text: MS UT; PC v. [Ludwig-Wilhelm-Stift (Damenheim) Baden-Baden]; Postmark, Baden[-Baden] 12[...]; Unpublished.

BadenBaden
– mercoledì

Cara Giulia

– vogliamo partire da qui il martedì che viene – 18mo – dunque dobbiamo arrivare a Firenze la sera di mercoledi, 19°. Saremo tutti due contenti di tornare, l'inverno commincia già qui in Germania. Stiamo tutti bene; anche la

Baronessa – mia suocera. Questa è la casa dove abita lei – ma noi siamo in un hôtel vicino. – Credo che gli amici della Villa Poggi ci manderanno un'automobile alla stazione, saremo a casa verso le sette della sera. Allora a rivederci fra pochi giorni.

[– Wednesday

Dear Giulia

– we want to leave here next Tuesday – the 18th – then we ought to arrive in Florence on Wednesday evening, the 19th. We shall both be glad to come back, winter is already beginning here in Germany. We are all well; the Baroness too – my mother-in-law. This is the house where she lives – but we are staying at an hotel nearby. – I think that our friends at Villa Poggi will send us a car to the station, we shall be home at about seven in the evening. So see you in a few days.]

4174. To Lilian Wilkinson, [12 October 1927]

Text: MS Schlaefle; PC v. [Ludwig-Wilhelm-Stift (Damenheim) Baden-Baden]; Postmark, Baden-Baden 12 10 27; cited in Sagar, Wilkinsons 71.

Baden.

Wed.

– This is the house where F[rieda]'s mother lives – quite nice. We are preparing to leave next Tuesday, 18th – stay the night in Milan, get to Florence about 6.0 on Wed. 19th. Would you like to meet us with the motor? – It is rather foggy here now – pity, because overhead there is sun. I am doing an Inhalation cure – sit in a white shroud and hood in the steam, or vapor rather, and look at other dim shrouded figures sitting across the room! – but I think it does me good. Still, we shall both be glad to be back – it seems so dark now. I'll write again definitely about the arrival: shall be so glad to see you all.

DHL

4175. To Giuseppe Orioli, [12 October 1927]

Text: MS NWU; PC; Postmark, Baden-Baden 12 10 27; cited in Moore, *Intelligent Heart* 369.

Hotel Eden. BadenBaden

Wed

Had your letter – glad you are safely back, but you don't say how you are. I'm doing an inhalation cure – sit in a white mantle and hood in a cloud of vapour, with other ghostly figures, for an hour every morning! But it does my bronchials good.

We want to leave here next Tuesday – so we ought to arrive in Florence on

Wednesday evening – 19th from Milan. I hope we shall see you soon. The Wilkses will order us a motor-car, I suppose. – If you see the Huxleys, tell them just when we shall be arriving – I don't know exactly where they are. – It begins to be foggy and wintry here, though not very cold – only the wintry darkness. We shall both be glad to be back at the Mirenda for a while, to pick up the real sunshine again. Is Reggie back? – and Douglas? – So just in a week from now we ought to be arriving in Firenze. Frieda is *pining* to get back – more than I am. But I want to paint another picture: a huge one.

à bientot!   D. H. Lawrence

4176. To Catherine Carswell, [13 October 1927]
Text: MS YU; cited in Carswell 228, 255, 259.

Hotel Eden, BadenBaden
Thursday

My dear Catherine[1]

Shame we havent written you. I had bronchial hemorrhages in July – rather bad – crept to the mts in Austria in early August – spent Sept. in the Isartal near Munich, F[rieda]'s sister's house – am doing a little Inhalation cure here – and next Tuesday we leave for the Villa Mirenda once more. I was pretty shaken – am still not myself – don't want to eat – but am much better – but much. A question now of putting on weight and getting the general condition up again. Basta!

We did have your card – but it came at a weary moment. Still I ought to have answered, later.

I'm glad you're getting along – a struggle as usual – I'd rather be penniless and struggle, than not *quite* penniless, and sick. Sporca miseria![2]

The Franchettis called one day with Maria Huxley.[3] He's rather nice, but spoilt little boy: she is spoilt little girl par excellence, but I might like her better than him. Anyhow they're just a bit ridiculous.

All well here – F's mother sorry to have missed you. – Glad the boy gets on well – I think he's a seltsamer Mensch – typo speciale. Aspettiamo![4]

Is there any news of Ivy?[5] one has to think of her sometimes. And your two

---

[1] Catherine Roxburgh Carswell, née MacFarlane (1879–1946), novelist and biographer, and her husband Donald (1882–1940), barrister, had been friends of the Lawrences since 1914; see *Letters*, ii. 187 n. 5. DHL took a special interest in their son, John Patrick Carswell (b. 1918); see Carswell 228.   [2] 'Bloody awful!'

[3] See Letter 4043 and p. 81 n. 4. Yvonne Franchetti was Catherine Carswell's cousin.

[4] 'a strange chap – a special type. We shall wait and see!'

[5] Ivy Teresa Litvinov, née Low (1889–1977), novelist and friend of Catherine Carswell, had known DHL since 1914. m. 1916, Maxim Litvinov (1876–1951), later Soviet foreign commissar, 1930–9.

brothers, how are they getting along?[1] Seems all a question of money. Hateful that is!

We'll see you again one day before long – perhaps you'll be coming to Florence.[2] Perhaps now the tide is going to turn for you, and you'll be richer. I believe so. Hope Don's book goes – what is it really?[3] We really must all chirp up, and have one of the jolly old times. We *must* chirp up, all of us.

Sempre! DHL

enclose very bad snaps of my pictures!!![4]

4177. To Franz Schoenberner, [14 October 1927]
Text: MS UT; Unpublished.

Kurhaus Eden, BadenBaden
Freitag

Lieber Schoenberner

Die Fotografien sind da, und sehr gut gedruckt – Vielen Dank, und lassen Sie mich nur zahlen.

Wir fahren Dienstag morgen weg, bis Mailand. Die Tage sind nicht mehr hell, trüb geworden. Man möchte die Alpen hinüberfliegen, wie die Schwalben.

Ich weiss nicht, wie lange wir in der Villa Mirenda bleiben – Wir sind eingeladen nach Egypten – aber ich kann noch nicht an der weiterer Reise denken.

Ich habe nach Amerika geschrieben, für das Hund-Stück für die *Jugend*: wie das klingt! Und es gibt noch eine kleine Novelle die meine Schwegerin könnte für Ihnen übersetzen. Sie kommt morgen, ich will mit ihr sprechen. Aber ich vergesse die *Jugend* nicht, sicher nicht.

Ja, kommen Sie einmal nach Italien mit der Frau Schoenberner. Auch

[1] The two brothers were: George Gordon MacFarlane (1885–1949), author of a vivid war novel, *The Natural Man* (1924) which DHL enjoyed (*Letters*, v. 315); and John Grant MacFarlane, mainly a farmer, who shared the house at 110 Heath Street, Hampstead, where DHL stayed on his return from Mexico in December 1923. (John is the brother referred to in Carswell 213.)
[2] Florence] London
[3] Carswell's *Brother Scots* (October 1927) is a collection of six biographical essays which 'give not only some account of a number of intrinsically interesting men but also a cultural picture of Scotland in the late years of the nineteenth century' (Preface). Favourably reviewed in *The Times*, 7 October 1927. See also Letters 4221 and n. 1, 4494.
[4] DHL described each picture on the verso of the photograph:
(a) [*Flight Back into Paradise*] 'Eve running back into Paradise – burning industrial town behind – Adam holds off old Angel at the gate – rather red – about 4½ft. by 3½ft.'
(b) 'Boccaccio' story of nuns and gardeners – pale colours about 4ft by 3.'
(c) 'Red willow trees. about 3ft × 2.'
(d) 'Resurrection. 1 metre square'
(e) 'Holy Family!'

wenn wir weg gehen, können Sie die Wohnung haben – nichts
imponierendes, sechs Zimmer und ein Bauernmädchen zu helfen.

Sagen Sie an Hans Carossa, mein Inhalieren ist nicht heiss: kalter Dampf.
Es ist gut für mich, ich glaube, aber gar nicht mirakulos!

Wieder vielen Dank für die Fotografien und alle ihre Freundlichkeit, und
Grüsse an die Frau Gemahlin.

D. H. Lawrence

[Friday

Dear Schoenberner

The photographs are here, and very well printed – Many thanks, and do let
me pay.

We leave on Tuesday morning for Milan. The days are no longer bright,
have turned dull. One would like to fly over the Alps, like the swallows.

I don't know how long we shall be staying at the Villa Mirenda – We have
been invited to Egypt – but I can't think yet about the longer journey.

I have written to America, about the dog article for the *Jugend*: that sounds
odd! And there is too a little novella which my sister-in-law could translate for
you. She's coming tomorrow, I want to talk to her. But I won't forget the
Jugend, certainly not.

Yes, do come to Italy one day with Frau Schoenberner. Even if we go away,
you can have the flat – nothing imposing, six rooms and a peasant girl to help.

Tell Hans Carossa my inhalation isn't hot: cold steam. It's good for me, I
think, but not at all miraculous!

Many thanks again for the photographs and all your kindness, and
greetings to your wife.

D. H. Lawrence]

4178. To Arthur Wilkinson, [14 October 1927]
Text: MS Schlaefle; cited in Pinto, *Lawrence After Thirty Years*, p.48.

Kurhaus Eden, BadenBaden
Friday

Dear W[ilkinson]

Many thanks for sending on those proofs[1] – you must be sick of me and my
mail – but never mind, not much longer. As for the delay, let 'em wait.

We want to leave here next Tuesday – arrive Florence Wednesday evening

---

[1] Possibly proofs of one or more of the following, all published in November 1927: review of
Trigant Burrow's *Social Basis of Consciousness*, in *Bookman*, lxvi. 314–17; 'Flowery Tuscany
II', in *New Criterion*, vi. 403–8; 'In Love', in *Dial* (see p. 46 n. 5); 'City of the Dead at
Cerveteri', in *Travel*, l. 12–16, 50 (Roberts C160–3).

at 5.10, from Milan: earlier than it used to be, unless the woman got it wrong. Anyhow the express from Milan, leaving there about 10.30. Would you hate to order us the motor, the same as when we came away? – and we should of course feel very welcomed home, if you and Lilian Gair were at the station, and came out with us: lots of room in the car, you know how little luggage we have! *But don't for a moment put yourselves out*: a postcard would order the motor-car, if you are busy or anything.

I thought you sounded not very gay, in your last letter. Was it the cold wind? Never mind, just you try fog! – But it's so-so here. – If you were coming with us in the car, would you hate to buy us bread, and butter, and cheese – I'll write to Giulia to have eggs and milk, and that'll do us the first evening. Oh, and please, a packet of Quaker Oats: I am given porridge in the morning. – Then we can sail out peacefully to San Polo. – But if you are busy, Giulia will get these things.

I'm not making any plans, beyond next Wed. One journey ahead is enough. I've got various bits of nagging literary work lying in wait for me – and I *feel* like painting a large picture of Adam and Eve driving the Lord God out of Paradise:[1] Get out of here, you righteous old bird! – But it's the knees of the gods.

The doctor says I'm really better than last year when he examined me. But with this catarrh of the bronchials and top of the lungs, you just have to go slow, and build up the general condition. I cough and puff uphill just the same – otherwise feel pretty well.

Then au revoir – we shall be glad to see you all, and hope we'll have a nice neighbourly winter.

DHL

Beastly those Poggi! Let's each buy a machine gun, against our respective landlords and their tribes and camp-followers.

The Huxleys are in Florence – so they wrote.

F[rieda] has got a lorgnette!

4179. To S. S. Koteliansky, [16 October 1927]
Text: MS BL; Postmark, Oos 16.10.27; Moore 1011–12.

Kurhaus Eden. BadenBaden
Sunday

My dear Kot

All right! though personally I don't like expensive limited editions, if it's a

---

[1] The water-colour, finished before 11 November (Letter 4201), was to be *Throwing Back the Apple* (*Paintings of D. H. Lawrence*, plate [24]); it was a small picture, 12″ × 9″.

good way to start, then let it be so. I'll try and write something suitable when I get back to the Mirenda, and I'll tackle Huxley and Douglas – though it's hard to get anything out of Douglas, he's so irritable and nervy and can't work much. You'll have to keep E. M. [Forster] up to the scratch – he's not dependable either.

Personally I think nothing of Gertrude Stein, and not much of Gerhardi. But they have the sort of limited edition public, I believe.

As for the 'Jimmy' story, you'd be perfectly welcome to it, only Secker is bringing out a[1] volume of short stories, my stories, in January probably, and including that, of course. We'll have to think of something else.

We leave on Tuesday morning early, and should be at the Mirenda by Wednesday evening.

Do you know anything of Murry, and his wife? – how she is?[2]

And do you know Campbell's address?[3] Perhaps I'll write to him.

I'm still doubtful of the 6d story series – so hard to get 'em going.

Will write from Italy.

DHL

We might get something decent from Compton Mackenzie, or Francis Brett Young.

4180. To Emily King, [17 October 1927]
Text: MS Lazarus; PC; Postmark [Baden]-Baden [. . .]; Unpublished.

BadenBaden
– Monday

So glad that Joan is through with her operation – you'll see, she'll soon be all right. We never got her those toys – the post is such a nuisance, much worse than in England. I only sent her a tiny picture book, which probably won't come. –

We leave tomorrow for Milan – twelve hours from here – but a lovely journey over the Gotthard – I begin to hate travelling, though. We should be at Florence on Wednesday evening at teatime, and our neighbours will meet us with a car. I hope I shall be all right at the Mirenda – if not we must go to a higher altitude. Ada thinks sanatoriums so wonderful – but does one get very much individual attention, especially individual cooking? It always seems to me like an hotel with rules and regulations, doctors, and milk to drink. – It is

---

[1] a] the   [2] See p. 47 n. 1.
[3] Charles Henry Gordon Campbell (1885–1963), Irish barrister, later 2nd Baron Glenavy of Milltown, was an old friend of Kot's and Murry's; he had known DHL since 1913 and, with Murry, was a witness at the Lawrences' wedding. m. 1912, Beatrice Moss Elvery. See *Letters*, iv. 28 n. 3.

sunny here, with a cold wind, and the trees all going gold and red, quite lovely.
But Frieda is awfully keen to get back to Italy, more than I am. But I'm not
going to do much work of any sort this winter – that's a vow I make – though
of course there are things waiting for me. – I'll write from the Mirenda.

Love   DHL

4181. To Johanna Krug, [17 October 1927]
Text: MS UT; PC v. [photograph of Frieda, Lawrence and perhaps Else Jaffe]; Unpublished.

[Hotel Eden, Baden-Baden]
[17 October 1927]

Die Else war hier mit der Marianne, der Friedel kam auch. Die Räder haben
nicht ganz glatt gegangen, aber das verstehst du. Geduld ist immer das beste
Oel. Krieg du dir auch eine grosse Flasche, für den Winter. Leider kann ich
dir so eine nicht schicken. Wir fahren morgen weg – sind Mittwoch abend im
Mirenda. Ich schreibe von dort – Grüsse Emil und danke ihm für seinen
Brief.

DHL

[Frieda Lawrence begins]
Dein *liebliches* Jacket kam heute, wir freuten uns so – über alles – gleich kam
mit ein Brief aus der Mirenda – alles alles Gute! Lorenzo schreibt noch –
[a third person, perhaps the Schwiegermutter, begins]
Vielend Dank! Wir sitzen und [   ]¹ Gedenken! Else, Marianne, und
Friedel waren hier! Bleibt gesund und vergnügt!
[Lawrence continues]
Ja, und du schickst wieder ein Paket! – aber noch zu viel. Sei nicht so nobel, du
verwöhnst uns alle.
[Frieda Lawrence continues]
Im neuen Schloss!
  Wir lassen Rebhuhne bei der Schwiegermutter! Oh!

[Else was here with Marianne, Friedel came too. Things didn't go altogether
smoothly, but you'll understand that. Patience is always the best oil. Get
yourself a big bottle too, for the winter. I'm afraid I can't send you one. We're
going away tomorrow – are in the Mirenda Wednesday evening. I'll write
from there – Greet Emil and thank him for his letter.

DHL

¹ Illegible.

[Frieda Lawrence begins]
Your *lovely* jacket came today, we are so pleased – about everything – a letter came with it from the Mirenda – all the very best! Lorenzo writes some more –
[a third person, perhaps the Schwiegermutter, begins]
Many thanks! We're sitting and [   ] memories! Else, Marianne, and Friedel were here! Stay healthy and cheerful!
[Lawrence continues]
Yes, and you've sent another parcel! – but too much again. Don't be so generous, you're spoiling us all.
[Frieda Lawrence continues]
In the new castle!
    We leave the partridges with the Schwiegermutter! Oh!]

4182. To Baroness Anna von Richthofen, [20 October 1927]
Text: MS UCB; Frieda Lawrence 263.

Villa Mirenda. Scandicci, Florenz.
Donnerstag

Meine liebe Schwiegermutter
    Wir hatten eine gute Reise – wenige Leute, keine Schwierigkeiten, und ich war nicht sehr müde. Ich habe nie die Schweiz so schön gesehen: ein stiller grauer herbst-tag, mit Gras so stark grün, beinah wie Feuer, und denn die Obst-bäume alle zarten Flammen, die Kirschbäume absolut kirsch-rot, Apfelbäume und Birnen gelb-rot und scharlach, und still wie Blumen: aber wirklich ein Zauberland. In Italien hat es ge-regnet. Heute aber ist milde Sonne und Wolken, warme Luft, und eine grosse Stille. – Die Nachtbaren waren da am Bahnhof, mit dem Auto – alles sehr freundlich – und hier die Bauern alle gesammelt auf der 'aia' – die Giulia strahlend, sie wird ganz hübsch. Sie hatte Feuer und kochendes Wasser – und wir waren da. Aber mir kam das Haus so fremd vor, nakt und leer und beinah unheimlich, als ob ich es nie gekannt hatte. Ich bin immer noch etwas fremd – die Frieda aber seelig. Ich weiss nicht was es ist mit mir, aber ich bin diesmal nicht zuheim, zuhaus in Italien. Doch ist es sehr nett, nur ein Gefühl. – In deiner kleinen Vase stehen Rosen und Jasmin– meine Bilder kommen mir hübsch vor – und ich höre an, an die Stille. Aber jetzt gehen wir zu den Nachbaren, zum Thee, und bringen die kleinen Geschenke. – Schon heut' morgen war dein Brief da. Es ist Schade dass die Ferne, solang es Ferne bleibt, so absolut ist. Wenn wir zu dir zum Thee kommen könnten, denn waren wir alle drei glücklich. – Aber wir werden näherer kommen, zu wohnen.

auf wiedersehen, bleibe lustig.   DHL

[Thursday

My dear Schwiegermutter

We had a good journey – not many people, no difficulties, and I wasn't very tired. I have never seen Switzerland so beautiful: a still grey autumn day, with grass such a bright green, almost like fire, and then the fruit trees all gentle flames, the cherry trees absolutely cherry-red, apple trees and pears yellowish-red and scarlet, and still as flowers: it really was a wonderland. In Italy it's been raining. Today though it's gentle sun and clouds, warm air, and a great stillness. – The neighbours were there at the station, with the car – everything very friendly – and here the peasants all gathered in the 'threshing barn' – Giulia radiant, she's growing very pretty. She had a fire going and water boiling – and we were there. But I found the house so alien, bare and empty and almost uncanny, as if I had never known it. I'm still a bit of a stranger – Frieda blissfully happy, though. I don't know what's wrong with me, but this time I'm not at home in our house in Italy. Actually it's very nice, only a feeling. – Roses and jasmine are standing in your little vase – I think my pictures look nice – and I listen to the stillness. But now we're going to the neighbours, to tea, and are taking them the little presents. – Your letter came this morning already. It is a shame that the distance, as long as it remains distance, is so absolute. If we could come to tea with you, then we'd all three be happy. – But we'll come nearer, to live.

auf wiedersehen, stay cheerful.   DHL]

4183. To Hon. Gordon and Beatrice Campbell, 21 October 1927
Text: MS UCin; Moore, *Intelligent Heart* 370–1.

Villa Mirenda, *Scandicci*. (Florence)
21 Oct. 1927

Dear Gordon and Beatrice

Here's a voice from the past![1] But Kot. said Beatrice was in London: and somehow I've been thinking about Ireland lately (does Gordon still say 'Ahrland', with gallons of tears in his voice?).

We've just got back here from Germany – and I've a suspicion that I'm really rather bored by Italy and the Italians; and I have an idea that next year I should like to try the wild Irish. Should I, do you think? Do you think F[rieda] and I would like to spend a year in Ireland – rent a little furnished house somewhere romantic, roaring billows and brown bogs sort of thing? Do you think we should? And is it feasible, practical and all that? somewhere where the rain leaves off occasionally. Of course Ireland is to my mind something like

---

[1] For DHL's last letter, in 1919, see *Letters*, iii. 334–5.

the bottom of an acquarium, with little people in crannies like prawns. But I've got a sort of hunch about it, that it might mean something to me, more than this Tuscany.

It would be great fun to see you both again, especially in native setting. I hear Gordon writes plays: furious tragedies, no doubt.[1] And Beatrice no doubt appropriately weeps, and the children sob in concert. My heaven, the children will be as big as I am![2] It's awful. I'm 42! No, things have gone so far, the plays will have to be comedies.

Do you still keep up with Murry? – he's licked all the gum off me, I'm no longer adhesive.

I'm serious about Ireland, next year. So write and stop me if I ought to be stopped. Meanwhile all sorts of greetings, tante belle cose from us both, and be sure and send a line in answer.

D. H. Lawrence –

4184. To Earl and Achsah Brewster, 21 October 1927
Text: MS UT; Brewster 150–2.

Villa Mirenda, Scandicci – Firenze
Friday. 21 Oct. 1927

Dear Earl and Achsah

We got back here yesterday – had your letter, Achsah, the last days in Baden. I hope the dentisting is done: miserable job. I've got a tooth started to hurt, so am in for it as well – miseria! Frieda had her whack in Baden.

Well what news have you got? – that sort of no news which *isn't* good news still? I hate to think of you suspended over the void, but apparently it is in your destiny. As for myself, I don't feel much terra firma under my feet. I wasn't a bit keen to come back to Italy. I don't know why, but Italy has sort of gone dead for me: seems sort of stupid. I have fits like that. Still, I suppose we shall stay here a few months, since here we are: then pull out, I don't quite know where to. But out of Italy anyhow. Frieda loves it here: but since I was ill, I look round at it all, and it means nothing to me, though it's quite nice. So between now and January or February I'll think of a move. We can't afford anything expensive: am afraid shall have to refuse the invitation to Egypt. But even that doesn't trouble me vastly. Am in a don't-care mood.

I don't feel a bit like work: yet shall have to tackle a few things. Secker wants to do my collected poems: that means typing them out and arranging and doing: then he's bringing out a vol. of short stories in January: and then I *ought*

---

[1] None has been traced.
[2] Patrick Gordon (1913–80), Brigid ('Biddie') Columbine (1914–44) and Michael Mussen Campbell (b. 1924).

to finish the Etruscan Essays, of which I've done just half. But I feel terribly indifferent to it all, whether it's done or not. – Four of the Etruscan Essays are to appear in *Travel* – beginning in November I think – with pictures. You see they have to go in a *picture* magazine. But they'll be cut down. – Then that resurrection story *The Escaped Cock*, suggested by a toy at Volterra at Easter – that the American *Forum* has bought – a weird place for such a story. I don't know which month they'll do it. They did my 'Nightingale' sketch in Sept, and seem to have got off with it very well. – As for the novel, *Lady Chatterley's Lover*, I'm keeping it under lock and key: I won't publish it, at least now.

I might begin a painting of Adam and Eve pelting the Old Lord-God with apples, and driving him out of paradise – but I've got no canvas, and shall never go to Florence – and I don't care either.

So there's David sitting on his thumbs.

So I hope you've really had a lucky streak, and come across something.

Perhaps in destiny Italy is finished for us.

I enclose ten Liras for the postage of the painting – perhaps the sight of that coy nymph and grinning man[1] – very orange, I remember them – might start me daubing a bit, if Earl wouldn't mind sending the canvas – I know posting things is an awful bore.

What is Harwood doing, amid the general irresolution? saying nought, like a wise child still?

Well send us a line, anyhow.

Love!   DHL

4185. To Martin Secker, 21 October 1927
Text: MS UInd; Secker 96–7.

Villa Mirenda, Scandicci – Firenze
21 Oct 1927

Dear Secker

We got back all right Wed. evening – tired, but not overmuch. It's warm and cloudy with bits of sun, very still, not much vegetation yet, after the drought: and the flies very pestering. I'm really not very keen on being here – but Frieda loves it. The space indoors, and the quiet, I like – but suddenly I don't care for Italy any more – have a sort of revulsion from it – it seems so stupid, somehow. Perhaps it's that illness I had here. I'm pretty well, but I can't go uphill without gasping – and of course every road here climbs straight up or goes straight down.

I had the list of stories in Baden. It seems to me all right: and unless you have a special reason, don't leave any out. I think the order in which you have

[1] See Letter 4114 and p. 133 n. 2.

them is pretty good – don't you? But no! Let us *begin* with *a lighter story*.[1]
1. 'Two Blue Birds'
2. *Sun.*
3. 'The Woman Who Rode Away'
4. 'Smile'
5. 'The Border Line'
6. 'Jimmy and the Desperate Woman'
7. 'The Last Laugh'.
8. 'The Man Who Loved Islands'[2]
9. *Glad Ghosts*
10. 'None of That'

———

I think this makes a better rhythm – they are rather hard stories to put together.
Remember us to Rina.

DHL

4186. To Arthur Wilkinson, [c. 25 October 1927]
Text: MS Schlaefle; Unpublished.

[Villa Mirenda, Scandicci, Florence]
[c. 25 October 1927][3]

Dear Wilkinson
I'm hugging my tummy once more – the sniffles went downwards – I'd better not go far from the house today!! Anyhow it's rather a grey day. – I can't understand my innards, since I'm back.

DHL

4187. To Norman Douglas, 26 October 1927
Text: MS YU; Unpublished.

Villa Mirenda. *Scandicci*, Firenze
26 Oct 1927

Dear Douglas
So you are still at Prato[4] – just because you've got a flat in Florence! That's

---

[1] Except that 'In Love' was placed eighth, and 'The Man Who Loved Islands' appeared only in the US edn, this was the order Secker adopted for *The Woman Who Rode Away* volume.
[2] Someone unknown (probably in Secker's office) put parentheses in red ink round this title on the MS; possibly the same person printed in red ink alongside the list between nos 8 and 9: 'MORE MODERN LOVE' (DHL's original title for 'In Love?').
[3] The conjectural date assumes that the note was written shortly after DHL's return to Villa Mirenda and that his eating 'more joyfully' on 28 October (Letter 4188) was relative to the abdominal disorder mentioned here.   [4] About 12 miles n.w. of Florence.

how we are! – I'm just back, so I'm feeling bored stiff by Italy, and wishing I was in any other country. But must stick it out a bit – everything costs so much, one dare hardly breathe, let alone travel.

This is a bit of business. A friend of mine, Jew, but a poor one, wants to become a publisher, on very little money: his peculiar paranoia. He wants to do it by publishing a series of little books, 8,000 to 10,000 words each – called *The Intimate Series* – limited edition of 400 copies maximum, at 15/- or £1. each copy. He wants you, and me, and Aldous Huxley, and E M Forster and Coppard etc. to give him a MS. – He'll pay you £25 or £30 down on account of royalties: and would like the MS. before Christmas. Now will you let me know – or let him know – if you can roll in the MS. – something a little more 'intimate' than you'd do for a magazine: let yourself go a bit – His address

S. Koteliansky. 5 Acacia Rd. St. Johns Wood, N. W. 8.

I'm trying to do a sort of story – not that I'm keen on limited editions, but because Kot and I have known each other so long, through long years of poverty.

Anyhow let me know, will you? And when you come back, come and see us, won't you.

Frieda sends her teutonic blessings with my nondescript.

Yrs   D. H. Lawrence[1]

4188. To Else Jaffe, [28 October 1927]
Text: MS Jeffrey; Frieda Lawrence 274–5.

Villa Mirenda, *Scandicci*, Firenze
Friday

My dear Else

I will send this to Baden – perhaps you will still be there. You will have had a lovely sunny week: here the sun is too hot, makes one tired, and feels like earthquakes. Still it is beautiful.

We got home safely with all the spoil – there are roses in the Wolfratshausen Glass you gave me, here on the table – and we drank the Kirsch from the little yellow glasses, when the Wilkinsons were here yesterday. I am much better, I eat more joyfully, and take the Brust-thee.[2] Imagine, one must let it boil slowly for hours. I do believe it is good, better than all the medicines. I am already doing a story,[3] and dabbing at my pictures of five negresses – called

---

[1] For Douglas's reply see p. 203 n. 2.   [2] Herbal tea for chest conditions.
[3] Possibly 'Autobiographical Fragment' (*Phoenix* 817–36) (named 'A Dream of Life' by Keith Sagar in *The Princess and Other Stories*, 1971) which contains a reference to October 1927 (*Phoenix* 835). It may have been intended as DHL's contribution to Kot's 'Intimate Series'.

The Finding of Moses – or, if the Schwiegermutter had to name it, Ein fürchterliches Schauerstück.[1] A la bonne heure.

I had a letter from Curtis Brown, saying that next year, in November, our contract with Kippenberg comes to an end, and then we can leave him and go to a different publisher. Also that he, Kip-, said in a letter of 1923, that he would gladly agree that you should do the translations. Curtis Browns have the letter. Now I have written Kippenberg to ask him what exactly he intends to do next year, with regard to my work. – We'll see if we can't have our own way in this matter, and you shall translate *The Plumed Serpent* if you wish, trotz Anton, trotz Katharina.[2] Vogue la galère![3]

Dark falling! We haven't made any fire in the stoves yet – it is so warm. Hope you are feeling well and easy. Love to the Schwiegermutter – the Schlips[4] came today – but I shan't wear it yet. Say thanks for me.

                                                                   Love   DHL

4189. To Nancy Pearn, 28 October 1927

Text: MS UT; Huxley 691–2.

                                             Villa Mirenda, *Scandicci*. Firenze
                                                                   28 Oct 1927

Dear Miss Pearn

Ages since I wrote you – but I thought something would be needing to be written. We were awfully pleased to hear from you and Mrs Angell, when we were in Bavaria, that you had two pleasant days here. But didn't you find the place a terrible bare barn, and the beds like the Great Desert of Gobi and the Little Desert of Gobi? Afraid you did! But we are such campaigners – Giulia had all to tell about you, how you didn't understand what she said, and she didn't capire una parola of what *you* said – they never get over it – and how you only ate a frittata di uova – and were always in the colombaia, come due piccioni, but that you were very cheerful, ridevano, ridevano, erano così allegre.[5] So there you are, you see, leaving footprints in the sands of the native mind.[6] – Tell Mrs Angell it's a pity she cant be on the tiles at this moment – such a good hot sun, and such stillness!

---

[1] 'A Terrible Horror-play'.
[2] 'In spite of Anton [Kippenberg], in spite of Katharina [Kippenberg]'. (Else Jaffe never realised the ambition which she had cherished for nearly two years and about which DHL had written to Kippenberg: see *Letters*, v. 332, 561.) DHL's letter to Kippenberg is unlocated.
[3] 'Come what may!'   [4] 'tie'.
[5] '... understand a word ... an omelette ... in the dovecote, like two pigeons ... they laughed, they laughed, they were so happy.'
[6] Cf. Henry Wadsworth Longfellow, 'A Psalm of Life' (1839), ll. 27–8 ['leave behind us/ Footprints on the sands of time'].

We've been back a week, and it's very lovely really – but since I was ill I'm out of patience with Italy – seems so stupid. But then nowhere else is any better. We had an invitation to Egypt – friends have a house there. But I'm afraid it would cost so much. – But I am *much* better – that's the chief thing, to me.

Would you answer this man as you think best. He had some other bits for another geog. book.[1] But I'm not sure if I like these anthology-compiling sort of people who get everything for nothing.

Pity you didn't come when we're here. Never mind – there are other times.

Tante cose from us both.   D. H. Lawrence

4190. To Emily King, [30 October 1927]
Text: MS Lazarus; Postmark, Firenze 31 . X 1927; Unpublished.

Villa Mirenda, Scandicci, Florence
Sunday 30 Oct.

My dear Pamela

I haven't had a line from you since we're back, but I suppose everything is all right. What a blessing if Joan's tonsils really make a difference to her! If I were you I'd give her some chalky solution for her bronchials – it helps to harden the tissue and make it resist chills. I take the French *Solution Pantanberge* – which is creosote and chalk, unsweetened[2] – then there's *Sirop Famel*, sweetened – another French one – In my opinion, they're very useful, these chalky solutions.

It's queer weather – today quite foggy – yet not a bit cold. We haven't had a fire yet. The sun in the afternoon is really hot, you sweat if you walk up the road. And the peasants complain it makes them so tired. Yet there's a mist every morning, and very heavy dew – curious, not Italian at all. The land and the people are exhausted still by the long hot dry summer. The stream is still dried up – the wells haven't got much water. Peasants had to sell their cattle to the butcher – no water and no fodder. It's quite a business.

I'm really better since I'm back – eating better. But the fog gets my chest a bit – and it would anywhere.

It's nice to be quiet and peaceful again, but since I was ill here, I've sort of lost my attachment to the place – to Italy altogether. If only England had a *bit* better climate, I'd come and live there again – in Devonshire, perhaps. But I dread the thought of perpetual rain and damp.

[1] William James Glover asked, in October 1926, if he could include two extracts from *Sea and Sardinia* in a school geography textbook (*Letters*, v. 554 and n. 1). Glover's letter on this occasion has not survived.

[2] DHL's favourite patent medicine for bronchial infection: see *Letters*, v.236 and n. 4.

How are you all? How was the Goose Fair? Was it really the last Goose Fair they'll hold in the Market Place?[1] If so, then I feel it's the end of Nottingham – there can't be a Nottingham without the old market.

I'm wondering so much how Gertie will be, when she's home at Ripley. Do tell me what you think of her. – And how's the shop? – even Ada complains of bad business!

Love to you all!   DHL

4191. To Ada Clarke, [30 October 1927]
Text: MS Clarke; Unpublished.

Villa Mirenda. *Scandicci*. Florence.
Sunday 30 Oct.

My dear Sister

We've been here ten days – I was expecting to hear from you, especially about Gertie, if she is home, and how she is. I feel it's a very important moment. Take care she doesn't start doing too much – she must above all not get tired. And I do hope the weather's decent.

Here everything is still exhausted after the long hot dry summer, the land and the people too. It hasn't rained much even yet – the stream is quite dry, not much water in the wells. Yet there is a mist every day, sometimes quite thick, and very heavy dew till midday. I suppose the land doesn't soak it up. It isn't like Italy, though. Florence lies half the time under fog – but we are mostly above it. It gets my chest a bit – but I'm better, eating with appetite. – I told you the Dobrées invited us to Egypt. If it weren't so expensive, I think I'd like to go, about Christmas. But the journey and everything is so dear, and we've spent so much already. I doubt if I can manage it. If not, we'll go to the mountains in January, to Cortina, in the Dolomites – not far. The Huxleys are going again. They say it did them the most marvellous lot of good last year, and want us to go with them. I believe it would be good and exhilarating – it's over 4000 ft. It's not sanatoriums I want, but some sort of tonic, freshness, something to take me out of myself a bit.

How is Jack? I hope he's not losing weight. You must weigh him from time to time, and pop him off to the sea for a bit, if he's going down.

It's quite warm here – we've had no fire so far – not wanted it at all. The sun, when it does clear the mist, in the afternoon, is so hot you can't sit long in it. The peasants say they feel so tired. What a topsy-turvy world!

Write and let me know about Gertie.

---

[1] Nottingham's annual three-day fair beginning on the first Thursday in October; it was originally held in the city's central square, subsequently on 'the Forest' (see Letter 4713).

The shirts are awfully nice but I'm wearing my old ones out here. – I suppose Master Bertram is his old self again – I'll order some little animal toys for them for Christmas, from Germany, shall I?

Love! DHL

Give Jack that Solution Pantanberge that Gertie took last year – it's awfully good for catarrh.

4192. To Aldous and Maria Huxley, [30 October 1927]
Text: Huxley 690–1.

Villa Mirenda, Scandicci, Firenze.
Sunday, Autumn, 1927.

Dear Aldous and Maria, –

Awfully nice of you to ask us so warmly to Forte: and we'd like to come, but for the weary fact of another removal at once. I feel dead sick at the moment of shifting about. But that won't last very long. Whatever flesh I've got on my bones isn't *Sitzfleisch*,[1] though it mayn't be much of anything else. – To-day – Sunday morning – it's quite a thickish fog – it is with you? – gets my chest a bit and makes me bark. Is it so by the sea? Almost every day the morning starts a bit foggy, and Florence is always deeply buried. Then the sun comes out so *hot*. – Under cover of the mist, the Cacciatori are banging away – it's a wonder they don't blow one another to bits – but I suppose sparrow-shot is small dust. And it's Sunday, *sacra festa*.

I don't find myself settling down very well here: feel, if I move, I'd like to clear out of Italy for good. I think I shall do so next year – and either try Devonshire or somewhere nearer home. Time to go home, I feel. – But if I'd any money I'd take a long sea-voyage first. But I haven't got any money – or a minimum.

Poor Kot, he'll be depressed about his 'scheme.' I haven't heard from Douglas yet – he's in Prato. But he's an erratic bird, I've not much hope of him. Poor Kot – I do what I can for him – but why should anybody want to be a publisher?

I'm glad Maria has met Mrs. Beeton: she's one of the few women worth knowing and cultivating.[2] Right-o! Maria! You wait a bit, and I'll be eating your puddings for you. God gives us a good meeting, as the Methodists'd say. – Though I'm sorry Rose has gone.[3] The boy must miss her terribly, lessons

---

[1] 'well padded'.
[2] Isabella Mary Beeton (1836–65), famous for her *Book of Household Management* (1861).
[3] See p. 120 n. 3.

or not! – Maria, have you greased the car? – I feel I don't want to do a thing, except curse *almost* everybody. Never mind! *Hasta la vista!*[1]

DHL

4193. To S. S. Koteliansky, 31 October 1927
Text: MS BL; Postmark, Scandicci 2.11.1927; Moore 1015.

Villa Mirenda. *Scandicci*. Florence.
31 Oct 1927

My dear Kot

Huxley said he was writing to you to say he's tied up to Chatto and Windus, and can't give you anything. And I enclose Douglas' letter – don't mind that he calls you a little Jew, it's merely Douglas.[2] – That's how people are! They're like fish that will only nibble at a fly that looks like a lot of diamonds. They do so love to say No! – because that gives them a sense of power. Myself I began a thing for you – but the thick morning fogs gave me a bit of cold again, and I've left off trying to work. But still, if you can get anybody else, I can have my MS. ready for Christmas for you. – Perhaps you might try A. E. Coppard – I know they 'collect' him. But I'm afraid you'll find most writers too cautious, too anxious for their own selves and pockets. If I said you were a millionaire just starting publishing, they'd rise at once.

Altogether the world is depressing – and I feel rather depressed. My bronchials are such a nuisance, and I don't feel myself at all. I'm not very happy here, and I don't know where else to go, and have not much money to

---

[1] 'See you soon!'
[2] Douglas replied to DHL's enquiry as follows (MS BL):

c/o Thomas Cook, Via Tornabuoni, Florence
29 Oct. 1927

Dear Lawrence
    Many thanks for yours of 26th. Yes; I am still in Prato, and my room looks due North. Great fun.
    I wish I could do something for your little Jew, but it is quite impossible. I am in the middle of distributing one privately printed book – have to do it all by myself – and printing another one; which is Hell. I was in Florence from 7 am to 10 pm yesterday at the beastly jobs. So sorry! I hope it will be a success, but the prognosis does not strike me as favourable. Five years ago, yes! The mania for privately printed books seems to be declining; in other words, people are coming to their senses again, which annoys me considerably just now. I wish they had waited a bit.
    Sure I'll come round and see you, as soon as I am through with this infernal crush of business. Much love to Frieda.

Yours ever   Norman Douglas

go anywhere with – I feel I don't want to work – don't want to do a thing – all the life gone out of me. Yet how can I sit in this empty place and see nobody and do nothing! It's a limit! I'll have to make a change somehow or other – but don't know how.

I'm sorry about Douglas and Huxley – but rather expected it. People are very small and muggy nowadays. Tell me if there's anything else I can do. Anyhow if you want my MS by Christmas I'll get it done – though it may be a bit *long*.

Ever!   DHL

4194. To Max Mohr, 31 October 1927

Text: MS HMohr; Max Mohr, ed., 'The Unpublished Letters of D. H. Lawrence to Max Mohr, *T'ien Hsia Monthly*, i (August 1935), 24–5.

Villa Mirenda. Scandicci. Florenz.

31 Okt. 1927

Dear Max Mohr

Had your letter today – and so you've actually sailed down the Danube on a raft! It sounds great fun: but when one comes to dead cities with exhausted people, the gilt goes off the gingerbread – But what a restless soul you are! No, you must learn to be more peaceful inside yourself, or one day you'll just explode like a rocket, and there'll be nothing left but bits.

It's awfully nice of you to take so much thought and trouble for *David*. But don't you bother too much about it, or you'll hate it and us in the end. – I know the translation is very unsatisfactory: my sort of German, which, like your English, must go into a class by itself. And of course the whole play is too literary, too many words. The actual technique of the stage is foreign to me. But perhaps they – and you – could cut it into shape. I shall be very much surprised if they *do* play it in Berlin. The public only wants foolish realism: Hamlet in a smoking jacket.

We shall be very pleased to see you in January, wherever we are. We may be here: we may be in Cortina: or we may just possibly go to Egypt, to Cairo, where we have friends. Would you come even there? and bring the Zieharmonika to play to the pyramids? I unfortunately can't yet promise to dance – my bronchials and my cough are still a nuisance. But I want so much to be *able* to dance again. And I think if we went somewhere really amusing, I should quickly be well. My cough, like your restlessness, is a good deal psychological in its origin, and a real change might cure us both. – The sun shines here, but the mornings are foggy. And I no longer love Italy very much – It seems to me a stupid country. But where is one to live, after all – I don't know if you would rather I wrote in my bad German – you must tell me. Tante belle cose alla Signora, anche alla figliuola, e non dimentichiamo la capra.[1]

Sincerely   D. H. Lawrence

4195. To Valentine Dobrée, 2 November 1927
Text: MS Brotherton; Unpublished.

Villa Mirenda, Scandicci, Florence.
2 Novem. 1927

Dear Mrs Dobrée

We were both very sorry to hear of your father so ill.[2] I do hope the operations are not very serious, and by now are successfully over.

Don't bother about us, anyhow – I'm sure you don't want two people descending on you the moment you get to Egypt. But it's a pity you can't come this way en route, to have a look round here.

Perhaps later we may manage to come out, and camp somewhere in your vicinity for a bit – I'm a trifle bored by Italy. I haven't heard from Dobrée – tell him we really will have a proper meeting some time, and see how we square out. I believe we should get on all right – my friends make me out more alarming than I am. But then people are so timid.

I do hope your father is shaping well.

Regards from us both   D. H. Lawrence

4196. To Martin Secker, 3 November 1927
Text: MS UInd; Postmark, Firenze 5 . XI 1927; Unpublished.

Villa Mirenda, Scandicci, Florence
3 Novem. 1927

Dear Secker

I'm disgusted at Compton Mackenzie taking upon himself to feel injured.[3] What idiotic self-importance! If it's like him, he ought to feel flattered, for it's very much nicer than he is – and if it's not like him, then what's the odds. – 'People are sure to recognise him –' And what if they do? Will it hurt him? – But as a matter of fact, though the circumstances are some of them his, the man is no more he than I am. It's all an imbecile sort of vanity. What does he think he is, anyhow? – the one perfect man on earth.

I *don't* want the story omitted. I would rather you never published the

---

[1] 'Best wishes to your wife, also to your daughter, and let's not forget the nanny-goat.' (Mohr's wife was Kathe, his daughter Eve.)
[2] Her father was Sir Alexander Brooke-Pechell Bt (1857–1937).
[3] See Letter 4029 and p. 69 n. 1.

book, than left it out, and yielded to such tommy-rot. Put the blame on me. Tell him he can write the worst story imaginable about me, and I shan't turn a hair. He could no more put *me* on paper than I have put him. What rot! One mustn't give in to it.

About the poems – I have only *Love Poems, Amores* and *Bay*: so you'd have to send me *New Poems, Look! We Have Come Thro.* and *BirdsBeasts.* – I shan't write them over – just arrange the rhymed poems in the first half – and leave the two unrhymed books distinct in the second.[1] But I'm in no hurry about this, if you aren't.

I may get a spurt on and finish those Etruscan essays – but at present am not inclined to do anything. I doubt if I shall settle down – I feel fed with Italy, fed stiff – and would move tomorrow if I'd plenty of money. It's hot weather – like summer – uncanny.

                                                        Saluti!   DHL

4197. To Baroness Anna von Richthofen, [6 November 1927]
Text: MS UCB; Frieda Lawrence 266–7.

                                        Villa Mirenda. Scandicci. Florenz
                                                                Sonntag
Meine liebe Schwiegermutter

Es ist schon wieder Sonntag, und der dritter seit wir hier sind. Das Wetter ist immer wie Sommer, so warm und klar, wir haben alle Fenster den ganzen Tag offen, und denken nicht an Feuer: auch Abends ist es ganz warm. Die Rosen blüthen, aber es gibt wenige Blumen, alles ist noch zu trocken, auch in den Brunnen sehr wenig Wasser. Du auch hast es schön, in Baden. – Sonntags muss ich immer an Baden denken, an die Musik im Kurpark, und an Malzbier in deinem Zimmer. Hier gibt's keine Musik, die dummen 'Jäger' schiessen nur die Spätze und Nachtigallen draussen im Wald, man hört es immer 'pop!' Malzbier gibt es auch nicht, und dein Zimmer liegt nicht fünf Minuten hinunter. Aber du wirst jetzt spazieren gehen, und wirst die Stiftsdamen in besten Kleidern unterwegs von der Messe entgegen kommen.

Die Nusch hat geschrieben – sagt, sie hat sehr viele Leute und geht viel herum. – Sie will hier in März kommen. Der Alfred schrieb auch, aus Ascona – ganz enzückt von den Paradies-tagen dort: ein netten Brief. – Die Frieda had wieder einen Klavier, jetzt will sie Händel spielen, den *Messiah* – aber ist noch nicht bis Alleluia gekommen. Ich male ein Bild, nicht sehr gross, von einem Tiger der auf einem Mann springt: so ein grinzenden Tiger! – Morgen sollen wir nach Florenz gehen, zum Mittagsessen mit Freunden – ich war noch nicht in der Stadt. – Wir spielen Karten mit den Nachbarn – Solo Whist

---

[1] In general the arrangement of *Collected Poems* followed this skeletal plan: the first four collections listed here appear in volume i as 'Rhyming Poems', the last two in volume ii as 'Unrhyming Poems'.

und Papst Joan und auch Patience. Weisst du, deine kleine Patience, die ein-zwei-dreie, sie heisst 'der Dämon:' sie kann es gut heissen, bei mir kommt sie nie aus.

Grüsse die Frau Kugler, auch die Halms. Hoffentlich geht es der Frau Oberin besser. Bleib du lustig; du sollst die Karten fragen, ob wir nach Cortina in Januar gehen sollen: 'lieben Kärtchen, sagt mir wohl –'

DHL

Für den Schlips habe ich noch nicht gedankt – es ist so hübsch – ich trage es heute zum Erstenmal.

[Sunday

My dear Schwiegermutter

It's already Sunday again, and the third since we've been here. The weather continues like summer, so warm and clear, we have all the windows open all day, and don't think of fires: it is perfectly warm in the evenings too. The roses are in bloom, but there are few flowers, everything is still too dry, very little water in the wells too. You too have it nice, in Baden. – I can't help thinking of Baden on Sundays, of the music in the Kurpark, and of the malt beer in your room. Here there is no music, those stupid 'hunters' only shoot sparrows and nightingales in the woods, one's always hearing the 'pop!' There's no malt beer either, and your room isn't just five minutes down the road. But now you'll be out walking, and will be meeting the Stift ladies in their best clothes on their way home from mass.

Nusch has written – says she has lots of people around and goes out a lot. – She wants to come here in March. Alfred wrote too, from Ascona – quite enchanted with the paradisal days there: a nice letter. – Frieda has a piano again, now she's trying to play Handel, the *Messiah* – but hasn't got to the Halleluia Chorus yet. I'm painting a picture, not very large, of a tiger who is jumping on a man: such a grinning tiger![1] –Tomorrow we're going to Florence, to lunch with friends – I've not yet been in the town. – We play cards with the neighbours – Solo Whist and Pope Joan and Patience, too. You know your little Patience, the one-two-three-er, it's called 'Demon:' it's the right name for it, mine never comes out.

Greet Mrs Kugler, the Halms too.[2] I hope the Mother Superior is better. Stay cheerful; you should consult the cards whether we should go to Cortina in January: 'dear little cards, tell me –'

DHL

I've not yet thanked you for the tie – it is so nice – I'm wearing it today for the first time.]

---

[1] The picture – *Jaguar Leaping at a Man* – is reproduced in *Paintings of D. H. Lawrence*, ed. M. Levy (1964).   [2] Unidentified.

4198. To Earl Brewster, [8 November 1927]
Text: MS UT; Brewster 152-4.

Villa Mirenda, *Scandicci*, Firenze
8 Novem.

Dear Earl

Frieda went in to Florence yesterday and got the ruddy nymphs.[1] Those people never notified us. – I think I like it almost best of my pictures – at the moment.

How are you, and did you find a villa? I have wondered all these days. It's all right for you to be suspended over the void! – but not for Achsah, I'm afraid. Myself I wish I were a bit more suspended too. We've got this flat till next May, but I'm sure I doubt if we'll stay half that time in it. I *am* somehow bored by Italy, and when a place goes against my grain, I'm never well in it. I do really think one is heaps better off in New Mexico – sometimes I pine for it. Let's go in spring – and you help me chop down trees and irrigate pasture on the ranch. I'm *sure* you'd be happier – if we were all there. After all one *moves* – and this deadening kind of hopeless-helplessness one has in Europe passes off. Let's all go in March – let's go. I'm sick of here. – India is largely illusion – besides, we aren't rich enough. – And let's make an exhibition of pictures in New York – what fun! For Easter, an exhibition of pictures in New York, then go west. We might afterwards sail to China and India from San Francisco – there's always that door out. Let's do it! Anything, anything to shake off this stupor and have a bit of fun in life. I'd even go to Hell, en route.

I've got a book on the Bagh Caves – not nearly so thrilling as the Ajanta caves – but interesting.[2] Did you know that in ancient Buddhism, the 'stupa' occupied the holy central position in the cave, or the temple: and when the Buddha figure was invented, the Standing Budda took the place of this stupa. Now it looks to me as if this stupa was just the monumental phallic symbol, like the Etruscan 'Cippus.' And the standing Buddha has still a phallic quality. They invented the seated Buddha later. My books say 'in the early caves the central cult object is the *stūpa* or relic monument'[3] – Do you know precisely what the stupa was? It looks just like the Etruscan phallic 'Cippus' in the illustration.

I did a little picture of a jaguar jumping on a man – but am not happy for working. It was a long strip of canvas left over, and cut on the skew. Now I can't afford to cut it down, to get it squared. Could I stitch or sew a bit on the top edge? Otherwise I'll have to cut my jaguar's ears off.

I doubt if we'll get to Egypt – if we're going to America in the spring. I

---

[1] See Letter 4184 and p. 133 n. 2.   [2] See p. 72 n. 4.
[3] *Bagh Caves*, p. 27. For illustration of 'the standing Buddha' see Plate VI a and b.

simply haven't enough money – it comes in slowly, much more than anybody would imagine.

I'll send you a copy of *Travel* with the first of the Etruscan sketches. It has got pictures, but disappointing because they're too small. But you'll recognise the whole thing. I think they're doing four sketches. – As for the rest, I doubt if I'll ever finish them – I just don't really want to do anything.

Achsah is right about this climate – it's not good enough. But lately it's been all sunshine – I'm feeling really better – I'm better when I grumble – like my old grandmother, who never was anything but worse and fading fast, for forty years, till she was dying, at 75, when she protested she felt a bit better, and a bit better: and so she passed out.[1]

There's no news – I've not been to Florence, and seen nobody but the Wilks. They are actually taking us a motor-drive to San Gemignano – It will remind me of the bus that brought me from Volterra.

Let me know where you are. Many thanks for sending the canvas. I had forgotten it was so big! What a shame you should have had to bother with it.

Well, here's luck. Let's pull out of Europe in the New Year. – But perhaps you're just moving into a 'sweet' villa.

Frieda sends her greetings – she says the man's head at the bottom of my picture is 'a young Earl.'

DHL

4199. To Marian Eames, 8 November 1927
Text: TMSC NWU; Huxley 692–3.

Villa Mirenda, Scandicci, Florence, Italy
8 Novem 1927

My dear Marian

Your Wedding card just come: imagine this sudden hop into matrimony![2] Anyhow I believe it's better than the theatre: I mean the matrimonial stage is a nicer one for you to shine on, than the theatrical. I hope you are feeling chirpy and all serene. You seemed to me a very nice and patient and long-suffering child, so you should make a real good wife, if the man doesn't spoil you. Anyhow here's luck! in a drop of Kirschwasser which happens to stand at my elbow.

---

[1] The reference is most probably to DHL's maternal grandmother, Lydia Beardsall, who died on 16 May 1900 aged 71 (not 75) years.
[2] Marian Eames, née Bull (1906–), daughter of Nina Witt by her first husband, Harry Adsit Bull (see *Letters*, iv. 332 n. 4). In September 1925 DHL expressed the wish that she would not go on the stage: 'it might spoil her' (*Letters*, v. 306). She married Hamilton Eames, nephew of the American operatic prima donna, Emma Eames (1865–1949): see Letter 4342.

Write and tell me who or what Hamilton Eames is, besides your husband.
Is he connected with the theatre? And my congratulations to him.

And how is your mother? I'm thankful she hasn't married that prize-
fighter, I forget his name[1] – I was wondering about her only two days ago,
whatever she is up to now! But I'm thankful to see that she is still Mrs. Witt.
And is it still Behaviourism and white rabbits and babies and reactions? or is
there a new *ism*? Anyhow better a new 'ism' than a new husband.

We came back here a fortnight ago – I was ill here in the summer, afraid I'd
leave my bones in the Campo Santo. Am still a bit groggy and not very well
pleased with myself: but painting pictures of large and ruddy nymphs and
fauns, to keep me in countenance.

We may come to America in the spring. If so, I hope we shall see you and
your husband – also Nina. Meanwhile all my unbishoply blessings on you,
and remember your mother's dictum: 'Nothing matters, so long as one keeps
one's heart warm'. She said that to me last time we were there. It's frightfully
true – but I suppose every different body means something different by it.

I'll send you one of my books,[2] having nothing else to send. My wife adds
her good wishes, and I hope we'll all meet soon.

D. H. Lawrence

4200. To Maria Chambers, 11 November 1927
Text: MS StaU; Moore 1019.

Villa Mirenda, *Scandicci*. Florence, Italy
11 Novem 1927

Dear Mrs Chambers[3]

Is it possible you really are the godmother of Rosalino – the actual Rosalino
of Oaxaca? Or do you mean, in the spirit merely? (pardon the merely). But if in
the flesh, do you know how he is, poor lad? The last I heard from Father
Rickards[4] he was in hospital, and not likely to live. Poor Rosalino, such a shy
gentle soul – it's an awful shame.

[1] His name was Leonard Rucker (1885–); when Nina Witt considered taking him as her third
husband in 1925, DHL thought he might be 'really rather interesting' (*Letters*, v. 237). (In
TMSC of this letter someone wrote above 'name': 'Len!!')   [2] See Letter 4342.
[3] Maria Cristina Chambers, née Mena (d. 1965), b. Mexico, went to USA at fourteen. m. Henry
Kellett Chambers, senior editor of the *Literary Digest*. She had not met DHL but became his
admirer when she read *Mornings in Mexico*. She persuaded her husband to reprint an abridged
version of the essay, 'The Mozo' (about DHL's Zapotec servant in Mexico City, Rosalino); it
appeared in the *Digest*, 24 September 1927, as 'A Look Inside a Mexican Indian's Head'.
[4] Fr. Edward Arden Rickards (1879–1941), Roman Catholic priest who befriended the
Lawrences in Oaxaca (see *Letters*, v. 177 and n. 2).

And did you really write the story in the *New Criterion*?[1] I wondered very much what woman it was knew the Indian so intimately. – And it is so well written too – but perhaps your husband helped you. Or are you so much at ease in English? How I detest Guadalupe anyhow! I mean Villa de G.

I haven't seen the *Literary Digest* of Sept. 24th – do send it me.

Perhaps if we come to New York in the spring I may see you and your husband, to talk about Mexico and to digest a little more literature.

Con tanti saluti e ossequiandola[2]   D. H. Lawrence

4201. To Hon. Dorothy Brett, 11 November 1927
Text: MS UCin; Postmark, [. . .]; Irvine, Brett 78–9.

Villa Mirenda, Scandicci, Florence.
11th.Novem. 1927

Dear Brett

Your letter today about the Ruffina–Peto scandal! What a nasty pudding she is, I wish Trinidad could get rid of her, for he is a nice soul in himself.[3] – Your picture of the singing Indians looks very nice, but I can't 'see' photographs – they mean so little to me. The frame shows best – one *must* have the colours, for the picture. I think the snaps of my pictures just ghastly. – And Bobchuli looks a gentle little thing – I do hope her face is quite better.[4]

We had Mabel's letter with your other one – glad she liked being at the ranch a few days. The autumn must have been lovely – it has been beautiful here, still and sunny every day, till today, when there has been some rain, and a cold wind. But it's been so warm all the time – we've never thought of a fire. – I am slowly getting to my real self – little by little. With me it's really a sort of asthma, and very difficult to deal with. All one can do is gradually to get robust enough to shake it off. Till I am pretty sound, I'd better not come very high up, because of the hemorrhages – which are bronchial, nothing to do with the lungs. But I hope by spring I'll be all right.

I've written to Earl telling him again to come out with us in spring to Taos. He's pretty fed up with things. I think they didn't get on at all with Mr Oliver Frost (Lucille's husband) at Cimbrone – so Cimbrone fell off their map.[5] Now

---

[1] Maria Chambers had published a story with a Mexican setting, 'John of God, the Water Carrier', in the *Monthly Criterion*, vi (October 1927), 312–31; in this issue it followed immediately after DHL's 'Flowery Tuscany I' and provided her with the pretext for introducing herself to him.   [2] 'With all good wishes and kindest regards'.

[3] Trinidad Archuleta had eloped with Agapeto Concha.

[4] 'Bobchuli, the lovely little racing mare' that Brett bought for DHL (*Lawrence and Brett*, pp. 300–1.)

[5] Lucy ('Lucile') Beckett m. 1926, Capt. Oliver Harry Frost; divorced 1941. (She had resumed her maiden name after divorcing her first husband, Count Otto Czernin, in 1920; see *Letters*, iii. 712 n. 1.)

they are again looking for a villa in Capri. They may come out with us in March, as a *pis aller*.

We've been back here three weeks – I'm not really working – did a smallish picture of a jaguar jumping on a man – and a water-color of Adam and Eve pelting the Lord with apples to drive him out of the garden. I may do that in oil – I hope you are right, that next year will be a better one, for health and finances both, for this has been a bad one. I'm disgusted with everything. You must send me the bill for taxes and the winter feed for the horses. Rachel writes she is keeping Azul:[1]

Tell Mabel I'll really get that cheque when I go to Florence: it's the agent's fault, they keep on declaring they know nothing.

You have a much better time of it out there than ever you'd get in Europe – it's awfully dead over here, in all the countries alike. I shall be glad to clear out. When I come I'll do things for the *Laughing Horse* – seems no connection here. I hear Murry's wife is said to be cured. Kot wants to become a publisher – start by publishing small books, limited editions at high prices! – I'll send this to Taos.

DHL

4202. To Idella Weatherwax, 11 November 1927
Text: MS UT; Postmark, Scandicci 12. 11. 27; Bynner 331.

Villa Mirenda, *Scandicci*, Florence
11 Novem. 1927

Dear Idella[2]

Your letter today – imagine your being married and moved far off to Aberdeen-Wash[ington]! What does your husband do up there, and how do you like it! And will *Palms* grow in such a northern climate, and produce real crops of nuts?

I've not written a poem, hardly, these last three years and more – not a jingle in me. Instead I paint pictures, here – which seems the right thing to do, in Tuscany of the painters. But I'll see if I can't warble some little lay for *Palms*.

We may come to America in the spring – though whether we'd ever reach your far edge, I don't know. Perhaps you'll be moving our way.

---

[1] Frieda's horse.
[2] Idella Weatherwax, née Purnell (1901–82), American poet whom DHL first met in Guadalajara, Mexico, where she lived with her father Dr George Edward Purnell (1863–1961); see *Letters*, iv. 435 n. 2. m. (1) 1927, John M. Weatherwax; (2) 1932, Remington Stone. 1923–30 she edited *Palms*, a magazine of verse; for DHL's publications in it see Roberts C54, C59, C66, C115 and Nehls, ii. 268–9. He contributed nothing to it after 1923.

How is your father? Is he still safe and sound in Guadalajara? What a long time it seems since Chapala!

Frieda sends her regards, with mine – also to your husband,

Sincerely   D. H. Lawrence

4203. To Else Jaffe, 14 November 1927
Text: MS Jeffrey; Frieda Lawrence 253–4.

Villa Mirenda, Scandicci, Firenze
14 Nov. 1927

Dear Else

Many thanks for the Beethoven *Letters*[1] – arrived today – not a literary man – and always in love with somebody – or *thought* he was – and in the flesh wasn't. But how German! – I mean the way he really *wasnt.*

Frau Katharina Kippenberg wrote they want to publish one of my books next year, and asks which I would suggest. I think I shall suggest 'Woman Who Rode Away', and 'The Princess' (from the English *St Mawr*) and a third story you haven't yet seen, 'None of That.' They'd make a smallish volume. Or would you suggest one of the novels – *The Lost Girl* or *Aaron's Rod*. I don't care.[2] Only we'll keep back *The Plumed Serpent*, and offer it *ready translated* to another firm, for 1929.[3] Do you think that's wise?

It has rained a bit here, but is sunny again – We're just going out for a walk – the country is full of colour, vines yellow, olives blue, pines very green. It is Monday, so the fusillade of cacciatori shooting little birds is quieter – it makes me so mad. – I am really quite a lot better – cough much less, especially in the morning – but haven't yet been to Firenze – think we'll go Thursday. – There's a queer sort of unease in the air – as if the wrong sort of spirits were flying abroad in the unseen ether – but it may be my imagination. Frieda strums away on her piano, and I have to listen for when she hits a wrong note. – I am dabbing at my poems, getting them ready for the *Collected Poems*. – Alfred wrote very nicely from Ascona. I hope we'll see you here in the early spring: if we are here: I feel sort of uncertain and unstuck. – I hope you're having more conferences and so on, if they amuse you. As for me, I play patience – and it hardly ever comes out.

Love!   DHL

[1] If the letters were in translation, the work was probably *Beethoven's Letters*, ed. A. Eaglefield-Hull (1926); if in German, *L. van Beethoven. Seine an den Verlag von Hoffmeister und Kühnel . . . gerichteten Briefe* (Leipzig, 1927).
[2] Else Jaffe's German translation of *The Woman Who Rode Away and Other Stories* was published in 1928 by Insel Verlag (Roberts D78).
[3] Cf. Letter 4188 and p. 199 n. 2.

4204. To Aldous Huxley, [14 November 1927]
Text: Huxley 693–4.

Mirenda.
Monday.

Dear Aldous, –

Many thanks for *Proper Studies*.¹ I have read 70 pages, with a little astonishment that you are so serious and professorial. You are not your grandfather's *Enkel*² for nothing – that funny dry-mindedness and underneath social morality. But you'll say I'm an introvert, and no fit judge. Though I think to make *people* introverts and extraverts is bunk – the words apply, obviously, to the *direction* of the consciousness or the attention, and not to anything in the individual essence. You are an extravert by inheritance far more than *in esse*. You'd have made a much better introvert, had you been allowed. 'Did she fall or was she pushed' – Not that I care very much whether people are intro or extra or anything else, so long as they're a bit *simpatico*. But, my dear, don't be dry and formal and exposition all that – What's the odds! I just read Darwin's *Beagle* again –³ he dried himself – and *tant de bruit pour des insectes!*⁴ – But I like the book.

We sit here rather vaguely, and I still haven't been to Florence. It's colder, and we warm up in the evening. Frieda, inspired by Maria, has launched into puddings: boiled batter and jam. I do bits of things – darn my underclothes and try to type out poems – old ones. Reggie and Orioli and Scott-Moncrieff and a young Acton came *en quatre*⁵ – I poured tea, they poured the rest.

We shall have to be seeing you soon and making plans for Xmas and Cortina: or rather New Year and Cortina. I think we shall go to Florence for Xmas – somewhere where we can eat turkey and be silly – not sit solitary here. Will you be in Florence, too?

I'm reading Beethoven's letters – always in love with somebody when he

¹ DHL had probably received a copy of the limited and signed edn of *Proper Studies* (November 1927). The book is a collection of socio-psychological studies greatly influenced by the Italian sociologist, Vilfredo Pareto (1848–1923). In one essay ('Varieties of Intelligence') Huxley discusses Jung's classifications, introverts and extroverts (pp. 42–53) and describes himself as 'a moderate extravert' (p. 46).
² 'Grandson' of the eminent biologist, Thomas Henry Huxley (1825–95) with whose work DHL had been familiar since 1907–8 (see *D. H. Lawrence: A Personal Record*, by E. T. [Jessie Chambers], 1935, p. 112).
³ *The Voyage of the Beagle* (1839) by Charles Darwin (1809–82).
⁴ '*so much noise for the insects!*'
⁵ Charles Kenneth Scott-Moncrieff (1889–1930), journalist (on *The Times*, 1921–3) and then translator of Proust, Stendhal and Pirandello, and from Latin, Old English and Old French. He lived in Rome and was renowned for witty, cultivated conversation (see *The Times* obituary, 3 March 1930). The 'young Acton' was (Sir) Harold Mario Mitchell Acton (b. 1904), author and aesthete.

wasn't really, and wanting contacts when he didn't really – part of the crucifixion into isolate individuality – *poveri noi.*

Love – whatever that is – to all!   DHL

I don't mean I didn't find the 70 pages good – they're very sane and sound and good – only I myself am in a state of despair about the Word either written or spoken seriously. That's why, I suppose, I wrote this, when I wasn't asked – instead of holding my tongue.

4205. To Emily King, 16 November 1927
Text: MS Lazarus; Unpublished.

Villa Mirenda. *Scandicci*. Firenze
16 Novem. 1927

My dear Pamela

I'm so sorry the tonsils have left Joan so knocked up. Really I think the stars are bad for us just now. But give her Horlicks at night – it's a very good thing.

Myself I've got on well this last month – I can walk to the top of the hills, and feel like getting a grip on life again. But one has to go slowly. Tomorrow, all being well, I'm going to Florence; for the first time since we are back; to lunch with friends. It's a fine sunny day today – Wednesday – but a cold wind. There was even a touch of frost in the night – which is very sudden, for last week was warm as summer. We've been back a month today – the time slips by so quickly. As you say, Christmas almost here. I want to write to Baden Baden for F[rieda]'s mother to send you some of those little animal toys, some for Joan and some for Bertie, all in a parcel to you. So you'll know what it is when it comes. But it will take some time.

And would you send me some tea, like that you sent before: a 2 lb packet, which is not so much to post. Perhaps you've got a tin for it. I enclose 10/-, which I hope will cover it. Did I ever say F's two sisters were both delighted with their tea?

I heard from Ada – glad Gertie sounds even so well as she does. If only she didn't cough! But perhaps she'll get strong enough now to do little things. – It's a pity trade is so bad. When is it ever going to pick up, with things as they are? They talk of a change of government, but I hardly see how it will help us to sell what people can't or won't buy. – I expect it will end in some sort of socialism – the English are not bolshevists, it's not in them.

I think we shall go in to Florence for Christmas. But don't think of sending anything, the post is such a weariness. – I want to escape making a Christmas tree for the peasants – there's such a host of them now, it wears one out:

Love from us both.   DHL

4206. To Baroness Anna von Richtofen, 16 November 1927
Text: MS UCB; Frieda Lawrence 255–6.

Villa Mirenda. *Scandicci*. Florenz
16 Nov. 1927

Meine liebe Schwiegermutter

Diesmal verlange ich etwas von dir. Die Nachbarin an der Ranch, die Rachel Hawk, will Spielzeuge für ihre Kinder. Sie will zwei Schacteln, einen Bauernhof und ein Dorf, nicht zu klein, und jede soll ungefähr 5 Mark kosten. Die Leute am Laden können es einpacken und schicken: zu

Mrs Rachel Hawk, Del Monte Ranch, *Questa, New Mexico. Ver. Staaten.*

Und als du da bist, kaufe du auch Tiere und Bäumle und Männer, die Allekleinsten, auch Hühner, und auch vielleich Häusle und Wägele u.s.w. für meine Nichte Joan und für meinen Neffe Bertie. Diese sollen alle zusammen ungefähr 10 Mark kosten – und sie können alle zusammen in einem Paket direkt vom Laden geschickt werden, zu meiner Schwester:

Mrs Emily King, 16 Brooklands Rd. Sneinton Hill, Nottingham

Ich schicke dir £2, das wird genügen – und vielleicht ein wenig übrig für den Dr Thomann, wenn er die Rechnung schickt. Du thusst es gern, nicht wahr? – im Laden dort am Augustaplaz – wo die grossen Autos stehen.

Wie geht es dir? Uns geht es wohl. Es ist kalt geworden, aber heute war sonnig den ganzen Tag – ich war oben auf den Hügel, sah Florenz da liegen, im Sonnenschein so hell und schon, die Liliestadt. Morgen sollen wir hingehen, zum Mittagessen mit Reggie in seinem Haus: das erstesmal das ich in der Stadt bin, seit wir Züruck kämen. Wenn es schön ist wie heute, geh' ich gern.

Wir sind beide fleissig – ich schreibe Novellen und typpe alle meine Gedichte, weil sie sollen gesammelt werden, in einem Band. Die Frieda hat heut' Abend sein Kittele fertig, sehr hübsch, aus dem violettfarben Samt vom Mantel der Nusch. Es ist wirklich hübsch, ein kurzer Janker mit silbernen Knopfen – sieht ganz Florentinisch aus, Renaissance. Abends machen wir Feuer im Ofen – Der Tag ist warm, die Sonne strömt im Zimmer herein. Aber der Abend ist kalt.

Der Max Mohr schreibt immer sehr freundlich, und will uns in Januar besuchen. Vielleicht werden wir in Cortina sein – wir gehen *nicht* nach Egypten. Aber wenn es uns beide so gut geht, bleiben wir hier in unserem eignen Haus.

Ich spiele immer eine Patience, abends, und ich denke, die Schwiegermutter spielt auch eine, grad' in derselben Stunde. Deine kommt mir viel besser aus wie die der Else. Wenn deine kleine: 'der Dämon' heisst, dann soll die der Else 'der Teufel' heissen.

Die Else hat mir Beethoven's Briefe geschickt. Aber was für ein abge-schnittener Mensch, er könnte an niemand nahe kommen: und sein Haus, was für eine Schlampus und eine Wahnhöhle! Der arme Grosser Mann! Gott sei dank, ich bin immer klein genug, meine Strümpfe zu stopfen und meine Tasse zu waschen.

Die Frieda schreibt dir: der Brief liegt schon zwei Tage da, halb fertig. Du wirst es endlich erhalten, wenn es kommt.

Sei gegrüsst, du ewiges Mère! Schade dass wir nicht Rosen dir schicken können, sie sind so schön.

DHL!

[My Dear Schwiegermutter

This time I'm demanding something from you. The neighbour at the ranch, Rachel Hawk, wants toys for her children. She wants two boxes, a farmyard and a village, not too small, each costing about 5 marks. The people at the shop can pack and send it: to

Mrs Rachel Hawk, Del Monte Ranch, *Questa, New Mexico. United States.*

And since you're there, buy animals and trees and people as well, the smallest there are, chickens too, and also perhaps little houses and carts etc. for my niece Joan and my nephew Bertie. These should all together cost about 10 Marks – and can be sent all together in one parcel direct from the shop to my sister:

Mrs Emily King, 16 Brooklands Rd. Sneinton Hill, Nottingham

I send you £2, that will be enough – and perhaps a little over for Dr Thomann,[1] when he sends the bill. You do it with pleasure, don't you? – in the shop on the Augustaplatz – where the big cars stand.

How are you? We are well. It's turned cold, but today it was sunny all day – I was up on the hill, saw Florence lying there, so clear and beautiful in the sun, the Lily town. Tomorrow we shall go there, to lunch with Reggie in his house: the first time I shall be in town since we got back. If it's as fine as today, I'll go with pleasure.

We're both working hard – I'm writing stories[2] and typing out all my poems, because they'll be collected in one volume. This evening Frieda has finished her little jacket, very pretty, out of the violet-coloured velvet from Nusch's coat. It is really pretty, a short jacket with silver buttons – looks very Florentine, Renaissance. In the evening we have a fire in the stove – The day is warm, the sun streams into the room. But it's cold in the evening.

---

[1] Unidentified

[2] One was *Rawdon's Roof* which was posted to Nancy Pearn on 17 November 1927 (entry in DHL's 'Memoranda', MS NWU); Rowena Killick acknowledged its arrival, at Curtis Brown's London office, on 24 November (TMSC UT).

Max Mohr always writes in a very friendly way, and wants to visit us in
January. Perhaps we shall be in Cortina – we are *not* going to Egypt. But if we
both stay so well, then we'll stay here in our own house.

I always play Patience in the evening, and I think the Schwiegermutter also
plays a game, just at the same time. Yours comes out much better for me than
Else's. If your little one is called 'Demon' , then Else's should be called
'Devil' .

Else has sent me Beethoven's letters. But what a cut-off man he was, he
couldn't get near anyone: and his house, what a hopeless mess, what a mad
hell-hole! The poor great man! Thank the Lord, I stay small enough to darn
my socks and wash my cup.

Frieda is writing to you: the letter has been lying about for two days, half
done. You'll get it at last when it comes.

Greetings, eternal mother! A pity we can't send you roses, they are so
lovely.

                                                                       DHL!]

4207. To Martin Secker, 16 November 1927
Text: MS UInd; Postmark, Firenze 17 . XI 1927; Unpublished.

                                          Villa Mirenda, *Scandicci*. Firenze
                                                            16 Novem 1927
Dear Secker

And if Mackenzie is, as you say, certainly identified in most people's minds
with the Man Who Loved Islands, what harm does it do him?[1] I may be
identified with the Man in the Moon, or with Mr Crippen,[2] in most people's
minds – but wherein does it alter me? Have we no existence apart from other
people's minds? – Moreover, will people's minds be adversely influenced
against Compton M. by my story? On the contrary. The Man Who Loved
Islands is a much purer and finer character than the vain, shallow, theatrical,
and somewhat ridiculous Mackenzie. If people identify him with my story,
they will inevitably have a deeper respect for him. For does he think people
don't already, and since years, find him ridiculous and mountebank,
personally? Of course they do. What was his whole island scheme but showing
off? The Man who loved islands has a philosophy behind him, and a real
significance. I consider myself I have done Mr Monty a great deal of honour.
If he can't see it, it shows what a cheapjack he is.

You needn't include the story if you don't want to. But remember, you

---

[1] Cf. Letter 4029 and p. 69 n. 1.
[2] Hawley H. Crippen (1862–1910), executed for murding his wife (see *Letters*, i. 505 and n. 7).

thereby lose part of my esteem. I should have respected you more if you'd asked *him*, as a personal favour, not to be so ridiculous and vainglorious and cheap in his behaviour.

I should be glad if you'd send me the list of contents you now propose.[1]

I shall include the story in the American edition.

Yrs D. H. Lawrence

4208. To Hon. Gordon and Beatrice Campbell, 16 November 1927
Text: MS UCin; Postmark, Firenze 17 . XI 1927; Moore 1021–2.

Villa Mirenda. Scandicci. Firenze
16 Nov 1927

Dear Campbell and Beatrice

Many thanks for the letter, cautious but encouraging. Was I a monster of impatience? – whether I still am, I don't know. *I* think I'm a very much sadder and wiser man – but I can still see you pulling long faces at me. No, but I'm patient. We've had this house nearly two years.

I really think, if we don't go to America to the ranch, we'll come to Ireland – about April. But I get so sick of Europe altogether (impatient too) that I feel I *must* go to America for an antidote. For America *is* somehow an antidote – so tonicky, and one *can't* be weighed down with problems there, one doesn't care. Then there's the ranch – the horses to ride – the space and the freedom. I remember your insisting that stone walls do not a prison make.[2] To me they make one absolute; I must move. – But of course America *is* tough and anarchic and soulless – but not as mercenary as Italy.

I should like to see you again – and Beatrice – and hear your melodious melancholy voice like a sort of bagpipe. I wish we could come in this very evening – you could drone and I could flourish, and the women could come in like kettle-drums – wouldn't it be fun? I'd love to have a bit of fun again, in the Selwood terrace and Bucks style[3] – and you'd *have* to weep because nobody loves you. Or perhaps you don't weep any more now you're going to be a Lord – You're not one already, are you?[4] I love to use a title when I can, so for heaven's sake let me know. – I don't care what anybody says about you – or even might say in Dublin. Yes, I'd listen to it all with joy – but there is a certain melancholy Gordon in a silk hat but a bathrobe first, with a Mrs

---

[1] See Letter 4185 and p. 197 n. 1.
[2] Richard Lovelace (1618–58), 'To Althea from Prison' (1649), l. 25.
[3] The Lawrences stayed in the Campbells' house at 9 Selwood Terrace, South Kensington, 24 June–15 August 1914 (and were married during this period); they then moved to Chesham, Bucks until 21 January 1915.
[4] Campbell succeeded to the barony of Glenavy on the death of his father in 1931.

Conibear singing in the basement – *what* was it she sang? 'Scenes that are brighter'?[1] – that Ireland knoweth not, nor politics either.

I think, you know, most probably we'll come. Won't you dread it! Never mind, Beatrice can handle us. Where is that sister, by the way, of Beatrices?[2] – And your Aggie? or was it Haggie?[3] My God, what fun! But the thing that will terrify me will be the grown-up children. *There* I'll be judged! I don't care. Let the skies fall! – Dear Beatrice, do please write us some news, he cant.

D. H. Lawrence

4209. To Richard Aldington and Dorothy Yorke, 18 November 1927
Text: MS Lazarus; Moore 1022–4.

Villa Mirenda. Scandicci, Firenze
18 Novem 1927

Dear Richard and Arabella

Your letters this morning – I was ill like the devil here in July – hemorrhages, but bronchial – and creeping about like a fly in Austria and Germany – and still feeble, too much cough – but better – poco a poco. I didn't write, feeling sort of disheartened altogether – but chirping up a bit. You shouldn't offer your hard-earned savings – my goodness, I damn well ought to have enough to live on – so I have, by living like a road-sweeper. But basta! But I saw the end of my days, and my only, or chief grief was, I couldn't spit in the face of the narrow-gutted world and put its eye out.

Scott Moncrieff said he'd write you. He has a nice side to him – but really an obscene mind like a lavatory. But obscenity must be either witty or robust.

We've been back a month – and I went to Firenze yesterday for the first time – the barrocino fetched us up from Vingone – but for all that, I am sitting[4] in bed this morning on the strength of it. Nothing enrages me like not getting well. I think I must have a robust temper, in spite of chests. We've had lovely weather – but now it's cold, with a bit of a frost fog.

Imagine, I met Kouyoumdjian – Michael Arlen – on the Lungarno yesterday.[5] He's taken a flat in Florence. Did you know him in the Bloomsbury days? He's thinner, perhaps sadder – otherwise much the same. But he too was ill – some sort of tubercular tumour – and has been curing at

---

[1] Mrs Conybear, the Campbells' housekeeper in London; her song was 'Scenes that are brightest' from the popular opera, *Maritana* (1846) by William Vincent Wallace (1812–65).

[2] Probably Marjorie Elvery who lived with the Campbells in London.

[3] Campbell had one sister, Violet Lilian Campbell (1888–).   [4] MS reads 'I sitting'.

[5] Dikran Kouyoumdjian (1895–1956), the original name of Michael Arlen, novelist; author of *The Green Hat* (1924), a bestseller which had been adapted for the stage, parodied, acclaimed and attacked and earned Arlen a considerable fortune. The Lawrences knew him from late 1915 when DHL liked 'the sound decency in him' (*Letters*, ii. 473 and n. 2, 474). m. 1928, Countess Atalanta Inarcati.

Davos. There's something about him I rather like – something sort of outcast, dog that people throw stones at by instinct, and who doesn't feel pious and Jesusy on the strength of it, like Cournos,[1] but wants to bite 'em – which is good. He's one of the few people I don't mind making their pile – just to spite 'em.

Dear Arabella, I had that apron on my mind. But they don't have them in Bavaria – and in Baden we were seeing doctors and doing a cure, and F[rieda] being dentisted, and altogether disheartened. But I have learned to play patience – I mean actually, at cards – so I play it. And when we come next within reach of a coloured apron, I'll send one.

I wonder if we shall go to the ranch in the spring – I believe I should feel better. I feel rather come down, after two years of Europe: and weary of Italy. But perhaps of myself most. That is, of being unwell.

Did you sell two editions of that pamphlet, Richard?[2] I saw it quoted somewhere. – But I find most people look on me as if I was a queer sort of animal in a cage – or should be in a cage – sort of wart-hog: sin amor y sin disprecio, as my dear song says.[3] – Well I hope you are happy in the Malthouse, and busy at things you like. We may go to Cortina in January 'curing.' Dobrée invited us to Egypt – but suddenly didn't write again – don't know why – sudden scare of the wart-hog and his grunts, I suppose – anyhow we won't go.

Nice little artichokes for lunch, Arabella – pity you can't be having one with us. How did your garden grow, this summer? Here it was so dry, they had to sell or kill the oxen – and still the wells are almost empty.

Awfully nice of you to offer an egg from your ill-laying goose. But I'm not hard-up – and when I am, if ever I am, I'll make richer people fob out.

DHL

4210. To Curtis Brown, 18 November 1927
Text: MS NWU; Curtis Brown, *Contacts* (1935), pp. 70–1.

Villa Mirenda, Scandicci, Florence.
18 November, 1927.

Dear C[urtis] B[rown]

I never thanked you for your note when you got back from America. Yes, I was ill, wearisomely – and though I did cures in Germany, I still cough too much and am rather feeble: which makes me very impatient. But I'm much better.

---

[1] John Cournos (1881–1966), Russian-born author and editor whom DHL had known since 1915. Cournos and his wife Helen (1893–) last saw the Lawrences in Florence in late March 1926 (*Letters*, v. 410 and n. 1).   [2] See p. 44 n. 1.
[3] The song has not been traced ['without love and without contempt' ('desprescio')].

I was sorry Barmby left, for all that.[1] I sort of felt I knew him and depended on him.

I want now to ask you about a new little thing. You know, probably you don't, I wrote a novel last winter that the world would call improper and all that. But it is a tender and sensitive work, and I think, proper and necessary, and I have it, so to speak, in my arms. It is no use thinking of publishing it publicly, as it stands: and I won't cut it. I thought of letting it lie by indefinitely. But friends in Florence urge me to print it privately, here in Florence, as Norman Douglas does his books – 700 copies at 2 guineas each – that is what he does.[2] Production is cheap, and myself and a friend[3] could easily do all the work ourselves. And I should make – with the gods – a few hundred pounds – even seven or eight – which would be a windfall for me. And no 20% tax.

It is not cheap, being ill and doing cures. And in January I am supposed to go up to the snow. You know the magnificent sums Secker makes for me – and Knopf. Not their fault, no doubt – nor mine. But without Miss Pearn I might be whistling, simply though we live.

So if this is a simple and decent way of putting the book into the world – and mind, one day I intend to put it into the world, *as it stands* – and also of earning some money to go on with, then I don't see why I shouldn't do it. Later, I could perhaps cut out parts and give the novel to Secker and Knopf. But I doubt if I should. Why should I? I'm sick of cutting myself down to fit the world's shoddy cloth.

Tell me what you think, will you? And what you think Knopf's and Secker's attitudes will be. I have no 'future books' contract with Secker, but I'm not sure of Knopf. Anyhow, I'd offer them the thing if I were letting it go for a normal publication.

Miss Pearn was afraid of damaging my magazine market[4] – but I'd send out no review copy – so I don't see how it would do that.

Tell me what you think, will you?

Sincerely,   D. H. Lawrence

4211. To Mabel Dodge Luhan, 18 November 1927
Text: MS Brill; Luhan 334–6.

Villa Mirenda. Scandicci. Firenze
18 Nov 1927

Dear Mabel

I enclose cheque for $48.00 – which is the equivalent of the Liras Orioli

[1] Nancy Pearn had told DHL on 21 July 1927 (TMSC UT) that Barmby was leaving Curtis Brown's New York office and being replaced by Edwin G. Rich 'who is well known in New York'.   [2] Douglas published his novel *In the Beginning* (December 1927) in this way.
[3] I.e. Orioli.   [4] See p. 29 n. 5.

gave me.[1] I draw the last remaining dollars out of an old account that I want to close, so if there is any hitch, don't be alarmed, it will only mean there's only 47 instead of 48 dollars in that bank. I think there are 49. – But if it's not right, I'll send you another cheque.

I was in Florence for the first time yesterday. Curious, something has gone out of me – towns mean nothing to me, only[2] noise and nuisance. I'm not interested in them. – I saw la Condamine for a moment – stuttering and faded[3] – and young Acton come up the other day. But the way they talk of Tony makes me so mad. 'I hear he comes to dinner in his war-paint!' – So I said: 'And why not? Doesn't your mother, and all the rest of your female friends? Tony is just as well bred.' – Dead and damnatory Florentine silence – nipped their little joke! Poor lot!

I met Michael Arlen too by chance – you know, *The Green Hat*. He too been sick, and looking diminished, in spite of all the money he has made: quite a sad dog, trying to be rakish.

The weather has gone suddenly cold and grey – very sudden. Gets my chest a bit. I bet you've got snow at Taos. I am busy getting my poems in order, to go into one vol – all the poems. My word, what ghosts come rising up! But I just tidy their clothes for them and refuse to be drawn. – I think I shall publish my last winter's novel *Lady Chatterley's Lover!* here in Florence, privately, myself – and rake in the badly-needed shekels and avoid all publicity. I must avoid publicity with it – it is so tender and so daring. I should print 700 copies only – at $10. a copy – and that ought to make me about 3 or 4 thousand dollars. There's an idea for you and your *Memories*, later on. I'll let you know how it goes – and you'll have to get me a few subscriptions, if I start.

I haven't heard from the Brewsters, whether they'll come with us in March or April to New York and then New Mexico. I think he would come – but Achsah in her long white robes and floating veils – oh, I'd love to see her in a side-saddle on an ambling pad – not Poppy – wafting between the plum-bushes toward the pueblo! *How* I'd love it! – We might have a joint, slam-bang exhibition of pictures in N. Y. – Achsah's acres of Jesus and the blue Virgin – always herself – Earl's charming landscapes and stiff white horse – my incorrigible nudes – and Brett's *Trinidad*. I think we'd baffle everybody – and certainly not sell a rag.

Don't build *many* more houses – they'll weigh on you at last, like Oscar Browning.[4] Stop in time! It's your lesson.

[1] See Letter 3995 and p. 37 n. 3.   [2] MS reads 'to, only'.
[3] Robert de la Condamine, a friend of Mabel Luhan's from her days at the Villa Curonia. See *Letters*, v. 642, 646; see also Rudnick, *Mabel Dodge Luhan*, pp. 36, 42.
[4] The allusion is obscure but DHL probably referred to Oscar Browning (1837–1923), Cambridge historian; he was chairman of the British Academy of Arts in Rome and died in Rome.

I hope Ida's better.[1] It will be fun to be back and see everybody and sort of take the lid off. One's got the lid on all the time here. And Spud's printing press may lay golden eggs yet.

Compton Mackenzie, after *swallowing* 'Two Blue Birds', was mortally offended at 'The Man Who Loved Islands', and Secker wants me not to print it in a book. I call that cheek – he should be so honoured! Oh small beer gone flat!

Look out for my story *The Escaped Cock* – in the *Forum* – don't know when – I want you to say what you think of it.

F[rieda] says she'll send more ribbons, Christmas coming.

a rivederci.   DHL

4212. To Giuseppe Orioli, [21 November 1927]
Text: MS UCLA; Moore, *Intelligent Heart* 371.

Villa Mirenda, *Scandicci*
Monday.

Dear Pino

Would you mind sending Carletto over to Michael Arlen with this note – I don't know his address – Borgo San Giorgio – and please ask Carletto to wait for an answer. He – Michael Arlen – was coming out on Wednesday – but Frieda's got a cold, in bed today, and Michael A. is terrified of getting a cold. So I must warn him. The Wilkinsons are staying the night in Florence, will bring out the note tomorrrow.

I am seriously thinking of publishing my novel in Florence: have already written to my agent about it: but you'd have to help me. Would you? I'll come and talk about it soon.

Did Arlen come in and see you? I believe he's lonely – and so sad.

a rivederci   D. H. Lawrence

4213. To S. S. Koteliansky, 22 November 1927
Text: MS BL; Postmark, Scandicci 24.11.27; Moore 1024–5.

Villa Mirenda, Scandicci. Firenze
22 Novem 1927

My dear Kot

Well how are things with you now? I was disheartened, because I had a cold and didn't feel myself, and nothing seemed worth while. But I'm bucking up

[1] Ida Rauh (1877–1970), American actress and sculptress; an old friend of Mabel Luhan's. Divorced wife of Max Eastman (1883–1969); she lived with Andrew Michael Dasburg (1887–1979), the American painter, 1922–8. See *Letters*, v. 159 and n. 1.

again now. And now Frieda is in bed these two days with a cold. But I expect she'll be up tomorrow: she's much better. It's this unnatural autumn – now hot like an orchid-house, hot and damp.

Have you done any more about your scheme? Judging from the notice of Forster's last book, he must be rather a piffler just now. And I read the *Celestial Omnibus* again – and found it rather rubbish.[1] Those things don't wear. But if you can get anything out of him, do. The devil will be, to get manuscripts: and it's entirely useless your beginning till you've got *four*: a series must at least begin to be a series.

I'm thinking I shall publish my novel *Lady Chatterley's Lover* here in Florence, myself, privately – as Douglas does – 700 copies at 2 guineas. It is so 'improper', it could never appear in the ordinary way – and I won't cut it about. So I want to do it myself – and perhaps make £600 or £700. Production is cheap here. And the book must come out some day. – But don't mention it, will you, among people.

Michael Arlen came to see us Saturday – ill poor devil – tubercular trouble. He's much thinner – not much changed – the Florence snobs cut him dead – he's absolutely persona ingrata now, after they made so much fuss of him. He turned all his money in America into a trust, can't touch it till he's 35 – now he's 31 – But then he'll have a large income, perhaps £100,000 a year. But what's the good! he's a sad dog.[2]

But tell me about the scheme, and what's to be done.

Huxley's *Proper Studies* is a bore!

                                                                                DHL

---

[1] Forster's 'last book' (published in October 1927) consisted of his Clark Lectures, delivered at King's College, Cambridge, and entitled *Aspects of the Novel*. DHL had read and commented earlier on *The Celestial Omnibus and Other Stories* (1911): see *Letters*, ii. 275–6. Kot had been unable to 'get anything out of' Forster who wrote on 19 November (MS BL) regretting that he had nothing to offer for Kot's publishing venture.

[2] After Arlen's visit on 19 November DHL wrote in his 'Memoranda' (MS NWU):

Kouyoumdjian came out to tea: has had a bad time with tubercular trouble, & a sad lost dog, in spite of all his money: says the Green Hat brought him 5,650 dollars one week: has turned himself into a trust, & can't touch any of his American money till he's 35 – now only 31. Wants to marry – but had a tubercular testicle removed – so it only means more tuberculosis: but wants a Greek or Georgian wife, something Oriental, being himself an Armenian: don't blame him, our women are juiceless: & he needs somebody to comfort him a bit, his fortune isn't enough. We talked my poverty – it has got on my nerves lately. But next day had a horrible reaction, & felt sort of pariah. People must feel like that who make their lives out of money. Definitely I hate the whole money-making world, Tom & Dick as well as en gros. But I won't be done by them either.

4214. To Henry Leach, 22 November 1927
Text: MS HU; Lacy, *Escaped Cock* 65–6.

Villa Mirenda, Scandicci, Florence. Italy.
22 Novem.1927

Dear Mr Leach[1]

I'm glad you are trying *The Escaped Cock* on your public. After all, you don't cater exclusively for flappers and self-opinionated old ladies – and it *is* a good story. I do hope to goodness the *Forum* will manage to nucleate what is otherwise an amorphous mass of intelligent people who want a little fresh air. The mass of magazines seem to me almost asphyxiatingly stuffy – the mind simply becomes stupefied by them. I do think the *Forum* is trying to open a window, and if people once begin to breathe fresh air, they'll want to go on.[2]

So here's luck – and best wishes from my wife and me –

Yours Sincerely   D.H. Lawrence

4215. To Max Mohr, 22 November 1927
Text: MS HMohr; Mohr, *T'ien Hsia Monthly*, i. 25–6.

Villa Mirenda. Scandicci, Firenze
22 Novem 1927

Dear Max Mohr

A very nice and clever letter you wrote in English – suddenly your English very good! You are a man who goes by fits and starts, I believe.

When are you going to Berlin? I was thinking you might like to see my wife's sister there. She was married to a Major in the old army, who made debts and scandals etc etc – and she (in your ear) was thereafter gay and demi-monde. Then, having turned forty, she wanted to repent and be respectable, so she got divorced from the Schreibershofen and married a very good, nice, estimable Herr Bankdirektor Emil Krug. So there she is, Frau Krug – poverina! – very respectable – and hating it like poison. 'Ich hass die Ehe! Aber was ist es mit der Ehe, Lorenzo, dass man es so hassen muss?'[3] – 'Fraid *I* don't know. But Emil is really intelligent and decent and nice – I really like him. So go and see them – –

Nymphenburgerstr. 9 II. Schöneberg.

I told Johanna I'd tell you. But don't give away what I said about her.

---

[1] DHL was replying to a letter (6 November 1927) forwarded to him on 17 November by Nancy Pearn. His correspondent was Henry Goddard Leach (1880–1970), American university teacher, author and editor. Leach edited the *Forum*, 1923–40. (See obituary, *New York Times*, 12 November 1970.)

[2] For the response by Leach's readers to DHL's story see Letter 4395.

[3] 'poor thing! . . . I hate marriage! But what is it about marriage, Lorenzo, that one has to hate it so?'

We shan't go to Egypt – costs too much. For heaven's sake don't imagine I've got any money – I'm as poor as a mouse. It's chronic with me: and shameful, really, that I make so little. Michael Arlen came in the other day – he made nearly a million dollars in America with *The Green Hat* and other things! Imagine! But he's sick, poor devil! – I think we may go to Cortina in January, to the snow: but perhaps we shall stay here, and go in April to the ranch – near Taos, near Santa Fe, in New Mexico. It's very fine there – nearly 3000 meters up – beautiful – and horses to ride. If we go, you must come too – but really. You'd love it for a while, at least. – But don't mention this either, for my Schwiegermutter weeps at the very sound of the word Ranch: it is so far off.

How is the Wolfsgrube now? Here it is warm and damp, like a hot-house: not nice. My wife is in bed with a cold: I cough, but no more than usual. With you I hope all goes well. Many greetings to your wife and la chiquita.

D. H. Lawrence

4216. To Ada Clarke, 22 November 1927
Text: MS Clarke; Unpublished.

Villa Mirenda. Scandicci, Firenze
22 Nov. 1927

My dear Sister

I was glad to have your letter and hear about Gertie and Jack. Sounds encouraging about G. – though one trembles at every change of weather. I went in to Florence Thursday, so of course it turned a bad day, and I got a bit of cold – but nothing much. Frieda been in bed these two days, also with a cold – but getting up tomorrow. – In Florence I met by chance Kouyoumdjian – who is now Michael Arlen – wrote *The Green Hat*. He has made quite a large fortune – nearly a million dollars – by the play chiefly – turned himself into a trust, and I don't know what. But poor devil he has had bad tubercular trouble – and after being so praised by the Mayfair Smart Set, they now hate him and openly cut him. So he's not very cheerful. You see he's an Armenian, and they hate having been taken in by him. I remember old Lady Esher writing to Brett[1] – 'a wonderful book, *The Green Hat* – and how he knows his Mayfair.' He's only 31 – and so forlorn.

I sent you a few books, thought Gertie might like them, they're quite simple. I'll send some more soon – my shelves are too full. I'm not doing much work – don't feel inclined – but always a bit. It's nasty kind of weather, hot as a hot-house, but literally: puffs of damp hot air like when you open the door of

---

[1] Brett's mother, Eleanor Viscountess Esher (d. 1940).

an orchid house. – I ordered some of those little German animal toys from
Baden, to be sent to Pam, and she's to share them with you when they come.
There were such pretty little ones. – Otherwise don't let's send any parcels for
Christmas, it *is* such a struggle with the post. Unless you'd like me to buy you
embroidered linen or tablecloths or anything – it's become much cheaper,
because fewer foreigners to buy it – and it's very nice here.

I do hope everything goes well – we're very quiet here.

Love!   DHL

4217. To William Roberts, 1 December 1927

Text: MS Roberts, W. H.; Postmark, Scandicci 4.12.27; Unpublished.

Villa Mirenda, Scandicci (Florence)
1 Dec 1927

Dear Mr Roberts[1]

Sorry I havent got a photograph myself – I don't like 'em. But ask Martin
Secker, he's got one and he's sure to lend it you willingly.

We've got some snaps, but I don't suppose they are of any use to you. If
they are, let me know.

Yours Sincerely   D. H. Lawrence

4218. To Alice Corbin Henderson, 1 December 1927

Text: MS UT; Postmark, Scandicci 4.12.27; Unpublished.

Villa Mirenda, Scandicci, Florence
1 Dec 1927

Dear Alice Corbin[2]

Glad to hear from you, and to know all serene. I wrote to my agents Curtis

---

[1] William Herbert Roberts (b. 1905), a Welshman, described himself (to the editors) as 'a bank-
clerk with literary aspirations in 1927'. He had written an article on DHL and believed its
chances of acceptance by a journal would be increased if it were illustrated. Hence his request
for photographs. See also Letters 4228 and 4427.

[2] Alice Corbin (1881–1949), American poet and editor. m. 1905, William Penhallen Henderson
(1877–1943). American painter and architect. Soon after arriving in USA in 1922, DHL met
her through Mabel Luhan (see *Letters*, iv. 290 and n. 4); the Hendersons' daughter Alice (1907–
88) m. 1922, John Ganson Evans (1902–78), Mabel Luhan's son by her first marriage.

   DHL was responding to the following letter, 2 November 1927 (TMSC UT), in which Alice
Corbin Henderson sought his permission to include three poems from *Birds, Beasts and
Flowers* in *The Turquoise Trail: An Anthology of New Mexican Poetry* (New York, 1928):

   Dear "David"; – or shall I say "Lorenzo" or Mr. Lawrence – ? –
   I'm going to ask a big favor of you which I hope you will grant me before you know what it is.
But here goes:

Brown, 116 West 39th St – New York – to arrange to let you have those three poems for your anthology.[1]

We are hoping to come to New Mexico in the spring – March or April – then we should see you. After two years of Europe, mostly Italy, one pants for a little space and *really* fresh air. Bit dead here.

Remember me to Henderson, and many greetings from us both.

D. H. Lawrence

4219. To Charles Wilson, 5 December 1927
Text: MS StaU; Unpublished.

Villa Mirenda, Scandicci, Florence
5 Decem 1927

Dear Mr Wilson[2]

I believe myself the miners who want to read anything would probably read me, if ever they got started. I'm a miner's son myself, so surely there's some sympathy.

But try them with *Sons and Lovers*, and some stories from *The Prussian Officer* – and perhaps that play which Duckworth publishes: *The Widowing of Mrs Holroyd*.

I'm making a New Mexico anthology which Houghton Mifflin will publish – and I want very much to include your *Men in New Mexico*, *Autumn at Taos* and *Red Wolf*, if you will give me permission. Of course, I will make all necessary arrangements with the publishers. Has Knopf taken over the book, or is it still Thomas Seltzer?

I think you will like my selection and I am counting on your poems, so please don't refuse me.

When are you coming back to New Mexico? Everything is very beautiful and quiet here now in the fall – cottonwoods golden and the first snow on the mountains.

Alice and her three daughters spent the summer here, Alice commuting between Buffalo and SantaFe; and John was here for a brief visit. They are all fine, and of course I loved having them here. Mabel is busy building in Taos, and seems happy. I have often regretted that things were so mixed up when you were here that I didn't see more of you and Frieda. Next time you come it will be different. But I suppose all experience counts. I am wiser, and I think *younger*, albeit a grandmother!

Anyhow I am happy, and will be still happier if you will let me use your poems.

With affectionate regards to you and Frieda, I am

Yours sincerely

[1] DHL's letter is missing.

[2] Charles Wilson (1891–1968), a free-lance journalist with an active interest in adult education; he was secretary of the local branch of the Workers' Educational Association (cf. Letter 4289). In pursuit of the miners' educational interests he invited visits from leading writers including, in September 1928, James Joyce (see *Selected Letters*, ed R. Ellmann, 1975, p. 336), and, in 1930, Aldous Huxley (see *Letters*, ed. Grover Smith, 1969, pp. 340–1). He was a keen trade unionist and in 1935 was adopted as the Independent Socialist candidate for the parliamentary constituency of Spennymoor, Co. Durham, but never contested the seat. He was known as 'The Pitman Poet', author of *The Poetical Works of Charles Wilson*, i. (1916), etc.

Men have got to learn not only to think for themselves, but to *feel* for
themselves, which is much more difficult, for feelings are even more
derivative than thoughts, and less susceptible to criticism and modification.

Good luck to you in your venture.[1]

D. H. Lawrence

4220. To Mabel Dodge Luhan, 5 December 1927
Text: MS UT; Unpublished.

Villa Mirenda, *Scandicci*, Firenze
5 Dec 1927

Dear Mabel

Just a hasty note in answer to yours about a start on the writing.

Don't be so scornful of the New York socialist years.[2] It wasn't bunk. It
wasn't even ideas. It was a passion, and a genuine one at the time – the anti-
social revolutionary passion. Of course you've gone back on it – and now, as an
accumulator of property, have a big resistance to it, and scorn it. – If you want
to write it, you've got to feel it again.

But read Upton Sinclair's *Money Writes*.[3] It is very good, in its way: and
true. He mentions Mabel Dodge quite heartfelt: when she had pawned all her
furniture: and again. That'll probably start you.

You can't write without sympathy – to that revolt-passion, which naturally
followed a diet of of Edwin. Taos being already anarchic, of course you don't
like the anarchic passion. But it's a real one.

But the streets of New York will yet run blood. Yours was one étape.[4]

But of course, you dont want all your new houses jeopardised.

[1] Miners in the county of Durham (including Willington, Wilson's home) suffered particular
hardship in the years following the General Strike; the *New Statesman* reported on 31
December 1927 that the miners were 'entering upon the third year of acute suffering without a
gleam of hope' (see W. R. Garside, *The Durham Miners 1919–1960*, 1971, p. 275). To occupy
their time, miners' groups sponsored the provision of non-vocational lectures (ibid., p. 299); it
is likely that Wilson's 'venture' was associated with such activities.
[2] During the later years (1912–13) of her marriage to Edwin Dodge, Mabel Luhan lived in New
York City and was influenced by radical friends such as Hutchins Hapgood, Lincoln Steffens
and John Reed to devote her energy to the work of the 'Lyrical Left' (see Rudnick, *Mabel
Dodge Luhan*, pp. 62ff.; Luhan, *Movers and Shakers*, New York, 1936).
[3] *Money Writes! A Study of American Literature* (New York, 1927). Sinclair recalls Mabel
Luhan's strenuous efforts on behalf of striking silk workers in New Jersey, which led to the
creation of the Paterson Strike Pageant in June 1913 at Madison Square Garden: 'we got up the
Paterson Pageant, and worked day and night over it, and bankrupted ourselves – how well I
remember that agonized final meeting, when Mabel Dodge pledged her furniture to get the last
five hundred dollars' (p. 58). He associates her with other radicals such as Reed, Ernest Poole
and Leroy Scott whose political integrity, like hers, was undamaged despite defectors from
their ranks (pp. 58–9).   [4] 'staging post'.

Ida's quite right – there's no male spirit in the men – it's all in the women, but not cosy yet in them: ill-sitting hen.

The anarchic passion tends to die down as one gets older. But one is always capable of a flicker or two, as of sex.

People coming – will write again.

DHL

very pretty pictures of the property.

4221. To Donald Carswell, 5 December 1927
Text: MS YU; Huxley 694–5.

Villa Mirenda, *Scandicci*, Firenze
5 Dec 1927

Dear Don

Many thanks for the book.[1] We've both read it, and both really interested. It's awfully good sidelights on recent history, and seems to me psychologically very sound. Only you don't allow enough for the emotional side of our reactions – poor Keir Hardie – and if your Lord Overtoun is sarcastic, which surely it is, then most people will take it for praise.

And you do admire a little overmuch English detachment. It often is mere indifference and lack of life. And you are a bit contemptuous of your Scotch: one feels they are miserable specimens, all told, by the time one winds up with Robertson Nicoll. It's because you underestimate the *vital* quality, and overestimate the English detached efficiency which is not very vital.

I got Cath's letter and wrote McGreevy, whom I've utterly forgot.[2] Tiresome, he is, fussing his little affairs round.

Cath's idea of a Burns book I like very much: I always wanted to do one myself, but am not Scotchy enough. I read just now Lockharts bit of a life of Burns.[3] Made me spit! Those damned middle-class Lockharts grew lilies of the valley up their arses, to hear them talk. If Cath is condescending to Burns, I disown her. He was quite right, a man's a man for a' that, and it's *not* a bad

---

[1] See p. 188 n. 3. The individual subjects of Carswell's biographical essays mentioned by DHL were: James Keir Hardie (1856–1915), a founder of the Independent Labour Party in 1913 and, later, MP; John Campbell White, Baron Overtoun (1843–1908), wealthy industrialist and philanthropist; Sir William Robertson Nicoll (1851–1923), journalist and religious editor, 'the cleverest, shrewdest Scot of his generation' (*Brother Scots*, p. 237).

[2] DHL's letter is missing. His correspondent was Thomas McGreevy, translator and critic; author of 'A Note on Work in Progress', *transition* xiv (Fall 1928), 216–19; *Richard Aldington* (1931); *T. S. Eliot* (1931), etc. See Richard Aldington, *Life for Life's Sake*, 1968, pp. 312, 318–21.

[3] John Gibson Lockhart's *Life of Burns* (1828 and frequently reprinted). Catherine Carswell's *Robert Burns* appeared in 1933.

poem.[1] He meant what he says. My word, you can't know Burns unless you can hate the Lockharts and all the estimable bourgeois and upper classes as he really did – the narrow-gutted pigeons. Don't, for God's sake, be mealy mouthed like them. *I'd* like to write a Burns life. Oh, why, doesn't Burns come to life again, and really salt them? I'm all for Keir Hardie, my boy. Did you ever *know* Sir G. Trevelyan, for example.[2] Pfui! 'I'm it, mealy mouthed it!' No my boy, don't be on the side of the angels, it's too lowering.

Germany sounds rather fun – but too far, too far. I'm supposed to go up to the snow in January, but am shirking it. See when January comes. The changing is such a bore. – I think we shall go back to the ranch in spring – March or April – . I'd like to be away from Europe for a bit.

We too have no news. Nothing goes very well – money dwindles – the govt takes 20% off what I do get – and Curtis Brown 10; Pax! What does one exist for, but to be made use of; by people with money.

Frieda sends her love with mine – do hope the boy is better – wish something nice would happen all round.

D. H. Lawrence

4222. To Nancy Pearn, 5 December 1927
Text: MS UT; Unpublished.

Villa Mirenda, *Scandicci*, Florence
5 Dec 1927

Dear Miss Pearn

I don't mind if the magazine people alter the end of the story a bit – as little as possible.[3] But *do please* keep me a complete MS. ticketed 'whole' – for those cuttings do spoil the artistic completeness of a story.

I was glad that editor of *World* liked the Etruscan essays: shows somebody still has a bit of sense. When will he begin to print.[4]

---

[1] 'For a' that and a' that', (1785), l. 12. Catherine Carswell later remarked: 'I had never said it was [a bad poem], but Donald had made a rather slighting reference to it in *Brother Scots*' (Carswell 261 n. 1).

[2] Sir George Otto Trevelyan Bt, OM (1838–1928), historian and statesman. Chancellor of Duchy of Lancaster, 1884; Secretary of State for Scotland, 1886, 1892; author of *The Life and Letters of Macaulay* (1876), *The American Revolution* (1899–1907), etc. DHL knew his son Robert Calverley Trevelyan (1872–1951) from 1913 (see *Letters*, ii. 116 and n. 1). His remark may have have been prompted by Carswell's reference, in the essay on Keir Hardie, to the 'sweet reasonableness such as Sir George purveyed' (*Brother Scots*, p. 178).

[3] Nancy Pearn had enquired on 2 December 1927 (TMSC UT): 'if the editor wanted to tone down the last few pages [of *Rawdon's Roof*] a bit, would you agree?'

[4] The four Etruscan essays which appeared in *Travel* (cf. p. 48 n. 1) were also published in the London *World Today* in February–March 1928 (Roberts C163, C165–6, C168). Nancy Pearn told DHL on 29 November 1927 that the editor of the *World Today*, Chalmers Roberts, had offered 'the none-too-bad price of Ten Guineas each' (TMSC UT).

Hear London is dark – it's greyish even here, but silvery.

Yrs   D. H. Lawrence

4223. To S. S. Koteliansky, [8 December 1927]
Text: MS BL; Postmark, Firenze 8 . XII 1927; Spender, *Encounter*, i. 34.

Villa Mirenda, Scandicci, Florence
8 Dec

My dear Kot

I was very much distressed to hear about Ghita – but thankful there'll be no ill consequences. I hope by now you've got her safely at the Cave, and she's about well, and all serene. Damn all motor cars: and I hope they've got to pay good substantial damages.

I suppose the Cave is not being abandoned, after all?

About the printing – dear Kot, what *is* the good of beginning with just one? My novel I'm writing all over again,[1] so that's in abeyance. But *how* can you begin the little books with just me? You'd begin and you'd end there. You've just got to *wring* a few MSS out of people, if you're going to start. The worst of it is, what people? They've all got commercial contracts.

Have you seen the German magazine *Querschnitt*?[2] It's a very good modern-popular sort of magazine. I believe, if one were going to do anything new and popular today, one would have to be quite bold, jump in with two feet, be unconventional, improper at times, print good nude pictures, and give the thing a kick. There's absolutely no public for merely 'good' stuff: there really isn't. The public wants pictures and bits of text. But *live* pictures. I'll send you a copy of *Querschnitt*. The good Jehovah has got to be a bit of a devil if he's going to do anything today. You'd far more easily find artists and draughtsmen for a magazine, than writers. Then the text becomes subsidiary – all the better – and you can put in snappy things of all sorts.

If we don't go to the ranch in the spring, I think we really shall go to Ireland:

Can you get from Gertler any explanation of Dobrées curious behaviour? He wrote very warmly in Sept, asking us to go to Egypt. I replied we'd like to, if we could. And since then, not a word from him – only a note from her, saying she hadn't been able to think of journeys – and evidently not badly wanting us. – She's a perfect right not to want us – but then in mere politeness he should answer my letter, and say, do we mind putting the thing off. – I'm

---

[1] The third version of *Lady Chatterley's Lover*.

[2] *Der Querschnitt* (Berlin) was a lavishly illustrated magazine – with pictures of buildings, authors, actresses, etc. – containing articles by well-known authors on past as well as contemporary literary matters.

surprised at his lack of manners. But I suppose there was some mischief made somewhere. However, I was polite, and so can they be.

I expect we'll be here for Christmas – weather dull, most other things too.

DHL

4224. To Emily King, 8 December 1927
Text: MS Lazarus; Postmark, Firenze 8 . XII 1927; Unpublished.

Villa Mirenda, Scandicci. Florence
8 Dec 1927

My dear Pamela

The tea came all right, 4/- duty. But it is very nice, such a nice bouquet, and I'm always so glad to have a bit of good China after a few months of India. It's so soothing, in comparison. Keep the odd $\frac{1}{4}$ lb – and we'll see how best to send it later.

I'm glad Joan liked the animals – do hope they were what she wanted.[1] It's a nuisance about her cough. But it's the air – the air itself is so bad. Even here it's been muggy and damp for three weeks, not dark or rainy, but not healthy either. And the bronchials simply wont stand up to the wrong sort of air. But today it is colder, with a N.W. wind, so perhaps we'll have a better spell. We need a little winter. The narcissus are in bud, they'll be in flower in another week, at this rate: and the anemones are up, green and flourishing. It's too soon – spring before Christmas.

I'm not sending any parcels this year – the post here is enough to drive you crazy. You can give me some little thing when I come in the spring. I enclose 30/-, and that's 10/- for each, and if the children like to have the money, let them have it. Really one gets sick of things, an endless accumulation of things, things, things. It's really better to be like our peasants, who have nothing but table, benches and bed. For the rest, as bare as the chickens of possessions.

I don't think we shall go in to Florence after all: the town only irritates me. We'll stay here, and have people out to us. The Huxleys will be in Florence for the Christmas week, so they too can drive us in. I expect we'll go to one or two parties, anyhow: and that's enough. We had promised to go up to the snow with the Huxleys – but they're going to Les Diablerets, over Lake Geneva, and I don't want to go there. I dont believe there'll be any real snow anywhere, yet – and those high places are awful in winter, with no snow. Better here. – But we might go later to Capri, to the Brewsters. We can see.

If we stay, we shall have to make a Christmas tree – the peasants are simply crazy for it, all being so sweet and doing all they can for us, in the hopes. I

[1] See Letter 4205.

suppose we shall have to do it. They don't have much colour in their lives, and really a Christmas tree is quite a miracle, to the children anyhow. They never forget it. But this year there's such a crowd – the old ones want to come, and nine new ones – Oh Lord!

I do hope Joan is better. Be wary at Christmas – I always think it's a dangerous time. Thank Peg for her letter – and tell her not to take German too seriously. If you learn it in the country you never realise all that grammar and syntax.

Love to all.   DHL

4225. To Ada Clarke, 8 December 1927
Text: MS Clarke; Unpublished.

Villa Mirenda, *Scandicci*, Florence
8 Dec 1927

My dear Sister

Christmas drawing near again – rather a bore, I dont really like it. Don't you festivate too much, or it hits back at you. I always think Christmas is a venomous feast. But the sound of the cakes and puddings is good: you've really been going it. I thought we'd go in to Florence for a day or two – but when I do go in, I don't like it. Then we thought we might go to Capri, to the Brewsters. But apparently after all we shall just stay on here, and not go away till January, if we go at all. We shall have to make a Christmas tree, which is rather a sweat. But the peasants are panting for it, I really daren't not do it. The old ones, who were sent away, have sent to ask if they can come – and the new family is nine – so it looks like a mob. However, it doesn't last long – and their lives are all work – so they may as well have it as anybody else. The children think the tree really grows in the sitting room, like a miracle. I guess Pietro will steal a young pine from the wood – about eight or nine feet high.[1] And the rooms here are big.

Did you get some little animals from Pem for Bertie? I hope they're the sort he wanted. Perhaps you'll keep them for him for Christmas. I'm not making any post parcels this year – it is *such* an effort. I enclose 30/- and perhaps you'll buy some little thing for Jack and Gertie from me. Or if Jack would rather have the money, give it him: he must have masses of toys. And don't you send anything, it's not worth it – I paid 4/- duty on about 1½ lbs of tea from Pamela: and 6/- on three books. This country's crazy.

The weather has changed a bit today – colder, and a wind. It's been so muggy, warm, and damp, but not rainy. I even found mushrooms, fine ones –

---

[1] Pietro stole such a tree for Christmas 1926: *Letters*, v. 616.

and in December. The flies too don't die, the brutes. We shall be much better for a spell of cold – perhaps it will come after Christmas.

Maria Huxley was here the other day. They are going up to Diablerets in Switzerland, high over Lake Geneva – want us to go. But I don't care for the region.

Michael Arlen was here a few times – man who wrote the *Green Hat*. He made pots of money, but has tubercular trouble, and is a sad dog. He's just off to San Moritz, to the snow: if there *is* any. There's not a speck on our mountains. But January is the time.

It's very trying weather, this muggy damp. I do hope G. keeps pretty well. If she gets through all right till Feb. she should sail along. One has to be so careful.

I'll get Jack some stamps in Florence – I've seen a shop.

> Love to you all.   DHL

4226. To Idella Weatherwax, 11 December 1927
Text: MS UT; Postmark, Scandicci 11.12.27; Bynner 331.

> Villa Mirenda, Scandicci, Florence
> 11 Dec 1927

Dear Idella

I had your letter two days ago – of course it found me in bed, and feeling limp. If I can rouse up during this week I'll do you a little article and get it off: but don't count on me, for anything less uninspired or uninspiring than myself just now I wouldn't want you to see. If the Lord sends me a flicker, I'll send you one. It's the best I can promise.

> all good wishes   D. H. Lawrence

4227. To Else Jaffe, 12 December 1927
Text: MS Jeffrey; Frieda Lawrence 257–8.

> Villa Mirenda, Scandicci, Firenze
> 12 Decem 1927

Dear Else

I can't help laughing at the end of Frau Katharina's letter – gets quite snappy.[1] However, that's that! I suppose by *Holy Ghosts* (imagine daring to pluralize it!) she means *Glad Ghosts*. I sent you a copy last year, didn't I? – little yellow book. I don't mind what they put in a vol. – I suggested 'Woman Who Rode' – and 'Princess' and 'None of That' – all more or less Mexican.

---

[1] Cf. Letter 4203 and n. 2.

But let her put in *Glad Ghosts* if she likes. Anyhow we've got her hipped.[1] Don't suddenly go and say you don't want to translate the things – or haven't time, or something – just when I've got it into order. It would be just like you.

Very grey and misty and unsatisfactory here. I am in bed, as the best place out of it all. But I'm all right – cough a nuisance still, but nothing extra. I'd get up if the sun would shine. Anyhow I'll get up this afternoon.

I'm writing my *Lady Chatterley* novel over again. It's very 'shocking' – the Schwiegermutter must never see it. – I think I shall publish it privately here in Florence.

We are staying here for Christmas and making a tree for the peasants. This year there'll be at least thirty of them. Dreadful thought. But Frieda wants it.

And we aren't sending out any Christmas presents – so please, Else, don't send us anything. The post is so tiresome here, and altogether one feels so unchristmassy. I'm sick of Jesus; and don't at all see why he should go on being born every year. We might have somebody else born, for a change. Toujours perdrix![2]

The Huxleys will be in Florence for Christmas, then going to Diablerets. I don't want to go there. Neither to San Moritz, where Michael Arlen has gone. I'd have liked to go to Egypt – but the fates seem to say no. So it's just San Polo!

The Schwiegermutter says you are having festas in Heidelberg, so I suppose you are wearing your best clothes and going it. Nothing like learning, for setting people on the hop!

Anyhow I hope you're having a good time, and the children too.

Love from both   DHL

4228. To William Roberts, [16 December 1927]
Text: MS Roberts, W. H.; Unpublished.

[Villa Mirenda, Scandicci, Florence]
[16 December 1927]

[In response to a request that Lawrence should send some snapshots of himself, he wrote sending a few and asking for two copies of Roberts' article when it was published.][3]

---

[1] 'out of temper, sulky' (Nottinghamshire dialect).
[2] Literally 'Always partridge!'. DHL used the phrase also in 'The Novel and the Feelings' (written in November 1925); see *Study of Thomas Hardy and Other Essays*, ed. Bruce Steele (Cambridge, 1985), p. 201.
[3] Information to the editors from W. H. Roberts. DHL's letter has disappeared.

4229. To Nancy Pearn, 17 December 1927
Text: MS UT; Unpublished.

Villa Mirenda, *Scandicci*, Firenze
17 Dec 1927

Dear Miss Pearn

Yes, do let the *Coterie* people have the *Escaped Cock* and print their hundred little books.[1] They were very nice about *Sun*, I remember, and I'm glad they're not dying.

It's bitter cold here just now – a change from the damp. We shall have a quiet Christmas: there will be the tree to make for the peasants, they love it so. Imagine it standing in a corner of the 'summer parlour' – which has a good hot stove going at this moment – and the room simply jammed with Contadini, and the children looking for space in which to play with their toys, and the fathers smoking toscani – cheroots – and the mothers sipping sweet wine. They're all being good as angels in anticipation. But Pietro hasn't yet stolen the pine tree from the pineta, for us.

I hope you'll have a nice time. All good wishes from us both.

Sincerely   D. H. Lawrence

4230. To Max Mohr, [18 December 1927]
Text: MS HMohr; Mohr, Briefe 528–9.

Villa Mirenda, *Scandicci*, Firenze
Sunday 17 Dec.

Dear Max Mohr

I hear from Johanna that you are in Berlin, buzzing round, as the Americans say. I'll bet you are enjoying it, really: you are a man who ought to buzz round, though not necessarily in Berlin. How are your affairs going? I hope you can squeeze a nice fat sum of money out of somebody, and we'll all set off to the ranch in the spring, when the daisies bloom again.

Here it has been foggy and unpleasant, and I have, naturally, coughed. But these last two days it is bitter cold, an ice wind, though the sun is warm. This is quite cold enough, without going to any Engadin.[2]

I have been very busy writing out my new novel, for the third time. I have done half of it now. It is so 'shocking', the most improper novel in the world!

---

[1] DHL was answering Nancy Pearn's letter of 15 December 1927 in which she assured him that the *New Coterie*'s financial difficulties had been resolved and the editor, Charles Lahr, was offering the same terms as for *Sun* in 1926: 'namely, Two Guineas a thousand provided this can include the same arrangements as before, i.e. the issue of a hundred booklets' (TMSC UT).

[2] A bleak, mountainous area in Switzerland near the Austrian border, known in the nineteenth century as a centre for 'air cure'.

that is, for the conventional smut-hounds, Schmutz-hunde. As a matter of fact, it is a very pure and tender novel. A la bonne heure! I don't know what your Wolfsgrubin would say to it: but I think she'd like it. – I can never publish it in the ordinary way, so I think I shall bring it out myself, here in Florence, privately, at 2 guineas a copy: M. 42. – Then I too shall have some money to go spree-ing off with. And if we don't like New Mexico for long, we can sail from San Francisco the other way round the world. The sister of a friend of ours married the Rajah of Sarawak in Borneo: an Englishman.[1] We might even go to Sarawak. I feel like moving: am sick of Italy, especially of Florence.

I told you Michael Arlen was here – now gone to San Moritz – lungs. He made such a lot of money with *The Green Hat* in America. Somerset Maugham also was here, but I didn't see him, as I don't like him.[2] My God, these writers, they are *dismal*! I belive the race of men is dying out: nothing left but women, eunuchs, and Robots.[3]

Have you left the Wolfsgrubinfrau behind in Bavaria? No wonder she sees you as the schwarzer Ritter,[4] riding on a fat black horse into the shades. But there are damn few shades to ride into, so she's pretty safe.

Let us know how you get on, and if you think you will come here in January. All the seasonable greetings, as the tradesmen say!

DHL

4231. To Rolf Gardiner, 18 December 1927
Text: MS Lazarus; Huxley 695–6.

Villa Mirenda, *Scandicci*, Florence
18 Dec 1927

Dear Rolf Gardiner

You never answered my last – did it annoy you? Never mind – take it as it comes. But write to me from time to time and tell me what you are doing and how you are getting on, because I'm always interested, even if I'm a Job's Comforter now and then. My own tiresome bronchials exasperate me, that's the worst of it. But they're rather better.

Anyhow I think if you could revive the old round dances and singing among the men of the mines and iron works, you would be doing a very

[1] Dorothy Brett's sister, Sylvia (1885–), m. 1911, Sir Charles Vyner de Windt Brooke (1874–1963); he was Rajah of Sarawak from 1917.
[2] William Somerset Maugham (1874–1965), novelist and playwright whom DHL considered 'a narrow-gutted "artist" with a stutter' (*Letters*, v. 157). They met on 5 November 1924 in Mexico City and DHL did not 'care for him' (ibid., v. 161).
[3] Recently entered the language from Karel Capek's play, *R[ossum's] U[niversal] R[obots]* (1923).
[4] 'black knight'.

valuable thing, an invaluable thing. But I do think you'd do better to work from a centre, and send out shoots and branches. I wish it could be done – really, health or not, I'd come and lend a hand. It's not talk that'll help nowadays – or only a minimum.

I have decided to give up this place in March or April: and if I cant face England, then I shall go back to the ranch in New Mexico. Anyhow there's space out there, and a desert to ride over.

I thought when I was in Germany, I thought there was a new sort of stirring there: a horrible disillusion, a grinning, awful materialism, but under it, a stir of life. It's too soon to look for results. – If I were talking to the young, I should say only one thing to them: Don't you live just to make money, either for yourself or for anybody else. Don't look on yourself as a wage-slave. Try to find out what life itself is, and live. Repudiate the money idea.

And then I'd teach 'em, if I could, to dance and sing together. The togetherness is important.

But they must first overthrow in themselves the money-fear and money-lust.

But anyhow send a line to say how your things are going.

Sincerely   D. H. Lawrence

4232. To Harwood Brewster, [18 December 1927]
Text: MS Picard; Brewster 155–6.

Villa Mirenda, *Scandicci*, Firenze
Sunday

My dear Harwood

So you have really found another home for a bit – and another of the beautiful pretentious sort! Are you saying hurray? – are you breaking no eggs about it.

How is Capri? Here, for some weeks, it fogged, and I naturally coughed. These last two days there is a wind from the heart of all the icebergs, so unspeakably cold – but the sun fairly warm. I'm pretty well, considering, though a bit cross. I spent yesterday and today doing a picture which I have just burnt – and it hasn't even made the stove any hotter. How's that for meanness!

We are sitting tight for Christmas, and making a Christmas tree for the contadini. As their name is legion,[1] with a few babies over, it's a job, and my spirit is rather faint. I'm afraid I get less altruistic (nice word) as I get older. Still, the tree isn't stolen yet from the pineta, and the toys are still to buy from

[1] Cf. Mark v. 39 ['My name is Legion: for we are many'].

the Quarant' Otto – a famous bazaar place here. So sufficient unto the day is the evil thereof.[1]

Which is our neighbours the Wilkinsons coming in to tea in about five minutes, the four of them. They are very thrilled, off to Rome tomorrow for a fortnight. Thank God I needn't go: cold Rome! But one day I think we shall trot down to Capri to see you: if we don't go to Switzerland up to the snow: dreadful thought, on a day like this!

I enclose ten bob for you for Christmas, and you are to buy with it exactly what you choose: a bottle of beer, and a pair of corsets for Rose, the darling, for she must be losing her figure by now; a handbag in the shape of a puppy-dog for your mother (all the rage! when you take your powder-box out of his tummy, he squeaks!) – and for your father, a wigwam. With what is left over, buy yourself a harp, so that you shall not forget your name is Schwannhild![2]

Tell your father thank you! for his letter, but I couldn't see wood for bho-trees. Ask your mama the reason of this long-drawn-out silence of hers. If the Villa Torricello is her Capri swansong, tell her I would fain hear a few notes of that truly rare, never-before-heard melody.

Apart from all this there is no particular news – and here are the Wilks! Leb'wohl, mein Kind![3] Don't forget me when you're boozing the champagne and devouring the turkey and the pheasants!

DHL
Your uncle in all but name.

4233. To Harold Mason, 18 December 1927
Text: MS BosU; *Centaur* 30–1.

Villa Mirenda, *Scandicci*, Florence
18 Dec. 1927

Dear Mason

How are you and yours! Long since we wrote!

I've been having a bad time with my bronchials, cursing my stars. But am a good deal better.

I've been thinking I'll publish my new novel myself privately here, as Norman Douglas does his, at 2 guineas – $10. – The reason is, I'm tired of never getting anything from the publishers – I'd like to be responsible to myself. But the real reason is the novel is so 'shocking' from the smut-hunting point of view, that no publisher would even dare have the MS in his office. From my point of view, it is an assertion of sound truth and healthy reaction against all this decay and sneaking perversity which fills most of the books

---

[1] Matthew v. 34.   [2] Cf. Letter 4107 and n. 1.   [3] 'Farewell, my child!'

today. I consider my novel pure in the best sense – and warm-hearted. But the Puritan will want to smite me down.

Do you think it will be all right if I print, as Douglas does, 750 copies at ten dollars – half for England, half for America? The thing I am most afraid of is your damned interfering censorship. Do you think there is much danger? Please advise me – and ask McDonald's advice for me too, will you?

I haven't done anything yet. In fact I am re-writing the book for the third time, and am half way through again. But I'd like to have the thing ready to mail by end of March, if I'm going to do it at all.

Because in April I think we shall give up this place, and perhaps come to America. I want so much to go back to the ranch. Only it's a bit high – near 9000 ft – for my unhappy bronchials – though they'll stand it if I can get them hardened up a bit. – I'd like to come back to America now. Europe pulls one down: it is very hopeless, and *energyless*, which is worse.

So I should like to come west in April. And if we do, then we shall see you again: and Mrs Mason: and the McDonalds: which will give me a good deal of pleasure, davvero!¹

Write to me then! and ask McDonald to write.

Yrs   D. H. Lawrence

Don't tell people promiscuously about the shockingness of the novel – least said, soonest mended.

DHL

4234. To Baroness Anna von Richthofen, [18 December 1927]
Text: MS UCB; Frieda Lawrence 232–3.

Villa Mirenda, *Scandicci*, Florenz.
Sonntag

Meine liebe Schwiegermutter

Hier ist wieder Weihnacht. Ich sage, der arme Kerl ist schon beinah zweitausendmal geboren, es ist genug. Er könnte wirklich in Ruhe bleiben, und uns in Ruhe lassen, ohne Weihnacht und Magenweh. Wir aber sitzen still, machen nur den Baum für die Bauernkinder: und sie denken, es ist ein Wunder, es wächst wirklich hier im Salon, und hat silberne Äpfeln und goldene Vögeln: für die ist es nur ein Märchen, gar nichts Christliches.

Du hast gehört, die Frieda will Sancta-sanctissima spielen – sie ist schon die heilige Frieda, Butter könnte nicht in ihrem Mund schmilzen: weil sie ein Bandelli-Kind in den Hospital gebracht hat. Aber Gott sei dank, das Kind macht Schwierigkeiten, und die heilige Frieda fängt sich wieder an sehr langweiligt und allzumenschlich zu werden.

¹ 'indeed!'

Grade jetzt waren die Wilkinsons hier – die Nachbarn – er mit Flöte und neuem Mantel. Sie fahren Morgen nach Rom, für 15 Tage. Gott sei dank, ich fahre nicht mit: es ist ein hundkalter Wind diese zwei Tage geblasen, und Rom ist ein steinkalter Stadt. Ich sitze hier im Ecke am Ofen, der sehr freundlich brummelt, und ich pfeife auf der Welt.

Die Else schrieb, vielleicht bringt sie dich nach Heidelberg für die Festetage. Aber geh' du nicht, bleib' fest da, und lass die Mistelbeeren [Frieda inserts:'*'] fallen auf den Dummen die sie wollen. [Frieda inserts: 'Mistletoe']

Die Wilkinsons haben mir ein Christmas pudding gebracht: es riecht sehr gut, ich ess' es gern.

Ich schicke dir ein Pfund, du kannst dir einen solchen kaufen. Nicht wahr? – echter Englischer pudding! [Frieda interjects: 'Ja nicht!']

Also leb' wohl! nicht zu viel saufen, tanzen, und kosen, sonst bekommst du einen richtigen moralischen Kather, und ich weine *nicht* mit.

Ade! du Germania unter'm Baum.   DHL

[Sunday

My dear Schwiegermutter

Christmas is here again. I say the poor chap has already been born nearly two thousand times, it's enough. He really could remain in peace, and leave us in peace, without Christmas and stomach-ache. We sit quiet though, only decorate a tree for the peasant children: and they think it is a miracle, that it really grows here in the lounge, and has silver apples and golden birds: it is simply a fairy-tale for them, not Christian a bit.

You've heard that Frieda wants to play the holiest of the holy – she is already Saint Frieda, butter couldn't melt in her mouth: because she has got a Bandelli child into hospital. But thank the Lord the child is being difficult, and Saint Frieda begins to be bored and turn all-too-human again.

The Wilkinsons just left – the neighbours – he with a flute and a new overcoat. They are going to Rome tomorrow, for a fortnight. Thank goodness I am not going with them: there's been a bitter wind blowing these last two days, and Rome is a stone-cold city. I sit here in the corner by the stove, which grumbles amiably, and the world can go to blazes.

Else wrote that she might take you to Heidelberg for the holidays. But don't you go, stay put there, and let the mistletoe berries drop on the stupid people who want them.

The Wilkinsons have brought me a Christmas pudding: it smells very good, I enjoy eating it.

I send you a pound, you can buy yourself one like it. Couldn't you? – real English pudding! [Frieda interjects: Don't!]

So farewell! don't drink too much, dance too much or flirt too much, or you'll have a really dreadful moral hangover, and be depressed, and I *won't* weep with you.

Goodbye! you Germania under the tree.   DHL]

4235. To Gertrude Cooper, 19 December 1927
Text: MS Clarke; cited in Lawrence–Gelder 171.

Villa Mirenda, *Scandicci*, Florence
19 Dec 1927

My dear Gertie

I was glad to hear from you and to know you are still chirping up a bit. The cough is probably bronchial – the chief point is to keep the temperature steady. But you'll have little ups and downs, bound to. – I don't wonder you feel sore against Feroze.[1] But those Orientals never have any real feeling. They are sentimental, and merely selfish. Don't bother about him any way, either forgiving or unforgiving.

We had damp foggy weather even here – so naturally I coughed a fair bit. On Saturday started a fierce wind, cold enough to blow the skin off your face: but it was sunny. But I stayed indoors by the warm stove, my bronchials won't stand ferocious changes. Today, when I was out just now, the vapour froze in my beard: never been so cold here. At the same time, there is no wind, and a hot sun, so that we don't need any fire. I sit in the sitting-room in the sun writing this, and my head is almost too hot. Yet the other side the house the water freezes if you spill it on the floor. What a world!

Christmas nearly here! – I hate these festivations really, but the children want them: so we shall make a tree for the peasants. I suppose you'll have quite a do at Torestin.[2] But mind you take it quietly, and don't eat things that may send the temperature up.

Our neighbours have given us one of their Christmas puddings, so we are quite set up. I expect a few friends will come out to lunch during the festa days.

We gathered a few narcisssus in the garden – and wild sweet violets in the fields. But this frost will stop all that. The broad beans were up nearly a foot – but today they are all hanging over, looking very sick. The peasants say they will revive, but I doubt it very much. The peas too were up six inches: they'll be a goner. But the wheat will be all right, it is tough.

[1] Dr Dhunjabhai Furdunji Mullan-Feroze (1874–1959), the Clarkes' family doctor (see *Letters*, iii. 313 n.2). He employed Gertrude Cooper for a few years to collect insurance money from his patients; she had to abandon this activity when she became ill (see ibid., v. 541 and n. 1, 583).
[2] Ada Clarke's house in Ripley.

Frieda will get you a little calendar like last year, in Florence tomorrow. Or if it's not too cold, I'll go in also, and get it myself. But nowadays I'm wary of trips to town.

Nice that you can go in the car to Pamelas: makes a change. How are the Booths?[1] And Edna, does she flourish now she's married. Pamela says the miners are only working two or three days a week. What do they say to it? What do the young fellows say? I should like to know how they take it.

Don't bother about money – if you need any, I can give you some. But Ada will tell me.

Have a nice pleasant Christmas, then.

Love. DHL

4236. To Nellie Morrison, [20 December 1927]
Text: TMSC NWU; Unpublished.

Villa Mirenda, Scandicci.
[20 December 1927]

Dear Nelly Morrison,

When you've finished retyping your 'story'[2] – is it the one that came out in that Scotch paper – if you'd care to let me see it again, with the alterations I suggested, I would give you a note to my agent, or to the woman who runs the magazine part – for it's she you want – and write to her myself. Then you'll get attended to.

And then, when you have time, would you consider typing a novel for me? I have the first half ready, and could send it to a regular typist here in Florence, but I know, that from her point of view, it is improper – not from my point of view. I should hate to be bothered with her exclamations. But if you do it, you must let me pay you the regular rates – ça va sans dire[3] – for it will be rather a sweat doing a long novel. And then, even you may be shocked. God knows, I don't understand people. Even Maria Huxley was a little shocked at one of my pictures. – 'these are things we usually keep private' – such cant! So just tell me simply. I shall understand perfectly if you feel you would rather not. I should die if I had to do it myself now.

Been a bit seedy this last week, but rousing up again. Frieda going to Florence this afternoon. I stay at home. Come soon and see us again,

DHL

---

[1] Harold and Lizzie Booth were close friends of the Clarkes; he was headmaster of a village school (see *Letters*, v. 377 n. 4); she and Ada Clarke visited DHL in Italy in February 1926.
[2] The story and 'that Scotch paper' have not been identified.
[3] 'that goes without saying'.

4237. To Arthur and Lilian Wilkinson, 22 December 1927
Text: MS Schlaefle; Unpublished.

Villa Mirenda, *Scandicci*, Firenze
22 Dec 1927

Cari Amici

Just a line to wish you a merry Christmas. I'm sure you're enjoying Rome –
yesterday on that lovely day – today is grey again, alas. But there's so much to
do in Rome. On a sunny day take a picnic lunch on to the Via Appia – past the
Tomba di Aeilia Metella – and look at the catacombs as you come back – I
always enjoy that. *Dont* go to Ostia. But the Rome museums are lovely –
Vatican, Terme, and Villa Giulia. Lots of fun, you'll have.

Yesterday the Huxleys came – and we're spending Christmas Day with
them at a friend's villa.[1] Otherwise no news. The Christmas tree isn't stolen
yet – but it hangs over our heads. We shall keep it till you come back, and then
you'll come and we'll light it up for the last time.

The portfolio is very nice indeed, and just what I want. Did you buy it or
make it? It's most professional. We like it immensely.

We're just going to Scandy to buy more things for Saturday: what a sweat.
The Huxleys urge us to go to Switzerland – they go Jan 2nd.[2] But it's a fag.

Well do have a real good time and come back gaily and we'll have another.
Auf wiedersehen.   D. H. Lawrence

[Frieda Lawrence begins]

Aldous does want to eat the plum pudding! *Lovely* Portfolio.
Have a good time.

Frieda

4238. To S. S. Kotelianksy, 23 December 1927
Text: MS BL; Postmark, Scandicci 25 12 27; Moore 1027–8.

Villa Mirenda, *Scandicci*, Firenze
23 Dec.1927

My dear Kot

Well here is Christmas once more – and such beastly weather you never saw
– first bitter cold, now clammy wet warm mist. Talk about the sunny south! –

---

[1] The Huxleys were staying on the Via S. Margherita a Montici in Florence with Costanza Fasola
and her husband Eckart ('Ekki') Peterich in consequence of the friendship between the Fasola
and Nys families. Maria Huxley and Costanza were particularly close after Maria left
Garsington. (The Fasolas owned a house in Forte dei Marmi where the Huxleys sometimes
stayed.)

[2] The Huxley family party consisted of Julian (1887–1975), the distinguished biologist, his wife
Marie Juliette (née Baillot), and their sons Anthony Julian (1920–) and Francis John
(1923–); Aldous and Maria, their son Matthew and his governess, Mlle La Porte. They had
rented the Chalet des Aroles at Les Diablerets in Switzerland.

and never any rain, the wells dry: only *damp*. At the ranch it is sun every day, and frosty nights!!!

I'm glad it's not so bad with Ghita, but my goodness, bad enough. Makes me furious, damned automobiles.

My dear Kot, I do think this is the low-water mark of existence. I never felt so near the brink of the abyss. But in 1928 something is *bound* to begin new: must. We're trampled almost to extinction – we *must* have a turn soon.

As for my novel, it's half done, but so improper, you wouldn't dare to touch it. It's the most improper novel ever written: and as Jehovah you would probably find it sheer pornography. But it isn't. It's a declaration of the phallic reality. I doubt if it will ever be published. But certainly no English printer would print it. When one is in despair, one can only go one worse. I am driven to le plus plus pis aller.[1]

Oh dear, why are you so Jehovahish! I could wish you a little Satanic. I am certainly going that way. Satanasso! It's a nice word. I'm weary of Jehovah, he's always so right.

So your scheme will have to wait a bit. But I think others besides ourselves are being driven to extremity. And when it reaches the limit, then surely something will begin. I'd come to England if there were anything to come for. I'd work in England if there were anyone to work with. But I don't want to found either a beshitten *Adelphi* or a noble magazine.

It's a low-water mark, it really is. As for Christmas, damn it. We're having in the peasants to the tree, Saturday night, and spending Sunday in Florence with people the Huxleys are staying with. Nothing more!

De profundis oremus omnes.[2]

DHL

4239. To Charles Wilson, 23 December 1927
Text: MS StaU; Unpublished.

Villa Mirenda, *Scandicci*, Florence
23 Dec 1927

Dear Mr Wilson

Thanks for your letter, and kind invitation to the north. Unfortunately my bad health makes me live chiefly abroad. But I shall surely be in England this summer, and then if there is a chance I should like to come to see you and the Durham men.

---

[1] 'the worst possible extreme'.
[2] Cf. p. 159 n. 2 ('Out of the depths let us all pray').

Meanwhile this climate seems just as bad as the English.

My home district, by the way, is the Notts-Derby, Erewash Valley coalfield: Eastwood, Notts, I was born in.

It depresses me very much to hear how badly the men are working.

But I hope you'll have a good Christmas.

Sincerely   D. H. Lawrence

4240. To Max Mohr, 23 December 1927
Text: MS HMohr; Mohr, Briefe 529–30.

Villa Mirenda, Scandicci, Florence
23 Dec 1927

Dear Max Mohr

Your letter today – First and foremost, of course we were pleased and amused by your wife's drawings: but sad that she sees you always riding away, riding away! Anyhow now you've come back: not, alas, a Goldener Ritter, but also, not a fallen one.

Don't bother about *David*. Only my wife is sad.[1] But I knew too well that you would never get past the commercial *Wurm* with it. I know, alas, even better than you do, the limits of possibility in the commercial-artistic world. And the limits get narrower and narrower. Soon we shall either have to start arse-licking or be squeezed out. But *courage! mon ami! Le diable vit encore!*[2] We are still alive and kicking. – If the sale of *Aaron's Rod* comes off, well and good: but M.10,000 they will *never* pay. Aspettiamo! Let us wait and see!

The weather here is atrocious, first cold as hell, now all warm clammy steam. Naturally I cough – but not so bad. Our friends want us to go to Diableret – above Montreux somewhere. But I feel like a pig in a garden: I don't know which gate to go out of, and I'm not going to be driven out. So I'll sit here till I make up my mind.

It is Christmas – the peasants have stolen us a handsome pine-tree – it stands there in the corner of this Salotta, with all the twinkle-things and candles on it, and looks very nice. Pietro and Giulia get so thrilled, dressing it up, that I get thrilled too. On Saturday evening we shall have all the peasants in, and they love it. But it's a bear-garden, I tell you.

It would be nice to come to your valley, if only it weren't so far. I hate journeys. Yet I still want to go to New Mexico in the spring, to the ranch: and that is a long journey.

It was awfully good of you to take so much trouble for us in Berlin, and a

[1] Frieda had translated the play into German.
[2] '*courage! my friend! The devil is still alive!*' (cf. *Letters*, iii. 305 and n. 1).

shame you are disappointed. Why did the *canaille* not take your comedy? Wasn't it swinish enough for them? Oh, if only they had but one arse, that I could give it a mighty kick!

Merry Christmas to you all three –   D. H. Lawrence

The contadina hasn't yet finished the Kittele for Eve[1] – it'll come for New Year I hope.

Your English is *very* expressive!

4241. To Nellie Morrison, [23? December 1927]
Text: TMSC NWU; Unpublished.

Villa Mirenda, Scandicci
[23? December 1927]

Dear Nellie Morrison

Just had your letter – many thanks. As to the paper, use whatever you like.[2]

Don't forget, if the task seems long and wearisome to you, or for any other reason you do not feel you can go on, let me know. I will try and get someone else to take it up.

Don't give yourself too much trouble, don't be too particular. If you make a mistake, just put xxx over it, and go ahead. We don't look for showy typescripts.

I shall be very grateful to you if you will help me in this business. At the same time, I should hate to put any burden on you. I am telling nobody you are doing it, so you need incur no sort of odium.

Let me know how you get on.

D. H. Lawrence

4242. To Giuseppe Orioli, [24 December 1927]
Text: MS UCLA; Unpublished.

Villa Mirenda, *Scandicci*
24 Dec.

Dear Pino

Many thanks for the bacon. I have, alas, already eaten it – and Frieda wouldn't have any, said it was *all* mine. It was very good, and made me think I was at the ranch.

I read *In the Beginning* with some little surprise and heartsinking. Never mind, so long as he sells it.

The photograph is for Carletto.

[1] The blouse was for Mohr's daughter, Eva.   [2] Cf. Letter 4236.

When will you come and see us then? The Huxleys are coming to lunch on Tuesday – but you'd rather come alone!

We've got such a big tree – and the peasant invasion is this evening. Come up, then! – Merry Christmas.

D. H. Lawrence

4243. To Margaret King, [28 December 1927]

Text: MS Forster; PC v. Assisi – Chiesa interiore di S. Francesco. S. Chiara – Particolare di un affresco; Postmark, Firenze 30 . XII 1927; Unpublished.

[Villa Mirenda, Scandicci, Florence]
28 Dec

So, Christmas over! We had quite a nice time – only 17 peasants to the tree, as it rained – but they were very happy and very nice. On Christmas Day the Huxleys motored us in to Florence, to friends – and we had another tree – but not so big and grand as ours, only finer. However, we ate turkey and pulled crackers, quite the regular thing. On Tuesday the Huxleys came out to us – and we had a plumpudding which our neighbours gave us. Great style.!

And so you are five bob risen! Good! We've got another German book for you.

DHL

4244. To John Clarke, 28 December 1927

Text: Lawrence–Gelder 171–2.

Florence
28 Dec. 1927.

Very many thanks for the pup – so you snipped him out all by yourself! Which is more than I'd know how to do. And such neat genteel handwriting! My dear Jack, I hope you're not getting too good to be true. We had quite a nice Christmas – seventeen peasants in to the tree, all very happy singing. Christmas day we were in Florence – the Huxleys motored us in to friends in a villa there – and we had another tree. Your mother hasn't written at all but I suppose she had my letter. What did you do with your ten bob?

4245. To Baroness Anna von Richthofen, [28 December 1927]

Text: MS UCB; Frieda Lawrence 234.

Villa Mirenda.
Mittwoch.

Meine liebe Schwiegermutter

So, alles ist beinah wieder normal! Der Baum steht noch da – wir müssen es

wieder anzünden, wenn die Wilkses von Rom heimkehren – vielleicht
Montag. Und wir haben noch die Resten vom Plum-pudding von gestern.
Sonst, sage ich, sind wir beinah wieder normal. Die Frieda auch hat ihre
Heiligtum für den Moment vergessen. Der Bub flog weg vom Hospital –
zuhaus – sein Padrone hat ihn wieder da gebracht, und ihm einen Rad
versprochen. So! Der Operation is gethan – gut: die Frieda geht morgen
wieder zum Besuch. Aber diesmal ist sie nicht mehr die eine und einzige
Heiligin – Der Padrone hat dem Dino einen Rad versprochen. Und der
Dante, älterer Bruder, sagt: Wenn mir jemand einen Rad verspricht, geh' ich
auch und lass mich operiert werden. – Aber, armer Kerl, er hat keine Ernia.

Das Wetter ist ein Sau-wetter – Regen und wenig Sonne. Abend ist die
beste Zeit, mit Feuer und Lampe und Stille. Die Frieda macht sich eine
Schürze, sehr bunt, alle Rosen und Vögeln.

Der Schlips hat grossen Erfolg. Ich habe es Weihnachttag in Florenz
getragen, sehr schön. Es ist viel schöner *an* wie auf. Der Badischer Kalender
liegt treu da, uns durch noch ein anderes Jahr zu bringen, mit allen Bildern.
Das letztes Blatt vom Alten hängt über dem Klavier – Schwarzweiss im
Schwarzwald.

Oh, liebe Schwiegermutter, lebe wohl noch ein Jahr, und habe ein lustiges,
glückliches 1928.

Grüsse der Else – ich schreibe ihr.

dein   DHL

Das Buch von Friedel ist so hübsch, wirklich hübsch.

[Wednesday

My dear Schwiegermutter

So, everything is almost back to normal! The tree is still standing there – we
must light the candles again when the Wilkses come home from Rome –
perhaps on Monday. And we still have the remains of the plum-pudding from
yesterday. Otherwise, I say, we are almost back to normal. Frieda has also
forgotten her saintliness for the moment. The boy flew out of hospital – home
– his padrone has taken him back again and promised him a bicycle. So! The
operation is done – good: Frieda goes to visit him again tomorrow. But this
time she is no longer the one-and-only saint – the padrone has promised Dino
a bicycle. And Dante, the elder brother, says: If someone promises me a
bicycle, I'll go too and be operated on. – But, poor chap, he hasn't a hernia.

The weather is dreadful – rain and little sun. Evening is the best time, with
fire and lamp and stillness. Frieda is making herself an apron, very gay, all
roses and birds.

The tie is a great success. I wore it on Christmas day in Florence, very nice.
It is much nicer *on* than off. The Baden calendar is lying faithfully there, to get

us through yet another year, with all its pictures. The last page of the old one hangs over the piano – black and white in the Black Forest.

Oh, dear Schwiegermutter, take care of yourself for another year, and have a jolly, happy 1928.

Greetings to Else – I'm writing to her.

your   DHL

The book from Friedel is so pretty, really pretty.]

4246. To Nellie Morrison, 28 December 1927
Text: TMSC NWU; Unpublished.

Villa Mirenda, Scandicci.
28th Dec 1927.

Dear Nellie Morrison

How is the labour of love? Not a labour of Hercules, I do hope. Anyhow don't hesitate to chuck it up when you've had enough. I sometimes have qualms. Anyway let me know.

We've still got our Christmas tree, quite handsome. I mean the tree itself, Nature's product. We had seventeen peasants on Christmas Eve, and they were very nice. But now, thank goodness, things are returning to the normal.

Come up one fine day if ever there'll be such a thing. I'll ask Orioli's boy to wait for a note. Frieda is doing her hospital visit this afternoon – I mean tomorrow, Thursday. Seems to me I'm going to sleep.

All the good wishes for the New Year from us both.

D. H. Lawrence

4247. To Nancy Pearn, [28 December 1927]
Text: MS Lazarus; Unpublished.

[Frieda Lawrence begins]

Villa Mirenda
28. XII 27

Dear Miss Pearn,

Your little cloth gave us *both* so much pleasure, you know Lawrence (rare bird among men in that,) *sees* such things, while I have a passion for *very* nice little clothes, can rarely indulge in that passion, and this is such a gay one – Where was it made do you think? Ireland or Sweden or where? Iulia told me of your visit, you seem to have had nothing but eggs to eat, you see I cook mostly, sometimes Lawrence – all she ever does is breakfast – I was sad you did'nt have really decent meals – The Mirenda looks so different now, the floors covered with thick, pale rush matting and fires –

We had the loveliest Xmas tree (I am sad to say stolen by Pietro), it's a huge cypress and Pietro and Iulia helped 'making it fine' and just jumped with bliss! Then we had *all* the peasants in, they sang and where certainly neither 'blasé' nor shy – Sunday we spent with friends and the Huxleys in Florence – The 'Wilkes' are in Rome for a fortnight – Lawrence is *much* better, but still it's always an anxiety and a strain, I think this peace and quiet is very good for him, our life has certainly nothing of the modern rush about it! One nice lunch we had, Michael Arlen, Douglas and a few others and nobody said anything nasty about any body else – I call that a triumph for once! I hope you are well and not working too hard –

Many, many good wishes for the new year – I still sleep in the hard hole of the 'matrimonio'!

Yours ever   Frieda Lawrence

[Lawrence begins]
Dear Nancy Pearn

Such a pretty little Sachet! but charming! I feel like creeping inside it myself and pretending I'm a clean napkin instead of a sorry rag. It's horrid weather, damp, and I cough, but not so bad.

I hope you had a jolly Christmas – and 1928 must be a real good warm-hearted year for you. You see if it wont be!

D. H. Lawrence

4248. To Alfred Knopf, 1 January 1928
Text: MS BraU; Unpublished.

Villa Mirenda, Scandicci, Florence
1 Jan. 1928

Dear Knopf

Thanks for your letter. As for the Etruscan Sketches – as you know, they are only one-half done – the other half would need a jaunt through middle Italy here – it's very cold – I cough – hotels are unwarmed in out-of-the-way places: so you see the chances. If I can get the MS in apple-pie order by end of March, well and good. If I cant – there you are, and there am I.

As for the novel, I am getting it typed: primo passo![1] It's improper – I intend it to be: essentially, of course, it *isn't*. But there I shall have to appeal to Mrs Knopf. I am thinking I may publish a private edition here in Florence – 700 or even 1000 copies at ten dollars: and so make myself a bit of money, which I badly need, and also bring out the novel uncastrated, which I fully intend. But I'd send you – or rather Mrs Knopf, she'll have more sympathy –

---

[1] 'the first step!'

a copy of MS or proofs – and if you like we can cut out the necessary amount of offence to let the book go through the ordinary channels. Let me know about this. I thought of changing the title to 'Tenderness.'

It isn't a long novel – about 80,000 I suppose: scene English Midlands.

But unless I publish it in some way *as it stands*, I'll never publish it at all. Of that also I'm decided.

I wrote that Secker was to wait for you before fixing date of publication for the short stories – *The Woman Who Rode Away*, and for everything else in future.[1]

I hope I'll be well enough and rich enough to come to America in April. I want to go to New Mexico again.

All good wishes to you and to Mrs Knopf for the New Year.

Sincerely   D. H. Lawrence

4249. To Nancy Pearn, 5 January 1928
Text: MS UT; Unpublished.

Villa Mirenda
5 Jan. 1928

Dear Miss Pearn

Will you type this out and give it to Jonathan Cape – he asked me for it – 6 guineas – and anything American extra.[2]

Bad weather – snow – then slush – now warmish fog. Sporca miseria!

DHL

4250. To Hon. Dorothy Brett, [6 January 1928]
Text: MS UCin; Postmark, Scandicci 6[. . .]; Huxley 696–7.

Villa Mirenda. *Scandicci*. Florence.
6 Jan. 1927

Dear Brett

So you are definitely down at Mabeltown, and the ranch is really shut up? I think it's good for you to have the change. You can't really turn into a hermit

---

[1] DHL's instructions have not been traced.

[2] Rowena Killick acknowledged this letter on 12 January 1928 (TMSC UT); she identified the MS to be typed as DHL's Introduction to Cape's edn of *The Mother* (*La Madre*) by the Sardinian writer Grazia Cosima Deledda (1876–1936) whom DHL found 'very interesting' in 1919 (*Letters*, iii. 338) and whose house he believed he found in Sardinia (*Sea and Sardinia*, 1921, p. 242). *The Mother*, trans. Mary G. Steegmann, was published in April 1928 (Roberts B25).

up there. And I guess you've got snow now. It even snowed here this week, but only lasted a day. So probably you are fairly deep in.

That's a bore about the Ruffian. She's a nasty piece of goods. But don't let Mabel scare you about counter-charges and all that. Mabel likes to make one's blood run cold, anyhow chill, now and then.

There's not much change here. Christmas came and went without much disturbance. We have a good big Christmas tree, ten feet or more, that Pietro stole in the wood; and on Christmas Eve we had seventeen peasants in. They sang, and were very nice. On Christmas day, Maria and Aldous motored us in to Florence to a friend's villa. – They have gone now to Switzerland, to the snow, and they want us to join them. I'm waiting to hear from them, what it's really like, and how dear it is. We *may* try it for a month.

Anyhow it is fully decided to leave this place for good in March or April. I don't want to keep it on. If my broncs will stand it, I really want to come to the ranch in April. But Frieda doesn't want to come. Still, we'll see! My cough is still a nuisance, and the weather is the devil: icy wind, then snow, then slush, then warmish fog, then feeble rain, then damp warmish days with weak wet sun: a bore. I just stay in bed a good deal. I feel that *somewhere* I'm really better and stronger. But my cough goes raking on. – It is, as Mabel says, partly a change of life one has to undergo.

I have been re-writing my novel, for the third time. It's done, all but the last chapter. I think I shall re-christen it 'Tenderness'. And I really think I shall try to publish it privately here, at ten dollars a copy. I might make a thousand pounds, with luck, and that would bring us to the ranch nicely. If only the fates and the gods will be with us this year, instead of all the time against, as they were last year. If only one were tough, as some people are tough!

I can see you make your life a good deal with the horses. I don't wonder. They're better – than people.

Well I do hope you'll have a good year, and that we shall come to the ranch and have good times. One pines for a bit of a real good time; if only things will fit.

                                                                                                   DHL

4251. To Ada Clarke, 6 January 1928
Text: MS Clarke; cited in Lawrence–Gelder 172–3.

                                                        Villa Mirenda. *Scandicci.* Florence.
                                                                                   6 January 1928
My dear Sister

I haven't heard from you all Christmas – only had just the little calender from Jack. Perhaps you wrote and it didn't come. Anyhow I hope you had my letter before christmas, with the little cheque for the children:[1] I haven't heard since before I sent it. – I hope everybody is all right. It's been pretty tough weather, to all accounts. Even here we had snow this week – then slush – then warmish fog – now a moderately decent day again. But the changes are trying, and don't improve my cough.

We had quite a nice time. The peasants came in on Christmas Eve – seventeen of them. We have a lovely big pine-tree that Pietro stole in the wood, ten feet or more tall: but the bits of Christmas things look very small on it. It is dense and green, and when the candles are lit, suggests a forest: very nice. The peasants sang to us, and were happy. On Christmas Day the Huxleys fetched us in to Florence to a friend's villa – another Christmas tree – and a good fat turkey. It was very pleasant. They came out here on the Tuesday to a good big fowl and a plum-pudding[2] which our neighbours the Wilkinsons gave us.

The Huxleys have gone to Switzerland, up to the snow, and they very much want us to go. If I thought it would really do me good, I would. Snow is marvellous for lungs, but bad for bronchials, and my chief trouble is my miserable bronchials. I shall wait a while still, and see.

I think we shall definitely give up this place in spring: it's not a good climate, always changing. Perhaps we may go to the ranch, just for the summer, if I can afford it: and try to sell it. I know we shall never *live* there. Then really I'd try Devonshire or somewhere for a time, and if it suits me, really make a home there. I feel I'd like a permanent place somewhere. One gets older – and my health really has been a nuisance. It would be better to settle down, if one could but find a place.

I think of Gertie in all the changes of weather – do hope she stands them.

Anyhow the year has turned. 1927 was a bad one, let's hope this will be better for us all. How are the pits working?[3]

Did you get the books I sent? with *The Peep-Show*, by Walter Wilkinson, our neighbour's brother?[4]

Write and let me know that things are all right.

                                                        Love!   DHL

---

[1] See Letter 4225.   [2] MS reads 'plum-puddings'.

[3] The coal industry was very depressed. Nottinghamshire miners were being laid off indefinitely, according to *The Times*, 6 December 1927; c. 600 men were suspended at Hucknall colliery on 18 January 1928 (*Times*, 20 January 1928); and mine-owners were proposing to reduce production in order to maintain prices.

[4] DHL probably sent his review copy of *The Peep Show* (cf. Letter 4017).

4252. To Spencer Curtis Brown, 6 January 1928
Text: MS UT; Unpublished.

Villa Mirenda. *Scandicci*. Florence
6 Jan. 1928

Dear Mr Brown[1]

I doubt if I could face the unending squalor of Viani's *Parigi*.[2] It would depress me so, I should never get through with it. Ask Scott Moncrieff to do it:[3] I believe he's in Rome now, but if you address him c/o G. Orioli, 6 Lungarno Corsini, Florence, that will find him. And he would do it well. – The book isn't quite so thrilling as the *Times* man found it. I expect he was chiefly thrilled at finding himself clever enough to read slangy Italian. The humour is a little monotonous: especially to anybody used to the Italians. And a good deal of the vogue the book had in Italy was due to its anti-French attitude. 'Mais oui! Mais oui! Mais oui! – like so many guinea-pigs!'

What a pity we are too far away to come to your wedding, to which we have received an invitation card! But all good wishes to you, and may it be a jolly marriage!

Yours Sincerely   D.H. Lawrence

I am sending the book back to you.

4253. To Rolf Gardiner, 7 January 1928
Text: MS Lazarus; Huxley 697–9.

Villa Mirenda. *Scandicci*, Florence
7 Jan. 1928

Dear Rolf Gardiner

Your long letter today – I'll answer it at once, while it's in my mind.

I had the Northumbrian report, and was interested.[4] The German Bünde has the sound of a real thing – but the English side seems not to amount to much. It's very difficult to do anything with the English: they have so little

---

[1] Spencer Curtis Brown (1882–1936), son of DHL's agent; see p. 262 n. 2.

[2] Lorenzo Viani, *Parigi* (Milan, 1925). DHL's attention must have been drawn to the review in *The Times Literary Supplement*, 18 March 1926, p. 212, in which the book was described as 'remarkable and unusual': 'in Italy . . . its vigour and freshness have been spontaneously recognized'. The reviewer warned that Viani wrote in 'local, not classical Tuscan' and that 'an Englishman who flatters himself on his knowledge of Italian' will often need a dictionary but even this will fail him because Viani's Italian is non-standard. In the vivid account of Viani's life in Paris there are censorious passages on the French with particular reference to galleries and Impressionist artists.   [3] See p. 214 n. 5.

[4] In September–October 1927 Gardiner organised a large-scale expedition in Northumbria for the German Bünde; it proved to be 'a turning-point' in the Bünde's history (Nehls, iii. 674 n. 149).

'togetherness,' or power of togetherness: like grains of sand that will only fuse
if lightning hits it. They will fool about and be bossed about for a time with a
man like Hargrave – but there's nothing in it.[1] Think of all the other
mountebanking cliques that exist – the Fontainebleau group and all the rest.[2]
The Germans take their shirts off and work in the hay: they are still physical:
the English are so wofully disembodied. God knows what's to do with them. I
sometimes think they are too sophisticatedly civilised to have any future at all.
– And you too, if you'll let me say it, are just a bit disembodied too: reaching
for earth rather than on it. You strive too much. I agree with you entirely: one
must be conscious. And also, one must have a centre of gravity, on which one
comes to rest. That is what you want. You never quite come to rest within
yourself. Patience, you are young. But perhaps you should spend part of your
time forgetting other people and not caring about them. Don't forget, you are
striving with yourself so hard, you hit other people in the eye fighting your
own phantasm. And they resent it. Your time is too mapped out. You need to
find a centre, a focal point within yourself, of real at-one-ness. At present you
strive and strain and force things a bit, and don't find it. Pazienza! Give
yourself time. Anything worth having is *growth*: and to have growth, one must
be able to let be.

It seems to me a pity you couldn't have made your farm a sort of little shrine
or hearth where you kept the central fire of your effort alive:[3] not all this hard
work business: not this effort. You ought to have a few, very few, who *are*
conscious and willing to be conscious, and who would add together their little
flames of consciousness to make a permanent core. That would make a holy
centre: whole, heal, hale. Even the German Bünde, I am afraid, will drift into
nationalistic, and ultimately, *fighting* bodies: a new, and necessary form of
militarism. It may be the right way for them. But not for the English. The
English are over-tender. They must have kindled again their religious sense of
atoneness. And for that you must have a silent, central flame, a flame of
Consciousness and of warmth which radiates out bit by bit. Keep the core
sound, and the rest will look after itself. What we need is reconciliation and
atoneing. I utterly agree with your song, dance and labour: but the core of
atoneing in the *few* must be there, if your song, dance and labour are to have a

[1] John Gordon Hargrave (1894–), founder in 1920 of 'Kibbo Kift, the Woodcraft Kindred',
and self-styled 'White Fox'. He provided Gardiner with a model of leadership and training
though Gardiner broke with him before Hargrave developed more obviously Fascist tenden-
cies (cf. *Letters*, v. 67 n. 1). In November 1927 Hargrave published his apologia: *The Confession
of the Kibbo Kift: A Declaration and General Exposition of the Work of the Kindred*. See Nehls,
iii. 77–80.   [2] Cf. Letter 4021 and p. 57 n. 4.
[3] Gore Farm which became the Springhead Estate, Fontmell Magna, near Shaftesbury; see
Nehls, iii. 674 n. 147.

real source. If it is possible. – The German youth is almost ready to fuse into a new sort of fighting unity, it seems to me: us against the world. But the English are older, and weary even of victory.

Well, enough of this! I'll let you know what I think of the *Kibbo Kift* book when it comes.

And do come and see us. I should like very much to talk to you: seriously, if you wish it, unseriously if you don't. I'm sorry there's nowhere really in this flat to put you up: it's not very comfortable: but I'm giving it up finally in April: done with it. – But you can come out by tram from Florence. And if you call at Pino Orioli's little bookshop, 6 Lungarno Corsini, he'll always give you any information – in English – about getting here or anything else. He's a friend of ours, and will be of yours.

If I don't go to the ranch, I shall try to go to Frankfurt this summer.[1] I believe my bronchials are beginning to behave better. I should very much like to meet Becker and Goetz, and to be at the camp.[2] But we can talk about it. – I have a sister-in-law and husband – bank-manager, but nice – in Schöneberg – Berlin.[3] My wife would like to see the real German youth too. We always go to Baden and Heidelberg: and there's a bit too much of the old stink there.

Let me know if you really think of coming here. The Huxleys – Aldous and wife – want us to join them in the snow in Switzerland. We *might* – just possible: but probably not. I want to keep my limited resources – financially this time – for the summer, to be able to move about then.

Well, don't be too affairé:[4] and don't expect too much of the world.

D. H. Lawrence

4254. To Nellie Morrison, 8 January 1928
Text: TMSC NWU; Moore 1032–3.

Villa Mirenda, Scandicci.
Sunday, 8th Jan. 1928

Dear Nelly Morrison,

I wasn't surprised when I got your letter, had rather expected it before. I felt, almost as soon as I'd given you the MS. that I had made a mistake. It's my fault entirely, not yours: to me the blame, not you.

It was very kind of you to have done so much, to have gone on, feeling as you say you did about it, just because of your friendship for me.

[1] DHL probably had in mind a visit to the Musikheim established by Gardiner at Frankfurt-on-Oder as 'a centre of social therapy through music, art and husbandry' (Nehls, iii. 666).
[2] Carl Heinrich Becker (1876–1933), sometime Prussian Secretary of State for Education; George Götsch (1895–1956), a close associate of Gardiner's, became director of the Musikheim; see W. J. Keith, *DHL Review*, vii (Summer 1974), p. 138 n. 6.
[3] Johanna and Emil Krug. [4] 'busy, restive'.

And remember, although you are on the side of the angels and the vast majority, I consider mine is the truly moral and religious position. You suggest I have pandered to the pornographic taste: I think not. To the Puritan all things are impure, to quote an Americanism.[1] Not that you are a Puritan: nor am I impure.

I'll call shortly and relieve you of the MS.. What a mercy you haven't seen the rest! I finished it today.

Every man his own taste: every woman her own distaste. But don't try to ride a moral horse: it could be nothing but a sorry ass.

All the same I am awfully grateful to you for having done as much as you did, and am really sorry I asked you to do something so distasteful to you. You must forgive me for that.

Meanwhile, for heavens sake, don't do any more. Pack the thing up for me when I call, I hope Tuesday or Wednesday. Then let us forget the whole show, stand as we did before, and leave the recording angel to write the last word.

DHL

4255. To Catherine Carswell, 10 January 1928
Text: MS YU: Carswell 270–1.

Villa Mirenda, *Scandicci*, Florence
10 Jan 1928

My dear Catherine

I wonder where you are – if in the Harzgebirge.[2]

I want a little help. I wrote a novel last winter, and re-wrote it for the 3rd time this – and it's very *verbally* improper – the last word, in all its meanings! – but very truly moral. A woman in Florence said she'd type it – and she's done 5 chapters – now turned me down.[3] Says she can't go any further, too indecent. Dirty bitch! But will you find me some decent person who'll type it for me at the usual rates? You'd do it, I know, if you were a person of leisure. But you're *not*. So turn over in your mind some decent being, male or female, whom I could trust not to let me down in any way, and who'd do the thing for me for the proper pay.[4] And write me soon. But not here. I think we shall go,

---

[1] Cf. Titus i. 15: 'To the pure all things are pure'. The parody of this original also appears in 'Cerveteri', *Etruscan Places* (1932).   [2] I.e. the Harz mountains in eastern Germany.

[3] See the preceding letter.

[4] Catherine Carswell recalled later: 'Though much wishing to do it I had been unable to undertake the typing of *Lady Chatterley* myself for Lawrence. But I . . . arranged to have it done for him' (Carswell 272). At least four typists, including Carswell herself, shared the work; one of them was probably her friend Ivy Turner Elstob (1898–1942).

either on Sat. or Monday, to Switzerland, to the snow. It's so damp here. You might send me a line c/o Aldous Huxley, Chalet des Aroles. *Diablerets.* (Vaud) Suisse. We intend to join them there and take a little flat they have in view: stay perhaps till end of February. I want really to try and get myself better – cough still troublesome – and I want to lay hold of life again properly. Have been down and out this last six months.

Then I think I shall publish my novel privately here in Florence, in March–April – 1000 copies, 2 gns. each: and so, D. V., earn myself a thousand pounds, which I can do very well with – rather low water. I'll call it 'Tenderness' – the novel.

But please don't talk about it to anybody – I don't want a scandal advertisement.

Hope the boy is real well – and you and Don. How is the Burns book.

I do hope I'm not bothering you. But I feel I must get another blow in at the lily-livered host. One's got to fight.

tante cose!   DHL

I *might* of course find a typist somebody in Diablerets.

Of course Curtis Brown, and everybody, doesn't want me to publish unexpurgated private edition – harm my reputation – Let it.

4256. To Nellie Morrison, [c. 11 January 1928]
Text: TMSC NWU; Unpublished.

Villa Mirenda, Scandicci
[c. 11 January 1928]

Dear Nelly Morrison

Will you please give the MS. to Orioli's boy who will wait for it? We are busy getting ready to go to Switzerland up to the snow for a month or so – leave in a day or two. I think it will do me good. Do come and see us when we get back. I'll let you know.

Very many thanks really for what you have done. As you won't tell me what I owe you, I will count the words myself, and send you the soldi. Don't refuse them, or you will offend me properly!

Ever   D. H. Lawrence

4257. To Else Jaffe, 11 January 1928
Text: MS Jeffrey; Unpublished.

Villa Mirenda, *Scandicci*, Firenze.
11 Jany 1928

Dear Else

It was damp and horrid so long here, that we have decided to go up to the snow in Switzerland – join the Huxleys at Diablerets, over Lac Leman – about

4,000 ft. – Meter 1300. I think we shall leave next Monday – and I'll send you an address from there. – Today is a lovely warm day – but it won't last.

I had the rose-leaf. Was I to eat it, because I'm a Golden Ass?[1] Plenty of ass, but not much gold!

Have the Kippenbergs made any decision about the next book? I think the tiresome Miss Watson has left from Curtis Browns.[2] – Tauchnitz is doing *England My England*.[3] – I have done my most improper and phallic novel again – now call it 'Tenderness'. I think I shall publish it privately here in Florence when we get back from Switzerland – in March. – We shall give up this house for good in April – enough of Italy!

I am a bit scared of the snow – but I hope it will do me good. Anyhow we ought to be back here during March and April. Will write from Diablerets.

Ever DHL

4258. To Rolf Gardiner, [11 January 1928]

Text: MS Lazarus; PC v. Assisi – Chiesa superiore di S. Francesco. S. Francesco fa scaturire l'acqua da una rupe (Giotto); Postmark, Scandicci 12.1.28; Unpublished.

Villa Mirenda
11 Jany.

Been such damp weather, we have decided to leave next Monday for Diablerets, (Vaud) Suisse to join the Huxleys in the snow – about 4000 ft. If you are passing, come there – c/o Aldous Huxley – Chalet des Aroles – till I send my own address.

D. H. Lawrence

4259. To Emily King, 11 January 1928

Text: MS Lazarus; Unpublished.

Villa Mirenda, *Scandicci*, Florence
11 Jan 1928

My dear Pamela

Your letter yesterday – the tea hasn't come – and if you didn't register it, I'm afraid it won't. They'll just confiscate it: as it is forbidden to send any

---

[1] In *The Golden Ass* (trans. William Adlington), III. xvii, Apuleius is told: 'if thou couldst get a Rose and eat it, thou shouldst be delivered from the shape of an Asse'; in the penultimate chapter he devours a garland of roses and is 'transformed from an asse to [his] humane shape'.

[2] DHL was wrongly informed: in 1928 Jean Watson was manager of the Foreign Department of Curtis Brown's London office; she later married Spencer Curtis Brown.

[3] *England, My England* was published by Tauchnitz on 28 April 1928; see William B. Todd and Ann Bowden, *Tauchnitz International Editions in English* (New York, 1988), No. 4825.

dutiable article in a letter. They just stole the letter Ada sent, with a hanky and tie. It's no good trying to evade them, they are brutes.

We have settled down after Christmas – and it's been such beastly weather, we have decided to go to Switzerland, up to the snow. We shall leave next Monday, I think – get to Diablerets, high over Lake Geneva, on Tuesday evening. I'll send you the address. – Of course, because we have decided to go, the weather has turned sunny and hot as March. But I doubt it won't last. The Huxleys are at Diablerets, and are getting a little flat for us.

Anyhow I'm not very fond of Italy nowadays. We shall give up this house for good, end of April, and perhaps look for a little place in Devonshire. But I want to try first what the mountains will do for me: 4,000 feet, they say, is just the right altitude.

Hope you're all feeling well. This is only a short letter.

Love. DHL

4260. To Ada Clarke, [11 January 1928]
Text: MS Clarke; PC v. Firenze – Madonna del S. Girolamo – Barrocci; Postmark, [Scandic]ci [. . .]; Lawrence–Gelder 177.

[Villa Mirenda, Scandicci, Florence]
Wed.

Had your letter – afraid the hanky has gone into an Italian pocket, and tie round an Italian neck. Now Emily sent $\frac{1}{4}$ tea by letter – it also does not arrive – no good! – It has been such damp weather, we have decided to go to Diablerets to join the Huxleys – in the snow, about 4000 ft. over Lake Geneva, Switzerland. We leave next Monday. I'll write from there and send an address. Everybody says its is the best thing for me, so one can but try. I dread it a bit. Hope you're all well.

Love! DHL

4261. To Hon. Dorothy Brett, [11 January 1928]
Text: MS UCin; PC v. Annunziazione, Beato Angelico; Postmark, Scand[icci] 12. 1. 28; Irvine, Brett 80.

Villa Mirenda.
11 Jany

Been such damp weather, we are going to Diablerets, Switzerland to join the Huxleys – till about beginning of March – I want to try the altitude, 4000 ft – and the snow, to see how I get on with them. – Your Christmas parcel hasn't come – we never sent out a thing – so tiresome the post. – We leave next Monday – dread the cold, but have hopes of the tonicky air and sun. Hope it's good weather at Taos. Remember me to everybody.

DHL

4262. To Earl and Achsah Brewster, 11 January 1928
Text: MS UT; Brewster 159.

Villa Mirenda. Scandicci, Firenze
11 Jany 1928

Dear Earl and Achsah

Very nice photographs of the family – look so nice and southern.

It was damp and horrid so long, we decided to join the Huxleys up in the snow in Switzerland at Diablerets, over Lake Geneva. I suppose we leave here Monday. I dread it a bit – but everyone says it is so good for me. And I *would* like to get myself solider this year.

I don't know quite what we'll do afterwards – but I shall give up this house in April – finally – and leave Italy – perhaps go to the ranch; if my bronchials will stand it: otherwise stay a time in Germany and England, and see.

I would really rather have come south – but everybody says the mountains, the mountains. So we'll try – 4000 feet.

I'll write and send address as soon as we get there.

tante cose!   DHL

4263. To Martin Secker, 11 January 1928
Text: MS UInd: Postmark, Scandicci 12.1.28; Secker 97–8.

Villa Mirenda, *Scandicci*, Firenze
11 Jany. 1928

Dear Secker

Been very damp bad weather here, and my health far from satisfactory – so we have decided to join the Huxleys up in Diablerets over Lake Geneva in the snow for a month or so. We intend to leave Monday. I'll send the address: or c/o Aldous Huxley, Chalet des Aroles, Diablerets (Vaud) will do. – Switzerland. – I suppose you'll be sending those proofs soon.[1]

Thanks for the poetry books. I've been typing out the early ones. I have been thinking it would be best to do the rhyming poems in one vol. I've typed out *Love Poems and Others*, and *Amores*, nearly, then with *New Poems* and *Bay*, that'll make a fairly big book. I've done a good bit of revising – should be a good book too. You might make *Collected Poems of D.H.L*, two vols. Vol. I. Lyrical Poems. Vol. II. Free-Verse Poems. Or put them all together if you like – but seems to me a bit clumsy. Anyhow I will let you have the complete MS. of the Lyrical Poems – that is, all the four vols. mentioned – the first four – in about a month's time, so you could approach Duckworth if you like.[2]

I also think I may bring out a private edition of my novel – now called

---

[1] Of *The Woman Who Rode Away* volume.   [2] See Letter 4157.

'Tenderness', twice re-written – here in Florence in spring – 1000 copies, 2 gns each – 500 for England, 500 for America. It's too improper to do publicly. But I'll send you a more-or-less expurgated typescript as soon as I can get it ready – and you can see what you think of it. I haven't yet got it typed.

We shall give up this house in April – perhaps go to the ranch. Remains to be seen how my bronchials go.

Remember me to Rina – hope you are better.

D. H. Lawrence

4264. To Max Mohr, [11 January 1928]

Text: MS HMohr; PC v. San Giorgio, Beato Angelico; Postmark, Scandicci 12 1 28; Unpublished.

Villa Mirenda.

11 Januar

Sie haben nicht wieder geschrieben! Und es ist hier so feuchtes Wetter gewesen, wir gehen nächsten Montag in die Schweiz, nach Diablerets, über den Genfer See – 1300 Meter. Hoffentlich wird es mir gut thun. Ich schreibe von dort – und schicke die Adresse – und vielleicht werden Sie kommen. Hat die Eva das Kittele?

viele Grüsse.   D. H. Lawrence

[11 January

Again you've not written! And the weather's been so damp here, next Monday we go to Switzerland, to Diablerets, above Lake Geneva – 1300 meters up. I hope it will do me good. I'll write from there – and send the address – and perhaps you will come. Has Eva got the blouse?

many greetings.   D. H. Lawrence]

4265. To Catherine Carswell, [13 January 1928]

Text: MS YU; PC v. Boulevard Thiers et Grand Hôtel; Postmark, Scan[dicci] 14.1.28; cited in Carswell 271.

Villa Mirenda.

Friday

Your cards today – sounds so nice: wish we'd come.[1] We were leaving for Switzerland on Monday – but suddenly I'm in bed with flu – misery – not bad, I hope – I still think we'll get away next week. I wrote you to London – but c/o Constable,[2] as I'd lost your address – and my memory, for I always

---

[1] Catherine Carswell was staying at Osteröde about 20 miles n.e. of Göttingen.
[2] DHL had directed Letter 4255 to Constable & Co. who published Donald Carswell's *Brother Scots*.

remembered it. Write to me c/o Aldous Huxley, when you get my letter – as I don't know your address. – Seems to me I always decide to go away a bit too late – or the flu gets me a bit too soon. It's my unhappy bronchials that lacerate so easily.

DHL[1]

4266. To Nancy Pearn, [14 January 1928]
Text: MS UT; Unpublished.

Villa Mirenda, *Scandicci*, Florence
14 July 1928[2]

Dear Miss Pearn

You will remember I sent a lot of photographs with the Etruscan Essays – they are all in America – get them from Mrs McCord, as *Travel* was returning them all, plus a few others – and *Travel* will have done with most of them by now, since their 3rd issue is out, they have only one number to appear, next month.[3]

So get them to send you *all* the photographs from New York – and do please keep them carefully, for if I finish the book.

We were off to Switzerland to the snow next Monday – but now I'm in bed with flu again – so sick of it – but it seems not very bad – So we shall go to Switzerland as soon as possible: I hope by next Wednesday or Thursday. Will send address.

Ever   D. H. Lawrence

all the best Tarquinia photographs are there.

4267. To Charles Wilson, 15 January 1928
Text: MS Martin; John Martin, *Consciousness* (Pegacycle Lady Press, 1974), p. [9].

Villa Mirenda. Scandicci. Florence
15 Jany 1928

Dear Mr Wilson

Many thanks for the calendar, which hangs on the wall here to keep me in mind of you and the men.

After hesitating rather a long while, I send the message – a bit shyly, for I'm no message-maker, really. Yet my god, it's time men woke up to themselves, and ceased to go on in industrial somnambulism as they have done. We only live once: and during that once, *never to live at all* – why it's monstrous!

[1] On the verso of the postcard DHL identified 'our rooms' on the picture of the Grand Hotel.
[2] DHL's error ('July' instead of 'January') was noticed in Curtis Brown's office and corrected in an unknown hand.
[3] Cf. p. 48 n. 1.

One can't change the world in a minute. But if one has a satisfactory system of values inside oneself, and something of an aim in one's life, it's a great deal.

The miners are all right. It's the industrial system which is wrong. And it's up to the miners to change it. Not by hating capitalism or anything else: but by just pulling the feathers out of the money bird, and determining, sooner or later, to have something quite different: neither capitalism nor bolshevism, but men. It wouldn't be very difficult to settle the material part of the problem, once enough sensible men tackled it.

And meanwhile we can all go ahead with the deepening and widening consciousness, which is the great job for each of us.

Sincerely!   D. H. Lawrence

4268. To Rolf Gardiner, [16 January 1928]
Text: MS Lazarus; Huxley 699–700.

Villa Mirenda, *Scandicci*, Firenze
Monday

Dear Rolf Gardiner

I read the *Kibbo Kift* book with a good deal of interest.[1] – Of course it won't work: not quite flesh and blood. The ideas are sound, but flesh and blood won't take 'em, till a great deal of flesh and blood have been destroyed. Of course the birthright credit too is sound enough – but to nationalise capital is a good deal harder than to nationalise industries. The man alternates between idealism pure and simple, and a sort of mummery, and then a compromise with practicality. What he wants is all right – I agree with him on the whole, and respect him as a straightforward fighter. But he *knows* there's no hope, his way – en masse. And therefore, underneath, he's full of hate. He's ambitious: and his ambition isn't practical: so he's full of hate, underneath. He's overweening, and he's cold. But for all that, on the whole he's *right*, and I respect him for it. I respect his courage and aloneness. If it weren't for his ambition and his lack of warmth, I'd go and kibbo kift along with him. But he'll get no further than holiday camping and mummery. Tho' even that will have *some* effect. All luck to him. – But by wanting to rope in *all* mankind it shows he wants to have his cake and eat it. Mankind is largely bad, just now especially – and one must hate the bad, and try to keep what bit of warmth alive one can, among the few decent. But even that's a forlorn hope.

But I wouldn't write a criticism in a paper against him. Rather praise him.

[1] See p. 258 n. 1. 'Kibbo Kift' aimed to establish reservations for camp training and Naturecraft, and thus to encourage self-reliance and the learning of handicrafts; movements towards international peace, 'Social Credit' and a World Council were supported; see Nehls, iii. 78.

Because his reaction is [. . .] on the whole sound. Only it is too egoistic, like all
modern things – even you are the same – and Goetz too, probably. The lack of
the spark of warmth that alone can kindle a little fire today. – Hargrave would
do all right for a *fight*.

I wonder how much following he has – Hargrave? I should say small, and
insignificant. There is a note of failure and rancour underneath. He doesn't
forgive you for leaving him. Still, he's a man. But not a leader for today. The
leader today needs tenderness as well as toughness: I mean a constructive
leader: Otherwise fight!

Of course I got a cold which prevents our leaving for Switzerland today.
But I hope we shall get off on Wed. or Thursday – be in Diablerets anyhow on
Saturday.

Yrs   D. H. Lawrence

4269. To Nellie Morrison, [16 January 1928]
Text: TMSC NWU; Moore 1035.

Villa Mirenda, Scandicci
Monday

Dear Nelly Morrison

We hoped to get away on Saturday, so of course I caught a cold which sent
me to bed instead for a day or two. But I am much better, so we'll go
Wednesday or Thursday.

I enclose the soldi, which please accept without further demur, or I shall be
enraged.[1] I didn't mind your not doing the novel, but I did mind the tone of
judgment. However, a la guerre comme a la guerre.[2] We need think no more
about it.

D. H. Lawrence

4270. To Martin Secker, [16 January 1928]
Text: MS UInd; Postmark, Scandicci 17.1.28; Secker 98–9.

Villa Mirenda, *Scandicci*, Florence
Monday

Dear Secker

Of course I got a cold which put me in bed and prevents our leaving for
Switzerland today. But I hope we can get off this week – be in Diablerets by
Saturday.

I was going over the poems. Would you get the *New Poems* typed out for

[1] See Letter 4256.   [2] 'we've got to take the rough with the smooth.'

me, one carbon copy, so I can alter them a bit, and get this whole first half into order. I am arranging it as a whole – i.e. the Lyrical Poems, contents of *Love Poems and Others*, *Amores*, *New Poems* and *Bay*. I have done the first two books – *Bay* is tiny: if you'd have *New Poems* typed for me, I'd have this MS. ready very soon: a complete thing in itself; – but we can print *Look! We Have Come through*, and *Birds Beasts* in the second section, pretty much as they stand: if you wish. I don't care whether it's two vols. or one. But as one, it will be pretty fat. And it's no good having too small a format, because of the long lines of some of the poems – looks messy.

And do you think there should be an introduction by somebody? In America Willa Cather told me Robert Bridges said I was the only living poet that counted – or to that effect.[1] He might do an introduction – if his Laureate lets him – and if you think it's worthwhile.

The proofs have not come.

Yrs   D.H. Lawrence

The proofs this minute come. I still think it ridiculous, and a little insulting to me, that you left out that other story.[2]

P.P.S.

I've just read the story: 'The Border Line': and the end is missing.[3] There should be two more pages or so. The man dies. Will you look at the MS. and see if the printer has lost any: and if the missing pages aren't there, ask Miss Pearn, and let me know at once. As it is, the story is pointless: and very hard to capture this 1921 atmosphere of Germany again. But it can't end like this!

Let me know at Diablerets.[4]

[1] The American novelist, Willa Cather (1876–1947) had met DHL in New York in February 1924 and in New Mexico in July 1925 (*Letters*, iv. 592 n. 2; v. 280 n.3). No independent evidence of the view attributed to the Poet Laureate, Robert Bridges (1844–1930) has been found; but see Letter 4346 and n. 3.   [2] See Letters 4029 and p. 69 n. 1, 4196.

[3] See Letters 4272 and n. 1, 4282.

[4] Secker replied on 20 January 1928 (*Letters from a Publisher*, 1970, p. 40; corrected from Secker Letter-Book, UIll):

Dear Lawrence,
   It is a mystery about that story "The Border Line". I am sending you the typescript supplied to us by Curtis Brown, from which you will clearly see that no one had any reason to suppose that it was not complete. I can only suggest that the original typist, whoever she was, lost the last page of your manuscript. Unless a duplicate exists, the only thing is for you to complete the story, if possible, in the page and a half which happen to be blank in the proofs.
   I am having "New Poems" typed out in duplicate and will send this to you in a few days. I still think the collection should appear in two volumes, but to be sold as a set. An introduction by Bridges would be very good indeed, and I will write to him about it.
   I hope you have got rid of your cold.   Yours

4271. To Arthur Wilkinson, [20 January 1928]
Text: MS Schlaefle; PC v. Route des Diablerets. Vers l'Eglise; Postmark, Aigle-Gare 20.1.28;
Unpublished.

– aigle
Friday evening

A lovely journey, brilliant sun on brilliant snow – but waiting here now for the
sort of tram to take us up to Diablerets. A bit slushy down here, mountains
rather grim, but a cosy tea-shop. Was quite an easy journey – the violets were
still sweet at Milan.

DHL

4272. To Nancy Pearn, 21 January 1928
Text: MS UT; Unpublished.

Chalet Beau Site, *Les Diablerets*, Vaud, Switzerland
21 Jany 1928

Dear Miss Pearn

Here we are – right in the snow. It's rather lovely, but one is a bit tremulous
at first.

Did Secker tell you that the end of the story 'The Border Line' is missing?
– there must be about four pages lost.[1] I wonder if it's the printer, or who? –
and if you can find the complete MS. – if not, I'll have to invent the thing
again – though it's completely left me. I'd utterly forgotten this story.

And will you tell me in which magazine it appeared? – and was 'Smile' in
the *New Statesman*?[2] I like to say in front where the stories have appeared, or
the editors are offended.[3] It is

'Two Blue Birds': *Pall Mall* or where?
Sun: *New Coterie*
'Woman Who Rode': *Criterion* (?)
'Smile' – *New Statesman*
'The Border Line'? –
'Jimmy and Desperate Woman'

---

[1] Nancy Pearn replied on 28 January 1928 (TMSC UT): 'We are in touch with Secker over
"The Border Line", so don't worry about it.' The story was first published in *Hutchinson's
Story Magazine*, September 1924 (Roberts C123).
[2] 'Smile' first appeared in *Nation and Athenæum*, xxxix (19 June 1926), 319–20 (Roberts C142).
[3] The other stories mentioned received their first magazine publication as follows: 'Two Blue
Birds' in *Dial* (see p. 69 n. 1); *Sun* in *New Coterie*, iv (Autumn 1926), 60–77 (Roberts C145);
'The Woman Who Rode Away' in *Dial* (see p. 76 n. 2); 'Jimmy and the Desperate Woman' in
Criterion, iii (October 1924), 15–42 (Roberts C125); 'The Last Laugh' in *Ainslee's*, lvi (January
1926), 55–65 (Roberts C136.5); 'More Modern Love' as 'In Love' in *Dial* (see p. 46 n. 5).

'Last Laugh' – *Criterion*?

'More Modern Love' – ?

Would you please give Mr Pollinger this address – and the other depts. too. Hope it's not a great bother. – So dazed with all this snow and altitude.

D. H. Lawrence

4273. To S. S. Koteliansky, 22 January 1928

Text: MS BL; Postmark, Les D[iablerets] 22 1 [. . .]; Moore 1035–6.

Chalet Beau Site, *Les Diablerets* (Vaud), Suisse

22 Jany 1928

My dear Kot

We got here Friday night – a rather lovely journey over the Simplon, sun and snow: but a bit long. Came tinkling from the station in a sledge. There are about a hundred tourists in the place, winter-sporting; but I'm not starting in yet. We've got a little flat in this chalet, cosy and warm. Outside there is good snow, dry – and it isn't cold, because there's no wind. I really like it, for a change, and I really think it will do me good. One needs a tonic, after Italy. – I suppose we shall stay a month at least – see how it suits me.

What about you? have you got a job yet? and are you flattening out your employer?

I am getting my novel typed out, and think I shall make a private edition in Florence, and an expurgated edition for Secker and Knopf. Meanwhile I'm collecting poems together for my *Collected Poems*. I'll sort of feel I've got everything behind me, when they are done, – and the novel. Then what next? Some sort of a new start? If we don't go to the ranch, I shall come to London at least for a time. But I am terribly sceptical of being able to do anything. The swine, as you call them, are too many: and vulgar finance and Beaverbrook are laying their hands on the last remaining remnants of freedom.[1] Well, let them! Perhaps when nothing independent remains at all, a few people will stir up. Meanwhile I see no signs.

I hope anyhow this place will be good for my health – that's all I'm here for. I'd like really to feel well again.

How are Ghita and Sonia?

---

[1] DHL probably had in mind the influence exerted by William Maxwell Aitken, Baron Beaverbrook (1879–1964) through his ownership of the *Daily Express* (from 1916), *Sunday Express* (from 1918) and *Evening Standard* (from 1923). Beaverbrook's earlier association with Lloyd George, who elevated him to the peerage in 1916, would also not endear him to DHL. But see Letters 4555 and nn., 4571.

4274. To Emily King, [22 January 1928]

Text: MS Needham; PC v. Les Diablerets en hiver. Le Grand Hôtel et les Diablerets (3222 m); Postmark, Les Diabl[erets] 22 1.2[. . .]; Unpublished.

Chalet Beau Site. *Les Diablerets* (Vaud)

Sunday.

We got here Friday night – after a long journey, but very lovely, brilliant sun on the snow. We are right in the snow here, about 3500 feet above the sea. We have a little flat in this chalet, very cosy, with good stoves – and it isn't really cold, because there is no wind. There's a fair amount of winter sporting, but I'm not starting in yet. I think it'll suit me.

Love.   DHL

4275. To Ada Clarke, [22 January 1928]

Text: MS Clarke; PC v. Les Diablerets en hiver. Le Grand Hôtel et les Diablerets (3222 m); Postmark, L[es Diablerets] 22 1.28; Lawrence–Gelder 178.

Chalet Beau Site. *Les Diablerets* (Vaud)

[22 January 1928]

Here we are, really in the snow – had quite a good journey from Florence – came tinkling along here in a sledge. There are about 100 people in the hotel – winter sporting – we have a flat in this chalet; like a ship, all wood and low ceilings. It isn't really cold, because there's no wind and the snow is dry. I think it'll suit me, really.

Love!   DHL

4276. To Martin Secker, [22 January 1928]

Text: MS UInd; Postmark, Les Diablerets 23.1.28; Secker 99.

Chalet Beau Site, *Les Diablerets* (Vaud)

Sunday

Dear Secker

Thanks for the MS of 'The Border Line' which came today. It is, unfortunately, as printed. But the end must be somewhere, as the story appeared in some magazine or other. I have written to Miss Pearn. – Do you mean you want me to squash the whole into the few lines on p. 133 and the blank p. 134? Is it important to use no more space? – because the original, I am sure, has three more pages. If I am to get it down to this bit, I shall have to alter all pp. 132 and 133 and condense them. Let me know.

Plenty of snow here: very white and still, and bit frightening. Yesterday was sunny, but today has clouded. I think it will snow again. One feels a bit queer at first – though we have a very cosy wooden flat in this chalet, like a ship. I think I shall really like it when we shake down to it – but I'm not trying ski-ing yet.

Hope the garden is looking up. Winter-aconites were out in Tuscany when we left.

DHL

4277. To Giuseppe Orioli, [22 January 1928]
Text: MS NWU; PC v. Les Diablerets en hiver. Le Grand Hôtel et les Diablerets (3222 m); Postmark, Les Diablerets 23.1.28; cited in Moore, *Intelligent Heart* 375.

Chalet Beau Site. *Les Diablerets* (Vaud)
Sunday.

Had a very good journey – Maggiore looking lovely, and brilliant sun on the snow above. Here is plenty of snow too. We've got such a nice flat in this chalet, warm, and all wood, like a ship. I think it will do me good, though one feels a bit shaky at first. Maria will do the 'worst' bits of the novel! Remember me to Douglas.

DHL

4278. To Giulia Pini, [23 January 1928]
Text: MS UT; PC v. [Les Diablerets]; Postmark, Les [Diablerets] 23 [. . .]; Unpublished.

Chalet Beau Site. *Les Diablerets*, Svizzera
[23 January 1928]

Abbiamo fatto un bel viaggio, molto bello, col gran sole sulla neve. Qui anche c'è molta neve, buona per lo sport. Abbiamo preso una di quelle piccole case di legna, tutta legna, a riscaldata con tre stufe insieme, bel calda. Ma fuori fa freddo: un freddo sano, però e la neve resta buona, asciutta.

tanti saluti!   D. H. Lawrence

[We had a good journey, very beautiful, with bright sunshine on the snow. Here, too, there is lots of snow, very good for sport. We have taken one of the small wooden houses, completely made of wood, and heated by three stoves together, so it's lovely and warm. But outside it's cold, a healthy cold, however, and the snow stays beautiful and dry.

Many good wishes!   D. H. Lawrence]

4279. To Else Jaffe, [24 January 1928]
Text: MS Jeffrey; PC v. Les Diablerets, l'Eglise Anglaise et Gd. Hôtel; Postmark, Les Diablerets 24 1 28; Frieda Lawrence, *Nur Der Wind*, p. 312.

Chalet Beau Site. *Les Diablerets*, Vaud
Dienstag

Wir sind hier seit Freitag Abend – in tiefem Schnee. Wenn die Sonne scheint ist es wunderschön, jetzt aber schneit es wieder. Wir haben eine so nette

holzerne wohnung in diesem Chalet – wie in einem Schiff, ganz anders wie
Irschenhausen – und gut warm. Aber wir zittern beide ein wenig, es ist so
fremd, wir sind so ungewöhnt, und schnee, tiefer Schnee, das ist so
ungeheuer. Ich bin wie ein grüner Papagei, ganz erstaunt. Aber doch soll es
uns gut thun – gesundlich: sonst ist es ein Wahn! Wie geht's dir?

DHL

[Tuesday
We've been here since Friday evening – in deep snow. When the sun shines it
is wonderful, but at the moment it is snowing again. We have such a nice
wooden flat in this chalet – just like a ship, quite different from Irschenhausen
– and nice and warm. But we are both trembling a bit, it is so alien, we are so
unaccustomed to it, and snow, deep snow, which is so overwhelming. I'm like
a green parrot, utterly astonished. But still it should do us good – in the way of
health: otherwise it's crazy! How are you?

DHL]

4280. To William Wilkinson, [24 January 1928]
Text: MS Schlaefle; PC v. [Les Diablerets]; Postmark, Les Diablerets 24.1.28; Unpublished.

Chalet Beau Site. Les Diablerets, Vaud.
Tuesday.

Well here we are, in deep snow – today blinding sun. It feels very queer, and
we neither of us know quite where we are. We've got a nice little wooden flat,
like a ship, in this chalet – very cosy and warm inside – very cold out: not many
people, only bob-sleigh contests and rather feeble ski-ing, nearly all the
chalets shut – great silence – I don't *really* like it! No mail yet from you.

DHL

4281. To Catherine Carswell, [25 January 1928]
Text: MS YU; Unpublished.

Chalet Beau Site, *Les Diablerets* (Vaud)
(Wed.)

My dear Catherine

I send you the first half – more – of the MS today.[1] Of that which is already
typed, I only want *one* copy. Of the MS book, I want *two* carbon copies. And
will whoever types it send it me in batches, as soon as a few chapters are done.

[1] Cf. Letter 4255 and n. 4.

What title: *Lady Chatterley's Lover*
   'My Lady's Keeper.'
   'Tenderness'.
Which do you prefer?[1]
I'll send rest of MS in a day or two.
Hot sun today – deep snow – am feeling better – was a bit queer at first.
Of *course* you *have no time* for yourself – Don is right indeed.

             Haste DHL

4282. To Martin Secker, [27 January 1928]

Text: MS UInd; Postmark, Les Diablerets 27. 1.28; Secker 99–100.

        Chalet Beau Site, Les Diablerets. (Vaud)
                     Friday

Dear Secker

I hope you'll soon send me the poems, because all the others of the first vol are done, and I want to put them together and let you have that MS.

Also as soon as you let me know about the story 'The Border Line' I'll send you the proofs. I wrote a new ending, but it takes about 4½ pages. If you can't put it in, I'll have to do something. I want to cancel[2] the last two pages printed, and substitute this new.

Would you send to my sister-in-law

  Frau Dr Else Jaffe-Richtofen, Bismarkstr 17, *Heidelberg*; Baden,

a copy of *St. Mawr*, and also a copy of the proofs of *Woman Who Rode Away*. The Insel Verlag wants to print a translation of *The Woman–*, and 'The Princess' and 'None of That' in the autumn, so they want the MS. And Else will do the translation.[3]

And could you send the same, 'Princess' and proofs – to

  Frau Katherina Kippenberg, Insel Verlag, Kurzestrasse, *Leipzig*.

Bright sun on the snow here – I have to wear dark glasses. It's a quiet place – very few people here; lots of chalets, but nearly all shut and covered with snow. I struggle up the hills, and pant a good bit, but I think it's doing me good. I'm not up to sports yet. Aldous, like a long stalky bird, all stalk and claw, goes mildly skiing in the afternoon. But it's a hard-working sport. You have to walk uphill with those enormous skis on your feet, for half an hour, to slither down again in ten minutes! There's some good bob-sleighing on the

---

[1] Catherine Carswell recalled: 'I did not care much for any of them, but have forgotten my own alternatives' (Carswell 272). [2] MS reads: 'want cancel'.
[3] Else Jaffe's translation of the volume included 'None of That' but excluded 'The Princess'.

276

[27 January 1928]

run, but that's a professional show. I'm going to content myself with gently tobogganing. Frieda quite likes it – but prefers the Mirenda. I'm not keen on snow, but I like the air. It makes me want to go back to the ranch.

Thanks for the papers you sent – how they patronise poor old Hardy.[1]

Hope Rina's having a decent time!

DHL

4283. To Frances Wilkinson, [27 January 1928]
Text: MS Schlaefle; PC v. Les Diablerets; Postmark, Les Diablerets 27.1.28; Sagar, Wilkinsons 72.

Chalet Beau Site.

Friday

Sunny weather, blinding snow, me in dark glasses. It seems quite difficult to believe that the Mirenda is still there. I trudge patiently up the hills, and pant – don't think of sports. Aldous goes mildly skiing – all stalk and claw – but doesn't get far before he slithers home again. No fun, struggling uphill with seven foot of ski on each foot. – We had the letters from your father and mother, but nothing forwarded as yet. Tell your mother I believe I'm the lost Freddy, fallen out of the shawls: that's how I feel on this snow. Makes me wish I was fat. I'll write a letter directly. No sound save sleigh-bells – and no motion, save a few people little as flies on the snow. Ugh!! Florish!

DHL

4284. To Hon. Dorothy Brett, [27 January 1928]
Text: MS UCin; PC v. [Les Diablerets]; Postmark, Les Diablerets 27.1.28; Irvine, Brett 80.

Diablerets.

28 Jan.

Had yours of New Years Day today. We've been up here a week – deep snow, sunny off and on. I think it's doing my broncs. good – but I gasp uphill on this snow. Aldous and Maria mildly ski without much joy, and we trudge a while, then go home. There are very few people – practically all the chalets shut and snowed over. We're in a cosy little chalet, but a bit boxy. Anyhow the altitude suits me all right – 3500 ft. – so I hope we'll get to the ranch – always patience!

DHL

The tie and hanky came the day we left Italy – so nice!

---

[1] Hardy died on 11 January 1928; he was buried in Westminster Abbey on the 16th, the pall-bearers including the Prime Minister, Barrie, Galsworthy, Housman, Kipling and Shaw. DHL may have found 'patronising' *The Times* obituary, 12 January 1928.

4285. To Else Jaffe, [31 January 1928]

Text: MS Jeffrey; Frieda Lawrence 269–70.

Chalet Beau Site – Les Diablerets, Vaud
Tuesday

Dear Else

We'll just go ahead with 'Rex' without bothering about Curtis Brown.[1] I'll just mention it to him when I write, and tell him I fixed things up myself. I think M.180 is quite a good price for *Jugend* to pay: and the usual arrangement is $\frac{1}{3}$ to the translator, $\frac{2}{3}$ to the author – so you get M. 60. Business, cara mia, business!

I wrote Secker direct and asked him to send to you and to Frau Katherina, both, copies of 'The Princess' (in *St Mawr*) and proofs of the vol of Short Stories *The Woman Who Rode Away*. I hope you will get these directly. In the stories, the end of 'The Border Line' is missing – printer lost two or three pages: so I'm having to write it in. But you'll understand the story is unfinished. – It's 'None of That' I want you to consider –

We had hot sunshine, and the snow was melting: but now today it is snowing again, a fine and crumbly snow. I must say, I don't like it. I am no snow-bird, I hate the stark and shroudy whiteness, white and black. It offends the painter in one – it is so uniform – only sometimes lovely contours, and pale blue gleams. But against life.

I've been busy doing my poems – have at last got all the early poems together and complete. What a sweat! But I shall publish the others, *Look!* and *Birds Beasts* as they stand. – Then I'll have to go through the novel, which I'm having typed in London. How glad I'll be when all this work is behind me, and I needn't give a damn any more. I'm sick to death of literature.

I think this place is a good tonic, but snow isn't good for bronchials: it just isn't, it scrapes inside.

I dreamed of Frau v Kahler last night. Are they all right.

That was such a good p.c. of Irschenhausen.

F[rieda] waiting to take the letter – so Wiedersehen!

DHL

---

[1] See Letter 4142 and n. 3.

4286. To Witter Bynner, 31 January 1928

Text: MS HU: Postmark, Les Diablerets 2 II.28; Huxley 701–2.

Chalet Beau Site. Les Diablerets (Vaud.), Suisse

31 Jany 1928

Dear Bynner[1]

Your letter, and the poems came today – and I haven't read the *Pamphlet* ones yet, only the little Chapalan slip, which I think have poignancy, and I like them. It's a fact, it doesn't matter what year it is. Time is where one is and with whom.[2] And I do think it's about now when one should be back in New Mexico under the turquoise.

But I've had a paltry time, being ill – since last June, I never got right – cough, bronchials very bad. So we came up here to see if it would do me good – the altitude – only about 3500, but fairly high for Europe – and the snow and sun. We've been here about ten days, and I'm no worse, anyhow. But I do wish I could get really better, I'm only half myself. That's why I never sent you *David*: I felt so limp and dragged. But I'm getting a copy now and will write in it and send it.

I feel about as you do about Europe – it isn't really there. I'd rather be at the ranch. But I've got to be well enough to take that journey. And Frieda doesn't much want to come: Brett and Mabel in her way: it's a weariness, and I wish I could get a sort of lift out, else I'm stuck. But I'll really see if we can't come, end of April: and yours was the first New Mexican hospitality, so I should like to come to you for a day or two. After all, as men, we get on right enough. I don't care a bit what you say of me – no doubt it's all true. But it's not really saying that matters, it's some kind of lingering feeling, as one likes the blue of turquoise. For the rest, I don't give a damn. Even if someone gave me a knock on the head with a lump of turquoise, I'd still like the blueness of the stone.

When will you really get your Chinese book out?[3] Probably I shall like the Chapalesque better – but we'll see. I've been collecting my poems together –

---

[1] Harold ('Hal') Witter Bynner (1881–1968), American poet and the prototype for Owen Rhys in *The Plumed Serpent*; a friend of the Lawrences from their early days in New Mexico (see *Letters*, iv. 316 n. 4). He recalled, in *Journey with Genius* (New York, 1953), pp. 331–3, sending DHL 'a careful little sermon about *The Plumed Serpent*' at the end of 1927. This letter and Letter 4336 constitute DHL's reply.

[2] With his 'sermon' Bynner sent a copy of *Witter Bynner* (New York, 1927), one of a series of *Pamphlet Poets*, ed. Hughes Mearns, together with 'a few chapala poems' (Bynner 332). In DHL's reference to 'Time' there is an allusion to Bynner's poem, 'Calendar':

> Why should I know or care what month it is?. . .
> If I watch the time, some of my friends will die,
> If I watch the time, I shall surely die myself. . .

[3] Bynner published a translation of a Chinese anthology, *The Jade Mountain*, in 1929.

Secker wants to do a *Collected Poems* of me. But what a job! I feel like an autumn morning, a perfect maze of gossamer of rhythms and rhymes and loose lines floating in the air. I did a novel too, which perhaps I'll publish privately in Florence – and then castrate for the public. I have most obviously left the balls in – and not even circumcised.

I don't know how long we'll stay here – perhaps till March – then go back to the Villa Mirenda, and clear up there. I'm giving it up, definitely. Enough of Italy this spell. Hope we'll get out to New Mex.

So au revoir!   DHL

4287. To Rolf Gardiner, 2 February 1928
Text: MS Lazarus; Unpublished.

Chalet Beau Site, Les Diablerets (Vaud)
2 Feby 1928

Dear Rolf Gardiner

Here we are in a little apartment in this chalet – and here I suppose we shall stay till about the end of the month. It's a fairly pretty place, and there's snow. But I rather hate snow: look on it however as a medicine.

We shall be pleased to see you if you come this way. Again the apartment is too small to put you up – like cabins on a ship – but the hotel is just near, I'd get you a room there, if you'd let me know. You take a little electric train thing up from Aigle.

Let me know when you think you'll come. We shall be glad to see you.

Yours Sincerely   D. H. Lawrence

4288. To Charles Wilson, 2 February 1928
Text: MS UT; Postmark, Les Di[abl]erets 2 II.2[. . .]; Unpublished.

Chalet Beau Site. *Les Diablerets* (Vaud), Suisse
2 Février 1928

Dear Mr Wilson

Very many thanks for your letter and for the case.[1] But I do wish you didn't send me a gift – but I shall always keep it as a token of regard from the miners, to whom so much of me belongs – and to your men at Willington my best and sincerest thanks.

I do agree with your letter. Men have got to be men first, before they can be supermen or men-like-gods.[2] Men-like-gods turn out pretty *Canaille*, if one is to judge from modern productions. I hear that H. G. Wells thinks Sir Alfred

[1] A nickel cigarette case (see next letter).
[2] John Hargrave's ambition was 'to develop "Men like Gods"' (Nehls, iii. 78).

Mond about the highest specimen of extant homo sapiens: because he can make more and more trusts, involving more and more money.[1] No no, men must develop their poetic intelligence if they are ever going to be men: the rest is a swindle. But ultimately the truly intelligent men must take over the control of the supplies: industries and money. We can't be forever at the mercy of Sir Alfred Mond.

We came up here to the snow, to try and get my chest a bit better: it was behaving badly. I suppose we shall stay till end of the month – end of February – then go back to the Villa Mirenda – and come to England, probably, early in May, when the weather is more hopeful. Anyhow I will let you know.

And again many thanks, also to the men, for the offering they sent.

I'll order you one or two of my books which you may not have.

Yours very Sincerely   D. H. Lawrence

4289. To Martin Secker, [2 February 1928]
Text: MS UInd; Postmark, Les Diablerets 2 II.28; Secker 100–1.

Chalet Beau Site. Les Diablerets (Vaud)
3 Feby 1928

Dear Secker

Many thanks for the typescript of the poems, which came very quickly. I have got vol I. MS all ready to send off. And Vol II. I shant alter, except very little – add a poem or two to *Look!*[2] But we'll print *Look!* and *Birds Beasts* in one vol together as they stand; and the few bits of poems done since, of no importance, we'll leave out. *Look!* and *BirdsBeasts* are so complete in themselves. – But the Rhyming Poems, Vol I. are a good deal done over. I can let you have the whole thing in a day or two.

I'm still waiting to hear from you about 'The Border Line'. When I hear just what you want – that is, if you definitely want me to use no more space than the $1\frac{1}{4}$ blank pages, or if I can run to four pages – then I'll send the proofs at once: and send the other copy to Alf[red Knopf].

---

[1] The reference is probably to Wells's *The World of William Clissold* (1926), volume i of which DHL reviewed in *Calendar*, iii (October 1926), 254–7. In this 'novel' – particularly in Book V – Wells advances the theory that great industrialists such as Sir Alfred Mond (1868–1930) would take part in 'an open conspiracy to realise the World Republic' (p. 736). Mond was director of numerous companies and the managing director of ICI; Liberal MP, 1906–28; author of *Industry and Politics* (1927), etc. Cf. *Letters*, i. 13, 152 n. 4.

[2] In *Collected Poems* DHL added the following to the 1917 *Look! We Have Come Through!*: 'Bei Hennef' (first published in *Love Poems*); 'Everlasting Flowers' and 'Coming Awake' (from *New Poems*); and 'Song of a Man who is Loved' (omitted in 1917 at the request of Chatto & Windus: see *Letters*, iii. 145 and n. 1, 148 n. 1, 164). See Roberts A43.

I'm having *Lady Chatterley* typed, and want to go over that MS here.

Would you send a copy of *Psychoanalysis and the Unconscious*, and *Fantasia, David*,[1] and *Sea and Sardinia* to

Charles Wilson, 2 Raby Terrace, Willington, Co Durham.

He has a class of miners, and they send me a nickel cigarette case, in token of admiration!!!

And would you send me here a copy of *David* please.

I saw from Cape's statement he sold already about 4,300 of *Twilight in Italy*. Not bad I think.

Here we had warm and blinding sun – yesterday snow and mist – today snow and rain and thaw and weirdness. It's very queer. I hate snow – hideous black and white – and it scrapes my bronchials. But I think it does my general condition good – tonics me up a bit. I wish I could get really well again.

Do you give me the copy of *Look!* – You can charge it to me, with the typing and other things.

Have you thought about the format of the poems? I like that of *Birds Beasts*, with that little print.

DHL

Did you send the things to my sister-in-law, and to Frau Kippenberg.

4290. To Rolf Gardiner, 3 February 1928
Text: MS Lazarus; Huxley 702.

Chalet Beau Site, Les Diablerets (Vaud)
3 Feby 1928

Dear Rolf Gardiner

Your letter just come – no doubt you had mine to Lansdowne Rd, to say we shall be expecting you. Do stay here the three days – 10 – 11 – 12 – we'll get you a room in a quiet chalet – there's deep snow – and the Huxleys are here – and probably there'll be Max Mohr, dramatist – German – quite nice. Anyhow we'll have a talk.

And don't let Goetsch or anybody make you do anything you don't want to do. Damn their discipline. If you've got to make mistakes – and who hasn't – make your own, not theirs.

And when you are in Heidelberg do go and see my sister-in-law

Frau Dr. Else Jaffe-Richthofen, Bismarkstr 17. Heidelberg.

She is very nice – has a son about your age at the university – knows everybody.[2] Jaffe was a Jew and professor – rich – and went and became

---

[1] *David*] *The Prussian Officer*
[2] For Gardiner's recollection of his meeting with Else Jaffe, see Nehls, iii. 178–9.

Finanzminister to the Bolshevik Bavarian Republic or whatever it was, in 1920 – and died of funk, poor chap. But Else is well worth knowing. I shall tell her to look out for you.

Let me know then just when you'll come, and we'll meet you at the station – and arrange a warm room for you.

Yrs   D. H. Lawrence

4291. To Hon. Beatrice Campbell, 3 February 1928
Text: MS UCin; Moore, *Intelligent Heart* 373–5.

Chalet Beau Site. Les Diablerets (Vaud), Suisse
3 Feby 1928

Dear Beatrice

Your letter came on here – where we came a fortnight ago, for my wretched chest – bronchials really to wreck a ship. They said – people, even doctors – altitude and snow. But snow's no good for bronchials, makes 'em worse: though the altitude is tonicky after Tuscany, which is relaxing. Well, there's my wail: I cough and pant, but sound worse than I am, maybe. I expect we'll stick it out here till about end of this month – then back to the Villa Mirenda, to wind up there. – There's deep snow here – a certain amount of winter-sport – none for me – and now it's snowing again – tinkle of sledge bells – me sitting on my bed, with a German feather-bolster over my feet – Frieda lying on her bed reading André Gide's *Corydon*, which is a damp little production:[1] and no sound in the white and crumbling world. We've got a flat in this chalet.

Well, there's the mise-en-scène – there's no drama. We still keep the Ireland idea. But we've got to drag our effects out of the Villa Mirenda. And moreover I've got on my conscience a novel I wrote, and which is much too shocking – verbally – for any publisher. Says shit! and fuck! in so many syllables. So if it's going to be published I'll have to do it myself – therefore think of bringing it out this Spring privately in Florence – 1000 copies, half for England, half for America – at two guineas. So perhaps earn some money, very welcome. But it's a good novel – love, as usual – and very nice too, but says all the things it shouldn't say. If I do that – publish it in Florence – it'll keep me there till end of April. Even so, May is a good time to arrive in Ireland.

We're really due to go back to the ranch in New Mexico – you know about it – owned by frieda – on the west side of Rocky Mts – altitude nearly 9000 ft – looking over the high plateau to Arizona – four horses, buggy, forest, all that. It's very lovely, and I'd be well there. But it's fearfully far and dear to get there

[1] *Corydon*, first fully published in 1924 (Paris); Frieda may have been reading the Paris edn. 1926. It consists of four Socratic dialogues in defence of homosexuality.

– 3 days in train, one in motor-car. Brett looks after it now. But I doubt if I'll
go so far. Ireland is much nearer. I'd like to see you all. Lord, how those
children have come on! Makes me nervous. Poor old Gordon! soon be a
grandfather!

Did you know I painted pictures last year – seven or eight big oils – nudes –
some people very shocked – worse than my writing.[1] But I think they're rather
lovely and almost holy. I always remember when you scolded me for making
Paul in *Sons and Lovers* paint dress-lengths.[2] I agree, after many years – it
would be rather boring. I did a picture of the Boccaccio story of the nuns and
the gardener – much more fun than batik.

Are there three children? somehow I only had track of Biddy and Paddy:
and now they're jazzers and golfers! Dio mio!

Is your hair still the same colour? F is a bit grey, and I found two white hairs
in my beard. C'est le premier pas qui coûte.[3]

I'd really like to come to Ireland, and see you all, and Liam O'Flaherty[4] –
and Dublin – and go to the west, I hope it wouldn't always rain, and I
wouldn't have a political aspect, and be shot or arrested. But I'd like to come,
and I think we will, once the Mirenda is wound up – in April – and that novel
more or less off my hands. Somehow I can form no picture at all of Ireland –
much more easily of Ecuador or Manchuria. But I think a country which
doesn't really exist and doesn't assert its non-existence violently any more – as
Italy does – must be rather a relief – Geographically nowhere, as you say.
Suppose one painted nudes in Ireland – not tough stucco John[5] ones – would
one be thrown in the Castle dungeons? Do the policemen wear orange trousers
and goose-feathers: no, orange is Belfast: green: green and pink policemen,
and money made of glass, and all motor cars pale pink by law? And a state
harpist at every street corner – and runes over all the house-fronts – and the
pavements with poems let in in little white pebbles – and lordly gentlemen in
bright collars of gold, like Malachi, and two-edged swords,[6] forcing every
civilian to pronounce six words in Erse before he passes on. That's how I
imagine it, so don't disappoint me. And in some streets no walking allowed,
forced to dance a jig from end to end. And ladies at night walking with their

[1] In addition to those listed in p. 188 n. 4, the pictures were: *Fight with an Amazon*, *Men Bathing*
and *Fauns and Nymphs*. (All are reproduced in *Paintings of D.H.Lawrence*, ed. Levy.)
[2] *Sons and Lovers*, chap. xii: 'Liberty's had taken several of his painted designs on various stuffs'.
[3] 'It's the first step that matters.'
[4] Liam O'Flaherty (1897–1984), Irish novelist; Edward Garnett had advised him about his first
novel to be published, *Thy Neighbour's Wife* (1923). *The Informer* (1925) brought him a
considerable reputation.   [5] Augustus Edwin John (1878–1961). Cf. *Letters*, iii. 176 n. 3.
[6] The kings of Midian, not Malachi, wore golden collars (Judges viii. 26, AV); in the Psalmist's
vision, the saints had 'a two-edged sword in their hand' (Psalm cxlix. 6).

white bosoms lit up with a necklace of tiny electric lights. And nuns in scarlet, and priests in lemon colour. Oh Ireland! And Gordon in a leopard-skin!

Never mind! au revoir   D. H. Lawrence

4292. To Earl Brewster, 3 February 1928
Text: MS UT; Brewster 160–1.

Chalet Beau Site. Les Diablerets (Vaud), Suisse

3 Feby 1928

Dear Earl

I dreamed so of Achsah in the night, I'd better write to you, lest you'll be thinking we've faded out entirely.

Here we sit, in the snow. Sometimes it's sunny and warm, sometimes it snows all day, like yesterday – sometimes it's very cold but dazzling sunny, like this morning. I'm not up to winter-sports – sometimes F[rieda] and I drag ourselves up the hill for forty minutes with a little toboggan, to slither down again in four minutes! Sport davvero! I trudge slowly up the snowy road, and gasp. Snow scratches my bronchials. But on the other hand, it *is* a sort of tonic, and builds up resistance. So I really feel better, even when my bronchials are more scratched. But I really hate snow,[1] it's very ungenial sort of stuff.

I've been busy getting my poems together for a collected edition – rather a sweat – but now it's done, and the MS is ready to go off. Something else behind me.

We've got a 4-roomed flat in this chalet, all wood, and low ceilings, just like a ship. Only sadly we can't sail on. But we can keep quite warm, with wood crackling in the stoves. I think Harwood would like it. She would even like ski-ing, toiling uphill once more with several pounds of timber at great length on each foot, to slither precariously down again in a few slippery and collapsible moments.

I think we'll stay till the end of this month, then back to the Mirenda for March and April – and then whither? – to the ranch if I'm really tough enough to face that long journey. But Frieda isn't very keen on the ranch. I am.

Maybe my sister-in-law from Berlin, and husband, will come to Capri end of March. If so, we might come down for a week, and see you. Which I should like. We must have some sort of conference before busting out of Italy to remote ends of the earth. – Anyhow meanwhile I hope you are all serene and very well.

Love from us both   DHL

---

[1] snow,] snow,

4293. To Max Mohr, 3 February 1928
Text: MS HMohr; Mohr, *T'ien Hsia Monthly*, i. 28.

Chalet Beau Site, *Les Diablerets* (Vaud), Schweiz

3 Feb. 1928

Lieber Max Mohr

Wir hatten gestern ihren Brief. Kommen Sie doch wenn Sie wollen. Wir haben leider keinen Platz in dieser kleiner Wohnung, aber wir finden Ihnen ein Zimmer oder in Hotel hier – es gibt nur einer, der Grand Hotel – oder in einem Chalet. Schreiben Sie nur und sagen was Sie wollen. – Es liegt tiefer Schnee – ist hübsch – ich aber kann keinen Winter-sport treiben, muss immer Schnaufen wenn ich gehe – besonders hinaufsteigend – und ich hasse Schnee. Aber Geduld! Es geht mir wirklich besser.

Sie müssen in Aigle umsteigen, und einen kleinen Elektrischen nehmen, bis hier herrauf. Und Aigle ist zwischen Montreux und Martigny.

Viele Grüsse an die Frau Käthe und an das Fräuleinchen Eva.

Auf Wiedersehen!   D. H. Lawrence

Upside-down!

[Dear Max Mohr

We had your letter yesterday. Do come if you'd like to. Unfortunately we have no space in this little flat, but we'll find you a room either in the hotel here – there's only one, the Grand Hotel – or in a chalet. Just write and say what you'd like. – There's deep snow – it's pretty – but I can't go in for winter-sports, always pant when out walking – particularly when climbing – and I hate snow. But patience! I'm really better.

You have to change at Aigle, and take a little electric train up here. And Aigle is between Montreux and Martigny.

Many greetings to your wife Käthe and to little Miss Eva.

Auf Wiedersehen!   D. H. Lawrence

Upside-down!]

4294. To Emily King, [3 February 1928]
Text: MS Lazarus; Postmark, Les Diab[lerets] 4.II.28; Unpublished.

Chalet Beau Site, Les Diablerets. (Vaud)

Friday

My dear Pamela

I was sorry to hear about the shop – Ada said £300 deficit, which is serious. Looks shady, somehow. I hope there'll be a satisfactory clearing up of the mystery. Otherwise I think really you'll have to join Sam in the shop, and help get things going a bit better. That'll never do. But what a nuisance just now. Let me know what the accountant says – something's wrong somewhere.

Here we go on with ups and downs – some days are bright sunny, some dark
and snowy. Today was lovely, very cold but good sun – now this evening it
snows again heavily. But after a good fresh snow the mountains do look nice –
so soft, against a blue sky.

Still for all that, I hate snow – even when it's good and dry as it is here. It is
so stark, so awfully white, and the whole landscape white and black is a bit
ghastly – these tall spruce firs hanging their paws down! No, snow isn't my
line – nor winter-sport. Anyhow I haven't tried any yet – except tobogganing,
which is easy. But you drag a toboggan uphill for forty minutes, and slither
down home in four – so its short sport. Frieda had her first try today with skis
– and I saw her most of the time swimming in the snow on her rear, trying to
get up and not succeeding, because of those great long skis. There's a lot of
work to winter-sport. Still, if I'm feeling better, I think I shall try ski-ing next
week. I can already walk a good deal better, and cough is easier – if only it
won't come back.

The Huxleys have a chalet a minute or two above this – there's Aldous and
Maria and their child and governess – then Julian, the professor, brother,[1] –
and his wife Juliette – and two children and nurse – and Rose, Maria's sister –
they're belgian – and Juliette is French Swiss – so it's a babel of French and
English. But they're very nice, and we go to lunch and tea, and they come here
– all very pleasant. Pity you couldn't have come – Peg would just have liked it,
trying her French. But I get so *bored* changing languages, I simply refuse.
Next week we've got a German dramatist coming from Bavaria to see us[2] – so
it will be German. I *hate* foreign languages.

We shall stay till end of the month, and perhaps longer, if it really suits me.
Today I feel quite a lot stronger, and I can't tell you what a pleasure it is. If
only I don't go back again, as I seem always to do.

Well – love to you all – and I hope things will turn out well.

                                                                    DHL

4295. To Ada Clarke, [3 February 1928]
Text: MS Clarke; Postmark, Les D[iablerets] [. . .]; Unpublished.

                                        Chalet Beau Site, Les Diablerets. (Vaud)
                                                                    Friday
My dear Sister
I was glad to get your letter – here doesn't seem so very far away from
England. It is a rather lovely place to look at, but snow is awful stuff, don't you
think? – so all over alike white. And me puffing uphill. But really I think I walk

[1] In 1928 Julian Huxley was Fullerian Professor of Physiology in the Royal Institution.
[2] Max Mohr.

Rolf Gardiner, 1928, from the painting on wood by Maxwell Armfield

Alfred Stieglitz, Lake George, 1919, from a photograph by Paul Strand

Bonamy Dobrée, c. 1929

Valentine Dobrée

Charles Wilson, 'The Pitman Poet', c. 1916

Crosby Gaige

Aldous Huxley, 1926, from the portrait by Sir John Collier

Maria Huxley, c. 1928

Juliette Huxley, c. 1930

Blair Hughes-Stanton, c. 1927

Max Mohr, c. 1929

D. H. Lawrence, Florence, 1928, from a photograph by Robert H. Davis

Norman Douglas, from the portrait by Desmond Harmsworth

Giuseppe Orioli

D. H. LAWRENCE

Will publish in unexpurgated form his new novel

LADY CHATTERLEY'S LOVER

OR

JOHN THOMAS and LADY JANE

limited edition of 1000 copies, numbered and signed,

at £ 2.0.0 net (of which 500 copies for America

at $ 10 net).

Ready May 15th. 1920.

D. H. LAWRENCE
c/o PINO ORIOLI
6, LUNGARNO CORSINI
FLORENCE (ITALY)

Please send me .... *copy (or copies) of*

LADY CHATTERLEY'S LOVER.

I enclose cheque (or notes) for

Signed

To be sent to ....

Order-form for *Lady Chatterley's Lover*, 1928

Enid Hilton, c. 1914

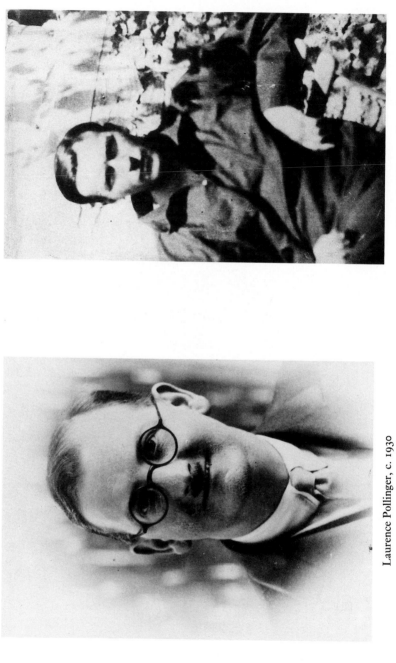

Richard Aldington, Port-Cros, 1928

Laurence Pollinger, c. 1930

better. Sometimes we take the toboggan and slither down home in about four minutes. And today Frieda tried skis for the first time, and spent a good deal of the afternoon on her bottom in the snow, unable to rise because of those thundering long sticks on her feet. When I feel just a bit tougher, I shall try too, and fall down just as often. But some people go like birds. The Huxleys, though, are only so-so: and Aldous looks a rare shoot, as he's 6 ft 4 and thin and half blind, and his skis are over seven foot long. But he does very well considering – better than the women. The brother is quite smart – Julian, the professor – also at skating. I must say I wish my chest would let me have a go too. But I'm too gaspy yet. And after all, you slowly drag up a hill on those skis for forty minutes, to slither down again in four – it's a lot of hard work for a bit of fun.

It was a lovely day – but now it's snowing again hard. The mountains look rather lovely in new snow, when the sun comes out. There's a little glacier shows its cold blue edge way up the Diablerets – at least it looks little from here, but I believe its big when you get there – seven hours.

That was a blow about that Bulwell shop. Of course Pamela ought to take a hand in the business. But I'm afraid she's too ladylike nowadays.

I've been collecting my poems together for a collected edition – a lot of work. I hope you keep all the first editions – they're all worth a guinea and more each now – so one day they'll be quite a nice little sum.

I do hope Gertie's well.

Love to all of you.   DHL

4296. To Catherine Carswell, 3 February 1928
Text: MS YU; Unpublished.

Chalet Beau Site. Les Diablerets, Vaud
3 Feby 1928

My dear Catherine

Thanks for your letter, and for looking after the typing for me.

I liked the Burns letter very much. How long is the poem?[1] I was thinking – Koteliansky very much wants to start publishing – doing smallish things privately, limited edition. He wanted to do my novel – but impossible in England. He wanted to arrange so that I had half profits. – Would you like me to suggest the Burns poem and letter to him? Seems to me a good thing to start with. And if you like, I could do a small introductory essay, as I am

---

[1] As becomes clear from Letters 4300 and 4353, and Carswell 261, the Burns letter was one of those to his friend Robert Ainslie and the 'poem' was the volume of bawdy verse (mostly not by Burns), *Merry Muses of Caledonia: A Collection of favourite Scots Songs* (c.1800; frequently reprinted). The proposal came to nothing.

'collected'. Or you could do it – just as you think well. And no doubt you could make some money out of it. The thing would surely sell a good many, to members of the Burns society. I wish I had a copy of the poem.

Let me know what you think about this, and I'll tell Kot. He'd probably start in and publish the poem and letter – are there other letters? – if I told him it was really a good thing. But of course he doesn't really like bawdy.

Snowing hard here. I hate snow. I really don't like it here: shut in in snow. I haven't the breath to do any sports – even to walk more than a little way. Wish I was well.

I thought the photograph of the boy too melancholy – prefer him sprightly.

DHL

Yes, I wanted three copies in all, of the novel – one for Florence, one for London, one for New York.

If you prepared the poem and letter for Koteliansky to publish, then he'd have to look on you as the 'author.'

4297. To Harold Mason, 4 February 1928
Text: MS (Photocopy) UT; *Centaur* 32.

Chalet Beau Site. Les Diablerets (Vaud), Suisse
4 Feby 1928

Dear Mason

Many thanks for your letter, which came on here – Rather gloomy! Poor old Rabelais, after all these years! It's too darned stupid.[1]

I'm going over my novel here – the typescript – and I'm going to try to expurgate and substitute sufficiently to produce a properish public version for Alf Knopf, presumably, to publish. But I want to publish the unmutilated version myself in Florence – 1000 copies in all – half for England. I shall send out *no* review copies. I shall make *no* advertisement – just circulate a few little slips announcing the publication. Then, perhaps, if I post direct from Florence to all private individuals before I send any copies to England, so that there can be no talk beforehand – perhaps that would be safest. I'm terribly afraid a crate might arouse suspicion, and the whole thing be lost. We might crate 50 copies to you – or more even, you[2] needn't look on them as *ordered*: perhaps to the other bookshops you mention too. But I daren't crate the whole

[1] See J. C. N. Paul and M. L. Schwartz, *Federal Censorship: Obscenity in the Mail* (New York, 1959), p. 47: c. 1928 'A rare edition of Rabelais, destined for A. Edward Newton, the Philadelphia bibliophile, was confiscated by Customs (the Post Office also condemned the work)'.	[2] even, you] even, if you

damn thing. What do you think? I'll be glad if you'll help me. But I'll send a
set of proofs. – Write to the Villa Mirenda, we shall be back there in early
March, I suppose. We are here for the time in the snow to see if it'll do my
chest any good. I think it does.

Will you please send by *book* post a copy of that porcupine to Aldous
Huxley, The Athenaeum Club. Pall Mall. London S.W.1. And also please
send a copy to me at the Mirenda. It's a shame it's still on your hands. It'll sell
one day – too late for all of us probably. And thanks for the money.

I shall send the MS to the printer as soon as I get it revised – but I don't
want to bring out the unexpurgated edition long before the public one –
perhaps I'll have to wait till June.

All good wishes – and don't be impatient with me.

D. H. Lawrence

4298. To Giuseppe Orioli, 6 February 1928
Text: MS UCLA; Moore, *Intelligent Heart* 375.

Chalet Beau Site. Les Diablerets (Vaud)
6 Feby 1928

Dear Pino

I think this place is really doing me good, I do feel stronger. I don't love
snow, exactly – it's so beastly white, and makes one's feet so cold. But
sometimes it's beautiful. Yesterday we drove in a sledge to the top of the pass,
and picnicked there, with Aldous and Maria and Rose, and Julian Huxley,
Aldous' brother, and his wife Juliette. It was brilliantly sunny, and everything
sparkling bright. I really liked it. It does put life into one.

I am just getting the typescript of my novel in from London; and Maria is
typing the second half. So in about a fortnight I think I shall have it all ready to
send to you. I am going to make expurgated copies for Secker and Alfred
Knopf, then we can go ahead with our Florence edition, for I am determined
to do it. I hope you are still willing to help me. I think in about a fortnight's
time I can send you the MS. to give to the printer.

If this place does me good, we may stay till the middle of March, but you
could start the novel going without me, couldn't you?

I hope you're all well and gay. Is Douglas still in Florence? Remember us
both to him. And has Reggie come back yet? Saluti anche a Carletto![1]

All good wishes!   D.H. Lawrence

[1] 'Greetings to Carletto as well!'

4299. To Arthur Wilkinson, [6 February 1928]

Text: MS Schlaefle; PC v. Mer de Brouillard, vue de l'Oldenhorn; Postmark, Les Diablerets 6.II.28; Sagar, Wilkinsons 72.

[Chalet Beau Site, Les Diablerets, Vaud.]

Monday

– Yours today – heaven knows what that Mrs Chambers has sent – she's the Mexican wife of the editor of the *Literary Digest*.[1] You might open the packet and look – and if you think I'd like it, send it me by registered post as *Manuscript*: 79 cents indeed! otherwise let it lie. Do hope it's not an awful bore. – We drove in a sledge, tinkletinkle, to the top of the pass yesterday – F[rieda] and I. – the others came on skis – and we picnicked on the pass, very high, very sparkling and bright and sort of marvellous – and some men did some fine ski-running. I liked it very much – and it sort of puts life into one. – But today it snows again!! But I can go quite nice long walks. – Sala da ballo,[2] my goodness!

DHL

4300. To Catherine Carswell, 10 February 1928

Text: MS YU; cited in Carswell 261.

Chalet Beau Site. Les Diablerets. (Vaud), Suisse

Friday 10 Feby 1928

My dear Catherine

I didn't acknowledge sooner the first three chapters of *Lady Chatterley*, which arrived safely, because your p. c. said a letter was following immediately. So I waited for that. However, it hasn't turned up – nor any more of the typescript. But I expect another batch will arrive soon. I hope so, as I want to get the thing off my hands. I hope the typist won't be too slow. Maria Huxley is going on with the second book of the MS. – here – so that will be a great help.

I enclose three pages that belong to the last chapter of the MS. book that you've got. Perhaps your typist will type them out, so that Chap. IX. is complete.[3]

When you send the next MS., will you enclose about 20 (*not* more) sheets of the paper the typist uses – and also a couple of sheets of carbon. One can't buy

---

[1] See Letters 4200 and n. 3, 4307. [2] 'Ballroom'.

[3] There was considerable confusion over how many chapters had been posted to Catherine Carswell for typing because the first notebook had two chapters numbered 'VI' and two numbered 'VII' and the last one was numbered 'X', but the second notebook (typed by Maria Huxley) began with another 'X'. So DHL thought he had sent nine chapters to London, but had in fact sent twelve.

anything here, and I'd like just a scrap of the paper, so that I can insert a page if I want to. You can send the things MS post.

I am thinking we certainly ought to get *The Merry Muses* printed privately, with an essay on Burns and the *Muses* by you – and *if you like*, a little essay on being bawdy, by me – but this last by no means necessarily. But probably you'll be writing shortly.

Shall I send some money for the typing now? It's the same to me. Only let me know. Be sure you keep count of postage and *all* expenses.

Had some brilliant sunny days, hot as summer, off the snow – but grey today. I expect we shall stay till end of month, and I *should* like to have the novel MS. complete and sent off before I leave.

Hope all goes well with you. Is J[ohn] P[atrick] a bit delicate? Where does it get him?

If you do your chaps. on Burns not too long, you could get them serialised before the book appears. Think of it.

Yrs   DHL

4301. To Martin Secker, 10 February 1928
Text: MS UInd; Postmark, Les Diablerets 10.II.28; Secker 102.

Chalet Beau Site. Les Diablerets. (Vaud), Suisse
10 février 1928

Dear Secker

I suppose you got the proofs of *Woman Who Rode* safely – I sent them a week ago. I hope the printer manages the insertion without trouble – it wasn't much.[1]

I sent the poems, all complete, to Curtis Brown, as Pollinger asked me to let them see the MS. I more or less arranged the setting out of *Look! We Have Come Through* and *Birds Beasts*.

I do hope you sent copies of *St. Mawr* and the proofs of *Woman Who Rode* to my Sister-in-law and to Frau Kippenberg – the Insel Verlag getting frantic, as they want to bring out the translations this autumn, and Curtis Brown was due to send them *St. Mawr* two months ago – and never did it.

I'm working away expurgating *Lady Chatterleys Lover* – can't think of a better suitable title. I hope I can let you have an expurgated MS in about a fortnight's time – and then you'll have to start a new expurgation, I'm afraid. But I hope not.

I want you to tell me when you would prefer me to bring out the Florence

[1] The proofs arrived in Secker's office on 10 February 1928; a copy went to Insel Verlag the same day (Secker Letter-Book, UIll). On the insertion see Letter 4282.

edition. I can have it ready, I think, by May. But would that suit you? You
would come out, I suppose, in September: along with Alf[red]. Would you
rather I were well ahead? – or not much in advance?[1]

We had some brilliant sunny days – but rather grey today. When the sun
shines, it's hot as summer, really. I think I'm better.

We'll stay, I suppose, till end of the month anyhow.

Hope all goes·well, no more floods in the garden – how beastly!

Yrs   DHL

4302. To Max Mohr, [10 February 1928]

Text: MS HMohr; PC v. Les Diablerets; Postmark, Le[s Diablerets] 10.II.28; Frederick I.
Owen, 'D. H. Lawrence and Max Mohr: A Late Friendship and Correspondence', *DHL
Review*, ix (Spring 1976), 156.

Chalet Beau Site. Les Diablerets (Vaud), Schweiz
Freitag

Haben Sie meinen Brief erhalten? – wir hören nicht von Ihnen. Der Hotel
hier ist geschlossen – keine Leute – aber man bekommt guten Pension in
einem chalet. Schreiben Sie denn ob Sie kommen.

DHL

[Friday

Did you get my letter? – we hear nothing from you. The hotel here is closed –
no people – but you can still get decent board in a chalet. So write if you're
coming.

DHL]

4303. To Hon. Dorothy Brett, 12 February 1928

Text: MS UCin; Postmark, Les [Diablerets [. . .]; Moore 1038–9.

Chalet Beau Site – Les Diablerets. Switzerland
12 Feb 1928

Dear Brett

Your letter yesterday about your teeth. Do you really think it was necessary

---

[1] Secker's views were conveyed to Curtis Brown on 9 February 1928 (Secker Letter-Book, UIll):

Many thanks for your letter, telling me of Lawrence's plans for the private publication of
"Lady Chatterley's Lover". As a matter of fact, apart from the difficulties and trouble in which
it will inevitably involve Lawrence, I regard this as an ideal solution, for we shall be able to go
ahead with an ordinary edition suitable for the commercial market without having to deal with
the author's natural reluctance to make any concessions in the matter of the text.

I hope it will be possible to arrange simultaneous publication with Knopf in the autumn.

The editions of the expurgated text were published by Secker and Knopf in 1932 (Roberts
A42d and e).

to have them *all* out? sounds to me very drastic. I think you might have gone a bit more gently. And whatever you think, I'm afraid you'll hate false teeth. I've got five, and I've always hated them. However, it may be all for the best. I'll have one of my big molars looked at when I get back to Florence. He may be causing me trouble, the brute.

We've been here three weeks – in deep snow. For two days it has snowed all day – today it seems to be raining: thaw. I must say I rather hate it: and my cough is as bad as ever: in fact I believe snow is bad for bronchials. But in myself I feel much stronger, and am much stronger – if this infernal cough would go down. I can't go uphill – simply pant. Bronchials are more devilish than you can imagine. Still, I'm stronger in myself.

Rolf Gardiner came up for three days to see us – the young man who does morris dances and all that. He's very nice, but not much in my line.[1] – Maria is going back to Florence on Wednesday, to get the car – then going on to England, where they're spending the summer. I expect we shall stay here until the 1st March, then go back to the Mirenda, to pack up and clear out of there. I'm glad to pull out of Italy. But in Florence I want to do my private edition of *Lady Chatterley's Lover*. I am making an expurgated version for the general public – but I do want to publish 1000 copies of the unexpurgated edition, and fling it in the face of the world. I expect you'll hate it really – but it's got to be done.

I've also collected my poems, for a collected edition, and I expect that will come out in the autumn – rather nice. And this spring they are bringing out the collection of short stories, *The Woman Who Rode Away*. I'll order you a copy – and Mabel. You know most of the stories: those you typed when we first came to Taos.[2] They're quite good, I think.

I'm working here over the typescript of my novel. Maria typed out the second half for me, and I was very grateful to her – am. But she makes far more mistakes than you do – oh, a simple chicken-pox of mistakes. – The first half is being typed in London, and damn them, they don't send it on.

Rachel just wrote that they are back in their old cabin. I hope things will settle down at Del Monte. If we get back, it would be nice to have them calm there, and the old man safely away.[3]

You sound pretty extravagant, getting a new car. I do hope you're not running hugely into debt. Be sure and let me know what I have to pay, taxes and horses and anything else.

---

[1] For Gardiner's account of his visit to Les Diablerets see Nehls, iii. 178–83.
[2] I.e. When Brett came with the Lawrences in March 1924; for the stories see *Letters*, v. 27 n. 2.
[3] The 'old man' was Alfred Decker Hawk (1862–1950), landlord to DHL when he was at the Del Monte Ranch during the winter of 1922–3, and Rachel's father-in-law.

Our coming back depends on my beastly cough. They say if I stay two months here – I've been three weeks – I ought to be very much better.

Well do take care, with those teeth, *don't* get chills. Let me know if it really makes you feel better, later on, to have them out.

I wish it were sunny here – thawing like hell now.

And au revoir.   DHL

4304. To Catherine Carswell, [13 February 1928]
Text: MS YU; Postmark, Les [Diablerets] 13.[. . .]; Unpublished.

Chalet Beau Site. Les Diablerets (Vaud), Suisse
Monday 12 Feby.

My dear Catherine

Many thanks for the two chapters of the novel arrived today. I was hoping your woman would have done more – is it a woman?[1] – Two chapters a week will take a long time – Could you tear out the 'safe' chapters, and give them to some regular typist bureau, which would get them done in a day or two? That would help a lot. Maria Huxley is working at the second half. – I should like to have the complete MS. here as soon as possible – certainly before the end of the month. – I enclose £5. on account of the typing – you will make me a proper bill. I'm afraid I've been a nuisance bothering you with this business when you are deep in your own work – I'm sorry.

Beastly weather just now – two days snowing, now awful thaw – my chest feeling rather raw. Bore!

I'm awfully sorry to bother you about that typing – I thought perhaps you knew someone, and it would be quite simple.

tante cose!   D. H. Lawrence

4305. To Else Jaffe, [17 February 1928]
Text: MS Jeffrey; PC v. Le Glacier des Diablerets; Postmark, Les Diablerets 17.II.28; Unpublished.

[Chalet Beau Site, Les Diablerets, Vaud, Switzerland]
Friday

– Secker said he'd sent the books to you and to Frau Kippenberg – I hope you have them safely. – Rolf Gardiner was here the week-end – he's deteriorated in these two years. Max Mohr also was here three days – but what a Schwätzer![2] – We had some horrid days of rain and mist and thaw – but fine again now. I think we shall go back to the Mirenda on March 1st. – though I dont really want to. But enough of snow!

DHL

---

[1] Unidentified, but see p. 260 n. 4.   [2] 'Gossip, gasbag!'

4306. To Martin Secker, [17 February 1928]
Text: MS UInd; Postmark, Les Diablerets 17.II.28; Secker 101-2.

Chalet Beau Site. Les Diablerets (Vaud)
Friday 18 Feb.

Dear Secker

I sent revised proofs off yesterday – all all right.[1] Thanks for sending to my sister-in-law and Frau Kippenberg. – Did you send those few books to the man in Willington Co Durham?[2] And please do send me a copy of *David* here: I've promised it so long to Witter Bynner, am ashamed. – And hold the other books for me, so I don't have to carry them round.

If only the typescript came quicker from London, I could let you have *Lady Chatterley* next week – in eight days. But I'm still waiting for four or five chapters, damn it! – It is frankly a novel about sex, direct sex. I think it's good, but you may not like it. I expurgate all I can – it's a pity one has to do it. You'll have to see what you think of the result. I think, considering what is published openly today, there isn't much risk. But if you think there is anything else that really needs taking out, let me know. But it would be best to risk the thing as it stands, I believe.

Another difficulty is the copyright. There is no copyright – I have it from Curtis Brown – for indecent, obscene, or blasphemous books. They may easily call the Florentine edition indecent, as it contains the improper words that are supposed to be indecency itself. I cancel them all for *your* edition. – Now if I can't copyright the Florence edition, I shall have to wait till August at least, and come out quite near to your edition. – The only other chance is, if you perhaps could print a little earlier, and copyright, say in June, and publish in September. Then I could come with mine in June. Is that feasible, do you know? You might perhaps mention it to Pollinger. We must manage it somehow.

We had some perfectly foul weather – mist, drizzle of rain falling on to snow a yard deep. Yesterday again was a magic of brilliancy – we sat out all the day, even had tea on the balcony with the Huxleys, in wild hot sunshine. It was impossible to believe the snow was there. I love these days. – Today is cloud and sun mixed. It may rain. It seems the winter is really over – there is most definite spring in the air, and the birds sing, and the river rushes. But the snow is white, white, and pretty deep.

How does Rina get on with *il Tonno*?[3] It's a silly book; but give it a bit of a playful tone, and the silly public may like it.

---

[1] Revised proof of *The Woman Who Rode Away* volume.   [2] See Letter 4289.
[3] Secker had wondered, in October 1926, whether DHL would translate Riccardo Bacchelli's *Lo Sa il Tonno* (Milan, 1923), but he found it utterly boring and refused (*Letters*, v. 562 and n. 4). The book never appeared in English.

I'd like to go to the ranch at the end of spring, if only I'm well enough.

I think we shall go back to the Mirenda about March 1st – though I don't really want to.

Yrs   D. H. Lawrence

4307. To Maria Chambers, 18 February 1928
Text: MS StaU; Schorer 60.

Chalet Beau Site – Les Diablerets. (Vaud), Suisse
18 février 1928

Dear Mrs Chambers

Your *Century* and letters came on here after us.[1] The story was nearly first-rate: but the gods didn't want you to be a writer: at least of fiction: they refused to put the bright spark at the point of your pen. The gods are very tantalising: they give so much, and then withhold the last bit. Perhaps they have some other destiny determined. – I sent the magazine back to you yesterday, by registered post, so you will have it safely. – Did you ever try writing straight autobiography? That would probably come more direct and more *you*, off your pen.

I had also the copy of the *Digest*, with Rosalino – and many thanks.[2]

We came here for my health – up to the snow. My bronchials have been so bad this last two years, I've been perfectly wretched. It's partly my age – I'm 42 – sort of change of life. I want very much to go back to our little ranch in New Mexico – near Taos. But the altitude is over 8000 ft., and the doctors say it's too high, till my bronchial tubes have hardened off a bit. I came up here to try to hurry them up – but it's a slow business. We may have to put off America till next year. But I *don't want to*. I'd like to come at the end of April or early May. If only the gods won't be spiteful to me. – I do feel better here. – So there we are! – Did you ever read *Reflections on the Death of a Porcupine* – that the Centaur Bookshop in Philadelphia published? – That's the ranch – and I do want to go back. And my wife and I, we should both like so much to come out and see you at Great Neck,[3] under the cherry tree in flower, en passant. And one day you and your husband might turn up at that little ranch in New Mexico. All possibilities – if only the gods were with us.

I've been busy getting my novel ready – *Lady Chatterley's Lover*, for lack of a better title. The vulgar public would find it too pure and undiluted as it stands: so I am having to impurify and dilute it for the market. But I want to

---

[1] It is not possible to identify the particular story which DHL had read; under her maiden name, Maria Cristina Mena published several stories in *Century*: see, for example, 'Doña Rita's Rivals', lxxxviii (September 1914), 641–52; 'The Vine-Leaf', lxxxix (December 1914), 289–92; 'The Sorcerer and General Bisco', lxxxix (April 1915), 857–66.

[2] See p. 210 n. 3.   [3] On Long Island, New York.

publish in Florence a pure and undiluted edition, for the non-vulgar public. We'll see!

I expect we shall go back to the Villa Mirenda early in March: for about six weeks. Then I shall give up that house, so that at least I am quite *free* to come to America. And if we can't come west, we shall probably summer in England and Ireland and Germany – so we might see you in London. Quien sabe?[1] I'm in despair, never able to say *I will come* or *I will go*, because of my wretched chest.

Did you find your soul? I've just about lost mine – but not in a bad sense. One's soul, alas, tends to be too cerebral.

Well, there's nothing to do but invoke the gods.

The Mirenda address is best.

tante belle cose!   D. H. Lawrence

4308. To Charles(?) Scott, 18 February 1928
Text: MS SIU; Unpublished.

Chalet Beau Site. Les Diablerets. (Vaud), Suisse
18 Feb 1928

Dear Mr Scott[2]

The photograph was so atrocious, and so utterly unlike either of us, I burnt it. But during the course of the summer I'll send you a decent one, and sign it. It's a promise. If you haven't got it by June, then write to me

c/o Curtis Brown. 6 Henrietta St. London W. C. 2.

and demand it.

The other, however, was a sheer libel.

Sincerely   D. H. Lawrence

Don't anyhow write to this address – we're moving about.

4309. To Rolf Gardiner, [20 February 1928]
Text: MS Lazarus; Huxley 703–4.

Chalet Beau Site. Les Diablerets, Vaud
Monday

Dear Rolf the Ganger

I'm sure you had a beastly journey – expect the Italian route would have been more bearable. But now you're evidently all right.

Max Mohr stayed till Thursday, and it was vile weather till he left, when it became most brilliant – and has stayed so. It's really rather lovely – still away

[1] 'Who knows?'
[2] It is assumed that the addressee was the same Charles Scott to whom DHL wrote about *Lady Chatterley's Lover* in March 1928 (see p. 335 n. 2) and who, encouraged by this letter in February repeated his request in August 1928.

outside the world, in a nowhere which I like. We think of staying two more weeks: or I do: my wife wants to go to BadenBaden for the last week.

I too was glad you came, I prefer to know my friends in the flesh. I think there's some sort of destiny in Gore farm.[1] We'll have to abide by it, whatever it is. Anyhow this summer I want to go down to look at it and smell it and taste it. Perhaps I'm due to go back to the Old England: and perhaps you are the whale that will spit forth my Jonahship on to the destined Coast.[2] We'll see! – We've all got a long way to go, yet – and I expect you'll embellish the inside of a few thousand railway-compartments still, before you come to earth. Max Mohr says we must all have roots. But at a certain point the business of the thistle is to roll and roll on the wind. Pazienza!

Frieda went and burnt the last sheet of your letter, so I lost the address to Ralph Coward:[3] therefore I can't send him his letter – unless you send me his address again. Otherwise I'll forward it to Holland Park.

Tonight the *Downland Man* book came: and it looks the kind of book I shall enjoy.[4] Awfully nice of you to send it; but caro mio, why do you spend your money? Don't do it any more. Let me buy the things. – I'm going to order the *Iron Age In Italy* – I believe it'll have something in it for me.[5]

Well, we'll meet somewhere or other, some time – and meanwhile we'll go on rolling, like thistle-down – that we used to call Angels when we were children. Non Angli sed Angeli![6]

So au revoir!   D. H. Lawrence

4310. To Bessie Freeman, 24 February 1928
Text: MS UNYB; Unpublished.

Les Diablerets. Switzerland
24 Feby 1928

Dear Bessie Freeman

What a queer creature you are – suddenly dashing all over the face of the earth! What is it? What possesses you? What is it you are rushing towards? Or is it something you are rushing away from?

Anyhow be careful and don't get typhoid – and then I don't suppose it much matters – where one is or where one is going to! So tomorrow as ever is you are setting off on a freight steamer for Beirut! I wish I were coming with

---

[1] Cf. p. 258 n. 3.   [2] Cf. Jonah ii. 10.
[3] Ralph Coward was one of Gardiner's collaborators; in 1929 he took over the farming at Gore Farm (Nehls, iii. 181). (MS reads 'Ralp'.)
[4] H. J. Massingham's study of prehistoric anthropology, *Downland Man* (1926) cost Gardiner a guinea.   [5] David Randall-MacIver, *The Iron Age in Italy* (December 1927).
[6] Words attributed to Gregory the Great when he saw fair-headed English slaves offered for sale in Rome ('not Angles, but Angels').

you. – I've had such a damned time with my bronchials, really almost to despair. So we came up here to the snow – and I am a lot better. But perhaps it's better for me to put off coming to America till next year: the ranch is a bit rough, and perhaps Taos is a bit strenuous. I envy you your nice long sea-voyage on a freight steamer. Tell me if it's nice: and I might see if I couldn't find a freighter to take me somewhere – east or south or west. I believe a quiet sea-voyage would make a man of me again.

I know nothing at all about Baghdad and modern Persia – but I believe it's quite easy to get to both places – by motor–car service. But Baghdad will surely be very hot. Now don't be rash, and ruin your health somewhere. What's the good!

Do write to me

> c/o Curtis Brown Ltd. 6 Henrietta St. *London W.C. 2.*

Do tell me about your journey, and Baghdad and Teheran. I really feel I'm mending now, and shall be able to set off again across the face of the earth in a little while. Then we'll meet somewhere.

Meanwhile I suppose we'll go back to the Villa Mirenda in about a fortnight – stay there till end of April – then??? – I'm going to try and bring out in Florence a private edition of my new novel, which the world will call very improper. I shall have to expurgate it for the public. Let me know where you are and I'll send you a copy if possible.

I'll write to Mrs Stevens[1] when we go to America: even show her my pictures, which people hate, but which I think are good – oils.

As for words of wisdom, I never felt more unwise in my life.

But send me a line c/o Curtis Brown, to say you are safe and sound.

> Love from Frieda   D. H. Lawrence

I don't forget our Apache trip.[2]

4311. To Bonamy Dobrée, 24 February 1928

Text: MS Brotherton; Unpublished.

> Les Diablerets. Suisse.
> 24 Feby 1928

Dear Dobrée

I did think you might have answered my letter from BadenBaden.[3] It was obvious Mrs Dobrée was too bothered to want visitors to Egypt – I could quite understand it – but you might have written and said so. We waited

---

[1] Mrs George W. Stevens ran the Toledo Art Museum, Ohio (see p. 335 n. 2).

[2] DHL visited Jicarilla Apache Indian Reservation with Bessie Freeman and Tony Luhan, 14–18 September 1922.

[3] Dobrée annotated DHL's letter at this point with the word: 'which?' DHL wrote from Baden-Baden, 6 October 1927, both to Dobrée and to his wife (Letters 4160 and 4161); Dobrée told Harry T. Moore (in a letter 28 November 1966, TMSC Moore) that he did not receive 4160.

actually for two months, thinking we might possibly come out. I had no idea Mrs Dobrée was taking her father out: she didn't say so.

The woman who rushed at you was no doubt a Mrs Crossthwaite, who asked me for a letter to you[1] – and I forgot all about it till a day or two ago. She is a sister of our neighbour at Scandicci – I only just know her – but she seems as nice as anybody else.

I feel much better up here – my damned bronchials really seem subsiding, so I'll be myself again soon, I trust. It's brilliant sun and white snow – though the snow is melting. But I like it. The Huxleys – Aldous and wife, also Julian – have[2] a chalet near, and are neighbours. But they're going away. And we'll return in a fortnight to the Villa Mirenda, for a bit. I'm giving the house up at the end of April: so if you come by Italy before then, come and see us. After that I don't know where we shall be.

But I want to bring out in Florence an unexpurgated edition of my new novel – too improper for the dirty public, I'll have to expurgate the public edition. And that may keep me in or around Florence for some little time longer. But I hope to have the private edition done by June.

I expect Egypt is irritating enough from the modern side. But I'd like to look at the pyramids and to go up the Nile: the old Egypt, spite of tourists, interests me and I'll have a look at it one day.[3] The very very old world was the best, I believe: before the 4th Dynasty.

If you let me know where you are and are going to be, we shall no doubt be within reach this summer of one another.

Regards from us both – also to Mrs Dobrée   D. H. Lawrence

4312. To Harry Crosby, 26 February 1928
Text: MS SIU; Postmark, Les [Diablerets] 27. II 28; Huxley 702–3.

Chalet Beau Site. Les Diablerets. (Vaud)
26 Feby 1928

Dear Mr Crosby[4]

Many thanks for your *Chariot of the Sun*. I'm glad somebody reaches a

[1] Nothing is known of Mrs Crossthwaite other than that she was Arthur Wilkinson's sister.
[2] have] have had
[3] His interest may have been stimulated by conversations with his uncle Fritz Krenkow (1872–1953), the Arabic scholar (see *Letters*, i. 7–8, 77 n. 1).
[4] Harry Grew Crosby (1898–1929), American poet and publisher of *de luxe* edns. m. 1922, Mary Jacob Peabody (named 'Caresse' by Crosby) with whom he founded the Black Sun Press, in 1927, at 2 rue Cardinale, Paris. Advisory editor, 1928–9, of *transition*. Author of *Shadow of the Sun* (1922), *Sonnets for Caresse* (1926), *Chariot of the Sun* (1927), *Transit of Venus* (1928), etc. Committed suicide, 10 December 1929. See Caresse Crosby, *The Passionate Years* (New York, 1955); Geoffrey Wolff, *Black Sun* (New York, 1976).

finger towards the real Ra. And dip your hand in Osiris too, since you're there.[1] It makes real poetry. I'm so glad when somebody waves a sunny hand towards me for once. And so thankful to catch a glimpse of a real poet in the real world: not a strummer on a suburban piano.

What is *The Enormous Room* – and by whom and when?[2] I never heard of it. As for a manuscript of mine – I burnt most of the earlier ones.

The Plumed Serpent lies in the cabin of the ranch in New Mexico: good sun there.[3] I suppose I could get it. And I think the MS of the story *Sun* is in Italy or London. I'll see. – But I never sold an MS. and I hate selling anything. How lucky you to be able to print just 48 exemplaires hors commerce – But if you like I'll sell you an MS. When I go back to Italy in a fortnight's time –
Villa Mirenda, *Scandicci*. (Florence)
I'll see what there is there, and let you know, and you can give me just as much 'gold' as you can easily spare, and I'll turn it into sun some way or other.[4]

But let us meet somewhere, shall we?

Sincerely   D. H. Lawrence

4313. To Earl and Achsah Brewster, 27 February 1928
Text: MS UT; Brewster 161–3.

Chalet Beau Site. Les Diablerets (Vaud).
27 Feb. 1928

Dear Earl and Achsah

We are still here – at least I am, for Frieda departed today to BadenBaden, to spend a week with her mother: and I remain alone in this little house – but I take the mid-day meal with the Huxleys. I expect to leave here March 6th, and meet Frieda the same day in Milan: so we ought to be back in the Villa Mirenda by March 7th. I hear the spring is very early in Tuscany, all the flowers out already.

Here too it is hot sunny weather – and a great deal of snow is gone from the south slope. But the north slope, and the Diablerets are still deep and white,

---

[1] Ra, the principal deity of ancient Egypt and one of the numerous forms of the sun-god; Osiris, the many-eyed, one of the chief Egyptian gods, represents the setting sun. Crosby had written to DHL from Egypt.

[2] A novel by Edward Estlin Cummings (e.e. cummings) (1894–1962), with introd. by Robert Graves (New York, 1922).

[3] Caresse Crosby later recalled: 'It was that January '28 on our trip to Egypt . . . that we discovered Lawrence and *The Plumed Serpent*. Harry found the copy of the first edition in a Cairo book shop and he read it as we churned up the Nile . . . He wrote to [DHL] about his own belief in the Sun God, described the impact of the Egyptian sun and asked Lawrence if he had any Sun story that we might bring out in a Black Sun Press limited edition. Harry offered, as bribe, to pay in twenty-dollar gold pieces, the eagle and the sun' (*The Passionate Years*, pp. 200, 227).   [4] See Letter 4365 and n. 1.

and the sledges still tinkle down the valley. But I doubt it won't last much longer – the snow. The days are very brilliant, and I'm sure it is quite as hot as Italy. But the nights are cold. I really rather like it: so out of the world, as if the world didn't exist. That just suits my mood at present – when I don't want to work or think much about anything. But if I stayed, I think I should want to begin to paint. – Which reminds me, Earl – if you have got those photograph nude studies within reach, do send me some, as promised. They will be useful to me, especially for water-colour studies. Send them, that is, to the Villa Mirenda: and if there are any good kneeling or crawling and reaching forward, send me those.

Well, our plans are very vague. The Mirenda is finished on May 6th – and I'm glad to be rid of it. What then, I don't know. Some work may keep me in Italy till June – and Frieda says she won't go to the ranch this year, but that she *will* go next year: in the spring. I'd like to go – and soon I must go. But perhaps it's a bit strenuous just yet. I'm much better, but not much good at climbing hills still. And I don't mind drifting around for a time – Germany, England, perhaps Ireland, for the summer: and for the winter, heaven knows. The Huxleys want us to motor with them in July over that country west of Marseilles – the coast between Marseilles and Spain. They think that might be a good spot. – But at the same time they say they'll come to the ranch with us next spring. Will you all come too? We'll be a host against Mabel! Or have you any other plans?

I'm glad you're both feeling so brisk and busy. It's just the opposite with me. I do nothing and don't care. But I'm reading a French book about Egypt[1] – pretty dry – it's all abstractions – they make the Egyptians as abstract as algebra, poor darlings: whereas they were beautifully concrete. I get so bored by science and the mental life business – it's all dry-rot.

When you write, send me Anna di Chiara's Paris address, will you? I owe her a long overdue letter.

My sister-in-law from Berlin isn't coming south after all – going to Finland or somewhere up north. The north Pole seems to be coming into fashion, and icebergs are the chickest things in resorts: Spitzbergen the new Nice.

But we might possibly get to Capri end of April – I might possibly sweat a few more etruscans on the way – Cortina Arezzo Chiusi Orvieto. We'll see. I feel we ought to have another conclave before we all bust abroad again.

Seems to me I'm your stormy petrel and harbinger of voyages.

My love to Harwood, if she's not growing too grown-up for it.

And au revoir to us all.   DHL

---

[1] Not identified.

4314. To Catherine Carswell, 28 February 1928
Text: MS YU; Postmark, Les Diable[rets] 28.II [. . .]; cited in Moore, *Intelligent Heart* 376.

Chalet Beau Site. Les Diablerets. (Vaud), Suisse.

28 Feb. 1928

Dear Catherine

Tomorrow is the last of the month, and the MS. isn't here: and people cabling and fussing about it. I do hope it'll come today or tomorrow. If not, will you please send me the whole thing, and send me my MS. back, and I'll get it finished here, or do it myself. I could no doubt manage what remains fairly quickly. Anyhow I must have the thing and get it off. I wanted the printer to have it in Florence this month. Fortunately Maria Huxley has finished the second half, so I only wait the four chapters you have. – As I say, if it's not done, will you send me what *is* done, and the MS., and I'll finish it myself.

Frieda has gone to Baden for a week – I suppose we shall meet in Milan this day week – and go on to the Villa Mirenda, and clear out of there. Then probably we'll come to England, so we shall be seeing you.

I do hope you are feeling better, and that the boy is all right, and Don. Don't put too much history in your Burns book – you can suggest it as you go.

tante cose! DHL

4315. To Catherine Carswell, 29 February 1928
Text: MS YU; cited in Carswell 255, 272.

Chalet Beau Site. Les Diablerets. (Vaud)

29 Feb. 1928

My dear Catherine

Many thanks for the chapters just come. I'm so sorry you've had flu – how wearisome that is! If only one could be really well, what a mercy! It's my one refrain.

Frieda is in Baden for this week. We are due to meet in Milan on Tuesday – 6th – and go on to Florence. So do let me have the end of the MS. if you can. I want to pack it up and post it away from here. But if you send by MS. post, please register, and *don't* enclose a letter. – I'm glad you won't be bothered by the thing much longer. – The typing is very nicely done – very few mistakes indeed. But do you agree with dont and cant and isnt, without apostrophe?

The weather here, after being brilliant has gone warmish, cloudy, and everybody suddenly has a cold. The snow is going – but the slopes opposite are still solid white.

Let me know what I still owe for the typing – and I do hope you'll all be well.

Yrs DHL

4316. To Max Mohr, 29 February 1928
Text: MS HMohr; Mohr, Briefe 530–1.

Chalet Beau Site – Les Diablerets (Vaud)
29 Feby 1928

Dear Max Mohr

So sorry you got the grippe in Switzerland: not in Diablerets, it hasn't come here yet. We had brilliant weather all the time till now, after you had gone. A shame you had it so horrid!

Today *Venus in the Fishes* has come, so I shall read it[1] – and many thanks – and I shall tell you what I think.

I am alone in this cabin, my wife is in BadenBaden. I suppose we shall meet in Milan next Tuesday, and go on to Florence. Here the weather is rather warm, and cloudy and neither winter nor spring nor summer: so perhaps Italy will be nice for a little while. I go for Mittagsessen[2] to the friends, the Huxleys, and we talk and talk, in French and in English. I must say I get tired of so much talk. What is the good of it! It is really much better to possess one's soul in patience and in silence:[3] and to dig the garden and tend the cow. – That was a charming photograph of the calf, and gave me a nostalgia for the land, for a Bauerngut.[4] – It's no good bothering about the world or man or civilization. It's all such a mess, that one must forget it, take one's mind off it. That is what you must do, deliberately: take your mind off the world, Berlin, publishers, Sodomites and everything – and live in a little world of your own. I insist on living *inside my own* Atmosphere – Ur-hülle.[5] Otherwise one dies, just dies.

I found crocuses on the hill here – and Juliette came with 2 gentians, very blue, and three primulas – Schlüsselblumen. But there is still a lot of snow – all the slope opposite is snow. It should go away.

Well I hope we shall meet in the summer – and at Wolfsgrube. Meanwhile many greetings to Madame and to you, and for goodness' sake, do cultivate calm, along with the potatoes.

Yrs   D . H . Lawrence

4317. To Frieda Lawrence, [1 March 1928]
Text: MS Jeffrey; PC v. Les Diablerets et le Culand; Postmark, Aigle-[Gare] I.III.28; Frieda Lawrence 268.

[Chalet Beau Site, Les Diablerets, Vaud.]
Thursday morning

No letter from you this morning – only one letter from Curtis Brown, asking

[1] Mohr's first novel, *Venus in den Fischen* (Berlin, 1927).   [2] 'Lunch' (mittagessen).
[3] Cf. Luke xxi. 19.   [4] 'Smallholding' (Mohr lived on a farm, 'Wolfsgrube').
[5] 'original skin'.

for the *Lady C.* MS. But I'm still waiting for the final two chaps. from that *woman*[1] – A warm morning, with warm dimmish sun. Our maid got the Grippe, so her sister is here. – I'm just going down to the station with Aldous – Diablerets coming to an end for us. I do hope we shan't get gripped going down to the valley – how do you feel it? Love to die Alte![2]

DHL

4318. To Martin Secker, [2 March 1928]
Text: MS UInd; Postmark [Les] Diablerets 2.III.28; Secker 103.

Beau Site. Les Diablerets. (Vaud)
Friday

Dear Secker

At *last* I have got the complete typescript of *Lady Chatterley* – am going over the final chapters, and hope to post the whole thing to Pollinger tomorrow. I find I simply don't know how much and how little to expurgate: so I'm not doing much. You must ponder it carefully, and if you want to take any bits out, then do so: but don't leave raw gaps, and don't make the thing lose its point. If you'd like me to alter any passages – re-write them, as I have done some whole pages – then you must send me the passages, marked, and I'll do my best.

I leave on Tuesday, 6th, for the Villa Mirenda: and to get the Florence edition started. Frieda is in BadenBaden – will meet me in Milan. Aldous left yesterday – en route for London. So Diablerets is nearly over. But it has done me good, and I've been happy here. But the snow looks a bit bleak now – time it went. It's no good for ski-ing. – It's a grey morning, warmish, after so much sun.

Well I hope you'll like the novel – don't be too timid about it, and we can trim it up to pass.

I'm thrilled about the poems. Shall you ask Bridges for an introduction?[3] – I was very irritated, Benn coming out with a sixpenny just now. That's Duckworth – because it must be nearly two years since they asked me about an *Augustan* six pennorth.[4]

Remember me to Rina and the boy. How goes the Tunny-fish?[5]

DHL

[1] See Letter 4319.   [2] 'the Ancient!' [Frieda's mother].
[3] See Letter 4270 and p. 269 n. 4.
[4] The selection of DHL's poems, in the series *The Augustan Books of English Poetry* (subtitled 'The Sixpenny Poets') was published by Ernest Benn in February 1928 (Roberts A38). DHL responded in a letter to Nancy Pearn, 17 January 1927, about Benn's approach which had first been made 'ages ago'; he added: 'Duckworth has two vols of my poems, and won't let Secker have 'em, – don't know if he'd let Benn' (*Letters*, v. 626 and n. 2).
[5] Cf. Letter 4306 and n. 3.

4319. To Catherine Carswell, [2 March 1928]

Text: MS YU; PC v. Les Diablerets en Hiver; Postmark, Les Diablerets 2.III.28; cited in
Carswell 272.

[Chalet Beau Site, Les Diablerets, Vaud.]
Friday

Many thanks for the MSS which came all safely. I am busy now going over it.
I leave here next Tuesday, 6th – for the Villa Mirenda, so write there. I do
hope all your colds are better. I rather dread descending to the low levels and
the germs.

DHL

4320. To Giulia Pini, [3 March 1928]

Text: MS UT; PC v. Skieurs à la montagne – Skiers of the Mountain; Postmark, Les
Diabler[ets] 4[. . .]; Unpublished.

[Chalet Beau Site, Les Diablerets, Vaud.]
Sabato –

Cara Giulia

Io parto di qui martedì e troverò la Signora a Milano: lei viene diretto di
BadenBaden. Dunque arriveremo mercoledì sera alla villa, verso le sei – spero
che gli amici della Villa Poggi verranno alla stazione coll'automobile. – Mi farà
piacere di vederti ancora, e vedere anche tutta la famiglia, ed i Salvestrini.
Tanti saluti, ed a rivederci, mercoledì sera.

D. H. Lawrence

[Saturday –

Dear Giulia

I am departing from here on Tuesday and will meet my wife in Milan: she is
coming straight from BadenBaden. So we shall arrive at the villa on
Wednesday evening, around six – I hope that our friends from Villa Poggi will
come to the station with their car. – I'll be happy to see you again, and to see all
the family too, and the Salvestrinis. Best wishes, and I'll see you on
Wednesday evening.

D. H. Lawence]

4321. To Giuseppe Orioli, [3 March 1928]

Text: MS NWU: PC v. Les Diablerets; Postmark, Les Diablerets [. . .]III.28; cited in Moore,
Intelligent Heart 376.

[Chalet Beau Site, Les Diablerets, Vaud.]
Sabato:

We are coming back on Wednesday – Frieda is in Baden, but we have

arranged to meet in Milano on Tuesday evening, so we shall be in Florence –
D. V. – on Wed. evening about 5.30. Perhaps the Wilkinsons will come to
meet us with a car. – *At last* I have got the complete typescript of my novel:
and I shall either post it to you on Monday, or bring it with me. All is ready!
We can begin. – So glad to see you all!

DHL

4322. To Rolf Gardiner, 4 March 1928
Text: MS Lazarus; Huxley 704–5.

Chalet Beau Site. Les Diablerets (Vaud)
Sunday 4 Mars 1928

Dear Rolf

The demon-drive must have been interesting – but as you say, sad: all the
old things have to die, and be born again: if they ever manage it. We're only in
the dying stage as yet.

So the Bünde patriots are trying to shove you out?[1] I suppose you'll leave
them in the end, but being shoved out is another matter. – I'm afraid the
whole business of leaders and followers is somehow wrong, now. Like the
demon-drive, even Leadership must die, and be born different, later on. I'm
afraid part of what ails you is that you are struggling to enforce an obsolete
form of leadership. It is White Fox's calamity.[2] When leadership has died – it
is very nearly dead, save for Mussolini and you and White Fox and Annie
Besant and Ghandi[3] – then it will be born again, perhaps, new and changed,
and based on the reciprocity of tenderness. The reciprocity of power is
obsolete. When you get down to the basis of life, to the depth of the warm
creative stir, there is no power. It is never: There *shall* be light! – only: Let
there be light![4] The same way, not: Thou *shalt* dance to the mother earth!
only: Let it be danced to the mother earth! – It's no good being pregnant with
the inert Austrians – They are en route to their death; and, let us hope,
resurrection.

We leave here – at least, I do, for Frieda is already in BadenBaden – on
Tuesday. We meet in Milan, and ought to be in the Villa Mirenda on

---

[1] Cf. Letter 4253 and n. 4.   [2] Cf. Letter 4253 and p. 258 n. 1.
[3] Benito Mussolini (1883–1945), Italy's Prime Minister, 1922–43, and Fascist dictator; Annie
Besant, née Wood (1847–1933), theosophist, who was also a political leader in India and
established the India Home Rule League (1916); and Mahatma Gandhi (1869–1948) who led
the Indian nationalist movement against British rule and implemented an effective policy of
non-resistance.   [4] Genesis i. 3.

Page 308 — 5 March 1928

Wednesday evening. So tell your sister just to send us a line when she is coming.[1] –Yes, one can ignore Fascism in Italy for a time. But after a while, the sense of false power forced against life is very depressing. And one can't escape – except by the trick of abstraction, which is no good.

I will send Ralph Coward his letter.[2]

Don't kick too hard against the pricks.[3]

D. H. Lawrence

4323. To Martin Secker, 5 March 1928
Text: MS UInd; Postmark, Les Diablerets 6.III.28; Huxley 705–6.

Diablerets
Monday 5 March 1928

Dear Secker

I posted off the MS. of the novel to Pollinger today – changed the title to: 'John Thomas and Lady Jane': which I hope you like, as it's much more suitable than the other.[4] I don't at all know how you'll react to the book: probably you'll hate it. Aldous Huxley and Maria liked it very much – so they said. Juliette, Julian Huxley's wife, went into a fearful rage over it – a moral rage. They're the only people who have read it so far.

The expurgations – I did a fair amount of blanking out and changing, then I sort of got colour-blind, and didn't know any more what was supposed to be proper and what not. So you must consider it. Don't all in a rush be scared and want to pull whole sections out. Just consider a bit patiently, in detail, what is *possible* and what isn't. I know it's not easy to judge. And then if there are little bits you can leave out without making obvious gaps, then I'm willing you should leave them out. But if you want any substantial alteration made, then consider the thing carefully, in detail, and mark it carefully in blue pencil, and send me the pages you want changed, and I'll do my best. I think we ought to manage to make it feasible.

I leave in the morning for Milan, where I meet Frieda. I do hope I shan't get any cold or anything going down, for I'm a good bit better now. – This evening it's trying to rain – warm spring rain on sodden snow. Just as well to descend for a bit.

Well I hope you won't hate the novel – though you easily may. It's a bit of a revolution in itself – a bit of a bomb.

DHL

[1] Margaret Emilia Gardiner (1904–). See Letter 4381.   [2] The letter has not been found.
[3] Cf. Acts ix. 5 (AV).   [4] For the origin of the title see Letter 4330.

4324. To Blanche Knopf, 5 March 1928
Text: MS BraU; Unpublished.

Les Diablerets.
5 March 1928

Dear Mrs Knopf,

I posted to Curtis Brown today the MS. of my novel: title changed to 'John Thomas and Lady Jane' which is much more suitable than the other, and which I hope you and Knopf will approve.

I somehow didn't get on very well with the expurgation: I somehow went quite colourblind, and couldn't tell *purple* from mere pink. So you'll no doubt have a bit of a shock. But I did blank out and alter quite a lot of bits: you're spared the worst. If you like the novel, and Knopf wants to publish it, then we can make some more alterations, if you think necessary. I don't mind if you leave out small bits: but for heaven's sake, don't make holes, and take out the meaning of the whole thing. And if you want me to alter anything serious, you'll have to mark the offences *in detail* – not *en bloc*, – and send me the pages. But I said the same to Martin Secker, so that if I alter any pages for him, I will at the same time send a duplicate to you, to see if it suits you: and we can keep the two editions more or less alike.

Meanwhile I am going back to Florence tomorrow, and shall start my private edition at once, so that it should be ready by May, or by June anyhow. No doubt you'll be thankful you're spared the unexpurgated MS. – But I do expect you not to take offence – you do care for my work, so you'll understand what I'm after, and take it in good faith. Knopf though may just dislike the novel. If so, I don't mind a bit if he doesn't publish it. I shall see his point of view.

Of the three women who've read the MS – apart from my wife – two went into a green fury, and the other into a queer delight.[1] But the first two would have liked to burn the whole thing – and perhaps me with it. Oh là-là! The only man who's read it – Aldous Huxley – liked it very much – or said so.

Well – tell me anyhow how you react.

Yours Sincerely   D. H. Lawrence

---

[1] The 'two' were Nellie Morrison (see Letters 4254 and 4255) and Juliette Huxley (see Letter 4323); 'the other' was Maria Huxley.

4325. To Hon. Dorothy Brett, 6 March 1928
Text: MS UCin; Postmark, Les [Diablerets] [. . .]; Lacy, *Escaped Cock* 66–7.

Les Diablerets
6 March 1928

Dear Brett

I am leaving here in the morning, going back to the Villa Mirenda for about six weeks. Here the snow is all going slushy – warmish spring weather, snow an anachronism. It's time to go down. The Mirenda ends finally on May 6th – so we'll be out by end of April, I expect. But I'm afraid my novel will keep me longer in Italy. At last I have the complete typescript – have posted a more-or-less expurgated script to London and to New York, each, for Secker and Knopf. Now I go to Florence with the unexpurgated. Let's hope I have luck there. – But I doubt if the thing can possibly be ready before end of May, so I'll have to stay and see it born. – It's a novel of sex: you'll probably hate it. Maria loved it: Aldous liked it, Juliette went into a white moral fury. So there you are.

Frieda says she won't come to America this summer – says my broncs aren't good enough for the long travel. But she says she *will* come early next year: and I believe the Brewsters will come too: and Aldous and Maria firmly declare they'll come with us. So that's that. It's a long time. But this seediness of mine started in Oaxaca,[1] and has had a long course to run. I feel at last it's beginning to heal from underneath, so if it will, what do a few more months in Europe matter? At the ranch, it only healed superficially. It broke down the minute I got to New York.

You must be having a rare job with your teeth. Tell me if it really really really makes a big difference. If it does, I'll think about *three* of mine – big back ones – that might possibly be doing me harm. But I'm a bit sceptical.

Don't accumulate a lot of bills. They'll only make your life a misery. But *do tell me* if there is anything I ought to pay.

About *The Escaped Cock*, I don't really mind if Spud prints it. I had thought myself it might make a nice little private-edition thing. But I had an idea I might add on to it perhaps another 5000 words. Of course I don't know if I could. I haven't yet seen the thing in print – my copy of *The Forum* will be in Italy.[2] – But that wouldn't prevent Spud from beginning, if he likes. Tell him to write me his idea in detail. And I suppose we'd have to tell Curtis Brown, and let him take his 10% of my share. Spud could write himself to

Edwin G. Rich, Curtis Brown Ltd,
116 West 39th St. New York City

[1] In February 1925.   [2] See p. 40 n. 1.

By the way, the English Curtis Brown is
6 Henrietta St. *Covent Garden*, W.C. 2.
and not Strand.

Frieda is in Baden this last week – I alone in this little chalet, but lunch and tea with Juliette and her mother and children in the other chalet.[1] Aldous and Maria have gone off to London. Diablerets is almost at an end. Juliette sends you many greetings.

Your paintings sound nice: hope Bobby proves a saleswoman.[2] I wonder what I'll do with my pictures when I leave the Mirenda. And I wonder when I'll start painting again. I've gone clean off it.

Perhaps in Italy I'll start and do the rest of my Etruscan Sketches. Did you, by the way, see *Travel*, with the four *Sketches of Etruscan Places* which they printed?[3] I think it's in the Oct. Novem. Decem. and January numbers. But the illustrations were disappointing.

Remember me to Mabel and Spud and everybody. I'll write again from Italy.

DHL

4326. To Baroness Anna von Richthofen, [7 March 1928]
Text: MS UCB; Frieda Lawrence 237.

Villa Mirenda. *Scandicci*, Florenz
Mittwoch Abend

Liebe Schwiegermutter

Frieda und ich sind in demselben Moment in den Bahnhof in Mailand angekommen, die zwei Züge zusammen, und die Gepäckträger haben uns denn in zwei Minuten zusammen gebracht. War das nicht gescheit?

Wir sind eben in die Villa Mirenda eingetretet: alles gut und schön hier – Freunde mit Blumen, die Bauern alle da zum Grüssen und Wilkommen – sehr nett und freundlich. Jetzt haben wir gegessen, und sitzen am Feuer eine Stunde, dann gehen ins Bett. Frieda ist glücklich, hier zu sein – geht herum und guckt alles an.

Nett ist die Krawatte, ich muss die Farbe am Tag sehen. – Bin so froh dass es dir so gut geht: ich komme auch im Sommer, und wir werden 'Erdbeern mit schlag' zusammen essen – nicht wahr?

So schöne Primmeln und Veilchen auf der Tisch unter die Lampe!

Also gute Nacht! DHL

[1] Melanie Antonia Baillot; Anthony and Francis Huxley.
[2] Bobbie Gillete (see p. 155 n. 1). DHL showed some interest in her literary potential (see *Letters*, v. 118–19) and held her and her husband in high regard (ibid., p. 135).
[3] See p. 48 n. 1.

Die Freunde gehen Morgen nach Florenz und werfen diesen Brief in die
Post. Du sollst nur wissen dass wir gut hier sind.

[Wednesday evening

Dear Schwiegermutter

Frieda and I arrived at the same moment at the station in Milan, the two
trains together, and the porters then brought us together within a couple of
minutes. Wasn't that clever?

We have just walked into the Villa Mirenda: everything fine and lovely here
– friends with flowers, the peasants all there to greet and welcome us – very
nice and friendly. Now we've eaten, and are sitting by the fire for an hour, then
go to bed. Frieda is happy to be here – goes round looking at everything.

The tie is nice, I must see the colour by day. – I am so glad that you're so
well: I am coming too in the summer, and we shall eat 'Strawberries and
cream' together – shan't we?

Such lovely primroses and violets on the table under the lamp!

Good night then!   DHL

The friends are going into Florence tomorrow and will put this letter in the
post. You should just know that we've arrived safely.]

4327. To Giuseppe Orioli, [8 March 1928]
Text: MS UCLA; Unpublished.

Villa Mirenda, *Scandicci*.
Thursday

Dear Pino

I forgot to say that Frieda's sister *Frau Dr Jaffé* is coming back to Florence
and may call in your shop to ask when we're coming in: – perhaps Saturday
she'll be there. So you can give her the news. We shan't come to Florence
before Monday or Tuesday. But tell her to come out here with Prof. Weber
whenever she wishes.

And when you come will you bring $\frac{1}{2}$ chilo of bacon, affettata,[1] from the
shop near Giuntina – he has it good – or from the Co-operativa, anywhere
where it's good.

Till Sunday!   DHL

[1] 'sliced'.

4328. To Juliette Huxley, 8 March 1928

Text: MS Huxley; Huxley 706–7.

Villa Mirenda, *Scandicci*. Florence
Thursday 8 March 1928

Dear Juliette

I had a very pleasant journey – so peaceful in Switzerland – but in Domodossola a lot of nervy Italians got in.[1] Frieda's train arrived in Milan just as mine did, and we met on the platform. Got home all right last night – all the peasants out to meet us, with primroses and violets and scarlet and purple anemones. Something touching about them. But I don't really like Italy: it's all in a wrong mood, nervous and depressed. And today it rains, rather dree,[2] and is colder than Diablerets. Impossible really to warm these great stone barns. So I've been painting a water-colour: torch-dance by daylight![3] How are Adam and Eve? – perfect now in a perfect paradise?[4] I quite miss them: had them in my eye so long, that I feel they must be waiting for me somewhere.

Frieda sends her regards, (oh, she says love!! – same thing!) and says she'll write and answer your letter. I'll try and keep her up to it. But perhaps you'd better begin another paradise in the meanwhile. – And she says – *Frieda* – that *I* left a picture in the bottom drawer of the wash-stand – the bottom-drawer was *her* drawer, declared empty when she left; so if you've time, do pick it up from old Ansermoz.[5] It's only a small canvas of a jaguar jumping on a man – *not* good, *not* finished, and I don't like it.[6] So there's no hurry about sending it, you can post it from London, if you'd be so kind – or even leave it till we come. No matter at all. Miserable thing!

I'm taking my novel to the printer tomorrow in Florence – if it doesn't Rain!

John Thomas and Lady Jane[7]
Were caught larking in the rain
Penalty! they're torn in twain!

---

[1] On the railway line n.w. of Milan, just across the Italian border.

[2] I.e. steadily, drearily (Nottinghamshire dialect).

[3] Later entitled *Fire-Dance*; reproduced in *Paintings of D. H. Lawrence*, plate [18].

[4] Lady Juliette Huxley explains in her autobiography, *Leaves of the Tulip Tree* (1986), p. 117: 'Touched by the subtle but definite influence of Lawrence, I wanted to embroider Adam and Eve in their paradise . . . Lawrence finished Adam's genital organs which I had fumbled, adding a black virile business to a perfectly sensible phallus. He obviously enjoyed this last touch and the collaboration which crystallised these precious moments.'

[5] Unidentified.   [6] See Letter 4197 and p. 207 n. 1.   [7] Cf. Letter 4330.

Tanti saluti e tante belle cose/choses![1] to your mother. – Not a sound from
Aldousells.[2] – Wish I was having tea on the Aroles terrace with you all.[3] – Post
is three miles away here, so must mail tomorrow. – Did you get *anything* done
in Aigle?[4] – those lovely hepaticas!

au revoir!   DHL

4329. To Edward McDonald, 9 March 1928
Text: MS UT; Postmark, Firenze 10.III 28; Moore 1042–3.

Villa Mirenda. *Scandicci.* (Florence)

9 March. 1928

Dear McDonald,

I wonder if by now you are bored by me and my books – and all the rest of
books! – but if you are, don't let me bother you. Probably Mason told you of
my wanting to print a private edition of my new novel 'John Thomas and
Lady Jane' – that's the title I want, instead of *Lady Chatterleys Lover*, which it
was previously – here in Florence. I took the MS. to the little printer today:[5]
very boldly. In Diablerets – we've just come back from there, in the
mountains, for my unhappy chest – I tried very hard to expurgate the two
duplicate MSS: but didn't get very far. I felt just blind to the purple of
impropriety. So I expurgated what I could – all the man's touching address to
his penis, and things like that – and sent on the MSS, one to Alf Knopf and
one to Martin Secker. They can fall foul of them if they like. But if they want
to publish, I don't mind expurgating more and more for them, so long as I can
publish my own immaculate and blemishless edition here in Florence – 1000
copies, 500 for America, at ten dollars: ready about May 20th. – Mason wrote
me rather scared about the censor and smut-hunting authorities: what do you
think? Do you think there is much risk in the mail? I want to mail to
individuals direct, but of course don't want those individuals to be let down.
Do, if you're not bored, write and tell me what you think. And give me any
wise hint you can.

Of course the book *isn't* improper: but it *is* phallic. I shall expect Mrs
McDonald anyhow to stand by it. If she did pour salt water on your sprouting
lawn, she won't pour any on my sprouting phallic seed. I shall expect you to
stand by it too. One may get awfully fed up – as you were: but for all that, one

[1] The word 'choses' was written interlinearly above 'cose'; neither was deleted.
[2] I.e. Aldous and Maria Huxley.
[3] The Lawrences invariably joined the Huxleys at tea-time in the Chalet des Aroles which they
had rented (*Leaves of the Tulip Tree*, p. 117).
[4] Juliette Huxley accompanied DHL to Aigle 'as the sudden change of altitude might have over-
tired him' (*Leaves of the Tulip Tree*, p. 125).
[5] The Tipografia Giuntina, directed by L. Franceschini at 4 via del Sole, Florence.

must fight. And the phallic reality is what one must fight for. So there! I was a bit abashed by Mason, because he told me that *The Bridge of San Luis Rey* was the best book that had been through the Centaur's stable in a year:[1] and I found it a dull dough-nut with artificial jam in it. Cookies! So I sort of feel I had better say no more to him about my own productions: though he's kind as an angel.

I want to come to New Mexico this summer, but my wife won't – says I'm not well enough. It's true I've felt rather Gummidgey[2] and 'low' and disheartened these last two years – but now I really think I'm picking up, getting my pecker up again,[3] and on the war-path therewith once more. So perhaps we might go to New Mexico in the winter – I want to. The world of man is all alike – a bad egg, which one would rather go without. Nevertheless, there is the other world, world without end amen[4] and a few people in it. So when we *do* come west, I shall try to see you and Mrs McDonald – and if you come to Europe – which isn't really a cheering thing to do – I hope you'll come and see me. We finish with this house at the end of April: then we shall be like the tramps of no fixed abode. But write me here before then.

Many greetings from both of us to you and Mrs McDonald.

D. H. Lawrence

4330. To Aldous and Maria Huxley, [9 March 1928]
Text: Huxley 707–8.

Villa Mirenda, Scandicci, Firenze.
9 March.

Dear Aldous and Maria, –

To-day I lunched with Orioli, and we took the MS. of the novel to the printer: great moment. Juliette, who read the MS. and was *very* cross, morally so, suggested rather savagely I should call it: 'John Thomas and Lady Jane'. Many a true word spoken in spite, so I promptly called it that. Remains to be seen if Secker and Knopf will stand it. – Afterwards, Juliette was *almost* reconciled to the novel: but she still thought: *what* if Anthony were 16,[5] and read it! – What indeed! However, to-morrow night I shall have a specimen page from the printer – and by Monday I may hear what Curtis Brown and Secker think of their expurgated (*sic*) MS. I'm prepared for anything – but

[1] The novel by Thornton Wilder (1897–1975) was published in New York, 1927; it won the Pulitzer prize in the same year.
[2] I.e. complaining, self-pitying, peevish (after Mrs Gummidge in Dickens' *Old Curiosity Shop*, 1850).   [3] I.e. recovering his strength and determination.
[4] The concluding phrase in the doxology from the *Book of Common Prayer*.
[5] See p. 246 n. 2.

shall go ahead here. – Saw Douglas to-day – but nothing new about him, still thinking of Jerusalem and preferring Chianti.

We wound up very nicely in Diablerets. Juliette and her mother and Mademoiselle all looked after me like angels, and we made a paradise with a woollen serpent![1] Juliette brought it to the station for a last word of advice – me as paradise-manufacturer – and nearly died of shame because Mademoiselle stood like an easel holding it for me to see – on the platform – and I cocked my eye – and all the station peeped and peeped at Juliette's Adam and Eve nude in lisle thread and pink wool!

To-morrow F[rieda]'s elder sister due to come. – House full of violets and anemones. Wilk[inson]s depart at end of month.

Disgustedly!   DHL

4331. To Martin Secker, 9 March 1928
Text: MS UInd; Postmark, Firenze 10 . III 28; Secker 105.

Villa Mirenda. Scandicci. (Firenze)
9 March 1928

Dear Secker

The proofs of the poems came today. On the thin paper, the type looks rather small. But if it is printed on good sound paper it will look more important again. – Do you want the index at the end printed in a double column?[2] I think myself it's all right, but will other people grumble?

Today I took the proofs of 'John Thomas' to the printer in Florence, and I shall have a specimen page tomorrow night. Then I want to print the little circulars and start sending them out:[3] the book should be ready by May 20th: that is, I ought to have the first hundred ready bound by then: and after that, about fifty a day. For the circulars, of course I must fix the title, so I hope 'John Thomas and Lady Jane' is acceptable to you. Let me know by return, as I must order the circulars next week: title and all.

I hope you'll take the novel in the right spirit. Aldous and Maria Huxley loved it: but Juliette, Julian Huxleys wife, went into a terrible moral temper over it: then afterwards was reconciled. The rage was a kind of envy, I found. But I hope you'll react pleasantly. The book is a kind of bomb: but a beneficent one, and very necessary. – If you don't like it, though, *don't print it*. I shall just go ahead with my Florence edition.

It's really colder here than Diablerets – the sun isn't so bright and fine.

[1] See p. 313 and n. 4.
[2] The double-columned 'index' is an itemised table of contents at the end of *Collected Poems*, vol. ii.   [3] A copy is reproduced among the illustrations in this volume.

Really, one winter you should try the mountains *–over 3000 ft –* it does pick one up. I feel much better. – Italy is rather depressed, poor, and no *forestieri*[1] coming.

DHL

Regards to Rina and the boy.

4332. To Earl Brewster, [11 March 1928]
Text: MS UT; Brewster 164–6.

Villa Mirenda. *Scandicci*. Firenze
Sunday

Dear Earl

We got back here Wednesday night – so it has rained ever since. I really think it is nicer in Switzerland: warmer even: at least I *felt* much warmer, and the sun was lovely. Italy enervates one, and so one feels the cold much more. As for the southern mode, it seems to me it is dead. Italy just makes me feel exhausted. I'm ten times the man, on the other side of the Alps.

' My sister-in-law Else came yesterday, with Prof. Alfred Weber: they've been as good as married, and as bad, for many years. Alfred is one of the best-known German professors, but myself I don't get much out of him, though he's really nice. But Else you will really like, both of you will like her, if she calls on you. She is Frieda's elder sister: Frau Dr Else Jaffe. – They have gone on to Rome today: and they may or may not come to Capri. But I gave her your address.[2]

As for the future, what's to be done? I'm almost sure the best thing would be to march off to New Mexico and have done with it. There one has sun, and altitude, and lovely landscape: and moderate expenses. But I'll have to stay here a bit, as I'm going to print a private and unexpurgated edition of my novel here. For the public it will have to be expurgated. It is a phallic novel, but very nice and tender. So I *must* issue it complete here – at ten dollars too! – I took the MS. to the printer. – I doubt I won't have the thing done till end of May, which means hanging around here, more or less. – I wasn't going to tell you, as it's not really in your line, or Achsah's. But you'd know some time.

So I might take some little excursion, between now and May. But not to Africa. Those Arabs don't interest me much. Anyhow it costs too much. And I doubt if Frieda will want me to go off alone. I might go to Cortina Arezzo Chiusi etc and finish the etruscan essays: but feel very vague. I don't feel a bit settled here – ready to leave almost any day. We may come to Capri for a little while. I'll have to rouse myself and make some sort of plan. But for the novel, I wouldn't stay here at all.

[1] 'visitors, foreigners'.
[2] The Brewsters were living in Torre Quatro Venti between Capri and Anacapri.

Many thanks for the photographs. Some of them are very nice and will no doubt be useful. Unfortunately most of them are deliberately – and artistically posed – which rather spoils the effect. I wish one could get absolutely natural photographs of naked people just walking about or jumping or sitting, with no idea of art. What are the other photographs like? – you said there were many. – The man comes out best – and one or two of the girl. But why pose like a Velasquez Venus, so obvious? If it's not asking too much, you might send me another batch, and I'll hunt through them, and send them you back, keeping one or two for use. But I'll send them all back safely. – I did a water-colour since I'm here – a torch-dance – two naked men – rather nice I think – not particularly 'natural'. Photographs are a great help with water-colours, where the figures are smaller than in oil, and more set in.

As for a show of pictures, somehow I don't care anyway. If we went to New York we might do it. But I've lost any interest I ever had in showing. Are you arranging a definite show, at a definite time? I wouldn't mind occupying a corner – but can't rouse myself to bother about it.

I'll order you a copy of my new book of stories, which should come out just now.[1]

And we'll meet before long, when this vagueness and indecision pass off.

I shall expect a grand meal from those young bacchanals when I come. Shall I be allowed bacon? – or is it strictly buttered leaves and grasses?

I'm correcting proofs of the poems. How it brings up the past! Shall be glad when it's over.

DHL

4333. To Mabel Dodge Luhan, 13 March 1928
Text: MS Brill; Luhan 336–7.

Villa Mirenda. *Scandicci.* (Florence)
13 March 1928

Dear Mabel

Here we are back from Switzerland – and I'm a good bit better. The altitude was good for me. Now I'm so busy with my novel. I want to call it 'John Thomas and Lady Jane' (John Thomas is one of the names for the penis, as probably you know): but have to submit to put this as a sub-title, and continue with *Lady Chatterley's Lover*: for the publisher's sake. But my own unexpurgated edition is being printed here now – quite thrilling. I want to have it ready by May 15th: and I want to post it direct from here, to those that buy it. I am doing 1000 copies, of which 500 for America, at $10. each. I shall

[1] *The Woman Who Rode Away.*

send you a few of the little order-forms, and do please send them out for me, to Buffalo and New York and places like that, to people who are likely to appreciate the book. It is frankly and faithfully a phallic novel, but tender and delicate, as I believe in it: and as I believe is necessary for us to become. It'll infuriate *mean* people: but it will surely soothe decent ones. Anyhow do help me all you can, as you promised. Then really I'll have some money to come to the ranch – for I mean to come. And I believe the Brewsters and the Huxleys will come along with us. Which would be fun. If we don't come in the summer, I wouldn't mind coming in autumn, as we did the first time. But I must get this novel off my chest first. – You might one day print your memoirs here in Florence, in the same way.

I expect you have some resistance inside yourself to the New York socialist phase of yours. What is it, I wonder? You can't really sympathise with the Mabel of those days. But why? – Unless you can sympathise with that Mabel you can't write that section.

I am sending some of the order-forms for *Lady Chatterley* to Bynner and Christine Hughes, for them to distribute – so don't overlap. But do give Spud as many as he really wants, for people in California and out-of-the-way places, to whom the book would be really attractive. – I'll send a few forms to Idella Purnell. – I shan't send out any copy until it's paid for – otherwise I'm left. – Well I hope I'll get through all right.

Yrs   D. H. Lawrence

4334. Christine Hughes, 13 March 1928
Text: MS UCLA; Postmark, [. . .]; Unpublished.

Villa Mirenda. Scandicci. (Florence)
13 March 1928

Dear Christine

So you think Brett is going crazy![1] But then I think Taos makes people seem like that, after a while.

I was in Switzerland up at the snow for a couple of months, and it did me a lot of good. I really begin to feel I *am* getting my strength back. – Now we are here again for a little while – and I'm busy printing a private edition, here in Florence, of my new novel *Lady Chatterley's Lover*. It has to be expurgated for the public: so I *do* want to bring out the thing complete. It's a phallic novel, frankly: but tender and delicate. And I believe in it. I believe the world is going crazy for lack of the real phallic feeling and consciousness – which is

---

[1]   Christine Hughes (cf. Letter 3995 and p. 38 n. 2) lived in Santa Fe, within a modest distance of her friend Brett in Taos.

more than mere sex. Sex can be any sort of cerebral reaction, mere cerebration transferred to the sexual centres. But the phallic reality is another reality. Anyhow I shall send you a few order forms, and do distribute them for me to one or two likely people, who *may* appreciate the book. I'm writing Bynner and Alice Corbin the same – and to Taos. I hope to have the book ready by May 15th: very nice, hand paper etc – but it's the inside I care about. But people have got to buy it, since it's worth it. I'm doing 1000 copies, 500 of them being for America: at $10. a copy.

We're in this house till May 6th: then God knows where. I want to come to New Mexico this year – perhaps, as you suggest, stay some time in Santa Fe. I think the Brewsters will come too: and probably the Huxleys. Quite a show of us!

How is Mary C[hristine]? I hope she's gathering herself together. After all, it's worth while to be an individual, not a mere heap of muddled qualities. It's worth while gathering oneself together. – And how are you – cheerful, I hope.

                                                          Yrs   D. H. Lawrence

Just about this time last year I came to Rome and stayed with you. – Do help me a bit with the novel – and fairly quick!

4335. To Alice Corbin Henderson, 13 March 1928
Text: MS UT; Postmark, S[candicci] 14 3 28; Unpublished.

                                        Villa Mirenda. *Scandicci*. (Florence). Italy
                                                          13 March 1928
Dear Alice Corbin,

I got today a copy of *Readings from the New Poets* – with your 'Music':[1] nice, but not one of your best, in my opinion. And I am far from thinking Masefield the finest living poet.[2] He's cheap. But there!

I'm going to send you a few little order-forms for my new novel, and will you distribute them for me to the right people, in Chicago preferably? I'm doing a private edition of the book here in Florence: for the public, it must be expurgated. It's a phallic novel, but tender and delicate, not to be taken lewdly. I do believe the phallic reality is good and healing, in a world going insane. I believe the phallic consciousness makes us gentle and really human hence my novel – and hence my desire not to have it expurgated, but to give it out whole.

I'm doing 1000 copies, of which 500 for America, at $10. To some people it will be worth it. I want to mail it direct from here to the purchasers. It should be ready by May 15th.

[1] See *Readings from the New Poets*, ed. W. Webster Ellsworth (New York, 1928), p. 143.
[2] John Masefield (1878–1967), an inventive but too prolific poet; later Poet Laureate.

And later on, I really want to come to New Mexico. Now I've been in Switzerland, at the snow, and it's done me a lot of good. So I'm sure New Mexico would help.

I do hope you're well – and everything going nicely. How is your anthology?[1]

Ever!   D. H. Lawrence

4336. To Witter Bynner, 13 March 1928
Text: MS HU; Postmark, S[candicci] 14 3 28; Huxley 711–12.

Villa Mirenda. *Scandicci* (Florence)
13 March 1928

Dear Bynner

I sniffed the red herring in your last letter a long time: then at last decide it's a live sprat.[2] I mean about the *Plumed Serpent* and the 'hero'. On the whole, I think you're right. The hero is obsolete, and the leader of men is a back number. After all, at the back of the hero is the militant ideal: and the militant ideal, or the ideal militant, seems to me also a cold egg. We're sort of sick of all forms of militarism and militantism, and *Miles*[3] is a name no more, for a man. On the whole I agree with you, the leader–cum–follower relationship is a bore. And the new relationship will be some sort of tenderness, sensitive, between men and men and men and women, and not the one up one down, lead on I follow, ich dien[4] sort of business. So you see I'm becoming a lamb at last, and you'll even find it hard to take umbrage at me. Do you think?

But still, *in a way*, one has to fight. But not in the O Glory! sort of way. I feel one still has to fight for the phallic reality, as against the non-phallic cerebration unrealities. I suppose the phallic consciousness is part of the whole consciousness which is your aim. To me it's a vital part.

So I wrote my novel, which I want to call 'John Thomas and Lady Jane'. But that I have to submerge into a subtitle, and call it: *Lady Chatterley's*

[1] See Letter 4218 and n. 2.
[2] DHL alludes to Bynner's letter to which Letter 4286 was partly a reply. Bynner's remarks to which he responds here read as follows (Bynner 332):

> You are forever hunting out in mankind some superior being (sometimes yourself) and attributing to him mystical or semi-mystical qualities of godly leadership. In this way you try to justify man's ways to God, or to yourself. There is always a spiritual tinge in it – an animal admiration – and often, arising out of that, a blur of spiritual admiration . . . For years, I have innerly believed that no man, not even the authoritative or prophetic leader, has any importance at all except as he foresees and furthers the ultimate amalgamation of all life into one total, completed consciousness which will somehow fulfill these imperfect and vain fragments of the totality, these individualities which we jealously restrict when, for right and happy growth, we should be enlarging them toward that final merged realization of the only self.

[3] *'Soldier'*.   [4] 'I serve' (the Prince of Wales's motto).

Lover. But I am printing here in Florence an unexpurgated edition of this tender and phallic novel, far too good for the public. The expurgated will come in the autumn. But this, the full fine flower with pistil and stamens standing, I hope to have ready by May 15th – 1000 copies, of which 500 for America, at ten dollars a copy. I shall send you a few little order-forms – and *do* please send a few out for me, to the right people. You can reach a lot of the right sort of people, in the universities. I shall mail direct from Florence, as soon as the book is ready: a good book. And why should the red flower have its pistil nipped out, before it is allowed to appear. – So I shall trust you in this.

We are in this house till May 6th – then I don't know where. I want to come to New Mexico – perhaps even earn a little money this way to come with.

tante belle cose!   D. H. Lawrence

4337. To S. S. Koteliansky, 15 March 1928
Text: MS BL; Postmark, Firenze 17 . III 28; cited in Gransden 32.

Villa Mirenda, *Scandicci* (Florence)
15 March 1928

My dear Kot

So long since I've written! but I was sort of hoping that something would turn up, some publication hope, to write about. But nothing! Only in Diablerets Aldous and I talked, that it would be good if a few authors joined together to publish their own books – the 'authors publishing company'. And they, the authors, provide the capital, and get a good man to run the show, on shares. Would that interest you? It's feasible, anyhow: and a good idea. – Aldous should be in London now, though I've not heard, and have only The Athenaeum Club, Pall Mall for his address.

Meanwhile my novel is with the printer here, being set up. I feel very bold. But I must do it. And I doubt if you could have got a printer to tackle it in England. English printers refuse to print words like 'arse' or 'shit' – just refuse. Which is nonsense. My novel, the second half, is phallic, and intentionally so. I believe in it. It can't be done publicly, so I do it privately. It will be on nice hand-made paper, and I hope will be handsome. – The printer's shop is an old fashioned little place – nobody understands a word of English – nobody can be shocked.[1] What a mercy! I hope to have the book ready by May 15th. I shall send you a few of the order-forms, and perhaps you

[1] Frieda later told Dorothy Warren: 'When the Italian, who printed Lady C (he didn't know one word of English) was warned that it was obscene, he asked how? And when he was told just "lovemaking," he said: "Well, we do that every day," in great astonishment' (Nehls, iii. 378–9).

would give them to one or two of your friends, like Schiff.[1] Then we'll see how it goes. It's a beginning anyhow.

We've been back a week. Diablerets did me really a lot of good. But *this* is a rotten climate. It's rained every day since we're back, and my chest is sorer. I can't stay here long: I suppose we'll have to summer somewhere up in Switzerland, to see if I can't make a cure of myself. Oh if only one were tough! But I'm so much better.

If we go to Switzerland in May, we shall most likely come to England in August. It's my health now that I must see after.

How are you all at the Cave? Ghita quite better? Grisha still there? – How is Gertler? – I often talked about him to Julian Huxley and Juliette, who really like him.

Tell me if there is any news.

Yrs   D. H. Lawrence

4338. To George Conway, 15 March 1928
Text: MS Moore; Postmark, Firenze 17 . III 28; cited in Moore, *Intelligent Heart* 359.

Villa Mirenda. *Scandicci*. Florence.

15 March 1928

Dear Conway[2]

I was so pleased with your book – thought you did it awfully well, and it gave me such a good glimpse into that early Spanish Mexico. I would have written at once, but was ill, and had to go away to Switzerland up to the snow. We have only just come back – and it did me a lot of good. But my chest is the very devil. The worst of being ill is one loses one's connection with nearly everything. But thank goodness I'm better. This is a bad climate, though: so we're leaving this house for good on May 6th. – probably we shall summer in Switzerland, and perhaps in autumn go back to New Mexico to the ranch. If so, when you are passing to Canada, you must come and see us. – It seemed a shame, Mrs Conway being in Europe, and as near as Paris, that we didn't see her. But I was disheartened with my health.

Now I'm busy here printing my new novel for a private edition here in Florence. You've been through it, so you'll sympathise with me. – I expect the

[1] Sydney Schiff (1868–1944), novelist (pseud. Stephen Hudson) and wealthy literary patron. Cf. *Letters*, iv. 565 and n. 3.
[2] George Robert Graham Conway (1873–1951), Scottish president of Mexican Light & Power Co. and Mexican Tramways Co., and an avid collector of Spanish colonial documents. He and his wife, Anne Elizabeth Conway (1881–1962), befriended the Lawrences in Mexico City (see *Letters*, v. 228 n. 1). In 1927 Conway published (privately in Mexico) an edn of *An Englishman and the Mexican Inquisition, 1555–1660, being an account of the voyage of Robert Tomson to New Spain, his trial . . . and other contemporary historical documents.*

publishers will publish an expurgated edition in the autumn. But I *must* bring
out the book complete. It is – in the latter half at least – a phallic novel, but
tender and delicate. You know I believe in the phallic reality, and the phallic
consciousness: as distinct from our irritable cerebral consciousness of today.
That's why I do the book – and it's not just *sex*. Sex alas is one of the worst
phenomena of today: all cerebral reaction, the whole thing worked from
mental processes and itch, and not a bit of the real phallic insouciance and
spontaneity. But in my novel there is.

I'm doing 1000 copies, on nice Italian hand-made paper – a nice book. It's
rather fun seeing it through, really. Didn't you find it so? The printer doesn't
know a word of English. – I hope, between America and England, I'll be able
to sell it. But I'm sending you one or two leaflets, and perhaps you'll give them
to anybody who might like the book – Donald Miller for example.[1]

With many warm regards to you and Mrs Conway from us both – and we'll
surely meet again before very long.

Yours Sincerely.   D. H. Lawrence

4339. To Dr Trigant Burrow, 15 March 1928
Text: MS (Photocopy) HU; Unpublished.

Villa Mirenda. *Scandicci* (Florence)
15 March 1928

Dear Dr Burrow

I had your letters, and the little books, and many thanks[2] – I was away in
Switzerland for my infernal chest – at the snow – am just back: and really a lot
better, feeling much more chirpy.

Now I'm busy printing my new novel here in Florence. It's such a nice
tender phallic novel, so of course, much too fine and sensitive for the gross
public. They'd cry dirt on it. So I'm doing it here in Florence. I shall send you
a few order forms, and I know you'll give them to a few people who may like
the book. As I say, it's a modern phallic novel, – the second half anyhow – but
tender and delicate. I think you'll like it, and be with it in spirit. The way to
gentle re-union is phallic, and through tenderness, don't you think? – between
men and women, and men and men, altogether. Phallic consciousness is so

---

[1] Donald Gazley Miller (1888–1953), American miner and engineer whom the Lawrences met in
Oaxaca in 1924 (see *Letters*, v. 163 and n. 5).
[2] The last surviving letters from Burrow were of 9 September and 21 December 1927 (see p. 115
nn. 1 and 2). The 'little books' are unidentified.

much deeper than what we call sex. I don't call my novel a sex novel: It's a phallic novel.

I hope too I'll get a bit of money by it, so we can come to New Mexico. – I don't earn my living – it has to earn itself. But if it'll earn me a bit of margin, good luck to it!

Hope you've had a gay successful winter in New York.

Sincerely   D. H. Lawrence

4340. To Emily King, 15 March 1928
Text: MS Lazarus; Unpublished.

Villa Mirenda. Scandicci. (Florence)
15 March 1928

My dear Pamela.

We've been back here a week – so it's rained every day, until today, when it blows. It really was much warmer up at the snow at Diablerets: and I felt better there. But we shall begin to pack up, and then go back to Switzerland. One may as well look after oneself. Though just now it's bad in the mountains, while the snow is going.

Ada ordered me some of that medicine of Aunt Ada's man, and the bill has come – but not the stuff.[1]

You haven't written, so I'm afraid you are hating the shop. But don't let it worry you, really. What's the point? One may as well be cheerful, even if the skies fall.

It's nearly your birthday – so you might write and tell me if I shall send you something from Florence, or just some money. There are all[2] sorts of embroidered tablecloths – and very nice soft hats of knitted silk straw – our peasants do them, very chic and nice, for the smart shops – but you know the sort of Florentine things – leather work, linen work, pictures, old jewelery, rather nice really – Tell me if you'd like anything.

And be sure to keep chirpy.

Love   DHL

Am ordering you the *Cavalleria Rusticana* book.[3]

---

[1] 'Aunt Ada' was Ada Rose Krenkow née Beardsall (1868–1944), wife of Fritz Krenkow (see p. 300 n. 3).   [2] MS reads 'There all'.
[3] Cape published DHL's translation of Verga's *Cavalleria Rusticana and Other Stories* in February 1928.

4341. To Curtis Brown, 15 March 1928
Text: Huxley 709–10.

Villa Mirenda, Scandicci, Florence.
15 March, 1928.

Dear C[urtis] B[rown], –

Thanks for yours about Gaige.[1] I thought that was gone – forgotten – so when Willard Johnson – the boy who did that *Laughing Horse* number of me in Santa Fé – wrote and asked me if he could do that story on his little press in Taos, I said 'yes.' He hasn't got a bean – so there's no money there. But I told him if he got ahead to fix up with the New York office. But perhaps he won't do it. If he doesn't, I shall write a second half to it – the phallic second half I always intended to add to it – and send it to you for Gaige to look at. Otherwise later I'll write a 10,000-word thing and send it. It's a length I like – and I hate having to fit magazines. Apparently the story appeared in the February number of *The Forum*, but they never sent me a copy, which is tiresome.[2] I wanted to see it.

My novel, *Lady Chatterley's Lover*, or 'John Thomas and Lady Jane', is at the printer's in Florence: such a nice little printing shop all working away by hand – cosy and bit by bit, real Florentine manner – and the printer doesn't know a word of English – nobody on the place knows a word – where ignorance is bliss! Where the serpent is invisible! They will print on a nice hand-made Italian paper – should be an attractive book. I do hope I'll sell my 1000 copies – or most of 'em – or I'll be broke. I want to post them direct to purchasers. I shall send you a few little order-leaflets, and you will find me a few purchasers, won't you? I shan't send the book unless the people send the two quid, else I'm left.

I haven't heard from [Secker?].[3] Maybe he's got a belly-ache. I can't help it. It's not my fault if people turn into withered sticks, with never a kick in them. I believe in the phallic consciousness, as against the irritable cerebral consciousness we're afflicted with: and anybody who calls my novel a dirty sexual novel is a liar. It's not even a sexual novel: it's phallic. Sex is a thing that exists in the head, its reactions are cerebral, and its processes mental. Whereas

---

[1] Crosby Gaige (1883–1949), American theatrical producer, publisher of fine edns and book collector (see obituary, *New York Times*, 9 March 1949). He was interested in publishing *The Escaped Cock* (see Letter 4377 and n. 1).   [2] See p. 40 n. 1.

[3] Huxley – who published and thus preserved this and some other texts for which no MS survives – deleted certain words and personal names to avoid giving offence. Occasionally (as here) Catherine Carswell's annotated copy of Huxley supplies the missing word or name; for the use of her marginalia the editors are indebted to John Carswell.

the phallic reality is warm and spontaneous and – but *basta*! you've had enough.

D. H. Lawrence

4342. To Marian Eames, 15 March 1928
Text: TMSC NWU; Huxley 712.

Villa Mirenda, Scandicci, Florence
15 March 1928

Dear Marian

I've not yet sent you the promised book:[1] but that was because I didn't have a nice one. Now I'm correcting proofs of my *Collected Poems*, and that seems very suitable. So as soon as I get copies, I'll write in one and send it you.

I was glad to hear you are gaily and hopefully embarked with a husband. Imagine Emma Eames being in the family! I do hope your husband will put out a few brave blossoms. The world badly needs a few courageous artists. The present lot have their tails sadly between their legs. When your husband writes, see that it's chirpy and defiant.

I'm going to send you a few order-forms for my new novel, which I'm printing here in Florence. It's a tender phallic novel: now you're married you'll understand it. I have to publish it here, as it's too phallic for the gross public. So if you can, give the leaflets to a few people who might like to buy the book. It's worth it.

And some time this year I do hope we'll be in New York en route to New Mexico, then we'll drink a pink and cheerful draught from the soda fountain, for our mutual healths, together.

Sincerely   D. H. Lawrence

Make your mother buy my novel: good for her, after so much behaviourism.

4343. To Harriet Monroe, 15 March 1928
Text: TMSC NWU; Harriet Monroe, 'D. H. Lawrence', *Poetry: A Magazine of Verse*, xxxvi (May 1930), 93, 94.

Villa Mirenda, Scandicci (Florence)
15 March 1928

Dear Harriet Monroe:[2]

Long since I heard from you – or even of you – since that day in Chicago:

---

[1] For this and some other references see Letter 4199 and n. 2. DHL never sent her any book.

[2] Harriet Monroe (1860–1936), American poet; founder and editor of *Poetry: A Magazine of Verse* (Chicago) in which several of DHL's poems appeared. She and DHL had corresponded since 1914.

and the ice on the shores of the lake, which I shall never forget, so wild and American still, with that wild forest of a city behind.[1] Something queer and terrifying about Chicago: one of the strange 'centres' of the earth, more so than New York.

I hope we shall go back to New Mexico some time this year, – and if so, that we shall again see you in Chicago. I feel it's time I connected up again with the west.

Meanwhile I'm busy here printing my new novel in Florence – 1000 copies, of which 500 for America. It is a nice and tender phallic novel – not a sex novel in the ordinary sense of the word. I don't know how much you sympathise with my work – perhaps not much. But anyhow you know it is quite sincere, and that I sincerely believe in restoring the other, the phallic consciousness, into our lives, because it is the source of all real beauty, and all real gentleness. And those are the two things, tenderness and beauty, which will save us from horrors. And I think with *Poetry* you've worked for those two things. And in my novel I work for them directly, and direct from the phallic consciousness, which, you understand, is not the cerebral sex-consciousness, but something really deeper, and the root of poetry, lived or sung.

So I shall send you a few order forms, and if you will give them to a few people who may care for the book, do so please. But if you don't want to be bothered, throw them away.

Yours sincerely,   D. H. Lawrence

4344. To Giuseppe Orioli, [16 March 1928]
Text: MS UCLA; Unpublished.

Villa Mirenda.
Friday

Dear Pino

If you get any proofs tomorrow, you could send them up by Windeam and Perceval, who are coming to lunch on Sunday.[2] I hope the printer has some ready.

Frieda's daughter Barbara suddenly appeared this morning – so we have visitors – *and vile weather.*

au revoir   DHL

---

[1] The Lawrences and Brett spent a day in Chicago with Harriet Monroe, in March 1924 (Monroe, *Poetry*, xxxvi. 93). Cf. *Letters*, v. 28.

[2] Robert Windeam's address appears in DHL's address book (MS UCB) as 16 Borgo San Jacopo, Florence; nothing further is known of him (cf. *Letters*, iv. 189). Deane Perceval, whom DHL had probably known since 1919 (cf. *Letters*, iii. 575), had been Secretary of the British Institute of Florence.

4345. To Maria Huxley, [16 March 1928]
Text: Huxley 714–16.

Villa Mirenda, Scandicci, Firenze.
Friday

My Dear Maria, –

Your letter yesterday. Glad you are happy in London. You wouldn't be wildly happy in Italy – it only rains – and was bitter cold and sleety – but now, thank heaven, is a bit softer and showery, not steady downpour. But I don't feel so brisk here – and chest more scratchy – don't like it.

Frieda's daughter Barbara suddenly arrived from Alassio this morning – for a fortnight or so. And F.'s sister Else is in Capri, and staying with us on her way back to Germany. And we are really clearing out of this house end of April. So I feel a bit confused.

No, I never said anything to Dorothy Warren about an exhibition – only Barbey talked to her of it.[1] I might do it – but I shan't sell the pictures – not till I'm strong. I've done three more water-colours:[2] not bad, but I'd rather do oils: one can use one's elbow, and in water it's all dib-dab.

The first batch of proofs due to-morrow. Secker wrote that he didn't see how the novel could possibly be expurgated for public sale – so I'll just go on with my private one. I'm only worried about copyright. – Did you get some of the little order-forms? – and did you notice the 1920 for a date! Pino overlooked it! You must get me a few orders if you can, or I'm broke. I've paid lire 4000 on account of the paper – nice hand-made paper, which will cost about 7000, I think! And I've made my design of a phoenix rising from the nest in flames, for the cover. Pino wouldn't have me let Bramanti wood-cut it:[3] said it would be much truer just cast and printed. Shall send you a specimen.

I think myself it's rather nice to be busy and practical on the outside – and day-dreams, as you call it, inside. The things one cares about are all inside, like seeds in the ground in winter. But one has to attend to the things one only half cares about. And so life passes away. I expect it is always so, in the winter of our discontent,[4] when the outside is mostly rather horrid and out of connection with the something else that struggles inside. Luckily the inside thing corresponds with the inside thing in just a few people. I think it is so with us. We don't fit very well outside – but the inside corresponds, which is most important.

June! What shall we do in June? Frieda says we must go back to

---

[1] See Letters 4108 and n. 3, 4144.
[2] The pictures were *Yawning*, *The Lizard* and *Under the Haystack*; they are reproduced in *The Paintings of D. H. Lawrence*, plates [20], [25] and [19] respectively.
[3] Unidentified.   [4] *Richard III*, I. i. 1.

Switzerland in May, and stay till mid July. Perhaps it would be wisest. But I'm not tying myself down to any plan.

Tell Juliette I expected to hear from her from London. I haven't got the Highgate address; will you send it me?

The French house sounds awfully nice – should very much like to see it.[1] I think it's rather a good solution.

The boy will be all right alone at school, after a week or so. Best for him. *Ora fa buio – buona notte!*[2]

DHL

4346. To Martin Secker, [16 March 1928]
Text: MS UInd; Huxley 714.

Villa Mirenda. Scandicci. (Florence)
Friday

Dear Secker

I was not surprised at your decision about the novel – Am going ahead with my edition – a little printer's shop in Florence where nobody understands any English, and some of the men, printers, can't even read. I shall make a nice book, at £2. – and hope I shall sell it, or I'm broke. I enclose you a few slips, and if you can get me one or two orders, benissimo! Write your order on one of the forms, will you – you may not want three copies.

I sent back proofs of the poems. Am interested to hear what Robert Bridges says.[3]

Barby suddenly turned up this morning from Alassio – and of course it still rains, but is not so cold.

Tell Rina, in case I forget, to take tram 16 from the Duomo to *Vingone* terminus. The inn is at the terminus. – But we'll be writing again before she comes – and if weather is decent we'll meet her in Florence. The inn charges L30 or L35 a day. – We shall be all busy packing up to leave – so it won't be so nice, alas!

Yrs.   D. H. Lawrence

---

[1] The Huxleys leased a house just outside Paris: 3 rue du Bac, Suresnes. DHL spent a week there in March 1929. (Matthew Huxley went to Frensham Heights School near Godalming.)

[2] '*Now it's getting dark – good night!*'

[3] Secker wrote to Bridges on 14 March 1928, inviting him to 'consider the idea of contributing an introduction' to *Collected Poems*; he offered to send a set of proofs 'for your full consideration of the question'; and concluded: 'I need hardly add that your introduction would greatly assist the public recognition of the author's work, and that your help would be greatly appreciated by Mr. Lawrence' (*Letters from a Publisher*, p. 41). Bridges' response has not been found.

4347. To Rolf Gardiner, 17 March 1928
Text: MS Lazarus; Huxley 712–14.

Villa Mirenda. *Scandicci*. Florence
17 March 1928

Dear Rolf

I expect you are back in England now – to winter again, for here even there's a bitter cold wind. I hope you are feeling cheerful. But don't *insist* on being cheerful: it costs too much from inside. I hope you weren't put out too by my remarks on leadership.[1] What I said is true to my experience. But you may not have got there yet – or it may not even be in your experience. Every man to his destiny. Only don't bluff yourself, because that way, you let yourself down.

When is your sister Margaret coming out? Here we are – if nothing drives us away – so tell her to come and see us when she will. If she will walk out, then *tram No. 16* from the Duomo to *Vingone*: to the very terminus and dead end ($\frac{1}{2}$ hour). Then there's another 25 minutes walk – straight ahead uphill from Vingone till you come to two cypresses, just beyond the house marked *Podere Nuovo*. Turn to the left there, and dip down into the little valley. Our house is the square big box on top of the poggio,[2] near the little Church of San Paolo.

[sketch map][3]

Now I want you to help me a bit. I wrote a novel –

Lady Chatterleys Lover

or

'John Thomas and Lady Jane'

– did I tell you? It is a phallic novel: a delicate and tender phallic novel. Secker thinks that even expurgated it could not be published publicly. *Bah*! So I'm publishing it here in Florence: have got a little printer to print it – nobody knows a word of English, on the place, so not a blush! – and I've made my favourite phoenix rising from a nest in flames (I rise up) for the cover – and it will be a nice book – 1000 copies, half of 'em for America, at £2. – I've got to sell it too: for I've got to live. So you must help me, because I know you will.

It is strictly a novel of the phallic consciousness as against the mental consciousness of today. For some things, you will probably dislike it: because you are still squeamish, and scared of the phallic reality. It is perfectly wholesome and normal, and man and a woman. But I protest against it's being labelled 'Sex'. Sex is a mental reaction nowadays, and a hopelessly cerebral affair: and what I believe in is the true phallic consciousness. But you'll see. – So I shall send you a bunch of the little order-forms, and you must get me

---

[1] See Letter 4322.   [2] 'knoll'.
[3] The sketch map gives rough directions from Vingone to the Mirenda.

what orders you can, because the book must be read – it's a bomb, but to the living, a flood of urge – and I must sell it. And it's part of the crusade that we are both out for, and una mano lava l'altra[1] – But I know you'll help me what you can. This is where I throw a straight bomb at the skull of idealistic Mammon. And of course it will in a way set me apart even more definitely than I am already set apart. It's destiny. Tu stai con me, lo so.[2]

DHL

4348. To Aldous Huxley, 17 March 1928
Text: Huxley 710.

Mirenda.
Sat., 17 March, '28.

Dear Aldous, –

Your letter and Maria's to-day – and first sound you've made since leaving Diablerets: those 2 post cards were ghosts. – It's a bitter cold wind here, and in Florence to-day like being in a knife-box. The printer is printing my novel. Secker won't do it – *meno male*[3] – but what about the copyright? Anyhow, I've got to sell my thousand, or I'm a lost soul. So you must help me. I'll send you a little batch of order-forms, and I'm sure you and Maria will make a few folks buy. That novel must be put down their throats. Mind you stand up for it, when the pigs begin to grunt, then to squeal, then to prance their feet in the porridge. It'll need a bit of backing. – Didn't you find a copy of my *Porcupine* at the club?[4] It was sent there. It's for Maria really – for the later ranch essays.

Let's go to New Mexico in autumn. Let's be amused.

I've said May fifteenth for my novel.

Damn everybody!

What is Julian's address?

We *must* put salt on the hypocritical and snaily tails, the good public.

Dear Maria, don't be downhearted.

Loeser is dead, in New York:[5] it killed him – *Son baie quelle, che dicono, che tanto cacca un bue, quanto mille mosche; perché ci sono più mosche che buoi!*[6]

DHL

---

[1] 'you help me, I'll help you'.   [2] 'You are with me, I know.'   [3] *'fortunately'*.

[4] See Letter 4297.

[5] Huxley had known Charles Loeser at least since July 1927. A wealthy American, Loeser had 'a house in Florence and a fine collection of pictures' (*Letters of Aldous Huxley*, ed. Smith, p. 288).

[6] '*When they say that an ox shits as much as a thousand flies they're being foolish; because there are more flies than oxen!*'

4349. To Laurence Pollinger, 17 March 1928
Text: MS UT; Unpublished.

Villa Mirenda. *Scandicci.* (Florence)

17 March 1928

Dear Pollinger

I have Secker's letter saying he thinks 'John Thomas' can't be done by him, in public edition.[1] Poor little Martin! how the devil must pinch him! I don't really mind a bit: only about the copyright. That's important. – Perhaps you might let Cape see the MS. – as you think best, when you've read it. Secker may be right, the thing may be too much of a naked man ever to be trimmed into unnakedness. Pah! – I don't care a straw about a public edition: only the copyright – But whatever you do, *don't* let the MS. stray about among publishers who hope for something bawdy. Let as few people see it as possible.

Of course Secker is a born rabbit – what he's doing publishing me at all is a mystery. After all, this perpetual state of funk is old-fashioned. Damn it, do you think the young are going to knock their knees together at the sound of the word *penis*, in terror! What rot! My novel is perfectly normal, and the phallic part of it is, or should be, part of every man's life, and every woman's. Then what the hell! Why all this bogey business? Why, they swallow the Marquis de Sade much more calmly:[2] and I defy any human being to find my novel anything but wholesome and natural. Bah, bogeys! People should have the phallic symbol branded on their foreheads, to cure them of their hypocrisy. But it's old-fashioned, it's out of date. And out of date it shall be, if I can have my way a bit.

But the printer is already printing here – and I've made my favourite design of the phœnix rising from the nest in flames, for the cover. I nearly put the motto: 'I rise up' – under the bird. But he who runs may read.[3] Avanti!

Many thanks for saying you'll send out the various copies of books of mine lying in your office. I enclose a list of addresses, and am very much obliged.[4]

I shall send you some of the little leaflets for 'John Thomas' next week. I must sell my 1000, or bust. 'io dico, che noi nasciamo di carne, e in su la carne muoiamo, la coda si fa, e la coda si disfa –'[5]

Yrs   D. H. Lawrence

---

[1] Secker's letter to DHL is unlocated; his letter to Pollinger, 14 March 1928 (Secker Letter-Book, UIll) makes his general attitude clear: 'I am returning the Lawrence typescript herewith which is of course quite unpublishable. I have written Lawrence fully on the matter, so that he is acquainted with our decision, and I have no doubt that Knopf will share our views. The proposed semi-private mode of publication is the only practicable one.'

[2] The marquis (1740–1814) became a byword for obscene writing.

[3] John Keble, 'Septuagesima Sunday', l. 1, in *The Christian Year* (1827) ['There is a book, who runs. .'].   [4] The list is missing.

[5] 'I tell you, we are born in the flesh, and die in the flesh, the tail is made, and the tail is destroyed –'

4350. To Giuseppe Orioli, [19 March 1928]
Text: MS UCLA; Unpublished.

Villa Mirenda, Scandicci
Monday

Dear Pino

Dont bother to send me any leaflets, as I am coming in on Thursday. We are lunching with the deaf Miss Moller.[1] But you might send these out:

20.   to L. E. Pollinger Esq. c/o Curtis Brown Ltd. 6 Henrietta St. London W.C. 2.

20.   Rolf Gardiner. 9 Lansdowne Rd. Holland Park. London W. 11.

20   Aldous Huxley. 3 Onslow Mews East. Cranley Place. London S.W. 7.

10.   Miss M. Beveridge. 20 Rossetti Garden Mansions, Chelsea. S.W. 3.

10.   Hon. Gordon Campbell. 'Clonard', *Terenure. Co. Dublin*, Ireland

Secker writes that it is impossible to publish the book in a public edition. I don't mind at all – save for the question of copyright. And Curtis Brown must see to that.

So we shall see you Thursday, unless it rains very much.

Yrs   DHL

4351. To Hon. Gordon Campbell, 21 March 1928
Text: MS UCin; cited in Beatrice Lady Glenavy, *Today We Will Only Gossip* (1964), p. 141.

Villa Mirenda. *Scandicci*. (Florence)
21 March 1928

Dear Gordon

Here we are back again in Italy – and this morning it is trying to snow. Bella vita! I suppose it's no better in Ireland.

I ought to stay here a couple of months now, for my novel. I'm having it printed – in Florence, in a little printer's shop where nobody understands a word of English, so nobody will be able to raise a blush. Isn't that nice! Imagine if the serpent in Paradise had whispered in Gaelic to Eve, when she only understood ancient Hebrew! What a lot of fuss might have been saved. – Secker wrote that he didn't think the novel could possibly be made fit for open publication, not even cut and modified. I didn't know it was as bad as that. And it isn't. But let him go to hell. Anyhow it is a phallic novel, and intended to be so, since I believe in the phallic reality, and in the phallic consciousness –

---

[1] According to DHL's address book (MS UT) Muriel Moller lived at 22 Lungarno Acciaioli, Florence; nothing is known of her except that DHL invariably spoke of her with affection.

which is by no means the same as what we call sex. Sex with us is a cerebral business, mental processes reflected down on to the physical activity, and therefore repulsive. But the phallic consciousness is true to itself.

Anyhow I hope you'll buy 'John Thomas' – and perhaps a few of your friends will too.

We haven't given up the hope of Ireland. Switzerland did me a lot of good, in health – and perhaps I ought to go back there for a bit. But not for long. Surely I won't have to think of my unhappy bronchials always.

Beatrice made you look so broken-down in her famous drawing, that I was quite sad. But then I know it is a weakness of the wifely eye, to see the husband as the sad sad weed of which *she* is the golden blossom. So I take off 60%, and remember your spats and cut-away coat of Conibear days.[1]

Well I *should* like to see you again, and Beatrice. And the Emerald Isle, I *should* like to see it for the first time. As for the children, they really are beyond me.

Yrs   D. H. Lawrence[2]

4352. To Gertrude Cooper, 21 March 1928
Text: MS Clarke; cited in Lawrence–Gelder 174–5.

Villa Mirenda. *Scandicci.* (Florence)
21 March 1928

My dear Gertie

I was glad to have your letter and know you are getting on. My supply of medicine came yesterday – more things than I wanted – five different ones. I am taking the capsules and the digestive powder – started last night. The

---

[1] Cf. Letter 4208 and p. 220 n. 1.

[2] Among the DHL MSS at UCB is one headed: '*March 13. 1928. Wrote letters to*'; there follows a list of persons to whom DHL wrote between 13 and 21 March. The list includes Letters 4333–6, 4338–9, 4341–3, 4347–9, 4351; those to the following addressees have not been found (identifying details, if known, are given only for individuals not mentioned elsewhere in this volume): Alfred Knopf; Edwin Rich; Idella Weatherwax; Mrs George W. Stevens (Toledo Art Museum, Ohio); Henry Kellett Chambers; Maria Chambers; Henry James Forman [author and political journalist] (the Harvard Club, New York); Mrs James Forsyth (Los Angeles); Mrs Elizabeth Hare [patroness of writers and artists] (Long Island, New York); David Rosenthal (*The New Student*, New York); George Bond [1925–7, Editor of] (*The Southwest Review*, Southern Methodist University, Dallas); Charles T. Scott; Edith Isaacs; Coburn Gilman; J. Elder Walker [Scottish engineer living in India whom DHL met on *R.M.S. Orsova*, April–May 1922 – see *Journal of the D. H. Lawrence Society*, iv (1987–8), 2, 63–6] (Darjeeling, Bengal); Genaro Estrada [acquaintance of DHL's in Mexico City and prototype for Garcia in *The Plumed Serpent*]; Miss Mary van Kleeck [Director of Industrial Studies for the Russell Sage Foundation, New York]; Anna di Chiara; Upton Sinclair; Millicent Beveridge. It is assumed that all were invited to subscribe for *Lady Chatterley's Lover*.

Umckoloaba doesn't seem to have any particular effect on me so far.[1] Perhaps it doesn't go for one's bronchials. But I'm a lot better.

It's the vilest weather – been bitter cold, and this morning was trying to snow – but had to turn into cold rain, which has lasted all day. Poor Italy! The peasants have already lost the first crop of peas, and the broad beans – frozen about a month ago. The second crop of peas is in flower, so of course they're trembling, for fear they shall be frozen too. But I don't think they will – I think it's going to turn warmer.

The country looks very brown and bleak – had no rain for months, till a fortnight ago. But the flowers are all out – the field dark with sweet violets – and grape hyacinths everywhere – and the scarlet and purple anemones, and the red tulips out in the young wheat. Yet somehow the flowers look lonely and a bit forlorn this year – the grass is not revived yet, brown, and everything brownish except the wheat.

Tell Jack I had his letter, and will send him an old brass cannon or a tank or something natty like that, in way of antiques. So he's started to keep a museum already! tell him to sit in the seat of importance, and be the greatest curio of all himself.

Frieda's sister Else came to see us the other day – now gone on to Capri. The Brewsters want me to go down too. I might. Yet it's a long way, and we shall be leaving this house at the end of April. I dread the thought of packing up – beastly job!

What a mercy if you can but get brisk and alert again. But you'll see you will. The wheel is coming round to our side again.

love to you all,   DHL

4353. To Catherine Carswell, 22 March 1928

Text: MS YU; Postmark, Firenze 22. III 28; [Donald Gallup], 'D. H. Lawrence's Letters to Catherine Carswell', *Yale University Library Gazette*, xlix (January 1975), 259–60.

Villa Mirenda. Scandicci. Florence.

22 March 1928

My dear Catherine

Here we are back again – and vile weather – yesterday trying to snow – but pouring with cold rain all the time instead. I suppose it's bad everywhere just now.

---

[1] Umckaloaba (a South African plant) was 'discovered' in 1897 by C. H. Stevens who, though not himself medically qualified, claimed that it had curative properties in many cases of tuberculosis. (It was administered in the form of drops or capsules.) It was subjected to tests and – certainly in 1928 – was prescribed by some doctors as a beneficial treatment. See Adrien Sechehaye, *The Treatment of Pulmonary and Surgical Tuberculosis with Umckaloaba*, trans. A. H. Grant (1930).

I am busy printing my novel with the little printer in Florence – they understand no English, so nobody has qualms. Secker writes he thinks it is impossible to make the book suitable for public publication. I don't care – I'll go ahead with my private one. The only question is copyright. – I shall make a nice book, on hand-made cream paper – and hope I'll sell it, or I'm broke. I'll send you one or two of the order-forms, and perhaps you know one or two people who might like the book.

We finish with this house at the end of April – Then probably we'll go back to Switzerland, to fix up my chest. Diablerets did it such a lot of good. And this climate does *not* suit it: I don't really like being here.

You must see how you like the look of my novel format – and then if you wish, no doubt Orioli would get the *Merry Muses* done for you here – probably make you more than Nonsuch. But perhaps you like Frances Meynell.[1]

I enclose the ten bob – and trust you are all well, these dismal days.

DHL

Give Gordon one of the order forms, will you?

4354. To Bonamy Dobrée, 22 March 1928
Text: MS Brotherton; Unpublished.

Villa Mirenda. *Scandicci* (Florence)
22 March 1928

Dear Dobrée

Tell Mrs Dobreé many thanks for her letter, and I'll write to her directly.

This is merely to send you one or two order-forms for my new novel. Secker says he can't see that it can be made fit for publication in the ordinary way, even cut. So I'm publishing it myself, in all its unfitness. And a little printer in Florence is setting it up: and I'll make a nice book: and I hope I'll sell it. It's a phallic novel, really, and most people will hate it. An attempt to set the phallic consciousness over against the withered mental consciousness. Not sex merely – because sex nowadays is a rotten cerebral affair, mental reactions reflected down on the physical, which thus becomes repulsive. But the phallus with its own consciousness, which is also us.

It's vile weather – sleet, cold rain. We leave this house end of April[2] – and in May go back, I think, to Switzerland, to the altitude, for a couple of months. It was so good for my health. – Then end of July I want to come to England –

---

[1] See Letter 4163 and p. 174 n. 2. (The Nonesuch Press did not publish *The Merry Muses*.)
[2] April] May

and perhaps in September sail for America, to go to the ranch. If not, we should like to come to Egypt next autumn.[1] But that's still far.

We must contrive to meet somewhere this summer – I really think I shall go back to the ranch before long – and the Huxleys say they will come too – Aldous and his wife – it's fun out there – and the world of people doesn't amount to much.

Regards to Mrs Dobrée from us both.   D. H. Lawrence

4355. To Max Mohr, [22–31 March 1928]
Text: MS HMohr; Mohr, *Briefe* 531–2.

Villa Mirenda. *Scandicci* (Florence)
22 March 1928

Dear Max Mohr

So, we are back again in Italy, and it is cold and rains every day, and I don't like it. Diablerets suited me very much better: though it was a shame you had such ugly days, and caught influenza into the bargain. I do hope you are better.

No, I didn't really like *Venus and the Fishes*: it is too modern for me: you know I am a bit 'altmodisch' really. And it is true, you have written drama so much, you are more concerned with the mechanism of events and situations, than with essential human character. That is where I think the novel differs fundamentally from drama. The novel is concerned with human beings, and the drama is concerned with events. A drama is *what happens*, and a novel is *what is*. And you don't care very much what *is*. You are not *really* interested in people: you don't care what they are, inside themselves. You only care for their 'figure', in the American and in the Italian sense – of what they're worth and what they look like. So you write novels as if your characters were puppets: much more so than when you write plays. – But perhaps the public will like it: I am no judge.

Here I am busy with my novel, which is being printed in a little printer's shop in Florence. I send you one or two leaflets, and if you know any rich man in Berlin who might buy a copy, send him a leaflet, will you. It is too dear for you to buy – Mark 40 – but later I shall give you one – not of this 1000, because I've promised not to give any of these away – but of the next lot, quite soon. For England, it is a very shocking novel: shocking! But that's because they are fools. It is really a novel contrasting the mental consciousness with the phallic consciousness. Do you remember saying that Rosanov is wrong, making *sex*

---
[1] autumn.] year.

the new great liberator.[1] But I think even Rosanov was trying to express the phallic urge and consciousness, not merely the sexual. It is quite true, sex today is all mental; intellectual reactions reflected down on to physical processes: and that is repulsive, hässlich und widerlich.[2] But the phallic reality is a free consciousness and a vital impulse, and is the great and saving reality.

I hope it's nice at Wolfsgrube. We shall stay here till May – then perhaps go to Switzerland. I don't know. I want to go to New Mexico. I don't like it here.

I do hope the novel of the 'Jungfrau Max' is going nicely and gaily.[3] If you write straight about yourself, no doubt it will be less 'dramatic.'

With regards to the gnädige Frau.[4]

D. H. Lawrence

31. March

Look, I wrote this letter nine days ago, and I thought you had it – but somebody put it under a book, and I've only just found it! Too bad! You may well wonder why I don't write. – I had your letter – you sound a bit sad. But *be* sad. It is far better to be sad than to laugh in a Lächle-Woche.[5] And I do hope the Pilatus play will amuse you, then you'll do it well.[6] I'm so afraid I may depress you by not liking *Venus*. But is no good unless one speaks the truth. And I do think your plays are more amusing than the novel.

DHL

4356. To Earl Brewster, 27 March 1928
Text: MS UT: cited in Brewster 166.

Villa Mirenda. *Scandicci*. (Florence)
27 March 1928

Dear Earl

Many thanks for the second batch of photographs. I painted from one of them a man pissing, which seems to me very touching and nice.[7] I should have written to thank you before, but thought you might write, or my sister-in-law might, to say she'd been to see you. But no news.

---

[1] Vasily Vasilyevich Rozanov (1856–1919), Russian critic and philosophical writer; advocated naturalistic religion of sex and procreation. Author of *Solitaria* (1912), *Fallen Leaves* (1913), *The Apocalypse of our Time* (1917–18). See DHL's review of *Solitaria* in *Phoenix* 367–71; for Rozanov's influence on DHL see G. Zytaruk in *Comparative Literature Studies*, iv (1967), 283–97.   [2] 'odious and repulsive'.   [3] *Die Heidin*, a novel published in 1929.
[4] 'gracious wife'.   [5] 'Keep smiling-Week'.   [6] The play is unidentified.
[7] Cf. Letter 4332. The painting, *Dandelions*, is reproduced in Keith Sagar, 'D. H. Lawrence's Paintings', *Words International*, i (November 1987), 30.

I sent you also a little bunch of my order-forms for my novel: thought Achsah especially might like to send one or two out to her most spiritual and purely pure friends. I'm sure Mrs Rhys Davids would profit by a course of 'John Thomas and Lady Jane'. But really, joking apart, if the things are going to make you blush at all, throw them in the fire. As I say, it's a novel of the phallic consciousness; or the phallic consciousness versus the mental-spiritual consciousness: and of course you know which side I take. The *versus* is not my fault, there should be no *versus*. The two things must be reconciled in us. But now they're daggers drawn. – If you've got Willa Cather's address, send her one.

I had a cable from Brett yesterday saying can I send my pictures to New York immediately for exhibition at the Weyhe gallery on May 1st.[1] Since it's so vague and sudden, I can't. Are there any Weyhe galleries? – But if anything matures, I'll let you know, and you can get some of your pictures and Achsah's sent at the same time for the same show. Or perhaps Brett has wired you too. She gives no address, no responsible person, nothing more definite than Weyhe galleries May 1st. I'm not risking it.

Pretty bad weather still. Yesterday was sunny, but today again grey and windy. Frieda's daughter Barbara is here, but departs back to Alassio tomorrow. Have you seen Else, F's sister?

Anna di Chiara wrote and ordered 5 copies of my novel – nice of her. She says she'll be back in Villa Giulia by middle May.[2]

I should like to leave here at once, but hang on for my novel. It does not suit my health. Is Capri any better, for weather.

Well do send a line, both of you, and let's put our heads together and scheme something. – A lot of people seem to be leaving Italy to go and live in French Tunis – say it's lovely.

                                                                              DHL

4357. To Dorothy Warren, 27 March 1928
Text: MS UN; Nehls, iii. 196.

                                        Villa Mirenda. *Scandicci*. (Florence)
                                                                  27 March 1928

Dear Dorothy Warren
     Barbara Weekley is here, and said you might like to exhibit my pictures.[3]

---

[1] Founded, in 1914, in New York City, by Erhard Weyhe (1882–1972).
[2] Anna di Chiara's house in Capri where the Brewsters had stayed in January 1927 (*Letters*, v. 626).   [3] See Letter 4108 and n. 3.

There are seven biggish oils, 1 yard x 1½ yds and so on – also three littlish ones – and six water-colours. – We're giving up this house 1st May, so I've got to pack my pictures and do something with them. So I might exhibit them – though really I'm not keen, and I dont want to sell them – unless one or two of the smaller things, and perhaps the waters. So what do you think? The oils are framed in plain wooden frames which I painted to fit the picture – buffish or greyish. I'd rather the pictures were left in their frames as they are. Only the waters need framing. But I can't afford a heavy expense. – Just let me know what you think.

I enclose a few order-forms for my nice new phallic novel. If you know anybody who'd like it, possibly, do please give them a form, if you'll be so good.

How are you after a fair number of years? Chirpy still, I hope – though people say, disillusioned. Well, that sounds romantic. And when you're through with it, you can just start being illusioned again, which is very nice.

We may be in England about August – when I shall come to your gallery, if it is open. Perhaps it shuts through the dog days, and you depart far off.

Meanwhile I hope things are going fairly gaily with you.

Sincerely   D. H. Lawrence[1]

---

[1] Dorothy Warren replied on 9 April 1928 (Nehls, iii. 200–2):

> I am delighted to have had news of you. I thank you very much indeed for your letter and for the notice of your book. I have ordered several copies and I have distributed the notices in quarters that seemed suitable. I run a book department in this gallery in cooperation with a friend, Prince Leopold Loewenstein, who is publishing German books in English, and buying English books for translation and publication in Germany. He would very much like to have the German rights of *Lady Chatterley's Lover*, if you have not already disposed of them. . . .
>
> I should really be delighted to make an exhibition of your pictures here, if you don't dislike the idea too much. When Barbara showed me the photographs I felt that I should like the paintings immensely and I wanted very much to see them. Please send them to me here as soon as it suits you to do so and I will keep them for you as long as you like.
>
> I do all my own framing. I keep my workman for that purpose. . . so please do not worry about the expense of framing the six water-colours. Have them on me, won't you?
>
> I wonder whether I am disillusioned. No one has raised the point to me before you did. I cannot remember having been conscious ever, either of possessing or of losing illusions, so how can I judge?. . .
>
> When I used to see you at at Ottoline's, in Hampstead, and the cinema parties (I wonder if you remember them, I enjoyed them so much) I was eighteen, and so full of ponderous reflections that I must have been very muddled or glib – probably both. Now I am monotonously articulate. I am thirty-two.. . .
>
> The latter part of April I shall be in Berlin arranging an exhibition there, but all letters will be forwarded.
>
> Please remember me very warmly to Frieda. She was always so kind to me.

4358. To Aldous Huxley, 27 March 1928
Text: Huxley 716–17.

Villa Mirenda.
27th March, 1928.

Dear Aldous, –

Your letter yesterday – glad you liked the porc. – I got yesterday two copies of *Scrutinies* – the book with my Galsworthy eassay in it.[1] Some of 'em hit fairly straight: but Edwin Muir, real Scotchy, is overpowered by Bennett's gold watch-chain.[2] I'd like to write an essay on Bennett – sort of pig in clover.

Your ideas of the grand perverts is excellent. You might begin with a Roman – and go on to St. Francis – Michael Angelo and Leonardo – Goethe or Kant – Jean-Jacques Rousseau or Louis Quatorze. Byron – Baudelaire – Wilde – Proust: they all did the same thing, or tried to: to kick off, or to intellectualise and so utterly falsify the phallic consciousness, which is the basic consciousness, and the thing we mean, in the best sense, by common sense. I think *Wilhelm Meister* is amazing as a book of peculiar immorality, the perversity of intellectualised sex, and the utter incapacity for any *development* of contact with any other human being, which is peculiarly bourgeois and Goethian.[3] Goethe *began* millions of intimacies, and never got beyond the how-do-you-do-stage, then fell off into his own boundless ego. He perverted himself into perfection and Godlikeness. But do do a book of the grand orthodox perverts. Back of all of them lies ineffable conceit.

Was in Florence yesterday – saw Douglas – looking very old – off in a week's time to Aleppo – or so he says – by Orient Express – do you remember its time-table in Diablerets? From Aleppo he wants to go to Baalbek – and then, presumably, to rise into heaven. He's terribly at an end of everything.[4]

I haven't got proofs yet of my novel, but they'll begin this week – and say they'll only take about three weeks. The phœnix is printed, very nice. I shall send Maria one. Orioli is very keen. I've got about two thousands liras in orders. Orioli thinks if we got on well with this book, perhaps he can do others, and the author give him a percentage. Not a bad idea. Might be the nucleus of the Authors' Publishing Society of which I spoke, however, to [Kot], so no

---

[1] See Letter 4027 and p. 67 n. 1.

[2] Muir stresses Arnold Bennett's 'materialistic philosophy' and the resulting limitations on his artistic 'competence', but concludes: 'The qualities which make him unsatisfactory as an artist make him also an interesting and original personality. He has brought to literature practical qualities which are seldom found there, but which, nevertheless, are interesting in themselves as well as humanly respectable' (*Scrutinies*, p. 27).

[3] Goethe's Wilhelm Meister novels, written at intervals 1777–1829; partly trans. by Carlyle as *Wilhelm Meister's Apprenticeship* (1824) and *Wilhelm Meister's Travels* (1827).

[4] For Aldington's and Frieda's accounts of this meeting with Douglas and the reconciliation after the contretemps over the Magnus *Memoirs*, see Nehls, iii. 699–700 n. 371.

doubt he'll bombard you.[1] I don't like his letters: sort of bullying tone he takes, with an offended Jewish superiority.

Did you get the order-forms? Do get private people to send money if you can – so that I can see if I can sell enough without the booksellers, who take a third commission in America, and a quarter in England – and then hold the book back and sell it for double the price. I hate middle-men, and want to eliminate them as far as possible. If I can carry this thing through, it will be a start for all of us unpopular authors. Never let it be said I was a Bennett.[2]

I was reading Aretino's *Ragionamenti* – sometimes amusing, but not *created* enough.[3] I prefer Boccaccio. We had one sunny day, but grey and windy again now – no fun – F[rieda]'s daughter here, but leaves to-morrow. The Wilks mere wraiths, having packed up every old rag, pot, pan and whisker with the sanctity of pure idealists cherishing their goods.[4]

Had a cable from Brett asking me to send my pictures to New York for exhibition on May 1st. Too short a notice.

Wish the sun would shine.

Even if we had to go to Switzerland, we could get away early in July, and go to Toulouse or wherever it is.

4359. To Laurence Pollinger, 27 March 1928
Text: MS UT; Unpublished.

Villa Mirenda. Scandicci. (Florence)
27 March 1928

Dear Pollinger

Very nice that somebody else does *Cavelleria Rusticana*.[5] I get a little tired of Alfred Knopf's striped trousers and ineffectual bounce. And Secker's tightness!

Poor old Garnett,[6] personally of course he'll like 'John Thomas', but he's as conventional as the King. If Cape thinks it impossible, don't show it to anybody else; unless just possibly Chattos – Chattos and Windus. But nobody else.

---

[1] See Letter 4337.

[2] Cf. 'Arnold Bennett. . . who is quite rich out of literature' (*Letters*, iii. 205).

[3] *I Ragionamenti* (1600), a prose fiction attacking the morals of recognisable Roman contemporaries, by Pietro Aretino (1492–1556).

[4] The Wilkinsons left Villa Poggi the next day, 28 March. They recorded in a diary: 'Lawrence sat amidst the wreckage, and smiled sadly for half an hour and at last all was ready and we. . . waved to Lawrence all down the hill' (Sagar, Wilkinsons 73).

[5] The Dial Press published the first American edn, in 1928; Cape had published the first English edn in February.

[6] Edward Garnett (1886–1937), DHL's first literary 'patron' (see *Letters*, i. 297 n. 2).

Did you get the order-forms? And will you give a few out for me? And if you want a copy of the book, will you fill in a form, and ask C[urtis] B[rown]. Because Orioli won't send out any copies without the money. And ask CB., when he's writing to Crosby Gaige, to put in an order-form – because I lost the address.

Beastly weather. If it really cleared up I might go a little tour here, to Arezzo, Cortina etc – and get the material to finish my Etruscan book. Safe stuff that! Even Knopf was quite brisk about it – wanted it quick sharp for this autumn! Won't get it!

D. H. Lawrence

Please tell the accounts dept. not to send any more to Diablerets –

4360. To Juliette Huxley, 27 March 1928
Text: MS Huxley; cited in Sagar, *Words International*, i. 25.

Villa Mirenda, Scandicci. (Florence)
27 March 1928

Dear Juliette

Your letter today – I didn't have your address, so couldn't send you a line. Frieda *now* thinks the tiger was on top of the wardrobe cupboard. What a surprise if he springs down on the next Beau-Chaletiers![1] Damn him, let him bide!

It's been beastly weather since we're back – cold and rain rain rain. Today still grey and windy. The flowers are all out – red tulips in the wheat, purple and red anemones, grape hyacinths and primroses and violets in great abundance. But what's the good of flowers unless the sun shines! I hate this great stark stone house, whose stoniness soaks up one's vitality. I preferred that little wooden cigar-box of Beau-Site. I cough more than in Diablerets, and feel peaked. Damn it all! But we only hang on a bit for my novel, which is being printed by a little printer, in Florence, in an old little shop where nobody understands a word of English, not even those basic foundation-words like fuck and cunt and shit. Ah, teach them to your mother, it's never too late to learn. – I am sending you one or two little order-forms, and if Julian has a bold friend who'll risk it, tell him to hand one out. – Secker has said he can't see a possibility of making the book fit for public presentation, even expurgated. But then he is himself an expurgated edition of a man: like so many others. It's much the greatest danger for men. – I just did a water-colour of a naked man pissing against a wall, as the Bible says.[2] It's most tender and touching, and I shall exhibit it in London, and perhaps you might embroider it to go on one side of the Adam and Eve, and I'll think of some other joy to go

---

[1] See Letter 4328.   [2] 1 Samuel xxv. 22, 34 ['that pisseth against. . .'].

on the other.[1] – As for the ibis, you have only to remember that it had once a quite weird exotic erotic symbolical meaning; to make it live *im Bild*.[2]

We ought to go to Switzerland in May – stay till mid-July – then probably come to England – and in autumn perhaps go to America. I feel like moving over the face of the earth[3] – don't belong here any more.

So you spring-cleaned like the devil – and I suppose polished up your soul and spirits at the same time, so that they shine. I feel I'd do with a shine-up just now. And how is your mother? Is she happier this time in our happy isle? And did you take any maids at all with you? And how are the children? And is Anthony going to school? And is he happy to be back in London? And does Marguerite weep *davvero*?[4] And is Julian too busy for words? Anyhow remember me to him.

And many greetings to your mother, and I wish we were going to tea in Aroles, with her jam and the Salami.[5] But there you are – and there we all are – talk about ends of the earth – fag ends!

Frieda *says* she'll write. She may even!

Tante cose!   DHL

4361. To Curtis Brown, 29 March 1928
Text: MS UT; Unpublished.

6 Lugarno Corsini, Florence
29 March 1928

Dear C[urtis] B[rown]

Thanks for your order and the two quid.[6]

I enclose a note from Aldous Huxley.[7] Seems to me impossible – my edition is already in the press, and order forms sent out to America –

---

[1] See Letter 4328 and n. 4.   [2] 'in a picture'.   [3] Cf. Genesis i. 2.
[4] Marguerite was nanny to Anthony and Francis Huxley (and probably the 'nurse' in Letter 4294); she came from Thielle, Neuchatel. Anthony was soon to go to Abinger Hill School.
[5] See Letter 4328 and p. 314 n. 3.   [6] A copy of *Lady Chatterley's Lover* cost £2 (or $10).
[7] Huxley wrote as follows, on 25 March 1928 (MS UT):

Dear Lawrence,
   A hasty note on a matter of business. This evening I mentioned your novel to my American publisher, G. H. Doran, who is over here now. He at once suggested the possibility of publication in America by a friend of his, Crosby Gaige, who has started a private press (as a side line – he is a theatre owner) and has produced a number of books with some success already. Doran thought that Gaige would be interested and pleased at the idea and that he'd have no difficulty in selling 1000 copies at $25 each. This ought to be fairly profitable and would also solve the copyright problem in U. S. A. Do you like the idea? or at any rate would you like him to make enquiries from Gaige as to whether he'd be prepared to undertake the job? If so let me know – by telegram preferably, as Doran is leaving on Saturday and would like to cable, so as to save time, before he goes. One word – *Yes*, if you want enquiries made of Gaige: *No* if you don't like the idea. You may prefer to do the whole thing in Florence. Any how, I thought you'd like to hear Doran's suggestion.

In haste.   Yours

Also John *Rodker* said he would like to print the commercial edition in London, but don't know what he's good for.[1]

If I don't inscribe your copy specially – I may have gone from here – I'll do it the first time you stick it under my nose in the office.

Looks like I'll sell the thing all right.

D. H. Lawrence

4362. To S. S. Koteliansky, 31 March 1928
Text: MS BL; Postmark, Firenze 2 . IV 28; cited in Gransden 32.

Villa Mirenda. Scandicci. Florence.
31 March 1928

Dear Kot

Orioli sent you some more leaflets – hope you have them. – And several booksellers, including Dulau, wrote asking for invoices.[2] We decided on 15% only. If they don't like it, I can't help it. Booksellers want 25% discount, then they hang on to the book and sell it for £4 instead of £2.[3] – I don't care vastly about them. It looks as if I'd sell the book alright, to individuals. – Orioli wrote Dulau and the others, the 15%. – I'll keep you No 1. if I can, and Farbman 17. But you know they should be shuffled, and taken at random, to be really fair. We are sending printed receipt-slips, saying amount received.[4] I can't alter the leaflets now – they are nearly all sent out.[5] We intend to bind the book in hard covers, and print on the cover a design of a phoenix rising from the nest in flames, which I drew, and which the printer has already cast. I'll send you a little slip with the design. – Do you remember my same phœnix on the seal I gave to Murry that Christmas when I came from Mexico?[6] I wish I had it back from him. 'Will[7] the bird perish, shall the bird rise.' No rising for *him.* – But it will look nice on the cover of the book. – I shall mail by registered book post – then there is no danger.

[1] John Rodker (1894–1955), writer, translator and, chiefly, publisher (his imprints included Egoist and Ovid Press). Published Eliot, Joyce and Pound among others. Associated with quasi-private edns of *Casanova* and similar books; hence, perhaps, his interest in *Lady Chatterley's Lover.* Cf. p. 569 n. 1. (DHL's letter was annotated at this point in Curtis Brown's office, probably by Pollinger: 'CB   I don't know this man.')
[2] The distinguished bookseller Dulau's Ltd. (founded in 1792), recently transferred to 32 Old Bond Street, W. 1, specialised in literature and natural history (see Bloch, *The Book Collectors Vade Mecum,* pp. 282–4).   [3] MS reads: 'instead £2'.
[4] DHL drafted the slip as follows (MS UT): 'Mr Orioli begs to thank you for your order for *Lady Chatterley's Lover*, with enclosed cheque for _____, and will forward the book by registered post immediately it is ready. 6 Lungarno Corsini, Florence.'
[5] Perhaps Kot had noticed the error in the leaflet which announced the publication date for the novel as 'May 15th 1920'; the adjustment to '1928' had to be made by hand (see among illustrations to this volume).   [6] Reproduced in *Letters,* iv. 551.   [7] Will] Shall

It's rather fun doing it – buying the special paper – going to the funny little printer's shop. – But I haven't bought the binding paper yet. Probably I'll get it from Milan. – Or do you think people would as leave have the book just sewn, in continental fashion? Of course that would be cheaper.

Yrs DHL

4363. To Barbara Weekley, [April? 1928]
Text: Nehls, iii. 189.

[Villa Mirenda, Scandicci, Florence]
[April? 1928]

[After Barbara Weekley returned to London on 28 March 1928 and was 'drifting in the way that was becoming a habit', Lawrence wrote] Don't throw yourself away; you might want yourself later on.

4364. To Nancy Pearn, 1 April 1928
Text: MS UT; Huxley 717–18.

Villa Mirenda, Scandicci. (Florence)
1 April 1928

Dear Nancy Pearn

Have you got by any chance the manuscript of *Sun* in the office? – an American asks me for it particularly, and offers $100[1] – So there's a windfall, if it exists. If it doesn't, povero me! – for I haven't got it, the MS. Would you tell me what MSS. there are of mine, in the office. I'm afraid I've burnt most of those left on my hands. – You remember *Sun* is the story the *Coterie* did, and printed 100 separate copies.

You hear I am burning my boats by publishing my 'shocking' novel here all by myself. I expect everybody will disapprove – you certainly will. So I shan't ask you to buy a copy.

It rains here – and rains! If it would leave off, I would go round and collect material for my final Etruscan Sketches. They at least are irreproachable. What it is to be always under reproach!

Sempre[2] D. H. Lawrence

Did the story 'The Lovely Lady' ever appear in Lady Cynthia's 'murder' book? If so, no one ever sent me a copy of the book.[3]

---

[1] See letter following.   [2] 'Ever'.
[3] On 'The Lovely Lady' see p. 21 n. 4. Nancy Pearn replied on 13 April 1928 (TMSC UT): '"Sun" is one of those we previously returned! Are you sure you burnt them all; and tell me, would it be cheating to write out the story again in your own fair handwriting to sell to the eager Yank? If not, why not?'

4365. To Harry Crosby, 1 April 1928
Text: MS SIU; Postmark, Firenze 2. IV 28; Huxley 718–19.

Villa Mirenda. Scandicci. Florence.
1 April 1928

Dear Harry Crosby

That was very nice of you, to send me that little pseudo-book full of red gold.[1] How beautiful the gold is! such a pity it ever became currency. One should love it for its yellow life, answering the sun. I shan't spend it if I can help it.

I have hunted for MSS – I'm afraid I burn most of 'em. I found 'The Man Who Loved Islands', which is a good story – came in the *Dial* and in the *London Mercury*: also 'Two Blue Birds' – from *Dial* and *Pall Mall*; also 'Smile', a slight thing of four pages, which I like: then 'None of That' – a story of an American woman and a Bull fighter in Mexico City – coming just now at the end of my vol. of short stories – a fairly long story:[2] Then the 'Scrutiny of the Works of John Galsworthy', just appearing in a vol. published by Wishart.[3] – What a pity, there is nothing exactly sunny! But I have written to London to see if the MS of *Sun* is there. And 'Man Who Loved Islands' is a good story. I should like so much to give you something *you* would like. Shall I send you 'Man Who Loved Islands' and 'Two Blue Birds' and 'Smile': and then *Sun* if it luckily turns up. Or perhaps a poem or two, those I changed for the *Collected Poems* which will appear this autumn?[4] – Tell me, will you. I am having the MSS which I've got bound in a simple cover, and I'll send you what you like: and certainly *Sun*, if it exists, as well.[5]

I enclose one or two little forms for my new novel, which I am printing here

[1] In his 'Memoranda' (MS NWU) DHL recorded: '1st April – Harry Crosby 19 rue de Lille – sent me $100, 5 beautiful gold pieces, for an MS.'
[2] On all these stories see Letter 4140 and p. 152 n. 3. ('Two Blue Birds' did not appear in *Pall Mall* until June 1928; see Roberts C154.)
[3] See Letter 4027 and p. 67 n. 1. The autograph MS (at UT) is entitled: 'A Scrutiny of the Work of John Galsworthy' (Roberts E181.3b).
[4] DHL's offer to send poems from 'those [he] changed' masks the fact that 'numerous poems were subjected to rigorous revision for the collected edition' (E. D. McDonald, *The Writings of D. H. Lawrence: A Bibliographical Supplement*, Philadelphia, 1931, p. 43).
[5] Among his 'Memoranda' DHL recorded under 1 April:
    Orioli takes MSS. to be bound: Printed proof of David
        MS. Rocking Horse Winner
            Two Blue Birds
            Smile.
            The Man Who Loved Islands
            Scrutiny of Work of John Galsworthy
            Things. None of That
            F's David in German
    Pino brought up first proofs of Lady Chatterley from Giuntina in Florence.

in Florence. It is a phallic novel – but good and sun-wards, truly sunwards, not widdershins nor anti! You might like it.

In May we shall go to Switzerland again, I think, for my health – But in early July we ought to be in Paris. I shall let you know of course. And in autumn I want to go back to New Mexico, where we have a little ranch, near Taos. You are American, are you? But do you always live in Paris?

Sincerely   D. H. Lawrence

4366. To Franz Schoenberner, 1 April 1928
Text: MS UT; cited in Schoenberner, *Confessions*, p. 288.

Villa Mirenda, Scandicci. (Florence)
1 April 1928

Lieber Schönberner

Da bin ich, noch im Land. Es regnet furchtbar, und regnet immer. – Wir bleiben hier nur bis Mai, dann gehen in die Schweiz. Wir waren zwei Monate in Diablerets: es hat mir so viel gut gethan, wir wollen wieder dahin. Aber hier bin ich fleissig, ich lasse meinen letzten Roman in Florenz drucken. Es ist zu schocking – shocking – für die Englische Verleger: also gebe ich es selber aus. Es wird jetzt gedruckt, in einer kleiner Buchdruckerei in Florenz, wo kein Mensch versteht ein Wort Englisch. Das ist sehr gut, niemand kann 'shocked' werden. Das Buch ist viel zu teuer für Ihnen – 40 Mark – ich schicke doch ein paar Zetteln; vielleicht kennen Sie einen Connoisseur. Und später schicke ich Ihnen einen billigeren Exemplar.

Können Sie mir sagen, was würde es kosten, meine Aquarellen in Farben gedruckt zu lassen. Eine Aquarelle 35 cm x 24 cm, was würde es kosten sie gedruckt zu haben, in guten Farben, vielleicht 500 Exemplaren? Sie können mir sagen, von der *Jugend*, nicht wahr? Es wäre sehr freundlich, mir es zu sagen.

Wie geht es Ihnen, und der gnädige Frau? ich hoffe gut. Mir geht's viel besser, und wenn das Wetter nur sonnig wäre, wäre ich ein ganzer Mann. Meine Schwägerin Frau Jaffe ist jetzt in Capri – es regnet auch dort. Sie kommt aber nächste Woche hier, und will bei uns ein Paar Tage bleiben.

Ich weiss nicht ob wir im Sommer nach Bayern kommen. Im Herbst wollen wir an die Ranch in New Mexico gehen. Aber wir werden uns wieder sehen, uns und die gnädige Frau und Hans Carossa.

tante belle Cose!   D. H. Lawrence

[Dear Schoenberner

Here I am, still in this country. It's raining frightfully, and always raining. – We're only staying here till May, then we're going to Switzerland. We were in Diablerets two months: it did me so much good, we want to go there again. But I'm busy here, I'm having my most recent novel printed in Florence. It is too shocking – shocking – for English publishers: so I'm bringing it out myself. It's currently being printed in a little printer's in Florence, where no one understands a word of English. That's very good, no one can be 'shocked'. The book is much too expensive for you – 40 Marks – but I send you a couple of leaflets: perhaps you know a Connoisseur. And I'll send you a cheaper copy later.

Could you tell me what it would cost to have my water-colours printed in colour. One water-colour 35cm x 24 cm, what would it cost to have it printed, in good colour, perhaps 500 copies? You can tell me from the *Jugend*, can't you? It would be very kind to tell me.

How are you, and your spouse? well, I hope. I'm much better, and if the weather were only sunny, I would be a real man. My sister-in-law Mrs Jaffe is in Capri at the moment – it's raining there too. But she's coming here next week, and wants to stay with us a couple of days.

I don't know if we'll come to Bavaria in the summer. In the autumn we want to go the ranch in New Mexico. But we'll be seeing each other again, we and your spouse and Hans Carossa.

All the best!   D. H. Lawrence]

4367. To Ada Clarke, [1 April 1928]
Text: MS Clarke; cited in Lawrence–Gelder 190–1.

Villa Mirenda. Scandicci. (Florence)
Sunday 1st April.

My dear Sister

I didn't write before, waiting to see what effect the medicine had on me: and I knew you'd see G[ertie]'s letter, of course. I duly take the Umckaloaba capsules, and can't see that they have any effect on me whatsoever. They don't upset me at all: the cough remains just the same: I'm certainly no worse: perhaps I'm rather better in general health: but as for my bronchials, they're going it pretty strong, as usual. So there you are! But I'll go on drinking the little brew till the box is empty: if persistence does it, let's try persistence. Thank God I feel I'm getting *stronger* this spring: though as I say, my coughing and spitting go on just the same. But it's something I'll have to shift from underneath, by increasing my strength against it.

If you'll send me Aunt Ada's address, I'll write her, though with some small hesitancy.[1]

Tell Jack yes, I was pulling[2] his leg about a brass cannon. But I'll keep my

---

[1] The letter is unlocated.   [2] pulling] putting

eye open for something small enough to send for his glass cupboard. He should put in that old hour-glass – I believe it's his – and they're quite smart antiques here.

It is the vilest weather imaginable. Today being Palm Sunday, it has poured all day. And we have had hardly any sun since we're back. The broad-beans and the first peas were frozen, and now the beans – the brown haricots – have most of them rotted in the ground, with the rain. Italy is awfully dreary when it rains for long on end. Yet I suppose we'll stay till early May.

Then I think we shall go back to Switzerland, anyhow for a couple of months. Diablerets made all the difference to me: gave me back my resistance. Then end of July, or early in August I want to come to England. I shall have to decide where we are going to live next.

Frieda's sister is coming for a few days on her way back from Capri. She's had beastly weather all the time. – Our neighbours the Wilknsons have gone: packed up and gone. Many people are leaving Italy. It's no longer a gay country: if anywhere is gay.

I painted six or seven water-colours, sort of series.[1] I might show them with my big pictures in a gallery in Bond Street, some time this summer. How folks will dislike them!

Did I tell you Martin Secker is going to publish my collected poems, in two vols: I don't know exactly when, but I've corrected the proofs. And he's got a vol of short stories ready.[2] Various things all at once! But I don't think I'm any more popular than I was. Not my destiny to be popular.

There are lots of flowers, in their own places – but the country still looks a bit blasted. But suddenly the pear-blossom is all out. Almond and peach are over. If only it wouldn't rain, and would be sunny! I hope it's nicer for you in England: I sort of believe it is.

Love. DHL

4368. To Muriel Moller, [1 April 1928]
Text: TMSC NWU; Unpublished.

Villa Mirenda. Scandicci
Sunday[3]

Dear Miss Moller

I'm so sorry you've not been well – but it is the weather to die in. I am lying a bit low.

---

[1] See Letter 4370.
[2] *Collected Poems* appeared in September 1928 (Roberts A43); *The Woman Who Rode Away* on 24 May (Robers A41).
[3] Dated with reference to Else Jaffe's arrival on 2 April 1928 (Letter 4370).

If it's decent weather, we should like very much to come to lunch. My wife may have her sister with her, and she speaks English perfectly well. – If the weather's bad, *I* shan't risk it – my chest is getting ticklish.

Let us hope for thursday, then – and if we come in about 12.30, you make lunch at any time that suits you.

Au revoir   D. H. Lawrence

4369. To Laurence Pollinger, 2 April 1928
Text: MS UT; Huxley 720.

Villa Mirenda. Scandicci. (Florence)
2 April 1928

Dear Pollinger

If you haven't sent over the MS. of *Lady C.* to Chattos office, please *don't* send it. I don't want any more publishers trying to cover their nakedness with 'large patches of sheer beauty' and sighing 'It's a great pity'. It is!

Instead will you either give the MS. to Aldous Huxley, or Mrs Huxley, should either of them call for it: otherwise post it to:

Aldous Huxley. 3 Onslow Mews East. *Cranley Place S.W. 7.*

And do you mind sending up the enclosed to the Foreign dept.[1]

Very rainy here.

D. H. Lawrence

4370. To Aldous and Maria Huxley, [2 April 1928]
Text: Huxley 720–2.

Villa Mirenda.
Monday, 2nd April.

Dear Aldous, –

Awfully good of you to go to Curtis Brown. They are furious in that office that I publish my novel: daren't say much – but their quotation of Johnny Cape, which I enclose, shows.[2] It seems to make 'em all very mad. Why, in God's name? One would think I advocated sheer perversity: instead of merely saying merely natural things. I'm beat by their psychology – don't understand 'em. But I can see they'll get the wind up. I shall ask Curtis Brown to send MS. to you – do you mind? Perhaps Maria will deposit it somewhere for me – and when I have got all proofs in Florence, we can burn it. Damn them all: Let [   ]³ put a sheer patch of beauty on his [   ]: I'll bet he's got an ugly one. – I'll have to leave out 'John Thomas', shall I? What a pity! But it's too

---

[1] Enclosure missing.   [2] Enclosure missing.   ³ See p. 326 n. 3.

late to leave it from the leaflets. – You were sent 25 leaflets the very first; wonder who took 'em? – one suspects everything. [   ] is forbidden to be sold in Italy, by Big Ben; and it is withdrawn by the publishers in England. So there's a mouse among the vestals once more! – 'For my own good,' they want me *not* to publish *Lady C. – not* to destroy my at last respectable reputation. Too late! I am embarked. You must stand by me, when the seas rise. Larboard watch, ahoy! All overboard but John Thomas. – Oh, captain, my captain, our fearful trip's begun[1] – 'John Thomas' – Hip – Hip!! for he's a jolly good fe-ellow –!

I've corrected 41 pages of proofs, and it was *almost* Maria's typing over again. Dear Maria, all those little mistakes you made, and I followed like Wenceslas's page so patiently in your footsteps:[2] now it's a Florentine printer. He writes dind't did'nt, dnid't, dind't, din'dt, didn't like a Bach fugue. The word is his blind spot.

Well, I painted a charming picture of a man pissing – I'm sure it is the one Maria will choose: called *Dandelions*, for short. Now I'm doing a small thing in oil, called *The Rape of the Sabine Women* or a Study in Arses.[3] – I might send my pictures to Dorothy Warren to exhibit – but I shan't sell 'em – unless perhaps the waters. Maria can have any one of the water-colours: they are seven: 'Adam Throwing the Apple', and *The Mango Tree*: those you know. Then *The Torch Dance, Yawning, The Lizard, Under the Haystack*, and *Dandelions*:[4] If I sell my novel, I might reproduce them in a portfolio, and sell that – 500 copies. I'm a lost soul to the publishers. But Maria can have any one of them, but if she'd rather have an oil she must wait a bit.

It's the most awful weather – pours and pours with rain. F[rieda]'s sister comes back to Florence from Capri to-day – it's rained all the while she was there – now she'll stay a bit with us, and it'll go on raining. My cough is as ever: but I'm no worse: really rather well, I think. Does me good to feel furious about the novel.

Dear Maria, do tell Lady Colefax to come to tea if she'd care to.[5] I don't

---

[1] Sir W. S. Gilbert, 'The Yarn of the Nancy Bell', in *The Bab Ballads* (1869) ['. . . trip is done']. Cf *Letters*, i. 293; v. 388.

[2] From the Christmas carol, *Good King Wenceslas*, ll. 29–30 ['Mark my footsteps, good my page,/ Tread thou in them boldly'].   [3] See *The Paintings of D. H. Lawrence*, plate [6].

[4] 'Adam Throwing the Apple' became *Throwing Back the Apple* (see Letter 4178 and p. 190 n. 1); for *The Mango Tree* see *Paintings*, plate [23]; for the other pictures see Letters 4328 and n. 3, 4345 and n. 2, 4356 and n. 7.

[5] Sybil, Lady Colefax, née Halsey (d. 1950). m. 1901, (Sir) Arthur Colefax (d. 1936). A friend of the Huxleys, a celebrated society hostess and perhaps unkindly described by Lady Cynthia Asquith (*Diaries: 1915–1918*, 1968, p. 366) as an 'indefatigable lion hunter'. *The Times* obituary, 26 September 1950, says that with her death disappeared 'perhaps the last London *salon* which had nothing to fear from comparison with the great literary *salons* of the past'.

know anything about her, but take your word for it. Tell her we shall be delighted, etc.

If we go to Switzerland in May, why shouldn't we have a little *giro* in France in early July – those Pyrenees – something *nice*. And I should so like to see the St. Cloud house and the Seine also.

DHL

Dear Maria – if you're passing by Curtis Brown's office with the car, will you call and demand the MS. of 'John Thomas', and carry it away from them. I don't want them to have it any more. And you can do what you like with it. – You ask for Mr. Pollinger. I've told him to hand it over.

I do wish you were coming in to tea – or we to you: for it rains, the country is motionless, there is no sound, the little narcissus in the jar smell wallow (?),[1] and we've not seen a soul to talk to happily since we left Diablerets.

DHL

4371. To Herbert Thring, 2 April 1928
Text: MS BL; Unpublished.

Villa Mirenda. Scandicci. (Florence.)
2 April 1928

Dear Sir[2]

I have asked Curtis Brown, my agent, please not to release Tauchnitz Edition rights until one year after first English publication, according to your suggestion.

Yours faithfully   D. H. Lawrence

4372. To Edith Isaacs, 2 April 1928
Text: MS WHist; Huxley 719–20.

Villa Mirenda – Scandicci. (Florence)
2 April 1928

Dear Miss Isaacs[3]

Many thanks for the book of *Theater Essays*. The first copy sent must have been stolen in the post.

---

[1] The question mark was Huxley's.

[2] George Herbert Thring (1859–1941), Secretary to the Society of Authors, 1892–1930; he was an expert on copyright law. DHL had corresponded with Thring when he was elected to the Society at the time of the suppression of *The Rainbow*; see *Letters*, ii. 433–5, 469. Though it appears that there may have been an earlier exchange of letters in 1928, none has been found.

[3] Edith Juliet Isaacs (1878–1956), editor of *Theatre Arts Monthly*, 1924–46, in which DHL had published 'The Dance of the Sprouting Corn' and 'The Hopi Snake Dance' (Roberts C122, C127); she had also edited *Theatre: Essays on the Arts of the Theatre* (Boston, 1927) in which these two essays were reprinted. See *Letters*, v. 115 n.4, 636 and n.1.

What a handsome book it is! and really very interesting. I think nothing is better, especially about the stage, than to hear all the different voices saying their say. One feels a bit bewildered at the end. But then, damn it all, one is a bit bewildered by the spectacle of life altogether.

I enclose a couple of leaflets for my new novel. It is frankly a phallic novel. But then I think it's the death of the phallic consciousness which is making us go so withered and flat, filmy, in our lives. Somebody says so in one of the essays – about the stage.[1] Essential drama is essentially phallic, and where the phallic consciousness is dead, there's no essential drama. – Of course I don't mean merely *sex*, the modern sex. That's a thing of mental consciousness and cerebral reactions, reflected down on to the physical, and rather repulsive.

But there, you don't want to hear all this. Again many thanks for the book.

Sincerely   D. H. Lawrence

P.S. We are giving up this house for good at the end of this month – But the Florence address – Orioli's will always get me.

4373. To Montague Shearman, 3 April 1928
Text: MS UT; Unpublished.

[Lungarno Corsini 6. Firenze][2]
3 April 1928

Dear Shearman[3]

Sorry I forgot all about that loan – but I did. Why didn't you remind me

---

[1] DHL may have had in mind Alain Locke's essay, 'The Negro and the American Theatre' (pp. 290–303) which describes 'modern drama' as 'an essentially anemic drama' (p. 291); it requires rejuvenation and could obtain it from the drama of Negro life with its 'use of the body to portray story and emotion' (p. 294). Or he may have alluded to André Levinson on 'The Negro Dance' (pp. 235–45); Levinson praised the 'wild splendor and magnificent animality', and the use of 'phallic symbol', in the *Revue Nègre* in Paris, 1925.

[2] The letter was written on notepaper headed: J. I. Davis & G. M. Orioli, Libreria Antiquaria, Firenze (1), Lungarno Corsini 6. and London, 30 Museum Street. Cf. p. 88.

[3] Montague Shearman (1886–1940), barrister and friend of Kot, Gertler, etc; keen book and art collector. He had given DHL £10 in February 1918; no mention appears to have been made of a loan (*Letters*, iii. 103 n. 5, 216). Shearman wrote to DHL on 30 March 1928 as follows (MS BL):
... Years ago you may remember or perhaps you have forgotten that in a moment of crisis I lent you a small sum of money (£10 in fact) which you promised to repay when things were better. This repayment at any rate has never happened.
So I suggest as an alternative that you might send me a free copy of the work that you are now advertising for sale. Or the work and £8?
... I just feel a little bitter tonight about a lost friend & a loan gone west but it is really the continued silence that is distressing.
Sincerely yours ...
P.S. You may possibly be interested to know that I am going to Mexico in July with the Plumed Serpent as a guide.

sooner? – Yes, I remember the Adelphi evenings perfectly, but had no idea
that you cared about seeing me again.

I hope you will have a good time in Mexico.

Sincerely   D. H. Lawrence

Enc. cheque for £10[1] – Don't bother about the book – I didn't send the
form.

4374. To S. S. Koteliansky, [3 April 1928]
Text: MS BL; Postmark, Firenze 3 . IV 28; Moore 1054.

Florence.
Tuesday

My dear Kot

What do you think of this letter of Shearman?[2] I felt rather mad – but sent
him his £10. at once. I can't remember the loan – and if he lent it, I'm sure he
gave the impression of *giving* it.

Curtis Brown and the publishers are very angry with me for publishing my
novel – they say it will only do me harm – etc etc. They'll put any obstacle in
the way they can.

Sad to think of Fox gone[3] – I can't believe he is no more in the Cave.

At last a day of sun.

DHL

4375. To Muriel Moller, [3 April 1928]
Text: TMSC NWU; Unpublished.

Florence
Tuesday

Dear Miss Moller

Now here is my sister-in-law, Frau Dr Jaffe, with her friend, Professor
Weber of Heidelberg – one of the best-known German professors – and *he* is
leaving on Thursday at 4.0. Now of course they want us to have a last lunch
together. So – shall we *not* come to you, and lunch all at the Orologio – or shall
we all four lunch with you – a fearful crowd? Or shall I try and split, and send
the two ladies to you, and we two men lunch in town? or let my sister-in-law
and Prof. Weber lunch in town?

A bit of a muddle. I feel four is *far* too much for you. Choose any way you

[1] MS reads: '$10'; that DHL intended £10 is confirmed in the letter following.
[2] DHL sent Shearman's letter of 30 March to Kot who kept it attached to DHL's.
[3] The Farbmans' dog.

like – perhaps you'd better have only the ladies. – I'll send you a book, as promised. – Send a reply to Orioli if possible – the boy will wait.

D. H. Lawrence

4376. To Muriel Moller, [5 April 1928]
Text: TMSC NWU; Unpublished.

Villa Mirenda.
Thursday

Dear Miss Moller

Awfully kind of you to invite the whole caboosh.[1] Now I've gone and got a bit of a cold, and am having to lie low: am so sorry I can't come. But the other three will be there at 12.30.

I don't know if *Mornings in Mexico* will interest you – perhaps not.

But anyhow it's not very *long*.

Do come and see us, now it's a bit more spring-like.

Sincerely   D. H. Lawrence

4377. To Hon. Dorothy Brett, 5 April 1928
Text: MS UCin; Postmark, [. . .]; Irvine, Brett 82–3.

Villa Mirenda. *Scandicci*. Florence
5 April 1928

Dear Brett

I didn't send my pictures to the Weyhe Gallery as I couldn't have had them there by May 1st – and I didn't know c/o who, nor anything. Perhaps we can manage later. I might possibly show them first in Dorothy Warren's gallery in Madox St. I've done a row of seven water-colors, to go with them. But I'm not fond of water-colour.

I'm very busy with my novel – buying paper, hand-made – correcting proofs – making a phoenix from a nest in flames, like that seal I gave Murry, for the cover stamp[2] – getting cover-paper – etc. It'll cost me about £300. I expect – possibly more – but I'm hoping. So far I've got orders for £70, which isn't bad. I do hope Mabel got the 50 leaflets, and that she'll send them out. I sent Bynner and Mrs Hughes and Idella Purnell – and I thought you and Spud would send some of Mabel's, – I really hope to have the book all ready by May 15th – unless the printer lets me down. – I shall send you a copy – don't send money, especially now you are so hard up. If you get in a real fix, you must ask me for a loan – especially if I sell my book.

---

[1] See Letter 4368 and preceding letter.   [2] See Letter 4362 and n. 6.

We are really leaving this house on May 1st. – and I'm glad. It never suited me. Tell Mabel and Spud and everybody *not* to write here, please – but

c/o Curtis Brown, 6 Henrietta St. Covent Garden W.C.2

until I send an address. I feel once we are rid of this house, it will be much easier to come to the ranch: for I am determined not to take another house in a hurry. Probably from here we shall go to Switzerland for a bit – for my broncs – then perhaps to England for a month – and most probably, at end of August, to Taos. That's how I think it will happen. Once we have no house in Europe, we'll soon be sick of messing around. – It depends a good deal on my novel: of course I've not had time yet for any orders from America. – The publishers have decided it is impossible to make the book fit for public sale – so my unexpurgated Florence edition will be the only one. I don't care a bit. – They – and Curtis Brown – are angry with me for publishing it – say it will damage my reputation. Let it. I'm tired of them all.

I wonder if Spud is doing *The Escaped Cock*. A man called Crosby Gaige wanted to do it.[1]

We've had most beastly weather since we are back – pouring rain. Now it's a bit finer, but not settled.

I do hope you're managing your teeth. What a curse of a mouthful they must be. – I've not had my doubtful molar out yet – I think it's the only unsound one – but I will.

Tell Mabel I'll write – I'll let you know all news.

DHL

4378. To Lady Cynthia Asquith, 5 April 1928
Text: MS UT; Unpublished.

Villa Mirenda. Scandicci. (Florence)
April 5 1928

Yes, we're still in the land of the living – just. I'm busy publishing my novel here in Florence – too improper, so they say, for regular publication. Anyhow I'm doing 1000 here, in a little Italian printing shop where nobody understands a word of English, so all's one to *them*. What's in a word! I don't suppose you'll care for the book – your husband might. But make Sir James and a few people like that buy a copy:[2] they deserve it. I'll have a few leaflets sent to you. But if you're afraid of blushing when it's too late, just put them in the fire.

---

[1] Neither Johnson nor Gaige published it; but see Letters 4447, 4543 and 4679.
[2] Sir James Barrie (1860–1937), dramatist and novelist, to whom Lady Cynthia had been secretary for nearly ten years (cf. *Letters*, iii. 272 and n. 1).

We leave this house for good end of this month: then presumably, to Switzerland for a couple of months, for my unhappy chest. Then, I hope to England – end of July, when there'll be nobody there. Then probably in Sept. to New Mexico, to the ranch. Had a lot of trouble with my chest this last year – chiefly bronchial, but vicious.

How are you all? – rolling in wealth, I hope. I'm throwing some of my few sprats hoping to catch a mackerel in the shape of £1000 for my novel. Imagine if I did it!

But I'd be still much happier if my cough would get better.

I hope we shall see you and Herbert Asquith this summer – the wheel's gone round towards a meeting again.

tante cose, from both.   D. H. Lawrence

4379. To Blanche Knopf, 5 April 1928
Text: MS UT; Unpublished.

Villa Mirenda. Scandicci. (Florence)
5 April 1928

Dear Mrs Knopf

Had your note. We are leaving this house *for good* on Apr. 30th. – so will you please cancel the address in the office.

c/o Curtis Brown, 6 Henrietta St, London W.C.2.

always gets me.

We shall probably be in London in August – and in Switzerland June and July. So let us know when you veer our way.

I suppose by now you've had your 'green fury' and got over it. The London people quite angry with me – but why? I feel most innocent. Perfectly normal and innocent novel! And people swallow such shady stuff!

Così è la vita![1]   D. H. Lawrence

4380. To Giuseppe Orioli, [5 April 1928]
Text: MS UCLA; Unpublished.

[Villa Mirenda, Scandicci, Florence]
Thursday.

Dear Pino

The MSS look awfully nice. They are all there. The German MS of *David* doesn't matter.[2]

---

[1] 'Such is life!'

[2] Among his 'Memoranda' DHL noted: '5 April. Got back above MSS [see p. 348 n. 5] from Pino, bound and very pretty'. The German translation of *David*, by Frieda, was never published (MS at UCB).

Would you send a few leaflets to
         The Lady Cynthia Asquith, *8. Sussex Place. Regents Park. N.W.*
I haven't one left! so give me some when I come down.

The bird I like very much, on the binding papers. It's very hard to decide
which one. Would you ask the man to print me fifty, in black, on a square of
cream-coloured paper. I want to stick them on my manuscripts when they're
bound, and then write underneath what the MS. is, and my name. So they
need to be smaller than these samples on coloured paper, but a little larger
than the square of my original drawing.

Curtis Brown is in a funk – thinks all the bad things are bound to happen.
They won't.

                                                                au revoir.   DHL

4381. To Margaret Gardiner, [ante 7 April 1928]
Text: Margaret Gardiner, 'Meeting the Master', *Horizon*, ii (October 1940), 184–5.

                                        [Villa Mirenda, Scandicci, Florence]
                                                    [ante 7 April 1928][1]

Your brother writes that you will be in Florence.[2] Do come and see us. You
must take tram No. 16 in Via dei Pecori, just near the cathedral. Come to the
very terminus – then walk on straight ahead uphill and don't turn till you see
two cypresses, close together as two fingers. Take the road to the left there –
dip down in the little hollow – our house is the big square box on the crown of
the hill. But let us know and we'll come at least part of the way to meet you, or,
if you prefer, send the peasant with the little trap, the barrocino. He'll rattle
you up in no time.

4382. To Ada Clarke, [7 April 1928]
Text: MS Clarke; Unpublished.

                                                            Villa Mirenda.
                                                            Saturday

My dear Sister

What a swindle that man![3] He sent me an invoice, so of course I sent him a
cheque for 35/-: which he acknowledged. If you had already paid him, that is
mean of him. But do write and get the money back, and *keep* it. No doubt he

---

[1] The letter appears to have been written before 7 April 1928 when DHL knew (and told other
    correspondents) that Frieda would be away from 11th. His letter implied that both he and
    Frieda would meet Margaret Gardiner.
[2] Cf. Letter 4322 and p. 308 n. 1. Margaret Gardiner's visit, fully described in her *Horizon* article
    (reprinted in Nehls, iii. 203–8), occurred during 11–16 April.   [3] Cf. Letter 4340.

has already cashed my cheque, or I'd stop it. But do please keep the 35/- – I don't want you to pay that medicine. And buy yourself something with it.

I take the umckaloaba: that is, I left off today, because my inside felt a bit tired of it, and hot. But I'll resume tomorrow or Monday. Perhaps it does me good: it's hard to say. My bronchials and the cough seem much the same, but in myself I am stronger, quite a lot stronger. – I think perhaps it *does* do me good underneath.

Frieda's sister Else is here till next Wednesday – came from Capri, where they had awful weather – and it's nothing to boast of here. The peasants say it will be a pasqua guasta – a spoilt Easter. It's the biggest festa of the year.

Frieda is going Wednesday to Alassio – near Spotorno – for a day or two, to see Barby Weekley. Then when she comes back we'll start and pack up here: leave the end of the month.

I hear a car – so expect it's people to tea.

au revoir   DHL

4383. To Arthur and Lilian Wilkinson, [10 April 1928]
Text: MS Schlaefle; cited in Sagar, Wilkinsons 73.

Villa Mirenda. Scandicci. (Florence.)
Easter Tuesday 1928

Dear Wilkses

Your card this morning – there was one from Paris too. We also had fearful weather – till two days ago; Sunday awful – but yesterday and today lovely – all pear blossom out, and plum and cherry. Today is the festa at Giogoli – the quarant'ore[1] – church lit up, and fireworks tonight – all the peasants trooped off. We were there yesterday – to visit the Bandelli, the peasants who moved from here over there – you know, just beyond the Villa Bombici. I drove with F[rieda]'s sister in the Bartolozzi barrocino – both our lot having gone to Florence – the old man Gigi drove us – it was very nice. Tomorrow F. is going to Alassio for a few days – her sister Else too – so I'll be alone. – Your poggi have been up once or twice, but not to stay for more than three days[2] – the old mother still has her tumour in the region of the liver to quote Gigi, and can't be operated because her heart is weak. I should say so. But there's been a reconciliation with the young son, the villain, and he and mother and young daughter lovingly here at the villa a day or two.

The sad news is that Gorgioli, the man at the inn at Vingone, died suddenly

---

[1] 'the forty hours' (i.e. the exposition of the Blessed Sacrament for forty hours following a major feast).   [2] See Letter 4178.

on Friday morning.[1] He seemed rather better – but kept on weeping. There was a grand funeral reaching from Vingone to the Quattro Madonna, and 200 candles. Somehow it was a shock to everybody, he seemed such a strong man. – And they had ordered all the food stuff for the Easter holiday-makers. – He has left Liras 90,000, including the house they live in – so the peasants say.

Beyond this no news. I am pretty well – going in to Florence tomorrow. – We're having tea on our grass, under the ippocastagni,[2] which are nearly in flower. – The grove of aspens above is a lovely feathery pinky colour.

We'll leave here at the end of this month: then probably Switzerland till July – then England in August – then if I can afford it, we'll go round the world by those Messageries Marittimes in the autumn, and to the ranch that way.[3] I must write to Mrs Francke.[4]

I hope you're having a jolly time – expect you are, now the sun shines. Write then – and we'll meet in England later.

Ciao!   D. H. Lawrence

4384. To Harold Mason, 11 April 1928
Text: MS UTul; Unpublished.

[Pino Orioli, 6 – *Lungarno Corsini* – 6, Florence – Italy][5]
11 April 1928

Dear Mason

Your letter today – awfully nice of you to think about me and my novel: and very good of George Busby to offer me financial help.[6] But I shall manage by myself, if I can. Of course I want to sell my 1000 copies – otherwise I am left looking rather sick. Because it seems the publishers think it quite impossible to publish the book in the regular way. So I've got to live on this private edition. But if my friends help me, I think I shall manage to sell most of them – the orders come in pretty well from England, none yet from America, as there is not time for an answer. – So if George Busby likes to help by ordering a few copies of the novel to give to his friends, who might not be able to buy it, I shall be glad.

I think by mailing all subscribed copies direct from Florence, we shall best avoid censor trouble. Perhaps later you might help with distribution. Anyhow I'm very much obliged for your offer. But you don't mention your terms. – We agreed to give only 15% trade discount in England – as the book is really

---

[1] DHL thought the event distressing enough to record it in his very sketchy 'Memoranda' (MS NWU): '5 April . . . The man died at Vingone inn.'   [2] 'horse-chestnuts'.
[3] The Messageries Maritimes is the leading French commercial shipping line.
[4] Unidentified.   [5] Written on headed notepaper, as is the letter following.
[6] Unidentified.

published for subscribers, not for public sale. Perhaps at this rate you will not want to order 25 copies: if not, just write me to *this* address. We are leaving the Villa Mirenda for good at the end of this month – the climate is bad for my chest. But I shall stay in Florence till the book is ready. I am correcting proofs and choosing cover-paper – have already bought the paper for the book – decent, hand-made, Italian.

I think in May we shall go to Switzerland for my chest again – and probably come to America in the autumn, if all goes well with health and fortune. – I'm awfully sorry you were landed with the *Porcupine*: yet they are good essays, I think. But perhaps you did not get hold of my public: it's difficult.

Well again, a thousand thanks for your kindness. I hope I shall see you before long: feel I shall. It's coming time for me to cross westwards again, I feel.

Many regards   D. H. Lawrence[1]

4385. To Mary Foote, 11 April 1928
Text: MS YU; Unpublished.

[Pino Orioli, 6 – Lungarno Corsini – 6, Florence – Italy]
11 April 1928

Dear Miss Foote.[2]

Well I saw my two *femmine* off today – don't feel like running round Florence. – I shall be in again on *Friday*: would you like to have tea with me here in town somewhere, or go out to tea to the Villa Mirenda with me? *Come Vuole Lei*.[3] – Or if you are busy elsewhere, of course don't bother. – But just leave a word with Orioli, will you?

---

[1] Mason replied on 26 April 1928 (TMSC Mason):

Dear Lawrence,
  We are enclosing herewith a list of addresses to which we wish the twenty-five copies of LADY CHATTERLEY'S LOVER sent upon publication. We find that this method of getting books through is usually successful and that copies sent to private addresses are subjected to far less scrutiny than a shipment of twenty-five copies sent direct to the Book Shop. It is quite all right to use some of the addresses more than once as there are not quite twenty-five in the list in spite of my misleading statement at the beginning of this letter. I suggest that you do not enclose bills in the packages but write us direct the minute the packages are in the mail and advise us to whom they have been sent and bill us at that time. I hope that we shall be able to do a bit more than this for you before the actual publication date but we are anxious to get the list into your hands in plenty of time so that there may be no delay in getting the books over here.
Faithfully yours

Appended was a list of fifteen individuals with addresses in Philadelphia or its environs; it included Mason himself, his partner David Jester and Edward McDonald.
[2] Mary Foote (1872–1968), American painter and friend of Mabel Luhan whose portrait she painted (*Letters*, v. 107 n. 4). Mabel Luhan had led DHL to expect Mary Foote in Florence in December 1926 (ibid., pp. 597, 603).   [3] '*As you wish.*'

My wife will be back on Sunday night.
Hope you are having a nice time.

D. H. Lawrence

4386. To Giuseppe Orioli, [12 April 1928]
Text: MS UCLA; Unpublished.

Mirenda.
Thursday

Dear Pino

Miss Moller and Miss Morrison are coming here to tea tomorrow – Friday
– so if there are any proofs will you send them out.

I'm better – but don't think I shall come in this week. Niente di nuovo.[1]

DHL

I've done the other proofs – wish the printer would hurry up.

4387. To Giuseppe Orioli, [12 April 1928]
Text: MS UCLA; Unpublished.

Villa Mirenda.
Thursday

Dear Pino

I already sent you a note to say Miss Moller is coming to tea tomorrow
afternoon – if there are any more proofs. – I shall come in on *Monday* if
possible.

I send the proofs now. I am almost sure the Giuntina haven't enough type
to set up all the book – and that they'll print the first half, and then distribute
the type. You might make sure: because I think we ought to print just a *few*
copies on ordinary paper – even if only 100 – to give away etc. Don't you think
so? – 100 or perhaps 200 on ordinary paper, if it doesn't cost much.[2] We could
change the title page and a word or two. – If they have to distribute the print of
the first half to set up the second half, we shall have to decide at once.

Perhaps you'd better keep these two letters.[3]

If we are afraid of American Vigilance we could send 100 copies to Mabel
Lujan, to keep for us.

Au revoir, then – come up if you can.

DHL

[1] 'Nothing new.'
[2] The earliest mention of the first edn of *Lady Chatterley's Lover* cheap paper issue (Roberts A42
    b); Roberts conjectures 'November? 1928' for the publication of the 200 copies.
[3] The enclosures are missing.

4388. To Witter Bynner, 13 April 1928

Text: MS HU; Postmark, Firenze 13 . IV 28; Huxley 722–3.

Villa Mirenda. *Scandicci*, Florence

13 April 1928

Dear Bynner

I got *Cake* and read it with a good deal of amusement.[1] It is often very witty, and in parts really funny. It's not particularly 'Mabel' – rather a type than the specific person – so she needn't 'get her hair off' about it. It's fault is perhaps in scattering the scenes over the earth, so destroying some of the unity, maybe. But it remains very amusing – and at last just spiteful, which of course tickles me. – But you notice the chief mischief of Mabel in your letter – her effect on the Dassburgs.[2] I don't mind her passion for cake – it's her passion for breaking other people's eggs and making a mess instead of an omelette, which is really dangerous. She seems to hate anybody to care for anybody – even for herself – and if anybody *does* care for anybody, she must upset it – even if she falls herself out of the applecart. – Do write a play about that – the helpless way a woman *must* upset any apple cart that's got two apples in it: just for the fun.

My health's a good bit better – and if I can sell my novel, and have some money, I want to start off sailing round the world with Frieda in the autumn – there's a grand cheap way, by the Messageries Marittimes – and land in San Francisco – and come on. And then really I think – Frieda certainly thinks – it would be better to stay in Santa Fe for some time, till we could go to the ranch. It would be fun. And perhaps one could have friends among men, instead of *ces femmes*. It would be nice to feel something stable – I begin to feel a bit battered, one way and another.

Do you by the way know how much Mabel got for the MS. of *Sons and Lovers*? Has she *really* sold it![3] News!

You'll help me what you can do with my novel, won't you. It seems to be rousing already a lot of gratuitous hostility. Povero me!

Well – pazienza! don't be irritated by m[e –]⁴ I'm really more good-natured than most people.

We leave the Mirenda for good at the end of this month – so write c/o Pino Orioli, will you. And I'm looking forward to a proper reunion, really.

---

[1] In *Journey with Genius* Bynner wrote (p. 336): 'In 1926 I had published a play called *Cake*, some aspects of which were said to be a satire on Mabel Lujan. The slant was sportive but not, I thought, malicious'. He could not explain why DHL did not receive a copy until 1928.

[2] See p. 224 n. 1.

[3] Mabel Luhan made a present of the MS to her New York analyst, Dr Abraham Arden Brill, in April 1925; it remained in his possession until his death in 1948 (*Sons and Lovers: A Facsimile of the Manuscript*, ed. Mark Schorer, Berkeley, 1977, p. [7]).   [4] MS torn; text from Huxley.

I think it's *very silly* of Ida and Andrew to be at outs and made mischief by.
People who have lived together had best stick together. You can only change
for the worse.

DHL

4389. To Emily King, 13 April 1928
Text: MS Lazarus; Postmark, Fi[renze] 13 . IV 28; Unpublished.

Villa Mirenda – *Scandicci* (Florence)
13 April 1928

My dear Sister

I've been waiting to send your cloth – Frieda got you a smallish tea-cloth,
sort of terra-cotta, and six napkins – but the post won't take it except as a
parcel, which is a great nuisance here – so I gave it to Frieda to give to Barby
Weekley, who will bring it you. She – Barby – is in Alassio, on the Italian
Riviera, not far from Spotorno – and Frieda has gone there with her sister Else
for a day or two – comes back Sunday night. I think Barby is leaving for
England almost immediately, so she can post you your cloth from London. –
F's sister Else stayed with us a week, on her way back from Capri, and was
very nice. She'll go on direct from Alassio to Heidelberg. – And on Monday
we shall start to pack up here, because at the end of the month we leave this
house for good. I'm afraid we shall just have to give most of the things away –
too expensive sending them.

We'll go to Switzerland I suppose in May, to stay a couple of months, for
my chest. I take Ada's medicine – and don't really see that it has much effect
on me of any sort. I don't suppose it's for bronchials, and my chief trouble is
bronchial – The lung trouble heals easily with me, but the bronchial
inflammation is very tiresome. And this is a bad climate for it. – I expect we
shall stay in Switzerland till July, then come to England. And perhaps in the
autumn go to Taos. It suits me there. But anyhow I shall see you first.

I had a post-card from Peg at Versailles – she seems to be having a nice time
– which is good. It would have been a pity if it had rained a lot and
disappointed her. Here it's a very poor spring – changing every day – a good
deal of rain – not a bit like Italy.

I know it's wretched for you being in a shop like that. But why didn't you
put your mind to it, when Sam was leaving Carlton, and get a *decent* business.
You should have been far more careful, when you stepped out of one hole,
about stepping into another. Now it's a question of watching carefully for an
opportunity for getting out of Bulwell into something really decent.
Otherwise you'll only go from bad to worse. – For God knows when the coal

trade will pick up again. *Why* did you take another shop depending on coal? – But there – things are difficult. The trouble is, I'm afraid they won't get better very quickly.

Miss Beveridge and her sister are arriving in Florence today – When they come back to England I'll send you some little thing by them too.

Love   DHL

4390. To Earl and Achsah Brewster, 13 April 1928
Text: MS UT; Brewster 167–8.

Villa Mirenda. *Scandicci*. Florence
13 April 1928

Dear Earl and Achsah

– Your letter, Achsah, came yesterday – and I infer from it you have Lucille and Manfred with you – the Reynolds girls and Harwood – but who is the sixth child?[1] Anyhow it's a crowd. – As for me, I am alone for a day or two, Frieda having gone off with her sister to Alassio, to see her daughter Barbara. But F. will be back Sunday night. Then we start packing up like the devil, and clear out of this house and this climate. There's no mistake, it's a poor climate. What with wind, rain, mist, scirocco and heaviness, it's a pearl. But at the end of this month we quit for good.

And I feel I ought to go to Switzerland. It did me a lot of good – and I'd better look after these bronchials of mine, they play the deuce with me. I'd have loved to go to Tunis and Kairowan with Earl – but what's the good, if one coughs all the way. So some time in May we'll go up to the mountains, and stop a couple of months. Then perhaps to England – and in the autumn I'd like to set out towards the ranch. If I can sell my novel and have some money, I'd like to go round the world again. The Messageries Marittimes has an arrangement whereby for about £120 sterling you can have a ticket round the world, good for a year, and you can stop off where you like, wherever their boats touch, and take the next boat on, or a month later take a boat – on from Egypt to India and so on – if possible to San Francisco – and from there to the ranch. If I have enough money, I'd like very much to do that. Otherwise we might go straight to the ranch. – But it would be so nice, just for a bit, to be drifting out of reach of mail and malice, no letters, no literature, no publishers or agents or anything – what a paradise! I'm awfully tired of all that side of the world.

---

[1] Manfred Czernin, Lucile Beckett's son by her first marriage to Count Otto Czernin, had remained with her after her divorce in 1920 (see *Letters*, iii. 712 n. 1). There were three Reynolds girls: Diana, Hermione and Pamela (cf. Letter 3983 and p. 22 n. 4). The 'sixth' is unidentified.

I painted a bit since I'm back – a few water-colors – and a little *Rape of the Sabine Women* – and I'm doing my Ravello *Fauns* up.[1] It's quite amusing to paint – if only one didn't have the feeling of other people looking on. That spoils it again. People keep coming – and they want to see one's pictures – and they *don't* like them, they don't really want to take the trouble of really looking at them, or at anything, they stand there half alive and make the whole thing seem like luke-warm fish soup. I'm fed with people – absolutely. That's why I'd like to move on a bit.

But if there's no other way, we'll try and dash down and see you in May – we are sort of due to have a family talk. – Earl, do you want those photographs back? if so I'll send them. – And what are your plans?

Now I'm going to Florence – not with much joy!

Au revoir, then.   DHL

4391. To Mary Foote, [13 April 1928]
Text: MS YU; Unpublished.

[Florence]
[13 April 1928][2]

So sorry about Wed. – I felt so limp after farewells and a lunch with a very deaf friend and very stammering man.[3] Am staying tonight in Florence; if you'd care to have a little meal with me somewhere about 7.0, benissimo. Otherwise do come to the Mirenda on *Tuesday*.

DHL

4392. To Else Jaffe, [14 April 1928]
Text: MS Jeffrey; PC v. Dintorni di Firenze – Panorama di Ponte a Vingone; Postmark, Firenze 16 . IV 28; Frieda Lawrence 271.

[Villa Mirenda, Scandicci, Florence]
Sat

Had your note from Alassio – glad you liked it there. I wonder if you are setting off today for Germany. I stayed the night in Florence at Oriolis, but came back to the Mirenda this afternoon. There is an atmosphere of departure, only departure and departure, which is a bit écoeurant.[4] I wish we were safely away, with no good-byes to say. – We shall meet some time during the summer somewhere nice and free and forgetful. Italy has too many

---

[1] See Letter 4114 and p. 133 n. 2.
[2] Dated with reference to DHL's arrangements for meeting Mary Foote, in Letter 4385, and see letter following.
[3] The deaf friend was probably Muriel Moller (cf. Letter 4350); the man is unidentified.
[4] 'sickening'.

memories, not enough spunk. I shall send your Füllfeder,[1] which I just discovered.

DHL

4393. To Giuseppe Orioli, [16 April 1928]
Text: MS UCLA; Unpublished.

[Villa Mirenda, Scandicci, Florence]
Monday,

Dear Pino

Would Carletto mind just meeting Frieda at the station, at 7.10 from Genova (Pisa) – and tell her everything is all right, and will she come straight out, Pietro will be at Vingone. Margaret Gardiner would like to go to the station too, just to see her – they've never met – and Margaret G. is leaving for England tomorrow.

Have done the proofs once – now am going over them again.

Hope you've had luck with your cheques and all. Shall come in in a day or two.

DHL

4394. To William Dibdin, [16? April 1928]
Text: MS UCLA; Unpublished.

[Villa Mirenda, Scandicci, Florence]
[16? April 1928][2]

Mr Lawrence asks me to say that his first book of poems was *Love Poems and Others* (Duckworth) *Amores* being the second book.[3] I have a copy of *Amores* in London, which you can get from Davis and Orioli, 30 Museum St. W.

---

[1] 'fountain pen'.   [2] The date is wholly conjectural.
[3] DHL appears to have drafted a letter, probably to be sent by Orioli, in response to the following enquiry (TMS UCLA); nothing further is known of William H. Dibdin. (In the Parliamentary Register for Bristol in 1929 his name is unaccountably given as 'Dibben'; his signature on the letter which follows is clearly 'Dibdin'.)

10 Glena Avenue, Knowle, Bristol, Eng.
4th April 1928.

Dear Sir,

I shall be pleased to receive particulars of your new book which I understand is soon to be issued in a limited edition. I am particularly interested in your work and have a collection of almost every book you have issued so far, with the exception of "Amores" a first edition of which seems very hard to find. Can you please tell me if this is your first book of poems? I suppose it is too much to ask whether you have a spare copy for disposal at the moment, if so perhaps you will be good enough to let me know.

Yours very truly,   W. H. Dibdin

The new novel is a full length book on hand-made paper – and apparently there will be no public edition.

4395. To Helen Bramble, 17 April 1928
Text: TMSC NWU; Huxley 726–7.

Villa Mirenda, Scandicci, (Florence)
17 April 1928.

Dear Miss Bramble,[1]

Many thanks for your letter and the copies of letters about the *Escaped Cock*. But what a lovely little anthology![2] I am delighted to have them. Now I know I've committed the unpardonable sin, I feel all right. I always was so afraid I might be saved: like ten dollars in the bank. No more fear of that! But oh, I do so want to know how many souls were *lost* through my maleficence: and the editor's. The more the merrier! Do you think Carrie J. Hill, who has nothing but sympathy in her dear old heart 'for us both' – one at a time, my dear – might be able to tell me? No wonder the *Forum* looks red, fiery and Mephistophelian.[3] Let it be more so. Long live the cloven hoof!

Of course you may have lost a few subscriptions pro tem. But believe me, those lost souls will either come back or send delegates. You won't lose in the long run. Deadness is what loses in the long run. Anything that makes 'em wriggle becomes at last indispensable. Vive le gai coq, et le coq gai!

I hope Carrie Hill will read my novel – and that it will fall into the hands of the son of nineteen, and that he'll read it aloud to the gaudy end before a stunned and aghast parent can stop him. Oh what a lot of hypocrites!

So I enclose a few order forms, and please send one to George Williamson, Litchfield, Mich. and to Carrie dear and a few others: I might even get them to lose their souls, instead of saving 'em: which would be *so* much more becoming.

Your sincere 'traitor and enemy of the human race'

D. H. Lawrence

---

[1] Helen Bramble was on the editorial staff of *Forum* which first published *The Escaped Cock* in February 1928. Cf. Letter 4214.
[2] *Forum* (subtitled *A Magazine of Controversy*) normally devoted many pages to readers' – often angry – letters. McDonald reported that 'for several months after the appearance of [*The Escaped Cock*] . . . a heated discussion concerning it was carried on in the correspondence columns of [*Forum*]' (*Bibliography: Supplement*, p. 97). By April several readers including Carrie J. Hill and George Williamson had protested. In the May issue, *Forum*'s editor declared: 'No story ever published by *The Forum* has aroused so violent an outburst of contrary opinions as "The Escaped Cock". . .' One irate reader described DHL as a 'traitor and enemy of the human race'.   [3] The magazine's front cover was printed in red-orange and black.

4396. To Maria Huxley, [17 April 1928]
Text: Huxley 723-4.

Villa Mirenda, Scandicci, Firenze.
Tuesday, 16 April 1928.[1]

Dear Maria, –

Quite a while since we heard from you. F[rieda] was in Alassio a week with her daughter Barbara – came back last night. Now we're going to begin to pack. I'm winding up my last picture, too, so I can have them shipped to London. I think I shall send them to Dorothy Warren – they might as well be shown. But I shan't sell them. I'm in the middle of the proofs – shall finish them this week – still haven't got a cover-paper – want to find a good *red* – phœnix in black. I send you one specimen with the bird – paper no good. Have a fair number of orders from England – and the first one from America yesterday. So they're beginning. After having the London people trying to pull me down and make me feel in the wrong about *Lady C.* – Curtis Brown's office *en bloc* – Secker – Cape –, I was quite pleased to have Mrs. Knopf's letter saying she liked it very much and they want to publish it. Really, people are swine, the way they try to make one feel in the wrong. – *The Forum* sent me letters written by people who read my story, *The Escaped Cock*, that *The Forum* published in February. Really, they're funny – I am an enemy of the human species, have committed the unpardonable sin, etc., etc. – and a story good as gold. And a woman who's been my friend for years told me on Saturday that my pictures were disgusting and unnecessary, and even old-fashioned.[2] Really, I shall have to buy a weapon of some sort. Wish I had the skunk's.

Did you enjoy the trip north? How well I know Lincoln – used to love it. Did you go to the flat dree coast, and Boston and King's Lynn? Or did you go to Southwell and Nottingham?

Roses are out – and iris just fluttering out. Are you feeling chirpy, both of you? We lunch with Lady Colefax at the Waterfields – who have inherited Janet Ross's place – on Monday.[3] *Beati noi!*

DHL

[1] 16 April 1928 was a Monday.
[2] Probably Mary Foote (see Letter 4406); or possibly Millicent Beveridge who arrived in Florence on Friday 13 April (Letter 4389) and was herself a painter.
[3] DHL had known Aubrey Waterfield (d. 1944), painter and illustrator, and his wife Lina (b. 1874) since 1913; he and Frieda visited the Waterfields' Castle of Aulla, near Spezia, in May 1914 (*Letters*, ii. 116 n. 1, 120). Janet Ross (1842–August 1927), Lina Waterfield's aunt, had bequeathed to her Poggio Gherardo, near Settignano, an imposing mediaeval fortress-dwelling. Lina Waterfield, in *Castle in Italy* (1961), recalled that she and her husband had not seen the Lawrences from 1914 to 1928: 'we were at Poggio Gherardo after the death of my aunt. They came to lunch with an old friend of ours, Sybil Colefax. Lawrence was looking far more ill than we had ever seen him, and he had lost much of his former vitality and sparkle' (p. 143). See ibid., opposite pp. 25 and 200, for photographs of Poggio Gherardo and 'Janet Ross at Poggio Gherardo' respectively.

I liked Lady Colefax – she seemed real – but looked as if she feared I might bite!

4397. To Harry Crosby, 17 April 1928
Text: MS SIU; Postmark, Firenze 19 . IV 28; Huxley 724–5.

Villa Mirenda. *Scandicci* (Florence)
17 April 1928

Dear Harry Crosby

Send your complete book of poems, and I'll write a little introduction for *it* – about 2000 words do you want?[1] I really like the poems. – Send it soon, so I do it before we leave here.

And I'll send you the MSS – 'Man Who Loved Islands' – and *Sun* – and a few poems. But I'm afraid the old MS. of 'Eagle' is burnt[2] – I might write it out for you. I'm taking the stories to be bound, as best they can be, here: will let you have them when the binder is through.

Thanks for the order for the book. – We leave this house May 1st: but c/o Pino Orioli will find me – 6 Lungarno Corsini, Florence.

And we'll meet in the summer – you say 'we' – are you also married?[3]

D. H. Lawrence

4398. To Alfred Knopf, 17 April 1928
Text: Moore 1055–6.

Villa Mirenda, Scandicci
17 April 1928

Dear Knopf

I was awfully pleased to get your letter saying you didn't find *Lady Chatterley* an abomination: and still more pleased with Mrs Knopf's letter. Because the London people have all been trying to make me feel tremendously in the wrong, and holding up pious hands afraid of touching pitch: which I don't forgive 'em, and shan't. – I shall write Mrs Knopf to London.

As you say, the situation has changed. Secker seems to have shrivelled up, as if somebody had put salt on his tail. I believe Chatto and Windus have the MS. now – but I doubt they'll make nothing of it. And I shall not let any other London publisher see it. Enough of their baby terrors! You must see what you

[1] DHL wrote the introduction for Crosby's *Chariot of the Sun* (in an edn not published until November 1931). The essay itself first appeared as 'Chaos in Poetry' in *Echanges*, December 1929 (Roberts B33, C194).
[2] The poem, 'Eagle in New Mexico' (published in *Birds, Beasts and Flowers*).
[3] See p. 300 n. 4.

can do – and if the thing can't be dished up for the public, it can't, and I don't care. But at least you won't have lifted shocked hands of virtuous indignation, like that London lot.

I am in the middle of proofs – hope to have done them all by next week. Then they'll begin to print.

Do you really want three copies? If you do, fill in one of the order forms and send it to Orioli, because he'll do the mailing.

We leave this house May 1st – for good. So address me c/o Curtis Brown, 6 Henrietta St, London W.C.2. And we really will meet somewhere in Europe during the summer.

4399. To Juliette Huxley, [17–18 April 1928]
Text: MS Huxley and TMSC NWU; Huxley 725–6..

Villa Mirenda. *Scandicci* (Florence)
17 April 1928

Dear Juliette

Had your letter from Wells' house.[1] Do you like staying there? Anyhow it's a change for you from Highgate. – I was so relieved when you said it was better with you and Julian now, and that something had come free. I'm so glad. After talking to you and your mother that evening in such a burst, I said to Frieda: I wish to God I'd kept my tongue still.[2] Now they'll say I've been making mischief again. – That has been the almost invariable result so far. But it's the people's fault. If they were decent enough, they'd come freer, like you. But they aren't honest, most folks. Why do you say I laugh at you? I may laugh at some things about you. I laugh at you when you say 'What if Anthony were sixteen, and read this novel!' – He'd be too bored at 16: but at twenty of course he *should* read it. Was your mind a sexual blank at sixteen? is anybody's? and what ails the mind in that respect is that it has nothing to go on, it grinds away in abstraction. So I laugh at you and shall go on laughing when you say: What if Anthony were 16, and read your novel? – What indeed! – But of course I don't laugh at *you*, nor at your mother either. For absurdities I laugh at everybody, including myself: and why not? But at the essential person I don't laugh. And of course, you ought to know it, and not have those silly misgivings.

I've been having a tussle with my novel: publishers, agents etc in London holding up hands of pious horror (because it may affect *their pockets*) and

[1] Easton Glebe, in Kent.
[2] Lady Juliette recalls that 'Lawrence was hard on Julian: he thought him "an expurgated version of a man; like so many others; much the greatest danger for men"' (*Leaves of the Tulip Tree*, p. 121).

trying to make me feel disastrously in the wrong. Now the Knopfs write from New York they like it very much, and hope to be able to get it into shape to offer to the public. I doubt they can't. But it's nice of them.

I'm in the midst of the proofs – hope to finish them this week. But I still haven't chosen the cover paper. The orders came in very nicely from England. Are you risking a copy, or not?

It's been nasty weather – not really nice since we came back. But today looks promising. Tomorrow Lady Colefax is due to come to tea. – I'm busy finishing off my pictures – think I shall send them to Dorothy Warren for her to exhibit in her Gallery in Madox St – she wants to. But don't go and see them – you'd only be in a rage as you were that morning in des Aroles.

We want to leave this house on the 30th – so we've not much longer. I may stay in Florence to see my book out on the 15th, then to Switzerland, to cure. I think we'll go to Vermala Montana, above Sierre (or is it Sion?)[1] – because it's a flat plateau and I can walk without gasping. My chest is so-so – but I'm better really.

Anyhow we'll see you during the summer – perhaps August. Remember me to Julian, and I hope the book goes gaily, and he'll feel nice and chirpy doing it:[2] and not try to do too many other things. – Frieda has actually written too. – How are the children? Is Anthony at school?

DHL

I suppose your mother is back in her Neuchatel. Remember me to her when you write.

The vegetable man from Aigle sent me his bill again – 39 frs. – but I wrote and told him you'd paid it.

[Frieda Lawrence begins]

Wednesday

Dear Juliette

Only today Lawr gave me your letter out of an old pocket. We often talk of you and it made me so terribly sad that you didn't seem happier, but now you will be more so; but England is such a difficult place to be happy in anyhow. Lorenzo is really better, but we will hop off to Switzerland and he will get much, much stronger. Yes, you must look at his pictures, you won't be so

[1] Vermala Montana is nnw. of Sierre.
[2] Julian Huxley was engaged on *The Science of Life*, with H. G. and G. P. Wells (it was published in fortnightly parts).

shocked after the novel. I feel that novel might really do some good in the world. There should be some glamour again in the relationship between men and women. We have grown so pettifogging. Is your mother with you still? She is real anyhow. I had a few beautiful days with my sister and Barby in Alassio. Do ask the children to come and see you – Miss Elsa Weekley, 49 Harvard Rd., Chiswick – I forget the telephone number. I send you this phoenix, it will rejoice your embroidering heart and I wish I had seen Adam and Eve.[1] What a good time Diablerets gave us! and that Lawr is better – I am not a letterwriter, so don't please think I am horrid not to have written, like that parrot who was supposed to talk and didn't 'I think all the more'.

With much love also to your mother Julian and the children   Frieda

4400. To S. S. Koteliansky, 18 April 1928
Text: MS BL; Postmark, Scandicci 21 [. . .] 28; Moore 1058.

Villa Mirenda, *Scandicci* (Florence)
18 April 1928

Dear Kot

Thanks for your letter and the Behrens order.[2] – We have now got about 150 orders – eighty-odd paid – only two from America, because they haven't had time – so these are all English. A good many people haven't ordered who will do so, I think – like E. M. Forster and his crowd – and W. J. Turner and so on. People don't like ordering far in advance. – Orioli says he will keep you no. 1. and no. 17, and let the rest go out promiscuously[3] – he's marked it down against your order. – I'm sorry about Ottoline.[4] – Tomorrow Lady Colefax is coming to tea, I'll get her to help. – And of course I want to see American results. – I had a letter from Mrs Knopf yesterday liking the novel very much, and wanting to publish it if they can get it possible for the public – So if they do it, no doubt they'll have English rights too. I think Chattos are considering the MS. now, but I shan't let it go to any other London publisher. If I can cover expenses before the book appears, I don't mind. I put £130 in the bank today – opening an English account here in Haskard and Casardi's.

---

[1] See Letter 4328 and p. 313 n. 4.
[2] In DHL's record of orders for *Lady Chatterley's Lover* appears the name of E. Beddington Behrens who sent a Westminster Bank cheque for £2 ('Memoranda', MS NWU). (Sir) Edward Beddington-Behrens (1897–1968), economist, was a member of the Secretariat of, and later a representative for, the League of Nations, and occasionally lectured at the London School of Economics.   [3] See Letter 4362.
[4] Lady Ottoline Morrell was very ill with necrosis of the jaw (cf. Letter 4494).

Dull weather here – rather gritty for the chest.

Awfully nice of you to take so much trouble.

Ever   DHL

I enclose you a phœnix – these I had printed just to use as *ex libris*.[1]

4401. To Orrick Johns, 24 April 1928
Text: MS UT; Unpublished.

Villa Mirenda. Scandicci (Firenze)
24 April 1928

Dear Orrick Johns[2]

Thanks for your letter and for telling me about George Macey.[3] I'll let my agent know in New York – it is always well to have a friendly publisher in mind. – How are you getting on with your work, by the way?

My health is pretty much the same: but no worse. We're in the throes of preparing to go, and not getting ahead very well. But I'll really be off to Switzerland early in May, to do some of my coughing there.

Perhaps before then we shall see you in town – and meanwhile many thanks.

Sincerely   D. H. Lawrence

4402. To Martin Secker, 24 April 1928
Text: MS UInd; Postmark, Firenze 24 . IV 28; Secker 105–6.

Villa Mirenda. Scandicci. (Florence)
24 April 1928

Dear Secker

What's the news by now? I heard from Pollinger that Knopf gave May 25th for the date of the short stories – so I suppose you are coming out with them then.[4] And the poems? – anything further settled?

I heard from Mrs Knopf that she liked *Lady Chatterley* and wanted to publish it, if they could arrange it so as to make it possible. Alfred wrote more or less the same. Remains to be seen if they can trim it down. I confess it seems to me a tough job – I don't know how to do it myself. But if they can do it, good for them.

---

[1] See Zytaruk [v] for a reproduction of the phoenix which is part of this BL MS.

[2] Orrick Johns (1887–1946), American poet. 1926–9 lived in Italy (partly in Florence) and had first met DHL in July/August 1927. Published three volumes of poetry, a novel and his autobiography – *Time of Our Lives* (1937) – in which he described his meetings with DHL (see Nehls, iii. 148–51, 686 n. 219).

[3] George Macy (1900–56), American publisher; DHL's address book (MS UT) records: 'Macy at Macy–Masius, 551 5th Avenue, New York'. He was later managing director of Nonesuch Press, London.   [4] Cf. p. 152 n. 3.

I told Orioli you said you wanted three copies, so he's sending you an invoice.

I've done rather more than half of the proofs – and ordered the binding paper – and made my phœnix design for the cover, and the printer has already made a block of it. – I hope we'll really be ready by May 15th – I think we shall, anyhow with the first batch of two hundred. – The English orders have come in very well – I think we shall soon have orders for all the English 500. The Americans have only just begun to answer – mail takes so much longer.

Frieda was away a week with Barby in Alassio – went to Spotorno, saw the tenente and the Capelleros and all.[1] She came back the other day, and we are spasmodically packing up – all at a loose end. I'm winding up my pictures, because I think I shall send them to Dorothy Warren to show in her gallery in Maddox St. She wants me to. More things for the British public to dislike and to balk at. But let 'em. – And I must do something with them, the pictures – if we give up this house.

The weather isn't very good – only half a spring. I wanted to go and do my etruscan giro and finish my etruscan book. But don't feel any too robust – and bad weather – and the novel to see to. – In the middle of May we intend to go to Switzerland again, fairly high, for a couple of months, for my health: then come to England about August. And if I get money for my novel, sail round the world. I think it would do me good. But we must see.

Regards from us both – and F. says many thanks for the papers that come so constantly.

D. H. Lawrence

The Phœnix rises from the nest in flames.[2]

4403. To Maria Chambers, 24 April 1928
Text: MS UT; cited in Maria Cristina Chambers, 'Afternoons in Italy with D. H. Lawrence', *Texas Quarterly*, vii (Winter 1964), 115.

Villa Mirenda. *Scandicci*. Florence.
24 April 1928

Dear Mrs Chambers
I never thanked you for the photographs and for the offer of the blood-stone. – No, I don't laugh at you about the stone. I'd rather people believed in a suave red stone than in some wretched abstraction. The principle of life is in stones too, and if in stones we can get into communication with it, then good,

---

[1] Luigi and Caterina Capellero were Rina Secker's parents whom the Lawrences first met in November 1925 (*Letters*, v. 336). The 'tenente' was Angelo Ravagli (1891–1976); he was to be Frieda's third husband (ibid., p. 337 and n. 3).

[2] DHL included an initialled phoenix reproduction with the letter.

it is surely healing. I'm certain the old people – the so-called palaeolithic people – felt the life-principle in massive stones, and got a vivifying response: and I'm sure for thousands of years man loved gold for its own golden life, its yellow life-stuff, and drew power from it: and that's how it came to have its value, which mankind can't get over. But the real value is religious, not monetary. – But don't break your stone. I'm a bit superstitious about those things. I feel it shouldn't be broken.

It is nice of you to set to about my novel. I am busy doing the proofs – hope to finish them this week. I made a design of the phœnix rising from a nest in flames, for the cover. It is a favourite symbol of mine: send you a copy. The printer made a block from my little drawing. – In my opinion my novel is worth working a bit for. I think you and I instinctively turn to the same thing, the life implicit instead of the life explicit. And the life implicit is embodied and has *touch*: and the life explicit is only ideas, and is bodiless. And my novel is an attempt to be in touch, to give the throb of the implicit life.

Did you see the story in the *Forum*, in February, I think, called *The Escaped Cock*? The editor just sent me the letters he received because of it: and I am delighted to think that I am 'a traitor and enemy of mankind', that I 'have caused many souls to be lost', and that I have 'committed the unpardonable sin,' that I am a menace to society etc etc.[1] You never saw such a batch of vituperative condemnation. And I thought it a perfectly harmless story – merely an attempt to show the resurrection *in the flesh*, instead of in vacuo and in abstraction. Of course if there is any point whatsoever in the resurrection it was the resurrection of the body. And if it was a resurrection of the man's natural body, then it was a strange and painful experience, and a somewhat bitter eye-opener. But there you are. The letters lament that there is no Inquisition.

We are waiting here till the middle of May, for my novel: and I am finishing off my pictures – oils and waters – because I think I shall exhibit them in London – and perhaps in New York in the autumn. People hate them so, there must be something in them. – In May we go to Switzerland again – up fairly high – for my health. I still cough too much and am a bit knocked out: but really getting stronger all the time again – gradually. I think we shall stay in Switzerland till end of July – then probably England for August – and then in autumn I want to sail away from Europe, and arrive ultimately in the ranch. Perhaps we'll come direct to New York, perhaps we'll sail the other way, by Egypt and India and the East, to San Francisco. Depends on my health. Alas, that one's health should have to be so much thought about!

[1] See Letter 4395 and n. 2. *Forum*'s editor was Henry Leach.

I send you one or two photographs – nothing very good – and you will say if you will be in England about August time.

tante cose!   D. H. Lawrence

4404. To Bonamy Dobrée, 24 April 1928

Text: MS Brotherton; Unpublished.

Villa Mirenda, Scandicci – (Florence)
24 April 1928

Dear Dobrée

A word to let you know our plans, as far as we have any. – Here till about May 20th – then Switzerland, till about July 20th – then probably England, till perhaps end of September. Then I don't know. If I sell my novel, and have money, perhaps we'll take a ticket round the world, by the Messageries Marittimes, which I hear are fairly cheap, and you can stop off wherever their boats stop – and take another boat on. So we could get off at Port Said and come to Cairo for a month or so, in the later autumn. I should like to do that. Then go on to India or somewhere. And end up at San Francisco, for the ranch.

I don't quite know what you mean by lust. If you mean simple physical desire, without any spiritual business, I agree entirely. But a simple physical desire argues a natural physical sympathy with the woman, if only for half an hour. And lust, as you can see it sometimes, surely, in an elderly Mohammedan, is entirely without natural sympathy, and ugly. – I do think one is simply made ill, nowadays, by women who 'love' one. One doesn't want all that conscious business – it turns my stomach. But one needs to be able to feel really gentle, really tender to the woman – if only for the half hour, and if one never sees her again. But without tenderness, lust, as you call it, hits back at you, and causes another insentience, sterility. – The worst of the 'wonderful' women is that one can never by any chance feel tender or gentle to them: they're a cut above it.

I think you'll like my novel – it's that line.

Poor sort of spring here!

D. H. Lawrence

4405. To Enid Hilton, 25 April 1928

Text: MS UCLA; cited in Moore, *Intelligent Heart* 355.

Villa Mirenda. *Scandicci* (Firenze)
25 April 1928

Dear Enid

You usually hover just when we're departing. – I never got very robust, after that illness last July – so had to go to Switzerland in the winter – January and February – and we're going again in the middle of May, for a couple of months. In January we stayed in Les Diablerets – above Aigle: and I liked it. But my trouble is climbing hills – I gasp. So I'd like a place with a bit of level walking – between 3000 and 4000 ft. up. They say Vermala-Montana is a good place, with a plateau, about 4000 ft. above Sierre, in the Rhone Valley. But there we'll have to stay in an hotel. You don't know of a nice *inn* where the peasants drink at evening; anywhere in Switzerland, at the right level, do you? – and where one gets good cooking. If you do, do tell me.

And if you get to Florence before we leave, of course come out and see us. You know where we are – tram No 16 from the Cathedral to Vingone – go to the very terminus. Then walk ahead about ¾ mile, keeping on the high-road, but the left branch at the pagoda – up to the two cypresses standing touching one another at the corner of the lane to the left.

[sketch]

Turn there, and dip down into the valley. The Mirenda is the big square box of a house on the hill in front of you, with the little church of San Paolo behind. – If we are away, you could come just the same – go to the peasants house and ask for Giulia, our girl – she'll have the key. – And you can stay at the little trattoria in Vingone, just where the tram stops, for about Liras 35 a day each. The man died at Easter – but the wife is nice and will look after you. And it's charming country round here – real country. – Our friends the Wilkinsons had a very decent pensione in Florence – and very cheap – but I've forgotten the address. You could write to Mrs A. S. Wilkinson, 25 South Parade, Chelsea and ask her. They were our neighbours here, but have gone to England.

We've had a poor spring, no steady sunshine as we ought to have – but also not a great deal of rain. Today was lovely. – If we come to England, it won't be till August anyhow.

I hope you'll get a nice holiday – and if you are in time, we shall see you both. Till then many greetings from us.

D. H. Lawrence

4406. To Hon. Dorothy Brett, 25 April 1928
Text: MS UCin; Postmark, Scandicci 26.4.28; cited in Huxley 727–8.

Villa Mirenda. Scandicci. (Florence)
25 April 1928

Dear Brett

I had your cablegram day before yesterday. But I promised to send my pictures to Dorothy Warren. It won't matter though – even if any are sold, they must be reserved till after the New York show. I expect the Warren will show in May or June – so that leaves plenty of time for them to come to New York. You say, show arranged for August. But whatever is the good of showing pictures in New York in August, when every single soul who looks at pictures will be away, mostly abroad? That looks a dud to me. I wish Mrs Hare would write to me personally, so that I know what she is actually doing. I wrote to her about my novel, and sent her some forms.[1] But she hasn't answered yet. Perhaps she will. And perhaps she will tell me about the pictures, what she is arranging.

I have got seven big ones: *A Holy Family, Willow Trees, Fight with an Amazon, Boccaccio Story*, 'Back into Paradise', *Resurrection*, and 'Nymphs and Fauns': they are all ready. Then I have smaller ones: 'Men Bathing at Dawn', *Finding of Moses* (five negresses), 'Cigarette', *Rape of the Sabine Women*, and 'Family in a garden'.[2] I'm just finishing the last – rather lovely nude. Then I've got seven water-colours – all nudes – all ready. Seems quite a lot to me. But most people seem to take offence at them. – Mary Foote was here twice. I liked her. At first she was inclined to jeer at my canvases – being the professional. Then she said they impressed her.

Do you think we ought to have a few of Earl's and Achsah's shown with ours? You know they have a whole bunch lying in New York waiting.

I shan't roll my canvases – don't trust them. They're painted with all sorts of paints. Must get them put in a packing case.

We have just a few orders from America for the novel – Stieglitz,[3] Brill – about eight, I suppose. No doubt the others will come in later. I have got enough orders so far to cover current expenses. I hope I'll pretty well sell the whole thousand. Your brother Maurice ordered a copy.[4] – Of course I shan't make 10,000 dollars. I have to pay for the thing – cost about 3,000 – out of my pocket: and postage; and then I must pay Orioli 10%. But if I sold them all I'd get about 6,000, which would be very nice.

We are staying here till about 15th May, till the book is out. I hope to god it will be ready, at least the first batch of 200, by that date. But so far I've only

[1] See p. 335 n. 2.

[2] 'Men Bathing at Dawn' eventually entitled *Men Bathing*; 'Cigarette' not known under this title; 'Family in a garden' became *Family on a Verandah* (*Paintings*, plate [12]); 'Nymphs and Fauns' later called *Fauns and Nymphs*.

[3] Alfred Stieglitz (1864–1946), leading American photographer; he had admired DHL's earlier writings (see *Letters*, iv. 499 and n. 1) and had subscribed for two copies of *Lady Chatterley's Lover* according to DHL's handwritten list of subscribers ('Memoranda', MS NWU). m. 1928, Georgia O'Keefe (1887–1986), American modernist painter.

[4] Maurice Vyner Baliol Brett (1882–1934), Assistant Keeper and Librarian, the London Museum, 1919–34. (DHL's list of subscribers includes the name of Oliver, not Maurice, Brett.)

done *half* the proofs: expect another lot tomorrow. And when the thing is printed, there's the binder to wait for. – I send you a phœnix rising from the nest in flames, which I drew to be stamped on the cover of the book. The printer has made a block of it.

Then in the middle of May we must go to Switzerland for my broncs. It did me so much good in the winter, I'll give it another couple of months try this summer. Then we must go to England for a bit. But in the autumn I really intend to sail towards the ranch. If I've got money, we might possibly sail in stages round the world, and land in San Francisco, as we did the other time. I don't mind arriving in the early winter in Taos. But once we leave here, now, I shall feel I am starting the voyage towards the ranch.

I'm so glad the cellar held up. Be economical, and get your debts paid off – they are a great bore. – I haven't heard from Spud about the story[1] – but the *Forum* sent me the letters they got on the strength of it, and apparently I am the enemy of the human race, have caused innumerable souls to be lost, have committed the unpardonable sin etc etc. Sounded like the *Adelphi*. – Tell Mabel I'll be writing her in a day or two.

a rivederci!   DHL

Did Mabel sell the MS of *Sons and Lovers*?

4407. To Earl Brewster, 25 April 1928
Text: MS UT; Brewster 169–70.

Villa Mirenda, Scandicci, (Florence)
25 April 1928

Dear Earl

So the Israelites are turned out of their little Canaan – and you think Constance is the next camp? – whereabouts on Constance – on the Swiss side, of course: and right on the lake? It can be very nice.

We think we might keep on the Mirenda – if you'd like it we certainly should. We shall leave *at latest* by May 20th – and shall be away at least six months. So if Achsah feels like camping for a summer here with Harwood, she's very welcome. Nice isn't very nice in summer. And here is rather lovely, really. Just let me know.

I hang on, waiting for proofs – have only done half, yet: wish the printer would hurry up. Orders come in pretty well – not in a rush – but all right. – I can go as soon as proofs are done and binding is settled – Orioli will do the rest. I'm not wildly keen on Switzerland, except just for my health. You don't know of a nice *inn* anywhere, do you, where the peasants drink at evening, and

---

[1] See Letter 4377 and p. 358 n. 1.

one can stay – about the same altitude as Diablerets – 3000 ft – 1000 meters – or a bit more: and if possible a bit of flat ground to walk on. I should like that so much better than an hotel with English old maids.

I doubt if we shall get to Capri – and you'll be flitting as we are. But we'll certainly meet this summer, Constance or elsewhere. I feel this time we're all being jerked off the nest – and the next settling will perhaps be different – though perhaps, the old roost. Who knows.

Brett cables an exhibition fixed – of our pictures – in New York for August. But she's so irresponsible, that till I hear from someone more weighty, I shall not move. But I think I shall send my[1] things to London, to Dorothy Warren's gallery – she wants me to. What else shall I do with them, if we clear out? We must talk about this exhibition business, when we meet – which will surely be before long. I suppose you don't want to send a few things to London? I could ask Dorothy.

I feel I don't much care where I go. The outside world doesnt matter quite so much as it did – it matters less and less – so long as one can sit peacefully and be left pretty much alone. One hardly wants any more to step out of the shadow of one's bô-tree. – But people still tell me Cyprus is a good island.

a revederci to you Achsah and Harwood and Earl.   DHL
Send you my phœnix, drawn by me, to be printed on the cover of my book.

4408. To Aldous Huxley, 25 April 1928
Text: Huxley 728–9.

Villa Mirenda, Scandicci, Firenze.
25th April, 1928

Dear Aldous, –

Lady Colefax sent in her cheque for ten pounds the same day as you sent yours for her. So I am sending hers on to you – have asked her – which settles it.

A lovely day – first *really* spring-summer day. We are staying on at least two more weeks: must see the book out: have only done *half* the proofs yet. Orders come pretty well – but nothing from the old crowd, E. M. Forster, or Clive Bell – only Hutchinson and Maynard Keynes.[2] The expenses, however, are covered. Wish the printer would hurry up.

[1] my] some
[2] In 1915 DHL 'rather' liked the critic Clive Bell (1881–1964) (*Letters*, ii. 435 and n. 5), but by 1927 he thought 'Clive Bell and Co. must be very wearing' (ibid., v. 651). St John ('Jack' Hutchinson (1884–1942), barrister, later defended Dorothy Warren in the case over the confiscation of DHL's paintings from her gallery in 1929. Hutchinson and his wife, Mary, had been known to DHL (through Kot) since 1916. DHL's impression of the distinguished economist, Maynard Keynes (1883–1946), was one of hostility and repulsion (see *Letters*, ii. 311 n. 1, 319–20).

We *might* keep on the Mirenda – but go to Switzerland now, of course.

I painted a little picture, *Finding of Moses* – which is really five negresses – now am doing a 'Family in Garden' – rather small – all nude, of course – ma in hammock, pa on his heels squatting – and two *bambini*. Guess Maria will want this one. Cable from Brett *not* to exhibit in London, as exhibition fixed for August, in New York. But think I shall ship the things to London.

I wish we knew of some *nice* well-fed inn in Switzerland – where the peasants drink in the *Gastzimmer* – it's so much nicer than an hotel with English old maids. Do you know of any such place? Does Julian? With a bit of level ground if possible. I'm pretty well, except on a hill. Tell me if you know of an inn.

It's still a rotten spring – country looks dead. – These two days there's a high wind ripping the blossom to bits – our front is strewn with broken buds of the *ippocastagni*. It's not a bit nice out of doors, so one stays in. But I think we'll be out of this house by the last day of this month – in two weeks' time[1] – then I hope I can leave my novel, and depart for Switzerland. Otherwise we'll go somewhere near, for a fortnight, till the novel is really out. I have it on my conscience. I expect by the end of the week it will be all set up. Then next week they'll start printing it on the hand-made paper. – So I'll leave out 'John Thomas' altogether – pity! – I heard from Curtis Brown they sent the MS. to Chatto's, so you could collect it. But do collect it for me when you can. I don't want the swine to have it another minute.

I think we shall go to Vermala Montana, above Sierre – because there is a plateau and one can walk on the flat, which is a relief to me. I hope it'll do me good, for I don't very much want to stick myself in Switzerland. I do hope I'll sell my novel. Then in the autumn I think we'll sail round the world, you can have a ticket by the Messageries Maritimes for about £120 – good for a year – stay wherever the ships stop – and go on when you like. – I want so much to get away from the world – books, publishers, agents, critics – all that sort of thing – to get away and forget everything for a bit. It's nothing but old chagrin makes me ill. – And end the *giro* at the ranch.

Lady Colefax writes, so we ask her to tea Thursday. Is she Lady Colefax or The Lady Sybil Colefax? Frieda wants to write you a *long* letter when she – Lady C. – has been.

But we'll really have a meeting nicely in summer. If you want to go straight to Forte – strange desire – I suppose you'd just pop up and see us on the plateau in Switzerland. But if you want to do a bit of a *giro*, so am I pining, pining to be amused, to forget and to escape the thousand natural snares.[2]

---

[1] The predictions should be regarded as alternatives and not as pointing to the same date.
[2] Cf. *Hamlet* III. i. 62.

How is Aldous? – If I can really get through with my novel, believe me, that's the thing to do: publish for oneself at £2. It's the solution for us small-selling authors.

How are you in London? I feel you're sick of it. It's wise you abandon the house idea there. But Italy's no happy land. Let's go to the ranch.

DHL

4409. To Arthur Wilkinson, [25 April 1928]
Text: TMSC Sagar; PC; Postmark, [. . .] 28.4.28; Unpublished.

[Villa Mirenda, Scandicci, Florence]
25 April

We leave here about May 15 for Switzerland.

4410. To Catherine Carswell, 26 April 1928
Text: MS YU; Postmark, Firenze 28.4.28; cited in Carswell 274.

Villa Mirenda. *Scandicci*. Florence
26 April 1928

Dear Catherine

Really! – you know Yvonne Franchetti – perhaps you don't know Maria Huxley – but another *lingua cattiva*.[1] Of course I never said anything more than expletives: That damned Catherine hasn't sent me any typing etc. But nothing malicious, why should I? – But you know what young spoilt women are – and Maria, I know, is *terrible* when she gets with a women like Yvonne: a public danger. She's really very nice, Maria: but with certain people her nerves go all to pieces, and she's a bit crazy. London does it to her too. Nay, when things are repeated, always judge the *repeaters*. What can it be but cattiveria which repeats, or pretends to repeat, malicious things? And why listen seriously to the cattivi? Of course the typing and everything was all right – only a bit slow – at which I, of course, fumed a bit – *quite* unnecessarily – ma – !

Didn't you get an acknowledgement of your cheque?[2] That's because it came *before* we got the slips from the printer. Orioli does all that business. But I was pleased you wanted the book. – Your brother Gordon hasn't ordered yet.

It goes pretty well – the orders from America only just coming in – just beginning. – I've only had *half* the proofs so far – and I do want to get it done

---

[1] '*wicked tongue*'.
[2] According to DHL's 'Memoranda' (MS NWU) Catherine Carswell was among the first subscribers for *Lady Chatterley's Lover*.

and get away. We must go back to Switzerland for a couple of months for my chest – it's no worse, but I'd better look after it. I want to leave at latest May 20th – So we shan't get to England till August. We are keeping on this flat, so if you'd like to come and camp here, do so, it'll be standing empty. And Giulia, our peasant girl, will help you all you want, for Liras 20 a week.

I'm sure the New Forest is fine – and I've never been, except through in the train. – I do hope you'll have some luck at last, with Don's play perhaps:[1] Money-luck. Though it's best to be well. I wish my chest healed up.

Perhaps I'll send my pictures to Dorothy Warren, to her gallery in Maddox St., to be shown. Make a few more enemies. But you'd like some of them. I'll tell you.

It's rather a spoilt spring here too – but not so very bad.

Things like Maria chattering depress me. One feels one should have no 'friends' – they do one so much harm; not really wanting to, but they can't help it.

DHL

4411. To Juliette Huxley, 26 April 1928
Text: MS Huxley; Moore 1060.

Villa Mirenda, Scandicci (Florence)
26 April 1928

Dear Juliette

Just a word to acknowledge your cheque, and to ask you if you know a nice *inn* in Switzerland, altitude 3 to 4 thousand feet, where you think Frieda and I would be happy – and where I might walk a few level yards. – We want to leave about 15th May – if only my book is out – and go direct to Switzerland.

And send me your mother's address, will you? One day I will write to her. I was quite happy with Madame Baillot.

I hope Maria doesn't repeat things maliciously. Just had a long indignant letter from a friend saying all that Maria said I'd said, carried on by Yvonne Franchetti, and home by a sister of the maligned[2] – and much worse than anything I *really* said, casually and explosively. It's too bad! Of course I say all sorts of things – you yourself know perfectly well the things I say about people – but they aren't malicious and méchant[3] things, just momentary. People who

---

[1] Donald Carswell's play, *Count Albany: An Historical Invention in One Act*, had been performed by the Scottish National Players in Glasgow, at Christmas 1927. It was not published until 1933.

[2] See previous letter. The sister of the 'maligned' Catherine Carswell was Fanny Oppenheimer (therefore also a cousin of Yvonne Franchetti).   [3] 'spiteful'.

repeat things are really wicked – because they *always* pour in vitriol, of their own.

We are keeping on this flat – so if ever you and Julian want to come and camp here, do. Our peasant girl Giulia – Julia – will help you all you need, and very cheap.

It's all a question of taking an open honest attitude to things. Usually one leaves things vague, and so one gets in a stew.

Regards from us both, and to Julian. D. H. Lawrence

So sorry about Ottoline. Send me her Gower St. address, will you?

4412. To Giuseppe Orioli, [26? April 1928]
Text: MS UCLA; Unpublished.

Villa Mirenda.
Thursday

Dear Pino

As Giulia was coming in to Florence to see her cousin, I thought I'd tell her to call and see if there were any proofs. – Send me also a few leaflets, will you: I haven't *one*.

I hope your thumb is getting better: you'll hardly be able to write, and it makes one feel so miserable.

Frieda definitely wants to keep on the house!!

Au revoir then. DHL

4413. To Ada Clarke, [27 April 1928]
Text: MS Clarke; PC v. Mattias Grünewald(?), Head of an Old Woman; Postmark, Firenze 28 4 [. . .]; Lawrence–Gelder 176.

[Villa Mirenda, Scandicci, Florence]
Friday

No, I'm not any worse – but my bronchials are a bit tiresome, as ever. But I'm better on the whole. – I'll order some more of those capsules now – the other things were only throat pastilles and cough drops – which I take if I need them. We want to leave for Switzerland in about a fortnight. But don't you go worrying about me – I'm fatter, and all right except for that asthmatic cough, my old friend – and I can do anything except climb hills. Pamela looks on the gloomy side – even of me, I'm afraid –

Love. DHL

4414. To Harry Crosby, [29 April–1 May 1928]

Text: MS SIU; Postmark, Fir[enze] 1.V 28; Huxley 730–1.

Villa Mirenda. *Scandicci* (Florence)

29 April 1928

Dear Harry Crosby

I had your note from Lausanne: so awfully sorry you are having things done to your throat. What's wrong? I do hope it's better.

I am sending you tomorrow the MSS, bound by the printer in Florence, nothing grand – but with my phœnix rising from the nest in flames, which I made to be printed on the cover of *Lady Chatterley*. But I coloured it a bit on your MSS covers:[1] do hope you'll like it. – *Sun* is the final MS and I wish the story had been printed as it stands there, really complete.[2] One day, when the public is more educated, I shall have the story printed whole, as it is in this MS. But I have no typescript copy, so one day, when the day comes, perhaps you'll have one made for me. Not now, or I shall lose it. – And at the end there are very few poems. 'Guards' has a third part which has never been printed – I didn't put it in my *Collected Poems*, which Secker is just doing. But I send it you because of the bit of night sun in it. And I send you 'Gipsy' with four verses; the last two verses I left out for the printed version, but they too have a bit of your sun.[3] 'The Man Who Loved Islands' had to be bound from the top, as I left no margins when I tore it out to send to London.

[1] See Letter 4380 for DHL's intention in using the phoenix.

[2] See Letter 4364 and n. 2. The MS sent by DHL to Crosby provided the text of the Black Sun Press edn of *Sun* (October 1928) (Roberts A35b). The bound volume (now at UT) is described in Carole Ferrier, 'D. H. Lawrence's Poetry, 1920–1928: A Descriptive Bibliography of Manuscripts, Typescripts and Proofs', *DHL Review*, xii (Fall 1979), 299 item 79.

[3] The MS versions of the two poems DHL mentions have never been wholly published. The third part of 'Guards' reads as follows (DHL's MS revisions are ignored in favour of what appears to be his final text):

Potency of Man

Silence of men in motionless scarlet, hark, hark to a silence now!
Guards erect with breasts bright red and the hair of bears at your brow,
Column and column of flesh erect and painted vermilion and silent-taut
What are you waiting for, taut attention, red-ones, silent of thought?

After-thought, afore-thought, pillars of potency, columns of blood
Emblazoned and silent under the sunset, nothing is understood.
It is yet to happen out of the stillness of men erect and in red
Red as the sun-rays standing at sunset in rows, when nothing is spoken or said.

Hark at the strange low breaths in hoarseness coming from under the caps of hair!
Breathing of men as the sun is retreating, roar of men with black cowls of the bear
And breasts of vermilion burning like torches lit by the sun for the thrust in the dark
Sun-dipped men with the sun allegiance burning upon them! Hark then, hark!

The sound of the sun in the male, vermilion breasts like clarions sounding at night

And I have done the Introduction to *Chariot of the Sun*, without waiting for the additional poems. I was afraid it might be too late for me to do it here, if I waited. – I am sending you the MS, which please keep, as I have got a type copy. But if you'd like it bound like the other two, send it to me c/o Pino Orioli, 6 Lungarno Corsini, Florence, and I'll have it done. – You can cut this introduction, and do what you like with it, for your book. If there is any part you don't like, omit it. I give you the thing along with the other MSS. If the publishers feel like paying a few dollars, all right. But not you.

And let me know if you'd like me to send the Introduction to my agent, to try on the magazines, or if you'd rather not. Probably no-one would print it – if they did, I'd better have the name of your publisher and date of publication of *Chariot*, you are keeping the same title? – are you keeping that engraving about the sun? If not, then strike out that sentence about it, in my introduction. – But if you'd rather the introduction were not printed except in your book, I am perfectly content. Only as a magazine-article it would be a bit of an advertisement for you.[1]

I do hope your throat is better, and not going to give you much more trouble. We shall be here, I suppose, till about 20th May, for my novel. Then we must go to Switzerland for my chest. You don't know a nice *inn*, do you, about 3000 ft. up, or a bit more, in French Switzerland? I hate the thought of an hotel with English spinsters, inevitable and sunless. We had an apartment in Diablerets – quite nice, but perhaps it would be nicer not to keep house for a

> Summoning all the rays that run dissolved in the veins of men, when the light
> Of days has left us, sun unto sun calling and answering out of the blood
> Of the sons of men and the fathers of courage, roaring the old delight
>
> Of men in potency all blood-potent clubbing their scarlet together, the red
> Scarlet sun-flame of each heart's maleness mounting together to one great sun
> Of the human heart-fire, masculine potent, making the night all warm, instead
> Of the grey of sunlessness seething the darkness with blood-born sun-rays, man-begun.

The last two stanzas of 'Gipsy' (again ignoring DHL's MS alteration) read as follows:

> Between thy moon-lit, milk-white thighs
> Is a moon-pool in thee.
> And the sun in me is thirsty, it cries
> To drink thee, to win thee.
>
> I am black with the sun, and willing
> To be dead
> Can I but plunge in thee, swilling
> Thy waves over my head.

For an early version of 'Gipsy', under the title 'Self-Contempt', see *Letters*, i. 196.

[1] See Letter 4397 and n. 1.

bit. And Diablerets[1] hasn't got a yard of level ground to walk on – all up and down – and I pant.

Regards from us both to you both, and I hope we shall meet – and that you are better.

> Sincerely.   D. H. Lawrence
> 1st May

I was just sending off this when the new poems came. No, I never had a sunstroke, so don't really like the poem. The others I like better – but *don't* print them in *Chariot*. They don't belong; they are another thing. Put them in another book. Leave *Chariot* as it is. I send my foreword – the *typescript* is the complete thing. It's good – but it won't fit if you introduce these new, long, unwieldly, not very sensitive poems. Do print *Chariot* as it stands. The new ones aren't so good.

> DHL

4415. To Alan Steele, [May 1928]
Text: MS UCLA; Unpublished.

> [Lungarno Corsini 6. Firenze]
> [May 1928]

Dear Sir[2]

The American post is[3] only just coming in, so we still have [. . .] a good deal of the American half of the edition unsubscribed. If you will let us know at once what number of copies you are likely to require, we will reserve them for you.

---

[1] Diablerets] Switzerland
[2] Alan W. Steele was a director of William Jackson Ltd, a London firm of 'Export Booksellers'. He had written to Orioli, 24 April 1928, as follows (TMS UCLA):

> Re "*LADY CHATTERLEY'S LOVER*".
>
> Dear Sirs,
>
> We would like to increase our order for this book by a further 35 (thirtyfive) copies, thus making our total order to date, 45 (fortyfive).
>
> We hope to still further increase this number in the near future, and we would like to point out that each copy is to fulfill a definite order, and that we cannot afford to have our numbers cut in any way.
>
> We should like to hear from you concerning your terms on this number, and also how you would like us to settle with you.
>
> We should be grateful also, if you would acknowledge this order, and reassure us that we are going to get our full numbers.
>
> Thanking you in anticipation,   yours very truly,
>
> P.S. We would be grateful if you would let us have the advance copy as soon as possible, so that we may review it in our "Bulletin".

DHL appears to have drafted this reply to Steele for Orioli; he wrote it on the verso of Steele's letter. (See also Letter 4450.)   [3] is] not

4416. To Giuseppe Orioli, [1 May 1928]
Text: MS UCLA; Unpublished.

[Villa Mirenda, Scandicci, Florence]
Tuesday[1]

Dear Pino

We are coming in on Thursday, lunching with Miss Moller and to tea with Mrs Otway.[2]

Will you let Carletto post my letters, and I'll pay when I come in – register the MSS to the boy who sent the gold.[3]

Enclose one order-form – have the cheque.

DHL

4417. To Else Jaffe, 4 May 1928
Text: MS (Photocopy) in Huxley following 772.

Villa Mirenda, *Scandicci*, Florenz
4 May 1928

Dear Else

I simply can't write biographical facts about myself. Will you answer this Bütow man, if you feel like it: and if you think it is worth while.[4] I have never heard of him. I must ask Curtis Brown if they have arranged with him about 'Islands'.

You have heard by now that we are keeping on the Mirenda. I took down the pictures and we began to pack: but Frieda became so gloomy, that I hung the pictures up again and paid six months' rent. Not worth while getting into a state about. So here we are, just the same. And probably we shall stay till the end of the month, as the proofs of the novel are *still* only half done. I wish the printer would hurry up.

I am asking people if they know of a nice Gasthaus in Switzerland, for me. I hate hotels-pensions, after a few days. I always want to kill the old women – usually English – that come in to meals like cats. We just had a very handsome Louis XV sort of a one to tea[5] – but American this time – and of course I'm bristling in every hair.

---

[1] Dated with reference to Letter 4414 in which DHL told Crosby that the MSS were to be sent 'tomorrow'.

[2] Mrs Otway might be the 'not so very old' lady referred to in the next letter. A later letter (December 1928) suggests that Mrs Otway was a friend of Orioli's; the lady in Letter 4417 lived 'on the Lungarno' and so did Orioli; moreover an Eva M. Otway appears twice in DHL's records of sales of *Lady Chatterley's Lover* (see p. 475 n. 3), and it is therefore probable that she was the Mrs Otway referred to here.   [3] See Letter 4365 and n. 1.

[4] Bütow is unidentified but evidently on the editorial staff of *Frankfurter Zeitung* (cf. Letter 4480).   [5] Mary Foote (cf. Letter 4419).

It is more or less summer too – the Kastanien in full flower – is yours too? The Bandelli peasants just brought us the first bacelli – Saubohnen[1] – which are tiny, and they eat them raw and think them wonderful. I like them because il bacello is one of the improper words. – We also eat green almonds boiled in sugar and water, like plums – and they taste like gooseberries. – We went to see an old Englishwoman – not so very old – who has a very elegant flat on the Lungarno, and was a cocotte – the expensive sort – but a real one. I must say, I find her very restful and smooth, after some of the others.

au revoir – tante cose!   DHL

4418. To Earl Brewster, 5 May 1928
Text: MS UT; Unpublished.

Villa Mirenda. Scandicci. Firenze
5 May 1928

Dear Earl

Just a note in answer to your letter – to say we are keeping the house anyhow for six months, and shall be pleased for you and Achsah to make what use you like of it, if only it will be comfortable enough. We shall leave sheets and blankets and linen – there are three bedrooms all right – all you need bring will be a little table silver. As you know, everything is rough – but it's pleasant in summer. When you are coming you must write to

Signorina Pini Giulia, *Scandicci*, per San Paolo (Firenze)

Pietro will fetch your bags and things from Firenze. We give him 20 Liras for a load from Florence – And he always drives us up from Vingone for five Liras. So Achsah need never walk – I think Giulia is perfectly trustworthy – she will do spesi[2] – or Pietro. Whenever Pietro comes to meet us in Vingone, we let him do the spesi in Scandicci first. We give Giulia 20 Liras a week – but she doesn't cook for us. She comes at 7.0, makes coffee, washes up and cleans a bit, and goes home about 10.0. Then comes again at 1.30 or so, and washes up. But if I were you, I'd have her from 7.0 till 2.0, and give her 50 Liras a week – and let her do the washing – anyhow all but sheets.

I am wondering what answer you have from the Brahmin.[3] Let me know. – We shall be here no doubt till end of month – printers delay. – I shall see if I can't get some of your pictures shown in London.

no time for more.   DHL

---

[1] 'the first beans – broad beans'; 'il baccello' can also mean 'penis'.
[2] 'shopping' (spese).
[3] Perhaps Dhana-Gopàla Mukhopàdhyaya (Mukerji) (1890–1936). Indian author and friend of the Brewsters (see Brewster 175; *Letters*, v. 77 and n. 5). The Brewsters later took him to meet DHL in Gsteig: see Letter 4563.

4419. To Mabel Dodge Luhan, 5 May 1928
Text: MS Brill; Unpublished.

Villa Mirenda, Scandicci. Florence
5 May 1928

Dear Mabel

Many thanks for sending out those slips – not many American orders, so far – but the English half doing very well. If the Americans don't turn up, I'll send the English all they order. We ought to hold some back, to be sold later. – Of course there's a delay in the printing, so I don't suppose we'll be able to post until end of the month, at the earliest. So I shall have to stay here till then. Then to Switzerland for a while – and I'm thinking to sail in the autumn.

Mary Foote was here, and I liked her. She seems quite gone on Jung – but anything to give her an interest in life.

Brett cables an exhibition of our paintings is fixed for August in New York. But can you tell me what is the earthly good of exhibiting paintings in New York in August – except in the hopes that the remaining lift-boys will go to the show to damp and cool their spirits. I had a note, too, from Mrs Hare in Santa Fe – but very brief and entirely vague. I wish you would tell me something straight and business-like about this show, if there is anything to tell. – Because I shall almost surely send the pictures to show in London this summer, and must arrange if they are to come on to New York. – With my novel safely through, and my pictures sent over the waters, I shall feel I have really wound up my European spell, and can start afresh. It'll be nice to break free again. – I've been a good deal better this spring than last, but it's slow work getting back to my old self, and the cough is tiresome. Still, I think I'm on the way all right – pazienza! How about you and your *Memories*? Mary Foote says she thinks that New York period of yours was one of your worst periods – that it was all a bit of a sham – that you were never really in it and never really felt anything about Socialism or the workers, that a crowd of nasty people sponged on you, and that your white bedroom was somehow bad taste. – I don't repeat, and *Mary Foote didn't say it*, in the least maliciously. I insisted on her saying what she thought. – So if she's right, you can only treat your New York experience in a spirit of self-criticism and perhaps irony. Or else just skip it briefly in an ironic chapter, and pass on to Taos!

Well – I'll try and send you some summer ribbons, before we go.

And one has to wait for the curve of destiny to bring us back to New Mexico – But it is curving slowly that way.

DHL

4420. To Emily King, [8 May 1928]

Text: MS Needham; PC v. Wolf Huber, Landscape; Postmark, Firenze 8 . V 28;
Unpublished.

[Villa Mirenda, Scandicci, Florence]
Tuesday

I wonder if Barby has sent you your cloth[1] – I think she is in England by now.
– We are staying on here till about the end of the month, I think. It's no good
going to Switzerland before the cold unsettled weather is over. Even here it's
not very sure – cloudy. – We are keeping on this house another year – it seems
simpler than scattering everything again – but I expect we shall be away a
good deal. Anyhow I expect we shall be in England in August and September.
– I do hope things are going fairly well for you – I hate to think of you
depressed.

DHL

4421. To Lady Ottoline Morrell, 8 May 1928

Text: MS UT; Postmark, Firenze 10 . V 28; Moore 1061.

Villa Mirenda, *Scandicci*, Florence
8 May 1928

My dear Ottoline

I was so sorry to hear of you ill and in all that pain – so was Frieda. But now
thank goodness you are a lot better, and soon one can think of you going nicely
around again and being there in the world. I do hope you'll keep well. I
consider people like you and me, we've had our whack of bodily ills, we ought
to be let off a bit.

I'm getting so cross with the printer, who is getting so cross with the paper-
makers, who no doubt are so cross with somebody else – because I can't get on
with my novel and send it out. I've only done *half* the proofs even now!

I trust we shall meet again one day, you and I, because I'm sure we're quite
fond of one another really, through all this long lapse. But the chief thing for
you for the moment is to get quite well.

tante belle cose! from us both.　　D. H. Lawrence

4422. To Mr Sanders, 8 May 1928

Text: MS Edmunds; Unpublished.

Villa Mirenda, *Scandicci*. Florence
8 May 1928

Dear Mr Sanders[2]

Many thanks for your letter and efforts on my behalf. But Curtis Brown has

---

[1] Cf. Letter 4389.　　　[2] Unidentified.

been my agent for some years: and he is negotiating *Lady Chatterley* with Knopf, my regular publisher. So I don't see what I can do at the moment. But I will keep you in mind.

And again thanks.

Yours Sincerely   D. H. Lawrence

4423. To Catherine Carswell, 9 May 1928
Text: MS YU; Unpublished.

Villa Mirenda. Scandicci, Florence
9 May 1928

My dear Catherine

Many thanks for offering us the studio for August. But don't hold it for us, as our plans are very vague – and probably in any case we shan't stay in London more than a day or two. It would have been very nice, all the same.

I am kept on here by the printer, who doesn't let me have the proofs – because he doesn't get the paper, which had to be made specially – and he's short of type. But I hope we'll get away by end of month – still don't quite know where in Switzerland we shall go. – It's poor weather for a Tuscan May – una primavera guasta.[1]

Everybody seems to be going to Brittany this year – or the Normandy coast. The Julian Huxleys asked us to join them there. – Whereabouts will you be? Anyhow it'll be the good fresh sea.

Nothing doing here – just waiting for those proofs.

DHL

4424. To Martin Secker, 12 May 1928
Text: MS UInd; Postmark, Scan[dicci] 14.5.28; Secker 106–7.

Villa Mirenda. Scandicci. Florence
12 May 1928

Dear Secker

I have written out a longer note for the *Poems*, which I enclose. I wrote it longer than this, as an introduction or foreword, then thought you would perhaps have trouble getting it in, so cut it down to half.[2] If this is still too long, you can cut it yourself to fit.

I'm rather glad there is no stuffy old Bridges introduction.[3]

Cold wind, snow on the mountains, and very like March.

---

[1] 'a ruined springtime.'
[2] For the longer 'foreword' (MS UCLA) see *Phoenix* 251–4; the shorter 'note' (MS IEduc) was published in *Collected Poems* (Roberts E73 and E73.1). Both MSS bear the date 'Scandicci 12 May 1928'.   [3] Cf. Letter 4346 and n. 3.

I'm putting a list of people for *Woman Who Rode Away*, at the back of this
letter. You won't mind sending them out, will you?

DHL

Send a proof of the foreword to Curtis Brown, for America, won't you?
The Woman Who Rode Away.

1. Mrs L. A. Clarke. 'Torestin', Broadway, *Ripley* (Derby)
1. Mrs S. King, 16 Brooklands Rd. Sneinton Hill, *Nottingham.*
1. Miss M. Beveridge, 20 Rossetti Garden Mansions, *Chelsea. S. W. 3*
1. Miss M. Harrison, 49 Bvd. Montparnasse, *Paris*
1. Aldous Huxley, 3. Onslow Mews East. *Cranley Place S. W. 7.*
1. G. Orioli, 6 Lungarno Corsini. *Florence*
1. Herrn Max Mohr, Wolfsgrube, *Rottach-am-Tegernsee*, Oberbayern
1. Herrn Emil Krug. Nymphenburgerstr. 911. Berlin-Schöenberg

4425. To Baroness Anna von Richthofen, [13 May 1928]
Text: MS UCB; Frieda Lawrence 261–2.

Villa Mirenda. Scandicci. Florence

Sonntag.

Meine liebe Schwiegermutter

Ich habe die Schlips, sie sind schön wie Rheingold. Aber warum für
Regenwetter? Heute trage ich den blau-und-roten – errinnerst du? – es ist nur
Baumwolle, ich glaube, aber du solltest sehen, wie es ist bunt und männlich.

Wir warten noch hier auf meinen Roman – es ist noch nur halb-gedruckt –
alles geht so langsam. Aber in fünfzehn Tagen hoffe ich, es wird fertig sein,
mindestens gedruckt. Es ist auch gut dass wir noch nicht in der Schweiz sind.
Der Wind kommt kalt, und auf den Bergen gegenüber liegt tiefer Schnee. Der
Tag heute war wunderschön, aber nicht wärmer wie ein sonniger Wintertag.
Und ich möchte nicht wieder in Schnee sein, wie in Diablerets. – Wir suchen
einen Gasthaus in der Schweiz: In den Hôtels sitzen so tausende Englishe alte
Jungfrauen, und sie langweiligen mich. In einem Gasthaus ist ein naturliches
Leben. Die Barby schreibt es gibt ein gutes, in Talloire, ganz in der Nähe von
Annecy, wo die Nusch war. Aber es ist in der Schweiz. Frage an die Nusch, ob
sie da war, in jenem Dorf, und wie es ist. – Sonst gehen wir nach Vermala-
Montana, wo die Else war. Aber es ist teuer. Es ist Schade dass der Klima hier
nicht gut ist – sonst ist alles so schön. – Die Frieda kann nach Baden kommen
wenn sie will; ich finde es doch etwas dumm, dass sie für 5 oder 6 Tagen
kommt, dann wieder weg. Schade dass wir nicht beide da sein können, wenn
die Nusch da ist. Aber für mich sagen alle Leute, die Schweiz, die Schweiz,
und ich, armes Tier, muss gehen. Später in dem Sommer aber komme ich zu
Baden.

Die Frieda näht sich Kleider: schon zwei Anzüge und einen Mantel. Die zwei Mädeln, Giulia und Teresina, kommen abends, und die drei nähen und schwätzen zusammen im Speisesaal. Ich sitze aber hier allein in der Salotta – zu viel Frauenzimmer für mich! – Frühlingsgemüse sind schon hier – Spargel, süsse kleine Erbsen, Saubohnen, und seit drei Wochen die neue Kartoffeln, und viele Artichoken. Es ist immer ein guter Moment in Italien, wann die Gemüse kommen. Als Obst haben wir Nespole – die gelbe Japanisches Mispeln – und die ersten Kirschen, aber nicht wirklich suss. Alles ist spät, dieses Jahr: und die Rosen viele viele, aber nicht glücklich blüten sie. Sie fallen in einem Tag, weil die Untererde immer noch zu Trocken ist, das Regen hat noch nicht gut und tief eingegangen. Nur sind die Poppies – Mohn – brennend rot im hohen grünen Korn – aber so viele wie ich nie gesehen habe, und so rot, es macht beinah Angst.

Errinnerst du die Zaira – die Maitresse des Majors hier – und den grossen weissen Hund Titi? Also, der Titi hat die Zaira gut und stark auf dem Arm gebissen, und ist geschossen worden: und die arme Zaira muss zuhaus bleiben – dort in Florenz – bis der Artzt sicher ist dass sie kein Rabies hat!! Ja, wenn die Zaira fangt an zu bellen und beissen, dann ist es wirklich zu viel. Die Frieda sagt: Noch einen Feind von mir gefallen! – Sie meint den Titi.

Die arme Ada Halm, sie war so nett, aber kam mir so klein und verloren vor, hier in Italien. Und die arme Frau Halm wirklich krank. Ich hoffe wohl sie sind wieder gut da in Baden. Geh du nicht nach Spanien oder Schweden reisend, Schwiegermutter, alte Damen sind beste in der Heimatstadt.

Also lebet wohl, Ihr beide, und wir sehen uns wieder, vor nicht langere Zeit.

DHL

[Sunday

My dear Schwiegermutter

I have the ties, they are as beautiful as Rhinegold. But why for rainy weather? Today I'm wearing the blue-and-red one – do you recall? – I think it's only cotton, but you ought to see how gay and manly it looks.

We're still waiting here for my novel – it is still only half-printed – everything goes so slowly. But I hope it will be ready in a fortnight, at least printed. It's good too that we're not yet in Switzerland. The wind blows cold, and deep snow is lying on the mountains opposite. Today was wonderful, but no warmer than a sunny winter's day. And I don't want to be in snow again, as in Diablerets. – We're looking for an inn in Switzerland. In the hotels sit such thousands of elderly English virgins, and they bore me. In an inn there is a a natural life. Barby writes that there is a good one in Talloire, very near Annecy, where Nusch was. But it is in Switzerland. Ask Nusch whether she was there, in that village, and what it's like. – Otherwise we'll go to Vermala-Montana, where Else was. But it's expensive. It's a shame that the climate isn't good here – otherwise everything is so nice. – Frieda can come to Baden whenever she wants: I think it's a bit stupid, though, to come for 5 or 6 days, then go away again. Pity we can't both be there when Nusch is there. But for me everyone says Switzerland, Switzerland, and I, poor creature, have to go. But later in the summer I'm coming to Baden.

Frieda is sewing herself clothes: two costumes already and an overcoat. The two girls, Giulia and Teresina, come every evening, and the three sew and chat together in the dining-room. I sit by myself here in the lounge, though – too many females for me! – Spring vegetables are already here – asparagus, sweet little peas, broad beans and for the last three weeks new potatoes, and lots of artichokes. It's always a good moment in Italy when the vegetables come. For fruit we have nespole – the yellow Japanese medlars – and the first cherries, but not really sweet ones. Everything is late this year: and many, many roses, but they haven't flowered happily. The petals fall in a day, because the subsoil is still too dry, the rain hasn't yet properly got in good and deep. Only the poppies – poppy – burning red in the tall green corn – but so many as I've never seen, and so red, it almost scares me.

Do you remember Zaira – the mistress of the Major here[1] – and the big white dog Titi?[2] Well, Titi bit Zaira good and hard on the arm, and has been shot: and poor Zaira has to stay at home – there in Florence – until the doctor is sure she hasn't got rabies!! Yes, it would be a bit much if Zaira started barking and biting. Frieda says: yet another of my enemies fallen! – she means Titi.

Poor Ada Halm, she was so nice, but to me looked so small and lost here in Italy. And poor Mrs Halm really ill. I very much hope they're safely back again in Baden. Don't you go journeying off to Spain or Sweden, Schwiegermutter, old ladies are best in their own hometown.

Then farewell, you two, and we'll meet again before long.

DHL]

4426. To Arthur, Lilian, William and Frances Wilkinson, 13 May 1928
Text: MS Schlaefle; cited in Sagar, Wilkinsons 73.

Villa Mirenda. Scandicci, Florence.
13 May 1928

Dear Wilkses All!

So glad Pino's measles are coming out all right. If they're a bit slow, make

[1] Raul Mirenda (see *Letters*, v. 459 and n. 1).   [2] Named Tito in Letter 4159.

him drink camomile tea, hot, lots and lots of it. Sure cure! – And Bim safe so far – and enjoying London and gadding round. – Here the wind has come so cold, I light a fire after supper – and snow on the mountains.

I talked to your peasants – very relieved to know Pino is better, and want you to come back. The Poggis were here last Sunday – I met them in the evening trailing home from a walk to the wood, and a more dismal sight of dreary bodies you never saw – one wretched shrimp of a man. But it was queer to see the light in your end window at night, as if you were there – and in the day the shutters open. I swear I hear the ghost of Pino's fiddle wailing. – Enrico says the Signora Poggi wants you to come back, and if you think you will ever return, you are to wire to her and she won't let the villa to anybody else – So there you are.

The white dog Titi bit Zaira badly in the arm, and was promptly shot, and Zaira is held up till the dottori are sure there's no rabies. Love me Love my dog![1] Anyhow no more Titi.

We are still here – probably till the end of the month. If we'd gone to Switzerland we'd have found ourselves sleighing again. Ugh! I don't want to see any more snow this spring.

We're having the first peas now – and [.][2] The artichokes very good this year, asparagus too. But the nespoli sour, and cherries few.

F[rieda] says she will write to Lilian Gair, so there ['s a] promise. So glad all goes well again.

DHL

4427. To William Roberts, 13 May 1928
Text: MS Roberts, W. H.; James T. Boulton, 'D. H. Lawrence: Study of a Free Spirit in Literature: A Note on an Uncollected Article', *Renaissance and Modern Studies*, xviii (1974), 6.

Villa Mirenda. *Scandicci*, Florence
13 May 1928

Dear Mr Roberts

Many thanks for the two copies of the *Millgate* with your article.[3] It's queer to read about oneself. When the 'gods the giftie gie us'[4] we see ourselves a different fish in every stream of consciousness, and sometimes a frog and

---

[1] English proverb. [2] MS torn.
[3] Roberts' article, 'D. H. Lawrence: Study of a Free Spirit in Literature', appeared in the *Millgate Monthly*, May 1928 (reprinted in *Renaissance and Modern Studies*, xviii, 1974, 7–16). The *Millgate* was a Co-operative Society journal, published in Manchester, broadly educative in purpose and popular in manner.
[4] Robert Burns, 'To a Louse' (1785), l. 43 ['O wad some Pow'r the giftie gie us/To see oursels as others see us!'].

sometimes a pelican. – But I must break your prophecy – about the verse of poetry – 'What is it internecine that is locked by very fierceness into a quiescence' – ¹ – What is it inside oneself, dangerous and deadly to oneself, which is drawn by its very intensity into tense quiescence? – we shall not know until it breaks forth from the surrounding envelope or tissue or condition, now gone corroded or decayed, into a new flowering. – In other words, since this poem, as re-written, in this present form, belongs to the war² – what was it inside one's breast that went so tight locked and numb, with weird hostility, then, in the horrors? – well, I don't know even now: but it was some savage spirit of life which babbled a bit in *Fantasia*, but which still hasn't made itself explicit. – But I consider the verse quite clear: especially in the context. You shouldn't nip things from their context. And you should never say: This is the best! – only: *To me* this is the best. – You don't know how many Americans say that the hymns in *Plumed Serpent* are the finest things I ever did. And that book belongs to the North American Continent.

I send a couple of the photographs.

Sincerely   D. H. Lawrence

4428. To Nancy Pearn, 13 May 1928
Text: MS UT; Unpublished.

Villa Mirenda. *Scandicci*. Florence
13 May 1928

Dear Nancy Pearn

I send you another article, 'Laura-Philippine'.³ If it won't do for the Olley

---

¹ After lengthy consideration of DHL's prose (with which 'it is captious to find fault'), Roberts turns to the poetry. DHL takes issue with the following passage in whch Roberts comments on lines from 'Débâcle' in *New Poems*:

And sometimes [DHL] writes this:

> What is it internecine that is locked
>   By its very fierceness into a quiescence
> Within the rage? We shall not know till it burst
>   Out of corrosion into new florescence,

the meaning of which, to quote Don Quixote, not even Aristotle himself could discover should he be raised from the dead for that very purpose. Such verbose obscurity is not in Mr. Lawrence's manner at all.
² The poem is found in a MS notebook (Roberts E320.1), where it is entitled 'Unwitting'; in another MS it becomes 'The Interim' (Roberts E320.2); in *New Poems* the title is 'Débâcle'; the text of the latter was printed unchanged in *Collected Poems*, the title becoming 'Reality of Peace, 1916'.
³ This sketch, based on Mary Christine Hughes, would be printed in *T. P's & Cassell's Weekly*, 7 July 1928 (Roberts C170) and collected in *Assorted Articles*.

man, it may for somebody else.[1] – No good my jotting down titles or suggestions – it's a sure way of making me *not* write 'em. But I'll trot in a four-pager now and then – and if you have any suggestions to make, do. I may as well earn this way – though I must say, I had gooseflesh when I saw that page with me in the *Evening News*, next the lady who knows why she couldn't marry a foreigner, because never a one asked her![2]

Keep track of these articles if you can, will you –[3]

D. H. Lawrence

I told *T. P.'s* I thought the best story in the world a certain one of Boccaccio's improper but charming tales from the *Decameron*.[4] How's that for *T. P.*? If only he'll print the tale, I'll translate it for him gratis. What a bean![5]

4429. To S. S. Koteliansky, [16 May 1928]
Text: MS BL; Postmark, Firenze 16 . V 28; cited in Gransden 32.

Villa Mirenda. Scandicci. Florence
16 May.

My dear Kot

Time I wrote you again. We are still here – are keeping on this house. The printer has at last got the *very nice* paper. Now he's printing the first half of the novel – 1000 copies on this paper – then he'll have to break up the type and set up the second half. Only enough type, and that rather ancient, for half the book. What a go! – But now he really won't be long – and the binder can start at once. I think we'll have 200 copies ready to send out by 7th. June.

We shall have to post everything registered book post: it's much the safest: though I may try to slip 200 copies into America in crates. The English have ordered already well over 400 copies: very nearly all their half. And the

[1] Arthur E. Olley, Literary Editor of the *Evening News*, had invited DHL (via Nancy Pearn who forwarded the letter) to contribute an article. On 26 April Nancy Pearn told DHL that if he could 'bear to tackle just those sorts of subjects which the Press adores', the consequent publicity could have 'immediate results in the way of increasing book sales' (TMSC UT). The first of DHL's articles in the *Evening News* had appeared on 8 May 1928 under the title 'When She Asks Why' (Roberts C169); DHL's own title had been 'The Bogey between the Generations'. At once on 8 May Nancy Pearn congratulated him on his journalistic success, also expressing the hope that further articles would follow.
[2] Beneath DHL's article came another headed, 'I Could Not Have Married A Foreigner', by the novelist G[ladys] B[ronwyn] Stern (1890–1973); she jocularly reflected on the problems facing an Englishwoman who contemplated marrying a foreigner.
[3] Between 8 May and 13 October DHL published seven articles in the *Evening News* alone (Roberts C169, C171, C174–8).
[4] With her letter of 8 May Nancy Pearn had enclosed one from *T. P.'s* (3 May 1928); it is now missing. Apparently DHL himself wrote to *T. P.'s*; that letter, too, is missing.
[5] I.e. 'a (good) chap!'

Americans are itching, but terrified I shan't get the book into the country, but I shall, and then they'll have to pay $15. instead of $10. He who hesitates pays more!

So we shan't get away probably till first week in June. But the weather is very bad in Switzerland now, so I'm just as well here. – We may stay in Paris a while in August – then you could come over. Otherwise we'll see you in England. I might take a house somewhere by the sea in England for September, and let my sisters come there: and then you could come too.

Dorothy Warren asked me to send her my pictures to show in her gallery. I've got seven big ones, four or five small oils, and seven water-colours. I wonder very much if I should send them. If you see Gertler, ask him what he thinks. I think there's a certain something in the pictures that makes them good – but you'd hate them.

It's very uneven weather here, rather cold, not right at all. But I suppose it's everywhere alike.

DHL

4430. To Juliette Huxley, 16 May 1928
Text: MS Huxley; Unpublished.

Villa Mirenda, *Scandicci* (Florence)
16 May 1928

Dear Juliette

Many thanks for taking so much trouble about Swiss addresses: and not to much purpose, apparently. The man from Arosa wrote that his house is shut re-building, and from Champex the enclosed. The man was evidently very much annoyed at getting a *British Empire* coupon,[1] so he sent his letter to me unstamped, so I should have to pay double, and unsigned, so we couldn't get at him: avec parfaite consideration![2] So small people are! But such people don't matter. – I'm sorry you had all that trouble in vain.

Now we hear of an inn in a nice village Talloire, about 30 miles from Geneva, and just inside Switzerland opposite Annecy on the French side. I know Annecy is nice: so I think we'll go there. Meanwhile we've at last got the paper for the novel – very nice paper – and the printer will print off the first half of the book, break up the type, and set up the second half – because he's only enough type for half a book. – But he won't be long, now he can really print. And I must wait till the thing is through – another fortnight or so. Anyhow I believe it would be horrid in Switzerland now, the weather is crazy. We may just as well stay quietly here.

---

[1] I.e. to cover return postage, valid within the Empire.   [2] 'with the greatest respect!'

I wonder it you'll get the Brittany house. We might look in on you on the way to England in August. That would be fun.

Maria says Julian has mysterious temperatures. It's probably the flu germ acting in a more subdued fashion. It seems to be that way with people out here this year – sometimes with intestinal trouble, more or less mild. Oh weird flu!

I'm glad Adam and Eve are framed in all their glory. I'll bet they look nice. What sort of frame? – And that you hide your lions and unicorns inside the cupboard is a joke.[1] I'll come and look at them before long, and roar or neigh with them. Do unicorns neigh? – or are they dumb beasts?

Are the children all right? – is Anthony at school? Do hope all goes well, and the temperatures are nothing.

DHL

Can't find the Champex note – he sent a list of hotels, and said 'Apply to one of these for their prospectus – avec parfaite consideration'.

4431. To Nancy Pearn, 21 May 1928
Text: MS UT; Unpublished.

Villa Mirenda – Scandicci. (Florence)
21 May 1928

Dear Nancy Pearn

I find it really rather amusing to write these little articles. If Mr Olley will tell me what he'd like, I'll try more or less to oblige.[2] I prefer it when they suggest the titles, it somehow tickles me more. As for being exclusively bound to the *Evening News*, I suppose it would be only for a short time. And then if we can make them go higher than their ten quid, good for us. Perhaps after all the public is not such a dull animal, and would prefer an occasional subtle suave stone to polish its wits against. Let us see!

I send a little article for the *What Women Have Taught Me* series.[3] Maybe

---

[1] See Letters 4328 and 4360.

[2] See p. 401 nn. 1 and 3. In Nancy Pearn's letter, 17 May 1928– to which DHL was replying – she conveyed Olley's delight at the first article and his enquiry whether DHL would write four more 'on agreed subjects, during which time he would not want you to write for any other paper'. In view of this condition Pearn had extracted an increased fee from Olley: 12 instead of 10 guineas.

[3] In her 17 May letter Pearn had told DHL that the *Daily Chronicle* planned to publish a series of articles by men under the general title, 'What Women Have Taught Me'. She asked him to contribute to the series: 'Would you do them about a thousand words – we could probably get Fifteen Guineas – remembering as you so cleverly did in the E[vening] N[ews] article, that you were writing for the G[reat] B[ritish] P[ublic] on this occasion' (TMSC UT). DHL submitted with this letter a five-page article which still remains unpublished, 'That Women Know Best' (MS UCB); its general thesis can be briefly summarised in DHL's last two sentences: 'Perhaps the things that one can unlearn from women are more effective than the things one can learn. How not to be too sure of right and wrong, for example.' On 15 June 1928 Pearn told DHL that the *Daily Chronicle* had accepted the article; the newspaper appears not to have published it.

they won't like it. Maybe too much tongue in the cheek. But try it on 'em. As you say, it's fun:

D. H. Lawrence

P. S. I send you 'Chaos in Poetry' which I wrote for a man I know to put in front of his vol. of poems.[1] I gave it him. But somebody some high-brow periodical might print the essay – it's rather nice – especially in America. The poems appear in the autumn, in Boston.

just got your note about *E. N.* articles – ask 'em to suggest topics.

4432. To Harry Crosby, [21? May 1928]
Text: MS SIU; Huxley 735–6.

Villa Mirenda, Scandicci, Florence
[21? May 1928][2]

Dear Harry Crosby

Your letter today – glad you liked the MSS. 'Man who Loved Islands' is one of my favourite stories.

Do a little *de luxe* or di lussissimo edition of *Sun* if you like.[3] But you'll have to decide how many copies you're going to print. And you give me 25% or 30% of profits, as the commercial de-luxers do: if there *is* any profit. If not, we'll consider it wine spilled to Phœbus Apollo.[4]

I dont think the little sun on your letter paper is good enough. I suggest one of the above.[5] You know the Aztec and Zuni 'cloud-tower' motive with the sun? There is the darkness. Your dishevelled marguerite won't do.

Do entirely as you like with the Introduction, end it where you like. I'll find 'sunwards' on my copy, and end it there.[6] I'll send it to the agent in London.

Which reminds me my agent may think he ought to make a contract and take a percentage all commercial and all, if you do a *Sun* de luxe. But it depends how many copies you print. You could put on it – sold only sunwards.

I'm so glad if you don't put any of those new poems in *Chariot*.[7] Don't lose

---

[1] See Letter 4397 and n. 1.

[2] It is difficult to assign a date to this letter; it appears to be written before Letter 4439 (despite Tedlock, *Lawrence MSS* 248).

[3] Crosby published 15 copies of *Sun* printed on Japanese vellum (Roberts A35c), as well as 150 'ordinary' copies (Roberts A35b).   [4] The sun-god.

[5] At the head of this letter DHL provided two sketches of his preferred design.

[6] Tedlock, *Lawrence MSS* 248–9 prints what 'may represent the revision' mentioned to Crosby; it ends: 'And because this little book of poems seems to me to be a pool of sun, in which conceited man is washing himself new again, it is to me a book of poetry, and the defects and nonsense are only the staggering in the pool.'   [7] See Letter 4414.

your delicacy and your sun-sensitiveness, and become Parisey, or look too much at hotels and Cook-tourists. What do they matter? You've looked too much at the world.

Are your bits of French always as you intend them to be? Il sera mort s'il ouvrait son cœur! – I say to myself 'il serait mort –'[1] But it's a very true saying.

We shall be here till end of the month. Then somewhere or other in Switzerland. I hope we shall see you and Caresse Crosby. I don't mind a chaos – though I'm fairly tidy by nature – if I feel sometimes the wind blows through the chaos. Those inert and dusty limbos of some people depress me.

tante cose!   D. H. Lawrence

4433. To Martin Secker, [22 May 1928]
Text: MS UInd; Postmark, Scandicci 23.5.28; Secker 107.

Villa Mirenda.
Tuesday.

Dear Secker

Put a photograph in front of the poems if you like: I don't care for photographs, but perhaps other people do.[2]

Have gone and got a bit of flu, and am in bed. Curse! But I'm doing the last proofs now, and next week we'll be off. Are you going to order a copy of the novel?[3] I'm not giving *any* of the thousand away, but if I do a cheaper edition, or any second edition, I'll send you one of that.

Yrs   DHL

4434. To Mark Gertler, 24 May 1928
Text: MS SIU and (Photocopy) HU; Postmark, [. . .]; Huxley 731–3.

Villa Mirenda – Scandicci – *Florence*
24 May 1928

Dear Mark

Kot said you'd like to see these photographs of my pictures – they're only snaps a neighbour took – there was another snap: – *Resurrection* – but I'm afraid I've not got it any more. There are seven big pictures – oils – a 'Nymphs and faun', all dark orange, not photographed. – also a *fight with an Amazon.* – I think I shall send them to the Warren for her gallery, because when we leave here – in about ten days – God knows when we'll come back, and it's no good just abandoning them. Would you take the big pictures off their stretchers and

---

[1] 'If he opened his heart he will die! . . . he would die –.'
[2] Secker did not include a photograph in *Collected Poems.*
[3] Secker sent a cheque for £5.2.0 in August 1928 (MS NWU).

roll them? – paint is a bit thick in places, it might crack off. But they'd need a *big* packing case. – I gave the seven water-colours and three smaller oils, on boards, to a friend to take to London for me: Kot's old acquaintance, Enid Hopkin, now Mrs Enid Hilton. She stayed in a little inn near here with her husband – and I admit they're both rather boring – if not very: but not *bad* people. If you felt like it you could call at her house – flat, that is, top floor – 40 Great James St., Bedford Row, W.C. 1. and look at the pictures she took. Perhaps you'll dislike them. I myself prefer the big oils. – The Hiltons won't be home, though, till 1st June – a week from now.

And would you tell me where you have your pictures photographed, and how much it costs? I'd like to have photographs of all these – but not if it's too expensive.

What do you do with the shiny places on your pictures, when you want 'em *not* to shine? Mine *do* shine – some all over, because there's so much oil in them. But I don't mind all over.

You'll be sick of my questions. – I am now doing the *last* proofs of my novel, so it won't be long. I expect some people will want to annihilate me for it: but I believe in it, it's got to be done. One's got to get back to the live, really lovely phallic self, and phallic consciousness. I think I get a certain phallic beauty in my pictures too. I know they're rolling with faults, Sladeily considered. But there's something *there*. Wonder how your work goes. I've seen nothing for two years – but that nude you were doing in Sept. 1926 seemed to me to have some phallic glow too.[1] – I hope we can send you your copy of the novel within a fortnight. Nice of you to order it.

I was so awfully sorry to hear of Ottoline so very ill. Poor Ottoline, when I feel she's down, my heart bleeds for her. After all, she's a queen, among the mass of women.

Of course I had to have a bit of flu, have been in bed some days. But am up again. I shall be really better at a higher altitude — when we get to Switzerland. Did you ever try the mountains – between 3 and 4,000 ft? It's really rather marvellous, if you stay long enough. I think we shall go to Annecy, just in France, south of Geneva, and look round from there. – I wish I really got well again – it's such a drag, not getting back to oneself. You know yourself how it feels. I do hope you're better, and feeling fairly chirpy.

We shall come to England, probably in August. Where will you be? – But we shall see you. We're not dead yet. We'll still show the world what's what.

[1] Probably *Reclining Nude*, reproduced in *Mark Gertler: Selected Letters*, ed. Carrington, facing p. 225.

Tell Kot I had his letter – and it's cold even here!

Frieda sends all sorts of messages.

D. H. Lawrence

4435. To Earl Brewster, 24 May 1928
Text: MS UT; Unpublished.

Villa Mirenda. *Scandicci*. Florence
Thursday. 24 May 1928

Dear Earl

Your letter just come. So you are already in Rome! We haven't budged yet, because of my novel. But I hear it's bitter cold in France, England and Switzerland, so just as well. It's none too warm here. – I'm just getting the last of the proofs of my book, so I hope it will very soon be ready, and we can go. I think ten days will see us off. Quite a good idea for you to come here a day or so before we go, and get the run of things. I'd say come now, but Frieda has been having a course of dentistry in Florence, and is rather upset and much too nervy and nervosa to look after anybody. She's in one of those woman's nervous states when the least thing extra to cope with is too much. I shall be glad when we get away to an hotel and she need do nothing and can stay in bed all day if she likes. Of course I had to get flu, and be in bed a few days – not bad, but a nuisance. Altogether life gets very trying sometimes – this being one of the times, for most of us, it seems. Today I am staying in bed because it's so cold.

But as soon as the trunks are packed everything will be off our minds, and I'd be glad for you to come. I'll write again on Monday or Tuesday and fix it up. If you get sick of the Rome pensione the little Osteria at Vingone is quite decent, and only Liras 25 a day. It's just at the tram terminus, you remember.

I think you'll find everything here that you need, though I'm afraid poor Achsah will think it rough and bare. Only, if it is easy to you, bring a bit of table silver – that's rather short, and I expect F. will take it along with her, in case we rent a chalet. But we leave all the linen, such as it is – and enough, I think.

I think we shall go to Annecy, in the French Alps, south of Geneva,[1] and look round from there. It's in France, but the Swiss border is near. – I'm looking forward to seeing you – wish we had a proper place and could put you all three up.

au revoir! DHL

[1] Geneva] Switzerland

I'm going to see if I can do something about your pictures in London – am waiting now to hear from Dorothy Warren.

4436. To Edward McDonald, 24 May 1928
Text: MS UT; Postmark, Firenze 25 . V 28; *Centaur* 33.

Villa Mirenda. Scandicci. (Firenze)
24 May 1928

Dear McDonald
      Very nice of you to get those orders, and send that cheque. I want to thank Mason too – but am waiting to talk to the agent here, about shipping in a hundred or maybe two, via Galveston or New Orleans. If it's to be done by nice Italian agency – I'll probably ship to the Centaur. – We'll mail the postal copies I hope next week. Printer has been very slow – Italian bit of a printing shop with no word of English, which leaves them unsullied, but not so the proof pages – Oh Lord. But I'm at the very last chapters now – and they print very quickly. They've only got enough print, type, for half the book – so the first half is already printed, and the type broken up and consumed into the second half. What a go! – We must have got at least 450 orders from England – nearly the English half booked – but not many from America. Of course not many *individuals* in America know – and the book-sellers are afraid of the mail – and the publishers' combine of course don't like my doing it a *bit*. – I have to call it *Lady C's Lover* – not one 'John T [homas]' would pass the customs – they won't even let me put it as a sub-title – but I'm persisting, and having a shot with 'Giantammaso and Lady Jane' for sub-title. – And shall Trelawney die?[1] – A few people's hair may curl, and a few may have it go up straight, but if I have to be a friseur among other things, soit! – I was better – but of course the flue nipped me, and I cough. We're going to Switzerland in ten days or so – once J.T. is ready to come out, with my phœnix on his cover, rising from the nest in flames. I'm afraid most people's nests are too wet to burn, nowadays! damp lot! How is Mrs McDonald – did the lawn ever grow again? I'll be writing to Mason tomorrow or day after. Once we get copies in to America, we'll charge more. Though I believe I'd be able to sell 'em all to England. – Douglas himself doesn't think much of *In the Beginning* – should have written 'Tail Ends' – but he's getting old and good.

D. H. Lawrence

[1] Robert Stephen Hawker, 'Song of the Western Men' (1825), l. 6 (Sir Jonathan Trelawny (1650–1721), Bishop of Bristol, was one of the seven bishops imprisoned by James II in 1688).

4437. To Lady Ottoline Morrell, 24 May 1928
Text: MS UT; Postmark, Sca[ndicci] 26 [. . .]; cited in O[ttoline] M[orrell], 'D. H.
Lawrence, 1885–1930, By One of His Friends', *Nation & Athenæum*, xlvi (22 March 1930),
860.

Villa Mirenda. *Scandicci*. (Florence)
24 May 1928

My dear Ottoline,

I'm most grieved to think you've had such a time and so much pain with
that mysterious illness: worse even than I thought. It puzzles me terribly why
these things should come. But do you know what I think? I think it's because
one isn't just vulgarly selfish enough, vulgarly *physically* selfish, self-keeping
and self-preserving. One wastes one's common flesh too much: then these
microbes, which are the pure incarnation of invisible selfishness, pounce on
one.

You ask me, do I feel things very much? – and I do. And that's why I too am
ill. The hurts, and the bitternesses sink in, however much one may reject them
with one's spirit. They sink in, and there they lie, inside one, wasting one.
What is the matter with us is primarily chagrin. Then the microbes pounce. –
One ought to be tough and selfish: and one is never tough enough, and never
selfish in the proper self-preserving way. Then one is laid low.

I've been in bed again this last week, but not bad, a touch of flu. And it's no
good going to Switzerland to be bitter cold. It's even cold here.

Yes, I'm sad about Garsington, very sad that it has gone.[1] While you still
had it I always felt in some way I still had it. If only one could have two lives:
the first, in which to make one's mistakes, which seem as if they *had* to be
made; and the second in which to profit by them. If it could only be so, what a
lovely Garsington we could all have, and no bitterness at the end of it!

But don't say you feel you're not important in life. You've been an
important influence in lots of lives, as you have in mine; through being
fundamentally generous, and through being Ottoline. After all, there's only
one Ottoline. And she has moved one's imagination. It doesn't matter what
sort of vision[2] comes out of a man's imagination, his vision of Ottoline. Any
more than a photograph of me is me, or even 'like' me. The so-called portraits
of Ottoline can't possibly *be* Ottoline – no one knows that better than an artist.
But Ottoline has moved men's imagination, deeply, and that's perhaps the
most a woman can do. And in the world today, full of women, how rare to find
one that can move the imagination! No, I wish, and wish deeply, there could
be Ottoline again and Garsington again, and we could start afresh.

---

[1] From 1924 Lady Ottoline lived at 10 Gower Street, London WC1.
[2] MS reads: 'sort vision'.

But we can start afresh anyhow, in a quieter, gentler way.

I'm doing the last proofs of my novel now, so in about a week I expect we shall leave. I hope the book won't shock you – but I'm sure it won't. You will understand what I'm trying to do: the full natural *rapprochement* of a man and a woman; and the re-entry into life of a bit of the old phallic awareness and the old phallic insouciance.

I do hope you are feeling a bit better each day. I'm a lot better really: only this bit of flu put me back.

Frieda sends her love and her sympathy, with mine.

D. H. Lawrence

4438. To Giuseppe Orioli, [24? May 1928]
Text: MS UCLA; Unpublished.

[Villa Mirenda, Scandicci, Florence]
[24? May 1928][1]

Dear Pino

Would you mind putting these cheques in the bank. You must endorse two of the English cheques. – I hope I have done the vaglia[2] properly. – And get me money for the Credito Italiano cheque, will you.

I hope I'll see you in a day or two. Bad luck to this flu. But this is the bulk of the proofs, thank God!

DHL

send me the 'Borderaux' from Haskard please.[3]

P.S. I hope you like Giantommaso – feel I must put him in. I've made a good many changes in these proofs – hope Giuntina will find 'em legible: I mean changes of the text, not just corrections.

I think we can leave out 'Privately Printed'.

4439. To Harry and Caresse Crosby, [25 May 1928]
Text: MS SIU; Postmark, Scandicci 26 [. . .] 28; Huxley 734–5.

Villa Mirenda. *Scandicci*. (Florence)
Friday 26 May 1928

Dear Harry Crosby and Caresse

My wife went to Florence yesterday and brought the Queen of Naples' snuff-box and three pieces of gold, from Orioli, to my utter amazement. But cari miei, it won't do. I'm sure you're not Crœsuses to that extent:[4] and

---

[1] Dated with reference to the letter following in which Frieda is said to have gone to Florence on 24 May. It is assumed that she took the proofs and this letter to Orioli.
[2] 'money order'.   [3] 'pay-in slips' ('Bordereaux'); cf. Letter 4453.
[4] See Letter 4365 for Crosby's earlier gift of gold.

anyhow, what right have I to receive these things? For heaven's sake, you embarass me! I hope to heaven you're quite quite rich, for if you're not, I shall feel really bad about it. Here I am, quite uneasy in my skin. Gold rollt mir zur Füssen![1] Gold – I feel almost wicked with it!

The wagon-lit man was a knave, and tried to bully Orioli out of 200 Liras, but only got one hundred. I wonder very much that he delivered the goods. – Why oh why did you send them![2] I considered myself paid in excess before, so now where am I?

But I shall buy some snuff and put it in the snuff-box and take it as my grandfather did: and offer worthy souls a pinch and a sneeze, with little finger lifted.

But at present I feel rather worried – for the first time I know what embarras de richesses means. Perhaps one day we can square it somehow.

Meanwhile very many thanks – but in future I shall tell you the price of my pen to a centime, and not a button more.

D. H. Lawrence

4440. To Blair Hughes-Stanton, 26 May 1928
Text: MS Hughes-Stanton; 'The D. H. Lawrence Letters', *Samphire*, iii (Spring 1978), 22, 24.

Villa Mirenda. *Scandicci*. Florence
26 May 1928

Dear Blair,[3]

Nice of you to order my novel. I'm getting to the last proofs now, and the printer is printing fast. So I hope soon we can send you your copy. And I hope you'll think it worth it.

So there is to be another bambino, to go with Judith: not a Holofernes, I hope.[4] It's a bit of a handful for you. But after all, I think perhaps the material responsibility of children saves one from a lot of useless worry about the world, the soul and the devil. I think children must make life warmer to one,

---

[1] 'Gold is rolling at my feet!'

[2] The unauthorised movement of gold was illegal; for Crosby's way of delivering the gold pieces to DHL (involving the sleeping-car attendant and, allegedly, the Duke of Argyll), see Geoffrey Wolff, *Black Sun*, p. 202.

[3] Blair Rowlands Hughes-Stanton (1902–81), distinguished wood-engraver, book illustrator and painter. He broke away (with Barbara Weekley among others) from the Royal Academy Art School and joined the seminally important school under Leon Underwood. Radical in art, politics and personality. Illustrated Cresset Press edn of *Birds, Beasts and Flowers* (1930) and *The Ship of Death and Other Poems* (1933). m. (1) Gertrude Hermes, 1925; (2) Ida Affleck-Graves; (3) Ann Ross.

[4] Judith Hughes-Stanton, b. 1926; Simon, b. 1928. (Holofernes, Nebuchadnezzar's general, was decapitated by Judith; see the account of her exemplary bravery in the Apocryphal Book of Judith.)

so you're really the winner. Perhaps if I'd have had children I'd have been a comfortable body with all my novels circulating like steam among all the safe people, and everybody pleased.

I expect we shall come to England in August, then surely we shall see you, as we think to stay six weeks or so.[1] I remember so well the beer and skittles in your basement (forgive the word, but it *is* too low down).[2] And if ever you all feel like coming and camping in this house, Judith and Holofernes and all, then here it'll be.

Many good wishes from us both   D. H. Lawrence

4441. To Giuseppe Orioli, [28 May 1928]
Text: MS UCLA; Unpublished.

Villa Mirenda.
Whit Monday

Dear Pino

We expected you yesterday – such a nice day. I am better, and think we shall come in tomorrow *afternoon* about 3.0, and bring the proofs. But they are so *few*! Why the devil dont the Giuntina finish setting up, and have it done!

I think we must give the binder his £4.30. He's a brute to ask more, but I suppose there *is* more work. The only thing is, will he raise the price every time you have a book to bind? – And why should the crisis in Italian industry make him charge *more*? But let us do anything to avoid further delay. Will he be quick, binding?

I enclose the two orders that came to me – one for 'Mrs Clutterley's Lover', 4 copies!!

Did you see Egidi? We will talk tomorrow.

DHL

4442. To Ada Clarke, 28 May 1928
Text: MS Clarke; Unpublished.

Villa Mirenda. Scandicci (Florence)
28 May 1928

My dear Sister

I should have written before, but kept waiting to see when we would go away. Then I had a bit of flu – quite mild. There was a sudden epidemic, and the peasants were all down, seven in bed at once. They had it worse than I. But

---

[1] or so.] ago.
[2] DHL's memory was of Hughes-Stanton's basement below his house in Hammersmith Terrace by the Thames.

the weather was so nasty – very cold wind, and spurts of very hot sun. On Saturday it thundered and lightened so much, and torrents of rain, that thank heaven it has cleared the weather up, and yesterday and today are lovely. I hope it is so in England too. – It's Whit Monday today – hard to remember here, because they don't make any festa of Whitsuntide at all. – Enid Hopkin was at the inn at Vingone for a fortnight or more – we saw them fairly often – quite nice, but she's a forlorn sort of little thing, with not much joy in life – and the husband is not exciting. They will be back in London Thursday. – I suppose you got *The Woman Who Rode Away*. I want to send you a couple of other books when I go down to Florence. – Emily says you are very busy – which is a good thing. I wish Sam were. – I think I may take a house by the sea in England in September, then you could come and stay – but I want to see how I get on in Switzerland first. – I'm really feeling better. My bronchial congestion seems to be loosening up at last, spite of a bit of flu. I don't take that umckaloaba medicine – it doesn't suit me, only irritates my bronchials – it's not that I want. – I expect you are all off somewhere in the car today – we drove over to some friends in a villa not far away yesterday – such a lovely day too.

I do hope everything goes nicely.

love   DHL

4443. To Emily King, [28 May 1928]
Text: MS Lazarus; Unpublished.

Villa Mirenda, *Scandicci*. Florence
Whit Monday

My dear Pamela

Whit Monday today, and a marvellous lovely day. I wonder where you are jaunting off to? Here they don't make a holiday of Whitsuntide – I only happened to notice it on the calendar, or I shouldn't have known. They celebrate Ascension – about ten days ago – and it poured with rain. – It's been awful weather, so cold, and bits of hot sun. But Saturday it thundered its head off, so now it's lovely again: very lovely. There are millions of poppies everywhere in the corn, the peasants are busy cutting the hay – they cut it all with sickles, and carry it in their arms to the wagon – the nightingales sing, and I saw the first firefly. So summer is really here. But never was such a cold horrid May in Italy as this year.

There was an epidemic of flu, and the peasants all have it – very miserable they are. I had it, but not badly, thank heaven. – It would have been useless, crazy to go to Switzerland to the ice again – and now the weather is so lovely, we may as well stay a bit. Then I'll go up the mountains and look after my chest: which really feels better, spite of flu.

Enid Hopkin and her husband stayed at the inn about a mile away, for a fortnight or more. They came up fairly often – and were nice: but she's an unsatisfied little thing, and he's rather dull. Now they're at the sea for a day or two, then back to London.

I suppose you had *The Woman Who Rode Away* – Secker said he sent it. We drove over yesterday to see some friends, not far, in a big, rather lovely villa. – I expect the Brewsters, from Capri, will come and stay here a while when we go. – Well I do hope the shop is doing fairly well – and you are all feeling cheerful. I hate to think of things going wrong.

Love to you all.   DHL

4444. To Giuseppe Orioli, [29 May 1928]
Text: MS UCLA; Unpublished.

Villa Mirenda
Tuesday.

Dear Pino

We must do something about the extra two hundred.[1] Either we must ask Giuntina to keep the last sedicesimo[2] of type, so that I can make a few real alterations in the last pages, and so call it a new edition[3] limited to 200 copies: or else we must put at the front: *Re-print from the original edition of one thousand; this re-print limited to two hundred copies.* – But we must make it clear, I think, what these 200 are. We must either print inside: *Second edition, limted to 200 copies.* Or we must put as above: *Reprint from orig. edit. etc.* – What do you think? The last pages of the book are taken up by a letter from J[ohn] T[homas] to Lady Jane. I could easily make that a little different, or even longer, for the two-hundred edition.

I hope to come in in a day or two. Have got up today.

DHL

Let me know what you think about this: and if you approve of the title-page.

Koteliansky was saying somebody in London was complaining about not having had a receipt from you for the money for the novel, but he didn't say who it was.

---

[1] Later in 1928 (probably November) a cheap paper issue of *Lady Chatterley's Lover* was published; the title-page and text are identical with the first edn of 1,000 copies; on p. [ii], facing the title-page, the statement of limitation is printed: 'Second edition limited to 200 copies' (Roberts A42b).   [2] 'sixteenth'.   [3] edition] edition of

4445. To Giuseppe Orioli, [31 May 1928]
Text: MS UCLA; Moore 1060.

Villa Mirenda.
Thursday

Dear Pino

Thank heaven we've got the last of the proofs. I return the others. – On the title-page we agree to cross out the sub-title. Is it necessary to put the name of some publisher or bookseller, as Giuntina says? If so, what shall you put? Yourself? – I don't really mind whether the Giuntina put themselves at the back or not – I suppose they want it. If they don't care, then we'll leave it out. But if they do care, we'll leave it. I don't mind really.

We want to come in tomorrow afternoon, and I'll bring the proofs.

No orders here either. America very slow!

Tomorrow then. DHL

If it makes it simpler, we can leave out 'Florence' on the title page, and just put 'Privately Printed' as Douglas did.[1]

4446. To Earl Brewster, [31 May 1928]
Text: MS UT; Unpublished.

Villa Mirenda. *Scandicci* (Florence)
Thursday

Dear Earl

Your letter to Frieda just come – and the final proofs too. So I think we shall leave next week – this day week probably. But do come all of you to Florence a day or two before we leave – we should both so like to see you. – The Pensione Casali, 11 Lungarno Serristori, has a nice garden. – Liras 45. – The Balestri, Piazza Mentana, near the Uffizi, is cheaper. – I doubt if the inn at Vingone has three beds. The Hotel Moderno, near Piazza Vittorio Emmanuele, has nice rooms but no food – about 20 Liras a day. You eat out. – I think the Casali might be a bit full – Americans – but not the others. Anyhow it's only a day or two. But if you can, you come on Tuesday and sleep here – wish we had room for all – and Achsah and Harwood might[2] stay at the inn or of course in Florence – or Achsah can come straight here and you and Harwood stay in the inn. Let me know. Am sending this down to Florence.

DHL

---

[1] The title-page in the published work reads simply: LADY CHATTERLEY'S LOVER/ BY/ D. H. LAWRENCE/ PRIVATELY PRINTED/ 1928. The verso of the title-page carries the statement: 'Florence – Printed by the Tipografia Giuntina, directed by L. Franceschini' (Roberts A42a).   [2] might] can

4447. To Willard Johnson, 3 June 1928
Text: MS YU; Lacy, *Escaped Cock* 67–8.

Villa Mirenda. Scandicci. (Florence)

3 June 1928

Dear Spud

Thanks for yours. – First and foremost, *don't* print *The Escaped Cock* as my agents say Crosby Gaige will put it in his privately-printed list and give me $1000. If he will, so much the better, and I can give you something else, if you like.

I shall tell Orioli to send [   ]¹ three copies of the novel – one for you, one for Joe² [   ] – remember me to him – and the other for [   ]ne's first wife. When they come, will [   ]lect the money and hand it over to [   ]³ pay horses feed and so on. – If only [   ]re they'd come in, I'd send you [   ]d copies to hold. – The English have subscribed their five hundred, but the Americans not very many. I suppose they don't know.

We leave here end of this week, for French Alps or Switzerland. Write me:

c/o Curtis Brown – 6 Henrietta St. W.C.2.

– Glad you have a house and a press. I expect we shall turn up during the autumn, then we must do some things together.

affectionately   D. H. Lawrence

4448. To Giuseppe Orioli, [4 June 1928]
Text: MS UCLA; Unpublished.

[Villa Mirenda, Scandicci, Florence]

Monday⁴

Dear Pino

Expected Carletto today – aren't the proofs done? Sending these by Adrian Stokes⁵ – I think title-page is all right – he can leave out 'Giuntina' now.

We do want to leave *Saturday*.

DHL

---

¹ MS torn.
² Probably Joseph O'Kane Foster (1898–1985) whom DHL knew in Taos; author of *D. H. Lawrence in Taos* (Albuquerque, 1972).
³ Brett's is probably the missing name: see Letter 4543.
⁴ Dated with reference to DHL's expectation that he and Frieda would leave Mirenda on 'Saturday': cf. letter following. This letter must be later than 4445 where DHL was questioning details about the title-page which, here, is 'all right'; it is likely also to precede Letter 4453 with its further mention of Adrian Stokes.
⁵ Adrian Durham Stokes (1902–72), writer and art critic; author of *Sunrise in the West* (1926), *The Quattro Cento* (1932), *Michaelangelo* (1955), etc.; see also his *Critical Works*, ed. L. Gowing (1978) and *Penguin Poets*, 23 (1973). From 1926 he had an extended stay in Italy during which he met Pound as well as DHL.

4449. To Enid Hilton, 4 June 1928
Text: MS UCLA; Unpublished.

Villa Mirenda, Scandicci. Florence
4 June 1928

Dear Enid

Here we still are. But the novel is all printed, and I am only waiting for the sheets to sign. We think we shall get off on Saturday. I shall write you immediately we have an address.

We had your p.c. of Fiascherino – dear old Fiascherino. I liked it so much – it is fifteen years ago![1] We had the same weather as you – thunder, then blazing sun. Now it's gone a bit muggy again.

I had your p.c. also from Chambery – and the pictures all right so far. I do hope you didn't have much trouble with them, and didn't have to curse them. Perhaps Mark Gertler, he is one of the modern painters, will call and see them[2] – you won't mind, will you? – and perhaps Frieda's younger daughter Barbara Weekley. If Barbara wants to take them away for a while, let her. But I think I'll have her bring them back to you, for she's a scatter-brained thing. I'm still a bit unsure what to do with the big pictures – think I shall have them packed and leave them a little while in Florence. Dorothy Warren seems to be staying away from her galleries for ever – still in Berlin[3] and likely to go bust, I hear.

The woman at the inn always asks after you – and wants to know if we have no more friends in viaggio. The fireflies are in the corn now at evening – very many – and still the poppies go on, redder than ever.

Many regards to you both from both – and I hope London is letting you down lightly.

DHL

4450. To Alan Steele, [4? June 1928]
Text: MS UCLA; Unpublished.

[Villa Mirenda, Scandicci, Florence]
[4? June 1928]

Dear Sir[4]

Owing to printer's delay, we shall not be able to send your copies of *Lady*

---

[1] The Lawrences lived at Villino Ettore Gambrosier in Fiascherino, Gulf of Spezia, 4 October 1913–8 June 1914.   [2] Cf. Letter 4434.   [3] Cf. pp. 341 n. 1 and 434 n. 3.
[4] As with Letter 4415 it appears that DHL was drafting a reply for Orioli, this time to the following letter from Steele to Orioli, 29 May 1928:

Dear Sirs,
   We have had no reply to several of our previous letters concerning D.H. Lawrence's new book "Lady Chatterley's Lover", but we sincerely hope that they have reached you safely.

Chatterley's Lover for another fortnight, or at the very latest, twenty days. I can't send you an advance copy, as the printer is only just finishing. But he *is* finishing.

As to a questionable nature, that is for every man to decide for himself. You may or may not find the book of a questionable nature.

But as soon as I have the first copies in from the binder, say in fifteen days time, I will send you a batch.

Am I to take it that your order for seventy copies stands, in any case?[1]

4451. To Curtis Brown, 4 June 1928
Text: MS UT; Unpublished.

Villa Mirenda. Scandicci. Florence
4 June 1928

Dear C[urtis] B[rown]

I'll do the other half of *The Escaped Cock* and let you see it for Gaige.

We leave here at the end of this week. I have just finished the proofs of *Lady C* – such a delay. But the first $\frac{2}{3}$ are already printed – only the end to print. So Orioli can start sending out in a fortnight. The English half is over-subscribed, but the Americans haven't come along so well. I expect they dont know.

Best wishes   D. H. Lawrence

4452. To Maria Chambers, 4 June 1928
Text: MS UT; Unpublished.

Villa Mirenda. Scandicci. (Florence)
4 June 1928

Dear Mrs Chambers

The photograph came along – rather like Duse long ago – but not so much of a tragic muse.[2] As for your autobiography, you should certainly write it, you seem to have it clear.

I've just finished proofs of the novel – so the first batch should go out in a

We would like you to make our order up to 70 (seventy) copies; this number represents our actual requirements at the moment of writing, but we hope that we may increase this at a later date.

Surely we should have received our advance copy by now? The book was announced for the 15th. May.

We want this copy badly, for we wish to see whether the book is of a questionable nature. Do you anticipate that there will be any difficulty concerning its entry into this country . . .

[1] See Letter 4552.
[2] Eleonora Duse (1858–1924), famous Italian actress whom DHL found fascinating: cf. *Letters*, ii. 595; iv. 485; v. 423.

fortnight. – If you sent Orioli ordinary American cheques for ten dollars, that's best.[1] That's net all right.

What shall I say about your coming to Switzerland? I'm not sure just where we shall be – perhaps in the French Alps, near Chamonix. But Europe's not so very big. And the fare from London via Paris would not be more than twenty dollars, second class, including food. Thomas Cook, the travel agent, makes you a ticket and tells you every mortal thing. It's very simple. – And a simple hotel costs about two dollars a day, including everything.

But now listen – what do you expect to find? Here am I, forty-two, with rather bad health: and a wife who is by no means the soul of patience. What can we do when you come? – talk a while, have lunch and tea, take a walk. And then? Even though we all get on aimiably and interestingly, you will only be disappointed. You think one day the heavens will open. They will never open. It would be a pity if they did. 'Il serait mort s'il ouvrait son cœur.' It would be better if there were things to do, as you say – cooking, milking the cow and so on. But what can one do in an hotel, besides talk? It would be much better at the ranch, where one can make a life. – So don't come to Europe chiefly to see me. If you come to have a pleasant trip, well and good. But if you come for the thrill of meeting me, you'll only be disappointed. If I could make a life with a milieu of its own, and a rhythm and a ritual of its own, then yes, that's a life. But what am I now but a stray individual with not much health and not much money? And one gets weary of talk, just talk. – I would like very much one day to have a place where we could live, and a few people could stay, to make a *life* together. But an hotel – And then of course my wife doesn't look on me as a shrine, and objects to that attitude in other people: at which one can't wonder.

We leave at the end of this week – and I'll write and tell you, as soon as we settle on a place. I want to find somewhere pleasant, about 3000 feet, but not all steep up and down.

It's very good of you to take so much trouble about the novel. I hope the book itself won't disappoint you.

I don't think Count Keyserling is taken very seriously over here. His silly book *Marriage* was chiefly read in America, practically not at all in Germany, and very little in England.[2] He doesn't amount to much – has no roots.

We'll see then, how the future works out.

D. H. Lawrence

---

[1] In his 'Memoranda' (MS NWU) DHL recorded receiving $10 from Maria Chambers on 2 July 1928.

[2] Count Hermann Alexander Keyserling (1880–1946), popular philosopher. His *Book of Marriage* (1927) was probably sent to DHL by Brett in February 1927 (*Letters*, v. 639 and n. 2).

4453. To Giuseppe Orioli, [6 June 1928]

Text: MS UCLA; Unpublished.

Villa Mirenda.
Wed.

Dear Pino

I can't help laughing at Miss Kent – she must be cracked – or has somebody done something to her?[1] I never even knew she was coming to see you – I asked Adrian Stokes please to give you the note, as he was coming in. But he didn't come. That young man was Adrian Kent, the woman's nephew – really a nice boy. I suppose he was feeling ashamed. I hardly know Miss Kent – she's been to tea once. She must have gone off like a lunatic – and an old maid. But you should have asked her please to speak English and please to remember her manners. I had no idea *she* was coming to your shop. – She must have something against you privately, do you think? I give people up.

Thanks for the bordereaux. Dont forget I owe you Liras 100 on the snuff-box[2] – and the 22 for trousers. I had forgotten. – I enclose cheque for Lit 4000, to you, for the Giuntina. My flue came back a bit, or I should have come in. – The Brewsters are here, but I think they'll go with us to Switzerland. So glad all proofs are here. I shall try to come in Friday.

DHL

4454. To Giuseppe Orioli, [7 June 1928]

Text: MS UCLA; cited in Moore, *Intelligent Heart* 380.

Villa Mirenda.
Thursday

Dear Pino

Here are all the sheets signed and numbered, up to 1000: then ten extra ones signed but not numbered, in case anything goes wrong – keep them apart – and ten blank ones. So glad that's all over.[3]

We want to go Sunday at about mid-day – by Pisa-Genoa-Turin. I should like to see you and have a little final talk about sending off the books, and paying and so on. Do you think you could come up on Saturday? – or Sunday morning with a car, if you like. I think we'll have a taxi to take us down – though it's too dear.

Anyhow fix it up with Frieda. Hope you've cooled down about Miss Kent.

DHL

---

[1] In a letter, 17 November 1928, DHL recalls Miss Kent's attacking Orioli 'in fierce Italian'. She lived in the Villa Bronciliano at Vingone; nothing further is known of her or her nephew Adrian.   [2] See Letter 4439.

[3] DHL's relief is reflected in his 'Memoranda' entry: '7 June 1928. Corpus Domini. finished last of proofs & signed all sheets for Lady C.' (MS NWU).

4455. To S. S. Koteliansky, [7 June 1928]

Text: MS BL; PC v.William Blake, *Illustration to Dante* (Drawing). Paradiso, Canto 25. SS. Peter, John and James, Dante and Beatrice; Postmark, Firenze 8 . VI 28; Zytaruk 343.

[Villa Mirenda, Scandicci, Florence]
7 June

Signed the last sheets for *Lady C.* today, so am free – expect you'll get your copy in about ten days. We leave on Sunday for the French Alps – muggy thunder here, no good. – Shall send address immediately we have one.

DHL

4456. To Max Mohr, 7 June 1928

Text: MS HMohr; Mohr, *T'ien Hsia Monthly*, i. 31–2.

Villa Mirenda, *Scandicci*, Florence
7 June 1928

Dear Max Mohr

I have been waiting to finish proofs and signing sheets of that novel *Lady Chatterley*. But thank God it is done at last, so we are leaving on Sunday, for the French Alps. We shall go to Grenoble, and from there I think, to Villard de Lans, about 1150 metres up.[1] I shall send you word from there.

Very kind of you to write to the[2] Fischer-Verlag about me. I am engaged to the Insel Verlag until November, then free. But Fischer would have to make arrangements through my agent:

Curtis Brown, 6 Henrietta St. Covent Garden, London W.C.2.

The photograph is charming, and the horse most modern-archaic. It's been a bad spring up here too – not so much rain, but cloudy and dull. But I'm sorry about your flowers, nipped by frost. Here too there is not much fruit – but the cherries are ripe, and very sweet, and big. The wild geizblatt[3] is finished – was very sweet – and the Nachtigall sings not much any more. Altogether it is not a gay year, and I am glad to be going away for a time. Very many greetings from us both to you three. I shall write from France.

D. H. Lawrence

4457. To Nancy Pearn, 7 June 1928

Text: MS UT; Unpublished.

Villa Mirenda, *Scandicci*, Florence
7 June 1928

Dear Nancy Pearn

Did you get MSS of 'Chaos in Poetry' and 'Mother and Daughter'?[4] And

---

[1] 15 miles s.w. of Grenoble.   [2] the] the the   [3] 'honeysuckle'.
[4] 'Mother and Daughter' was published in *Criterion*, viii (April 1928), 394–419.

did a woman – Allanah something – from Chelsea, ask to see them for her new Paris venture?[1]

We leave here on Sunday for the French Alps – so don't write here any more. And please tell the other depts, will you? – It's muggy thunder-weather, rather horrid, and eight of our peasants – the nearest – down with flu – bronchial. Time for me to clear out.

Shall send an address the moment we settle.

D. H. Lawrence

4458. To Laurence Pollinger, 7 June 1928
Text: MS UT; Unpublished.

Villa Mirenda, Scandicci, Florence
7 June 1928

Dear Pollinger

Thanks for the cuttings – does Gerald Gould possibly imagine he's clever.[2] – Also for the copies of *Woman Who Rode*.

Today I have signed the last sheets for the novel, so I'm free. The printing is nearly done. I expect you'll have your copy within ten days.

But we are leaving on Sunday for the French Alps, somewhere near Grenoble. So don't write here any more. I'll send address as soon as we have one.

Yrs   D. H. Lawrence

4459. To Ada Clarke, [7 June 1928]
Text: MS Clarke; PC v. Allart Van Everdingen (1621–1675) *Landscape*; Postmark, Firenze 8 . VI 28; Lawrence–Gelder 183.

[Villa Mirenda, Scandicci, Florence]
Corpus Domini[3]

We think to leave here on Sunday, for the French Alps near Grenoble. The Brewsters are in Florence, and will go with us. Very muggy thundery weather here – it will be nice to get a bit higher up. We shall look round for a place about 3000 feet, and I shall write you as soon as we have an address. Nearly your birthday too.

love   DHL

---

[1] Allanah Harper, editor of *Echanges* (Paris) which began in October 1928 (cf. Letter 4533).
[2] Gerald Gould (1885–1936), poet, critic and journalist (Associate Editor, *Daily Herald*, 1919–22). He had reviewed several of DHL's works (see Roberts A7, A21, A24, A26, A29); his general view may be deduced from the remark in his *English Novel of To-Day* (1924) that DHL and Joyce were the 'two living writers who exercise the most sinister influence on the contemporary novel'. It is not known what pronouncement DHL was reacting to here.
[3] Normally called 'Corpus Christi' (cf. p. 420 n. 3).

4460. To Nancy Pearn, [12 June 1928]
Text: MS Lazarus; PC v. Chambéry – Rue de Roche. La Savoie; Postmark, Grenoble 14 VI 28; Unpublished.

– Grenoble
Tuesday
we are going tomorrow up to
Hotel des Touristes, *St. Nizier de Pariset*, nr. Grenoble, Isère, France.
It seems very nice there. Do be kind and give the address to the other depts. –
So hot down here in Grenoble.

D. H. Lawrence

4461. To Ada Clarke, [13 June 1928]
Text: MS Clarke; PC v. Costumes de Savoie (Tarentaise); Postmark, Grenoble 14. VI [. . .]; Unpublished.

[Grenoble]
[13 June 1928]
Hotel des Touristes, *St. Nizier de Pariset*, près Grenoble, Isère, France
We're going up to this place tomorrow. So write there – very lovely – about
3500 ft. up – looking far off to Mt Blanc. It's hot down here in Grenoble.

love   DHL

4462. To Emily King, [14 June 1928]
Text: MS Needham; PC v. Dauphiné – Couvent de la Grande-Chartreuse, Vue intérieure de la Cour d'Honneur; Postmark, Grenoble 14 VI 28; Unpublished.

[Grenoble]
Thursday
We are going this evening up to the
Hotel des Touristes, *St. Nizier de Pariset*, près Grenoble, Isère, France
Shall write from there – it's about 3500 ft up – nice – the Brewsters are with
us. Very hot in Grenoble.

DHL

4463. To Baroness Anna von Richthofen, [14 June 1928]
Text: MS UCB; PC v. Costumes de Savoie (Tarentaise); Postmark, Grenoble 14 VI 28; Unpublished.

[Grenoble]
[14 June 1928]
[Frieda Lawrence begins]
Hoffe einen schönen Platz für L[awrence] gefunden zu haben – gefällt ihm
Brewsters sind mit uns

[Lawrence begins]
   – Hotel des Touristes, *St Nizier de Pariset*, bei Grenoble, Isère, France.
                                                        Grüsse dir.   DHL

[Hope to have found a nice place for L[awrence] – he likes it Brewsters are
with us
[Lawrence begins]
   – Hotel des Touristes, *St Nizier de Pariset*, near Grenoble, Isère, France.
                                                    Greetings to you.   DHL]

4464. To S. S. Koteliansky, [14 June 1928]
Text: MS BL; PC v. Grenoble. – Vue Générale et la Chaîne des Alpes; Postmark, Grenoble
[. . .] 4. VI. 28; Zytaruk 343.

                                                                Grenoble,
                                                                Thursday
We are going up this evening to
   Hotel des Touristes, *St Nizier de Pariset*, nr Grenoble, Isère, France
   It's about 3500 ft up – edge of a plateau – queer country, lovely air – down
here it's hot. Will write.
                                                                    DHL

4465. To Martin Secker, [14 June 1928]
Text: MS UInd; PC v. Dauphiné – Vue Générale du Couvent de la Grande-Chartreuse;
Postmark, Grenoble 14.VI.28; Secker 108.

                                                                [Grenoble]
                                                                Thursday
We are going up this evening to
   Hotel des Touristes, *St Nizier de Pariset*, nr Grenoble, Isère, France
   Hot down here in Grenoble – but that is 3500 ft up – on the edge of a plateau –
queer country, rather lovely.
                                                                    DHL

4466. To S. S. Koteliansky, [15 June 1928]
Text: MS BL; Postmark, Grenoble 15.VI 28; Zytaruk 344.

                                                                St Nizier
                                                                Friday
Dear Kot
   This place won't do[1] – So don't write here. We are moving on to
Switzerland – I will send address.
                                                                    DHL

---

[1] For the explanation see Letter 4478.

4467. To Giuseppe Orioli, [15 June 1928]
Text: MS (Photocopy) HU; PC; Postmark, Grenobl[e] 15.VI 1928; Unpublished..

[St Nizier]
Venerdì –

Caro Pino –

Non restiamo qui, dunque non mandar qui le lettere. Andiamo in Svizzera, e ti scriverò l'indirizzo domani. Ma aspetta che ti scrivo.

D. H. Lawrence

[Friday –

Dear Pino –

We are not staying here, so don't send the letters here. We are going to Switzerland, and I'll send our address to you tomorrow. But wait until I write.

D. H. Lawrence]

4468. To Martin Secker, [15 June 1928]
Text: MS UInd; Postmark, Grenoble 15.VI 28; Secker 108.

St Nizier.
15 June

Dear Secker

This place won't do after all – we are moving on to Switzerland – Will send address.

D. H. Lawrence

4469. To Nancy Pearn, [15 June 1928]
Text: MS UT; Unpublished.

St Nizier
15 June

Dear Miss Pearn

This place won't do after all – we are moving on to Switzerland. Please cancel the address altogether – am sorry to be a nuisance.

D. H. Lawrence

4470. To Ada Clarke, [18 June 1928]
Text: MS Clarke; PC v. Chexbres Grand Hotel et les Alpes; Postmark, Ch[exbres] [. . .]; Unpublished.

Grand Hotel, *Chexbres-sur-Vevey*, Switzerland.
Monday

We came on here to be decently warm and comfortable. It's a big hotel, but pleasant, above the lake of Geneva, with lovely views. The Brewsters are here too – and Frieda is going for a week to Baden. Hope you didn't write to the other place. Thought of you on your birthday.

DHL

4471. To Emily King, [18 June 1928]

Text: MS Needham; PC v. Chexbres et les montagnes de la Savoie; Postmark, Chexbres 18 VI 28; Unpublished.

Grand Hotel, *Chexbres-sur-Vevey*, Süisse
Monday

We've come on to a fairly big hotel here above the Lake of Geneva – the other place too high and comfortless – here anyhow one has decent comfort. It's quite lovely as far as view goes – and a lovely day, though rather cold.

DHL

4472. To Giuseppe Orioli, [18 June 1928]

Text: MS (Photocopy) HU; PC; Postmark, Chexbr[es] 18.VI 2 [. . .]; Unpublished.

Grand Hotel, *Chexbres-sur-Vevey* – Vaud, Svizzera.
lunedì

Mi pare che resteremo qui qualche settimana. Spero che non abbia mandato lettere all'altro albergo – a St Nizier – perché non ho fiducia a loro, per rispedirle. – Scrivo italiano che 'l Carletto possa capire anche.

D. H. Lawrence
[Monday

It seems as if we are staying here for a few weeks. I hope you sent no letters to the other hotel – at St Nizier – because I don't trust them, to forward them. I am writing in Italian so that Carletto also will be able to understand.

D. H. Lawrence]

4473. To Martin Secker, [18 June 1928]

Text: MS UInd; PC v. Chexbres – L'Eglise et les Alpes; Postmark, Chexbr[es] 18.VI 28; Secker 108.

Grand Hotel, *Chexbre-sur-Vevey*. Switzerland
Monday

I think we shall settle down here a bit – it's a biggish hotel, but decently comfortable – the other place too high and cold and raw. I hope you didn't write there – I don't trust them to send on the letters. It's nippy here, but rather lovely – and good for one!

our regards to you all.   DHL

4474. To Nancy Pearn, [18 June 1928]
Text: MS UTul; Unpublished.

Grand Hotel, *Chexbres-sur-Vevey*, Suisse.
Monday

Dear Nancy Pearn

Apparently we shall stay here a week or two – so it's an address. Did anybody write to the St. Nizier place? – because I don't at all trust them to forward things. – Shall send you a story in a day or two. – Chilly here, but rather lovely.

DHL

4475. To S. S. Koteliansky, [19 June 1928]
Text: MS BL; PC v. Chexbres – L'Eglise et les Alpes; Postmark Chexbres 19.VI.28; Zytaruk 344.

Grand Hotel. *Chexbres-sur-Vevey*, Suisse
Tuesday.

We got here Sunday, and are pretty comfortable, so I expect we shall stay a while. We are only 1800 above the sea – but the weather is rather cold, so it's quite enough for the moment. It's a lovely view across the Lake of Geneva. Frieda has gone off today to Baden for a week. Am anxious to hear from Florence.

DHL

4476. To Enid Hilton, [19 June 1928]
Text: MS UCLA; PC v. Lac Léman – Famille de Cygnes; Postmark, Chexbres 19.VI.28; Unpublished.

Grand Hotel – *Chexbres-sur-Vevey*, Suisse.
Tuesday.

The St. Nizier place was too bleak – we have come on here – to a biggish hotel, but comfortable enough, and a lovely view across the Lake of Geneva. So I expect we shall stay a while. Did you write to the other place? I don't trust them to forward letters. – Frieda has gone off to Baden for a week. Rather chilly weather, but fine. How are you both?

DHL

4477. To Juliette Huxley, [19 June 1928]
Text: MS Huxley; PC v. Lac Léman; Postmark, Chexbres [. . .]; Unpublished.

Grand Hotel. *Chexbres-sur-Vevey*
Tuesday.

At last we've got an address to send – not very high up, about 1800, but enough for the moment, as it is cold – The hotel is fairly big, but comfortable –

so one just vegetates, or tries to. F[rieda] has gone off to Baden for a week – but our friends from Capri, the Brewsters, are here. How are you all?

D. H. Lawrence

4478. To Giuseppe Orioli, [21 June 1928]
Text: MS UCLA; Moore, *Intelligent Heart* 380–1.

Grand Hotel. Chexbres-sur-Vevey, Suisse.
Thursday

Dear Pino

Letters forwarded from Florence today – and your handwriting, I think: so you are there, are you? Have you been to England? or are you going?

We are in this biggish hotel, with the Brewsters – well looked after, 9 francs a day including tea – and about 2000 ft. above Lac Leman. So we're all right for a bit – *and if you come to England this way, stop off at Lausanne and see us.* It's above Vevey, quite near Lausanne. – That St. Nizier place was very rough – and the insolent French people actually asked us to go away because I coughed. They said they didn't have anybody who coughed. I felt very mad. But it's much better here – dull, but comfortable. And it's no good shivering with cold and being uncomfortable. The Brewsters are here – Frieda has gone to BadenBaden for a week, Aldous has telegraphed that he and Maria will join us next Tuesday or Wednesday – from Paris. So we are not likely to be lonesome, as the Brewsters say. – They are very nice, the Brewsters, look after me so well: I ought to get quickly fat, fatter than you or Frieda. – By the way, be sure to give Maria a copy of *Lady C.* when she turns up. And if a man Charles Wilson from Willington,[1] Durham wrote for a copy, send him one, I know him. I'm so anxious to know what milady is doing, and what you are doing about her. People pelting me with letters now, to know when they'll get her. – Somehow I feel it will be safe to post to England, day by day: start about a week after the American copies have gone off. But once you start sending out, go straight ahead, until something stops you. I am very anxious to hear from you, what is happening. Wish I could have stayed on till the thing is out, and posted.

It has been cold here, real cold – but warmer today. Write me a line!

DHL

---

[1] Willington] Darlington

4479. To Harry Crosby, 21 June 1928
Text: MS SIU; Postmark, Chexbres 22 VI.28; Unpublished.

Grand Hotel – Chexbres-sur-Vevey. Suisse

21 June 1928

Dear Harry Crosby

Here we are in a dull hotel with dull people in a dull country – but good friends are here too – and the air is good – and the view is still beautiful – so I am pretty well content. I suppose we shall stay a week or two, then perhaps move up the mountains a little higher – my woful bronchials! – How are you and where are you and where are you going? – I have got all my gold with me! – and my wife is in BadenBaden with her mother swelling round with the ex-queen's snuff-box.[1] So you see what a gilt edge you've given us!

Tell me which way you are veering, we might meet. – Was doing a story with mixed suns in it:[2] call down wrath on my poor head.

D. H. Lawrence

4480. To Frieda Lawrence, [21 June 1928]
Text: MS UT; Frieda Lawrence 224–5.

Grand Hotel. Chexbres-sur-Vevey

Thursday morning

Had your p. c. this morning – glad you found Nusch there. I guess you'll schwätzen schwätzen[3] all the day. – Today is better here – am sitting on my little balcony to write this – Achsah has already sent Earl down with a cup of ovaltine – and it is sunny in snatches. – I worked over my Isis story a bit – am going to try it on Earl. Last night we sang songs, 'Twankydillo' etc.,[4] up in Achsah's attic. Everything very quiet and domestic.

Had a few letters forwarded from Florence this morning: enclose the Curtis Brown.[5] Ask Else what she thinks about a complete break in November with Insel Verlag.[6] Of course it is insolence on their part that they won't tell my agents what they are doing with my books. They should of course write Miss Watson about the proposed book of short stories.[7] Ask Else about it – what they are really doing. And ask her if she kept that short biography of me which

---

[1] Cf. Letter 4439.   [2] DHL was writing Part II of *The Escaped Cock*; cf. Letter 4500.
[3] 'chatter chatter'.
[4] 'Twankydillo' begins: 'Here's a health to the blacksmith . . . ' (see *Cecil Sharp's Collection of English Folk Songs*, ii (1974), 206–7).   [5] The letter is missing.
[6] See Letter 4188 and p. 199 n. 2.
[7] The 'book' was to be Else Jaffe's trans. of *The Woman Who Rode Away and Other Stories* (cf. Letter 4285).

she did for the *Frankfurter Zeitung* man.[1] If she did, you might look it over and send it to Miss Watson, *in English*, for this Kra man.[2] I simply can't write biographies of myself. Damn them all. – A sort of lamentable letter from Cath Carswell – no money etc – and still fussing about what Yvonne Franchetti said about that typing. Then a letter from the irrepressible Durham miner man – wanting *Lady C.* very much – nothing else – no word from Orioli though it's his handwriting on the envelopes. Nothing from Huxleys either, save their telegram. Madame will have a double room for them. Wish they'd bring the car, we could look at places a bit higher. I told you they arrive next Tuesday or Wednesday. – There is nothing forwarded from that St. Nizier place.

I think of you in the Schwiegermutter's room with Nusch there. Has die Anna got any flowers? Buy her a nice pot from me. And buy something for Nusch, for 20 Marks. I want her to have something for a quid. Only not schnecken nor foie gras. – I can now smell Braten[3] of some sort. – Perhaps we shall go to Vevey this afternoon. We want to go to Gruyère when you come back – also to Le Pont, which is M. Stucki's other hotel about 3000 ft. up, with three little lakes. Might go there. But he leases it in summer to another hotelier. What are Nusch's plans.

Love to you all – the Goddesses Three.[4]   DHL

4481. To Catherine Carswell, [21 June 1928]

Text: MS YU; PC v. Chexbres. – L'Eglise et les Alpes; Postmark, Chexbres 22 VI 28; cited in Carswell 274.

Grand Hotel – *Chexbres-sur-Vevey*, Suisse
[21 June 1928][5]

Your letter came here today – we got here Sunday – a biggish hotel over Lac Leman – quite comfortable, and not expensive: nor thrilling either, but expect we shall stay a while, as it seems good for my bronchials. – I'll order you *Woman Who Rode Away* – it may amuse you. Been very cold, but sunny today and warmer.

Ever.   DHL

[1] See Letter 4417 and n. 4.
[2] Philippe Soupault (1897–), French poet, novelist, biographer and one of the founders of Surrealism; he was the *directeur littéraire* of the Parisian publishing house, Kra (Nehls, iii. 702 n. 408). See Letter 4539 and n. 1.   [3] 'snails . . . roast'.
[4] DHL may have had in mind the song 'Goddesses Three' (Venus, Minerva and Juno) which Achsah Brewster remembered singing at Gsteig (Brewster 290).
[5] Dated by DHL's reference to the letter from Catherine Carswell in the preceding letter.

4482. To Max Mohr, [21 June 1928]

Text: MS HMohr; PC v. Lac Léman – Famille de Cygnes; Postmark, Chexbres. 22.VI[. . .];
Unpublished.

Grand Hotel. Chexbres-sur-Vevey, Schweiz.

[21 June 1928][1]

At last I can send you an address – we are settled for the moment in this hotel
above Lac Leman – only about 600 meter – but enough for the moment. My
wife has gone to BadenBaden for a week – but we have friends in the hotel.
How are you? I do hope you're feeling better, and the 'Jungfrau Max' goes
well.[2] Went down to Vevey this afternoon – a lovely lake and warm sun.

Many greetings.   D. H. Lawrence

4483. To Rolf Gardiner, [22 June 1928]

Text: MS Lazarus; PC v. Lac Léman; Postmark, [Che]xbres 22 VI 28; Unpublished.

Grand Hotel. Chexbres-sur-Vevey, Suisse.

[22 June 1928]

Got here Sunday – usual run of hotel, above Lac Leman – but quite nice – and
good for me. – The novel ought to be sent out from Florence any day now. –
Saw Adrian Stokes a few times. Send me a line and remember me to Margaret,
hope to see you later.

DHL

4484. To Giuseppe Orioli, [22 June 1928]

Text: MS UCLA; PC v. Chexbres et les montagnes de la Savoie; Postmark, Chexbr[es] 22 VI
28; Unpublished.

[Grand Hotel, Chexbres-sur-Vevey, Suisse]

Friday

Had your letter and enclosures today – shame you couldn't get to England.
How much of the binding paper did they cut wrong? for how many copies! Oh
how tiresome people are! It's rather nice here. I think I shall send my pictures
to London – so if Pietro appears with them on the barrocio, will you go with
him to Egidi's? Where *is* Michelino? Did you put down John M. Weatherwax,
323 North 'B' Street, *Aberdeen*. Wash. U.S.A for five copies? He is quite safe.
Will write tomorrow.

DHL

Also Willard Johnson. Taos. New Mexico for three copies – also safe.

---

[1] Dated through DHL's mention, on 21 June, of a visit to Vevey 'this afternoon' (Letter 4480).
[2] See Letter 4355 and n. 3.

4485. To Laurence Pollinger, 22 June 1928
Text: MS UT; Unpublished.

Grand Hotel. *Chexbres-sur-Vevey*, Switzerland
22 June 1928

Dear Pollinger

We're settled down here for a bit – think it's good for me. Did they send me[1] all the Knopf presentation copies of *The Woman Who Rode Away* to your office? a great bore! I wrote asking Mrs McCord if she'd send them out for me, then found she'd quit.[2] – If they're there – and they should be *ten* – would you be so good as to have them posted from your office. I enclose a list of addresses.

I hear the first 200 copies of *Lady C.* are ready and being sent off to America. Hope there's no fuss. England has subscribed over six hundred. – You ought to get your copy directly.

Sincerely   D. H. Lawrence

Copies of the American edition of *Woman Who Rode Away* to be sent out:

---

1.   Hon. Dorothy Brett, c/o Del Monte Ranch. *Questa*, New Mexico, U.S.A.
1.   Mrs Mabel Lujan. *Taos*. New Mexico.
1.   G. R. G. Conway Esq. Marsella #47. *Mexico. D. F.*
1.   Miss Barbara Low. 13 Guilford St. Russell Square, W.C.1.
1.   Mrs D Carswell. 3 Parkhill Studios, Parkhill Rd. N.W.3.
1.   Miss Idella Purnell. Galeana #150. *Guadalajara*, Mexico
1.   Harry Crosby Esq. 19 rue de Lille. *Paris*
1.   Dr. E. D. McDonald. The Drexel Institute, *Philadelphia*. Pa.

4486. To Giuseppe Orioli, [23 June 1928]
Text: MS UCLA; Unpublished.

Grand Hotel. *Chexbres-sur-Vevey*. Svizzera
Saturday

Dear Pino

I have written to Giulia to send in my pictures to you,[3] safely wrapped in the blankets. Will you take them to Egidi – or go over with Pietro when they come – and have Egidi pack them in a box, ready to send them to England. Two galleries want to show them:

Dorothy Warren, *The Warren Galleries. 39A Madox St. London W.1.*
and also

[1] me] you   [2] See p. 181 n. 2.   [3] The letter is unlocated.

M. Thompson Bowen. Secretary, The Claridge Gallery. 52 Brook St.
Grosvenor Square, *London W.1*.[1]

I am not quite decided which to send them to, but will either write or wire the address next week. The pictures that are framed, send them in their frames. And will you please pay Pietro sixteen Liras, and send to Giulia six postage stamps, 1.25, so that she can write to me. Take it from my money.

I want to pay Egidi in advance. Will you pay him for me? But *don't* let him charge to the gallery on delivery. And you can take the money from *Lady C.* or I will send a cheque, as you like. I am asking that boy Adrian Kent to go over to the Mirenda and see that the pictures start all right with Pietro. Perhaps you will see that Pietro takes the blankets back safely.

I am looking forward to my copy of 'John Thomas'. Do you still feel scared of the authorities? You got the p.c. with addresses: *five copies* to

John M. Weatherwax, 323 North 'B' Street. *Aberdeen*. (Washington) USA
three copies to

        Willard Johnson. Taos. New Mexico. U.S.A.

one copy

        Mrs Mabel Lujan. Taos. New Mexico.

one copy

        Hon. Dorothy Brett. Taos, New Mexico.

It is hot sun here, very hot, but air good and fresh. Frieda is still in Baden. When you get through with 'J. T.' perhaps you'll join us. You won't mind helping with the pictures, will you? Hope you're feeling pretty well, and not minding all the bother with 'Lady Jane'. – Scandalous that you didn't get your passport! Send me a line – and remember me to Reggie.

                                     DHL

4487. To Arthur Wilkinson, [23 June 1928]

Text: MS Schlaefle; PC v. Chexbres. – L'Eglise et les Alpes; Postmark, Chexbres 23 VI 28; Unpublished.

               Grand Hotel. Chexbres-sur-Vevey
                               Sat.

Here we are – guess you know the place – not so grand as all that, but very nice. The Brewsters are here, all three, toning up after Capri Scirocco. Frieda has whipped off to BadenBaden for a week. I am feeding and loafing – and feel all right – even take sun-baths. – And how are you all? and is anything happening to you? – The Huxleys turn up next week, en route to Forte from

---

[1] The gallery was owned by Mrs Ena Mathias (Nehls, iii. 222, 700 n. 384).

Paris. – It's brilliant sunny weather, but cool air. Good to be out of Italy for a bit. Write.

DHL

4488. To Dorothy Warren, [23 June 1928]
Text: MS UN; Nehls, iii. 221.

Grand Hotel. *Chexbres-sur-Vevey.* Switzerland
Saturday 24[1] June 1928

Dear Dorothy Warren

I have just heard from Barbara Weekly that you are back and expecting my pictures. But the Claridge Gallery wrote for them, and I replied *almost* promising to send to them, at once, as they want to show from July 12th to 28th; – their July show having fallen through. I'd rather really send[2] them to you; but let me know at once when you would show them, as I have promised to send them to New York in autumn. If you don't let me know immediately – for you seem to leave long lapses between your answers – I shall send the things to Claridges. I am not pledged to them, though.

The water-colors and the three smaller oils ought to be in London – I don't know if Barbara has seen them – she doesn't mention them. But she could get them and show them to you. The big pictures are packed, in Florence, waiting to be forwarded immediately I send an address.

My friends E. H. Brewster and his wife Achsah Brewster, well-known painters really, have got some things in London; about twenty canvases I think, ranging around 30 × 35 inches. If you have room I should like you to show some, at the same time as mine. You could see the canvases and decide. Let me know.

Sincerely   D. H. Lawrence[3]

---

[1] 24] 22   [2] send] show
[3] Dorothy Warren replied at length on 26 June 1928 (Nehls, iii. 221–3):

Dear Mr. Lawrence,
   By now I hope you will have received my telegram. I understood from our last correspondence that you agreed to my exhibiting your pictures in my gallery, and that you would dispatch them from Italy on or about May 1st. I only returned from Berlin, where I was holding an exhibition of young English painters (Barbara amongst them) at the end of May, and found your work had not arrived. I had intended to show it now, but of course I had to carry on without it.
   I know nothing about your arrangements with the Claridge Gallery, except what you have written and what Mrs Mathias said when she rang me up yesterday. Please be advised by me. Do not show from the 18th of July until the 28th. Ten days is certainly not long enough to give any show a chance, and it is much too late in the season. The only daily papers which are important as regards art criticism would hardly have time to bring out their notices ... and the weeklies would have no time at all to publish anything about the show until it was over. I always

4489. To Mabel Dodge Luhan, 24 June 1928
Text: MS Brill; Unpublished.

Grand Hotel. Chexbres-sur-Vevey, Switzerland
24 June 1928

Dear Mabel

I had yours about Orioli, enclosing the letter from 'Sister' – Rose Clarke's sister, did you say?[1] Anyhow, from the tone of her letter she was[2] a thoroughly objectionable person, and if she put Orioli's back up, I don't wonder. I'm very glad he wouldn't sell her any books – too many impudent American females stroll in to buy the shop for fifteen cents and their noble patronage – I don't suppose he said a word against you, or the bitch would have repeated it. And don't be alarmed that you were swindled over those few books – you weren't – an odd incomplete 1st edition Amer. Henry James is worth about four dollars.[3] – So keep cool and don't go to the trouble of forwarding trivial letters

do three-weekly shows and sometimes I extend them even beyond that period . . . The very best month of the whole year for picture-shows is November oddly enough, in spite of the almost complete absence of day-light. October is also good, when people return from holidays and are anxious to see what is going on. Although I should like to arrange your exhibition for November, as I feel it will be an important event and should be treated accordingly, I could do it in early October, so that the pictures could be in America by early November. I need hardly tell you that I am longing to have your show. I really have been looking forward to it tremendously, and I should do everything in my power to make it a success. Do you remember the little picture you painted of the flight into Egypt which used to hang over the mantelpiece in Byron Villas? I always loved it and I remember it quite vividly. I am longing to see what you have been doing since.

While I was in Germany I was badly let-down. Letters were neither answered nor forwarded to me. I left instructions for 10 guineas to be sent to Florence for 5 copies of your book, and I have only just discovered . . . that this was not done, so I have sent the cheque myself. A stringent and sweeping reform has taken place, and everything is running so smoothly it is almost too good to be true! . . .

I really appreciate your saying that you would like to show with me, and I want to feel quite sure that you really mean it. I am collecting some work of yours from an address that Barbara has just given me on the telephone.

With regard to the Brewsters, where can their work be seen? I have often heard of them from Lucile Beckett (now Lucile Frost). Until I see your pictures it is difficult to judge exactly how much I could hang with them. I can show between 40 and 50 smallish pictures, but yours are mainly large and I hate the sort of thickly hung show that one always sees in London galleries, which makes one feel that almost anything can be crowded in somehow with a lot of good will and no taste. I tend to show fewer pictures on my walls than is usual in other galleries. However I will do what I can about the Brewsters if they will get in touch with me. Please let me know how you feel about an early October date? One could open on the 2nd, which would be a Tuesday. I try to open on Tuesdays always because it is a good day. I should like to have at least three weeks clear for you, but if you want the pictures to go to America, I could close on Saturday October 20th, which would be two days short of three weeks, if that would suit you.

Yours Dorothy

[1] Rose ('Tante') Clark had been Mabel Luhan's art teacher in school at Buffalo; she lived for a time in the Villa Curonia (Emily Hahn, *Mabel*, Boston, 1977, p. 42). Her sister is unidentified.
[2] was] put. O   [3] See Letter 4021.

from spiteful old maids. – As to the New York period – you know best. If you can do it and make it interesting and alive, that's all that matters.[1]

I expect Orioli has sent you a copy of *Lady Chatterley* by now. I ordered you a *Woman Who Rode Away* from New York, but the fools sent all the Amer. copies to me to London, so it'll come on to you from there.

We are here about 1000 ft. above Lake of Geneva – lovely view. It suits me, and my bones seem to be shaping up, so I may be able really to set forth in the autumn. I shall be very glad if I can – but must get the beastly cough down a bit first. – Frieda is in BadenBaden – the Brewsters are here with me – and the Huxleys arrived yesterday from Paris: so we're quite a party. Brett said you had high blood-pressure – I expect you'll have to go to a lower altitude for a bit. But I hope you're having a nice summer.

love,   DHL

4490. To Hon. Dorothy Brett, 25 June 1928
Text: MS UCin; Postmark, Chex[bre]s 25.VI 28; Irvine, Brett 85–6.

Grand Hotel, Chexbres-sur-Vevey, Switzerland
25 June 1928

My dear Brett

Well here we all are – Achsah and Earl and Harwood – and Aldous and Maria arrived last night – and Frieda comes back from Baden this evening: quite a tea-party, as you say. We have your letters, so picture you up there at the ranch. I do hope the Indians will all behave, so you have no more fuss, as last year with Ruffina.[2] And what about Trinidad's hands? are they better? – You have never told me what the charges were for horses' feed this winter. I asked Spud, when he gets the three copies of *Lady Chatterley* he ordered, to pay you the $30. But do let me know if there is anything else – and the taxes too! Do ask Mabel to ask the man who pays her taxes, about those for the ranch. – The first 200 copies of *Lady C.* are to be ready to be sent off today – so you should have yours soon. I do hope there is no bother with the authorities. What a curse that would be! I'm afraid I should lose all the copies sent. – I ordered you a copy of the *Woman Who Rode Away* stories from New York – but they tiresomely sent the batch all to London – so your copy will have to come on to you from England. Still, you'll get it. It seems to be selling fairly well in England, but the American papers don't like it.[3]

This place seems to me to be good for my broncs. It's not very high – only

[1] See Letter 4419.   [2] See Letter 4201 and n. 3.
[3] For confirming evidence see the summaries of American reviews in *D. H. Lawrence: An Annotated Bibliography of Writings about Him*, ed. James Cowan (De Kalb, 1982), i. 85, 87–8, 90, etc.

about 2000 – but a lovely view over the Lake of Geneva. And I find I can take sun-baths again. So perhaps I'll get my beastly cough reduced, and if so, we can set out. – It is true, Achsah is really afraid of leaving Europe any more – she is not so strong as she was. And even Frieda seems afraid of New Mexico – I don't quite know why. But on the whole I think you have a good time there. So I don't see why we shouldn't all face it.

I am sending my paintings to London – but not decided yet between the Warren's Gallery and Claridges. Anyhow they'll all be ready to come to New York in the autumn, if that show is really fixed up. Though I feel again I don't care about showing. I had a nice letter from Mrs Hare. – Anyhow have a good time!

DHL

4491. To S. S. Koteliansky, 27 June 1928
Text: MS BL; Postmark, Che[xbr]es 28.VI.28; Zytaruk 345.

Grand Hotel. Chexbres-sur-Vevey, Switzerland
27 June 1928

Dear Kot,

I hear from Florence the first copies of *Lady C.* are ready, and a good many will go off this week. Orioli will mail them as they come from the binder — it's no good holding them – the post office won't register a mass at once. So people will get them in turn. But we shall send to America first. And now let's trust in heaven.

Aldous and Maria are here for a few days – not so chirpy as they were in Diablerets – but I expect that is big cities like London and Paris. Frieda is back from Baden. I am pretty well – much better than last year, thank heaven. This hotel is very comfortable and pleasant – only about two thousand feet up – Probably in July we shall move up somewhere, over the 3000 line. But one does feel better in Switzerland. – This afternoon Maria motored us to the Castle of Chillon – but those show-places bore me. – I am thinking definitely of sending my pictures to London, but am hesitating between the Warren Gallery and Claridge's. Must decide directly.

The weather is mixed – was very hot – then thundered – now is cool. But the hotel anyhow is pleasant. – I can't say definitely about coming to London. If the altitude suits me *very* much, the doctors say I should stay up till end of Sept. But if it doesn't make a terrific difference to me, we shall probably come to England end August. And we *may* go to Egypt in the winter.

Hope you're all right – now I'll be all anxiety till *Lady C.* is safely delivered.

DHL

Do let Orioli know immediately you get *Lady C.*

4492. To Nancy Pearn, 27 June 1928
Text: MS UT; Unpublished.

Grand Hotel. Chexbres-sur-Vevey, Switzerland
27 June 1928

Dear Nancy Pearn

The Olley man wrote and said could he have one of the four articles this week for the *Evening News*? Naturally it's doubtful if he'll *get* it this week. But I enclose the MS of 'Insouciance' – could you have it typed and sent to him at once?[1]

Had your letter about *Eve*. I'll see if I can do a little story.[2] – By the way, did that Miss Allanah Something make any decision for her Paris magazine?

Do please keep these newspaper articles for me somewhere: I'm sure to lose them. But if 'Laura Philippine' and the other have appeared, could I see them?[3]

Your letters to the Villa Mirenda wandered on at last. Nice of you to be so pleased about my hopes of sales and Arnold Bennett's little boost.[4] But I believe I'm more likely to make my living by your 'periodical' efforts, really.

By the way, do you think the newspaper articles could be sold also to America? That would be really hot dog!!

Hot here – now today thundery. Aldous Huxley and Maria here for a few days – going back to Italy. They are a bit discouraging about London. You know Mr Olley wants me to write 'Why I don't like London!' Why London doesn't like me is more to the point. I'll send you that in a day or two – little article, I mean.[5]

D. H. Lawrence

4493. To Lady Ottoline Morrell, [27 June 1928]
Text: MS UT; PC v. Château de Chillon & les Dents du Midi; Postmark, Chexbres 27.VI.28; Unpublished.

[27 June 1928]

[   ][6] So glad to hear you are getting better – we are sipping Kirsch, above

---

[1] The essay appeared in *Evening News*, 12 July 1928, under the title 'Over-Earnest Ladies'; it was collected in *Assorted Articles* as 'Insouciance' (Roberts C171).

[2] Nancy Pearn wrote on 25 June that *Eve: The Ladies Pictorial* would welcome a short story for 'a Christmas opening' (TMSC UT).   [3] Cf. Letter 4428 and p. 400 n. 3.

[4] Bennett briefly reviewed *The Woman Who Rode Away* volume in *Evening Standard*, 7 June 1928. He commented that DHL 'can be formidably unreadable; nearly all his books have long passages of tiresomeness. But he is the strongest novelist writing today' (*D. H. Lawrence: The Critical Heritage*, ed. R. P. Draper, 1970, p. 340).

[5] 'Dull London' was published in *Evening News*, 3 September 1928 (Roberts C175). The title on DHL's MS is 'Why I Don't Like Living in London' (Roberts E107).   [6] Illegible.

Lake Leman – pity you aren't here in a flowery shawl, to sip with us. Ma speriamo.[1]

> D. H. Lawrence
> Frieda
> Maria
> Aldous

4494. To Ada Clarke, [27 June 1928]
Text: MS Clarke; Postmark, Chexbres 28.VI.28; Unpublished.

> Grand-Hotel – Chexbres-sur-Vevey, Suisse
> 27 June

My dear Sister

I had both your letters here – glad to know all goes decently well. Poor G[ertrude Cooper], if only she can live quietly and peaceably, that's enough. She can't expect to be robust. – I am pretty well – Switzerland suits me – it really is my bronchials, not my lungs. We are here only about 2000 feet up – but in July I want to move above the 3000 feet level, as that is better. The Brewsters will come with us, I think – they are here now in this hotel. Aldous and Maria Huxley are here too, but only for a day or two. They are on their way to Italy by motor. – We have just come back from Chillon – but those castle show-places bore me rather. And I don't like motoring.

The doctors say that if the 3000 feet altitude makes a real difference to me, I ought to stay three months and give it a fair chance. I must see. If I can't come to England, perhaps you can come out here. It's quite near from Paris – about nine hours – and I can pay for you.

Frieda came back from Baden on Monday night – says her mother seems older, not so chirpy. She's been having rheumatism, a new thing for her.

Hope you liked Don Carswell's book. I found it a bit *slow*.[2] Catherine seems to be in a horrid nervous and irritable state – woman of fifty! My heaven when a woman's over forty, she needs to watch herself and keep herself in shape – nervously as well as physically. So many go to pieces then. Lady Ottoline has been *very* ill with gangrene of the jaw bone. – I was glad you had a jolly birthday. I'll find you something pretty somewhere. There goes the dinner gong!

> love! DHL

---

[1] 'But let's hope so one day.' (Four individual signatures follow and the card was addressed by Maria Huxley.) [2] See Letters 4176 and p. 188 n. 3, 4221.

4495. To Giuseppe Orioli, 28 June 1928
Text: MS UCLA; cited in Moore, *Intelligent Heart* 381.

Grand Hotel. *Chexbres-sur-Vevey*, Suisse
28 June 1928

Dear Pino

Lady Chatterley came this morning, to our great excitement, and everybody thinks she looks most beautiful, outwardly. I do really think it is a handsome and dignified volume – a fine shape and proportion, and I like the terra cotta very much, and I think my phoenix is just the right bird for the cover. Now let us hope she will find her way safely and quickly to all her destinations. When you send to America, send a line to Dr McDonald, Philadelphia and to Mabel asking them to cable when they get the book: and when you send to England, the same: I already asked Koteliansky and Barbara Low to notify you immediately they receive the book. – I do hope there is no fuss. – I was wondering if you couldn't post to England by parcel post – to people like Jackson.[1] The post comes monstrous dear, – and then all the trouble of packing each book separately! My copy arrived beautifully.

What am I to do with those *vaglie* when you send them? Can I cash them here? Or must I just return them to the people who sent them, and ask for a cheque?

The Mirendas are fools, barricading the house. But I am still undecided between the two galleries. It's very nice of you to see to the business for me.

Aldous and Maria left this morning for Turin, over the Grand S. Bernard. They were very nice, but depressed, I thought, and made me a bit depressed. – Did you like Rosalind – Mrs Popham?[2] She's an old friend of ours. I am sorry we missed her. We motored to Chillon yesterday – and had tea in Montreux. I thought of Reggie. Be sure and tell him to come and see us. – Am feeling so anxious now for 'John Thomas'' safety. Brewsters send their greetings to you –

affectionately.   DHL

[1] See p. 390 n. 2.

[2] Rosalind Popham, née Thornycroft (1891–1973), friend of DHL since 1912–13. m. (1) 1913, Helton Godwin Baynes (1882–1943), divorced 1921; (2) 1926, Arthur ('Hugh') Ewart Popham. See *Letters*, v. 475 n.2.

4496. To Emily King, [28 June 1928]

Text: MS Needham; PC v. Château de Chillon & les Dents du Midi; Postmark, Chexbres 28.VI 28; Unpublished..

Chexbres-sur-Vevey.
Friday[1]

Had your letter yesterday – yes, it's a pretty place, but only about 2000 ft. – We want to move up to 3000 later. Frieda is back from Baden – said she found her mother older, getting smaller. Aldous and Maria Huxley were here for a day or two. They've just left for Italy – motoring over the Gd. St. Bernard. We motored to Chillon yesterday – quite interesting in its way. It's not very far away. The Brewsters are here – will probably move with us when we move up a bit. They are very nice. – The weather goes from hot to cold, very variable, but not unpleasant. And I'm better here than in Italy. I shall write a letter directly – hope Joan's cold is better.

Love.   DHL

4497. To Nancy Pearn, 28 June 1928

Text: MS UT; Unpublished.

Grand Hotel. Chexbres-sur-Vevey, Switzerland
28 June 1928

Dear Nancy Pearn

Here's another article for the *Evening News:*[2] I may as well get the four done: and hope they'll suit.

Sincerely   D. H. Lawrence

4498. To Enid Hilton, [28 June 1928]

Text: MS UCLA; PC v. Chexbres; Postmark, Che[x]bres 28.VI.28; Unpublished.

Grand Hotel. Chexbres-sur-Vevey, *Suisse.*
[28 June 1928]

Did you have my other cards? I've not had a word from you since you are back – but hear of you in Ripley, so know you *are* back all right. What about the pictures?[3] – It's pleasant here, but only about 2000 ft – shall go higher later. Frieda went to Baden for a week – Aldous and Maria Huxley have just left for

---

[1] The departure of the Huxleys and the visit to Chillon 'yesterday', combined with the postmark, confirm the date (as with the preceding letter) as Thursday, 28 June 1928.

[2] DHL's letter was annotated in Curtis Brown's office: 'Men Must Rule', the original title of the essay published in *Evening News*, 2 August 1928, as 'Master in His Own House' (Roberts C174, E230). It was written on this subject in response to Olley's suggestion for an article on 'Man Must Be Master Again' (letter from Nancy Pearn to DHL, 14 June 1928, TMSC UT).

[3] See Letter 4434.

Italy – they stayed a few days with us – and we have other friends, from Capri.
I'm pretty well – send me your news – how was your father?[1]

affection to both.   DHL

4499. To Giuseppe Orioli, [30 June 1928]
Text: MS UCLA; Unpublished.

Grand Hotel. Chexbres-sur-Vevey, Svizzera
Sat.

Dear Pino

Yes, it seems to me the 200 copies are all right in brochure – so you can let
Giuntina do them.[2] We must decide what we shall charge for them.

The only thing I don't quite like about *Lady C.* is the white label on the
back – it looks so staring. I wish it toned down to the cover more: wish we'd
used the same cream paper as the book is printed on.

I enclose Wells' worry.[3]

By the way, Martin Secker says he really wants three copies:

Martin Secker. 5 John St. Adelphi, London W.C.2

Did he ever fill in a form.

We went motoring to look at a place higher up, and it's given me a
headache.

Let me know if you've got the pictures. I'm almost sure I shall send them to
Dorothy Warren.

affectly.   D. H. Lawrence

4500. To Laurence Pollinger, 30 June 1928
Text: MS UT; Unpublished.

Grand Hotel. Chexbres-sur-Vevey, Switzerland
30 June 1928

Dear Pollinger

Thanks for sending off the books.

I have almost finished the second half of *Escaped Cock* – very nice – but
maybe Crosby Gaige will think it fierce and be scared of it. It's not very fierce
anyhow. Will send it along in a while.

D. H. Lawrence

---

[1] Willie Hopkin.   [2] See Letter 4444 and n. 1.
[3] The enclosure is missing and the remark is unclear.

4501. To Unidentified Recipient, 1 July 1928

Text: MS YU; Unpublished.

Grand Hotel – Chexbres-sur-Vevey
1 July 1928

Dear Sir

Aaron's Rod is not one of a series. The only sequence in my books is *The Rainbow*, and *Women in Love*: the latter is a sort of sequel to the former.

Yours faithfully   D. H. Lawrence

4502. To James Read, 2 July 1928

Text: MS YU; Unpublished.

c/o Curtis Brown – Ltd. 6 Henrietta St. *London. W.C.2*, England
2 July 1928

Dear Mr Read[1]

Thanks for your letter about the ranch at Lobo. My wife, who owns the place, says she doesn't want to sell it just now – but may later. We hope to come over before long, then we could talk about it.

Yours Sincerely   D. H. Lawrence

4503. To Giuseppe Orioli, [4 July 1928]

Text: MS UCLA; PC v. Chexbres. la Dent de Jaman & les Rochers de Naye; Postmark, Chexbres 4.VII 28; Unpublished.

[Grand Hotel, Chexbres-sur-Vevey, Suisse]
Wed

Many thanks for yours – am glad the pictures are there – have decided to send them to

Miss Dorothy Warren, The Warren Gallery. 39*a* Maddox St. *London,*
W.1.

So will you give the address to Egidi. –

We think of leaving tomorrow, to go higher up – not so very far – will let you know. The Vaglie are in Berne, and they ask where I want them paid – they must wait a bit – it is 40 dollars. But I'll send you the names immediately I have them. How is the packing and posting going? – I am very anxious the things should arrive safely. Aldous and Maria will be in Forte by now – but have not heard. Hope it's not too hot for you. Saluti to Carletto.

DHL

No great hurry about the pictures as Dorothy plans to exhibit them in October – which is a good time.

---

[1] James B. Read, manager of the First State Bank of Taos.

4504. To Giuseppe Orioli, 4 July 1928
Text: MS UCLA; cited in Moore, *Poste Restante* 96.

Grand Hotel. Chexbres-sur-Vevey, Suisse.

4 July 1928

Dear Pino

Your letter this evening – I enclose cheque for £40 sterling – Haskards will give you the Liras equivalent – and you will tell me how it goes.

We leave here Friday to look for a place higher up. Will send address. – I sent you address for pictures –

The Warren Gallery, 39a Maddox St. *London W.1*.

But no great hurry, Dorothy is not showing the pictures till October – better then.

Must go down to dinner. Hope this cheque is right, in sterling – if not send it back.

affectly   DHL

They will forward from this address all right.

4505. To Hon. Dorothy Brett, 4 July 1928
Text: MS UCin; Postmark, Chexbres 4.VII 28; Irvine, Brett 86–7.

Grand Hotel. Chexbres-sur-Vevey, Switzerland

4 July 1928

Dear Brett

Your long cable about Lawrence Gomme forwarded today from London.[1] – Damn Lawrence Gomme! – why should I answer his self-important letters?[2] He's not paid a cent for his 50 copies, so let him keep still – he's out to lose nothing.

Please don't spend money cabling *anything* – it only annoys me. I can manage this affair myself. The book is being posted by mail – we'll watch if it

---

[1]   Laurence James Gomme (1882–1974), 'Consulting Bookseller' on 5th Avenue, New York, and an expert in old and rare books. Born in England, he joined the staff of Bretano's, NY; later was first President of the Antiquarian Booksellers Association of America.

   Brett had been in touch with Gomme since at least 27 April 1928 when she wrote asking him to contact DHL: 'Will you write to him about his new book yourself and will you also help him and tell him what to do if the censor makes a fuss. I have told him you will help him if the Government interferes' (MS UN). Brett was following up the initiative taken by Mabel Luhan; they and Gomme had mutal friends in Ted and Bobbie Gillete (see p. 448 n. 3).

[2]   Gomme had written to DHL on 4 May 1928, ordering ten copies and ten for Terence Holliday; he enquired what discount he could expect and advised: 'If the book is of such a character that it could be censored at the New York port of entry it would be useless attempting to send it by freight or express' (TMSC UN). Having received no reply Gomme wrote again on 28 June; see Letter 4526 and p. 456 n. 1. On the same day he told Mabel Luhan that he had 'orders now for about 50 copies' (TMSC UN).

arrives all right – if it does Mr Gomme gets his fifty at once – if not, we'll find some other means of sending them. And Mr. Gomme can stew in his own importance. But don't bother me about him or anybody.

When Spud gets his three copies I asked him to pay you the $30 – you can pay the cable out of that. – But *don't cable* me – I hate it. There is nothing to cable about.

The same with the pictures. I am writing to Mrs Hare direct, that I can't let the pictures be in New York until November.[1] That is simple. So don't fuss there either.

DHL

4506. To Hon. Dorothy Brett, [4 July 1928]
Text: MS UCin; PC v. Chexbres. – L'Eglise et les Alpes; Postmark, C[hexb]res 4.VII 28; Irvine, Brett 87.

[Grand Hotel, Chexbres-sur-Vevey, Suisse]
4 July.

– I am sending my pictures finally to Dorothy Warren – and she is planning an exhibit for *October*: so don't let Mrs Hare fix anything for that month – the pictures will be free for November, which is the best month. But I'm not very keen on sending to New York. – Aldous and Maria were here – have gone on to Forte dei Marmi for the summer – seemed a bit depressed by London and Paris. – It is hot, and we want to move a bit higher up the mountains, all of us. I feel better here. – Am awfully sorry about Violet, but you know I can't stand *him*, at any price.[2] Do hope you have your copy of the book by now – both books![3]

DHL

4507. To Giulia Pini, [4 July 1928]
Text: MS UT; PC v. Château de Chillon & les Dents du Midi; Postmark, Chexbres 4.VII 28; Unpublished.

[Grand Hotel, Chexbres-sur-Vevey, Suisse]
4 luglio.

Cara Giulia
La tua lettera è venuta ieri sera – l'hai scritta molto bene. Sono contento che i quadri sono spediti finalmente a Londra – e che voi state tutti bene. – Ci sono stati qui gli amici di Forte dei Marmi, coll'automobile, e abbiamo fatto dei giri

[1] The letter is unlocated.
[2] Violet Murry was seriously ill with pulmonary tuberculosis; Middleton Murry had abandoned virtually all other activities in order to nurse her.
[3] *Lady Chatterley's Lover* and *The Woman Who Rode Away and Other Stories.*

– anche a questo castello sulla cartolina. Ora sono partiti per Forte – e forse ver anno alla villa. Se vengono, e vogliono stare due o tre giorni nella villa, tu farai tutto ch'è necessario.

Tanti saluti da noi due, a tutti.   D. H. Lawrence

[4 July.

Dear Giulia

Your letter arrived last night – it's very well written. I am glad that the paintings have been sent to London at last – and that you are all well. – Our friends from Forte dei Marmi have been here, with their car, and we went on some trips – also to this castle on the postcard. Now they have left for Forte – and perhaps they will come to the villa. If they come, and want to stay two or three days at the villa, you will do whatever is necessary.

Best wishes from us both, to everybody.   D. H. Lawrence]

4508. To Dorothy Warren, 4 July 1928
Text: MS UN; Nehls, iii. 224.

Grand Hotel. Chexbres-sur-Vevey, Switzerland.
4 July 1928

Dear Dorothy Warren[1]

Well I have ordered the pictures to be sent on to you – so they'll arrive in due time. They are seven – and four of them in simple wooden, painted frames. I prefer them in those frames painted to merge out the atmosphere of the picture – much better than gold or black frames. So will you let your man do the others about the same – But the water-colours, I don't mind how they are framed. – When you have the pictures, let me know how you like them. Probably you will like them better as you get used to them. They are quite simple, with no tricks: but I consider they are, what very few pictures are, organically alive and whole. All the modern smartness only succeeds in putting pictures together, it practically never makes a picture live as a whole thing.

I was sorry to break with the Claridge people – especially as they were going ahead. But October is really a better time. And then I felt they were just commercial. After all, I know you, and the thing is more personal. But you are an unstable person – you disappear and leave no trace, you don't answer letters when you say you will, everybody says you are going bust, and altogether it's like riding to the moon on a soap-bubble. But do be wise for a little while longer. – I didn't put any price on the pictures – must think about

[1] DHL was responding to Dorothy Warren's letter, 26 June: see pp. 434–5 n. 2.

it. What would you suggest? – I'm not anxious at all to sell the big ones – I have only those seven – but the little ones I care less about.

The Brewsters have about twenty pictures in Lucille Beckett's – Lucille Frost's charge, at Marble Arch. I wish you would look at them and show them when there is a chance. I'm sure they are better than most people's pictures.

Well – please let me know when the pictures come – I am having carriage paid in advance – and how you like them. Don't lapse into the void, or I shall have to come over to London and rescue the things.

all good wishes   D. H. Lawrence

4509. To Laurence Pollinger, 4 July 1928
Text: MS UT; Unpublished.

Grand Hotel. Chexbres-sur-Vevey, Switzerland
4 July 1928

Dear Pollinger

Thanks for sending on that cable – but if only folks wouldn't fuss! Why can't Mr. Gomme sit still and wait for his 50 copies – he's not paid for them, so he loses nothing. Damn busybodies!

We're moving a bit higher up the mountains on Friday – very hot here.

Sincerely   D. H. Lawrence

4510. To George Macy, 5 July 1928
Text: MS UT; Unpublished.

c/o Curtis Brown Ltd. 6 Henrietta St. *London W.C. 2*
5 July 1928

Dear Mr Macy

I had your cable today. – The first copies of *Lady Chatterley* are already sent off to America – but not many. What I can do is to guarantee that, if you publish a limited edition in New York, not more than two hundred of my edition shall come to America – that is, only those copies that are already paid for. The unpaid-for orders I need not fulfil, but the others I must, having begun.

If you want to go on with this, will you please consult Rich of [Curtis Brown's office.][1]

If you decide to go on with your limited edition, will you please cable to that effect to Orioli – his address is (telegraphic)

AVORIOLOR – FIRENZE

---

[1] MS torn (for Rich see p. 222 n. 1).

I will tell him not to send to America more than 200 copies of the book, before July 25th. And you can write me c/o him:

c/o G. Orioli, 6 Lungarno Corsini, *Florence.*

or else to Curtis Brown, as above.

4511. To Giuseppe Orioli, [5 July 1928]
Text: MS UCLA; Unpublished.

Grand Hotel. *Chexbres-sur-Vevey*, Svizzera
Friday[1]

Dear Pino

Your espresso just come. The Macy Masius people are publishers who want to get hold of some of my work. – I have answered them, I cannot withhold my edition entirely from America, as the first copies are sent off: but that, if they wish to publish a limited edition of *Lady C.* in America, I will guarantee that *not more than two hundred copies* of my edition shall be sent to that country. This will allow us to send all that are paid for – and will leave us a free hand as far as England is concerned. I ask them to wire you their answer.

Now as to mailing. Will you send a copy[2] *at once* to:

1. Dr. E. D. McDonald, Philadelphia
1. Harold T. Mason. The Centaur Bookshop. Philadelphia
1. Alfred A. Knopf. New York
1. F. E. Gillett. N. York[3]
1. Lawrence Gomme – New York (he ordered 50 copies, unpaid)
1. Alfred Stieglitz. New York
1. Witter Bynner. Santa Fe.

and I will send a note to all of them except Stieglitz, (I haven't got his address) asking them to wire you the moment the book arrives. I[4] enclose a note to him.

Then I think you might send three or four copies every day to America, especially to the Philadelphia people – copies that are paid for, of course. We must take some risk.

Then send to England to people we know, who are not likely to talk – and to people like Dulau. Send as soon as possible: we must get the thing going.

Send also to Anna di Chiara, Capri, her five copies: and to Mabel Harrison in Paris: and the Beveridges in England or Scotland – we can ask them to wire. Though Paris is safe. Anyhow let's get started.

---

[1] In view of the following four letters, all written after this to Orioli and dated 5 July 1928, it is presumed that DHL wrote 'Friday' (instead of Thursday) in error.   [2] a copy] extra copies
[3] Frederick ('Ted') W. Gillete, husband of Bobbie, née Hawk (p. 311 n. 2).
[4] arrives. I] Will you write a word to Stieglitz – or I (For the 'note' see the letter following, posted in Florence by Orioli.)

I sent you £40 sterling on Haskard[1] – hope they cash it all right for you.

This in haste.   DHL

4512. To Alfred Stieglitz, 5 July 1928
Text: MS YU; Postmark, Firenze 7.VII 28; Unpublished.

Grand Hotel. *Chexbres-sur-Vevey*. Suisse
5 July 1928

Dear Alfred Stieglitz

We are mailing you a copy of *Lady Chatterley* today.[2] Would it be too much to ask you, when you receive it, to send a telegram to Orioli – whose telegraphic address is

AVORIOLOR.   FIRENZE.

just saying: *Received.*

I should be infinitely obliged – and then we should know the book was coming in all right.

I hope to see you before long – we want to come to America, to that little ranch.

greetings!   D. H. Lawrence

4513. To Harold Mason, 5 July 1928
Text: MS (Photocopy) UT; *Centaur* 34.

6 Lungarno Corsini. Florence.
5 July 1928.

Dear Mason

We are mailing your copy of *Lady Chatterley* today – when you get it, would you be so good as to wire *Received* to Orioli. – His telegraphic address is

AVORIOLOR. – FIRENZE

I am so anxious to know the book arrives safely.

I was awfully grateful to you for getting me orders and being so kind about this venture. Let's hope we pull it off.

Sincerely   D. H. Lawrence[3]

---

[1] Cf. Letter 4504.

[2] Stieglitz was among the earliest American subscribers: he paid $20 in cash on 25 April 1928 ('Memoranda', MS NWU).

[3] Mason replied on 31 July 1928 (TMSC Mason):

Dear Lawrence:

By this time, you have heard from McDonald the story of what befell the two copies of LADY CHATTERLEY'S LOVER. So far as we know, the copy addressed to me reposes in the hoosegow [jail]. I have not been notified officially of its arrest but the fact that McDonald has had his copy for ten days is proof enough of what transpired.

4514. To Edward McDonald, 5 July 1928
Text: MS UT; Postmark, Ch[ex]br[e]s 5.VII 28; *Centaur* 34.

6 Lungarno Corsini. Florence.[1]

5 July 1928

Dear McDonald

We are sending off your copy of *Lady Chatterley* today. Would you be so good as to wire Orioli when you get it, so we know the book is coming in. His telegraphic address is

AVORIOLOR. FIRENZE

– and just say *Received*.

I am most anxious the thing should arrive safely.

Sincerely   D. H. Lawrence

You have been too courageous for our timid and dove-like postal inspectors who have been scared stiff by the naughty words you employed. It is, really, too sickening but I know the devils and know them well and there isn't the remotest chance, at least as far as Philadelphia is concerned, of getting the book through direct. You would simply be throwing them away at great expense and we, on the other hand, would find ourselves in difficulty if copies were addressed to the Centaur Book Shop. Nor do I think that we could count upon a sufficient percentage of copies percolating through to private addresses. There is only one thing to do as far as we are concerned. If our allotment can be got into the hands of our English agent, William Jackson, 18 Took's Court, Cursiter Street, Chancery Lane, London, E.C.4, he will give a parcel of them into the hands of our very good friend on the American Merchant, who will see that they are brought over customs and mailed us quite innocently enough from New York. It will take months to get twenty-five (25) copies over but I do not know of a better way unless you do. It may be that copies addressed to Professor McDonald would be regarded leniently by the customs or it may be that his copy came through on a fluke. We shall probably never know unless the experiment is tried again but I am exceedingly pessimistic and this feeling is the result of tackling customs officials and postal inspectors for six years. I know the way their minds work and I am without hope of ever persuading them that an honest and fearless piece of work is not simply a dirty piece of obscenity (if there is such a thing).

I hope you can get them into England without any trouble whatever because this will mean that eventually we shall have them. I am sorry that my views are so pessimistic but I cannot feel otherwise. Do let me know what you will do. We have many people who are waiting for the book and somehow they must not be disappointed.

I am very anxious to read it and will borrow McDonald's copy, giving up hope of owning one myself for the present.

To this Orioli replied on 17 August 1928 expressing surprise that only one copy had arrived since he posted three on 7 July (one to McDonald) and three on 10 July, all to the Philadelphia area; eight were posted on 25 July (including one each to David Jester and Mason himself) and eleven more on 28 July. Orioli continued: 'If all these copies are undelivered, do you think we could get them back from U.S. Customs? Anyhow I have sent your letter to Lawrence. The book in England has gone very well and all copies order have been delivered without any trouble. Also in some other part of the U.S. the book has passed through undisturbed . . .'

[1] 6 . . . Florence] Grand Hotel – Chexbres-sur-Vevey – Suisse

4515. To Laurence Gomme, 5 July 1928
Text: MS UN; Unpublished.

> 6 Lungarno Corsini. Florence.
> 5 July 1928

Dear Mr Gomme

We are mailing you a copy of *Lady Chatterley* today, registered. Would you be so kind as to send a cable, deferred, when you get it. The telegraphic address is

> AVORIOLOR. FIRENZE

and you would just say: *Received.* – Then your other copies will follow on: I hope all quite safely.

> Yours Sincerely   D. H. Lawrence

4516. To Earl Brewster, [6 July 1928]
Text: MS UT; PC v. Gstaad (1053 m.); Postmark, Gsta[ad] 6.VI [. . .]; Unpublished.

> *Hotel National.* Gstaad.
> Friday

Came into showery rain here – and a clap of thunder – place quite pleasant in a small touristy way – the air really fresh and good – hotel not so nice as yours, but all right – 10 frs. Hotels not at all full – few people here – but no chalet in sight as yet – I believe it's going to be a bit difficult to find what we want – however, we'll scout round tomorrow and let you know – now it rains!

> Hope you're all gay.   DHL

4517. To Earl Brewster, [7 July 1928]
Text: MS UT; PC; Postmark, Gs[taad] 7 VII [. . .]; Unpublished.

> *Gsteig bei Gstaad.*
> *Sat.*

Came here this morning and have steadily hunted for chalets. I think we have a small one for ourselves, about a mile out – we settle it finally tomorrow, but I think we shall take it. There is another one still, across the valley, that we can look at tomorrow for you, but I'm afraid it's small – We have asked at the hotels – the Bear is full – the Sanetsch, rather small, not elegant, will give you three small rooms, quite nice, one with balcony – and tea included, for 9 francs. The other hotel, the Victoria, newer, rather smarter, but of course not big, will give you one double and one single room, balconies – quite nice – pension 9 frs *without* tea – they wouldn't give it in. – This is a little place, about 4000 feet, pretty, bits of snow not far above – and lovely fresh air. The air really is good – I've walked such a lot. It's about 8 miles from Gstaad. –

Will you write *at once* to me in Hotel National. Gstaad, and say what you will do. We have said we will come out on Tuesday to our chalet, if we fix up tomorrow – which I suppose we shall. – You might even get Madame to telephone a message to us tomorrow evening or Monday morning – as you like – or just write. – You can have a taxi meet you at Gstaad station – but I doubt it won't get your trunks on. – Don't take *too* much hand luggage, very little room in that electric train from Montreux. – Hope I've said all clearly.

DHL

I think better the Victoria.

4518. To Earl and Achsah Brewster, [8 July 1928]
Text: MS UT; Brewster 172–3.

Hotel National. *Gstaad.*

Sunday evening

Dear Earl and Achsah

We have decided to go out to the chalet tomorrow, Monday evening, at six oclock – it saves another day in this dull hotel. We went to Gsteig this morning and fixed up. The chalet must be about a mile from Gsteig village, and climbing up all the way, alas – I panted, but it wasn't so bad – a most lovely morning. We picnicked out there – it's quite a pleasant little place, with kitchen and a good-sized living room, (good-sized for here, that is) and a goodsized bedroom downstairs – and one room, which I didn't see, upstairs. We pay 300 frs. for the ' Season' – which is till middle or end Sept. – not dear, but quite enough, for what it is. Yesterday we saw a *very* nice chalet – but alas, it had been let for three weeks *the very day before* – and it was charming, and big enough for us all. – I want Achsah to see ours before we look at anything for you – she may find it too peasanty and primitive, and may prefer the hotel. She's hardly a chalet person. – It's quite high up, 4000 ft and more – the upper world – rather lovely – has a bit of the Greater Day atmosphere.[1] The people *seem* very nice – perfectly simple and naïve – poor as mice – odd. – They were straining the honey in our barn – you'll eat some.

Well I expect you'll write or telephone before we leave. If you arrive Tuesday at mid-day – same train we took – and if we know, one of us will try to come in to meet you. The Hotel Viktoria will send in their motor, if they know in time – and they can perhaps get all your luggage on. Otherwise the post

---

[1] Almost certainly an allusion to his story 'The Flying-Fish' which DHL would read to the Brewsters during their stay in Gsteig (see Brewster 288). The beauty and timelessness of the 'Greater Day' are evoked by a quotation from the *Book of Days* compiled by an ancestor of the story's principal character (*St. Mawr and Other Stories*, ed. Brian Finney, Cambridge, 1983, p. 209).

autobus leaves the station for Gsteig at about 2.0 oclock – you could eat at the hotel next the station, if you had to wait for that bus.

Would you mind asking Madame to cash this cheque for me, and you bring me the money. – If you aren't coming, ask the porter to post it to me in a registered letter – I'll send you the stamps. And please give this note with address to the porter – I ask him to give my mail to you to bring, if you are coming.

We have only seen Gsteig on sunny days, and it's lovely then – I hope you won't hate it, if it rains.

au revoir to you all.   DHL

The address is: Kesselmatte. *Gsteig bei Gstaad.*

The altitude gets me a bit – one will have to go softly.

4519. To Giuseppe Orioli, [8 July 1928]

Text: MS NWU; PC; Postmark, Gstaad 9.VII.28; Unpublished.

Kesselmatte, Gsteig bei Gstaad, Bernese Oberland. Svizzera
Sunday.

Dear Pino

We have taken a little chalet high up here – about 4000 feet – not very much below the snow. It is very pretty, and cheap – but rather lonely, and we've only seen it on sunny days. I hope we shan't want to die, if bad weather comes. – The Brewsters are still in Chexbres – I don't know if they will join us. – The altitude makes my chest a bit sore and gasping – but it's bound to do so at first.

I have written now to Chexbres for the post to be sent on – am so anxious to hear about *Lady C.* and her carryings on. Let me have a line. Pity you can't come here – it's about $2\frac{1}{2}$ hours from Montreux, but on the north side, German speaking.

Grüsse   DHL

4520. To Nancy Pearn, [9 July 1928]

Text: MS Lazarus; PC; Postmark, [Gst]eig 9 VII 28; Unpublished.

Kesselmatte, Gsteig b. Gstaad (Bern), Switzerland
[9 July 1928]

So, we've made another move – taken a little peasant chalet here on the mountain, till end of September. – so I suppose this is the address for the summer. The place is about 4000 ft. high – and quite lovely to look at, among the tops of the mountains. But so far we've had fine weather – if it pours with rain, which God forbid, I hope we shan't die of gloom. There are still quite lovely flowers up here: the snow isn't so very far above. Perhaps I can do an

Eve story among the mountains – a new line for me.[1] – I've not had my mail
for some days, so don't know if there's anything to answer. But I get it
tomorrow. I must do the fourth of the *Evening News* articles – I did the third –
will send it along.[2] – Where are you going for your holiday this year? – and
when? I hope it'll be a jolly one. There aren't many visitors in this region yet,
but by end of the month everywhere will be full up.

Yrs   D. H. Lawrence

4521. To Earl Brewster, [9 July 1928]

Text: MS UT; PC v. Gstaad b. Gstaad. Spitzhorn & Sanetschpass; Postmark, G[staad] 9
VII.[. . .]; Unpublished.

[Kesselmatte, Gsteig b. Gstaad, Switzerland]
Monday morning

Your letter and message both this morning – the motor of the Viktoria will be
there at 12.0 on Wednesday, then – and Frieda too, I expect – I shall stay on
my mountain because of the climb – but great fun to see you.

DHL

4522. To Enid Hilton, [9 July 1928]

Text: MS UCLA; PC v. Gstaad (1053 m.); Postmark, [. . .] 10 VII 28; cited in Moore, *Poste
Restante* 96.

Kesselmatte, Gsteig b. Gstaad (Bern)
Monday

Well we've left the Grand Hotel, and in contrast got a little peasant chalet here
quite alone, high up on the mountain 4000 ft. – and a mile away from the
village. We only came in at teatime, now it's nightfall, and feels queer, like
being in another world. – So glad to hear of your move up too.

Will write.   DHL

4523. To Emily King, [9 July 1928]

Text: MS Needham; PC v. Gsteig b. Gstaad. Spitzhorn & Sanetschpass; Postmark, [. . .];
Unpublished.

Kesselmatte, Gsteig b. Gstaad (Bern)
Monday.

We came here at tea-time – and now it's nightfall – we have taken a little
peasant chalet to ourselves, away on the mountain about a mile from the
village – and 4000 ft up. It's very lovely – only I hope the weather will stay

---

[1] See Letter 4550 and n. 1.   [2] See Letter 4531 and p. 461 n. 1.

good, or we shall be forlorn souls. But the Brewsters are coming to stay in
Gsteig village. I shall write you properly now.

DHL

4524. To Ada Clarke, [9 July 1928]

Text: MS Clarke; PC v. Gsteig b. Gstaad. Spitzhorn & Sanetschpass; Postmark, [. . .];
Lawrence–Gelder 178–9.

Kesselmatte, *Gsteig b. Gstaad* (Bern)
Monday.

We have been very bold, taken a little peasant chalet away up on the mountain,
4000 ft – we two alone – the peasants have moved across to their hay hut across
the valley. We only came this afternoon – now it's the first evening, and feels
queer. The Brewsters are coming to stay in Gsteig village, about a mile away,
in the hotel. When do you go to the sea?

DHL

4525. To Martin Secker, [9 July 1928]

Text: MS UInd; PC v. Gsteig b. Gstaad. Spitzhorn & Sanetschpass; Postmark, [. . .]; Secker
108.

Kesselmatte, *Gsteig b. Gstaad* (Bern)
Monday

We have been very bold – taken a little peasant chalet on the Pillon pass, about
4000 ft up – F[rieda] and I alone – and now we want to sit here for a month or
two to see if it won't make a new man of me. It's quite lovely to look at – snow
not far above – but a wee bit rough and perhaps a bit alone. We only came this
evening – now there's the last flush on the rocks above, and it's rather chilly.
How are you all?

DHL

4526. To Giuseppe Orioli, 11 July 1928

Text: MS UCLA: cited in Moore, *Intelligent Heart* 384.

Kesselmatte, *Gsteig b. Gstaad* (Bern), Svizzera
Wed. 11 July 1928

Dear Pino

I had your letter of 7th today, and the two cheques (Whittmore, and
Norton).[1] You forgot the bordereau for the £40 in Liras – send it when you

---

[1] Thomas Whittmore (£2) and E. Lucy Norton (£2-2-0) are recorded in DHL's 'Memoranda'
(MS NWU); nothing further is known of them.

write, so I keep a check on everything. – I had a cheque £2. from Maria, and one £4. from Aldous – both dated April!!

Will you answer this Gomme man![1] What a bore he is!

I do hope the books all arrive safely – it'll be so thrilling to know that the people get them.

It is so quiet up here – and quite lovely, alone in our own little chalet 4000 ft. up. – Tell Reggie Montreux is very hot just now.

tante cose!   D. H. Lawrence

4527. To Emily King, [11 July 1928]
Text: MS Lazarus; Unpublished.

Kesselmatte, Gsteig b. Gstaad (Bern).
Wed

My dear Pamela

Well here we are, settled in in our little chalet – and most of the time alone. The woman and girl go off to the hay at 4.0 in the morning,[2] and come in in the early evening – then they wash up for us and do the evening meal – more or less. It's a very pretty place – I wish you could see it. Would you venture to come for a fortnight if I sent you the money? We have a room upstairs you could have. But it's rather a long journey.

I think it's going to do me good. At first the altitude, 4000 ft, makes one feel a bit queer – but one gets used to it. And the long days so still and clean are lovely. They made me a table and seat under the pine-trees, so there I sit in the mornings, and try to paint a bit. But I am too[3] hazy yet to get anything done.

The Brewsters arrived today – they are staying in the hotel. They would like to find a chalet too, so I suppose Frieda will hunt with them, as they don't speak a word of German – and it is German here – Over the pass, about eight miles, is Diablerets, and it's French there. I don't go very far because of the climbing – its all up and down, and I simply gasp going uphill. I do hope that will get better.

---

[1] Gomme's letter, 28 June 1928 (TMSC UN) had reached DHL via Curtis Brown's London office. He reminds DHL of his earlier letter, 4 May (see p. 444 n. 2) to which he had received no reply; he increases Holliday's order to fifteen copies; and he asks when the book is likely to be published. Gomme concludes: 'Mr. Gillett sent you an order in April for a copy to be sent to him personally and I believe enclosed a check for the full amount of the book. He and Mrs. Gillett send you their regards and hope to have the pleasure of seeing you on your way through to Taos.'
    Orioli responded on 23 July (MS UN) on DHL's behalf. He told Gomme that an initial batch of four copies had gone to Holliday and six to himself. 'In a few days I shall send a few more parcels untill order is complete.'   [2] Frau Kathe and Lena Trachsl (cf. Letter 4530).
[3] MS reads: 'to'.

I don't know what your plans are for the holiday – will you go to the sea with Joan? – or will you boldly set out and come here? You must do as you really wish. Anyway I enclose five pounds towards the holiday fund.

We've taken this place till end Sept – and probably if it really suits me, we shall stay on. I must try to get my bronchials healed a bit. – But I am having an exhibition of my pictures in a private Gallery in London in October – and they say I ought to be there. I don't care much either way – but probably we shall come to England at the end of September for a week or two. If only my health were better, I'd be there now. I don't particularly *want* to be in Switzerland. But the doctors say this is where I ought to be – so we'll try it. – I really want to try to get rid of this beastly cough – it's no worse – and no danger in it – but it is such a nuisance.

love.   DHL

4528. To Ada Clarke, [11 July 1928]
Text: MS Clarke; Postmark, Gsteig 12 VII 28; Unpublished.

'Kesselmatte', *Gsteig b. Gstaad* (Bern), Switzerland
Wed

My dear Sister

Well we've been two days in our little chalet, and it's very nice – so still, and so peaceful with the quiet of the high mountains. I'm beginning to feel a bit adjusted this evening – the altitude affects me for the first day or two. But now I seem to be more *here* – and I think we ought to be all right. It's a nice chalet, with balconies, and a kitchen, and a very nice big living room – then one bedroom downstairs, and one up. I wish you could have come, it is such real mountain upland, quite lovely in its way. We are not more than eight or nine miles from Diablerets – but over the Pillon Pass – Here everything is German – Diablerets is all French. I really prefer the German side – it's fresher. Chexbres, lovely as it was, was stuffy and rather enervating.

We've taken the house till end September, and if it suits me I suppose I must stay. I do so want to get rid of my tormenting cough – and the doctors say I should stay up at this altitude for three months, without going down. Not that I believe infallibly in doctors – but one may as well give it a try. I want to come to England end of September, to see you all – and then Dorothy Warren is giving a private show of my pictures in her gallery off Bond St. in October – and I might be there the first day.

I asked Pamela if she'd like to come out for a fortnight – if she seems to fancy it, just give her a shove. I sent her £5, and I'd send her the rest of the fare – it would cost her nothing here. But don't bother her unless she's up and doing. I'm sorry you can't come – I suppose you won't – Anyhow I'll see you this autumn.

The Brewsters arrived today, like fluttered chickens. They are staying in the hotel in Gsteig – about a mile away – but alas, a steep mile, and I cant climb. But they'll be out here every day. – And there's a peasant woman and girl to do the washing up and the rough work, so we're by no means lonely.

I'm glad you're having a sensible quiet three weeks at Mablethorpe – much better than your crowds. I do hope it'll be good weather. – I enclose the two quid for the Children – their holiday allowance – and two quid for you, anything you might fancy.

Love   DHL

4529. To S. S. Koteliansky, 12 July 1928
Text: MS BL; Postmark, Gsteig 13.VII.28; Zytaruk 346–7.

Kesselmatte, *Gsteig b. Gstaad* (Bern)
12 July 1928

My dear Kot

Well here we are, having made a new move – this time into a little peasant chalet on the mountain about a mile above Gsteig village – and not many miles – six or seven – from Diablerets, but on the other side of the Pillon Pass. It's very peaceful, the stillness of the high mountains – and the people, the peasants, seem very nice – more alive than the French Swiss round Chexbres. We've got the place till end Sept. – and I really ought to stay and not come down – it's about 4000 ft – and really see if I can't cure my cough which is still a curse – though I'm pretty well in myself. But I can't climb hills either. I think I can be quite happy here for a while, drifting around in the meadows and the pine woods. I like to be a good deal alone. And we're not by any means isolated – our friends the Brewsters, from Capri – who were with us in Ceylon – are staying in the hotel in Gsteig village, and they come up. So let's hope I really can get better, I'm so sick of not being well.

I want to come to England end of September – Dorothy Warren is going to show my pictures in early October – and I want to see my sisters and everybody. I'm not sure what we shall do in the winter. Have you seen Dobrée? is he in London?

Have you got your copy of the novel? – Orioli is sending them out. I am so anxious to know they arrive. – I don't suppose you'll like the book – but never mind – every man his own say, and some things must be said.

Will you stay in the cave all summer –? and Sonia and Grisha and Ghita? –

Where will they be going? – How alone you will be, even foxless![1] Imagine that that young rascal should now be only a memory!

I hear Murry is writing again to Brett – lamentoso – and she is inviting him out, en famille, to New Mexico. – Do you have any news of him?

A thunderstorm, and massive rain suddenly! How are you?

DHL

Orioli sends out the books twenty or so a day, as they come from the binder. If we sent a great mass at once, they are much more likely to be held up and inspected by the authorities. A few at a time should pass unnoticed, especially if nobody raises their voice.

4530. To Juliette Huxley, 12 July 1928
Text: MS Huxley; Moore 1067–8.

Kesselmatte, *Gsteig b. Gstaad* (Bern).

12 July 1928

My dear Juliette

At last I can send you a line and a sort of address. We hunted round from Chexbres for somewhere to go – it was nice there, but not high enough, too hot. At last we are settled in here – in a nice little peasant chalet on the mountain about a mile from Gsteig village, about 4000 ft. up and I suppose about four or five miles from where we picnicked on the Pillon pass in February: in all the snow! Now the buses run over! I think this side is nicer than the Diablerets side, fresher, more unspoilt. Gsteig is quite small and quite charming, and not so very dear. We pay 100 frs. a month for this chalet – nice big rooms – that is, a kitchen, a good-sized living-room and bedroom downstairs, and another bedroom upstairs. There are two rooms upstairs, but in one they store their things – the peasants. At present they are supposed to be living in their other chalet across on the north side, with the cows. But the woman, Frau Trachsl, appears about tea-time and sleeps here with the Lena, her adopted girl of fourteen. But I don't mind, they are very nice, and like to do anything we want. The people here really seem nice, not greedy at all.

Maria and Aldous called at Chexbres with the car for three days. They were very nice, but I thought they seemed a bit depressed. Now however they will be cheered up – Maria writes very gaily from Forte, so they'll be all right.

We've got our friends the Brewsters, from Capri – we were with them in Ceylon – staying in the hotel in the village. They come trudging up to see us – I haven't descended yet to Gsteig, since we came in, because of the climb

[1] See Letter 4374 and n. 3.

back. Of course there are no level walks – but I potter around among the trees, and they have made me a little table and bench where I sit and dibble away at a painting of men catching horses – just a little thing.[1] Now there's just been a thunderstorm and an hours heavy rain – which the peasants badly wanted – so now there's that wet peace in the world, of the dripping pine trees. – It seems very near to Diablerets – not only in miles – I almost feel that Eve is waiting for me to put a few stitches in her arm, and that we are going to have your mothers jam and wurst for tea.[2] Instead of which I'm having a cup all by myself – Frieda is thinning by abstaining.

Have you got your copy of the novel? – You ought to have it by now. I think it is very appropriate that I should be on this mountain when it arrives in the world – it was on this mountain I launched the very first launching of it.[3] – And I feel so safe up here, from all the slings and arrows that will come back at me.

We've taken this house till[4] end Sept. – if we stay so long. I want to come to England then. Dorothy Warren is giving a show of my pictures beginning Oct. – she's got the small ones now – call and tell her to show them you!

Lively remembrances from us both, also to Julian.

DHL

Do go and see my pictures – Maddox St. – if it amuses you – 7 water-colors and 4 oils – small.

When are you going away?

I still can't climb hills – *must* stay here and try and get my cough better.

4531. To Nancy Pearn, 12 July 1928
Text: MS UT; Unpublished.

Kesselmatte. *Gsteig b. Gstaad* (Bern)
12 July 1928

Dear Nancy Pearn

Thanks for yours – and for *T.P.'s* with 'Laura Phillipine'. What a rag of a paper, *T.P.'s*! And how solemn Aldous, on the first page![5] And then: 'Is God Good?' I suppose it depends.

I enclose the other two articles for the *Evening News*. If Mr Olley doesn't like them, let him not print them. One doesn't want to force him against his taste – the latter being a purely mysterious quality.

---

[1] Cf. Letters 4593, 4641 and p. 549 n. 2.   [2] Cf. Letter 4328 and n. 4, p. 314 n. 3.
[3] Cf. Letters 4321 ('All is ready! We can begin'), 4323 and 4324, all written from Les Diablerets.
[4] till] for
[5] Cf. Letter 4428 and n. 3. A picture of Huxley accompanies his article, 'What To Teach Our Boys'. Following the article (on p. 330) is a column headed, 'Is God Good?', which consists of readers' replies to an earlier piece with that title.

I do think the Americans should have had a look at 'Laura Philippine' – it's the kind of thing they like – *Vanity Fair* might have done it.

Sudden thunder here in these mountains, and a head full of electricity.

Yrs   D. H. Lawrence

Enc. 'Matriarchy' and 'Ownership': please have them typed and sent over to the *Evening News*.[1]

4532. To Giuseppe Orioli, [13 July 1928]
Text: MS UCLA; Unpublished.

Kesselmatte, *Gsteig b. Gstaad* (Bern)
Friday

Dear Pino

I enclose the order for *three* from

Mrs. Christine Hughes. *Santa Fe*, New Mexico.

I also enclose her cheque and the other for $10.[2] When you go into Haskards, will you put these to my *Lira* account?

I hope you are sending off the parcels to England as fast as possible – and that everything is going well. What a relief it will be when all are gone!

You are only sending to America those that are *paid for*, aren't you?

Ever   DHL

4533. To Harry Crosby, 13 July 1928
Text: MS SIU; Postmark, Gsteig 14 VII 28; Huxley 737.

Kesselmatte, *Gsteig b. Gstaad* (Bern), Switzerland
13 July 1928

Dear Harry Crosby

I had yours from Venice – glad you are sunning yourself. We are up here in a peasant chalet, to get my cough better – and propose to stay till end Sept., if we don't get too bored.

I just heard that a person Miss Allanah Harper has accepted your little foreword article – called 'Chaos in Modern Poetry' – for her new magazine which is to start in Paris in October, – and be devoted to international literature or something of the sort.[3] I think her mag. appears quarterly – or 6

---

[1] 'Matriarchy' was published in *Evening News*, 5 October 1928 with the title, 'If Women Were Supreme'; it was collected under DHL's original title in *Assorted Articles* (Roberts C177). 'Ownership' was rejected by Olley (cf. Letter 4725) and was unpublished until its inclusion in *Assorted Articles*.

[2] In his 'Memoranda' (MS NWU) DHL recorded the $30 from Christine Hughes immediately followed by Maria Cristina Chambers's cheque for $10.

[3] The news about the acceptance of the article reached DHL in Nancy Pearn's letter, 9 July 1928 (TMSC UT); 'Chaos in Poetry' was published in English and French in *Echanges*, December 1929 (Roberts C194).

monthly – and the second number is to be all French – the 3rd all German –
the 5th no doubt Lattvian or one of the 'coming' languages – and the 20th
probably Hittite. Anyhow is October all right? and do you want to
communicate with the lady? – I've lost her address, but you can get her
    c/o Curtis Brown Ltd. Magazine Dept. 6 Henrietta St. London W.C.
I think her 'version' is again a little different from yours – and I think better –
and I don't believe I mentioned the 4 Seas; or is it 7 Seas? When does your
book appear? – *Write and tell her.*

    Don't bother with the *Sun* story unless you feel quite determined about it. –
If you do, tell me how many copies you propose to print, when, where, and
how much, and I'll write to Seck[er] and Knopf for their respective
permissions.[1] They'll probably want to fleece *you* if you write. – I'll do a sun
graph if I can. What else?

    Your copy of *Lady Chatterley* was sent to Paris end of last week, I hear.
Have you got it? I hope so.

    I send this to Paris, as you put no address on your letter, and I can't address
you c/o The Sun. It may even be raining in Venice – as here, with thunder. – I
wish I was well.

                                                                    D. H. Lawrence

4534. To Maria Huxley, [13 July 1928]
Text: Huxley 736.

                                                        Kesselmatte, Gsteig b. Gstaad.
                                                                        Friday evening.

The [Brewsters][2] came to tea and [Achsah] as near being in a real temper as
ever I've seen her. She said: I don't know how it (the place) makes you feel,
but I've lost *all* my *cosmic consciousness* and *all* my *universal love*. I feel I don't
care one bit about *humanity*. – I said: Good for you [Achsah]! – but it was as if
another horse-fly had bit her.

    So now you know what's wrong with Switzerland, why you can't stand it,
and why it's good for health.

4535. To Giuseppe Orioli, [15 July 1928]
Text: MS UCLA; PC v. Gsteig b. Gstaad & Mittaghorn; Unpublished.

                                        [Kesselmatte, Gsteig b. Gstaad, Switzerland]
                                                                            Sunday

Thanks for yours enclosing bordereaux and one cheque. Yes, do give a copy to

[1] See p. 404 n. 3.   [2] See p. 326 n. 3.

Giglioli, with my compliments.[1] – I hope the other 25 books are in England now: if they are, try one parcel, parcel post, on Jackson or some bookseller you know. It will make it much easier for you if you can send parcels with five copies. – Been hot even here, but today a lot of rain and thunder, and turned colder. So perhaps the weather has changed. – I haven't quite got used to the place yet – and to the altitude – hope it'll do me real good when I have. The Brewsters come to see us, else we'd be a bit lonely on this mountain.

DHL

4536. To Martin Secker, 17 July 1928
Text: MS UInd; Postmark, Gsteig 18.VII.28; Secker 109.

Kesselmatte, *Gsteig b. Gstaad* (Bern)
17 July 1928

Dear Secker

Your letter today, and the *Illus. News*, for which many thanks. Am glad you are having a good time down in Norwich. Here the altitude has got me a bit, so I'm lying low till it's adjusted.

About the poems – you know I hate signing copies. Besides, if I sign a hundred, and you get one guinea[2] extra for each one, of which you give me 15% – then you make 85 guineas, and I 15 guineas, just for the signature – which isn't good enough. Of course I know there's bookseller's commission – but I guess you'd sell a fair number direct. No, it's not good enough. At the price, I'd rather not sign any. If I sign any, we must divide the proceeds of the signing – else let them go unsigned.[3]

Yrs   D. H. Lawrence

4537. To Nancy Pearn, 17 July 1928
Text: MS UT; Unpublished.

Kesselmatte, *Gsteig b. Gstaad* (Bern)
17 July 1928

Dear Nancy Pearn

Here is the review for *Vogue*.[4] But for disappointing you in your efforts on

---

[1] See Letter 4065 and n. 2.   [2] one guinea] two guineas
[3] In addition to the ordinary edn, Secker issued a special edn of *Collected Poems* (also in September 1928): 100 copies each signed by DHL, at two guineas.
[4] Nancy Pearn told DHL on 11 July 1928 (TMSC UT) that *Vogue* (London) had invited him to write a review article on four books sent under separate cover. She asked him to remember that *Vogue* was 'a terribly refined and pleasant journal'. The review appeared in *Vogue*, 20 July 1928; the books reviewed were: Robert Byron, *The Station: Athos, Treasures and Men*; Clough William-Ellis, *England and the Octopus*; Maurice Baring, *Comfortless Memory*; W. Somerset Maugham, *Ashenden, or The British Agent* (Roberts C172).

my behalf, I wouldn't have done it – for they were a dull lot of books – except *Athos.*

Tell them they can cut it down if they want.

And I could never rise to the fatuous idiocy of Humbert Wolf, whoever he is.[1] Imagine their sending me him as a pattern! Tell them to go to simpering simpleton's hell.

D. H. Lawrence

You remember they want this stuff by 20th.[2]

4538. To Giulia Pini, [18 July 1928]
Text: MS UT; PC v. Landschaft bei Gsteig; Postmark, G[steig] 18.[. . .]; Unpublished.

Gsteig b. Gstaad – Svizzera.

18 luglio

Cara Giulia –

Faceva molto caldo laggiù al lago, dove eravamo – siamo venuti più in alto sulla montagna, a più di mille metri, ed abbiamo preso una piccola casa di legno, come questa che vedi sulla cartolina. Qui siamo soli, la signora ed io, con una donna di servizio. Gli amici però stanno nel piccolo paese laggiù, in un albergo, e vengono ogni giorno. Di mattina, fa bellissimo tempo – e di sera piove, ogni giorno. La ragazza ci porta le fragole selvagge che raccoglie nei boschi. – Spero che non sia troppo caldo a San Paolo.

Molti saluti a tutti.   D. H. Lawrence

[18 July

Dear Giulia –

It was very hot there on the lake, where we were – we have moved higher up on the mountain, to more than a thousand metres, and we have rented a small wooden house, like the one you can see on the postcard. My wife and I are alone here, with a housemaid. Our friends, however, are down there in the little village, in an hotel, and come every day. In the mornings, the weather is

---

[1] Humbert Wolfe (1885–1940), poet, critic and civil servant; he had reviewed several of DHL's earlier works (Roberts A23, A27, A29, A38); he also edited *The Augustan Books of English Poetry* and wrote the preface for DHL's own contribution to that series (cf. *Letters*, v. 2).

[2] Nancy Pearn replied on 19 July 1928 (TMSC UT):
Dear darling Mr Lawrence,
    You never for a moment really thought anybody meant you to take *Humbert Wolfe* as an example!! It was merely one which came first to hand, and was sent by the editor as giving an idea of the *form* of their reviews in the sad but possible event of your not being a reader of her priceless publication. Too bad that they sent you boring books! . . .

wonderful – and in the evenings it rains, every day. The girl brings us wild strawberries that she picks in the woods. I hope it is not too hot at San Paolo.

> Best wishes to everybody   D. H. Lawrence]

4539. To Jean Watson, 18 July 1928
Text: MS UT; Unpublished.

> Kesselmatte. *Gsteig b. Gstaad* (Bern), Switzerland
> 18 July 1928

Dear Miss Watson.

With great reluctance I have forced myself to write out a draft of an autobiography – Let the Kra – Kra – Kraaa! read *Sons and Lovers* and *The Rainbow* and he's got all he wants – and be damned to him.[1]

Will you please have this typed out, and two carbon copies made. And will you please send one carbon copy here to me, and give one copy to Miss Pearn – she keeps most of my reference stuff – and one copy to the Kra. Then I hope we'll have provided against the future. – I feel rather cold about French publicity of me.

What are you doing about the Fischer Verlag?[2] They say he's an old swindler – S. Fischer – call him Saü Fischer – and he's simply ancient – but I suppose he's 'alive.' Anyhow the Insels need a sound dig in the ribs.

> Sincerely.   D. H. Lawrence

4540. To Giuseppe Orioli, [19 July 1928]
Text: MS UCLA; Unpublished.

> Kesselmatte. *Gsteig b. Gstaad.* (Bern)
> Thursday

Dear Pino

I have your letter of 17th with bordereaux and Haskard's enclosed. I feel pretty sure the English parcels are all going through – if one goes, the rest will, in every batch. I think we ought to post to England as quickly as possible – get them in before anybody starts any fuss. Why not ask someone you know, some

---

[1] Jean Watson had forwarded Philippe Soupault's renewed and now very pressing request for an autobiographical sketch (see Letter 4480 and p. 430 n. 2; Nehls, iii. 231); she urged DHL to comply. She concluded her own covering letter: 'Our Paris representative points out that Kra makes a great feature of his introductions, and that a good one would be extremely valuable publicity for your work in France. I have collected all the information I can from "WHO'S WHO" and various other reference books, but apparently they want something more detailed and personal. Neither Secker nor Miss Pearn have nothing which meets the case' (Nehls, iii. 232). DHL wrote the 'Autobiography' partly on the back of the letters from Soupault and Watson; it is printed in Nehls, iii. 232–4 and as 'Autobiographical Sketch' in *Phoenix II* 300–2.   [2] See Letter 4456.

bookseller who has ordered a number of copies, to send you a telegram each
time he receives a copy, and to charge the telegram to me on the invoice. So
you send him a copy every day or every two days, and as long as his telegram
arrives, all is well. – Because as soon as information is laid against the book,
they will hold up *all* books from Florence. So get them off as quickly as
possible.

Whom did you give a copy of the second edition to? – you left the name
blank – but I suppose it is that professore who wrote the article about the
Serpente Alata. If Douglas would like one of the sec. edition too, give him one
with my regards. But we won't send out any yet.

I have heard only from Barbara Low, that she has her copy.

It has gone cooler here, after torrents of rain – so perhaps the same has
happened to you.

Let me know when we shall pay the rest of the Giuntina bill, and I'll send a
cheque.

How many copies have you actually sent off now? – I do wish I was there to
help.

How is Carletto bearing up through it all?

Grüsse.   DHL

4541. To Dorothy Warren, 20 July 1928
Text: MS UN; Nehls, iii. 230–1.

Kesselmatte, *Gsteig b. Gstaad* (Bern), Switzerland
20 July 1928

Dear Dorothy

Have you got my pictures yet from Florence? they were forwarded to you
some time ago. Be sure and let me know as soon as they arrive. – You have the
little ones, Mrs Hilton told me you sent and fetched them. – Let me know
what you think of them, will you? And tell me your ideas of framing and the
prices to put on them. I asked you this before, but you didn't answer. Please
answer now, as it annoys me when you do not so much as trouble to reply.

It may be I should like the small pictures taken over to show to some
American friends who will not be in London. If so, I should ask Mrs Hilton to
call and take charge of them for the time. So if she should arrive with a note
from me, will you please deliver all the small pictures over to her: or if you are
away, have them delivered?

I am doing one or two more small ones here, which I will send along later,
all being well.[1] I might even finish another biggish one, quite different. We are

[1] See Letters 4596, 4636.

due to stay here till towards end of September, for my health: then I intend coming to London.

I hear that Alfred Stieglitz is doing the show in New York: he is a very good man. I wrote and asked them to arrange for November. – I don't really mind if I don't have a London show, since Stieglitz is arranging this in New York. So you needn't bother if you dont want to.

But let me hear from you, and do answer my questions. Hope everything is going nicely with you.

Yours   D. H. Lawrence

4542. To Enid Hilton, 20 July 1928
Text: MS UCLA; Moore, *Intelligent Heart* 382–3.

Kesselmatte, *Gsteig b. Gstaad.* (Bern), Switzerland
20 July 1928

Dear Enid

I was glad to hear from you and you so happy with your removal. Did I tell you I believe that is the very house we lived in, in 1917 in the Aldingtons' rooms on the first floor, on the front and Arabella had an attic at the top – it was very jolly, I liked it very much.[1] I hope you can stay there in peace.

I was a bit sorry you yielded up the pictures so easily to Dorothy Warren's messenger. I don't altogether trust her – I knew her of old, she is Lady Ottoline's niece – and she hasn't answered my letter. And now the Mirenda pictures, the big ones, have gone off to her. – If I don't hear from her satisfactorily, I will give you a letter to her and you can just go and demand the small pictures back from her. Then we shall have some hold over her. I've told her I may do this.

We are here in a small but very nice peasant chalet on the mountain just over the German side of the Pillon pass from Diablerets. It's very nice – we have two nice big rooms downstairs, all old broad planks of pale wood, scrubbed and soft-coloured, about 200 years old: then a pleasant kitchen, and another good room upstairs – then the balconies – and the steep meadows, and spring, and barn – all for 100 francs a month. It's quite cheap and very easy – they leave chopped wood, and we pay for it at the end of the month as we consume it – and they let us have butter and eggs and milk and honey. We are about a mile from Gsteig village, towards the Pillon – and about 4000 ft up. One summer you should really try a holiday[2] here; ask the post-office woman in Gsteig: her boy has a rather rough chalet, in fact two together, across the

---

[1] Enid Hilton was living in 44 Mecklenburgh Square; the Lawrences occupied Hilda Aldington's flat there c. 20 October–30 November 1917.   [2] holiday] summer

opposite mountain, and he'd let them *both* together for 80 frs. a month – they're smaller and rougher than this, but great fun to camp in. – They are so cheap because the peasant holders abandon them in summer, when the hay begins to come on, and they move to the higher alps with the cows, and shut in these meadows for hay. Our peasants are just across the valley on the north side, with their cows, in their other house. But they send the girl to wash up and clean for us. It is really very nice – and if I could tramp the hills, it would be perfect. But it *is* steep. – This woman, of our house, is Frau Käthe Trachsel, and I expect, if you wanted to come, say in June, when the flowers are lovely – late June and early July – she would no doubt let you have kitchen, sitting room – a nice big room – and nice big bedroom – for 80 frs. a month. There is a second darker kitchen where they camp when they come. They are *very* nice – and dont overcharge – but they speak German – it is all German this side. In early July there is nobody in Gsteig at all. The mail bus runs between Gstaad and Gsteig, over the Pillon to Diablerets. – I'm hoping it's going to do my health a lot of good. – I do hope you and Lawrence are happy in the new quarters. – Orioli is sending out the novel, and when he's about through, in a week or fortnight, I shall ask him to send you a copy of the 2nd edition. So it'll come along all right.

Our friends the Brewsters are staying in the village in the Viktoria. They come up to tea. – I wish you had a chalet across the valley.

many regards from both to both.   DHL

4543. To Hon. Dorothy Brett, 20 July 1928

Text: MS UCin; Postmark, Gsteig 23.VII.28; Lacy, *Escaped Cock* 68–9.

Kesselmatte. *Gsteig b. Gstaad.* (Bern). Switzerland
20 July 1928

Dear Brett

Here we sit in this little chalet about 4000 ft. up. It is a pleasant little place, very peaceful – and the house is very nice, so attractive inside, with the plain scrubbed wood everywhere – about 200 years old. It's a bit like the ranch – but I wish the ranch-houses were so nicely floored and walled. – You must have been doing a lot – what with your cellar and the bridge for the stream – and you seem to have a regular Pueblo of Indians up there. However do you feed them all? – especially as you say it's been so hot. But I suppose it makes it easier that you can go down to Taos for week-ends.

The Brewsters are still in the hotel in the village. They come sweating up to tea – and sometimes Earl comes and paints in the morning. I try to do just little things – small little panels – but I haven't got much art in me here. Perhaps it's just as well – as the chief thing is my health. I can't come to

America, I can't really go anywhere, while my cough is as bad as it is. It's really very trying – and I can't climb hills to save my life. It all makes me feel a bit sick of things. So now I must stay here about three months and see if this won't make a real change for the better. It's really very nice and peaceful here – but of course I wouldn't have come to Swiss mountains for *choice*. They aren't my spirit's home, by any means.

I hope you have the book by now. A whole batch has been sent off to America. I hear quite a lot of people have got their copies in England – but silence about the contents, except Kot thinks it is a pity I ever published such a book. I don't think so.

My pictures have gone off to Dorothy Warren. I told you she fixed her exhibition for Oct. 4th – and the pictures were to be in New York, all of them, by Nov. 1st. I do hope that'll do. You are doing a lot of work – and lately I'm doing nothing. But I suppose there'll be enough.

I send fifty dollars for horses and taxes etc. And Spud will give you another thirty when he gets the three copies of *Lady C.* – I haven't raked in much yet – most people haven't paid for the copies they've ordered, and they won't, till they get them. – And I haven't given Crosby Gaige the second half of *Escaped Cock* though I've written it, and I think it's lovely. But somehow I don't want to let it go out of my hands. It lies here in MS. – not typed yet. – I've done a few newspaper articles to keep the pot boiling. – A man wrote from Taos wanting to buy the ranch for $2000 but I said we weren't selling just now.[1] I must anyhow see it again. Hope you're having a good summer.

DHL

4544. To Giuseppe Orioli, 23 July 1928
Text: MS UCLA; Unpublished.

Kesselmatte. *Gsteig b. Gstaad* (Bern)
Monday 23 July 1928

Dear Pino

Yours with the three cheques this morning. I sent them back to you signed – when you go in to Haskards, will you put the dollars to my *Lira* account, the pounds to my *sterling* account, as usual.

You didn't send me the binders bill. Send it, and I will return it to you with cheque. Was it just Lit. 4000.00?

I'm so glad the books are arriving all right. Now we have to see about America. – And then those who haven't paid must pay.

---

[1] See Letter 4502.

How glad you will be when it is all done, and you can get up to Vallombrosa. Too bad you are in all that heat.

You had my other letters with cheques I signed and returned to you?

We are going on very nicely here – never too hot. What a pity you can't come for a while.

Have you got the MS. of *Gastone de' Medici* from Acton?[1] You'll have to be thinking of a new venture for autumn.

Herzliche Grüsse.   DHL

4545. To Giuseppe Orioli, 24 July 1928
Text: MS UCLA; Unpublished.

Kesselmatte. Gsteig bei Gstaad (Bern)
24 July 1928

Dear Pino

Yours enclosing the bill for binding has come this afternoon. I return the bill and cheque for four thousand Liras. You will add the twentytwo from money in hand.[2]

I enclose also the two cheques signed. Put them to my sterling account, will you, in Haskards.

Thanks for the two bordereaux. – Has Robert Mountsier sent his cheque again, signed?

Tell me how many copies you have sent to America, and how many to England. Don't bother to copy the list. Just add up and tell me the total.

How long is it since you sent the first copies to America? Isn't it time you had a cable or two from there? You sent at the very beginning a copy each to Alfred Knopf, Alfred Stieglitz, Dr E. D. McDonald, Harold T. Mason, Lawrence Gomme – didn't you? I wrote to each of these: asking them to wire as soon as they had the book. I think we'd better wait, now, till we hear from them. Then as soon as we have wires from America, we can send out all those copies ordered by reliable people like the Centaur Press. But let us wait till we hear that some of the first lot are safely arrived.

I am sure you want to get away to Vallombrosa. What is Carletto doing? Is he staying in Florence? If so, you could trust him to send away the copies you leave ready. If the things are going into America safely, we ought to send the safe orders, as soon as we are sure.

But if those Macey Masius people should cable, that they will do a limited

---

[1]   Orioli published a subscribers' edn of 365 copies of *The Last of the Medici* [an anon. *Life of Gian Gastone de' Medici*], trans. Harold Acton, introd. Norman Douglas, in 1930.

[2]   The transaction appears in DHL's 'Memoranda' (MS NWU): 'To Orioli for Lenzi the binder – July 24. cheque for Lit. *4000 £44* stg (bill of Lit. 4022. for 1,005 copies)'.

edition over there, then we won't send to America more than 150 or at the most 200 copies in all. We ought to hear from them in a day or two.

It is much cooler here – I wish it were with you.

If only the people will pay quickly, then I can pay you too. As soon as we reach £1000 I will give you £100, and count the rest later, as it comes in. At present I have received £427··13··6 in English cheques, $604 in dollar cheques, also about £58. sterling received in cash (English, Italian and dollars): which makes it in all £606··13··6. And I have paid out about Liras 16,000. – which is about £174 stg. Now there is the rest of Guintina's bill to pay. If you like, I will give you £50. now for yourself, and £5. now for Carletto –

If we sell them all and get paid for them – but we won't do that – we'll keep some to gamble on – let us wait a bit.

DHL

I have enclosed £55 – cheque – £50. for you and £5. for Carletto. Just a beginning, anyhow.

DHL

4546. To Martin Secker, 24 July 1928
Text: MS UInd; Postmark, Gsteig 25.VII.28; Huxley 738.

Kesselmatte. Gsteig bei Gstaad (Bern)
24 July 1928

Dear Secker

It occurs to me we've never made the agreement yet, for the poems, and I've no business to go behind Curtis Brown's back. So I shall write to Pollinger now about it.

And I shall tell him I want also the $33\frac{1}{3}$% on the 100 guineas extra for signing. If the booksellers get $33\frac{1}{3}$% (they never asked me for more than 25%, and they got only 15%) then you get $33\frac{1}{3}$% and I get $33\frac{1}{3}$% – which seems very fair, since these signed copies cost you nothing extra. And really, you ought to give me this $33\frac{1}{3}$ guineas down, for signing the books. Why should the government get 20% for what is not royalty at all? – I shall write this to Pollinger.

Many thanks for the books: I have great fun reading Hardy's stories again: what a commonplace genius he has: or a genius for the commonplace, I don't know which. He doesn't rank so terribly high, really. – But better than Bernard Shaw, even then.[1] I'm afraid *The Intelligent Woman's Guide* I shall

---

[1] Secker probably sent Hardy's *Short Stories*, published by Macmillan in March 1928, as well as Shaw's *Intelligent Woman's Guide to Socialism and Capitalism* published by Constable in June.

have to leave to the intelligent woman: it is too boring for the intelligent man, if I'm any sample. Too much gas-bag. Still very many thanks, and shall I send them back to 5 John St. or to Bridgefoot?

I hope you've got your copies of *Lady Chatterley* – I know all those paid for are sent out[1] – and in England, received all right. I think it's quite a handsome book.

One goes up and down in health here – it's always like that, the first weeks of altitude. But I can eat well and sleep well: it's only the walking uphill that's a failure still. Yet I think I manage even that better.

I'll keep Palling in mind, in case we want to go there one day.[2] It sounds the right sort of place. I do want to come to England end of Sept. Dorothy Warren is supposed to be showing my pictures the first three weeks in October – If I'm feeling pretty well, I might go back to Italy and finish my Etruscans.

Glad you had a good holiday.

DHL

4547. To Laurence Pollinger, 24 July 1928
Text: MS UT; Unpublished.

Kesselmatte. *Gsteig bei Gstaad* (Bern), Switzerland
24 July 1928

Dear Pollinger

Secker has been writing about the *Collected Poems*, which he has ready to publish in autumn, apparently 2 vols at a guinea the set. We haven't made any agreement for these yet, have we? – Do we put the royalty at 15%, as for the novels? – this is a much more highly-priced book, comparatively.

Secker wrote he wants me to sign the first leaves of 100 copies, which he will then sell at *two guineas* a set, and on this hundred copies he will give me twenty per cent. – But I say, he must give me equal shares on that 100 guineas clear which is made simply by the signatures – costing him nothing. He says booksellers take $33\frac{1}{3}$% – then, say I, he can take $33\frac{1}{3}$ guineas, and give me also $33\frac{1}{3}$ guineas on this hundred, seeing it is money made purely by my signing. – What do you think? Why should I just sign money into his hands, or anybody's? – And further I say, he ought to give me those $33\frac{1}{3}$ guineas down, as fee for signing, and reckon the whole sales at the fixed percentage, signed copies the same as unsigned. For why should the government take 20% for my signature – which is not royalty at all. I'm tired of being always worsted.

---

[1] According to DHL's 'Memoranda' (MS NWU) Secker's cheque for £5·2·0 was not written until 16 August 1928. [2] On the Norfolk coast about 18 miles n.e. of Norwich.

And why does he give booksellers $33\frac{1}{3}\%$? They never asked me more than 25% – and didn't get it, either.

I hope you've got your copy of *Lady Chatterley* – all have been sent out, and most people have received theirs.[1] You will see I made her quite handsome materially, whatever you may think of her spiritually. – I am now waiting to hear that the dear creature is landed safely in America.

Well write me about the poems.

Sincerely   D. H. Lawrence

4548. To Emily King, [25 July 1928]
Text: MS Lazarus; Unpublished.

Kesselmatte. *Gsteig b. Gstaad*. (Bern)
Wed.

My dear Pamela

You must make up your mind if you'd care to come, because you must get a passport and arrange trains. We've a room upstairs with two beds, you can have any time. The altitude is just over 4000 feet, and it makes one feel pippy at first – for a few days – sometimes for a week. It is a pity Peg. would only have ten days – wouldn't the man make it 17? You see the journey will take about two each way.

You come Paris (Gare de Lyons) Vallorbe, Lausanne, Montreux, and there change and get the electric train, two hours, up the mountain to Gstaad – where you find a motor to bring you here. – Or if it's a bit more convenient, you go the same way from Paris, but instead of getting out at Montreux, sit on in the big train another half-hour to Aigle: and at Aigle change and take a different little electric train up to Diablerets: and at Diablerets we'd meet you with a car. – If you come this way, it means you must cross Paris by taxi from Gare du Nord to Gare de Lyons – but it's very easy.

Otherwise I believe you can get a train direct from Calais to Berne – and come to Gstaad from Bern. But it'll be 12 or 15 hours from Calais here, I'm afraid. You can ask Cooks.

If only it weren't the long journey, you would like it so much. And if you stay a night in Paris, in an hotel, that shortens your time still further.

I really do want to come to England at the end of September – and I really think I shall: perhaps by BadenBaden. I want to see you all – and to see about my pictures.

It's quite lovely here – but I never really walk – and I'm afraid you wouldn't get far either. Yet it's very nice among the trees and in the meadows, and the weather is on the whole lovely.

[1] Pollinger paid for his first two copies on 2 April 1928 ('Memoranda', MS NWU).

Frieda was thrilled by the *Guardian* and the accounts of the new university
– I suppose we shall see it one day.[1]

If you come by Montreux, or Aigle, you should arrive there in full daylight,
as the journey by Lake of Geneva and Castle of Chillon is very lovely – and
from Montreux the little train goes sheer up for nearly 3000 ft, winding up
above the Lake. Chillon is just beyond Montreux – you can see it.

What have you decided about Joan?

Love   DHL

4549. To Richard Aldington, 25 July 1928
Text: MS ColU; Delany, *DHL Review*, ii. 206–7.

Kesselmatte. *Gsteig bei Gstaad* (Bern), Schweiz
25 July 1928

Dear Richard

I really don't know what makes the English dead, unless they like it, and
find it genteel. They think life a little 'loud.' But if, as you say, they're not
dead when it comes to the point, perhaps time will lead them gently to the
point.

We have got a little chalet up here, about 4000 feet – not exactly for choice,
but, if possible, to reduce my nuisance of a cough. So far, I see no difference in
the cough – we've been here 17 days. We have got the place till end Sept. It's
very nice – very peaceful – steep meadows, pines, waterfall, mountain-tops,
patches of snow, harebells, wild strawberries, hay. Gsteig is a pretty tiny
village just filling up with tourists – but I never see it, because of the climb
back, of about a mile. But in case you ever want high air, Alps, and a chalet,
this is quite a nice place: you can have a rough but decent little chalet for 80
francs a month for two persons – linen, cutlery and all – in fact two chalets,
one thrown in – on the mountain opposite us. The peasants are in the high alps
with the cows, during the summer.

I want to come to England during the autumn – at the end of September –
partly because I think of having a show of my pictures, waters and oils, in
Dorothy Warren's gallery in Madox St., in first half of October. What are you
and Arabella doing? – going gaily off to Spain or somewhere there? – I hear
you are having good weather, that the flowers are wonderful in English

[1] Emily King had probably sent a copy of the *Nottingham Guardian*, 10 July 1928, the day when
King George V opened the new building (subsequently the 'Trent Building') of University
College, Nottingham. The *Guardian* printed photographs (p. 2), and an account of the royal
programme (p. 9). The munificence of Sir Jesse Boot was prominent (see also *The Times*, 9 and
10 July: see *The Complete Poems of D. H. Lawrence*, ed. Vivian de Sola Pinto and Warren
Roberts, 1964, ii. 1002).

gardens, and vegetables A.1. All of which is very comforting, and I hope it makes you feel nice and lively again. How is Arabella? I think she ought to have a chalet to amuse herself in – and if you stayed abroad long enough, you might really utter the ultimate revelation. Not that anybody would take any notice – the Word is even deader than the English.

Herzliche Grüsse from both.　DHL

4550. To Nancy Pearn, 26 July 1928

Text: MS UT; PC v. Gsteig b. Gstaad & Sanetschpass; Postmark, [. . .]; Unpublished.

[Kesselmatte, Gsteig b. Gstaad, Switzerland]
26 July 1928

– Am sending you to day MS. of a story 'The Blue Moccassins' for *Eve*.[1] Will you have it typed for me – and please send me the MS. book back here – I didn't want to tear it out this time[2] – I may as well make nice MS. books. – Brilliant hot sun here – so I expect it's the same in England. Are you going away just now?

D. H. Lawrence

4551. To Giuseppe Orioli, 28 July 1928

Text: MS UCLA; Moore 1069–70.

Kesselmatte. *Gsteig b. Gstaad.* (Bern)
28 July 1928

Dear Pino

Your letter with two bordereaux and these four cheques which I here return signed – will you put them to my sterling account.

I hope you have my letter with Lenzi's bill, cheque for Lit. 4000.00, and cheque for £55. st[erlin]g. for you and Carletto: and Mrs Otway's cheque signed.[3] You should have it by now.

I'm so glad everything is arriving – and very glad indeed the Amer. copies are in. Yes, now send *all* American orders that seem to you quite safe: especially those Centaur ones. This is a good moment – everyone away on holidays.

---

[1] The story was published in *Eve: The Lady's Pictorial*, Special Christmas Issue, 22 November 1928 (Roberts C178.5). For the Brewsters' account of the two versions of the ending, see Brewster 291 (see also Roberts E50).

[2] DHL wanted to preserve intact the 'copy-book with green emerald corners' given him by the sixteen-year-old Harwood Brewster and 'inscribed on the fly-leaf: "Merry Christmas to Uncle David"' (Brewster 291). It was returned by Nancy Pearn's secretary, Rowena Killick, on 8 August 1928 (TMSC UT).

[3] Eva M. Otway sent a cheque for £2 (dated 25 July 1928) and a further cheque (10 August) for the same amount.

Tell me how many copies sent *altogether*. – We might send a hundred copies to Willard Johnson. Taos – or to the Centaur – to hold for us: or 50 to each. What do you think?

Mabel is a bitch – she already wrote me a snorty letter because some American old maid acquaintance had been in your shop and said you spoke 'slightingly' of Mabel Dodge and her books – and that you had two 1st edit. Henry James worth God knows how many dollars from Mabel's library. I replied to Mabel she shouldn't listen to second-hand reports, and she should try for once not to be so idiotically self-important – I wrote her a nasty letter – I'm sick of these God-almighty blown-out women.[1] Don't bother about her.

I've heard from several people they have got the book and like the outside very much: but nobody has criticised the inside – except Koteliansky, who thought it was a pity I wrote such a book, it would do me harm. Same old[2] Jewish song! We'll see what harm it does me.

When you have time would you send me those two books that a nuisance of a fellow – Charles Wilson, Willington – sent me to sign. Giulia's father brought you the parcel. – Did you send him a copy of *Lady C.* with invoice for £2. he is quite safe?

Charles Wilson. 8 Cumberland Terrace. Willington, Co. Durham.

Will you also send another copy to Pollinger.[3]

I do hope you are not exhausted. You must leave it all now and go to Vallombrosa.

I find it very hard to get used to the altitude here. I really feel weaker and more upset than I do at the Mirenda – so does Frieda. I hope we'll soon get adjusted.

Have Giuntina's finished everything now? – send me their bill.

love from both.   DHL

4552. To Alan Steele, 28 July 1928
Text: MS Unlocated; Unpublished.

Kesselmatte. *Gsteig b. Gstaad* (Bern)
28 July 1928

Allan W. Steele,

for William Jackson Ltd. 16 Tooks Court. Chancery Lane, E.C.4

28 July 1928

Dear Sir

Will you please deliver to the bearer of this note all the copies of *Lady Chatterley's Lover* that were sent to you from Florence before you cancelled

---

[1] See Letter 4489.   [2] old] of
[3] The copy was for the publisher George S. Harrap (see p. 480 n. 3).

your order. There should be either[1] seventy-two or seventy-four copies in all
– Mr Orioli says sixty-six copies by registered book mail, and one parcel-post
package of eight copies – making seventy-four. But elsewhere he said
seventy-two.

With thanks for your courtesy.

Yours faithfully.   D. H. Lawrence[2]

4553. To Enid Hilton, 29 July 1928
Text: MS UCLA; cited in Moore, *Intelligent Heart* 383.

Kesselmatte, *Gsteig b. Gstaad* (Bern), Switzerland
29 July 1928

My dear Enid

Now I'm in more trouble. A beastly firm of book-exporters ordered eighty
copies of *Lady Chatterley's Lover* – now it turns out that they have a Wesleyan
connection – they've read the book – and cancelled the order hastily – after
Orioli has already posted to them *seventy-two* copies from Florence. Now
unless we're quick they'll send the things back to Florence – may even refuse
to accept them from the post-man. So I want somebody to go and collect
them. – But I warn you, the book *is* shocking – though, course, perfectly
decent and honest. The authorities *may* suppress it, later – they've done
nothing so far. And in that case you'd have to keep it a dead secret, that you
had these copies. – So speak of it first to Lawrence – and then, if you feel like
risking it, telephone the Jackson people and ask them if they have the copies
ready for you to fetch away: say *Mr D. H. Lawrence has asked me* – ask for Mr
Steele etc. I enclose a note to them. The manager is *Allan. W. Steele*, for
'William Jackson. Books. Ltd' – 16 Tooks Court. Cursitor St. Chancery
Lane, E.C.4 and their telephone is *Holborn 5824.*

If it's all right, take a taxi and fetch what parcels they have. I *believe* there
are two copies in each registered parcel. – But they won't have received all yet,
I don't suppose. Probably the eight copies sent in one parcel by parcel post
will still take some days. So, if all have not arrived, you can telephone them
another day and get the rest, if they've come – seventy-two copies, Orioli said
– but also he said sixty-six copies registered – and a parcel of eight – makes
seventy-four. You will see.

If you fetch them, open one of the small parcels and take a copy for yourself
– it is yours. Keep the others just as they are, and then, when we get more
orders from London, you can just dab on a new address and post or deliver the
parcel. Will you do that?

[1] either] eight   [2] This letter was enclosed with the next to Enid Hilton.

I enclose cheque for two pounds, for present expenses – and feel like a conspirator.

Ever.   D. H. Lawrence

But talk it over with Lawrence first.

You'll see I mention no name to the Steele man – If you don't want to do this – or if Lawrence doesn't want you to – you might just send this letter to S. Koteliansky – 5 Acacia Rd. St Johns Wood.

4554. To Giuseppe Orioli, 29 July 1928
Text: MS UCLA; Unpublished.

Kesselmatte. Gsteig b. Gstaad. (Bern)
Sunday. 29 July 1928

Dear Pino

That Jackson fellow is a *cur*. Why didn't he say his order was provisional. How can he cry off like that!

However I have written him to say will he hold the copies till a friend of mine calls for them. – And I have written Enid Hilton to ask her to go and fetch the parcels in a taxi, and keep them for me till I ask for them to be distributed. She lives in 44 Mecklenburgh Square, W.C.1. – fairly near – and I think she'll do it all right. – I didn't give Jackson's her name – we'll leave her nameless. But I think she's all right. If not, I must ask Koteliansky.

But damn and blast that Steele fellow – the dog. He's the first real rebuff we've had – let's hope there'll be no more.

I do hope you have my letter with cheques for Lenzi's bill and for yourself and Carletto. If not Haskards must hold back any cheque made out to you and not presented by you.

At last I got the $40. for those four Vaglie. But the post office didn't give any name of sender, or anything – I do hope you have their names.

I suppose now you've gone on sending to America. If nothing worse happens than the beastly Jackson, I don't mind.

ever.   DHL

You write to Steele – the Jackson man – also, and tell him to do as I request.

Mrs Enid Hilton. 44 Mecklenburgh Square, London W.C.1.

but if she fetches the books, we'll let her fulfil the London orders – you can forward them to her.

4555. To Lord Beaverbrook, 29 July 1928
Text: MS BBK Papers; Unpublished.

Kesselmatte, *Gsteig b. Gstaad* (Bern), Switzerland
29 July 1928.

Dear Lord Beaverbrook[1]

I'm glad you got your copies of the novel from Florence safely.

I haven't got any copies of *The Rainbow* – all mine have been stolen away from me. But if you mean the first – Methuen – edition, Pino Orioli got a copy for £5. the other day – I can ask him to look out for one for you. – If you would like the American edition, I think you can buy it in London anywhere – in one of those little dollar editions. It's a little bit expurgated.

Yours Sincerely   D. H. Lawrence[2]

4556. To Giuseppe Orioli, 30 July 1928
Text: MS UCLA; Unpublished.

Kesselmatte – *Gsteig b. Gstaad.* (Bern)
30 July 1928

Dear Pino

Your letter tonight, with news about *Foyle* and *Stevens and Brown:*[3] it never rains but it pours. Why didn't you give me the address of Stevens and Brown?

---

[1] Beaverbrook (who was a patron of writers and artists) had written to DHL on 31 March 1928 (TMSC BBK Papers):

Dear Mr. Lawrence,
    I understand that you are bringing out a new novel in May. Will you be good enough to put me on your list of subscribers for three copies?
Yours sincerely

On 21 July he wrote again, with his cheque for £6 (TMSC BBK Papers):

Dear Mr. Lawrence,
    Many thanks for your books. I enclose cheque.
    Will you let me have a copy of Rainbow, or tell me where I can get one.
    I had a copy many years ago, but it has disappeared from my library, and I would like to have it to complete my collection.
Yours sincerely

[2] Beaverbrook replied on 1 August (TMSC BBK Papers):

Dear Mr. Lawrence,
    Replying to your letter, if you can get me an unexpurgated copy of "Rainbow" from Orioli for £5, I would be very glad to have it.
Yours sincerely

[3] Foyle's returned six copies (see letter following); the 'American Library and Literary Agents', B. F. Stevens & Brown Ltd (4 Trafalgar Square), wrote to Orioli as follows on 25 July 1928 (TMSC UCLA):

Dear Sir,
    We have duly received yours of July 20th, and the 28 copies of Lawrence's book, but did not

Are they London? Yes, I see they are. – I am writing now to Koteliansky to ask him if he will fetch away the 36 copies. Will you write to him also at once – and to Stevens and Brown? – I don't think Kot. will refuse.

If you ask Boris[1] to deliver the three copies to L. E. Pollinger, of Curtis Brown, that will be good.

I will send the money for Giuntina tomorrow.[2]

Will you please put the enclosed signed cheques to my sterling account.

Giglioli wrote and thanked me for the book, and enclosed his bill for £1.345.00. Not cheap! But I prefer to pay him.

I want you to have 10% on all my profits –

I only heard from Richard Aldington – he liked the book very much, and thought it a feather in the cap of the 20th Century.

Did you send Jacksons 72 or 74 copies? You said 66 registered and 8 in a parcel: that makes 74. – Yet you say 72.

What fun! We must get those copies safely hidden!!

Glad Carletto was pleased. – Do tell me how many copies in all you have sent away.

> Affecy   DHL

I sent you his letter asking for one more copy – would you ask Boris to deliver him these two more copies at Curtis Brown's office![3]

telegraph you as to their arrival as on examination of a copy we found at once that it was a book which we could not handle in any way. All our copies were ordered for American clients, and we are sure that, like us, they had no idea that the book would be such as it is.

Please do not send the other copies ordered, and instruct us by return what you want us to do with the 28 copies which we refuse to accept.

> Yours faithfully

[1] Boris de Croustchoff, a Russian bibliographer whom DHL had met through Philip Heseltine (see *Letters*, ii. 448).

[2] In his 'Memoranda' (MS NWU) DHL recorded: 'paid July 31st 1928 Liras 15,000'. For precise details of the cost covered by this payment, and recorded in the 'Memoranda', see Michael Squires, *The Creation of Lady Chatterley's Lover* (Baltimore, 1983), p. 222.

[3] What is positioned here as a postscript was written by DHL at the end of a letter from Pollinger (DHL's letter is written on its verso) which he enclosed for Orioli. It read:

Dear Lawrence,

O.Kyllman, Chairman of Constable and Michael Sadleir have just been in to see me, and I proudly placed in front of them "LADY CHATTERLEY" in her handsome dress. They were so taken by my enthusiasm for the book – materially as well as spiritually – that they asked me to get them each a copy of the book. I told them I was afraid that this would be impossible but I would write to you.

The copy I enquired about yesterday was for George S.Harrap, who came in here late yesterday evening.

If you can possibly lay your hands on three copies and get them across to me, I will collect the three two guineas and mail the cheques to you.

I didn't think the Italians could produce such good looking books.

> with haste   Yours sincerely,

4557. To S. S. Koteliansky, 30 July 1928

Text: MS BL; Postmark, Gsteig 31.VII.28; Moore 1070–1.

Kesselmatte. *Gsteig b. Gstaad* (Bern)

30 July 1928

My dear Kot.

Now the fun begins – the dealers – some – are beginning to refuse to accept the books they ordered. Today I heard from Orioli that Stevens and Brown, Booksellers, London – he doesn't give me the address – say they must return the thirty-six copies they ordered, and ask to be informed *at once* what they shall do with them. They had already received 28 copies at the time they cancelled their order – but also the remaining eight were on their way from Florence.

Would you hate to fetch away those thirty six copies for me? I should be so glad. You could ring up the bookshop and tell them you were speaking on behalf of Mr. Orioli of Florence, and Mr. D. H. Lawrence – and that Mr Lawrence had written asking you to fetch away thirty-six copies of his novel, the order for which they had cancelled.

I enclose £2. for taxi and expenses – but of course, don't do it if you have any qualms. – I can have the books fetched away from your house in a day or two if you wish. Not that there is any risk so far.

I enclose a note to Stevens and Brown.[1] You needn't tell them your name.

Foyles also sent back six copies – and another man some – Damn them all, hypocrites.

DHL

Did you receive your last copy, No 17? I do hope so.

4558. To Gertrude Cooper, [30 July 1928]

Text: MS Clarke; PC v. Gsteig b. Gstaad & Mittaghorn; Postmark, Gsteig 31.VII.28; Unpublished.

Kesselmatte. Gsteig b. Gstaad. (Bern)

Monday

My dear G[ertrude]

– I was glad to hear from you from Brighton, and to know it was doing you good. But it's a slow business – and a weariness. My cough is the devil, and doesn't get much better, Switzerland or not. And I tell you I gasp climbing the bit I do climb, up these mountains. Everywhere is steep, steep – and I just can't climb. So I don't get far. But it's very pleasant and peaceful here, and I hope I'll really get tougher. I am simply tired to death of being an invalid –

[1] Unlocated.

more or less. – Today Ada sent snaps of her garden – and one of the tea-party, where you look really quite bonny. But photographs show just what they think they will. – How queer Aunt Ada and Uncle Fritz look – sort of a bit bundly and come to pieces! It must be fourteen or fifteen years since I saw them. No, not so much – Mountain Cottage – ten years.[1] I remember your cousins so well, my regards to them. I want to come to England at the end of September. Let's hope we'll all be bouncing by then: so keep on getting fat. There's still a bit of snow on the mountains just across, and evening is chilly.

Love from both.   DHL

4559. To Ada Clarke, [30 July 1928]

Text: MS Clarke; PC v. Sanetschfall, Gsteig b. Gstaad; Postmark, [. . .]28; Unpublished.

[Kesselmatte, Gsteig b. Gstaad, Switzerland]
Monday

– Your letter with the photographs – very pretty, your garden lovely – queer Aunt A[da] and Fritz look – so many years since I saw them. – I am sending you some books for the holidays – nothing very thrilling, hope they come in time. Cooler here now, but lovely weather – hope you'll have a good time at the sea.

Love   DHL

We look across at this Fall.

4560. To Laurence Pollinger, 30 July 1928

Text: MS UT; Unpublished.

Kesselmatte. *Gsteig b. Gstaad.* (Bern)
30 July 1928

Dear Pollinger

Nice of you to make people want *Lady C.*[2] I sent your first order to Orioli in Florence: he is still posting American orders.

But now I hear that a miserable firm of booksellers in London have refused their 36 copies ordered – they are shocked. So I am having these collected, and your three copies can be brought round to you directly – at least I hope so – by hand.

Secker says he'll send me a cheque for 33⅓ guineas for signing those poems – a special cheque. I suppose you had my letter about that –

Would you ask Mr. Joseph why he sent this cheque to me instead of paying

---

[1] ten years] eighteen (Fritz and Ada Krenkow stayed with the Lawrences at Middleton-by-Wirksworth in early August 1918; see *Letters*, iii. 267).   [2] Cf. p. 480 n. 3.

it into my account in the usual way?[1] – And I have no English stamps – perhaps he wouldn't mind dabbing one on and sending the cheque to the Westminster Bank – Aldwych.[2]

So glad you like *Lady C.* – but she was a struggle to get dressed and ready for presentation, I can tell you.

D. H. Lawrence

4561. To Giuseppe Orioli, 31 July 1928
Text: MS UCLA; Unpublished.

Gsteig b Gstaad.
Tuesday morning. July 31st 1928

Dear Pino

I have gone through Giuntina's bill – seems all right. I have kept a copy – you keep the original. I enclose cheque on Haskard for £76 sterling, which should cover the Liras 7,000.[3]

I do hope there'll be no more bookseller's 'returns' – and no police trouble. Be sure to write to Koteliansky.

I have sent Giglioli his money. Really, I much prefer to pay him. One doesn't want to have those things unpaid.

I believe it's going to turn hot again.

DHL

What else have we to pay now? – some more postage, I suppose.

4562. To Aldous and Maria Huxley, 31 July 1928
Text: Huxley 738–9.

Kesselmatte, Gsteig b. Gstaad.
31 July, 1928

Dear Aldous and Maria, –

I should have written before, but have been under the altitude – felt perfectly wretched, and made design for my tombstone in Gsteig churchyard, with suitable inscription: 'Departed this life, etc., etc. – *He was fed up!*' However, last Friday – or Thursday afternoon, I forget which – I decided to live a little longer – and to-day I walked down to the village, and what is much worse, up again. It's like climbing to the Diablerets glacier. However, here I am, with a crick in my neck I admit, and Achsah *et famille* will be drippingly arriving to tea just now. The sun is sharply hot, the wind quite

---

[1] Michael Joseph (1897–1958), a director and general manager of Curtis Brown Ltd, 1926–35; subsequently founded his own publishing house (see *Letters*, v. 523 n. 2).

[2] DHL had maintained an account at that branch since June 1914 (see *Letters*, ii. 189 n. 3).

[3] Giuntina's total bill was for 15,000 liras (cf. p. 480 n. 2); 7,000 represented DHL's payment 'to complete his bill of Lit. 15,000' as his 'Memoranda' expressed it.

cool. But the sun sort of dissolves one's corpuscles. I daren't try another sunbath, not for a minute. So I rather envy you your red colour all over – or pansy-bronze or calceolaria or burnt-monkey-musk, whatever it is – and I would willingly dangle myself before a shark if I could swim in the deep sea and sit in the southern sun naked and undiminished. In fact, if I don't actually sit on a muck-heap and scrape myself with a tin lid, it's because I haven't the energy.

I suppose all the ordered copies of 'Lady Jane' are in England: so the booksellers have hastily written to say we must take back their copies at once, they couldn't handle the *Lady*, and I must cancel their orders, and will we remove the offence at once. That is in all 114 copies we have to fetch back. Of course, these children of God haven't paid. – Then there are rumours that the police are going to raid the shops: I suppose people hope they will. At the same time, the first batch has arrived safely at its various destinations in America.

I believe I have lost most of my friends in the escapade, but that is a small loss, alas! I never had any. Richard Aldington writes he gets a great kick out of it, and it's a feather in the cap of the XX century. It's a fool's cap anyhow, why should I put a feather in it. An American young man writes: But oh, your friends, Lorenzo! By their reactions shall you know them![1] – I shan't, because they'll keep them severely dark. I have unkindly set my foot down, and won't either give it or lend it to the [   ]'s[2] and of course, buying is beyond their idea.

I see the white flutter of our spotless friends away down on the high-road – poor dears, such a climb! Heaven is not reached in a single bound![3] No indeed, [   ], it isn't, and it was an American who first registered the fact.

Well, I feel there's not much of me left. What little there is gives you the Easter Kiss and hopes we'll crow in chorus once more, one day, like risen Easter eggs.

DHL

4563. To Emily King, [31 July 1928]
Text: MS Lazarus; Unpublished .
[Frieda Lawrence begins]

Gsteig bei Gstaad
Tuesday
Dear Pamela

It was so thrilling to get Peggy's letter – we did wonder if you really would

---

[1] Cf. Matthew vii. 16, 20 ['By their fruits ye shall know them'].   [2] Cf. p. 326 n. 3.
[3] Josiah Gilbert Holland (1819–81), American novelist, poet and moralist, in his poem 'Gradation' ['. . . reached at a . . .'].

come – It's such perfect weather cool and fresh and sunny, I hope to goodness
it will keep – Really your brother's cough seems better, I hope it's lasting the
improvement, it's so terrible always this anxiety, never any peace – Do bring
me two meridian vests, please, large women's and 2 pair of knickers – Also you
might bring an eiderdown for your brother – sew it in a cushion and use it for
travelling, you escape duty and you'll need a cushion travelling through the
night. It will be cooler in the night, day travelling might be terrible – Have
some mineral water with you in the carriage. You will be so tired – I wanted to
meet you Spiez[1] but cannot get there so early, so we meet you at *Gstaad* in a
car – Elsa and Barby will be in Somerset or I would have asked them to see you
off in London – But Peggy is so efficient – I want the eiderdown *single bed*,
plain green would look well in his room at the Mirenda – Your brother is just
washing his hair – We seem to have floods of Americans, friends of the
Brewsters – had an Indian writer Mukerje to tea – this is a very simple place,
not as 'grand' as the Mirenda, but if it's fine weather you'll enjoy it – Peggy
wont need any german, everybody speaks french or english –

So we are looking forward to your coming – Do bring me also 3 pairs of
good silk and wool stockings, pale grey or biscuit – Yes, you may need warm
clothes, but at present it's warm – nothing 'smart' out here!

A rivederci   Frieda

[Lawrence begins]
I hadn't realised Frieda wanted so many things – but the eider-down makes a
good travelling cushion. – The £5. is for you, and the two pounds is for the
things Frieda wants. – I'll pay the rest when I know how much.

4564. To Richard Aldington, [31 July 1928]
Text: MS Lazarus; Moore, *Intelligent Heart* 383.
[Frieda Lawrence begins]

Kesselmatte, Gsteig bei Gstaad, Bern
Tuesday

Dear Richard,
Your appreciative letter of *Lady C* came at the right moment – Lawrence
was lying on his bed, looking furiouser and furiouser ever minute – People
seem so *horrified at* it! But I feel pleased! Anyhow one has shocked them for
once and is'nt so shocked and hurt oneself! like I was over the *Rainbow* – And
in the end, the very end not even the run or the long run, it's a triumph, so
there! And I think Arabella will agree – It would be fun to see you both again
soon – Lawrence is really getting better – but it's slow work – We sit here cool

---

[1] On the Thuner See, 25 miles n.e. of Gstaad.

and still in a chalet – very primitive and the sun shines every day – Miracles of days!

Our love to you both   Frieda

Yours was the first *pleased* letter and only about 4 more!

[Lawrence begins]

The rest a few pellets of icy disapproval, and the most, frost-bound silence. Oh, I am so glad to lose the fag end of my friends! especially the old-maidy sort.

4565. To S. S. Koteliansky, [1 August 1928]

Text: MS BL; Postmark, Gsteig 2.VIII.28; cited in Moore 1073.

Gsteig.

Wed.

My dear Kot

Your letter this evening. I asked Enid Hilton (Hopkin) to fetch the Jackson books. She lives 44 Mecklenburgh Square now, and I think she's room. – And I think they'd be safe there. – But I haven't heard from her yet if she would do it.

I asked you to get the Stevens and Brown books – 36. My sisters don't know that I'm publishing that novel – I don't want them to know – it would only upset them. Anyhow, if you will get the 36 copies for me, I'll ask Richard Aldington to fetch them in a taxi – down into the country – Malthouse Cottage, Padworth, nr Reading. Berks. You could let him know.

But I don't believe they will suppress the book – so till they do there's no risk.

Perhaps you might send two copies to

L. E. Pollinger. Curtis Brown Ltd. 6 Henrietta St. Covent Garden.

He asked for two. – And Simpkin and Marshall wrote to Orioli for more copies.[1] –

This in haste.   DHL

4566. To Giuseppe Orioli, [1 August 1928]

Text: MS UT; Unpublished.

[Kesselmatte, Gsteig b. Gstaad, Switzerland]

[1 August 1928]

[Frieda Lawrence begins]

[   ][2] and the hot sun were very trying, but at last I believe he is getting

---

[1] Simpkin, Marshall Ltd (4 Stationers Hall Court, London E.C.4) were the largest wholesalers of English books in the world.   [2] Part of the MS is missing.

stronger, the fighting does his soul good! And I fairly flourish on it like a dandelion in the sun! The Brewsters come to tea, Achsah always in white and her soul is so white too, like white of egg, and they call Lawr 'David,' and she paints him as a blue eyed *Eunuch*! This is a long letter from me – The women in the village are all anxious to do things for me, they are all very good and protestant, but they like me; I think it's the love of the saint for the sinner!! The chalet is very plain and simple and terribly clean, and lovely saucepans in the kitchen, and a very shy little wild calf of a Lina, who waits on us, she is terrified of L. – brings us lovely wild strawberries and 'Alpenrosen' – the weather is gorgeous and we have such sunsets, it's wonderful too and I wish you could pay us a visit! But L says you have no passport –

Tante belle e bellissime cose   Frieda

Greetings to Carletto

[Lawrence begins]

Wednesday

– I have your registered letter with the cheques. – I am a bit anxious that you have no cable from Centaur or McDonald: they would anyway be more suspect than the others, and their copies may be detained. Do you think we should go on sending to America? I don't want to *lose* a lot of copies. – I will let you know as soon as I hear from Enid Hilton about the Jackson books, and from Koteliansky about the Stevens and Brown. I will ask Enid Hilton to take two more copies to *Pollinger* at Curtis Browns.

DHL

4567. To Else Jaffe, [1 August 1928]

Text: MS Jeffrey; PC v. Gsteig b/Gstaad; Postmark, [Gst]eig 1. VIII.28; Unpublished.

[Kesselmatte, Gsteig b/Gstaad, Switzerland]
[1 August 1928]

[Frieda Lawrence begins]

Du wirst doch so nett sein und zu meinem Geburtstag hier sein? Wie war A[lfred]'s Geburtstag? Du kommst wohl von Bern nach Spiez – es giebt eine Montreux-Interlaken Bahn – Es hat Lawr sehr angegriffen die Höhe, aber ich hoffe es geht ihm besser – Viele Grüsse

F –

[Lawrence begins]

Ich möchte – I want to give Frieda a fountain pen for her birthday – will you buy it for me – a nice one.

DHL

[Frieda Lawrence begins]
[You'll be so kind as to be here for my birthday? How was A[lfred]'s birthday?
You'll certainly come from Bern to Spiez – there's a Montreux-Interlaken
line – the height has been very bad for Lawr, but I hope he's getting better –
many greetings

F –

[Lawrence begins]
I would like – I want to give Frieda a fountain pen for her birthday – will you
buy it for me – a nice one.

DHL]

4568. To Richard Aldington, [1 August 1928]
Text: MS UTul; Unpublished.

Kesselmatte – Gsteig b. Gstaad. (Bern)
Wednesday

Dear Richard
So glad you liked *Lady C*. Apparently I'm going to have trouble with them.
Some booksellers are returning them – shocked – and there is a rumour of
suppression – but rumour merely.
Stevens and Brown wrote to ask us to collect their 36 copies – which they
return. I asked Koteliansky just to fetch them for me. But I believe he'll be
scared to hold them. Could you put them in your cottage if necessary? I really
don't think there's any actual risk. If you would, do write to
S. Koteliansky – 5. Acacia Rd. St. Johns Wood. N.W.8.
and tell him. I sent him some money for taxis – and I'll send you some more. –
Then if you can get them, take a copy for Arabella – she hasn't written yet – It
is a great bore, people's hypocritical funk. – This in haste for post.
Of course Kot may not collect the things.

DHL

Kot. is in the telephone book under Bourse Gazette. I've written him about
you.

4569. To S. S. Koteliansky, 4 August 1928
Text: MS BL; Postmark, Gsteig 6.VIII.28; Moore 1072–3.

Kesselmatte. *Gsteig b. Gstaad*. (Bern)
Sat. 4 Aug 1928

My dear Kot
I was very glad to have your express and to know the books are safe. By the

same post I heard from Enid Hilton that she has the 74 books from Jackson in her flat.

Now I suppose Richard A[ldington] will write you about taking your copies down to the country. But will you send two more copies to L. E. Pollinger, of Curtis Brown's – making four in all – and one copy to Bettina von Hutten, 19 Whitehead's Grove. Chelsea. – Is that the Baroness von Hutten?[1]

I do wish you hadn't sent back my cheque. Will you, since you are so proud, keep an account of what I've cost you, and tell me.

I am writing now to Enid Hilton to ask her if she knows of some safe place, where to store the books. For the life of me, I can think of nowhere except Richard A. As I told you, my sisters know nothing of this venture, and I don't want to tell them. – But I shall ask Enid to keep about two dozen copies in her flat, to distribute for me. I don't think there's any risk – at least not yet.

I wouldn't trust Miss Beach in Paris for a moment.[2] We must find some safe place to deposit the things, in England. You might speak to Richard.

I myself shall raise the price before long. What would you suggest about that?

Where are you going, in the country? I hope it'll be nice.

I'm very grateful to you for taking this trouble for me. I expect we'll get it all smoothed out one day. I believe Orioli sent to most of the booksellers without pre-payment – and some seem to be deferring their paying – hoping, I suppose, to sneak out if the thing is suppressed. What a world!

DHL

Have you got your last copy – no. 17?[3]

Be sure to let me know immediately if there is any move to suppress – and let Enid H. know, will you?

4570. To Enid Hilton, [4 August 1928]
Text: MS UCLA; Unpublished.

Kesselmatte. *Gsteig b. Gstaad*. (Bern)
Saturday

My dear Enid

I was so glad to have your letter and know that sixty, at least, of the books were there. But that Steele is a scoundrel. He should hand over the books to you *at once*, or pay at once. What he is doing, he is hanging on, hoping the book

[1] Baroness Bettina von Hutten (1874–1957), expatriate American, popular novelist and story writer. m. 1897, Freiherr von Hutten zum Stolzenberg (divorced 1909).
[2] Sylvia Woodbridge Beach (1887–1962), expatriate American, founder and owner of the celebrated bookshop, Shakespeare & Company, in Paris; patron of James Joyce and publisher of *Ulysses* (1922), she played a central rôle in 'literary Paris' in the 1920s and 30s. See Noel R. Fitch, *Sylvia Beach and the Lost Generation* (1984).   [3] See Letters 4362, 4400.

will be suppressed, and then *he needn't pay* – and, of course, he won't hand over more than a few copies to the police. The rest he gets for nothing. I am anxious to get your second letter. I enclose a note to the fellow: also a receipt, which you can give him when you have the books.[1]

I'm so glad you're doing this for me. – Will write about the pictures later.

DHL

Use the enclosed only if necessary – and fill in the number of copies received.

[Frieda Lawrence begins]

Dont get into any trouble – you seem such a small thing for a conspirator.

F.

4571. To Giuseppe Orioli, [4–5 August 1928]
Text: MS UCLA; cited in Moore, *Intelligent Heart* 384.

Kesselmatte. Gsteig b. Gstaad. (Bern)

4 August 1928

Dear Pino,

Today I heard from Kot. that he has collected the 36 copies from Stevens and Brown, and has them safe in his house. – I am having them taken down to the country.

I also heard from Enid H[ilton] that she has got the 74 copies from Jacksons safely in her flat. So that is all right. I am getting her to deposit 50 safely somewhere.

I have asked Kot. to give two copies to Pollinger, and to send one to *Baroness v. Hutten* – I presume it *is* the Baroness. I will ask her to pay me direct.

Has Boris sent out the six Foyle copies? I heard from Pollinger – he has not received anything yet. Make sure of Boris.

Don't send out any copies to England or America: only to France or Italy etc. *Send all orders to me, here*, and I will forward them to Enid H. But we must have cash in advance: or on delivery. – What do you suggest?

So America seems to have gone wrong! What a blow, if all those copies are lost! – and if we have to re-fund the money! Oh curse their prudery! We can now only wait.

How many people are there who have not paid? Do you think some of the brutes are waiting, hoping the book will be suppressed, thinking then they *need not pay*? We must make them.

Kot. was very nice – he will help all he can. But we mustn't let anybody *steal* the books from us, if we can help it.

---

[1] The enclosures are missing.

I enclose Lord Beaverbrook's letter – get him a *Rainbow* if you can.[1]

Now do have a good peaceful cool time in Vallombrosa. Tell Carletto I will send him a post-card in answer to his.

All serene here, save for anxiety about her ladyship.

Affectionately DHL

Thanks for the 'Chas. Wilson' books – I got them safely.[2]

Sunday.

– Just got your letter with Holland cheque.[3] Will you send all orders to *me* here – and I'll forward to Enid H. – so she receives no Italian letters.

4572. To Dorothy Yorke, 4 August 1928
Text: MS StaU; Schorer 62.

'Kesselmatte', *Gsteig b. Gstaad.* (Bern), Switzerland
Sat. 4 Aug 1928

My dear Arabella

Your letter came on yesterday – and the cheque – which I'm sending back to you, as I want you to take a copy from the 30. odd which Richard will rescue for me from Koteliansky, I am sure. Kot. has got them safely. Perhaps he has written.

I was awfully pleased that you liked the book, both of you. I'm afraid it's cost me the beaux restes[4] of my friends – a rugged remnant, anyhow. And I'm really very glad you like to read me, Arabella. Believe me, I get far more insults and impudence about my work, than appreciation: so when anyone comes out a bit whole-heartedly, I really feel comforted a great deal. I must say, I don't find much generous appreciation. It's usually superior disapproval, or slightly-mingy, narrow-gutted condescension.

I want R. to keep these copies quite quietly, and tell nobody, and just let them lie till I have a use for them. So far, there's not the slightest risk. The book is not suppressed, and is as free as any other book. But some of the booksellers, swine, are in a funk and making these returns.[5]

If we come to England, be sure we'll come to the cottage. I *know* you *really* like us both – but I felt a bit doubtful about Richard. Men so easily seem to

[1] See p. 479 n. 2. [2] See Letters 4551 and 4585.
[3] Vyvyan Beresford Holland (1886–1967), biographer, short-story writer, translator; author of *The Mediaeval Courts of Love* (1927), *Son of Oscar Wilde* (1954), *Oscar Wilde* (1960), etc. DHL noted in his 'Memoranda' (MS NWU) that Holland's cheque for £2, dated 29 July, was 'sent to Emily'. (Holland is credited with two earlier cheques: 18 June and 17 July, both for £2.)
[4] 'the fine remainder'.
[5] Aldington wrote to Kot, 8 August 1928, and quoted this paragraph verbatim; he was asking Kot to send the copies of *Lady Chatterley's Lover* 'by passenger train as soon as possible' (TMSC Moore).

have a mysterious grudge against me – I'm always up against it. But now I think R. really likes us too – without that reservation which I felt before. Anyhow I hope so. – And if I am a fool, and say out my impressions to almost anybody – still, I don't think I'm either ungenerous or dishonest.

So I hope we'll meet this year. I do wish I were better – I've been down all this year. If only I'm better we might do something together in the autumn.

Frieda sends her love, with mine.

DHL

Kot. has been *very nice* about the books.

4573. To Enid Hilton, 4 August 1928
Text: MS UTul; Huxley 740–1.

Kesselmatte. *Gsteig b. Gstaad.* (Bern)
4 Aug. 1928

My dear Enid

Yours today, to say you have the books safely – Hurrah! I was afraid of that Steele – as I wrote you, in my unnecessary letter this afternoon. – Don't be troubled about being Cordelia. But I *do* wish you hadn't given your father's address. Better a fake one. You are under *no* obligation to give Jackson's your name. You may give them any name you please. The only person you are responsible to is to me. – But though Jackson has no right to disclose your name to anyone except *me*, if I demand his receipt; – he may kindly inform the police, should there be any trouble. There is no trouble so far – no risk whatsoever – the book might as well be any common book on the market, in that respect. So you are perfectly safe. The only trouble would be *if* the book were suppressed, *if* Jackson's gave the police your address, *if* they followed it up to your Daddy – then they might descend on you and seize the books. That is all they could do. You are in no way against the law.

But I shall write to Jackson's and give them my receipt and ask ·hem to post yours to me. And then I think we'd better try and think of a place where we can deposit the books, safely. At the moment I can think of nowhere. I'd send them to Ada, but I'm not telling my sisters about this venture. It would only shock them. Have you any idea of a place – some safe place where the things could lie till we needed them? If you think of a place, just box fifty copies and transfer them to it. You can have someone fetch the box, and you needn't know where it goes. It would be safer.

Then the odd twenty copies you could send out as I ask you. I'll tell Orioli to send me[1] the orders, and I'll forward them to you.

---

[1] me] you

And I *want* you to take a copy – later on I'll write in it: to Enid, for her help in time of trouble. And then later it will become more valuable.

Meanwhile I'm most awfully grateful. And tell Lawrence not to trouble: nobody is under any obligation whatever to give their name on request: the only danger would be if you did it to *defraud Jackson's* – which you don't in the least – so you can call yourself what you like, and give the moon for your address, and you don't infringe at all on the law.

DHL

Orioli has a bunch of orders in Florence – I asked him to send them to me, and I'll forward them to you. So keep 20 or 30 copies by you.

4574. To Laurence Pollinger, 4 August 1928
Text: MS UT; Unpublished.

Kesselmatte, Gsteig b. Gstaad. (Bern), Switzerland
4 Aug. 1928

Dear Pollinger

Thanks for yours about Secker, and for putting that cheque in the bank.

The bookseller is Stevens and Brown – terrified for their reputation. And another brute, Jackson, writes he wants to return the things. Damn all their white livers, the brutes. How dare they go back on their orders. But I wish I knew of some safe place in which to store the excess copies. There seems to be a scare of suppression and police search. But people are always scared. – I got a friend to collect the Stevens and Brown copies – but I'd better not give his name. I've asked him to send you in all five copies – three you ordered, two you can hold for me, in case anyone wants one. And would you pay the cheques in to my account in the Aldwych Westminster. Saves bother. – But let me know if you've had the books.

Lord, what fuss, always fuss!

D. H. Lawrence

4575. To Margaret King, [5 August 1928]
Text: MS Needham; PC; Postmark, Gsteig 6.VIII. 28; Unpublished.

Gsteig
Sunday

My dear Peg

Your letter just come – what fun that you are coming! You may just as well come Lausanne–Montreux – it is prettier that way. But ask about the trains back – it may be more convenient to go back Spiesz–Bern–Calais. Or you might go Diablerets, Aigle Lausanne. There is a bus from here to Diablerets.

494 *[6 August 1928]*

– Don't bring much luggage – the less the better – bring ½lb tea each. It's been quite hot here, with a cool wind, and no rain. But you never know if it will turn chilly – so bring one set warm underthings. Ivy might meet you at the Gare du Nord and go across with you to Gare de Lyons, have dinner on the station, it's quite nice. You only have just the one night in the train – not so bad – It'll be dawn on the Jura. – You don't have to get out at Vallorbe – frontier – they come into the carriage for passports and customs. – I'll write a letter to your mother directly.

Love   DHL

4576. To Enid Hilton, [6 August 1928]
Text: MS UCLA; Huxley 741.

Kesselmatte. Gsteig b. Gstaad.
Monday

Dear Enid

Richard Aldington says he'll house some copies – so if you feel like putting forty copies in a box and sending them – or even taking[1] them down – by passenger train, to him at

Malthouse Cottage. Padworth, nr. Reading, Berks.

that would relieve you of a lot. You might send him a note.

So sorry to be bothering you. I'll send you orders to distribute directly they come from Florence, and arrange with you about it.

DHL

4577. To Giuseppe Orioli, 6 August 1928
Text: MS UCLA; PC; Postmark, Gsteig 6 VIII 28; Unpublished.

[Kesselmatte, Gsteig b. Gstaad, Switzerland]
Monday. 6 Aug. 1928

Dear Pino

I wrote you to Florence – this is duplicate. – All books are safe, with K[oteliansky] and with Mrs H[ilton]. Now will you send me all orders *here*, and I will forward them to Enid H. and have them sent out from the Jackson lot. I don't trust Jacksons. – And we'll have payment on delivery. Send me the orders as soon as you can.

Hope you are having a good time in Vallombrosa – here it is suddenly quite cold, though sunny. Perhaps you are freezing!

Love from both.   DHL

[1] taking] putting

4578. To Laurence Pollinger, 6 August 1928
Text: MS UT; Unpublished.

Kesselmatte. Gsteig b. Gstaad. (Bern)
6 Aug 1928

Dear Pollinger

Elkin Matthews can have *Rawdon's Roof* if they like, but if I am going to sign the thing they must pay me twenty-five guineas instead of twenty – I loathe signing – and 20 gs. is less than 15%.[1]

If they agree, I would like to look over the story – I would send it back the next day. And if they'd prefer it a bit longer, no doubt I could expand a little, as I always try to nip things down, writing for magazines.

Sincerely   D. H. Lawrence

4579. To Martin Secker, [7 August 1928]
Text: MS Lazarus; PC; Postmark, Gsteig 7.VIII.28; Unpublished.

[Kesselmatte, Gsteig b. Gstaad, Switzerland]
7. *August.*

I signed the sheets yesterday and sent them back – signed 102, two extra in case of mishap.[2]

Do you want to see *The False Prince* – the German book I wrote you about?[3]

DHL

4580. To S. S. Koteliansky, 8 August 1928
Text: MS BL; Postmark, Gsteig 9.VIII.28; Zytaruk 352.

Kesselmatte. Gsteig b. Gstaad. (Bern)
Wed. 8 Aug. 1928

My dear Kot.

I'm glad you will keep the 36 copies by you. Richard A[ldington] said he had written for you to send them down there[4] – but I presume you didn't.

Now Orioli says he has sent you[5] some orders to distribute. Perhaps you

---

[1] Elkin Mathews published *Rawdon's Roof* as No. 7 of *The Woburn Books* series (Roberts A40); 530 numbered and autographed copies were published (though DHL told Mathews in February 1929 that he had signed 531 sheets).   [2] See p. 463 n. 3.

[3] The book, by Harry Domela, was *Der Falsche Prinz* (Berlin, 1927). Published by the avantgarde publishing house, Malik-Verlag, it chronicles Domela's success in passing himself off as the heir to the German throne, together with his diverse experiences as a farm-hand, the inmate of a jail, unemployed, etc. The memoir is that of a déclassé who authentically strips the veneer off German society at both the exalted and the lower levels.

[4] See p. 491 n. 5.   [5] he has sent you] you have sent him

have done it already. If not, send on the orders to Mrs Lawrence Hilton, 44
Mecklenburgh Square, W.C. 1. – and ask her to do it. I don't trust the
Jacksons either, and would much rather have that Jackson lot distributed. I
have already asked Enid H. to send 40 copies in a box down to Richard. And I
have asked Orioli to send all orders here to *me*, and I'll forward them to Enid
H. He has another two dozen or so, he says – And if you hear of any action
against the book, you'll let me know at once, won't you – and Enid H. too –
and Richard.

I'm sending the cheque again. I beg you please to pay *all* expenses out of it.
Don't please send it back again.

Did you send the two copies to Cornish Bros. of Birmingham? Orioli says
he sent you their order for two copies, and then wrote to you they had *cancelled*
it. – Dirty swine. – If you have *not* sent them the order, will you forward them
their money back (I enclose cheque). But if you *have* sent their order, perhaps
you can get the books back before you refund. I really think Orioli is too meek
about accepting the cancelling of orders. I am trying to make Jacksons refund
postage.

Well, you are probably gone away to the country by the time this reaches
London. I hope you'll have a good time. It's marvellous weather here.

I'm most awfully sorry to give you such a lot of trouble. But now I hope it
will be finished. And do pay all postage and everything from my cheque.

DHL

Cornish Bros. – Booksellers. 39 New St. Birmingham

4581. To Giuseppe Orioli, [8 August 1928]
Text: MS UCLA; PC; Postmark, Gsteig 9.VIII.28; Unpublished.

Gsteig.
Wed

Your Monday's letter today. Have written Kot. about Cornish Bros. and sent
cheque to him. – Now I hope you'll let me have all orders as soon as possible,
that I can hand them over to Mrs. H[ilton]. Kot. is going away into the
country tomorrow – Thursday – for about a fortnight.

I am trying to make Jacksons pay postage. They *all* ought to pay postage on
returns. – And now I think we ought to say cash on delivery – especially if
Mrs. H. delivers by hand.

Am glad you are at Vallombrosa. Here the sun blazes, but wind is cool,
quite cool – it is extraordinary weather, so fine. Hope you are feeling well.
Poor Carletto, he'll still be hot!

DHL

Lord Beaverbrook said if you could get him a copy of *The Rainbow* for £5. – he'd be glad.

4582. To Enid Hilton, 8 August 1928
Text: MS UCB; Unpublished.

Gsteig.

8 Aug 1928

Dear Enid

If Mrs Aldington asks you for a copy of *Lady C.*, do send her one at once, as I had her cheque[1] – but am not sure if Koteliansky has forwarded the copy or not. – He – Kot – has gone away to the country for two weeks. – I hope to be able to send you about thirty orders tomorrow – or the next day – to distribute. Hope all is well.

DHL[2]

4583. To Richard Aldington, [8 August 1928]
Text: MS Lazarus; Unpublished.

[Kesselmatte, Gsteig b. Gstaad, Switzerland]
Wed

Dear Richard

I wonder if you got that copy of *Lady C.* for Arabella. If not, send the enclosed to Enid Hilton. 44 Mecklenburgh Sq. I expect Kot. kept the 36 copies – so perhaps you'll be taking some from the other lot.

Anyhow we'll never say die. You must stick to it that you think the book a good book – and a feather in the cap of the 20th century!! Don't go back on it. Don't, like all the rest, be minchione. The whole be-shitten world is minchionato, even the apparent perky ones. But I tell 'em all what I think of 'em. Tutto il male non viene per nuocere.[3] Whatever happens, let me live game and die game – the ghastliest of all is to let them minchionare one.[4]

If you take some of the books please keep them and *don't* try to peddle them. Don't tell anybody you've got them. Let them be the nest-egg. And when the book rises in price, we'll think about selling them then. But be mum.

Meanwhile hell have all hypocrites and narrow-gutted pigeons.

DHL

---

[1] See Letter 4572. (DHL referred to Arabella Yorke as 'Mrs Aldington' though she was not married to Richard Aldington.)
[2] This letter was enclosed with the one following to Aldington.
[3] 'It's an ill wind blows no one any good.'   [4] 'take one for a ride'.

4584. To Mabel Dodge Luhan, 9 August 1928
Text: MS Brill; Luhan 337–8.

Kesselmatte. Gsteig b. Gstaad. (Bern), Switzerland
9 August 1928

Dear Mabel

I'm glad you got *Lady C.* and that you liked it. I'm anxious about the other copies sent – about 200 in all – to America, as several people sent cables saying 'don't send.' – It went into England all right, though there was a great scare in London – police were reported to have a warrant to search for it. However nothing has happened so far; and perhaps it won't, if nobody raises a dust. But most people seem to hate the book: some dealers have returned their copies – and altogether there is a lot of fuss and nuisance. Makes one hate hypocrisy and prudery more then ever – and people as a bulk.

We sit here in this little chalet near the top of the mountains – been here nearly five weeks – and until this week I felt no better. But this week I really begin to feel a difference, and can begin taking short sun-baths – they only made me worse before. If only I can get a real start, to shake off this accursed cough, I ought to come along all right. But this last year I don't seem to have been able to get back to myself. Now let's hope I can. Anyhow it's useless thinking of coming to New Mexico or anywhere far, till I get this cough down.

The Brewsters are in the hotel in the village – at present with *four* American spinster friends[1] – quite nice women, but Oh God! the meaninglessness that simply stares at one out of these women of fifty. They seem to have outlived any meaning they might ever have had, and are just rattling, rattling insistent spectres. Awful! They give me the jim-jams. If only they wouldn't *insist* on being there! If only they'd fade into the nothingness they really are! Then they might emerge again somehow. As it is, they rattle with the insistence of skeletons.

We are due to stay here till end Sept. – and shall, I suppose, if it really does me good. Pray God it may! I'm supposed to go to London to see my pictures exhibited, first two weeks in October – and I may, or may not. Here I just dibble at tiny pictures, and potter about among the trees. – A bad few years for everybody. But let's hope we'll all get steady on our legs and manage with a bit of real equilibrium, afterwards. Poveri noi! Anyhow the weather is superb.

Now I'll go and hunt my spectacles, which I lost this morning! Hope you're feeling well.

Regards to everybody   DHL

---

[1] See Letter 4596.

4585. To Charles Wilson, 9 August 1928

Text: MS NYPL; PC v. Sanetschfall, Gsteig b. Gstaad; Postmark, Gsteig 10 VIII 28;
Unpublished.

Kesselmatte. *Gsteig b. Gstaad*, Bern
9 Aug 1928.

Dear Mr Wilson

Your card came today and I thought it would say you had the books. I wrote
in them and sent them off to you last week: and I *told* the girl to register them –
probably she didn't. What a blow if they are lost! I believe it is ten full days
since I sent them. Do let me know the moment you get them. Of course it's
just the kind of parcel that would be likely to be stolen. *St. Mawr* and *Plumed
Serpent* it was. I am getting better – but they insist I must stay here till end of
September at least – which is rather boring. – Did you by the way receive a
copy of *Lady Chatterleys Lover?* I believe one was sent. Probably you are
shocked, like most other people: but take a second breath, and get over it.
Nothing really natural is shocking. It is pleasant here, and very fine weather –
but I'd come to Paris and England if I could. One can have too much of
mountain tops. – I do hope you have the books.

DHL

4586. To Enid Hilton, [10 August 1928]

Text: MS UCLA; Unpublished.

Kesselmatte, *Gsteig b. Gstaad.* (Bern)
Friday evening

Dear Enid

Had your note – my regards to your Father and 'Betty'.[1]

I enclose Orioli's letter and list of orders.[2] I would rather they paid on
delivery – but don't insist on those who are *good* – There's only one
questionable. – Kot says the safest way is by parcel post, and he puts inside a
slip:

Sent by Pino Orioli, 6 Lungarno Corsini, Florence.
That leaves you nameless.

But of course if you are to deliver and get payment on delivery, it would
have to be done by hand. I leave it to your discretion. Of course you'd take a
taxi – don't lug parcels about. I'll send more money. – Books to the country of
course must be posted.

Kot. says *he* can take forty of your copies, to *hide* them. He'll let you know if
it's necessary. We might wait a bit. If you've sent a box to R[ichard]

---

[1] Olive ('Lizzie') Hopkin.   [2] The enclosures are missing.

A[ldington], then that's done.

Will you write to Orioli to tell him you have delivered the books – and result – when you've done it. And about payment.

I'm awfully grateful to you for looking after the business for me.

I wish you both were in the chalet across. It's such lovely weather – today we went over the pass to Diablerets. Now it's six oclock, and a still, full sunlight on *your* mountain and chalet.

Tell me how you get on with the books – love from us both to both.

Keep as *mum* as possible about having the books in your possession.

DHL

4587. To S. S. Koteliansky, 10 August 1928
Text: MS BL; Postmark, Gsteig 11.VIII.28; Zytaruk 353.

Kesselmatte. Gsteig b. Gstaad. (Bern)
10 Aug 1928

My dear Kot

Many thanks for yours. I have today sent Enid H[ilton] a list of twenty copies to send out. Hope she does it safely. – She *may* have sent some copies down to Richard A[ldington] – if so, I expect we shall soon exhaust what are left with her. But I'll let you know. – Only if anything *definite* happens in the confiscation line, you might make sure her lot is safe. Otherwise don't you trouble any more. I'm awfully sorry you've been bothered so much. – Now there is that final bit of a nuisance with Cornish Bros – Oh dear!

I'm sorry you're not going to the country – it might have done you good. But perhaps you'll get your trip yet.

hastily.   DHL

4588. To Giuseppe Orioli, 10 August 1928
Text: MS UCLA; cited in Moore, *Poste Restante* 96.

Kesselmatte, Gsteig b. Gstaad. (Bern)
10 Aug 1928

Dear Pino

I have forwarded your letter with orders to Enid H[ilton] – asked her to collect on delivery if possible – and to let you know the result *direct* – and where she has not been able to collect the money, will you send the invoice at once, to the people concerned. But wait for her letter.

Yes, this way seems to me good – send me your list of orders and the labels, and you keep the *letters* containing the orders.

Kot raises a little more scare. He sent out the 12 copies – also to Cornish

Bros. I wrote and asked him to recover those two, and I sent him cheque to re-fund.

Did Boris send out the six Foyle copies?

How many people have not paid for Copies received? Kot. says he will go and deal with them if necessary.

Hope we'll soon get straight. – Am glad you're in the freshness. We went to Diablerets today – so different from winter. – Do hope there's no fuss with the authorities about *Lady C.*

Love from both. DHL

Don't take too much notice of Kot's alarms – he *is* like that.

4589. To Enid Hilton, [11 August 1928]
Text: MS UCLA; Unpublished.

Gsteig – b. Gstaad. Switzerland
Saturday

Dear Enid

I hear Kot. called at your house, but you were out. He is anxious about your having so many copies.

Will you do this today: take a dozen copies along to Mr. L. E. Pollinger, of Curtis Brown, 6 Henrietta St. Covent Garden. – They are my agents. He will sell them.

But also take him this enclosed letter,[1] ask to see him, tell him how many copies of the book you've got, and then take his advice about handing a certain number over to him to hide and sell – but don't give him more than twenty-five or so, as I shall continue to send orders to you to distribute – that is, don't give him more unless he says there's danger in your keeping them.

DHL

4590. To Giuseppe Orioli, [11 August 1928]
Text: MS UCLA; cited in Moore, *Intelligent Heart* 384.

Gsteig.
Saturday

Dear Pino

I sent this man a note telling him you would forward him a copy if he sent cheque for £2.[2]

[1] Missing.
[2] DHL had received (via Curtis Brown) the following enquiry dated 8 August 1928, from Martinus Nijhoff, bookseller in The Hague (TMSC UCLA):

Boris has *not* left a copy with Pollinger. Has he collected those six Foyle copies? And what has he done with them? If he has not collected them, we must ask Mrs. H[ilton] to get them *at once*. Kot is out of town.

DHL

4591. To Bonamy Dobrée, 12 August 1928
Text: MS Brotherton; Unpublished.

Kesselmatte. Gsteig b. Gstaad. (Bern)
12 August 1928

Dear Dobrée

We expect to be here all September, in case you should care to look us up. You can come Montreux to Gstaad by the Berner Oberland Railway: or from Aigle to Diablerets, and thence by post-bus. But as you say, it is very hilly, no level walks – and altitude does affect one. Though it's a quiet and pretty place.

I don't mind what you say about *Woman Who Rode Away*. If you saw the American reviews you would understand, one is used to anything and everything. Twenty years of putting books into the world leaves one quite callous. And I enjoy slanging a book when it gets my goat. But I rather feel, in your criticisms – few I've seen – that you don't react direct – rather take an attitude and display that, rather than your own feelings. It's sort of modern – and makes criticism so boring – no first-hand feeling or experience, always an attitude.

Amusing how people disliked *Lady C.*[1] I'm afraid I've lost $\frac{9}{10}$ of my few remaining friends. But such friends are well lost, like dead limbs from a tree.

Don't let us arrange a visit to Egypt – I think, being four people, we don't know one another well enough to risk a staying visit. But we may come for all that and stay in some hotel or pension, and come to tea when you ask us, and perhaps make little jaunts. Anyhow I do *not* want to stay in Italy this winter. When I've sat here in comparative solitude for three months, then I shall feel like shifting round a bit. Why not to the pyramids!

Dear Sir,
   I am told you have published in Italy *Mrs. Chatelet's Lovers*. I am anxious to get a copy and will consider it as a favour if you will tell the publisher to send me a copy of if you will kindly inform me where I can get it.
   Thanking you in anticipation. . .

DHL's 'note' in reply is unlocated; his letter to Orioli was written on Nijhoff's.
[1] Presumably Dobrée had received his copy of *Lady Chatterley's Lover* and had commented on it; his cheque was dated 14 April 1928 ('Memoranda', MS NWU).

It's marvellous weather here – and I paint a bit, and we have some friends in the village. Time slips by like a sleep. I think the place does me good.

Hope you are both having a nice summer.

Yrs   D. H. Lawrence

I've not seen the *Criterion* – probably someone will send it along.[1]

4592. To Enid Hilton, [13–14 August 1928]
Text: MS UCLA; Unpublished.

Gsteig.
Monday night

Dear Enid

Another order, three copies, J. E. Cornish Ltd. 1 Ridgefield. Manchester. Will you please send them off.

Tuesday

Yours just now to say the books are stowed away – and Richard writes he has got the batch safely – wonder if you've been able to send out the orders – Here's another one. If you haven't enough forward to Richard, he'll send out for me. Keep account of *all* your expenses, mind!

DHL

4593. To Harry Crosby, [13 August 1928]
Text: MS SIU; Postmark, Gstei[g] 15.[. . .]; Huxley 747–8.

Kesselmatte. Gsteig b. Gstaad. (Bern)
Monday

Dear Harry Crosby

Yours this evening. Many thanks for the books. I'm very much interested in modern painting – but I doubt that's not a good book you sent. I expect to have an exhibition of my paintings in London in Oct. – and probably in New York in November, in Alfred Stieglitz's gallery. When we come to Paris in Oct. I'll give you a little painting I did of men catching sun-horses – quite tiny – but I always half meant it for you. Perhaps we shall go to New York in late autumn. But I hope we'll see you before then.

I enclose a drawing of the Sun, from a Maya design.[2] You can blank out the

---

[1] Dobrée had published 'William Congreve: A Conversation between Swift and Gay at the House of the Duke of Queensberry, near London, June 1730', in *Criterion*, vii (1928), 4, 7–17.

[2] The drawing enclosed was inscribed: 'To Harry Crosby from D. H. Lawrence. The Greater Sun, with the daily sun as his breast-gem.' It was used as a frontispiece to the Black Sun Press *Sun* (Roberts A35b).

lettering if you like. But you may not like the design. I do though. Anyhow keep it if you like it.

I only get depressed about my health – if only I am well I'm a quite happy soul. But I do get tired of not being well: it's three years now I'm shaky, since we came back from America last time.

Imagine a race-horse! But what a tricky thing to ride! I've never ridden except in New Mexico, where we've got four or five horses – value 50 to 70 dollars apiece. But I love them, and wish to God I was there unsaddling at the little saddle-house now evening is falling. Will you ride your Sunstroke in the Bois – or will you race him at Newmarket? Bella bestia![1]

What luck to find a sun-maid! not a raisin but a real lass![2] Americana anche! proprio d'oro, o soltanto dorata? beato tu![3]

I'll tell Knopf and Secker and my agents that you are doing 100 de luxe *Suns* late autumn at 125 francs French – Do write the Miss Allanah Harper – and compare the MSS, yours and hers.[4] Make her give you proofs. And take any bits out of hers that you like, especially at the end. I believe it's better.

Savage rumours that *Lady Chatterley* is to be suppressed in London: and that it is stopped from entering America. Lieb Ding![5] – Better read it – it's a direct phallic book, i.e. the direct *nocturnal* connection of a man with the sun – the path of the dark sun.

D. H. Lawrence

I've got a nice canvas of sun-faun and sun-nymphs laughing at the Crucifixion – but I had to paint out the Crucifixion –

If the sun is too complicated, I'll try a simpler one. This is meant to be done in three colours, but it would probably look all right in black and white half-tone.

4594. To Martin Secker, 14 August 1928

Text: MS UInd; Postmark, Gsteig 15.[. . .]28; Secker 110.

Kesselmatte. Gsteig b. Gstaad. (Bern)
Tuesday. 14 Aug. 1928

Dear Secker

We decided we couldn't translate *The False Prince* as it was too depressing

---

[1] 'Fine animal!' DHL is pictured with 'Sunstroke' in Caresse Crosby, *The Passionate Years* (1955), plate 30. According to Harry Crosby's diary (*Shadows of the Sun*, ed. E. Germain, Santa Barbara, 1977, p. 210), the Crosbys bought the 'yearling (terribly cunning and young and fiery) and his name is "Sunstroke"', on 15 August 1928.

[2] The pun involves the well-known brand of 'Sun-Maid raisins', and the 'lass', Josephine Noyes Rotch (1908–29) who became Crosby's mistress and died with him in 1929 (see Wolff, *Black Sun*, p. 208ff.).   [3] 'American as well! real gold, or only gilded? lucky you!'

[4] Cf. Letter 4533 and n. 3.   [5] 'The dear thing!'

and a bit scaring. But I found it very interesting, really, as a document of that underworld.[1]

Thanks for the $33\frac{1}{3}$ guineas.[2] I am looking forward very much to the poems. When do you think you will bring them out?

I agree about the label on the back of *Lady C*. – I don't like it. –

A friend in Paris, Harry Crosby, wants to do a little edition of the short story *Sun* – a hundred copies only, more or less *de luxe*. He wants to do it because he bought the MS. from me, and found the printed version so much expurgated, he wants to print it whole. Let me know if you have any objection. I think he'd do it late autumn, *if* he does it –

Lovely weather always here – and I think it does me good: if only it weren't so *steep*. I simply can't get up and down these slopes. Otherwise it's really a very nice place.

I've been painting a bit, but not much else. I think if we go back to Italy in October I'd like to finish my Etruscans. Aldous said they'd motor us round.

Hope all goes well.

Viele Grüsse   DHL

4595. To Alfred Stieglitz, 15 August 1928

Text: MS YU; Postmark, Gsteig 16.[. . .]28; Huxley 742–3.

Kesselmatte, Gsteig b Gstaad. (Bern), Switzerland
15 August 1928

Dear Stieglitz

Many thanks for sending that cable to Florence.[3] I'm glad you liked *Lady C*. She seems to have exploded like a bomb among most of my English friends, and they're still suffering from shell-shock. But they're coming round already: and some few already feeling it was good for 'em. Give them time. – There are rumours of suppression in England, and rumours of ban in America. But I can't help it. I've shot my shot, anyhow: I shot an arrow into the air tee-de-dum![4]

Don't be alarmed about the pictures – they're quite good. Anyhow they *contain* something – which is more than you can say of most moderns, which are all excellent rind of the fruit, but no fruit. And because a picture has subject-matter it is not therefore less a picture. Besides, what's a deformed guitar and a shred of newspaper but subject-matter? There's the greatest lot of bunk talked about modern painting ever. If a picture is to hit deep into the senses, which is its business, it must hit down to the soul and up into the mind

---

[1] See Letter 4579 and n. 3.   [2] See Letter 4546.   [3] See Letter 4512.
[4] Longfellow, 'The Arrow and the Song', l.1 ['. . . air,/It fell to earth, I knew not where'].

– that is, it has to mean something to the co-ordinating soul and the co-ordinating spirit which are central in man's consciousness: and the meaning has to come through direct sense-impression. I know what I'm about. As for their space composition and their mass-reaction and their arabesques, if that isn't all *literary* and idea-concept, what is? Such a lot of canary-cages, and never a bird in one of 'em! What, I ask you, is Roger Fry? – a literary gentleman, or a painter?[1] My God, look at his pictures! The pen is mightier than the palette in *his* case.[2]

But I'm not really keen on exhibiting, so don't go to any trouble. Dorothy Warren is supposed to be showing my things in London in first half of October – that is, if I don't go and stop her – which leaves the pictures free for November. But as I say, I don't really care whether the canvases come to New York or not. Only if you show me, at least have a look at Brett's things and see if you don't like them.

I want to come to America in late autumn anyhow, to go to the ranch. So I hope we shall meet. How *did* O'Keefe take the book?

Sincerely   D. H. Lawrence

4596. To Earl Brewster, [15 August 1928]
Text: MS UT; cited in Brewster 175–6.

Kesselmatte. Gsteig b. Gstaad (Bern)
Wed. morning

Dear Earl

Hope you're having a good time in Paris with Mukerdji. Here it's just the same, but a bit more cloudy. I'm beginning to feel a bit fed up with it, and wish we could go away. I reckon my health is just as good anywhere else.

I painted *Contadini* on the panel you gave me.[3] – Oh, if there are in Paris nude photographs that I could use in my sort of painting – natural ones – buy me some if you have time. But don't bother of course. I have never seen but two of the famous Paris 'obscene' post cards, and they were just ugly. They need not be, surely.

We had dinner at the Viktoria last night, said goodbye to the Barkers. At

---

[1] Roger Eliot Fry (1866–1934), art critic and painter associated with the Bloomsbury group; responsible for influential exhibitions of Post-Impressionist paintings (1910 and 1912), and for increasing interest in modern French painting.

[2] Cf. Edward George Earle Bulwer-Lytton, *Richelieu*, II. ii. 308 (1839): 'The pen is mightier than the sword'.

[3] The whereabouts of this small oil painting which particularly caught the attention of one reviewer of the Warren Gallery exhibition are unknown (see Nehls, iii. 334, 715 n. 185).

least they have a certain quiet. Adelaide Kirk, how she did rattle! – and how I
hate that song 'The Four Marys' since Belle, or Bell, mewed it![1]

We'll be expecting you back Sunday – and then we can be casting round in
our minds plans for late autumn and winter. At the moment I incline towards
the ranch and the simple life.

Poor Achsah had tooth-ache, and is going to Gstaad this morning to have
the aluminium filling taken out. Sporca miseria!

Frieda had such a grand birthday feast at the Viktoria on Saturday, such a
pile of gifts, and she was so *moved*. I of course was the mocker at the festival.[2]

Somebody sent me *Transition* – American number – that Paris
modernissimo periodical, James Joyce and Gertrude Stein etc.[3] What a stupid
olla podrida[4] of the Bible and so forth James Joyce is: just stewed-up
fragments of quotation in the sauce of a would-be-dirty mind. Such effort!
Such exertion! sforzato davvero![5]

My regards to Mukerdji, the indiarubber ball. Tell him he's all right so
long as he keeps his bounce. It would be fatal if he went slack.

Tante cose!   DHL

4597. To Maria and Aldous Huxley, 15 August 1928
Text: Huxley 741–2.

Kesselmatte, Gsteig b. Gstaad (Bern).   .
15 August, 1928

Dear Maria and Aldous, –

Nothing particularly new here. – Last week I was better, and sun-bathed –
this week I've got a cold and feel all hot inside. It's a beastly climate really,
hot and cold at once. I'm getting sick of it, hope we can leave in first half of
September. But my sister is coming with her daughter for a fortnight end of
this month. Then when she goes we can go – presumably to Baden-Baden for
a bit – and possibly England. I have it in my mind I want to go back to the

---

[1] 'The Four Maries' is a Scottish folk-song.
[2] Achsah Brewster recalled that DHL made the occasion on 11 August 'a gay festival' (Brewster 290).
[3] From Harry Crosby (cf. p. 300 n. 4, Letter 4641), DHL had received no. 13 (Summer 1928) of *transition: An International Quarterly for Creative Experiment*, ed. Eugene Jolas, the journal published in Paris and made famous particularly by the contributions of Joyce, Kafka, Picasso, Gertrude Stein, Allen Tate and many other leading artists and writers. In the 'American Number' Joyce printed further 'Continuation of a Work in Progress' (pp. 5–32); Stein contributed 'An Instant Answer or A Hundred Prominent Men' (pp. 118–30). The issue was concluded with an 'Inquiry among European Writers into the Spirit of America' to which DHL refers disparagingly in Letters 4597 and 4641; among the contributing writers DHL would notice the 'Kra man', Philippe Soupault (cf. Letter 4480 and p. 430 n. 2).
[4] '*pot-pourri*'.   [5] 'really excessive!'

ranch – but absolutely – in November. Perhaps we might first go and look at some Etruscan things, for a little *giro* – Arezzo, Cortona, Chiusi, Orvieto, Norta, Bieda – places just north of Rome. What do you say? – But I begin to feel I want to go back to New Mexico. I shall never be well any more in Europe – so dead! Nothing to re-act to. I am still unaware of the fate of 'Lady Jane' in America – some copies arrived – then we had cables saying 'wait.' So we are waiting. Not that there is any hurry any more; all the English copies having arrived safely. It has been good fun, really, and worth it. Though the money hasn't all come in, by any means. But I feel I've had another whack at 'em – a good satisfactory whack – and it's for them to feel *minchione*,[1] not me. How they love to make one *minchione*, with their decayed disapproval. But their turn, not mine. How glad I am to have lost certain of my 'friends' through 'John Thomas' – like the Israelites who fell dead when the Magic Serpent was erected.[2] May they all fall dead! Pfui!

Aldous, will you please write me out the words of 'I'll give you one – O!' after *four*?[3] I know as far as 'four for the Gospel Writers'. But 5, 6, 7, 8, 9, 10! I don't know.

I had a copy of *Transition*, that Paris magazine – the Amer. number. My God, what a clumsy *olla putrida* James Joyce is! Nothing but old fags and cabbage-stumps of quotations from the Bible and the rest, stewed in the juice of deliberate, journalistic dirty-mindedness – what old and hard-worked staleness, masquerading as the all-new! Gertrude Stein is more amusing – and some of the Americans quite good. But for prize *jejune pap*, take the letters from Frenchmen at the end – the sheer rinsings of baby's napkins. How feeble the Frenchy mind has become!

DHL

4598. To Emily King, [16 August 1928]

Text: MS Lazarus; PC; Postmark, Gsteig 16.VIII.28; Unpublished.

Gsteig.
Thursday

My dear Pamela

So we shall expect you on the 26 – Sunday week, at about nine in the morning. Do hope you won't be too tired – but it's only one night. Don't bother to bring the eider-down after all, as we shall most probably come to England later. But it wouldn't matter as far as customs goes – you can bring

---

[1] '*fools*'.

[2] DHL appears to allude to the 'fiery serpent' Moses was instructed by God to make from brass and erect in the wilderness; it ensured that Israelites who suffered snake-bites should *not* die (Numbers xxi. 6–9).   [3] The song is 'Green Grow the Rushes O'.

anything you use personally – like a cushion – or even an eider-quilt, in place of these great bolsters here. Customs is perfectly easy – I don't think you need wash the undies, if you fold them a bit carelessly with your own things – as if you were going to use them. They never bother about simple things one *does* use: only cigarettes and scents and so on. – Last night the weather broke, and now for the first time since we are here it is a rainy day, and rather cold: the first day in six weeks. I do hope it won't last. It would be awful if you came and it poured. – But it's been dry now for over two months here – which is unusual for the Alps. – I expect the Brewsters will still be here when you come – and Frieda's sister wants to come about Sept. 15th. But I think we shall be leaving about then — go to Baden and then, I think, England. – I'm sorry Joan isn't well – but she'll soon get all right at Ripley. Don't get into a stew about the journey – it's as easy as wink, and everybody perfectly nice. Then we must pray to the Lord about the weather.

love! DHL

4599. To Ada Clarke, 16 August 1928
Text: MS Clarke; Postmark, Gsteig 17.VIII.28; cited in Lawrence–Gelder 179–80.

Kesselmatte. Gsteig b. Gstaad. (Bern), Switzerland

16 Aug 1928

My dear Sister

Well you've been gaily at Mablethorpe for a fortnight, and I hope having a good time. If the weather's good, I know you are. Pamela grizzles a bit that Joan can't go to the seaside: but I really do *not* see why you should be saddled with her every year. And if she's so nervy etc, as Pamela says – well really, Emily should try not to work on the child's nerves herself. They are definitely coming – leaving Saturday week. I do hope everything will be nice for them. Last night we had three thunder-storms in one, so today it is cold and rainy: the first day for six weeks. It's been very dry here for two months – most unusual for the Alps – I'm terrified the weather will break, and be beastly while Pamela and Peg are here. It will be just a catastrophe, for there's nothing to do but sit and stare at rocks and rain and pine-trees and grass-slopes. A bit of new snow fell last night.

Frieda asked Emily to bring an eider-down sewed up in a cushion – a green one for a *single bed*, for me – just simple cotton, I don't want silk and show. I thought if it's not too dear you and Pam might give it me for my birthday. But Pam seems a bit nervous about bringing it – fear of Customs – though there's no need: and I really do want to come to England end of September – so perhaps we had better get it when we are there. No use carting it round – for I expect we shall go to Baden for a bit – Friedas mother seems not so well – a bit of diabetes – and rather depressed, for her – she's usually so cheerful.

I had a letter from Gertie – poor G., it's hard work! But I hope she was fairly happy sitting on the sands in the sun. And let us pray heaven she'll have a good winter.

Today it feels like autumn, and the turning of the year. The peasants bring us bilberries – and soon it will be cranberries. – We drove over the pass the other day to Diablerets. It looked so different in summer, you wouldn't know it was the same place. But a lot of not very pleasant tourists – I really preferred it in winter. In summer it's nicer on this side. – The Brewsters had four American spinster friends at the hotel – quite nice though – and Mukerdji, a Hindu writer who lives in America. He was quite amusing – but Hindus seem a bit false to me, over here.

I'm pretty well in myself, but my cough is a nuisance as ever, and I simply cannot climb these slopes. I suppose I shall just have to put up with it, and leave them unclimbed. Anyhow I don't care so much any more about walking and going to see places.

Is Jack doing the fancy swimming and diving in the Mablethorpe pool? – just let me know when he breaks a record. As for Bertram, he's taking life pleasantly, I know: no thorns on his rose.

Love.   DHL!

4600. To S. S. Koteliansky, [17 August 1928]
Text: MS BL; Postmark, Gsteig 18.VIII.28; Zytaruk 354–5.

Gsteig b. Gstaad.
Friday.

My dear Kot.

Your card from Falmouth this evening. It's a pity if Cornish Bros. send all the way back to Florence. I ought to have suggested that they were sent to *me*, c/o L. E. Pollinger of Curtis Brown Ltd. Pollinger would have taken them in for me – and been quite safe. He is very friendly. However, I suppose it is too late now. I would have told Pollinger to hold the books for me.

Enid sent 32 copies to Richard, who has them safely. The others she has mostly distributed, according to orders – and collected cash in most cases. Mrs Lahr took another twelve copies, and paid on the spot: seems very nice.[1] I think, if Enid has distributed my final orders, she will have only one copy left. And I asked Richard to distribute ten: leaves him 22. Will you do the next

[1] Esther Lahr, née Archer. m. 1922, Charles Lahr (1885–1971), publisher and bookseller, founder and editor of *New Coterie* (see *Letters*, v. 572 n. 1).

batch of orders? – or shall Richard? – Pollinger has sold nine copies for me –
nett – very nice. He may dispose of more. – Or do you think we can begin
again sending out orders from Florence? – Foyle's kept their six copies after
all: after cancelling order. They said they saw the little notice in the *Star*!!¹

There is no further news from America.

Here we had heavy thunder and rain, so now it is quite cold. But I don't
mind. – My sister Emily, elder sister, is coming with her daughter of 20 – they
arrive on the 26th – Sunday week. I do hope it will be fine weather. By Sept. 15
I think we shall have had about enough of here – then probably go to Baden
for ten days – then I want to come to England.

That Bettina von Hutten – Baroness or not – hasn't paid yet.

Enid was awfully good and smart delivering the things. – Orioli says it is
bad business to demand payment on delivery from people we know are pretty
safe – only with comparative strangers one should do it.

Did you have a nice holiday? My word, how I remember Falmouth! staying
near there with the Murrys, in war time: and Murry trying to drown us all, one
Sunday afternoon, when we were rowing on that river and a sudden storm
blew up.² That will always be war region to me.

DHL

4601. To Enid Hilton, 17 August 1928
Text: MS UCLA; Unpublished.

Kesselmatte. Gsteig b. Gstaad. (Bern)
Friday 17 Aug 1928

Dear Enid

You are a jewel distributing those books so well. And now this morning I
have the two cheques, £17 from Lahr, £3 ·· 8 ·· o from Rota. Will you please
place the cash to my account in the Aldwych branch of the Westminster Bank.

I take it you have so far delivered:

---

¹ The following entry in 'The "Star" Man's Diary' appeared in the *Star*, 7 August 1928:

  I am told that there is a brisk inquiry among 'book-fanciers' – as I term those connoisseurs
  whose main idea is the £.s.d. of collecting – for the latest D. H. Lawrence, which has just been
  printed privately in Italy, and was issued at two guineas.
  Only a thousand copies were struck off, and each copy is autographed by Mr Lawrence. The
  title of the book is 'Lady Chatterley's Lover', and the treatment is as frank in some ways and as
  obscure in others, as anything Mr Lawrence has written.
  Personally I rather doubt if the book will enhance the reputation of this distinguished writer,
  though its literary quality is – need it be said? – of the highest.

² The incident may have occurred on Sunday, 30 July 1916, when the Lawrences were staying
  with the Murrys in their cottage at Mylor near Falmouth (cf. *Letters*, ii. 639).

Murray (Ramsgate)	3 copies		
Rota	2	,,	
Sotheran	3	,,	
Mrs Hutchinson[1]	1	,,	
Lahr	12	,,	in all
Miller and Gill	4	,,	
	25 copies		

If you give Pollinger 5, this makes 30. Then with Allen's six, you have only *three* over: your total being 39, Richard having 32. Is that right? You had 72 copies from Jackson, didn't you? – Orioli says Mrs Varda of the Varda Bookshop wants two more copies: I suppose that is in addition to the two you are leaving her. She is a friend of Orioli – and I know her. So if she wants four, take them out of the Allen six. Also send those other three from the Allen six, if you have not forwarded the order to R. I mean the order I sent[2] you on Tuesday.

This will leave you with two copies (exhausting Allen's six). Will you please send one copy to

Miss Daisy Bendex,[3] 19 New Cavendish St. W. 1. (paid)

This leaves you with one copy only. I'll send the rest of the orders to Richard.

Send me the Rhys Davies book when you've read it. Is it the Buddhist scholar Rhys Davies?[4]

I'm so grateful to you for doing all this. I'll write you again about the Allen six. We can get them from R. if necessary. But let such people *wait*.

4602. To Enid Hilton, [17 August 1928]
Text: MS UCLA; PC; Postmark, Gsteig 19 VIII 28; Unpublished.

[Kesselmatte, Gsteig b. Gstaad, Switzerland]
Friday evening.

Thanks for yours – O[rioli] will send invoice to Elkin M[athews].

You send a word to Varda – Mrs – and ask her if you should post to her.

Write to Richard to send the six for L[ahr] – or to you, or direct.

---

[1] Bertram Rota (1903–66), expert in rare books especially modern English literature; his bookshop was in Davis Street. Henry Sotheran Ltd, founded in 1816, operated from 43 Piccadilly. For Mary Hutchinson see p. 383 n. 2.   [2] MS reads: 'send'.
[3] Unidentified.
[4] DHL was confusing the novelist and short-story writer, Rhys Davies (1903–78) who had recently published *The Withered Root* (November 1927), with Caroline Rhys Davids, the Buddhist scholar (cf. Letter 4009 and p. 50 n. 3).

Where did Alice order[1] – from O.? Tell R. to send it.

No, Emily will stay with us – no one in yours all summer. I'm better – think we'll come to England end Sept. We'll tackle Dorothy about the pictures in a day or two – I heard from a woman she'd *seen* one of the pictures – but not which. – Don't bother for a while about the new road –

DHL

4603. To Dorothy Yorke, [17 August 1928]
Text: MS StaU; Schorer 61–2.

Kesselmatte.
Friday

Dear Arabella

You've got your copy of the book now, of course – and I hope you'll like it. I feel I've shot it like a bomb against all their false sex and hypocrisy – as my Florentine doctor said,[2] against all their a-sexual sexuality. So let's hope it'll explode and let in a bit of fresh air. As for me, I feel a bit feeble and a poor rag, and I hate it.

My sister Emily with her daughter Margaret is coming tomorrow week to stay a fortnight. Hope it won't rain! She's never been out of England. – Then I think we shall be getting sick of here, and shall go to BadenBaden for a fortnight or so – then, I hope, to England.

And in the late autumn, let's really go somewhere. Would you go to Egypt if we went? we might find some way of doing it cheap – and there *are* quite nice modest pensions in Cairo. Let's go to Egypt in November, en quatre – and go sometimes and see the Dobrées, and go up the Nile and look at the desert and perhaps get shot in Khartoum like General Gordon.[3] – Frieda of course, woman-like, pines for more islands – Majorca and Minorca – but I'm not keen on islands. The other thing is the Mediterranean shore of Spain. I'd like to go to Madrid to the Prado. But I *don't* want to stay in the Mirenda this winter.

I'm glad you write poems. Do send me some to see. Are they printed yet?

And you must go and see my pictures when they're on show in Oct. – I just did a nice one of contadini.

Have you got lots of flowers, and beans and carrots. We have phlox in a tiny fenced garden, and salad and a few turnips and red currants. – There aren't many Swiss here anyhow – and only peasants – and more like queer earth creatures than anything – very queer – but quite nice.

DHL

---

[1] Perhaps Alice M. Flewins whose cheque (drawn on a London bank) was dated 19 May 1928; she may have been known to Enid Hilton. [2] Dr Giglioli. [3] In 1885.

4604. To Richard Aldington, 17 August 1928
Text: MS Lazarus; Unpublished.

Kesselmatte. *Gsteig b. Gstaad* (Bern)
17 Aug 1928

Dear Richard

Could you send out at once the following orders:

Henry Young and Sons. 12 South Castle St. Liverpool.	1.	copy
G. Jardin. Bookseller. 27 Oxford St. Manchester.	1.	copy
T. S. Mercer. 4 Gerard St. W. 1.	3.	copies
Alfred Rozle and Willan Ltd. 139 Victoria St. E.C.4.	1.	copy
H. K. Beazley and Co. 19 Churton St. Victoria. S.W.1.	3.	copies

I enclose Orioli's four only labels for the parcels. And Kot. said it was best to send by parcel post, and put inside:

sent by Pino Orioli, 6. Lungarno Corsini. Florence

When Kot. comes back I'll get him to send out orders from his 19 copies. Mrs Hilton has exhausted hers – she may forward an order to you. – I enclose cheque for £1. for postage and expenses – and I do hope it doesn't bore you terribly. Arabella of course has her copy. This will leave you with 22.

We had a terrific thunder-upset, and it turned cold. But the sun is out again today, warm.

Hope I don't bother you too much.

DHL

4605. To Giuseppe Orioli, 17 August 1928
Text: MS UCLA; Unpublished.

Kesselmatte. Gsteig b. Gstaad. (Bern), Svizzera
17 Aug 1928

Dear Pino

Your letter now, with cheques from Foyle and Beazley. I'm so sorry you've had toothache. Achsah Brewster has it too.

I have written now to Richard Aldington to ask him to send at once to

Henry Young.	1.	paid
G. Jardin.	1.	not paid
T. S. Mercer.	3.	paid.
Rozle and Willan.	1.	? ?
Beazley.	3.	(You say not paid – but I have their cheque from you –)

The Varda and the Pollingers Mrs H[ilton] is attending to. So send all invoices necessary. Pollinger has already paid for 3 copies £6. don't send him invoice.

You will have heard from Enid that she sent:

F. E. Murray – Ramsgate. –	3 copies	(paid)	
Bertram Rota.	2 ”	”	(£3··8··0)
Sotheran.	3 ”	(”)	(£5··2··0 cash)
Mary Hutchinson.	1 ”		
Mrs Lahr	6 + 2 + 4 = 12 copies, all paid (£20··8··0)		
Miller and Gill.	*4 copies not paid* – send invoice		
	total 25 copies		

Truslove and Hanson were *cancelling* their order – so Enid took their two copies to Lahr (paid). Varda was shut – twice. But Enid will call again and deliver the 2 + 2 copies. J. A. Allen and Co. 16 Grenville St. W.C. 1. were nasty and did not pay, so Enid kept back their six copies. *Have they paid the first two?* If they have, and want the other six, let me know, and *send the invoice* to me, and we'll collect on delivery.

Will you please send at once *three copies* to
    Miss Allanah Harper, 101 *bis* rue de la Tombe, *Issoire. Paris*
    (*paid* – I have her cheque)
Whenever you suggest we collect on delivery, send me the invoice at the same time as the order.

Kot is a very real Jew, as you say.

Enid has no more copies in London – she sent 32 to R. A. because of Kot's alarms. So now I'm asking R. to send out. But when Kot comes back we'll ask him. No word from him since I sent the Cornish Bros. cheque (Birmingham) to him to refund.

Lahr's seem very good: made a very good impression on Enid.

How many copies have you got in Florence?

I do hope the toothache will be better. It's the effect of the heat. We feel a bit limp, though it is pretty cool here.

I wrote and told Jackson's they ought to re-fund the postage – and I asked them for Enid's receipt, sending mine in its place. Behold their solicitor's answer. They are frightened really. I shall give them another slap directly – dirty dirty swine!

Kot is away in the country.

I'll tell you next time the total of all money received. Secker of course is another Jew.

That Bettina v. Hutten (Baroness?) has not paid the copy Kot sent her. She was staying same place as Archie Douglas – has he paid?[1]

If there is anything I owe you, take it from payments or cheques made to you.

DHL

4606. To Nancy Pearn, 20 August 1928
Text: MS UT; Unpublished.

Kesselmatte, *Gsteig b. Gstaad*, Switzerland
20 August 1928

Dear Nancy Pearn

If that Mr Olley would print articles half as fantastic as his own letters, he'd be a gem! – But damn them, they are so *afraid* of their public, they can only balk, balk, balk!

Now let him have 'Why I don't like London':[2] and if he's afraid of it, I'll write one, 'Why I don't like him'!

Did *Vogue* print that review? – I'll bet not![3]

DHL

4607. To Carlo Linati, 20 August 1928
Text: TMSC Bonsignore; Giuseppe Gadda Conti, 'Una Lettera Inedita di D. H. Lawrence', *English Miscellany*, xix (1968), 337.

Kesselmatte. Gsteig b. Gstaad (Bern), Svizzera
20 August 1928

Dear Carlo Linati,[4]

I have your letter today. Do you mean you wish Treves to have the translation rights to 'The Ladybird' and 'The Fox' and pay nothing at all? I'm afraid my agents, Curtis Brown, won't agree. They are very much against granting the right to publish works, without any payment whatsoever. However, I will write to them. I shall be very happy to have you translate those two *novelle*, if it interests you. But the French, the Germans, even the Spanish pay me either a fee or a royalty. It is not a great deal, and makes not much difference to me personally. But my agents insist, and are very stern with me.

I will ask Jonathan Cape to send you a copy of *Mastro Don Gesualdo* in the

---

[1] Son of Norman Douglas; he paid for two copies by cheque dated 20 August 1928 ('Memoranda', MS NWU).   [2] See Letter 4492 and n. 5.   [3] See Letter 4537 and n. 4.
[4] Carlo Linati (1878–1949), Italian critic, had written on DHL and on Pound (*Letters*, v. 90 and nn. 2 and 3). His translation of 'The Fox' and 'The Ladybird' was later published by Treves (Milan) in 1929 (Roberts D112).

English translation – and also *Cavalleria Rusticana*, which came out this year.[1]

Meanwhile I hope you'll be able to go ahead, and that the series of translations from the English will succeed.

With all good wishes   Yours sincerely   D. H. Lawrence.

4608. To S. S. Koteliansky, [23 August 1928]
Text: MS BL; Postmark, Gsteig 23.VIII.28; Zytaruk 355.

Gsteig.
Thursday

My dear Kot

Many thanks for yours. I'm sorry the motor holiday was expensive, but motor holidays always are. Was everywhere very crowded? did Cornwall seem very spoiled? I've been thinking so much about it lately – I loved Cornwall.

Would you mind sending these two copies to Simpkin Marshall – they are paid. I asked Richard to send out about 18 or 20: and I'm sending him the provincial orders. Soon we'll have no books in England. I've asked Orioli to tell me how many he has left in Florence. *Do you think it's quite safe to post to England from Florence?*

I do wish you didn't send the cheque back – why are you so obstinate?[2]

I had a fluttered and 'interested' p. c. from Barbara. How the flutterings bore me! – My sister Emily and her daughter arrive Sunday morning. No word from O[rioli] about Cornish Bros.

DHL

4609. To Giuseppe Orioli, [24 August 1928]
Text: MS UCLA; Moore 1078–9.

Kesselmatte. Gsteig b. Gstaad. (Bern), Svizzera
Friday. 24 Aug.

Dear Pino

I have your letters – and return various enclosures. I'll put down what I have done.

1.   A. L. Humphreys. Devonshire Club. St James St. S.W.1.[3] – I asked

---

[1] Cape published DHL's translation of Verga's *Mastro-don Gesualdo* (first published in 1923) in the *Travellers' Library*, March 1928 (Roberts A28b) and of *Cavalleria Rusticana* in February 1928 (Roberts A39). DHL knew of Linati's interest in Verga (*Letters*, iv. 232).

[2] See Letters 4569, 4580.

[3] Arthur L. Humphreys (1865–1946), founder of *Books of To-day and To-morrow* which he edited 1894–1924; retired in 1924 as senior partner of Hatchard's; author of several books on booksellers, local history, etc. (*The Times* obituary, 22 March 1946). His cheque for £12 was dated 20 August 1928 ('Memoranda', MS NWU).

him to send cheque to you, saying you would then deliver books. When
you get the cheque, will you ask *Kot.* to deliver, as R[ichard]
A[ldington] will be about used up.

2. I enclose letter from John Clark, with order for Toronto and London.[1]
    Have asked R. A. to send in the London order, you send the Toronto.
    Send invoice for four.

3. All the other orders I have sent on to R. A. Enid has used up all her
    copies. I hope Richard has sent out the Foyle six – (really five, as Enid
    had delivered Pollinger's) – but I haven't heard yet. – Yes, Richard has
    just written to say he has sent out all orders – now I forward him the
    new lot.

4. I don't know what to do about America. It is evident some arrive, some
    don't. I enclose the mad Mrs Chambers' letter – you will see.[2] That
    bookseller *might* be a police spy! – And Willard Johnson. Taos, hasn't
    got his copies. What *shall* we do about America – wait a bit longer?
    Write to Holliday, ask him if he has any other suggestion for getting his
    copies in to U.S.A.[3] I don't think we should post any more to America
    until we are sure *none* are being held up.

5. I think we must begin to send orders from Florence to England. I will
    let you know what copies Richard has left – but they will be very few.
    And Kot. will only have 17, when he has sent the last two to Simpkin

---

[1] See letter following.   [2] The letter is missing, but see Letter 4613.
[3] Terence Holliday, a New York bookseller, would have received the letter dated 3 August 1928
from William Jackson, the London exporters; it is possible that Jackson's letter with Holliday's
addendum (TMS and MS UCLA) had now reached DHL. The two missives read as follows,
the first from Jackson to Holliday:

Dear Sirs,
    Re your order for 20 copies of the new D. H. Lawrence book "LADY CHATTERLEY'S
LOVER". After careful consideration we have decided to have nothing whatever to do with
this book as it is of a thoroughly obscene and disgusting nature.
    While we hate to turn away business and to disappoint any of our clients we feel sure that it is
to the interests of both to leave out this book, for we beleive that when the authorities discover
the nature anyone found handling the book will get into serious trouble.
    Incidentally, we have no doubt whatever that the U.S.A. customs would prohibit its entry
into the country in which event we would both be caused endless trouble and expense.
    Trusting you will agree with the step we have taken.
                                                                    Yours very truly

My dear Mr. Lawrence, –
    This from our London agent from whom we of course ordered some of your book. Needless
to say, I do not agree with him. May we secure the additional twenty from you?
                                                            Sincerely   Terence Holliday

and Marshall. We might keep those, and try posting from Florence when we have¹ an order from someone we know and can trust.

6. Have you received the two copies back from Cornish Bros. Birmingham? I sent a cheque to Kot. for them, and he wrote them, that as soon as he heard that you received back the two copies, he would let them have the cheque.²

7. What about that one copy of Truslove and Hanson, not paid? They said to Enid H. that they had cancelled the order for it. We must make sure – and they must either return it, or pay.

I return the letters you sent – and send some of mine – I don't want any back.

It turned quite cold here, we had to warm the house – but today it seems a bit scirocco again, stuffy.

My sister with her daughter of twenty arrive on Sunday morning, to stay about a fortnight. I hope it'll be nice weather. The Brewsters are still in the village – with a Hindu friend who massages me.³ We shall stay here anyhow till the 15th September – then go to Baden for a bit – and then perhaps to England, perhaps not. Richard Aldington is offered a fortress on an island off the French coast⁴ – off Toulon or St. Tropez – and he wants us to winter there. Perhaps we'll look at the place on our way back to Florence in October.

I do hope it won't be hot in Florence – but there seems a change everywhere now, for cooler weather. When does Carletto come back? We shall have to be turning our thoughts to autumn and winter.

affectly.   DHL

---

¹ have] know   ² them . . . cheque.] you know.
³ 'A Hindu friend, Boshi Sen, visiting us, gave Lawrence massage, with skilful fingers, running lightly up and down Lawrence's spine, thumping, patting, slapping, moving the head about, rubbing the mop of hair, twisting his neck' (Brewster 288–9). Boshi Sen was a scientist whom the Brewsters met in Calcutta in 1926 and with whom they shared a bungalow in Alinora, United Provinces.
⁴ See Letter 4636; the Lawrences stayed on Ile de Port-Cros 15 October – 17 November 1928.

4610. To Giuseppe Orioli, [24 August 1928]
Text: MS UCLA; Unpublished.

[Kesselmatte, Gsteig b. Gstaad, Switzerland]
[24 August 1928][1]

Ordered R[ichard] A[ldington] to send two to Ludgate Square. *You* send two to Canada.

Send invoice for 4 copies to Ludgate Square.

4611. To David Garnett, 24 August 1928
Text: MS NYPL; Postmark, [Gste]ig 25.VIII.28; Huxley 746.

Kesselmatte. Gsteig b. Gstaad. (Bern)
24 Aug 1928

Dear David

I'm so glad you like *Lady C.* – and glad you tell me, so many people are beastly about it. I'm ordering you a copy.[2]

I should like to give your father a copy, if he'd care for it.[3] Let me know, will you, and if to send to the Cearne. In my early days your father said to me 'I should welcome a description of the whole act' – which has stayed in my mind till I wrote this book. – But your mother would disapprove.

Do you live there at St Ives? and in a Hall? grand dieu! – I wondered if you still were at your bookshop – must be a bore – they haven't paid yet for their copies of *Lady C.*[4]

We may be in England end of Sept – and should both like to see you very much. I always look on the Cearne as my jumping-off point into the world – *and* your father as my first backer. Do you remember swimming in the Isar?[5]

tante cose!   D. H. Lawrence

---

[1] This letter was enclosed with the preceding; it was written at the foot of one from John Clark (export bookseller), 12 Ludgate Square, E.C.4, dated 20 August 1928 (TMS UCLA):

Dear Sir

I have orders for your book which I understand you are publishing personally entitled LADY CHATTERLEYS LOVERS. I shall be glad if you will have two copies sent immediately to: –

The Mackay Book Shop. 47. Richmond Street West. TORONTO. CANADA.

and two copies to this address letting me have Invoices so soon as you have despatched the books. On receipt of the Invoices I shall be very pleased to send you my cheque.

Not knowing your address I am sending this through our good friend Mr Martin Secker.

Yours faithfully

[2] DHL would soon receive David Garnett's cheque for £2·3·0, dated 22 August 1928.
[3] See Letter 4359. (The Cearne at Edenbridge, Kent, was the home of Edward Garnett and his wife, Constance, 1861–1946, the celebrated translator of Russian literature.)
[4] David Garnett's home was Hilton Hall, Huntingdon, nr St Ives, Cambs. Shortly after the war he – with Francis ('Frankie') Birrell (1889–1935) – opened a bookshop in London. Messrs Birrell & Garnett sent a cheque for £8·10·0 dated 3 September 1928.
[5] In 1912; see *Letters*, i. 429.

4612. To Nancy Pearn, 24 August 1928

Text: MS UCB; Tedlock, *Lawrence MSS* 223.

Gsteig b Gstaad.
24 Aug 1928

Dear Nancy Pearn

Here's the article on the 'Cocksure Woman'. Since he wants a slap at the ladies, he'd better have a little one for the men at the same time.[1]

D. H. Lawrence

He can cut it if he likes – but do keep me a complete copy!

4613. To Maria Chambers, 25 August 1928

Text: MS StaU; Schorer 63.

Kesselmatte. Gsteig b. Gstaad. Switzerland
25 Aug 1928

Dear Mrs Chambers

Orioli sent me on your letter. I'm awfully sorry you haven't got your copies of *Lady C.* It's very curious, some copies seem to have got through the mail and customs, some seem to be stopped. But if once the authorities have an order to stop the book, they'll stop it, and confiscate every copy they can lay hands on. Which is a great nuisance, as it means the copies sent are entirely lost, stolen, in short, by those base swine – and I don't in the least know how we are to get through the copies of those who have paid and not received them. It must be done in some way. But don't go round talking to booksellers: they even may be police agents. Please don't do anything – the quieter one keeps, the better. All the English copies went through safely, and many booksellers are handling the book – carefully, of course. Many of my friends are mortally offended by the openness of the novel – but many, on the other hand, seem really grateful for it. By their reactions shall ye know them.[2] Those that are offended show their own dirtiness, or their own deadness. There are so many living dead.

We've been up here for two months now – about 4000 ft. I think I'm better – though the improvement is not startling. But I think I'm slowly veering round. Yet I don't want to start on a long voyage till my cough is better – it is such a nuisance. Probably Alfred Stieglitz will make an exhibition of my

---

[1] DHL had been invited by Arthur Olley to write on 'Women are Cocksure but Never Quite Sure' (Pearn's letter to DHL, 11 August 1928, TMSC UT). DHL's letter is written at the end of the MS entitled 'Cocksure Women and Hen-sure Men', the essay which was rejected by Olley (cf. Letter 4734) but published in the American magazine *Forum*, January 1929 (Roberts C181). Achsah Brewster recalled that, after reading the article to her and Boshi Sen, DHL predicted: 'But they won't publish it even though they have asked for it!' (Brewster 289).

[2] Cf. Letter 4562 and p. 484 n. 1.

pictures in November. I should like to come to America this autumn – but this infernal cough – which is not a death cough at all, but an unspeakable nuisance – is for the time master of my movements. I think in about three weeks we shall go to BadenBaden – then probably to the sea, the Mediterranean. Orioli's address finds me.

I do wish that by chance your copies of the novel may slip through. If not, we must devise a way. Surely there are some sporting fellows somewhere.

If you want to know how the ranch is getting on, write to the friend in charge of it:

Hon. Dorothy Brett. *Taos*, New Mexico.

She'll tell you all the news. – I hear Mrs Gillett is back.

Hope you are well, and the heat has passed.

D. H. Lawrence

4614. To Dorothy Warren, 25 August 1928
Text: MS UN; Nehls, iii. 237–8..

Kesselmatte. *Gsteig b. Gstaad* (Bern), Switzerland
25 August 1928

Dear Dorothy

Now you must write by return and tell me:

1. If you have the big pictures safely from Florence.
2. How you like them – also the small ones.
3. What are your plans concerning them.

For my part, I don't care whether you make an exhibition of them or not. So many people seem mortally offended by *Lady Chatterley* that perhaps a picture show might only carry the offence further. Not that *I* care about offending them. But you may. Personally, I think such skunks should be offended to the last inch. However, you are in business, and must have your own opinions. – Which reminds me, you never ordered any copies of the novel, as you so plainly said you would. Not that it matters, except one wonders if you ever do what you say you will.

Alfred Stieglitz says he wants to make an exhibition of my things in New York in November. But I expect I shall be in England in September, so I can ship them off myself. If I hadn't heard from a woman that she'd seen you, and seen some of my pictures at your gallery, I should doubt whether you really existed.

The man of the Leicester Galleries wanted to see my pictures, with a view to showing them.[1] Lucille Frost wrote about it – but I said there was nothing to be done at the moment.

---

[1] Oliver Brown (1886–1966) joined his father at the Leicester Galleries in 1903, became a partner in 1914. Enthusiast for modern art, staged major exhibitions of British and European artists. In March 1928 mounted exhibition of Gertler who may have prompted the approach to DHL.

However, I must hear from you now –
I've got a very nice panel of Italian peasants which I did here.[1]

Sincerely   D. H. Lawrence[2]

---

[1] Cf. Letter 4596 and p. 506 n. 3.

[2] Dorothy Warren replied on 29 August 1928 (Nehls, iii. 238–40):

Dear Lawrence,

Thank you so much for your letters. I have been so exhausted, ill and over-worked that I had to rest a while and that is why I haven't written before. I am so sorry! On top of all this my secretary has also been away ill.

All your pictures arrived safely and I like them immensely. The water colours are already framed; I enclose samples of the papers which we have used for the mounts. The mounts are perfectly simple, just plainly cut out and I think they look lovely. The frames are plain Hazel pine moulding. I am now framing the oils, I quite agree with you that they should have extremely simple mouldings so that I am doing them in 3″ flat plain wood showing ½″ flat plain slip. If, when you see them, you do not like the slip it is an easy matter to remove them. I find the slip important, because, without looking fussy, it gives a very slight recession, but not enough to make a shadow on the canvas.

It would be a mistake to hang anything else with your pictures, they need extremely careful and wide spacing but there will be room for anything else you like to bring or send in September. I should love to see the panel of Italian peasants.

With regard to the opening day, I should suggest Friday, October 5th. to Friday October 26th., which is exactly three weeks, as the earliest possible date. That would mean that your pictures could be put back into their cases and started off for America by the end of October so that you could reckon for their arrival in New York certainly by the middle of November. If it were not for the American show I should prefer to open on Tuesday, October the 9th. as there are more people back in London in the second week than in the first.

Of course I anticipate prudish objections and attacks on myself and my Gallery. All that will have to be faced and it won't be a very new experience, although it is one to which I am not absolutely hardened! But I think your pictures fine and free and individual so that I want to show them.

It is extremely difficult to fix selling prices, as I expect you will understand one must be either prohibitive and regard them as of "Bibliophile" value or else one must present them as a first exhibition of a painter new to the public at reasonable prices. There is no middle course. In taking the latter course, both painter and dealer have to consider the fact that the painter intends to make his career by painting and work his prices up proportionately to his selling fame. Esthetic and commercial values have less and less in common these days which makes the task of pricing difficult. I should think the water colours ought to average between 12 gns. and 15 gns. apiece. About the oils I really don't quite know, you must let me hear what you think.

From a commercial point of view it might not be a bad idea to put a prohibitive price on those you do not want to sell, although that means, of course, that if the prices are given, one is bound to sell, but then if this occurs, the prices of other works go up automatically.

I am very sorry about the muddle with regard to *Lady Chatterley*. I do want three copies for which I enclose 6 gns., but please will you have them addressed to:

Prince Löwenstein/The Warren Gallery/39a Maddox Street/London, W.1

as a great many books come here for him from abroad and I think it would be better.

The Assistant I had here while I was in Germany made such a muddle of everything that it has taken me all my strength, time and energy to straighten things out and ascertain what orders of mine were, or were not, carried out.

I hope to get away for a fortnight during the last half of September, but I shall be in or near London until then in case you should come here.

Yours,

4615. To Charles(?) Scott, 25 August 1928
Text: MS UIll; Unpublished.

Gsteig b. Gstaad. Switzerland
25 Aug 1928

Dear Mr Scott

We've had no luck with snapshots this year – I send you what scraps I can find, and hope they'll do.[1]

Yours Sincerely   D. H. Lawrence

4616. To Dr Anton Kippenberg, [25 August 1928]
Text: MS Sverlag; Unpublished.

Kesselmatte. *Gsteig b. Gstaad.* (Bern), Schweiz.
25 Okt. 1928

Dear Dr Kippenberg

I have your two letters, forwarded from Florence. I shall be pleased to write a short sketch for the Hans Carossa book.[2] But I am not very sure how much a Druckbogen is – I take it, between 2000 or 3000 words. Or is it shorter?

Curtis Brown had already written to me to say he wanted to transfer the German rights of my books to another publisher – presumably Fischer of Berlin. And I had already answered him, since he was so insistent on making a transfer, why do the thing *en bloc*? Why must one publisher have the exclusive rights to an author's work? It seems to me unnecessary. You did not mind when a Berlin publisher brought out *Jack im Buschland.*[3] Why can't Curtis Brown arrange to let Fischer have some books, if he wants them, and you some, if you want them? – But he says that is very unsatisfactory.

Curtis Brown insists on making a transfer of my German rights. When he asked me about it, a year or so ago, when he and I were both annoyed because you did not give us any answer to our questions, I agreed that it would suit me if he approached another German publisher. Now I can't go back on it. But I will again put forward my suggestion of letting two publishers divide the books, if they wish. Though much good an author's suggestions are, between publishers and agent! –

Anyhow I hope we can settle something satisfactory, and am

With all good wishes   Yours Sincerely   D. H. Lawrence

---

[1] Cf. Letter 4308.
[2] DHL contributed his essay, 'Hymns in a Man's Life'; translated by Frieda it appeared as 'Kirchenleider im Leben Eines Mannes' in *Buch des Dankes für Hans Carossa* (Insel Verlag, c. September 1928) (Roberts B25.5). DHL's error in dating this letter is confirmed by his subsequent letter to Nancy Pearn, with which he enclosed the completed essay, on 2 September (Letter 4635). For Hans Carossa see Letter 4145 and p. 156 n. 1.
[3] Else Jaffe's translation of *The Boy in the Bush*.

4617. To Giuseppe Orioli, 27 August 1928
Text: MS UCLA; Unpublished.

Kesselmatte, *Gsteig b. Gstaad* (Bern), Svizzera
27 Aug 1928

Dear Pino

If there is a letter from New York, from Macy Masius or the Vanguard Press, addressed to Villa Mirenda, open it and read it.[1]

The Vanguard Press say they want to publish and distribute *Lady C.*, subscribed edition, $10. – of which I get 10%. They cannot *print* in U.S.A. – therefore they want to photograph the existing book and reproduce it that way. For this purpose they need three copies, two to photograph from, one for case of accident. Is the print of our 200 edition just as good as the other? If so we'll send those. And we must make a false cover. Do you think Giuntina would print you three covers, and three title pages: *Joy Go With You – by Norman Kranzler.* (*The Ponte Press*). If he would do that in an hour, then tear off three of the existing paper covers and the title-pages, stick these on, and mail the three copies to me here, quick. – If there happen to be three sets *unbound*, send me those without further trouble. But I'm afraid you[2] have no sets unbound.

I want the Vanguard Press to do this edition, otherwise sure as life the book will be *pirated* in U S A, and we shall be done in the eye. Also they can supply our American orders, and we can keep our books for this side – for it seems *useless* to mail copies to America.

Will you put this enclosed cheque to my sterling account?

We'll have some fun yet with the devils.

DHL

Of course setting up the book by photography will cost them a lot – but they are rich.

I wrote you Saturday enclosing all returned letters.

4618. To Laurence Pollinger, 27 August 1928
Text: MS UT; Huxley 748–9.

Kesselmatte. *Gsteig b. Gstaad.* [(Ber]n),[3] Switzerland
27 Aug 1928

Dear Pollinger

I received the enclosed from the Vanguard Press this morning.[4] I think Rich should have forwarded their communications.

---

[1] The Vanguard Press, New York, was founded in 1926; it was primarily a literary house and acquired a reputation for its interest in provocative and slightly sensational books.
[2] you] I   [3] MS torn.   [4] The enclosure is missing.

I want them to go ahead with *Lady C.*, so have cabled them as they suggest: *Withold, Knopf two, sent.* It seems the U.S. mail is holding up some, at least, of the copies I sent – so I can send no more, and those held up will be lost. I am determined to stand by *Lady C.*, and to send her out into the world as far as possible. I perfectly understand that C[urtis] B[rown] and Rich are against her, thinking she will do me harm, and probably disliking her anyhow. But I stand by her: and am perfectly content she should do me harm with such people as take offence at her. I am out against such people. Fly little boat! Therefore if the Vanguard will distribute her in U S A, well and good. It suits my aims.

About Knopf, I don't care very much either way. Rich seems to want to play into his hands. Before *The Woman Who Rode Away* I owed Knopf two more books. I concluded *The Woman* was a book. But no, Rich says I still owe two. Now to the Vanguard he says *three*. That won't do. I'm not having it. – I know that the Knopf people don't care for me, except for Mrs Knopf. They want me to be a good little boy. They sell damn few – no more than Secker. And they're not doing anything about it. Why should they mind losing me? Why should I mind losing them? It's not money – I don't want any money from them, as Rich suggests. But I damn well will have my books put into the world without diffidence, especially that pseudo-genteel diffidence of A[lfred] A K[nopf], so absurd. I liked poor little Seltzer so much better, only he didn't know how to fight.[1]

But I won't *write* to the Vanguard, beyond this cable, which commits me to nothing but *Lady C.*, until I hear from you: *that is, if you will reply by return.* If CB. is back in the office, of course you will give him this letter.

I finished the second half of *The Escaped Cock* – about 10,000 words – rather lovely – but I feel tender about giving it out for publication – as I felt tender about *Lady C.* This story is only a tiny bit 'fierce', as CB. puts it. I can't make up my mind about having it typed and sent out. Possibly Crosby Gaige wouldn't like it – not that I'd care a bit. Only why expose my sensitive things gratuitously? And this story is one of my thin-skinned ones.

Nothing further from Elkin Matthews about *Rawdon's Roof* – and I am rather relieved. I really would rather *not* sign 500 sheets. He can have the story *unsigned* for the usual £15. I'd much prefer that.

I have notice of two *exchange* cheques, £4. and £2. – That means three more copies of *Lady C.* paid in to my acc., I suppose. Many thanks. The 'returned' lots are nearly all gone.

                                                    Yrs   D. H. Lawrence

[1] Thomas Seltzer (1875–1943), DHL's chief publisher in USA until the two men parted company in 1925.

I think the Vanguard are right about piracy danger – and their $10. edition won't hurt mine. – Please send me the Baker letter back.[1]

DHL

4619. To Juliette Huxley, 27 August 1928
Text: MS Huxley; Unpublished.

Kesselmatte. Gsteig b. Gstaad. (Bern)
27 Aug 1928

Dear Juliette

Well what luck! – to get away to a nice place, then have both the lads down with whooping-cough! I hope to heaven you didn't catch it, and that the sore throat meant nothing. But whooping cough is a great curse.

I wish we would have come to the sea. I really get rather sick of these eternal mountains standing there *en bloc*. But yesterday arrived my sister and her daughter, to stay fifteen days – which runs us into the second week in September. We are due to stay till the end of the month, but really, I think, we'll pull out about the 15th. or 17th. – and go to Baden Baden for ten days or so. Then I'm due to come to England. But really, people in England make me so mad what with one thing and another – especially *Lady C.* – that I feel I'd be downright ill if I saw those dirty cliffs of Dover just now.

We went to Diablerets one day with the post-omnibus, and had tea at the hotel. It wasn't nearly so nice in summer – seemed *dark* – and the hotel crowded with a horrid common sort of motor-bike people, everybody in a rather nasty humour. We hadn't time to go Beau Site, but saw the little red Swiss flag flying there – and children playing around des Aroles. We bought quite a lot of goods at the store from the long-nosed man – he wanted to know why we were at Gsteig and not at Diablerets. He seemed terribly bored and tired in his shop. It was much jollier in winter. On top of the pass where we picnicked that brilliantly cold Sunday morning I couldn't recognise a thing. There was a big new hut with restaurant and thousands of things for sale, and dozens of motors and chauffeurs and guides – awful – just like America.

But here it is really quiet – nobody – and the tourists already mostly departed from Gsteig.

I am pretty well in myself, but the cough is just about the same infernal nuisance. I get so tired of it. – The peasants are very much sunk into the earth, like moles or voles, creatures. But they don't seem greedy – and our Frau Trachsl is really quite good to us. And we do have a little world to ourselves. But my cough torments me just the same.

---

[1] Jacob Baker, director and managing editor of Vanguard Press.

I have lost a good many friends over *Lady C*, but such friends I am thankful to lose. Some people again have written very nicely, really. And I keep the flag flying.

I wish we could have come to that Brittainy sea – it draws me much more than these mountains.[1] Ah, well! I'll let you know our movements. That Dorothy Warren does *not* write to me. She's terrible. If you are in London do go to her in Madox St. and know the reason why, and find out for me what exactly she is doing with my pictures. – And I hope above all the whooping-cough is *quite* gone.

saluti e tanti ricordi   DHL

4620. To Enid Hilton, [28 August 1928]
Text: MS UCLA; Lacy, *Escaped Cock* 69.

Kesselmatte. Gsteig b Gstaad (Bern)
Tuesday

Dear Enid

The Aldingtons are going off to Italy for the winter on Friday. I asked them, if they have any *Lady C*'s left, to send them to you. They may have about five copies.

Can you type – and have you got a typewriter? If so, would you do me a story – about 10,000 words – which I don't quite care to send to the professional typist?[2] I'll pay the proper rates, of course.

Emily and her daughter are here – and today it's pouring rain. They stay till Friday week. I expect we shall leave on Sept 15th – or thereabouts.

I had your last letter and list of all you sent. I do wish we'd never sent any to R[ichard] A[ldington]. Kot is such a fusser. Hope all goes peacefully.

tante cose!   DHL

4621. To Richard Aldington, [28 August 1928]
Text: MS UT; Unpublished.

Kesselmatte. Gsteig b Gstaad (Bern)
Tuesday

Dear Richard

So you are off directly to Vallombrosa! I do hope you'll find the man better – it'll be nice at Vallombrosa, now. No, I shan't envy you riding in the embassy car – kind of thing I like to avoid.[3]

I expect Arabella will have sent off the other ten books – which will leave

---

[1] The Huxleys had been staying at Port Blanc in Brittany.
[2] *The Escaped Cock*; cf. Letter 4618.   [3] Cf. Letter 4625 and n. 3.

only five. Would you keep them till the last *convenient* day, because Orioli will probably send me more orders this evening, and if so, A. might just pop the books in the post. But if you *don't* hear from me in time, would you send the five to Mrs Hilton. No good leaving them lying all winter in Malthouse.

I think we'll stay here till Sept 15th. Then

c/o Baronin v. Richthofen, Ludwig Wilhelmstift, BadenBaden

for ten or fifteen days. Then if you're really going to the island, we can join you.[1] But you'll never come up to Paris if you cross to the island from Toulon – will you?

We *might* have to go to England end of Sept – but my desire is small.

In Florence call and see Pino Orioli – 6 Lungarno Corsini.

Write all the news about the island, and your movements.

                                                                                    DHL

4622. To Earl Brewster, [28 August 1928]
Text: MS UT; Unpublished.

                                                                            Kesselmatte.
                                                                        Tuesday night[2]

Dear Earl

Of course I forgot everything – do hope the cheque's right – and that you won't curse, having the books at the last moment.

You will write of course from Geneva – and we're not going far apart, we can soon nip together again –

                                                                   so au revoir   DHL

4623. To S. S. Koteliansky, 30 August 1928
Text: MS BL; Postmark, Gsteig 31.VIII.28; Zytaruk 356–7.

                                            Kesselmatte. Gsteig b. Gstaad, Switzerland
                                                                            30 Aug 1928

My dear Kot

Thanks for yours. Am glad rumours have gone quiet. I wonder what 'influential people', indeed?

Those Cornish Bros. stopped their cheque – it was returned to Florence unpaid. And they have *not* returned the two copies – not so far. Oh swine of people! So please burn my cheque to them.

Did you send the six copies to the A. L. Humphreys at the Devonshire Club, James St. SW1. – ? – I thought we'd better draw on your little lot for him, as he paid the £12. in advance.

---

[1] Cf. Letter 4609 and p. 519 n. 4.
[2] Dated with reference to the Brewsters' departure on 29 August 1928 (cf. Letter 4636).

I enclose a letter from Miss Sylvia Raphael.[1] I had her cheque and ordered her a copy, either from Enid or R[ichard] A[ldington], some weeks ago. I begged R. a. to send me his list of copies he'd sent out, people he'd sent to, but he didn't do it. And tomorrow he and Arabella are leaving for Italy – to be away all winter. If he sent out all orders I forwarded to him, he would have not more than five copies left. These I asked him to send back to Enid. – But I don't know what's happened.

Would you send this one copy to Miss Raphael.

The Vanguard Press in New York want to do a limited edition at $10. – for subscribers only. As they can't *print* it in U.S.A., they want to do it by the photography process – and give me 10%. I suppose, considering all their expense and risk, it's worth it. At least one can supply orders. The U.S. authorities are holding up some copies. There was a paragraph in a California paper saying the book was obscene and the customs were not allowing it to go any further.[2] But some copies have got in – we know of about 14. But Orioli sent 140 or so – probably most of them lost. Damn!

I want him to tell me how many copies we have left, but he[3] doesn't do it. But he is back in Florence now. He has started sending a few copies to England again. I shall ask him to send you another twenty, two copies per day. Shall I put it that way? If you'd rather have it otherwise, write him direct. We won't ask you to send out any more, now he is posting from Florence.

My older sister and my niece are here – but somehow I feel a bit remote and depressed. They are so far from my *active* life. And it pours with rain. And I've got a bit of cold, and write this in bed. And altogether, I wish the Lord would make a new man of me, for I'm not much to boast of now.

                                                                                    DHL

Let Barbara write to Orioli for a copy!

[1] DHL misread the signature: Enid Raphael (1901–?45) had ordered a copy of *Lady Chatterley's Lover* and paid by cheque dated 30 July 1928; she wrote as follows on 20 August from 38 Hill Street, Mayfair (MS BL):

Dear Mr Lawrence
   You were good enough to write me a letter when you acknowledged my cheque for "Lady C's lover –" & said you thought the book would arrive in a day or two. That is now however some time ago & I have had no sign of the book's arrival – *Please* let me know if there are difficulties in sending it to England – I am probably going to Le Touquet for a few days sometime & if there are, could have it sent to me there –
   I am sure I shall not be shocked! I have read a few pages in a copy that a friend of mine had & so thirst to have my own copy –
   I have read all your works & appreciate & enjoy them so much –
                                                                        Yours sincerely
DHL's letter to Enid Raphael, acknowledging her cheque, is unlocated.
[2] See letter following, n. 1.   [3] but he] but damn him, he

4624. To Giuseppe Orioli, [30 August 1928]
Text: MS UCLA; Unpublished.

[Kesselmatte, Gsteig b. Gstaad, Switzerland]
[30 August 1928]

Under my signature write in a copy:

With all good wishes
to Frank A. Curtin.

2 Sept. 1928

Then probably the book won't have to go through customs. Then take the book to the Amer. Express and ask them to send it to the address given. We'll see if it arrives – but I doubt *it won't*.[1]

We must wait and see if the Vanguard Press are doing an edition: if they are, we must turn over orders and money to them. We can do nothing from this side unless somebody helps. That swine Jackson might have done something. But since this man wants to risk a copy through American Express, try it.

DHL

[1] DHL was following the advice offered by Frank Curtin, a lawyer from Fresno, California, who wrote to him on 11 August 1928, and on whose letter DHL wrote his own to Orioli. Curtin wrote as follows (TMS UCLA):

My dear Mr. Lawrence:

The copy of Lady Chatterley's Lover which I ordered from you last June has got as far as San Francisco, but I feel it will get no further, having been notified a few days ago by the custom authorities to whom it was turned over by the mail authorities that they are holding a "grossly obscene" book addressed to me and sent from Florence, Italy.

Well, that is my loss, not yours, but I believe that if you would send a book by American Express rather than by mail my chances of eventually receiving it would be much better.

I am therefore enclosing to you herewith my check in the sum of $11.00 with the request that you send to me one copy of the book by American Express.

Sincerely.

Express Address: 305 Rowell Bldg., Fresno, California.

I enclose clipping from this morning's Fresno Republican which may interest if not amuse you.

The original enclosure has disappeared but the clipping from the *Fresno Morning Republican*, 11 August 1928, undoubtedly read as follows:

Postal Officers Confiscate Books Headed For Fresno

A Fresno book dealer is going to be short five copies of a privately printed book, D. H. Lawrence's "Lady Chatterley's Lover."

Customs officials at San Francisco yesterday seized the books, which were privately printed in Italy, as unfit for the United States mails, it was announced yesterday. All the copies are autographed by the author and are valued at $10 each. The mail examiners opened the package and then turned them over to the customs.

The name of the Fresno dealer was not made public. Officials said he would be allowed to send the books back to the consignor and thereby retrieve the $50.

I have written to the man – You send book.[1]

DHL

Richard Aldington and wife are coming to Vallombrosa – this week-end. I'll tell them to look in on you.

4625. To Giuseppe Orioli, 30 August 1928
Text: MS UCLA; cited in Moore, *Intelligent Heart* 384, 407.

Kesselmatte, Gsteig b. Gstaad. (Bern), Svizzera
30 Aug. 1928

Dear Pino

Damn the Americans – damn and damn them. – But those Vanguard people anyhow seem to have spunk. I hope they'll do an edition, for the sake of supplying the book over there. *Don't* post anything to America. And I shall not cash any more dollar cheques unless the books have gone. – Yes, Mrs Chambers, whom I have never seen, save a *large* photograph, looks quite handsome – poor thing.

I have written Frank A. Curtin – if he doesn't get this copy, we'll try to supply him from the Vanguard.

Do keep the ten copies if you like.

But I do want to know how many copies we have left in all.

We must be careful sending to England. Ask Murray kindly to let you know by return when he has the book. I don't want to lose any more copies. – Kot. is silent lately. I don't know if he sent Simpkin Marshalls' their two copies.

Thursday night. I enclose Kot's letter. I think it is a good idea to have some copies in England. You might send him twenty copies, two a day; at your leisure.

The three *Joy go with you*'s have not come yet,[2] but I have your letter tonight with the bordereau. – You mustn't send any more copies to America, because I have promised the Vanguard Press in my cable, to *withold*. We must turn our orders over to them. I shall send Mrs Chambers her cheque back.

I begged Richard Aldington to let me know exactly what orders he had sent out – but he's not answered. And they leave tomorrow for Vallombrosa, to stay with a man called Randall, who is secretary to the embassy to the Vatican.[3] They will be at Hotel Foresta. But I do wish I knew if they'd fulfilled all orders. Because today I had a letter from Miss S. Raphael. 38 Hill

[1] On 6 December 1928 Curtin acknowledged DHL's letter of 30 August; DHL's letter to Curtin is missing.   [2] See Letter 4617.
[3] (Sir) Alec Walter George Randall (1892–1977) was 2nd Secretary to the British Legation to the Holy See, 1925–30; later he was Ambassador to Denmark.

St. Mayfair, whose cheque I had in July, saying she's not had her copy – and I know I ordered it her, from the English lot; not from Enid, though.

Birrell and Garnett haven't paid their first two copies yet, have they?[1] They are down on your list, not paid.

Do please count the number of copies you still have, and tell me. I think, when we raise the price, you must say to the people – '*Mr Lawrence has disposed of all his copies. I have fifty – or a small number – which I bought for my shop and which I am willing to sell at £2··10··0 net. or £3. net.*' – or something like this. Dont you think.

I am going to count the money again exactly. I believe the gross receipts are about £980 – counting all the money in sterling – and the total expenses, counting your £50 – are just about £300. I'll send you another £25. or so, when I next write.[2]

It has been pouring torrents of rain this last three days. I've got a bit of cold, and am in bed. My sister and her girl are here – and somehow it depresses me terribly – they are so far from my active life, everything they say seems wrong, somehow. And I have to hide *Lady C*. like a skeleton in my cupboard. – The Brewsters have gone down to Geneva – had enough of here. I feel I have too.

I wonder if you went to Forte.

DHL

4626. To Charles Lahr, 30 August 1928
Text: MS UNYB; Moore 1083.

Kesselmatte, *Gsteig b. Gstaad*, Switzerland
30 Aug 1928

Dear Mr Lahr

Many thanks for *The Withered Root* – which Mrs Hilton sent on to me, and I have read.[3] It seems to me good, and real, and there is a certain grim unconscious humour about the revival business. But the first half is best. Because I don't think Rhys Davies manages *young* women very well. They are a bit mechanical. And since one *knows* how the revivaling must turn out, there needed a counterbalance to all the nonsense of it, in the end. But the end is sloppy and enervating – so easy *to let go* like that. Mr Davies does just what he dislikes his characters for doing – he sloppily lets himself go in an emotional relaxation – Death is so *easy*, in novels. It never kills the novelist: though it is pretty risky for the artist. Could that miserable Reuben never get his pecker up? He should be called Rhubarb, he gives one a belly-ache. I am so sick of

[1] Cf. Letter 4611 and n. 4.   [2] Cf. Letter 4637.   [3] Cf. Letter 4601 and n. 4.

those modern inspired young heroes with weak, rhubarby guts. Why do young men never conceive a hero with a bit of fighting spunk.

But I was glad to have the book, and to feel that weird depressing Welsh flavour of dark slate subsoil.[1] So many thanks, also to Rhys Davies (I thought it was some unknown work of the Bhuddist Scholar I was getting).

Yours Sincerely   D. H. Lawrence

4627. To Giulia Pini, [30 August 1928]

Text: MS UT; PC v. [Swiss chalet]; Postmark, Gsteig 30.VIII 28; Unpublished.

[Kesselmatte, Gsteig b. Gstaad, Switzerland]
30 agosto.

Cara Giulia,

Abbiamo ricevuto la tua lettera – spero che ti senta ora tutto bene di saluti. Qui piove da annegare il mondo, e fa freddo. C'è mia sorella e sua figlia, e non possiamo uscire – che mi dispiace. Oggi sono partiti gli amici – ma noi restiamo ancora venti giorno.

Molti saluti   DHL

la casa è la bottega dove facciamo le spese.

[30 August.

Dear Giulia,

We have received your letter – I hope that you have completely recovered by now. Here it is raining fit to flood the world, and it is cold. My sister and her daughter are here, and we can't go out – which disappoints me. Our friends left today – but we are staying another twenty days.

Best wishes   DHL

the house is the shop where we do our general shopping.]

4628. To Enid Hilton, 31 August 1928

Text: MS UCLA; cited in Moore, *Intelligent Heart* 388.

Kesselmatte. *Gsteig b. Gstaad* (Bern)
31 Aug 1928

My dear Enid

I was glad to have your letter, to know all is well, in spite of that wicked white dust of the Foundlings.[2] Poor Foundlings – demolished too.

---

[1] The novel is set in the coal-mining valleys of South Wales; Reuben Daniels is born and dies there; he is acclaimed 'the Great Evangelist', the leader of a religious revival. Rhys Davies later defined the 'highflown theme' of his novel as 'warfare between religious spirit and carnal flesh, with spirit a heavy loser' (*Print of a Hare's Foot*, 1969, p. 119). The reviewer in *The Times Literary Supplement*, 8 December 1928, shared DHL's lack of enthusiasm for Davies' presentation of character.

[2] The Foundling Hospital in Mecklenburgh Square (where Enid Hilton lived) had been demolished and a new site for it acquired in Berkhamstead.

Many thanks for putting the cash in the bank. I have the Archer cheque.[1] If they want more they must write to Orioli. I heard tonight from Mrs Aldington – she has apparently four copies left. If you get them, as I asked her to send them to you, will you please post one copy at once to:

Henry Young and Sons. Ltd. 12 South Castle St. Liverpool.

And will you take the other three copies to Dorothy Warren at her Warren Galleries in Madox St. In case she is out, address the parcel to

Prince Leopold Loewenstein, The Warren Galleries, Maddox St. W. 1.[2]

But I heard from her today, very nice – she has all the pictures – she says the water-colors are framed, and look lovely.[3] Tell her I told you to ask her to show them to you. – She says she's been ill – I know she's awfully nervy. But get her to show you the pictures, if she's not being tiresome.

Emily and Margaret are here – and though I am glad to see them, it worries me and depresses me rather. I am not really 'our Bert'. Come to that, I never was. And the gulf between their outlook and mine is always yawning, horribly obvious to me. They stay till the 7th. or 8th. – and I think we shall stay one more week after that.

Kot suggests we send you about twenty copies of *Lady C.* from Florence, to *store* for a while – not to send out. Because they say I ought to hold back some copies till the price rises to £3. instead of two. Shall I do it?

If you *don't* get the four copies from Arabella, would you send the order over to Kot. 5 Acacia Road. N.W. 8 – and ask him please to send at once.

A lot of new snow on the mountains – colder – and dark now, I can't see any more.

Goodnight DHL

The three Warren books are *paid*.

4629. To Dorothy Warren, 1 September 1928
Text: MS UN; Nehls, iii. 240–1.

Kesselmatte. Gsteig b. Gstaad. (*Bern*), Switzerland
1 Sept. 1928

Dear Dorothy

I was very glad to hear from you, and to know at least you are in the land of the living – and keeping up the fight. Don't for heaven's sake get into the way

---

[1] Esther Lahr (who traded under her maiden name, Archer) sent a cheque dated 13 August 1928, for £13·12·0, to Enid Hilton, for copies of *Lady Chatterley's Lover* ('Memoranda', MS NWU).

[2] Prince Leopold of Löwenstein-Wertheim-Freudenberg (1903–74), b. Salzburg, Austria; came to England, 1926, naturalised British, 1936; associated with the world of publishing and authorship. m. Diana Gollancz. (*The Times* obituary, 11 September 1974.)

[3] Cf. p. 523 n. 2.

of being ill! That's what I've done – and heaven, I'd give anything to be well.

I've asked Mrs Hilton to bring round the three copies of *Lady Chatterley* for Prince Loewenstein – she had a few in store for me, these are the last. Do show her the pictures when she comes.

We'll put a high and prohibitive price on all the big pictures, for I really don't want to sell them. Something like five hundred pounds. And then the small pictures and the water-colours you can price as you think best. Only the small picture *Close-Up* – Frieda wants to keep it,[1] so we'll either have to mark it sold, or price it high. – If, as you say, any-one offers the prohibitive price for a big picture, we shall have to let it go. But somehow I can't associate my pictures with money.

I will ask Alfred Stieglitz to let you know his date, so that if you want to open Oct. 9th instead of 5th, you could do so if his date allows.

I certainly don't intend to make my living by painting – far from it. I intend to paint simply and solely for the fun of it, and damn the consequences.

I shall send you my small panel of *Contadini* – and some others, directly. I am pining to see the pictures in their frames – pining. But my health is a nuisance – my cough a curse – God knows if I ought to come to England.

Anyhow I hope you are well and chirpy. Don't get downhearted, that's the worst. And it's good for you to have a fight for your gallery – as it's good for me to fight for my things, as I have to. Yet one does mind being insulted, bitterly.

Sincerely   D. H. Lawrence

4630. To Alfred Stieglitz, 1 September 1928
Text: MS YU; Postmark, [. . .]; Huxley 749–50.

c/o Curtis Brown Ltd. 6 Henrietta St. Covent Garden, London W.C. 2.
1st Sept. 1928

Dear Alfred Stieglitz

Would you please let me know by return whether you think of making a show of me and Miss Brett this autumn or winter.

Because Dorothy Warren wants to open her show of me alone on Oct 5th. or on Oct 9th. – the latter for preference, if you are in no hurry – and to keep it till Oct. 26th. or till Oct 30th. – just three weeks. She would then ship the pictures to you, if you want them: So please let me know by return. And if there were any hurry, please send a line direct to

Miss Dorothy Warren, The Warren Gallery, 39a. Maddox Street,
London. W. 1.

---

[1] Frieda confirmed this in a letter to Dorothy Warren, 31 August 1928: 'I want to keep the *Resurrection, Boccacio* and the *Kiss* [*Close-Up*]. I was very sad to let the pictures depart. I had watched them being born and they were part of one's life' (Nehls, iii. 240).

But as I wrote you to Lake George, I don't mind *a bit* if you don't make a show. I'm not very keen on sending anything to U.S.A., if the truth must be told. So please let me know by return, whether to send the pictures to New York or not.

It appears the U. S. mail is holding up *Lady Chatterley*. Poor weak-minded fools! There was a fuss and a threat in London – but nothing done so far – so I shall be able to sell out my edition over here, without bothering about America. So your copy will no doubt rise considerably in value, and you'll have lost nothing by me.

But I'm glad you liked it – it's a test of people.

Yours Sincerely   D. H. Lawrence

I've lost your New York address.

4631. To Earl, Achsah and Harwood Brewster, [1 September 1928]
Text: MS UT; Brewster 176–8.

Kesselmatte. *Gsteig b. Gstaad*
Saturday

Dear Earl and Achsah and Child

Had your letters. Yes, those were three awful delugious[1] days. But yesterday was marvellous – all new snow, even on the waterfall mountains, and brilliant, brilliant – and vivid clear everything, with real high sunshine – for the best day we've had. Today is fine too – clear, snow melting, air a bit sharp. This is how it *should* be. Pamela and Peg have gone off to the waterfall, so we have a little breathing space. Oh dear, visitors! How nice the mornings are when there is nobody!

I expect our two depart this day week – the 8th – and if the weather keeps decent like this, I want to stay on another week, till 15th or possibly 17th, which is Monday – because I think F[rieda]'s sister Else wants to come here for a day or two. Then we'd go to BadenBaden direct, and stay ten or twelve days. Then I'm a bit vague. Dorothy Warren is showing my pictures from Oct 5th. till 26th. – having them all framed fresh – the waters are done, and she says they look lovely, framed. Of course I'm pining to see them, and to see how they look, hung. So I *might* go over to England for a week. But perhaps I shan't. If I don't, I'd go down to look at that island, about Oct. 1st. You might look in *Baedeker*, if you have a *Southern France*, and see what it says: Island of Port-Cros – though Arabella writes St. Cros – off Toulon or St. Tropez. If you can find it, tell me what it says. – We'd stay a week or so on the island, to

---

[1] The word is DHL's invention; it is not recorded in Sir James A. H. Murray and others, eds., *A New English Dictionary on Historical Principles*, 10 vols (1894–1928).

make sure. Then in second half of Oct. I'd like to finish the Etruscan places –
Arezzo, Cortona, Chiusi, Orvieto, Rome – take about ten days – Aldous and
Maria said they'd motor us. Then, if the island had turned out well, go back
there for some winter months. If not, then somewhere else – Sicily, Spain –
chi lo sa!

That's what I have in my mind. What the gods intend for me, I know not. I
don't even know if I'd be well enough to do the etruscans. But I really hope so.

Now what about you? I guess you'll soon be tired of Geneva – though
perhaps not. Baden is certainly more easy to loaf in, to hear music, to read all
the newspapers in the world, to have good walks, to drink water, to see plays –
in German. But it will cost you about 12 Mark – a Mark is the same as a
shilling – 12 M. per day each. Not cheap. But what is cheaper? – unless you go
into France.

So meet us when and where you will. Even go first and look at the island, if
it amuses you. There is an hotel. Or if you'd like to go to Baden, let me know
and we'll fix up rooms.

You remember that *clay* medicine that you once put on your ear? Since
Boshy suggested hot mud on my chest, I feel that might do me good, your
clay. If you could get it in Geneva, ask the shop to send it, C.O.D. – they send
things C.O.D. in Switzerland all the time.

Anyhow I know that you're well tubbed – and I hope decently fed. I
washed my hair this morning, in the sun.

Lebewohl!   DHL

4632. To Laurence Pollinger, 1 September 1928
Text: MS UT; Unpublished.

Kesselmatte. Gsteig b. Gstaad. (Bern)
1 Sept. 1928

Dear Pollinger

Shame to bother you on your holiday! Is it nice down at Margate? – I've not
been there since before the war.[1]

I wrote to Jacob Baker of the Vanguard that I had sent the cable and books,
and would he make the contract with Rich.[2] I told him Rich varies my
obligation to Knopf, saying one letter *two full-length books* and another *two
novels.* – They can settle between them what it really is. – I promised nothing.

Personally, I don't care for Liveright.[3] And the Viking Press[4] have of mine

[1] In July 1913 (see *Letters*, ii. 30ff.).   [2] DHL's letter is unlocated.
[3] Liveright, a nephew of Seltzer's and New York publisher.
[4] Viking Press, founded in 1925, the largest US publisher of poetry, fiction, biography, etc. B. W.
Huebsch was Vice President.

The Rainbow, New Poems, and *Look! We have Come Through*. I had their statement[1] last week, and they had sold eight copies of each book – total royalties $4.20 – income tax deducted $3.60 – cheque to C[urtis] B[rown]'s office 60 cents. This makes me mad. I send the statement back to Rich,[2] and I asked him to try and get back the rights of *New Poems* and *Look! We Have Come Through*. It infuriates me to have my poems treated this way. Knopf has refused to take up the *Collected Poems* for the U. S. A. So I told Rich I would try and do them myself. I won't have them in the humiliating state they are in over there, odds and ends. Secker's edition will be quite nice (by the way, no contract yet for that). So if no publisher takes up the *Collected Poems* over there, I will try and do them myself, as I did *Lady C*. If there is difficulty with copyright I can probably add enough new stuff. But anyhow the books are severally copyrighted.

So I don't feel very drawn to the Viking Press – and I don't like Liveright. I feel this Jacob Baker is a twisty customer – I don't like his 'my friends' touch, and his using 'my friends' to get my future books for the Vanguard. But if he's hot and alive, he's better than moribund Vikings or ready-made Knopfs.

Will you write your suggestions to Rich, as to the contract with the Vanguard?

I'm really sorry to bother you on your holiday.

Would you tell me though how many *Lady C*'s you have paid into my account – is it six copies so far? I have to keep check for Orioli.

I hope it's fine at Margate. Here we had three awful days – result brilliant new snow on the mountain, and huge waterfall, and brilliant new days, but autumn, and cow-bells, the cows coming down to lower pasture.

DHL

'Spes Bona' is priceless![3]
Don't you think 10% royalty on a $10. is little?

4633. To Enid Hilton, 2 September 1928
Text: MS UCLA; Huxley 750.

Kesselmatte. *Gsteig b. Gstaad*. (Bern)
2 Sept. 1928

Dear Enid

I am sending you today the MS. of *The Escaped Cock*: the two parts. I wrote the first part a year and a half ago, and it came out in the American *Forum*, and brought down most fearful abuse on my head. So I had to do a second part.

---

[1] statement] returns   [2] Rich] CB
[3] The name of the boarding-house where Pollinger was staying.

I wish, if you can trust your friend, you would ask her to type it for me: typing is a fearful bore really. I would like one true copy, one carbon copy. There is no desperate hurry. And when it is done – if it is done in time, – send me the typescript here. We shall be here till the 15th. at least. And send me a proper bill. I want the whole thing typed.

I may give Emily a couple of small oils to bring to England – panels like the *Finding of Moses*. If you like you might meet her at Victoria on Sunday next – 9th. – at 18.43, by the boat train from Newhaven, and take the pictures for Dorothy Warren. But if you are doing anything that day, *don't bother in the least*, Emily can post the things from Nottingham. Margaret, her daughter, is a reddish haired girl of 19. – They will leave St. Pancras about 9.0 oclock, for Nottingham, that night.

You'll think there's no end of me!

DHL

4634. To Franz Schoenberner, 2 September 1928
Text: MS UT; Unpublished.

Kesselmatte, *Gsteig b. Gstaad*. (Bern) Schweiz
2 Sept. 1928

Lieber Herr Schönberner

Meine Frau wollte das Stück für Hans Carossa übersetzen: ich hoffe es geht. Wollen Sie die Englischen Worte die sie nicht kennt auf Deutsch, bitte übertragen lassen.

Tun Sie bitte mit dem Artikel wie Sie wollen. Kürzen oder verändern ganz wie Sie wollen. Wenn es zu viel Englisch gibt, sie können es übersetzen lassen, oder herausschmeissen.

Und wenn der Artikel gar nicht gefällt, sagen Sie mir nur, und ich will einen neuen schreiben. Aber ich weiss nicht warum, der Hans Carossa macht mich an Kindheit und Kirchenlieder denken: vielleicht weil er so zart ist.

Wir sind hier bis 15n Sept – denn nach BadenBaden. Und in Oktober wieder nach Italien. Wie geht es Ihnen, und ihrer Frau? – ich hoffe gut, gut. Mir geht's besser.

Viele Grüsse   D. H. Lawrence

[Dear Mr Schoenberner

My wife wanted to translate the piece for Hans Carossa; I hope it works out.[1] Would you please have the English words translated which she doesn't know the German for.

[1] See Letter 4616 and n. 2.

Please do what you want with the article. Shorten it or alter it just as you like. If there is too much English, you can have it translated, or chuck it out.

And if the article isn't liked at all, just tell me, and I'll write a new one. I don't know though why Hans Carossa makes me think of childhood and hymns; perhaps because he is so delicate.

We are here until 15th September – then to BadenBaden. And in October back to Italy. How are you, and your wife? – very well, I hope. I'm better.

Many greetings   D. H. Lawrence]

4635. To Nancy Pearn, 2 September 1928
Text: MS UT; Unpublished.

Kesselmatte. *Gsteig b. Gstaad.*

2 Sept. 1928

Dear Nancy Pearn

Did you get the 'Cocksure Women' article? – I sent it a week ago?[1]

A few of the poems were published before the war – in the *English Review* and the old *Westminster* chiefly. I don't remember very well which – 'Dreams Old' and 'Dreams Nascent' – 'Snapdragon' – 'Love on the Farm' have appeared[2] – but none of *Look!* and none of *Birds Beasts* – and few of the others.

I enclose an article I did really for a German book for Hans Carossa – but somebody might like it in English.[3] The German has gone off to Munich. Do as you like with this English version. If anybody wants it they can cut it if they like – do what they darn well please.

DHL

4636. To Aldous Huxley, [2 September 1928]
Text: Huxley 744–6.

Kesselmatte, Gsteig b. Gstaad.

Sunday, after Tea.

Dear Aldous, –

Many thanks for the *One-O* words.[4] It is a great success with the Brewsters,

[1] See Letter 4612 and n. 1. Nancy Pearn acknowledged the arrival of the article (and 'Hymns in a Man's Life') on 5 September 1928 (TMSC UT).
[2] 'Dreams Old' and 'Dreams Nascent' first appeared in *English Review*, iii (November 1909), 561–2 (Roberts C2), and 'Snap-Dragon' in *English Review*, xi (June 1912), 345 (Roberts C14); these poems were collected in *Amores* (1916). 'Love on the Farm' was first printed in *Love Poems and Others* (1913) under the title 'Cruelty and Love' (Roberts A3).
[3] 'Hymns in a Man's Life' was published in *Evening News*, 13 October 1928 (Roberts C178).
[4] Cf. Letter 4597 and p. 508 n. 3.

and a Hindu called Boshi, who tells us at great length the Sanscrit meaning of it all. – But they've gone – all gone last Wednesday – the Brewsters to Geneva – because Achsah hates Switzerland. So they sit in an hotel and look as if they were keeping the league leagued up: and I believe they hate it.

For a change, we have [Emily][1] and her daughter [Margaret] and it is really rather suffering – and [Emily], poor [Emily], she can't help feeling that ninepence is exactly half as good again as sixpence. If I wearily protest that ninepence is nothing to me unless it's ninepence worth of life, she just looks at me as if I'd said nothing. How I *hate* the attitude of ordinary people to life. How I loathe ordinariness! How from my soul I abhor nice simple people, with their eternal price-list. It makes my blood boil.

However, they leave next Friday, back safely to England, dear England, with its eternal 'expensive' and 'not at all dear, you know.' The English are *actually* the most materialistic people in the world. They're deader and pennywiser than any Americans: and I can stand them less.

However, to horse! we think to stay here till the 17th of this month – then to Baden for about a fortnight – and then, but that I'm fed up to the nose with Englishness just now, I'd go to England. Dorothy Warren is showing my pictures from Oct. 5th to 26th – she says they are framed and look lovely. I'm *pining* to see them framed and hung. But whether I shall have the strength to put my nose into that stink-pot of an island, I don't know. I very much doubt it.

Richard Aldington says he is offered by Paulhan,[2] editor of the *Nouvelle Revue Française*, his house, an ancient fortress, a vigie, on the isle of Port-Cros, about ten miles off Hyères on the Riviera – and Richard wants us to go there. Frieda is pining for sea in winter. We may go then about Oct. 1st and look at the place. There is a little hotel. – Having looked, we'd come on to the Mirenda. And if it would suit you I'd like to do those Etruscans in the last half of October. But don't, of course, disturb yourself a hair's breadth for us. If one did the Etruscan places, I suppose it would take 10 to 14 days. And will you go on to Sicily? You don't want to be there till November – it's really best in January when the almond blossoms. Now it will be pretty dried up. But I love Sicily. – But if we like the Port-Cros island I think we'll go there for the three winter months – very warm and fine pine-forest on the island (which is about 5 × 2 miles, I think) no gendarmes – 13 families fishermen – and *chi lo sa!* – Not many miles from Monte, glittering Monte!!

But one might be happy there. I like Richard Aldington and Arabella – they

[1] Cf. p. 326 n. 3.
[2] Jean Paulhan (1884–), French critic and essayist, edited the highly influential *Nouvelle Revue Française*, 1925–40.

     543

are in Vallombrosa at the moment. We'll see, anyhow. I don't feel quite at the point when I can go to the ranch. I'm pretty well in myself, but cursed with the same cough. I wish we could all have houses on the island for the winter. But you are so difficult with people – the poor [Brewster]'s! I thought on the island I might paint nice out-door nudes. I ought to have been at Forte, oughtn't I? – I've only painted one or two little things here – one nice board, of *contadini* – And now figures on the sand at the sea.[1] There's something very dramatic about paint. Really, why don't you begin? – I never forget that I owe Maria a picture. If only she were there and seized one that she liked! But for myself, I feel I've not yet painted the picture for her – something a mixture of Watteau and Boucher,[2] with lotus flowers and decorative nudes that nobody will blush at. I'll do it one day.

Do stay at the Mirenda if ever you want to – but write to Giulia first – Signorina Giulia Pini, Scandicci, per San Paolo (Firenze). Because the *padroni* may have taken the key to Florence. – Only the beds, Maria, the hard beds! – And think of it quite bare of pictures!

Orioli said he might come to Forte for a week-end – then you'd hear all about *Lady C.* – That beastly [   ], why doesn't a shark eat him – not fit for anything else. How I *hate* ordinary people.

Here it's turning to autumn. We had three awful deluge days – then a brilliant morning, brilliant new snow, brilliant new world – and slopes all bubbled over with pink autumn crocuses – very lovely. This evening it's sulking and trying to thunder: cow-bells ting-ting-ting – very still in all the world, and somehow far. Even our visitors have subsided in comparative stillness.

Am reading again *Chartreuse de Parme* – so good historically, socially and all that – but emotionally rather empty and trashy.[3] Had of course to rescue F. – who is painting autumn crocuses in water, and *naturally* rubbed her paper with milk roll instead of stale bread, to thin off her pencil marks. Of course milk roll is so much better class! nice and greasy.

Night falling – mist on the mountains – stewed rabbit and onions in the kitchen – wish you were here for a party! –

DHL

[1] The picture was entitled *North Sea* (*The Paintings of D. H. Lawrence*, plate [10]). It was later given to Maria Huxley.
[2] Antoine Watteau (1684–1721) and François Boucher (1703–70) were both painters of elegant pastoral scenes (though Boucher's pictures lack the poetic subtlety of Watteau's).
[3] The novel (1839) by Stendhal (Henri Beyle) (1783–1842) about the life and intrigues at a small Italian court 1815–30. DHL knew the novel by November 1916 (see *Letters*, iii. 21).

4637. To Giuseppe Orioli, 4 September 1928

Text: MS UCLA; cited in Moore, *Intelligent Heart* 384.

Kesselmatte. *Gsteig b. Gstaad.* Svizzera

Tuesday. 4 Sept. 1928

Dear Pino

Yours with the two Amer. cheques just come. – You will have had mine. – Sounds to me as if the Gotham were trying a swindle. Just the kind of thing they might do – and very easy too – just say the books did not come through.[1] What swine! And I am told that when the authorities hold up books, they sell them secretly at huge prices! Wouldn't they just!

R[ichard] A[ldington] sent his last 4 copies to Enid – who is sending *one* to Hy. Young, Liverpool, as you asked – and *three* copies to Dorothy Warren (£6. *paid*). She is The Warren Galleries, 39a Maddox St. W.1. as you know. – *All* the orders you sent to me are sent out.

I won't send Simpkin's order to Kot. till I hear he has delivered the A. L. Humphreys six copies. I believe he will now have only ten copies left: if he sends Simpkin's five, he will have only five. We must send out all orders from Florence. Enid has now nothing – R. A. nothing. – Yes, Enid has *two* copies only, holding for Varda, who ordered 4, but her shop is closed till Sept. If she is open this week, Enid will deliver the two. – I know Kot. hates delivering. And if Varda wants more you must send them.

As far as I can make out, the *total* money received up to today, with those you sent and Prince Bibesco's[2] £2. is

Sterling	£769.11.9
dollars $829.50 =	£166 sterling.
Various cash, in sterling	£78.0.0
gross total in sterling	£1013.11.9
my profit is	£713.11.9.

So I owe you on the 10% scale another £22.[3] I enclose cheque for £26. – of which one pound for Carletto.

If I have received a total of £1013.11.9, that will mean we have received the money for *about* 560 copies.

---

[1] David Moss of the Gotham Book Mart, New York, had sent two cheques each for $37.50 (17 and 22 August 1928); a third for $10 came later (dated 19 September 1928) ('Memoranda', MS NWU).

[2] Prince Antoine Bibesco (1878–1951), Roumanian diplomat whom DHL had encountered on many occasions since 1915 (see *Letters*, ii. 453 and n. 3).

[3] The '£22' should read £25 to make DHL's arithmetic correct. This is confirmed by an entry in his 'Memoranda': 'to *Pino Orioli, £25 for his 10%* – and £1. for Carletto £26. Sept 4th.'

Do count the copies that remain, and tell me how many.

Dorothy Warren has my pictures and some newly framed. She says they look lovely! She is showing them from Oct 5th. to 26th. I expect there'll be more hubbub then!

Have you had the two copies back from those swine in Birmingham – Cornish Bros?

Wonder if you went to Forte. Quite cool here – but today a lovely day – went to Diablerets this morning.

Put the cheque to my Lira account, will you?

DHL

I hear Douglas was very mean to Brooks about *Birds Beasts of Greek Anthology.*[1]

I went and forgot Carletto – so had to make him out a separate one.

I believe New York is letting its copies through – perhaps hoping we'll send more.

4638. To S. S. Koteliansky, 5 September 1928
Text: MS BL; Postmark, Gsteig 6.IX.28; Zytaruk 358–9.

Kesselmatte. *Gsteig b. Gstaad.* Switzerland
5 Sept 1928

My dear Kot

Thanks for yours received today, with Cornish Bros cheque, and list. I got a list from R[ichard] A[ldington] – he had only four copies left, and he sent them to Enid: who had just got orders for four from me – which clears up that bunch entirely.

Orioli wrote that Simpkin and Marshall wanted five more copies, and wanted them delivered by hand if possible, and they wish to pay on delivery. Do you mind doing it? If Enid had any copies I'd ask her.

I hope Orioli is sending you the twenty copies. He still has not told me how many copies remain in Florence. – Of the American 140, I'm afraid about half were unpaid. But some Americans are paying as they receive their copies. I'm afraid we shall lose a number there, though.

If I don't let the Vanguard print, then someone else is *sure* to pirate the book. You know Joyce was pirated, in sections, in spite of Sylvia Beach's

---

[1] Norman Douglas dedicated his privately printed *Birds and Beasts of the Greek Anthology* (Florence, 1927) to John Ellingham Brooks (1863–1929), English expatriate whom he and DHL knew in Capri (see *Letters*, iii. 443 and n. 2). He chose to render the Greek text in Brooks' execrable verse and, with conscious or unconscious irony, to phrase the dedication thus: 'To his friend J.E.B. whose verses have enlivened this dismal discourse'. For the reaction of a writer who knew Douglas and Brooks, see Richard Aldington, *Pinorman* (1954), pp. 176–8.

frantic efforts.[1] – And if the Vanguard print a 1000 at $10. – I don't see I break faith with the purchasers of my edition. I didn't promise that no other edition should ever be published.

My sister and daughter leave on Friday. It is sad to say I rather suffered from them. But a gulf comes as one grows older. And nowadays I can't bear to be stuck among several women, alone. It just seems to annihilate one.

I expect we shall leave here for good on the 17th. – go to BadenBaden for ten days or a fortnight – then I really ought to come to England. Dorothy Warren is showing my pictures from Oct 5th. to 26th. She has had them framed, and says they look lovely. Of course I'm pining to see them framed and hung. Yet I don't know if I can drag myself to England. – I think she will put about 15 gns. on the water-colours – and something a bit more on the small oils – but on the big pictures I want her to put a real high price, like £500., because I really don't want to sell them. I have so few, and we got so fond of them, as they hung in the Mirenda.

Are you all alone in the Cave? – I think it must be rather nice.

DHL

4639. To Martin Secker, 5 September 1928
Text: MS UInd; Postmark, Gsteig 6.IX 28; Secker 110–11.

Kesselmatte. *Gsteig b. Gstaad.* Switzerland
5 Sept. 1928

Dear Secker

We are still here. My elder sister, Mrs King, and her daughter of 19 have been with us this last two weeks – but they leave on Friday. I think they liked it here. Yesterday we went over to Diablerets – lovely going over the pass.

I got the agreement for the *Poems* today, and am returning it signed. When exactly will you bring them out? I'll send you a list of people for my six. Don't send me my copy till I get somewhere settled.

We think to leave here on the 17th. – and go to BadenBaden till end of month or thereabouts. Then I ought to come to England, because Dorothy Warren is showing my pictures from Oct. 5th. to 26th. – She has got them all and had them new framed – making them look lovely, she says. I'm pining, of course, to see them framed and hung. But even so I don't know if I shall drag myself to England – though I think Frieda will come. – But you won't like the pictures.

I want to go with Aldous and Maria to do the rest of the Etruscans in the second half of Oct – they said they'd motor us. But nothing is fixed.

[1] Cf. p. 489 n. 2.

Would you send a copy of *Mornings in Mexico* and a copy of *Fantasia* to
    Boshi Sen Esq, c/o American Express, 6 Haymarket. S. W. 1.
He is a Hindu who was here with the Brewsters – a nice man, a scientist,
working at the University of London – and he used to give me Hindu
massages.

It's rather lovely autumn weather here – the peasants are mowing the grass
for the second time. I suppose it's nice in England now.

The women just trooped in with muddy feet and gentian flowers –

                                       au revoir   DHL

4640. To Harold Mason, 6 September 1928
Text: MS BosU; *Centaur* 34–5.

                        (Kesselmatte. *Gsteig b. Gstaad*. Switzerland)
                  better c/o Pino Orioli. 6 Lungarno Corsini. Florence
                                       6 Sept 1928

Dear Mason.

It was good of you to take so much trouble about *Lady C.* – all to no avail, I
am afraid, but many thanks all the same. Your suggestion about William
Jackson was no good.[1] Those canaille ordered 80 copies – received them – had
a funk and cancelled the order. However, I got the books back from them,
have sold them all, and have Messrs William Jackson well in mind for a future
occasion. – I believe Orioli shipped in all about 140 copies to America. How
many are lost, I don't know. But we know a fair number arrived. The other
day the Gotham Book shop of New York wrote that they had received *five*
copies – which is curious, seeing that ten copies were sent, in *five parcels of two
copies each*. By what mystery did one parcel get split? – Or is the Gotham
adding one to the subtraction of the customs officials?? – What a feeble set of
fools your customs officials are! Imagine being under the thumb of such
morons! But one day America will be under the thumb of a nigger Klu-Klux –
and she'll have asked for it.

There was a rumour of suppression in England – I hear a certain
'influential' person known to me moved for it. But there was sufficient
pressure against it, so nothing has happened – and I have sold something like
600 copies to England – besides the steady orders from Paris. So it looks as if I
shall sell out my edition pretty soon. I am in no hurry, really, now the bulk are
gone. – I suppose Americans who want copies will get them from European
dealers, and pay through the nose. Which is very nice for European dealers,
but very much like having your nose out of joint, for the Americans.

---

[1] Cf. pp. 449–50 n. 3.

Anyhow we are not sending another copy to America, neither one way nor another. It's not good enough – and Europe will take them all.

Autumn is coming on – we shall go back to Italy in October, I suppose.

Regards to you and to Mrs Mason.

sincerely   D. H. Lawrence[1]

4641. To Harry Crosby, 6 September 1928
Text: MS SIU; Postmark, Gsteig 7.IX.28; Huxley 751.

Kesselmatte. Gsteig b. Gstaad. Switzerland
6 Sept 1928

Dear Harry Crosby

Secker wrote he was willing for you to publish *Sun*, but he wants you to present him with a copy when it comes out. He's a sly dog at getting his picking. But please yourself whether you *do* send him a copy or not. – I haven't heard from Knopf yet.

The *Modern French Painting* book turned out better when I really read it.[2] I was prejudiced by the amazingly feeble and inadequate choice of illustrations – but preposterous. Yet the man Jan Gordon is on the whole sound and sane and quite good – even if he talks down to his reader as if to an eternal Slade student.

Some of the things in *Transition* I found really good and amusing. But James Joyce bores me stiff – too terribly would-be and done-on-purpose, utterly without spontaneity or real life. Gertrude Stein amuses me for while,

---

[1] Mason replied on 25 October 1928 (TMSC Mason):

Dear Lawrence:

I have been intending for weeks to write you about LADY CHATTERLEY'S LOVER and to tell you, first off, that I think it is really a magnificent book. I read it, every word, borrowing a copy from McDonald, one of the few that filtered in to his professors at the Drexel Institute.

You have heard, by this time, the unfortunate story of the copies that were sent to the private addresses, not one of which came through. I do not wonder that you are exasperated beyond measure at the stupidity of our Customs authorities. I did not even get through the copy sent me, mentioned in your letter written immediately after the publication of the book, but I mean to own a copy of the first edition some day as I must add it to my complete collection of your works. I have just finished a book recently issued over here entitled TO THE PURE. It is a study of this ridiculous censorship question and shows graphically how absurd the whole thing is. It leaves one baffled and inarticulate.

I have talked to a number of people who have read your book and I have yet to hear a dissenting voice. Every one likes it and likes it immensely. It is, indeed, a work of great beauty and strength and there are pages of it that have never been excelled, in my opinion.

I hope that you will not feel too bitterly about it to return to this country . . . I am hoping that you will not be discouraged and that you will keep on with the splendid writing . . .

Ever yours

[2] Jan Gordon, *Modern French Painters* (1922).

but soon palls. Some of the other things, *not* the most ambitious, made me laugh. But the feeblest of all feebles were the sayings of the French wise men at the end, about America.[1] Really the French are crumbling to sheer puerile inanity. They have the minds of domestic cats.

My sister is going through Paris, and will post you there your little picture – *Sun-men catching horses*.[2] It is nothing – so just put it in the fire if you don't care for it. I think it's quite a nice trifle, that's all.

We stay here till the 17th., then to BadenBaden for a fortnight or so – then probably to France, maybe to England. When do you sail for America?

I hope Sunstroke is looking shiny and stroked.

Sincerely   D. H. Lawrence

4642. To Edward McDonald, 6 September 1928
Text: MS UT; Postmark, Gsteig 7.IX.28; Moore 1086.

(Kesselmatte. Gsteig. b. Gstaad. Switzerland.)
c/o Pino Orioli. 6 Lungarno Corsini. Florence
6 Sept. 1928

Dear McDonald

Many thanks for your various letters and cable. It is curious, as you say, what happens to *Lady C.* – some copies get through, some don't – the same in Santa Fe. I am afraid we have lost a certain number, thanks to the feeble-minded industry of your officials. It is amazing how pusilanimous the Americans are – they sit down to any-thing: and to such tyranny of cretins and morons. My God, if ever your country has a war on its own – which it will have before you die – what a hell it will be for you citizens! It's a rod you've made for your own backs: tyranny of imbeciles and canaille.

There was a stir in England to get the book suppressed – But also there was a stir the other way. So nothing has happened. Therefore I have distributed safely all the orders there – and I think we shall fairly easily sell out the whole edition. I don't think there are two hundred copies left – not more, certainly. And there was no trouble. And the orders still come in from London and Paris. I suppose, if Americans want the book, they will have to pay dear for it to European booksellers. That's all it amounts to. What clever American business!

No, I didn't try to teach you any words you didn't know. I didn't want to teach you anything. Why should I? I wanted to give you a book written from one, at least, of the main roots of life. I consider I did so. I guess Mrs McDonald got more than two new Anglo-Saxon monosyllables out of it.

[1] Cf. Letter 4596 and p. 507 n. 3.   [2] Nothing further is known of this picture.

But thanks for taking so much trouble for me. And tell me if I am in default anywhere.

Sincerely   D. H. Lawrence

4643. To Hon. Dorothy Brett, 8 September 1928
Text: MS UCin; Postmark, Gsteig 9.IX.28; Irvine, Brett 90–1.

Kesselmatte. Gsteig b. Gstaad. Switzerland
8 Sept. 1928

Dear Brett,

Your letter today with the various 'items.' – About the gold, I expect you found all there is to find. But if you want to do anything about it, send the necessary paper along, and Frieda will sign it. Remember the ranch is not mine.

About Trinidad, that's a very nasty business, and looks to me as if there was more than Rufina behind it. Who is putting Rufina up to all this beastliness? – some enemy of Tony's, I suppose – or some 'party.' Very nasty business.

About selling the ranch, anyhow Frieda will do nothing about it without coming over herself. I wrote the same to Mr Read.[1]

About *Lady C.* – The Americans are what they are – and I know all about it. About 140 copies in all were sent – some have arrived – we are waiting to hear *how many* have not arrived. I am afraid the booksellers who have been sent orders unpaid, may *pretend* they haven't received their copies, even when they have: so as not to pay. Do you know how many copies Gomme received? If so, please tell me. – There is no sign of him over here.[2] – We have stopped sending anything to America for the last three weeks – or month – and shall send no more. – So far, the Amer. customs have returned no copies to Florence. I'm afraid the milky angels do that selling at huge prices, which you talk of: on their own account. – So far as I am concerned, I cannot suddenly start charging huge prices for a book I offer at £2. I think I have sold about 600 or 650 in Europe – of which some 560 are paid for. There are the 140 to America, many of which are unpaid and probably a dead loss. Leaves me just about 200 copies. – I expect we shall raise the price in a while – but nothing startling. I have made so far about £700 clear – which is not bad, but not the vast sums you dream of.

[1] See Letter 4502.
[2] Mabel Luhan had doubtless passed on to Brett (and thence to DHL) information from Gomme's letter to her of 20 August 1928 (TMSC UN): 'I [Gomme] am leaving for Europe at the end of this week and expect to be in Neuchatel Switzerland around the 6th of next month. Is D. H. anywhere near there. I would like to meet him and discuss the question of his book with him if it be possible.'

We leave here in about ten days time, for BadenBaden – a fortnight there. I am better generally, but the cough about the same. I think we shall winter by the sea – perhaps on an island off the S. of France, with friends – perhaps Spain. Or we may go to Egypt. They say it is very good to alternate altitude with sea. Don't you come over to Europe. In any case I don't want to come to America just now – too much dirty American fuss of all sorts over *Lady C.* – I feel I don't want to set eyes on the country. But it's no use your coming over here – we shall probably be moving about anyhow. And there's nothing to gain by it.

What you might try to do at the ranch one day is to get somebody to find the *sights*, and trace out the proper square of the holding. You know there is only a wiggly piece of it fenced in. The proper ranch is square, and $\frac{1}{2}$ mile × $\frac{1}{2}$ mile. Old Willy Vandiveer[1] *might* know the sights. Ask Mabel if she knows.

Well, I feel dead off America and everything American at the moment. How glad I am John Collier hated *Lady C*. He always was a worm.[2]

Dorothy Warren is showing my pictures from Oct. 5th. to 26th. As I don't want to sell, I am putting £500. on the big pictures. The little ones go at more usual rates. Don't care a damn if I don't sell a thing. I was waiting to hear from Stieglitz definitely in the matter. Long effusions from him and O'Keefe over *Lady C.* – but nothing definite about the pictures. I shan't send them anyhow to America now.

Cows all coming down from the high alp pastures, tinkling myriads of bells – means summer is over. – Remember me to Mabel. I'm sorry about Spud's books.

Do you know if Ted Gillett got his copy?

DHL

4644. To Nancy Pearn, [8 September 1928]
Text: MS UT; PC; Postmark, Gsteig 10 IX 28; Unpublished.

Gsteig.
Saturday

Could you please send a typescript copy of 'Hymns in a Man's Life' to Herrn. Franz Schoenberner, Elizabethstrasse 8iv, *München*, Bayern.
Germany

---

[1] Vandiveer] Berryman (Vandiveer was the blacksmith at San Cristobal.)

[2] John Collier (1884–1968) and his family lived next door to the Lawrences in Taos; he was an American social worker and organiser of the Indian Defense Association (see *Letters*, iv. 332 and n. 1). His wife, Lucy Wood Collier, had ordered two copies of *Lady Chatterley's Lover* via Laurence Gomme; they were sent to her on 8 August but before they were delivered she cabled Gomme on 10 August: 'Situation complicated Stop relative subject my order make no shipments until you hear from me' (TMSC UN).

I don't know at all if I shall come to England this autumn – but the thought of broadcasting makes my blood run cold anyhow.[1]

Where are you going for your holiday?

D. H. Lawrence

4645. To Laurence Pollinger, [8–10 September 1928]
Text: MS UT; Unpublished.

Kesselmatte. Gsteig b. Gstaad. Schweiz
8 Sept. 1928

Dear Pollinger

Many thanks for your letter. I shall be glad to get my American side straightened up a bit, but especially the poems.

I have received the contract from Elkin Matthews for *Rawdon's Roof* today – and *why* did I ever say I'd sign 500 books for £25! Now I suppose I shall have to. But never again that signing business.

I notice 6 gns. for change of cheques today – which means 3 copies of *Lady C.* from you. – Did you get the 3 copies from Mrs Hilton? – because all her lot were gone – and paid for. Of the 108 'returned' copies, only five are left – and those ordered. We have to post from Florence now. – But probably you'd get your three out of the last five. – People have paid up pretty well – Orioli sees after all that, so I don't know exactly. But there must be about 600 paid. – Some sent to America are lost and unpaid, alas – I dont know how many – 60 or 70 maybe – maybe more. – So there are not many copies in Florence, especially as Orioli wants to take some over to speculate on! – I wish I knew how many copies have got into America – I *hope* about 70 or 80. – On the whole it's gone very well, and been exciting, what with one thing and another. Anyhow I enjoyed putting it through, and dropping a little bomb in the world's crinoline of hypocrisy.

I sent *The Escaped Cock* to be typed. I'll let you have a copy when it comes back. But I'm not keen on giving it to Crosby Gaige. Somehow I am dead off the Americans, at the moment.

I wish I could wriggle out of signing those 500 Elkin Matthews copies.

I didn't know there was another little twig on the family tree. Is it masculine or feminine, ♂ or ♀?[2] I think children are a great help, they give an immediate importance to life, and block out a lot of depressing vistas. I say so, having none – only 'vistas democratic'!

[1] Nancy Pearn wrote to DHL on 5 September 1928 (TMSC UT): 'The B. B. C. is still keen for you to broadcast: especially so since those articles appeared in the "*Evening News*" . . . We have found that broadcasting really is quite a useful and dignified bit of publicity.'
[2] Pollinger's second son, Russell Martin, b. 15 July 1928 (his first son, Gerald John, b. 1925).

English September can be lovely, with a big moon. Here it's just wheeling round to autumn, the mountains a hub for the sad ceaseless clouds. We've had ten weeks sun, though. We leave this day week, the 17th. (it's now Monday) – for BadenBaden.[1]

4646. To Dorothy Warren, 10 September 1928
Text: MS UN; Nehls, iii. 242.

Kesselmatte. *Gsteig b. Gstaad*. Switzerland
10 Sept. 1928

Dear Dorothy

I sent you two more panels to London – nice ones I think.[2]

There is such a fracas and an alarm in America over my novel, such a panic, that I must postpone any thought of showing my pictures there. I'm sure the Customs in New York would destroy them! So that's off. I wouldn't risk sending the pictures across the Atlantic this year, not for anything.

This leaves you free to do as you like in England, as regards the time of your show. Some of my 'friends' write that this is the very wrong moment to show pictures of mine in London, it will provide an opportunity for all my enemies, that it will do me a lot of damage, and do your gallery a lot of damage etc. etc. – I don't give much for such Job's Comforters myself. Nor do I tremble at the thought of my 'enemies', dear Lord! But you think it over and do as you really think best. Barkis is willin',[3] as far as I'm concerned, to agree with any decision you make. But I don't feel like being 'frightened,' either. Haven't my enemies been doing their damnedest for twenty years! Keep 'em running.

I hear you are in Austria – but I hope this will be sent to you from London. After the 17th. my address will be:

c/o Frau Baronin von Richthofen, Ludwig-Wilhelmstift, *BadenBaden*
Avanti, arditi![4]   D. H. Lawrence

4647. To Ada Clarke, 10 September 1928
Text: MS Clarke; Lawrence–Gelder 180–2.

Kesselmatte. Gsteig b. Gstaad. Switzerland
10 Sept. 1928

My dear Sister

Well Pamela has been, and gone. I was glad to see her. But it's a bit upsetting too. I wish things were a bit rosier for her. She said very little – but I

---

[1] MS incomplete.   [2] *Contadini* and *North Sea*, both done in Gsteig (cf. Letter 4633).
[3] Proverbial, originally from Dickens, *David Copperfield*, chap. v.   [4] 'Onward the brave!'

could feel it was rather a *cul de sac*. The Lord knows what that Sam will do. He's not fit to have a shop with a lot of stock. He's only fit for milk or fried fish, with no stock hardly. If he has fifty shops, they'll all go wrong. Very depressing!

Peg has improved in appearance, at least. But she's hardly a man's woman. My god, these mincing young females all mincing together in a female bunch, they little know what a terrible blank they're preparing for themselves later, when this mincing young female business wears itself out. Are *all* young Englishwomen instinctively homosexual? looks like it, to me. Of course I'm only speaking of the instinct, not of any practice. But that instinct sends a man's feelings recoiling to the ultimate pole. My God! – what a ghastly mess 'purity' is leading to! – But don't say anything – this is absolutely between you and me.

The eiderdown is very nice and very warm, and many thanks for it – or for your share of it. – I'm glad you feel good and brisk – but don't put on too much steam – I'm terrified now of days of reckoning later. Talk about the dangerous age, it's a limit! So take care of yourself, no matter how bouncing you feel. – Poor Bertie, I sympathize with him, a prisoner already. I think it is quite wrong for young children to have so many hours schooling. Three hours in the morning would be *quite* enough, up to the age of eight. But I suppose one has to do as the world does: else be exceptional. As for myself, I take my stand on exception.

Today it's blowing up grey and autumnal. We've had good weather, very, for the mountains. But I'm about ready to go. We leave on the 17th., for BadenBaden. Else, F[rieda]'s sister, is coming this week-end – on the way to Nice. I don't think I shall come to England. The thought of it always depresses me. I think I shall probably go to the south of France, and join Else, and Richard Aldington and Arabella, on the 1st. Oct. – and Frieda will come to England for ten days or a fortnight. I want her to see my picture show. Dorothy Warren opens it either on the 5th. or 9th. of Oct. The first two days will be by invitation only. I can have her send you a card if you wish. – But I'd advise you *not* to go. You won't like the things. Best leave 'em alone. – But the show will be open to the public till about end of October.

The cows have now *all* come down from the high alps – summer is over – time to go. – I do hope G[ertrude] will keep all right.

Love.   DHL

4648. To Maria Chambers, 11 September 1928
Text: MS StaU; Schorer 63.

Switzerland.
11 Sept. 1928

Dear Mrs Chambers

I am sending you back your two cheques of $20 each. It is useless trying to post *Lady C.* to U.S.A. – all held up and dead loss. I'm so glad you got your two copies.

I am furious at the fuss made over there in U.S.A. – even worse in St Louis and San Francisco and Sante Fe than in New York. My God – don't people *know* what's natural and what isn't.

We leave here next Monday for BadenBaden. I shan't dare send my pictures to New York now – they'd be confiscated too. What hypocrites!

D. H. Lawrence

4649. To Baroness Anna von Richthofen, 11 September 1928
Text: MS UCB; cited in Frieda Lawrence 278.

Kesselmatte. Gsteig b. Gstaad. Schweiz
11 Sept. 1928

Meine liebe Schwiegermutter

Ich habe deinen Brief und den Schlips – einen schönen. Ja, wir kommen bald. Die Else soll hier Samstag kommen – 15n. – und bis Montag bleiben. So fahren wir alle zusammen bis Gstaad, am 17n – und Frieda und ich sollen da in Baden an demselben Abend sein. Nur wenn die Else noch zwei Tage hier bleiben möchte, denn bleiben wir bis Mittwoch. Aber ich glaube doch wir kommen Montag – und möchten in den *Eden* gehen, zwei Zimmer wie letztes Jahr.

Heute schreibt mir der Brewster aus Genf, sie fahren heute nach Basel und wollen auch nach Baden kommen – können da sein vielleicht an Donnerstag. Sie möchten auch im Eden bleiben. Vielleicht wirst du telefonieren und fragen ob sie zwei Zimmer haben für die drei, Vater, Mutter und Mädchen von 16 Jahren. Ich will dem Brewster schreiben, er soll direkt an den Eden oder telegrafiern oder schreiben, um zu sagen den Tag der Ankunft. – Er ist Mr. E. H. Brewster. – Vielleicht wirst du die *Preise* fest machen. Die Brewsters sind Vegetarians, essen kein Fleisch.

Hier ist es wunderbar still, seit meine Schwester und Nichte fort sind. Sie waren Freitag weg – und ich hatte eine Postkarte aus Paris. Hier waren sie Vergnügt: meine Schwester aber ist ein wenig trüb, der Mann ist ein Nichtsle. – Wir hatten auch die sommertagen. Heute aber ist es Herbst, die Wolken drehen die Gipfeln den Bergen herum und herum, still und grau und nieder, so still, es macht beinah Angst. Hier in den Bergen braucht man Sonne.

Es wird nett sein in Baden, wenn die Brewsters auch da sind, und wir gehen zu Konzerten und Theater zusammen. Aber sie sollen nicht zu viel zu dir kommen, sonst ermüden sie dich. Ich komme aber, und – wir trinken einen ruhigen Thee, und spielen einen Whist mit der Frau Kugler. Wie geht es ihr, auch?

Ich glaube die Else fährt mit Zug hier – und trifft den Alfred mit Auto in Lausanne oder irgendwo. Ich möchte nie von hier bis Nizza in Auto fahren – es macht furchtbar müde. Es ist aber das neues Spielzeug, sie werden stolz darüber sein.

Wir essen Kilos von Weintrauben – die Frieda macht Traubenkur – auch Wachholderkur, – und Gott weiss was.

Hörst du kein Wort von der Nusch?

Also Lebewohl – und auf baldigen Wiedersehn

DHL

[My dear Schwiegermutter

I have your letter and the tie – a nice one. Yes, we're coming soon. Else should arrive here on Saturday – the 15th. – and stay till Monday. Then we'll all go together to Gstaad, on the 17th and Frieda and I should arrive in Baden the same evening. Only, if Else should want to stay here two days longer, then we'll stay till Wednesday. But I really think we'll come on Monday – and would like to go in the *Eden*, two rooms like last year.

Today Brewster writes to me from Geneva, they are going to Basle today and would also like to come to Baden – could perhaps be there on Thursday. They would also like to stay in the Eden. Perhaps you would telephone and ask if they have two rooms for the three of them, father, mother and a girl of 16. I'll write to Brewster that he should either telegraph or write direct to the Eden, to tell them the day of arrival. – He is Mr. E. H. Brewster. – Perhaps you could fix the *prices*. The Brewsters are vegetarians, eat no meat.

Here it is wonderfully quiet, since my sister and niece left. They went on Friday – and I had a postcard from Paris. They enjoyed themselves here: my sister though is a bit depressed, her husband is a little nonentity. – We had summer days, too. Today though it is autumn, the clouds are wrapped round and round the mountain peaks, still and grey and low, so still, it is almost frightening. Here in the mountains one needs sun.

It will be nice in Baden, if the Brewsters are there too, and we go to concerts and the theatre together. Though they shouldn't come to you too much, or they'll tire you. But I'll come, and – we'll drink a quiet tea, and play Whist with Mrs Kugler. How is she, too?

I think Else is coming here by train – and meets Alfred with the car in Lausanne or somewhere. I would never like to travel by car from here to Nice – it's dreadfully tiring. But it's the new toy, they'll be proud of it.

We eat kilos of grapes – Frieda is doing a grape-slimming-course – also juniper-berry-slimming-course, – and God knows what.

Do you hear nothing from Nusch?

So farewell – and see you soon.

DHL]

4650. To Earl Brewster, [11 September 1928]
Text: MS UT; Unpublished.

Kesselmatte.
11 Sept.

Dear Earl

Just have your wire – have written my mother-in-law to ask for rooms for you in Hotel Eden, Baden – and to fix prices. You must write or wire the hotel the day you want to arrive – write

Frau Baronin v. Richthofen, Ludwig-Wilhelmstift, *BadenBaden*
and tell her too. She understands enough English. I hope the hotel will have rooms. I said you might arrive Thursday.

Else arrives Sat. for the week end – on her way to Nice – she will leave Monday morning with us, and F[rieda] and I ought to be in Baden Monday night: so see you soon. Today it rains.

Haste – the boy is waiting.

DHL

4651. To Enid Hilton, 12 September 1928
Text: MS UCLA; Moore, *Intelligent Heart* 388–9.

Kesselmatte. Gsteig b. Gstaad. Schweiz
12 Sept 1928

Dear Enid

Very nice of you to look after my family – hope they were appreciative. –

Don't give the two *little* pictures to Dorothy Warren.[1] I don't want to show them. Just keep them for the time. – I don't mind a bit if she doesn't show *Dandelions.* I want her to do what she really thinks best. – I wrote her I didn't mind now if she postpones her show, as I can't send the pictures to New York.

---

[1] Cf. Letter 4646 and n. 2. The MS is annotated (probably by Enid Hilton): 'Italian Peasants already in *Catalogue*' (cf. Letter 4668).

Of course they've made a fuss over the book – confiscated what they could lay hands on – luckily not so very many. So I'm afraid they'd follow up by confiscating the pictures. So I shan't risk sending them – not I. – Therefore Dorothy can choose her time. – I should like to have all the pictures *photographed*, if it's not too wildly expensive, and keep the copyright for reproduction myself. You might ask D. W. about that when she comes back.

Imagine those booksellers making money like that on *Lady C*! I hear in America the price is $50. Oh Lord, one is always swindled. But we are going to put up the price now on the remaining copies.

I suppose you saw Kot, and heard all his alarms. He is like that. He thinks because Gertler and a few like that will say nasty things about my pictures, it means all the world. It doesn't.

We leave here next Monday 17th., and the address is

  c/o Frau von Richthofen, Ludwig-Wilhelmstift, *BadenBaden*

I suppose we shall be there a fortnight. Then if D. W. is showing the pictures in early Oct., Frieda will come to London. But I shan't – I can't stand England. I shall go to the South of France, en route for Italy.

Wonder what Alice Dax thought of *Lady C*![1]

Mountains are beginning to be misty and a bit damp and silent and autumny – time now to go. Thanks so much for looking after things so well. Remember me to L[aurence].

                                                              DHL

4652. To Alfred Stieglitz, 12 September 1928
Text: MS YU; Postmark, Gsteig 14.IX.28; Huxley 752.

                                             Kesselmatte. Gsteig b. Gstaad.
                                             12 Sept. 1928
Dear Stieglitz

Your long 14-pager today. I'm afraid my friends have been bothering you about those pictures. Too bad! I didn't want it at all. I am *not* hard up – have plenty of money to go on with – don't want to sell my pictures at all, really, because I rather love them and want to keep them. I'd miss them much more than a few thousand dollars would make up. – Don't gasp at my 'thousands'. – I am showing them in London because friends wanted me to – and we are giving up the Italian villa – and – vanity, I suppose. Or mischief. More arrows

[1] Alice Mary Dax (1878–1959), militant feminist and socialist whom Enid Hilton would have known as prominent in Eastwood affairs (see *Letters*, i. 2, 44 n. 3). Alice Dax had told Enid Hilton's mother, Sallie Hopkin: 'I gave Bert sex' (Moore, *Intelligent Heart* 93); she later referred to the occasion as the 'one short memorable hour' when they were 'whole' (*Frieda Lawrence: The Memoirs and Correspondence*, ed. E. W. Tedlock, 1961, p. 245).

in the air, and let's hope one won't fall in my own eye, like Harold at Hastings.[1] – But it would be useless to send them to America now – too much stupid fuss over *Lady C.* – Why so much fuss over simple natural things. They ought to censor eggs, as revealing the intimate relation of cock and hen. Though they don't necessarily – so there –?

However, don't bother, it would only be foolish of me to ship pictures to New York this year. Some other year, maybe. But why think of other years!

Thank O Keefe for her letter – I should like to see you both – and to see some of your work. But that too will have to be another year. I shan't come to America now. Too much fuss. I hate foolish fuss.

Sincerely   D. H. Lawrence

4653. To Giuseppe Orioli, [13 September 1928]
Text: MS UCLA; Unpublished.

[Kesselmatte, Gsteig b. Gstaad, Switzerland]
[13 September 1928]

Send him a copy when you get his money[2] – but tell him you are afraid all *mail* steamers go to N. York – Perhaps you could let Egidi send it by a boat to Texas – carriage to be paid on delivery. Do that, and see how it turns out. Ask him to

---

[1] Cf. Letter 4595 and n. 4. King Harold was killed at the Battle of Hastings (1066), allegedly by an arrow from an English archer.

[2] DHL was responding to a note scribbled by Orioli on a letter which he had received from Philip Brooks, 71 Bedford Street, New York. Orioli wrote: 'Please send back this. I have not received his money order yet. Shall I send a copy to this *galantuomo* at the original price. Let me know. Pino.' Brooks' letter – on which DHL also wrote his own – reads as follows:

Dear Sir:
   There seems to be a conspiracy on foot to keep Mr. Lawrence's audience from reading his "Lady Chatterley's Lover". My English agent found the book "demoralizing", and having miraculously survived the effects of reading it, turns protector to the rest of mankind and warns us away from it. He seems to have the sympathy of the book-selling league in England and this country. Some of our dealers here find it so vile that they refuse to sell it for anything less than $50.
   The foregoing is merely a preliminary to my placing an order for a copy with you directly. I have had a money order for the equivalent of $10 sent to you to-day. I trust that this is sufficient to cover the cost of postage. If it is not, will you please advise me and I shall cheerfully forward the balance. Will you mail my copy of "Lady Chatterley" to the following address:
   Miss Minetta G. Littleton, 6845 Avenue O, Houston, Texas, U.S.A.
As there may be difficulty in passing the U. S. Customs at New York it may be well to see that the package is sent via some steamer going to some of the southern ports in the United States. I hope that this will not increase your difficulties any; I merely want to take these extra precautions as I am extremely anxious to have a copy of the book for my library.
   I hope that your publishing venture may enjoy the success which I believe it deserves.
Sincerely yours,

let you know if he gets the book. Might be a good way of sending – and we lose nothing.

Tell him this is the *last copy* you are sending.

4654. To Giuseppe Orioli, [13 September 1928]
Text: MS UCLA; Unpublished.

[Kesselmatte, Gsteig b. Gstaad, Switzerland]
[13 September 1928]

Have written him to consult my agents[1] – and told him I asked you to send him *one* copy at $10. – plus post – but I have no more copies.

You must put on his copy *MAY BE OPENED.*

Write to the Holliday Bookshop, when you get their order and money, that these are the *last* of my copies – Hence it is $21. from you, per copy.

4655. To Giuseppe Orioli, [13 September 1928]
Text: MS UCLA; Moore 1090–1.

Kesselmatte.
Thursday evening.

Dear Pino

I have your second letter saying you have 255. copies in hand: also the bunch of bordereaux. Tell me about the cheques at the beginning of my other letter.

---

[1] DHL received the following letter, dated 23 August 1928, from Pascal Covici of the publishing house Covici, Friede Inc., New York:

Dear Mr. Lawrence:

Fortunately for me, I procured a copy of your book, "Lady Chatterley's Lover," before the Custom House started confiscating the book.

Sincerely, I believe it to be the most vital piece of fiction I have read in the last ten years. It would be a tragic loss to literature if your book would not be brought out in some way or other in America. Besides, it will be a total loss to you in a financial way. I believe, and hope you will agree with me, that "Lady Chatterley's Lover" would not lose any of its power and strength and beauty if some of the phrases that seem to offend our Custom House officials were taken out.

If you would consent to change some of the phrases, I should be very proud and happy to have the firm bring your book out this year and give it a wide circulation. Won't you please let me hear from you at your earliest convenience?

Under separate cover I am sending you a copy of our catalog and Remy de Gourmont, which I recently brought out. Mr. Ezra Pound can tell you of my enthusiasm for your work.

In the meanwhile could you mail me, by first-class mail, 10 copies of the book as printed in Italy? I think we can get by if you will send them to me as per my directions. Mail them one at a time and use jackets of some other book, and address the first five to:

Pascal Covici, 17 East 84th St. New York City, N.Y.

and the others to my office:

79 West 45th St. New York City, N.Y.

DHL wrote to Orioli on this letter; his letter to Covici himself is unlocated.

I didn't want to raise the price till we were down to 200 copies. So we will let the Holliday have his copies, if his cheque turns up all right. That leaves 220 copies – of which three to Pollinger – leaves 217. *You* write to the Covici saying you, not I, can let him have the ten copies, sent by *letter* post – very expensive – one at a time,[1] according to his instructions – but as I am sold out, your price to him will be twenty dollars. Ask him to write or else cable if he wants the books on this condition. – Meanwhile send him *one* copy by letter post as he says, and the invoice. If he gets the one he'll order more – and on this *one* copy charge only $10 net plus post. Letter post, remember. Giuntina could print you 20 wrappers to fit.

Yes, send twenty copies to Kot. But wait till you hear he has the first parcel, before you continue. Are you sure they are going into England all right?

I enclose Kot's letter – you'll see he still is scared.[2] And he is scared stiff of my having a picture exhibit just now. Says my enemies are waiting to pounce on me.

Don't send me the Covici parcels of books – look at them and see what they are.

I'm sure that business of your nephew was a great shock – but I'm so cross with *him*.

I believe we shall be *very slow* selling 200 copies at £4··4··0. We might let private individuals have them at £2··2··0. – But we'll wait and see what the result of your present letters is.

We are all right. *We leave on Monday*.

Love. DHL
P.T.O

Have Giuntina print you a dozen false wrappers, on solid white paper, in solid black print.

The Way of All Flesh
by
Samuel Butler

Giotto Edition
Price One Guinea

---

and the same on the back. Make it look imposing and life-like. You may be able to use these for yourself. And try the Texas dodge with one copy.

---

[1] sent by . . . time] sent as two packages by Egidi, on a ship sailing to Texas
[2] The enclosure is missing.

4656. To Earl Brewster, 13 September 1928
Text: MS UT; Brewster 178–9.

Kesselmatte.
13 Sept. 1928

Dear Earl
I should have written again, but wasn't sure if you'd be gone.

My mother-in-law writes the *Eden* is full till Oct 1st. – so she has telephoned to the[1] *Hotel Löwen*, Lichtenthal, (bei BadenBaden). It is about seven minutes on the tram from Baden – and quite a nice level walk – and a nice hotel – 8 Mark a day pension, with big sunny room. Will you wait for us till Monday? We leave here Gstaad 9.57 in the morning, but you must look up the time of arrival in Basel – I suppose about 4.0 in the afternoon – as we have no time-table. – My sister-in-law has *not* written from Zürich to say when she will arrive and leave. But we'll telegraph if we are delayed on Monday.

Now can I thank you for the birthday letters and the gifts, all *so* nice, but why spend money, especially you Achsah, with those grand handkys? But it was nice to be remembered, after all. You and my two sisters and Frieda's mother – that was all. But then I'm not a celebrator.

It's very quiet here, the clock ticks – no cuckoo since Harwood left – and the cow-bells ting-ting-ting. *All* the cows are down from the high alps, all the men are home in the chalets, the place is dotted with cattle, and simply shimmering with endless bells. Frau Trachsl pretends to weep because we are going. The weather is mixed – hot sunny morning – then bits of rain and weird phantasmal wreathings of clouds, finally lit up lurid with shafts of evening light. It's quite changed. The crocuses have come again above the *mown* green grass, very lovely, long pale bubbles. I painted a flower picture – also two others on Earls panels – *North Sea* and *Accident in a Mine*.[2] Show you them – but sent *North Sea* to London. Have a most amusing story of mine in Amer. *Bookman* – called 'Things' – you'll think it's you, but it isn't.[3] I shall bring it along. – Hope Chatterji will find something *thrilling* for you.[4] – Else suggests *Salem*, a school in Bavaria, for Harwood.

– All the meadows are mown again – some still hay-making, rather damply.

If you want to go *before* we do to Baden, write my mother-in-law. – Harwood, the Etruscan embroidery is done, save the background.[5] – Achsah,

---

[1] the] to   [2] In *Paintings of D. H. Lawrence*, plate [9]. See also Brewster 289.
[3] 'Things' appeared in *Bookman* (New York), lxvii (August 1928), 632–7. Despite DHL's disclaimer, the story was clearly based on the Brewsters.
[4] Most likely Jagadish Chandra Chatterji about whose *Kashmir Shaivaism* (1914) DHL and Brewster spoke when at Kesselmatte (Brewster 175).
[5] Probably the 'panel – a design adapted from an old Etruscan design – in the brightest of colour' which the Wilkinsons remembered DHL embroidering in June 1926 (Sagar, Wilkinsons 65).

I wrote an article – 'Hymns in a Man's Life' – but it's gone away.

Au revoir then   DHL

4657. To Nancy Pearn, [13 September 1928]
Text: MS Foster; Tedlock, *Lawrence MSS* 229.

[Kesselmatte, Gsteig b. Gstaad, Switzerland]

[13 September 1928]

Article for the *Evening News*, if they want it.[1]

DHL

Please note address after Saturday *15. Sept.*:

c/o Frau von Richthofen, Ludwig-Wilhelmstift, Baden-Baden. Germany

4658. To Giulia Pini, [14 September 1928]
Text: MS UT; PV v. Gsteig b. Gstaad & Oldenhorn; Postmark, [. . .] 15 IX 28; Unpublished.

[Kesselmatte, Gsteig b. Gstaad, Switzerland]

Venerdì –

Cara Giulia

Ho ricevuto la tua lettera, e scriverò fra due-tre giorni. Lunedì partiamo di qui per andare alla Madre della Signora, a BadenBaden. Oggi ho mandato un libro che tu guarderai fin'che torniamo in Ottobre. Qui fa freddo, e voglio scendere delle montagne.

tanti saluti   D. H. Lawrence

[Friday –

Dear Giulia

I have received your letter, and will write in two-three days. We leave here on Monday and go to my wife's mother's, at BadenBaden. I sent a book today so that you can have a look at it until we return in October. It is cold here, and I want to go down from the mountains.

best wishes   D. H. Lawrence]

4659. To S. S. Koteliansky, 15 September 1928
Text: MS BL; Postmark, Gsteig 17.IX.28; Moore 1091–2.

Gsteig.

15 Sept. 1928

My dear Kot.

Orioli was away from Florence for a time because of a family tragedy – but

---

[1] This note was written at the end of the MS of 'Red Trousers'; the article was published, under the title 'Oh! For a New Crusade', in *Evening News*, 27 September 1928 (Roberts C176).

he is back now. I have asked him to send you 20 copies. He writes that there are about 210 copies left, that is 190 when yours are gone. And feeling very fierce because the book is selling for $50 in New York – there can't be very many copies there to sell – he has written to people ordering copies that the edition is sold out, Davis and Orioli have bought the remainder, and the price is four guineas.[1] Since he's done it he's done it, I don't care very much: especially as it is the *Americans* who are now rushing to order. We'll see how it goes off.

I wrote Dorothy Warren she could postpone the show if she likes, as I cannot think of sending the pictures to New York now. I'm afraid the silly ass has shown them to half London already. But if she wants to make a public show in Oct., let her. I've always had the same enemies. As for the painters, if my pictures aren't ten times better than Roger Fry's, then he's welcome to Fry them to his heart's content. My pictures are alive – and the little whipper-snappers will hate them for it. – Bah, if I'd spent my life considering my enemies, I should be a dumb dead fish long ago.

I sent you a stupid book which was sent me – *Why We Misbehave* – I thought, as it is only just published, and at $4 or $5, you might perhaps sell it in Charing X Rd one day when you're selling books you don't want.[2] If not, throw it in the dust-bin.

We leave here on Monday for BadenBaden. I think we shall stay in
Hotel Löwen, Lichtenthal, bei *BadenBaden*.

Autumn here now, chilly, cloudy – time to go. I doubt I shan't come to England – damn England. I didn't know Enid had her tragedy up her sleeve – or had a tragedy at all. Her husband isn't thrilling, but quite nice. Perhaps she was only being impressive.

Gute Nacht!   DHL

4660. To Emily King, [15 September 1928]
Text: MS Needham; PC v. Basel. Amazone an der Rheinbrücke; Postmark, [Gst]eig 17.IX.28; Unpublished.

[Kesselmatte, Gsteig b. Gstaad, Switzerland]
Sat. afternoon

– Glad you had a nice journey home, and the crossing decent. We leave on Monday for Baden – the Brewsters are waiting for us in Basel, to go along.

[1] J. I. Davis and Orioli were in partnership from 1911, specialising in incunabula, early Italian literature and modern first editions; they set up first in Florence and then, in 1913, also in London (Museum Street, Bloomsbury).

[2] Samuel Daniel Schmalhausen, *Why We Misbehave* (New York, 1928). A year later Schmalhausen wrote trying (in vain) to interest DHL in his latest theories; on that occasion he described *Why We Misbehave* as 'the first attempt in America to interlink the various dynamic and vital psychologies and to apply . . . the artist's approach to human nature'.

Here it is real autumn, rather chilly, with clouds all tangled in the mountain tops. The cows have just been let into the home field, so of course they've all rushed straight under the windows, and such a clashing of bells you never heard – deafening! Frieda has gone to Gstaad to meet Else – they'll be home by the bus at 6.0. Frau Trachsl weeps that we're going – they really dread the long lonely dark months. Lina got a jug of cranberries – the first this year.

I'll write from Baden.

Love.   DHL

4661. To David Higham, 15 September 1928
Text: MS UT; Unpublished.

Gsteig b. Gstaad.
15 Sept 1928

Dear Mr Higham[1]

I return the Elkin Mathews agreement signed.[2] I wish they'd let me off signing 500 sheets – they can pay me less. – Ask them if they want me to go over the MS. before they send it to the printer. I've only thought of it as a magazine story.

Address me to BadenBaden – c/o Frau von Richthofen. Ludwig-Wilhelmstift.

Yours Sincerely   D. H. Lawrence

4662. To Giuseppe Orioli, [16 September 1928]
Text: MS UCLA; cited in Moore, *Poste Restante* 96.

Gsteig.
Sunday.

Dear Pino

I am sending you the lists of copies sent out from London – they are all accounted for. Only I rather think we've sent Henry Young, Liverpool *two copies* when he only wanted one.

We are not leaving till Tuesday, as my sister-in-law is here and wants to stay till that day.

My agent in New York is very unwilling to make a contract with the Vanguard Press – and I don't mind if he doesn't. – So that leaves us free to send copies to U.S.A. if we get payment in advance.

I think we shall stay in Baden at
Hotel Löwen, *Lichtenthal*, bei Baden-Baden. Germany.

---

[1] David Higham (1895–1978), at this time on the staff of Curtis Brown's London office; in 1935, with Nancy Pearn and Laurence Pollinger, he formed an independent authors' agency.

[2] See Letter 4645.

Real autumn here, and I shall be glad to be off. They want me to finish the
Etruscan book this autumn. Perhaps I shall. It means a giro to Arezzo and
Cortona, Chiusi, Orvieto, Bieda etc.

Hope you're feeling all right – don't get depressed.

DHL

If you get any dollar cheques for me, put them to my *sterling* account – not
to the Lira account.

DHL

4663. To Alfred Stieglitz, [17 September 1928]
Text: MS YU; Postmark, Gsteig 17.IX.28; Unpublished.

Gsteig b Gstaad. Switzerland
17 Sept.

Dear Stieglitz

A hurried note, as we are just leaving for BadenBaden. Got your letter
about the Holliday book-shop etc. – They are all cowards – curious what
skunks people are.[1] And Holliday has an order for 35 copies in Florence – but
I doubt we shan't send them. I am nearly at the end of my 1000 – and Davis
and Orioli have bought the last remainder and are going to put up the price. –
I asked Orioli to send you a copy in a false wrapper. I hope it'll come through.
How those New York people *tremble*! that is the most astonishing thing about
Americans – they tremble with fear. – In the end, you will be governed by a
Nigger Klu-Klux. That is my prophecy for U.S. – no real spunk left: except a
bit in the women.

I'm afraid we've lost a fair number of copies in America. And those
booksellers who have received copies unpaid – I know of one or two – are
seizing the opportunity for delaying payment, or pretending they haven't
received the copies.

DHL

4664. To Lilian Wilkinson, [17 September 1928]
Text: MS Schlaefle; PC v. [Swiss chalet]; Postmark, Gsteig 17.IX.28; Unpublished.

[Kesselmatte, Gsteig b. Gstaad, Switzerland]
17 Sept.

I did get your letters for my birthday, here. So nice of you to remember! – I
wrote envelopes for the Nencioni long ago – five or six. – We leave in the

---

[1] See p. 518 n. 3. In his 'Memoranda' (MS NWU) DHL recorded a cheque for $297.50, dated 10
September, 'sent to London' from the Holliday Bookshop, but not received by him when this
letter was written.

morning for BadenBaden – and I'll write from there. Frieda will probably come to England in Oct. – I think Dorothy Warren will be showing my pictures in her gallery in Maddox St. – you must go and greet them! Just turned cold here – quite wintry – time to go. – The Pini (Giulia) are turned out from the Mirenda poderi[1] – so I suppose we shall give up too. I shall go to S. of France for Oct. – You'll see Frieda in London.

Viele Grüsse   DHL

your p.c. came on from Scandicci.

4665. To Giuseppe Orioli, [17 September 1928]
Text: MS UCLA; Unpublished.

[Kesselmatte, Gsteig b. Gstaad, Switzerland]
[17 September 1928][2]

Dear Pino

My answer on back of this – sent to him direct – that[3] the 'gentleman' is by no means a certainty.[4] Meanwhile I enclose Stieglitz's letter. If you send him a copy, wrap it in another wrapper. He is safe for the money. – I don't think we should put up the price for Europe till we are below 200. But unless we know the people well, we should demand cash in advance. Do you know Passmore? And is Dracott safe? Birrell and G[arnett] are safe.[5]

To Americans who order from N. Y. etc – say my edition is exhausted, Davis and Orioli bought up the remainder and are selling at $21. – But we'll sell another 50 or so to Europe at the usual price. – So cold here – we leave in the morning.

DHL

Have sent you two other letters this week-end.[6]

turn over

---

[1] Cf. Letter 4671.

[2] Dated from the reference to the Lawrences' departure; they left Gsteig on 18 September 1928.

[3] My answer . . . that] I'm answering Holliday myself – that his books are put aside and can be sent when cheque is received – that

[4] DHL's letter was written at the foot of Holliday's (5 September 1928) to him; this read:

My dear Mr Lawrence:
    Yesterday I received a visit from a gentleman who claims that he has been authorized by you to print for America an edition of a thousand copies of your new novel. I should be glad to know if this information is correct and also whether you have shipped the 35 copies we have on order from you.
Sincerely yours

    DHL's answer to Holliday, of which he wrote a copy for Orioli, constitutes the letter following.

[5] The name of Walter Passmore was deleted, without comment, from the list of 'Dollar Cheques for *Lady C.*', in DHL's 'Memoranda' (MS NWU); E. Dracott sent cheques totalling £8·10·0 in August and September 1928; for Birrell and Garnett see p. 520 n. 4.

[6] Someone – probably Orioli – wrote on Holliday's letter: '*of course not shipped.*'

4666. To Terence Holliday, [17 September 1928]
Text: MS UCLA; Unpublished.

[Kesselmatte, Gsteig b. Gstaad, Switzerland]
[17 September 1928][1]

The 'gentleman' who is authorised to print 1000 copies for Amer. is not yet authorised, – as far as I know.[2] At least I have seen no contract – and heard nothing.

Orioli sent me on your letter. I am nearly at the end of my edition – Davis and Orioli have bought the remainder, not many, and will sell it on their own account. No copies have been sent to America at all, for the last five weeks. About your order, I don't know. I told Orioli to reserve you 35 if you sent remittance and instructions how to deliver. But it is no good my holding up my European sales. If the remittance and instructions come quickly, you can have the 35 copies: the last I shall sell to America. But if there is any delay, I shall be sold out, and you can deal with Davis and Orioli if you wish. I am tired to death of hypocrisy and fuss.

It may be those people will print 1000 copies for New York – it depends on my agent Curtis Brown also. Myself I feel very indifferent, and don't really care if America never sees another copy of the book. I can easily dispose of my few in Europe – and quickly. And Orioli will do as he likes – perhaps prefer to hold his. I am tired of America and the knock-kneed fright in face of bullying hypocrisy. It's not my affair.

DHL

4667. To Maria Huxley, 22 September 1928
Text: Huxley 752–3.

Hôtel Löwen, Lichtenthal, Baden-Baden.
22 Sept., 1928.

Dear Maria, –

No news from either of you for a long while – and I wrote Aldous. We are here since Tuesday – and good weather. F[rieda]'s mother here in hotel with us, *and the Brewsters!* We all drove in two grand 2-horse landaus yesterday to the *altes Schloss* and through the forest for three hours – everybody in bliss. It's rather cold – and Germany is queer – prosperous and alive – different from other people – makes me feel a bit queer inside. We go to the *Kurhaus* and drink hot waters and listen to music and – eat, of course.

I never know quite where I am, in Germany. We leave 1st October – Frieda

[1] This undated MS is headed: 'Copy of my letter to Holliday'.
[2] The man was Jacob Baker of Vanguard Press.

for England, I for South of France, where I shall stay a bit with F.'s sister Else, and join the Aldingtons to look at the island – Port-Cros. What are you doing, now autumn is here, fat red apples on the trees by the road, and yellow leaves dripping? Hope you got *le Dieu des Corps* – the French improvement on *Lady C.*[1] Very cold potato, I thought.

DHL

4668. To Enid Hilton, 22 September 1928
Text: MS UCLA; Huxley 753–4.

Hotel Löwen, Lichtenthal, bei BadenBaden
22 Sept. 1928

Dear Enid

Thanks for your letter and the typescripts, which arrived safely this afternoon.[2] They are quite all right, and I enclose cheque. Don't send me the MS. itself while we are on the move – it's only another thing to carry round.

Quite pleasant here – rather chilly today, but sunny. We eat too much and talk too much – and listen to music in the Kurgarten and so on. I don't mind Baden for a bit, but it soon palls.

The picture *Contadini* is of two Italian peasants – as the word itself says. They can call it *Italian*[3] *peasants* instead of *Contadini* – which as you know, means the same thing.[4]

I expect Frieda will come to England on the 2nd or 3rd – and I shall go to S. of France. Meanwhile don't you take too much notice of the horridness of England – shut your eyes and ears all you can, and keep an inside quiet.

And thanks so much for looking after these things for me.

DHL

Let me know if there is any change in the date of the show.

4669. To Giuseppe Orioli, [22 September 1928]
Text: MS UCLA; cited in Moore, *Intelligent Heart* 389.

Hotel Loewen, Lichtenthal, bei BadenBaden, Germany
22 Sept.

Dear Pino

We got here all right Tuesday night. Baden quite pleasant. We stay till 1st Oct. – then I shall go to South of France, F[rieda] to England for a bit.

[1] Volume ii of the novel *Psyché*, by Jules Romains (1885–) was entitled *Le Dieu des Corps* (Paris, 1928); it was later translated by John Rodker as *The Body's Rapture* (New York, 1933).
[2] See Letter 4633.   [3] Italian] to   [4] See pp. 553 n. 2 and 557 n. 1.

How is everything in Florence? – Pollinger wants *four* copies of *Lady C.* – are you sending Kot. his?

I feel sort of out of connection with everything here – don't *really* like it. – The Brewsters are here, *of course.* – It's a bit chilly, and I don't feel quite right in my skin! But it's not long. – Hope all is well – you had my letters, 3, from Gsteig?

DHL

4670. To Harry Crosby, [22 September 1928]
Text: MS SIU; Postmark, Baden-Baden 22. 9. 28; Unpublished.

Hotel Löwen, Lichtenthal, bei BadenBaden, Germany
22 Sept.

Dear Harry Crosby

I hope you had those first proofs all right – I sent them from Switzerland to Rue Cardinale.[1] We are here till 1st Oct. – then I think I shall go south, to Hyères – somewhere down there. When do you sail for U. S. A.?

D. H. Lawrence

4671. To Giulia Pini, 22 September 1928
Text: MS UT; Huxley 754.

Hotel Loewen, Lichthenthal, bei BadenBaden, Germania.
22 settembre 1928

Cara Giulia

Siamo qui a Baden Baden con la madre della Signora. Sono belle giornae di autonno, un po' fresche, le foglie degli alberi già gialle e rosse. Ogni giorno ci sono concerti di musica, belli, nel grande giardino, e ci andiamo bevere il thé al fresco. Alla signora Baronessa, la suocera, le[2] piace molto quando noi siamo qui, e facciamo, come ieri, lunghi giri in carrossa a due cavalli, come le hanno ancora in questa città, lunghi giri fuori, fra i boschi. Allora la vecchia signora è contenta.

Ci dispiaceva molto sentire che i padroni vi mandano via. Ma io l'aspettavo. Quando il fattore voleva far seminare l'erba, era chiaro che volevano mandare via una famiglia. Ma pure voi restate ancora un poco, e ci rivedremo. Poi andiamo via finalmente anche noi. Spero veramente che troverete un altro podere, ed una casa buona, e buoni padroni. E' una cosa un poco difficile – ma pure, cercando si trova un buon posto.

Scrivimi una parola per dire ciò che succede. Siamo qui fino al 1° Ottobre – poi la signora va in Inghilterra per quindici giorni, io l'aspetto nella Francia.

[1] The Paris address of the Black Sun Press which was producing *Sun.*   [2] MS reads: 'si'.

Non voglio fare il lungo viaggio. E poi ritorniamo in Italia, nel mezzo di Ottobre.

Spero veramente che tutti stanno bene, e che abbiano sentito di un buon posto per l'anno venturo.

Molti Saluti   D. H. Lawrence

[22 September 1928

Dear Giulia

We are here at Baden Baden with my wife's mother. We are having pleasant autumn days, rather cool, the leaves of the trees are yellow and red. There are music concerts daily, very nice, in the big garden, and we go and have tea in the fresh air. The Baroness, my mother-in-law, is very pleased when we are here, and, as we did yesterday, take long trips in a two-horse coach, as they still have them in this town, long trips out, among the woods. Then the old lady is happy.

We were sorry to hear that your landlords are sending you packing. But I expected it. When the farmer wanted the grass sown, it was clear that they wished to get rid of one family. But then, you stay a little longer, and we'll see each other again. Then we too will depart in the end. I do hope that you will find another farm, and a good house, and kind masters. It is a bit difficult – but then good employment can be found if one looks around.

Drop me a line to tell me what happens. We'll be here till the 1st of October – then my wife goes to England, I'll be waiting for her in France. I don't want to make a long journey. And then we'll return to Italy, in mid-October.

I do hope that everybody is well, and that they have heard of a good place for next year.

Best wishes   D. H. Lawrence]

4672. To Ada Clarke, 24 September 1928
Text: MS Clarke; PC v. Hornisgrinde, 1166m (Schwarzwald); Postmark, Baden-Baden 24.9.28; Unpublished.

Hotel Loewen. Lichtenthal, bei BadenBaden
24 Sept. 1928

We've been here a week, and I've not sent you a card. We are in this hotel, F[rieda]'s mother with us too – and the Brewsters. I leave with the latter for south of France on 1st October – Frieda is coming to England for a fortnight or so. It is suddenly quite cold here, and inclined to rain – I shan't be sorry to go south. How is Bertie getting on at school?

love to all   DHL

4673. To Martin Secker, [24 September 1928]

Text: MS UInd; PC v. Schloβ Eberstein im Murgtal bei Baden-Baden; Postmark, Baden-Baden 24.9.28; Unpublished.

Hotel Löwen – Lichtenthal, bei BadenBaden
24 Sept.

We are here till Oct. 1st – then F[rieda] is probably coming to England, for the picture show – and I am going to S. of France. You didn't tell me when you are bringing out the poems. Have you got them ready? – or are you waiting longer? – It turned quite cold here – and turned my thoughts south. But I think we are definitely giving up the Mirenda – wonder where we'll pitch!

How are you all? Send a line –

DHL

4674. To Laurence Pollinger, 24 September 1928

Text: MS UT; Unpublished.

Hotel Löwen, *Lichtenthal, bei BadenBaden*
24 Sept 1928

Dear Pollinger

I am sending you today the typescript of *The Escaped Cock*, for Crosby Gaige. As I said before, I don't mind a bit if he doesn't want it: then I shall print it myself. But if he does take it, he should pay more than a 10% royalty.

Rich seems to be getting rather into a stew with Jacob Baker of the Vanguard Press. I am keeping entirely out of it, if I can, and letting them settle between them. I don't care whether the Vanguard prints me at all or whether it doesn't. But I still don't see why Rich finds 'the Knopf imprint' so 'extremely valuable.' Valuable in what way?

We are here till Oct 1st – then I am going to S. of France. It's already cold in Baden, and going to turn rainy, I believe – showery now.

I hope Orioli sent you the three copies – I asked him from here to send a fourth.

Is it bitter to be back at the desk?

D. H. Lawrence

4675. To Dr Anton Kippenberg, 24 September 1928

Text: MS SVerlag; Unpublished.

Hotel Löwen, Lichtenthal, bei BadenBaden
24 Sept. 1928

Dear Dr Kippenberg

It seems there is nothing to be done now but to finish the agreement that is between us, and to make no further renewal. I am sorry about it, but it is the only way, and I hope you don't really mind. So that the contract between us ends finally at the end of October, next month.

Yours Sincerely   D. H. Lawrence

4676. To Giuseppe Orioli, [25 September 1928]
Text: MS UCLA; Moore, *Intelligent Heart* 390.

Hotel Loewen, Lichtenthal, bei BadenBaden

Tuesday – 25 Sept

Dear Pino

I haven't heard from you, but I suppose you waited to hear from me. We are staying here till next Tuesday morning – 2nd October. Then I think Frieda will come direct to Florence, by Milan, arriving Wednesday evening. We want to give up the Mirenda, I am sure it is bad for my health, because in these other places I am better than I am there. Then the Maggiore – or the Zaira – is sending away the Pini family – Giulia, Pietro, all of them – and there is sure to be a great emotional stew. I can't stand it. So Frieda will come and pack up the few things – they are nearly all packed – and give up the house. – *But please don't tell anybody* – so nobody need fuss round her. I shall go to S. of France – the Aldingtons are having an old fortress on the island of Port-Cros, about 19 Chilometri off from Hyères near Toulon. It is very warm there, and no people, only 14 families of fishermen. So if we like it we will stay the winter, and if you can, you must come. Perhaps they will give you a passport for there. – I have no news, except that Beazley, London W1. wrote he would like to pay me direct for the three copies he received. I wrote he could send a cheque to me here, or pay the money into my bank.[1] I'll let you know. I have not heard if Edward Garnett received the copy I sent him from Gsteig. I hope so. – It has been *very* cold here.

love. DHL

4677. To Maria Huxley, 25 September 1928
Text: Huxley 755.

Hôtel Löwen, Lichtenthal, b. Baden-Baden.

25th September, 1928.

Dear Maria, –

Had your letter – so sorry it rains – guess it's left off. Here it was bitter cold – but is warmer now. Our plans too are a bit changed. The Mirenda people are sending away our peasants, Giulia, Pietro and family – and there's sure to be a

---

[1] DHL's letter is missing. For Beazley's reply see p. 603 n. 1.

great emotional stew. And I really feel the Mirenda is bad for my health. So Frieda intends to come direct to Florence, leave here next Tuesday, 2nd, arrive Florence 3rd, and finish the bit of packing – it's nearly all done – and give up the house for good. It ought only to take a few days. If you are in Florence, go and give her a bit of moral support – she'll probably be in a bit of a stew too. I, coward, am staying out of it. – I shall go on Tuesday to S. of France. That Island Port-Cros is 19 kms. off Hyères, and may be a nice place to winter, no people, no villas, one small hotel, 13 families fishermen and the Vigie – fortress. It may be nice. Also F.'s sister Else is down just there till 8th Oct. So I'll try it – and Frieda can join me somewhere there. The exhibition of pictures is put off till Nov. – and F. will go to London to see it, I shan't. She may see you in Paris *en passant*. Meanwhile do stay a day or two *en passant* on that bit of Riviera near Hyères, and see me – and F. if she's already back. I wonder when you'll start. It was so cold here, but not much rain – now is a bit warmer. Only six more days here – so much food! We are now going to the *Fischkultur* for tea. Hope they won't give us ants' eggs. – I may be able to send you my pictures to your Paris house after all – am *not* sending them to U.S.A. I guess you'll like Suresnes once you settle in. We are staying home.

Love to both.   DHL.

4678. To Giuseppe Orioli, 26 September 1928
Text: MS UCLA; Unpublished.

Hotel Loewen. Lichtenthal, b. BadenBaden
Wednesday 26 Sept 1928

Dear Pino

Had yours this morning with McGoff cheque and bordereau for Galignani and the Toronto man.[1] – I cross them both out on the unsent list.

You didn't tell me about those entries I wrote to you about from Gsteig – Birrell and Garnett etc – whether you had sent them me *double* or not. I don't want to enter the same money twice.

Your last letter to Gsteig gave Simpkin and Marshall £10, and Albert Dowling £5··2··0. But the bordereau gave Simpkin and Marshall £8··10··0, and Albert Dowling £5-0-0. I suppose the bordereau is right, and Dowling knocked off 2/-.

I put down Liras 184. for the copy you sold to the Milanese: suppose that's right.

---

[1] Galignani was a Parisian bookseller. The 'Toronto man' was Roy Britnell (1900–83), owner of the city's most famous bookstore founded by his father Albert Britnell (1864–1924); his cheque for $8.50 was dated 1 May 1928. McGoff is unidentified.

Do send Kot his 20 copies. – But do[1] you think we need send Mrs Hilton
the 30? Probably we might just as well keep them in Florence. Or are you
getting tired of the business? If you are tired of it, we can send them to London
and find somebody to distribute – but *not* Davis and Orioli!

I enclose Mrs Chambers letter, in case you didn't read it.[2] Quite amusing
really! What swine Americans are!

I sent you a line yesterday to say we are leaving next Tuesday morning –
2nd. Somehow I don't feel very happy in Germany this time – for one thing, it
was so cold. I shall be glad to get away, if only to the S. of France. I shan't
come to Florence now, unless it is necessary. But later I will come and finish
my Etruscan essays. – Aldous and Maria want to go straight to their house in
Paris, next week or so. I think they are a bit hard up. So we shan't motor to the
Etruscan places.

You can keep me an *unnumbered* copy of *Lady C.* for my personal copy.
That leaves only three.

Is Kot. receiving his copies all right?

How are you feeling now? I hope you aren't depressed by that nephew. You
must really try to come to S. of France for a change, when we get settled there.
Anyhow I expect you'll see Frieda next week.

love from both   DHL

Did you have that wrapper made?[3]

4679. To Maria Chambers, 26 September 1928
Text: MS StaU; cited in Schorer 64.

BadenBaden.
26 Sept 1928

Dear Mrs Chambers

Your letter came on this morning from Florence. Orioli says he received it
with the seals broken, and opened. So who is reading your mail?

I must say the American attitude to *Lady C.* is rather disgusting. The
English are bad enough, but still there's quite a lot of intelligent appreciation
there – even enthusiastic. Whereas all the Americans either squirm and look
sickly, or become sordidly indignant. Anyhow I'm glad you put in a blow or
two for the lady. – You got your two cheques back safely, I presume. Orioli
isn't sending any copies to U.S.A. – but there is talk that a man in New York
will print 1000 copies for private subscription. I don't know if it will come off
– and don't care either. If you happen to go into the Skylark Bookshop in New

---

[1] do] you   [2] The enclosure is missing.   [3] Cf. Letter 4655.

York, find out if they had their three copies sent them – but[1] don't put yourself to any trouble, and *don't* run athwart the precious authorities.

I told you we shan't come to America this year – and I shan't send my pictures. So the show in London will be a little later – I suppose November – and I shan't go there either. I am leaving here next week for the South of France, to join some friends there. Germany doesn't make me feel happy this time – though it seems very prosperous. But it chills something in one's marrow – or one's soul.

I finished *The Escaped Cock* – with a second half in which there is the real resurrection of the flesh. An American said he wanted to do a limited edition of it. I don't suppose he will. But I don't care at all – I can do it myself.

At present I feel a bit of special disgust with the civilised human species – especially the Transatlantic section of it. *So* unclean and ignominious. So absolutely unbrave.

But patience! patience!

D. H. Lawrence

4680. To Emily King, [26 September 1928]
Text: MS Needham; PC v. [Lichtental bei Baden-Baden]; Postmark, Baden-Baden 26.9.28; Unpublished.

[Hotel Löwen, Lichtental, bei Baden-Baden]
Wed
We had your letter – I was all right on the journey – but it's been very cold here. We leave next Tuesday – myself for south of France, Frieda for Florence where she will get rid of the Mirenda, then join me. The exhibition of my pictures is put off till November, which is a better month. Frieda will come to England then – but I shall not.

Love to all. DHL

4681. To Enid Hilton, [27 September 1928]
Text: MS UCLA; PC v. Lichtental bei Baden-Baden; Postmark, Baden-Baden 28 9 28; Unpublished.

[Hotel Löwen, Lichtental, bei Baden-Baden]
Thursday
Had your letter – imagine *T.P.'s* coming out so comparatively bravely![2] But I

[1] but] and the
[2] *T.P.'s Weekly*, for the week ending 29 September 1928, carried a review by John Rayner entitled: 'The Lady and the Gamekeeper: Mr D. H.Lawrence's New Book from Florence'. Following his assertion that in earlier novels DHL speaks of sex in 'a tortuously mystic way', Rayner stated that in *Lady Chatterley's Lover* 'no veils are drawn. Everything is as open as the night.' He continued:

have a fair number of *fors* as well as many *againsts*. D[orothy] W[arren] wired me, but as usual her promised letter has *not* followed. I leave for South of France on Monday morning. Frieda will go straight to Florence and get rid of the Mirenda – then join me. I do think Florence doesn't suit me. Glad you are better.

DHL

4682. To Ada Clarke, [27 September 1928]

Text: MS Clarke; PC v. Baden-Baden – Lichtental; Postmark, [Baden-B]aden [. . .]; Unpublished.

[Hotel Löwen, Lichtental, bei Baden-Baden]
Thursday

Had your letter – so glad G[ertrude Cooper] is feeling stronger and getting about a bit. I leave here for South of France on Monday morning – shall send you the address. Frieda is going direct to Florence, to get rid of the Mirenda. We must try another place, that suits me better. The picture show is being postponed a bit to a better date – also Dorothy Warren is getting married in Vienna.[1] So Frieda will come to England later.

Love   DHL

4683. To Arthur Wilkinson, [27 September 1928]

Text: MS Schlaefle; PC v. Lichtental bei Baden-Baden; Postmark, Baden-Baden 28 9 28; Unpublished.

BadenBaden – Lichtenthal.
Thursday

Again on the move – I leave next Monday for south of France, where we *may* stay the winter. Frieda will go direct to Florence to give up the Mirenda – finally decided. It will only take a day or two – then she'll join me somewhere near Hyères – and she will come on to England end of Oct. or so, for my picture-show – which is postponed a bit. – So you see we are in the air. But I told you the Maggiore is sending our peasants away. Too much fuss. How are you?

DHL

Mr Lawrence has carried realism to a pitch seldom aspired to in the whole history of literature. And the result is a fine novel, bold and – stark is the only word to describe it. And it is so amazingly uncynical . . . The prose is really beautiful . . . Mr Lawrence writes so forcefully, he is not trivial, he takes you with him to the ends of the earth. And either you wake up afterwards and say: "neurotic, supersexual, and generally nasty". Or you are his for life, and swear there is none like him.

[1] She married Philip Coutts Trotter in November 1928; he – a specialist in Styrian Jade – became her partner in the Warren Gallery.

4684. To Juliette Huxley, [27 September 1928]
Text: MS Huxley; PC v. Lichtental Jm Klosterhof; Postmark, Baden-Baden [. . .]9 28;
Unpublished.

Lichtenthal. BadenBaden.
Thursday

Your letter came on this afternoon – so awfully sorry about that whooping cough. Spell of bad luck. – I leave here on Monday morning for south of France. Frieda is going straight to Florence to get rid of the Mirenda – try a better climate. The picture-show is postponed, perhaps till Nov. – Frieda will come to England, but I shan't, to see it. I'll send you an address when there is one.

DHL

4685. To Richard Aldington, [27 September 1928]
Text: MS Lazarus; Unpublished.

[Hotel Löwen, Lichtental, bei Baden-Baden]
Thursday 28 Sept 1928

Dear Richard
    I don't know if you'll get this in time, but it is to say I shall probably go to the Grand Hotel, Le Lavandou near Hyères for a day or two with my sister-in-law – but will meet you in Hyères if you let me know just where and when. I'll send you a line also poste restante, Hyères.
    Been so cold here – so I've got a cold – sickening – I hope to leave Monday morning.

au revoir   DHL
    One can sail from Le Lavandou to Port-Cros, I think.

4686. To Laurence Pollinger, [28 September 1928]
Text: MS UT; PC v. Baden-Baden – Lichtental; Postmark, Baden-Baden 29 9.28;
Unpublished.

BadenBaden.
Friday

Thanks for the *T.P.* cutting – a sport, that man. We are leaving here on Monday for S. of France – I'll send an address later – would you stop this address in the other depts.

D. H. Lawrence

4687. To S. S. Koteliansky, [29 September 1928]

Text: MS BL; PC v. Baden – Lichtental; Postmark, Baden-Baden 29 9 28; Zytaruk 362.

[Hotel Löwen, Lichtental, bei Baden-Baden]

29 Sept

– I am leaving on Monday for South of France – not quite sure where. Frieda is going direct to Florence to get rid of the Mirenda. I shan't go back there – it really doesn't suit my health. I shan't go to Paris just now, but later we may, and I'll write you. The picture show is postponed a while – I think Frieda will come over. – Has Orioli sent you the books? Did you see the article in *T.P*'s. Will send address.

DHL

4688. To Giuseppe Orioli, [30 September 1928]

Text: MS UCLA; cited in Moore, *Poste Restante* 97.

Lichtenthal. b. BadenBaden.

Sunday 30 Sept.

Dear Pino

Just got your letter with bordereau and cheque from Hollidays.[1] You didn't enclose copy of Holliday's letter – and I would very much like to know how *he wanted the books sent*. If he wanted them posted to New York, it seems quite useless: and if you have not sent them off, let me know, and he can have his cheque back.

Tell Mary Foote and the others that I refuse to be responsible for the action of the U. S. A. govt. Their books were sent *registered* – they must now apply to the post-office for delivery: or to the American government. I have done all in my power. I will *not* supply books free to the American government. Send them the registration slips – the scontrino or bigliettino, whatever it is called.

The Sitwells, of course want to be important at any price, poor souls.[2]

No, don't send to London more than Kot's 20 copies. And if you have sent 35 to Holliday, 10- to Passmore, 10- to Galignani – with 20 to Kot – you will have less than 180 copies – and we can raise the price.

I am sending this to Florence, although you will be gone. And Frieda will arrive Wednesday night – everything is arranged. I have written to Carletto to

---

[1] Cf. Letter 4663 and n. 1.

[2] It is conceivable that the Sitwells had read *Lady Chatterley's Lover* (Osbert Sitwell was a friend and admirer of Orioli) and were already claiming that DHL had used Osbert and Renishaw as models for Sir Clifford Chatterley and Wragby Hall (see John Pearson, *Façades*, 1978, pp. 222–32).

meet her if possible, and take her to your flat for the night, so she will not be all alone that night at the Mirenda. It's a great pity you will be away. But Frieda will still be there, in the Mirenda or in Florence, when you come back on 11th. or 12th.

I am leaving tomorrow morning for Hyères, near Toulon. I shall write and tell you what it is like there. Here it *rains*.

Grüsse   DHL

Did Mary Foote lose *both* her copies? – or only one? Did you send her *own* copy to America?

4689. To Harry Crosby, 30 September 1928
Text: MS SIU; Postmark, Baden-Baden 1.10.28; cited in Moore, *Poste Restante* 97.

Lichtenthal – BadenBaden.
30 Sept 1928

Dear Harry Crosby

I am leaving here tomorrow – going Strassburg-Lyon direct, so shan't come through Paris. I'll send you an address when I have one. – Many thanks for your invitation. My wife may be coming through Paris shortly – in about two weeks' time. She will probably stay with the Aldous Huxleys, who are just going to their house at Suresnes. But she would like very much to see you, if you are not gone off to America. – I shall let you know.

I am not sending my pictures to New York. They have made such a fuss about *Lady C.* – confiscating all they can lay hands on – that I'm afraid they might confiscate my pictures too. But the exhibition comes off in London some time in October.

I send the final proof of *Sun*. Am very much interested to see what it will look like when it's ready.

tanti saluti!   D. H. Lawrence

4690. To Emil Krug, 30 September 1928
Text: MS UT; Unpublished.

Lichtenthal, b. BadenBaden
30 Sept 1928

Lieber Emil

War es denn du der den Baumkuchen schickte? Ach, und es ist schon nur eine Erinnerung, alles gegessen. Es war aber gut, and für mich etwas neues. Die letzten Stücke haben die Schweicharts zum 'dessert' gehabt, und geschmeckt. Und alle lassen danken.

Ich reise morgen weg – über Lyon (Strassburg) – nach Toulon. Die Frieda geht Dienstag nach Florenz, bleibt eine woche dort, giebt die Mirenda auf, denn kommt zu mir. Wir haben Englische Freunde die wollen den Winter auf dem Insel Port-Cros, in der nähe von Hyères bleiben, und wollen dass wir mit-wohnen, in einer alter Festung. Ich gehe um zu sehen wie es ist. Aber ich glaube wir bleiben jedenfalls dort in der Nähe von Hyères oder St Raphael – bei Toulon – diesen Winter. Es sollte warm sein, und frei, und Ihr könnt da kommen im Fruhjahr für die Sonne. Es ist besser wie den Baltic.

Baden ist immer gleich, nur viel mehr Fremden. Es war ganz nett hier im Löwen – der kalte Wind hat aber mich erkältet. Heute aber regnet es, und es ist warm und dunkel.

Der Schwiegermutter geht es gut. Sie ist aber viel mehr ruhelos wie früher, kann nicht lang still sein, und vielleicht hat ein wenig Angst wegen ihre Gesundheit. Sie bleibt hier mit der Frieda bis Dienstag, dann zieht wieder ins Stift. Ich hoffe sie wird einen guten Winter haben.

Also adieu! ja, einmal kommen wir nach Berlin zu deinem Haus – ich danke dir.

In November komm ich vom Insel Verlag los, und gehe an Fischer, Berlin. Mein Agent in London wollte es: sagt Fischer ist besser. Insel ist wirklich zu hoch-kragener Classik für mich.

Auf wiedersehen, denn – auf der Riviera.   D. H. Lawrence

[Dear Emil

So was it you who sent the Baumkuchen? Ah, and it is already only a memory, all eaten up. But it was good, and for me something new. The Schweicharts[1] had the last pieces for 'dessert', and appreciated it. And everyone sends thanks.

I go away tomorrow – via Lyon (Strassburg) – to Toulon. Frieda goes to Florence on Tuesday, stays there a week, gives up the Mirenda, then she comes to me. We have English friends who want to spend the winter on the Island of Port-Cros, near Hyères, and want us to live with them, in an old fortress. I'm going to see what it's like. But I reckon that in any case we'll stay near Hyères or St Raphael – near Toulon – this winter. It should be warm, and free, and you could come there in the spring for the sun. It's better than the Baltic.

Baden is the same as ever, only many more strangers. It was really nice here at the Löwen – but I got a cold from the cold wind. Today though it's raining, and is warm and murky.

---

[1] Unidentified.

The Schwiegermutter is well. But she is far more restless than before, cannot stay still for long, and she is perhaps a little worried about her health. She stays here with Frieda till Tuesday, then moves back into the Stift. I hope she'll have a good winter.

Goodbye, then! yes, some day we'll come to Berlin to your house – thank you.

In November I get free of the Insel Verlag and go to Fischer, Berlin. My London agent wanted to: says Fischer is better. Insel is really too classy and classical for me.

Auf wiedersehen, then – on the Riviera.   D. H. Lawrence]

4691. To Giulia Pini, 30 September 1928
Text: MS UT; Unpublished.

Hotel Löwen – Lichtenthal, b. BadenBaden.
30 settembre 1928

Cara Giulia

La signora parte martedì, e arriva a Firenze mercoledì sera, un poco dopo le cinque. Ma forse resterà la notte a Firenze, – forse no. Se viene a San Paolo la sera stessa, dovrebbe essere là alle sei o alle sei e mezzo. Se non arriva prima delle sette, verrà giovedì mattina.

Io non vengo, perché abbiamo deciso di non guardare la casa. Io resto nella Francia, al mare. La Signora porterà via i bauli, quando avrà fatto tutto in ordine, e verrà da me al mare. Non ci sarà molto da fare, alla villa – dunque la signora resterà soltanto quattro o cinque giorni.

Tu non mi hai scritto per dire se abbiate trovato un posto e una casa nuova. Vorrei veramente sapere: a vorrei che fosse una buona casa e un buon posto. Non c'è tempo di mandare una risposta qui. Ma scriverò dalla Francia.

Chissà ora quando ci rivedremo! Ma prima di andare in America voglio venire ancora a Firenze, forse nella primavera: e poi verrò a trovarvi.

Scrivo adesso anche al Maggiore per dire che vogliamo finire con la villa, e che la signora resta pochi giorni.

Mi rincresce anche molto di non venire ancora a San Paolo, e di dovere dire addio! a voi tutti. Ma se mi mandi l'indirizzo della nuova casa, dove andate, nella primavera verrò a farvi una visita.

Ora vi saluto, e penso con vero dispiacere a San Paolo, che non ci vengo più.

Tu affmo   D. H. Lawrence
credo che la Signora resterà a Firenze mercoledì sera, e verrà giovedì mattina alla villa.

[30 September 1928

Dear Giulia

My wife is leaving on Tuesday and will be in Florence on Wednesday evening, just after five. Perhaps she'll spend the night in Florence, – perhaps she won't. If she comes to San Paolo the same evening, she should be there at six or six-thirty. If she doesn't get there before seven, she'll come on Thursday morning.

I am not coming because we have decided not to look for a house. I'll stay in France, at the seaside. My wife will take away the trunks, when she has put everything in order, and she'll join me at the seaside. There won't be much to do at the villa – so my wife will stay only four or five days.

You did not write to me to say whether you have found a job and a new house. I'd love to know: and I hope they will be a good house and a good job. There isn't enough time to send a reply here. But I will write from France.

Who knows now when we shall see each other again! But before going to America I want to come to Florence again, perhaps in the spring: and then I'll come and see you.

I am also writing to the Major[1] now to say that we don't want the villa any longer, and that my wife will stay only for a few days.

I am also very sorry not to come to San Paolo again, and to have to say good-bye! to you all. But if you send me the address of the new house where you are going, I'll come and visit you in the spring.

Now I'll say good-bye, and I am thinking with real regret that I'm not coming to San Paolo any more.

Your most affectionate   D. H. Lawrence

I believe my wife will stay in Florence on Wednesday evening, and will come to the villa on Thursday morning.]

4692. To Baroness Anna von Richthofen, [1 October 1928]

Text: MS UCB; PC v. Strasbourg – Nid de Cigognes; Postmark, [. . .]; *Letters,* iv. 587.

Strassburg[2]

– 9 Uhr Abends

Denke dir, der Bub vom Löwen ist zu spät mit dem Grossgepäck gekommen, wir haben den Zug verloren, könnten erst an 2.0 Uhr abreisen – jetzt fahren um 10.25 von hier, und reisen durch die Nacht. Ich aber habe Schlafwagen, die andern sitzen im Coupé. Schlimm! Wir kommen aber wohl an.

DHL

[1] Raul Mirenda.

[2] This postcard was erroneously printed as if written on 20 February 1924; the opportunity is now taken to place it in its correct position in the chronological sequence. The 'others' to whom DHL refers were the Brewsters who travelled with him to southern France and then 'continued [their] way to Nice and on to Italy' (Brewster 298–9).

[Just think, the boy from the Löwen came too late with the large luggage, we missed the train, couldn't depart till 2.0 o'clock – now leave here at 10.25, and travel through the night. But I have a sleeping-car, the others sit in the coupé. Awful! But we will indeed arrive.

DHL]

4693. To Earl Brewster, [3 October 1928]
Text: MS UT; PC v. Strasbourg – Cathédrale, Portal Central; Postmark, [. . .]; Brewster 181.

Le Lavandou.

[3 October 1928]

– Else was at the station – but we were too late to see you – This is a nice quiet little place – We went out in a fisher-boat – with motor – to the island Port-Cros – It is rather lovely, all tangled forest like Corsica – but the hotel is 'chic' – quite a lot of high-browish people there – and the whole place a bit artificial. The Vigie – fortress – is an hour's stony walk uphill – and no way except to walk. – Tomorrow the Aldingtons come and I decide if we shall stay at the Vigie for two months – not more – or whether we stay on this coast, which is really very pleasant. The Huxleys are here – Else and Alfred leave tomorrow. I'll send an address tomorrow, when I've made up my mind.

DHL

4694. To Baroness Anna von Richthofen, [3 October 1928]
Text: MS UT; PC v. Strasbourg – Cathédrale. Les Vertus Ecrasant Les Vices; Postmark, [. . .]; Unpublished.

Le Lavandou
– Mittwoch

Hier sind wir alle zusammen – die Huxleys auch. Es ist sehr nett hier. Heute sind wir in einem Fischerboot an das Insel gegangen – ein nettes Insel, aber es würde schwer sein, mit keinem einzigen Laden – alles muss vom Land kommen – von Hyères – zwei Stunden weg, in Schiff. Ich denke es waren zu viele Schwierigkeiten. – Die Else reist morgen weg – will dir besuchen auf der Ruckreise. Ich schicke dir eine Adresse morgen.

DHL

[Wednesday
Here we are all together – the Huxleys too. It is very nice here. Today we've been to the island in a fishing-boat – a nice island, but it would be difficult, with not a single shop – everything has to come from land – from Hyères – two hours journey by boat. I think there'd be too many problems. – Else goes away

tomorrow – wants to visit you on the journey back. I'll send you an address tomorrow.

DHL]

4695. To S. S. Koteliansky, [5 October 1928]
Text: MS BL; PC v. [La Corniche des Maures, Le Lavandou: Tartane à la Plage d'Aiguebelle]; Postmark, Le [Lavandou] 5–10 28; Zytaruk 363.

Le Lavandou, Var
[5 October 1928]

Nice down here by the sea, sunny and fresh and so easy-seeming. Frieda is in Florence – I am alone for the moment. I may go over to the island of Port-Cros, so will send address in a day or two.

DHL

4696. To Emily King [5 October 1928]
Text: MS Needham; PC v. La Corniche des Maures – Bormes-Le Lavandou – La Plage de la Favières; Postmark, Le [Lavando]u 5[. . .]28; Unpublished.

Le Lavandou
– Friday

I like it down here by the sea – sunny and warm – I am all alone for the moment – Else and the Huxleys all have left – but Arabella and Richard Aldington are due to arrive – and F[rieda] will come next week. We may go over to island of Port-Cros – so will send address when I'm sure. Am feeling well.

DHL

4697. To Earl Brewster, [5 October 1928]
Text: MS UT; PC v. [La Corniche des Maures, Le Lavandou; La Fossette d'Aiguebelle]; Postmark, Le La[vandou] 5[. . .]; Brewster 182.

Le Lavandou
– Friday.

The Huxleys and Else have all gone on, so am quite alone for the moment. But it is very pleasant lounging on the sands and seeing the men play boccia.[1] It feels very pleasant and easy. No sign yet of the Aldingtons – so plans rather vague still. Will write when they materialise. I wonder how you are. Send me a line here –

Grand Hotel. Le Lavandou. Var.

I am feeling pretty well here.

au revoir   DHL

[1] 'bowls' ('bocce').

4698. To Ada Clarke, [5 October 1928]
Text: MS Clarke; PC v. [La Corniche des Maures, Le Lavandou: Vue Générale de St. Clair]; Postmark, Le Lava[ndou] 5[. . .]; Lawrence-Gelder 183–4.

Le Lavandou
– Friday

Nice down here by the sea not far from Toulon. The others have all left – Else and the Huxleys – but am expecting Arabella and Richard Aldington – and Frieda next week. We may go over to the island of Port-Cros, so I'll send address in a day or two, when I am sure. Am feeling very well.

DHL

4699. To Earl Brewster, [6 October 1928]
Text: MS UT; PC v. [La Corniche des Maures, Le Lavandou: La rade à travers les pins]; Postmark, [Le] Lavandou [. . .]10 28; Unpublished.

Saturday

– Still no word of the Aldingtons – so shall stay on here as yet. – I want Frieda to stay the night in Nice when she comes next week, so look out for her letter.[1] Wonder if your plans have developed at all – mine are perfectly vague still. But it's quite pleasant here – seems freer and really more friendly than Italy. I just stroll along the coast and watch the men play boccia. – Hope you've sent me your news.

DHL

Grand Hotel, Le Lavandou. Var.

4700. To Else Jaffe, [8 October 1928]
Text: MS Jeffrey; PC v. Ile de Port-Cros (Var), Une jolie auberge provençale qui s'encadre a sa place dans le paysage; Postmark, [. . .]10 28; Unpublished.

Le Lavandou
– Monday

Am still here – no word from Frieda – but I hope she'll come soon. It's lovely weather, and pleasant among the people. The Aldingtons are on the island, telegraphed that they like it and for me to come. But I'll wait for Frieda. How are you?

DHL

---

[1] The Brewsters were staying in the Hotel Vauban, Nice.

4701. To Baroness Anna von Richthofen, [8 October 1928]
Text: MS Jeffrey; PC v. Ile de Port-Cros (Var), Et la féerie devient plus intime: Une Vallée verte invraisemblablement touffue L'Égarée sur la route; Postmark, Le Lav[andou] 8. 10 28; Frieda Lawrence, *Nur Der Wind* p. 321.

Le Lavandou
– Montag

Ich bin noch hier – höre noch nichts von der Frieda – ich warte hier bis sie kommt. Es ist wunderschönes wetter, und ich bin wohl – ein freundlicher Ort dieses. Aber jetzt soll die Frieda kommen. Wie geht's dir?

DHL

[– Monday
I'm still here – hear nothing yet from Frieda – I'm waiting here till she comes. The weather is lovely, and I'm fine – a friendly place this. But Frieda ought now to come. How are you?

DHL]

4702. To Giuseppe Orioli, [8 October 1928]
Text: MS NWU; PC v. Ile de Port-Cros (Var), Le Château-Fort qui abrita les amours d'Hervé et de Flora; Postmark, [. . .]; Unpublished.

Grand Hotel. Le Lavandou. Var
Monday

– By now you will be back – I hope everything went off all right. I am sitting here waiting for Frieda – thought I'd have heard from her today, but not a sign – so shall wait on. I think we shall go over to the island. Address
La Vigie, Ile de Port-Cros, Var.

The Aldingtons are there, and seem to think it is all right. So write me. It's lovely weather – and very pleasant here.

DHL

4703. To Earl and Achsah Brewster, [10 October 1928]
Text: MS UT; cited in Brewster 181.

Grand Hotel. Le Lavandou. Var.
Wednesday. 4.0 pm

Dear Earl and Achsah

Yours just come, and also one from Frieda – and the very first word I've had from anybody since I got here. The post is atrocious. And now there's a strike on this idiotic little railway, which doesn't seem big enough to have a strike, damn it. But they are *supposed* to be running one train – if they dare call it a train – per day each way – so the train which leaves St. Raphael at about 3.0, which Frieda should catch, *ought* to run all right. Do ask Cooks on the day F. arrives. If the strike gets worse, and that train doesn't run – but I think it will – then do wire me, and I'll go to Salius d'Hyères, and Frieda must go on then to Toulon directly on the main line, and from Toulon to Salius d'Hyères by the P[aris] L[yon] M[arseille], which isn't striking. Otherwise I'll be waiting here.

Yes, the weather, the sun, the light are lovely. Man is everywhere vile.[1] They are just beginning to mess this coast up – but the messing seems to proceed rapidly, once it starts. Little villas 'tout confort' – yes my word. Very comforting to the eye! I think we shall go over to the island end of this week – if F. comes and sea is still. I hope she'll turn up soon, I'm getting a bit bored – have churlishly refused to talk to *anybody* – I'm sick of people – there are about ten in the hotel. We'll try the island – perhaps we might find a corner in it – though I saw high-brow visitors striding on every path – too precious for words, that Perle of an island. – I *do* hope the school suits[2] – I feel very vague about really settling anywhere – perhaps Frieda will push me. Anyhow I feel we'll meet before long.

DHL

4704. To Enid Hilton, [13 October 1928]

Text: MS UCLA; PC v. Ile de Port-Cros, [Et la féerie] devient plus intime: Une Vallée verte invraisemblablement touffue L'Égarée sur la route; Postmark, [Le Lavan] dou [. . .]; cited in Moore, *Poste Restante* 97.

La Vigie. Ile de Port-Cros, Var.
Sat.

Have yours of 29th – no, not a word from D[orothy] W[arren] – F[rieda] joined me last night from Florence – and on[3] Monday we go over to the island – write there – Could you find out what booksellers are charging now for *Lady C.*

Lovely and sunny here – hope you had a good holiday.

DHL

---

[1] Cf. 'From Greenland's Icy Mountains' (1827), the hymn by Bishop Reginald Heber ['And only man is vile']. Cf. *Letters*, iv. 110.
[2] Presumably a reference to a school for Harwood Brewster though, in 1928, her studies were supervised by Richard Reynolds (see p. 22 n. 4). Perhaps the Brewsters were already contemplating Dartington Hall School in Devon, where Harwood went in 1929.
[3] on] for

4705. To Else Jaffe, [13 October 1928]

Text: MS Jeffrey; PC v. Ile de Port-Cros (Var), Cloches de Pàques, Voies aériennes dans l'Ile en fleurs; Postmark, [. . .]; Unpublished.

La Vigie, Ile de Port-Cros. Var.

Samstag

– Die Frieda ist gestern abend angekommen – in auto von St. Raphael, diese dumme kleine Eisenbahn macht einen Streik. Die Aldingtons schreiben vom Insel, es sei wunderschön – sie mögen es sehr, und wollen dass wir gehen. So gehen wir Montag, wenn das Meer still ist! – Ich bestelle dir jetzt die *Collected Poems*.

Love DHL

[Saturday

– Frieda arrived last night – by car from St. Raphael, this stupid little railway is on strike. The Aldingtons write from the island, it's very beautiful – they like it very much, and want us to go. So we're going on Monday, if the sea is calm! – I'll order you the *Collected Poems*.

Love DHL]

4706. To Emily King, [13 October 1928]

Text: MS Needham; PC v. Ile de Port-Cros (Var), L'opulence de ce paradis terrestre, la pureté de l'air et la splendeur de la lumière défient toute comparaison; Postmark [. . .]; Unpublished.

La Vigie. *Ile de Port-Cros*, Var. France

Sat

– Frieda came last night – we expect to join the Aldingtons on the island on Monday, so write there – All well here – lovely sunshine.

Love DHL!

4707. To Earl Brewster, [13 October 1928]

Text: MS UT; PC v. Cavalaire (Var). – Place de la Poste; Postmark, [. . .]; Unpublished.

[Grand Hotel, Le Lavandou, Var.]

Sat

F[rieda] arrived last night – couldn't get to Nice on Friday, stayed night in San Remo – and had to drive in a taxi from St. Raphael here – nearly three hours! The Aldingtons write they love the fortress and are waiting for us every day – so if it's fine we'll go over Monday – write

La Vigie. Ile de Port-Cros. Var.

There's only mail three times a week. What news?

DHL

4708. To S. S. Koteliansky, [14 October 1928]
Text: MS BL; PC v. Ile de Port-Cros (Var), La Château-Fort qui abrita les amours d'Hervé et de Flora; Postmark, [. . .]; Zytaruk 363.

La Vigie – Ile de Port-Cros, Var.
Sunday

We are going over to the island tomorrow, and this is to be the address. Send me a line.

DHL

4709. To Martin Secker, [14 October 1928]
Text: MS UInd; PC v. Ile de Port-Cros (Var), La Château-Fort qui abrita les amours d'Hervé et de Flora; Postmark, [. . .]; Unpublished.

La Vigie. Ile de Port Cros, Var
Sunday

We are going over to the isle tomorrow – will you send me a copy of the poems there.

DHL

4710. To Harry Crosby, [14 October 1928]
Text: MS SIU: PC v. Ile de Port-Cros (Var) Une jolie auberge provencale qui s'encadre a sa place dans le paysage; Postmark, [Le La]vandou [. . .] 10 [. . .]; Unpublished.

La Vigie – Ile de Port-Cros, Var
Sunday

We are going over to the island tomorrow and this is to be the address – but I'll write a letter.

D. H. Lawrence

4711. To Giuseppe Orioli, [20 October 1928]
Text: MS UCLA; Unpublished.

La Vigie. *Ile de Port-Cros*, Var. France
Sat.

Dear Pino

I sent you the address on a p.c., but have no word from you. We came here last Monday – a funny fortified place on the top of the island, no people – only inside the enceinte are ourselves, and Richard and Dorothy Aldington – and another friend, Brigit Patmore[1] – and a Sicilian man Giuseppe to do the work[2] – aged 28 – and a donkey Jasper to bring up the goods from the little port, an

---

[1] Brigit Patmore, née Ethel Elizabeth ('Brigit') Morrison-Scott (1882–1965), author. b. Ulster. m. 1907, John Deighton Patmore. She became Aldington's mistress. (See *Letters*, v. 589 and n. 1.)   [2] Giuseppe Barezzi.

hour away below. We all get on very well, and like it – and I think we shall stay till about Christmas.

Frieda arrived from Florence with the most beastly bad cold – Carletto's cold – and of course I caught it, and have felt pretty rotten. But now it is going away: I hope clean away.

Any more news of *Lady C.* – ? If the Holliday Bookshop don't get the first five copies, I'll send back the money for the remaining thirty copies, and we'll keep them – I am waiting for your letter.

I wish I could think of something *pure* to publish now. Don't do Douglas' limericks at the moment – nor *Gastone*.[1] I'll ask Aldous – but he never has anything. We'll see how my pictures are received in November – might do those in black and white.

I'll send you my *Collected Poems* directly.

belle cose!   DHL

4712. To Harry Crosby, 20 October 1928
Text: MS SIU; Unpublished.

La Vigie. Ile de Port-Cros. Var.
20 Oct 1928 Saturday

Dear Harry Crosby

The sheets came today, and I have signed them – but unfortunately there is no mail leaves the island now till Tuesday, so that will explain delay – but I shall try and rush the boy down to today's boat if I can. You don't say when you sail, but if you land Nov. 8th. – it must be soon. I'll do my best anyhow.

I think we shall stay here till about Christmas, so write to me and tell me all news from New York. Tell me how people are feeling about *Lady C* there now. And what about *your* poems, and this *Harper's* magazine?

The design for *Sun* looks very nice, I think – By the way Knopf wrote saying certainly you could print it – and making no stipulation. – As for the money, mind you take away all your expenses and everything before you begin sharing with me.

When will you be back in Paris? I suppose we shall meet one day. If you give me your address, I'll sign a copy of my poems – *Collected Poems* – and send to you.

Best wishes from us both to you and Mrs Crosby – and buon viaggio!

D. H. Lawrence

[1] In 1928 Orioli published a limited edn (110 copies) of *Some Limericks collected for the use of students and ensplendour'd with introduction, geographical index and with notes explanatory and critical by N. Douglas.* For *Gastone*, see Letter 4544 and p. 470 n. 1.

4713. To Emily King, 20 October 1928
Text: MS Lazarus; Postmark, Ile de Port-Cros 23 OCT 28; Unpublished.

La Vigie. *Ile de Port-Cros.* Var.
Sat. 20 Oct 1928

My dear Pamela

Your letter came Thursday, and was the first I received on the island. We only get mail on Tuesdays, Thursdays, and Saturdays, and only then if the sea is smooth enough for the boat to come.

Frieda arrived from Florence with the bad cold she usually gets travelling, and of course she gave it me – so I've been feeling rather cheap. But it's nearly gone.

The Vigie – the watch-place, – is rather fun. It isn't a castle at all – only a fortification on the top of the tallest hill of the island, a thick low wall going round enclosing a couple of acres of the hill-top – and a moat outside, dry of course – and inside the rooms built along the walls, a sitting room and four bed-rooms on the south side, a big dining hall, and kitchen, pantry, and the little room we use for eating in, on the N. E. side. It was all abandoned – so that inside the enclosure is all wild lavender and stinking nanny and arbutus and tiny pine-trees really very nice. Outside, below, the island is all green pine forest – umbrella pines – then the blue sea, and the other isles, and the mainland. There are no people on the island, only a few fishermen and the hotel on the little bay, an hours walk. – There is an Italian, Giuseppe, 28 years old – who fetches everything up on the little donkey Jasper – and he washes dishes and makes beds and sweeps floors and chops wood – there isn't a great deal of scrubbing done. The women just do the cooking among them – Frieda and Arabella and Brigit Patmore – a friend of the Aldingtons whom we've known a long time. – It is quite fun, and I think we shall stay at least till about christmas time. All the food has to be ordered, and comes by boat – but we get plenty – and good fish.

Yes, I had your other letter, and Pegs – and the kodaks – I thought I looked horrid – but those of the Trachsl's were excellent. I'm not working at all – just doing nothing. It'll take me some time to settle down here, with other people – we are so used to being alone. Tell Peg I'll send her some typing when I have any. – It must have been a grand fair, there on the Forest.[1]

Love to you all   DHL

---

[1] Held on 4–6 October 1928, Nottingham's Goose Fair had been transferred to a site known as 'the Forest' not far from the High School which DHL attended as a boy. See Letter 4190 and p. 201 n. 1.

4714. To Earl and Achsah Brewster, 20 October 1928
Text: MS UT; Brewster 182–3.

La Vigie. Ile de Port-Cros. Var.
Sat. 20 Oct 1928

Dear Earl and Achsah

Earl's letter just now and the telegram – and all the magazines – for which many thanks. Why ever didn't you wire me for 1000 francs – I could have sent them in an envelope in a minute. – Frieda arrived with a raging Italian cold – and of course passed it on to me, so I've felt very cheap this week. But it's much better. – The vigie isn't a castle but a top of a hill with a moat and low fort-wall enclosing a bare space, about 2 acres, where the wild lavender and the heaths grow. The rooms are sort of cabins under the walls – windows facing the inner space, loop-holes looking out to sea – a nice large sitting-room – a bedroom each – then across, a great room where we throw the logs, and a kitchen, pantry and little dining room. It's very nice, rather rough, but not really uncomfortable – and plenty of wood to burn in the open fireplaces. The Italian Giuseppe, a strong fellow of 28, fetches all provisions on a donkey, once a day. We get practically everything – except milk – and plenty. But all has to be ordered from the mainland. Giuseppe does all the housework except cooking – which the women take in turns. Richard and Arabella are very nice, and so is Bridget Patmore, we get on very well, and it's quite fun, but I've felt so limp with my cold – real influenza cold – poor Achsah, how I sympathise! – Whyever didn't you wire me for money. I do hope Achsah is really better – dont travel till she is. Where are you going to anyhow? is Capri inevitable? – I think we shall stay here till towards Christmas. The island is all green pine-tops seen from above – then blue sea and other islands. It's nice because one is quite alone – but of course I don't want to live here. There are no other houses – only the hotel and the few fishermen at the bay – and it took me a long hour to get up from there, so I doubt I'm perched, as at Kesselmatte. Anyhow I don't care. I don't think I shall do much work here – but it's better for me. – I've got a copy of my poems for you, which I'll send when I'm sure you are staying somewhere. – If you go to Capri, see if you cant get 2nd class wagon-lit from Ventimiglia – I *know* you can Genoa to Rome, and saves a lot of exhaustion – gets you to Rome about 7.0 a.m.

All feels very vague – I don't know where we shall ultimately go – and I get scared when this influenza begins biting again. – But tell me what you are doing.

Love from both to three   DHL

4715. To Nancy Pearn, 20 October 1928
Text: MS UT; Unpublished.

La Vigie. *Ile de Port-Cros*, Var. France
Sat. 20 Oct 1928

Dear Nancy Pearn

I sent Pollinger this address on a p. c., but since I have nothing from 6 Henrietta, perhaps he didn't get it.[1] Do you mind sending it round to all the depts. – I think we shall be here till Christmas, anyhow. – We are with friends in an old fortification on top of the island of Port-Cros – across from Hyères – not far from Toulon. It's quite fun – only ourselves – all the rest of the island pine-trees.

I hope you had a good holiday. Send me all the news.

Ever   D. H. Lawrence

4716. To Enid Hilton, 21 October 1928
Text: MS UCLA; cited in Moore, *Poste Restante* 97.

La Vigie. *Ile de Port-Cros*. Var.
Sunday 21 Oct 1928

Dear Enid

I got your letter only yesterday, saying you would be in Toulon. It wasn't dated either, so I don't know when you were there – probably last week, when I was all alone in Le Lavandou, and should have been so glad to see you!!

We came here last Monday – quite fun – but we both had vile colds, which Frieda brought from Italy. But they are getting better – and we can have good fires of pine-wood in the open chimneys of this funny place.

I suppose the bookseller in Milan didn't want his name to come up in case the book *should* be held up in customs. Oh Lord! – I'll write later about Orioli's sending you twenty copies.

Hope you had a good time. It's sea-foggy here today – and so still.

DHL

4717. To Giuseppe Orioli, [21 October 1928]
Text: MS UCLA; Moore, *Intelligent Heart* 391.

[La Vigie, Ile de Port-Cros, Var.]
Sunday

I think if I were you I would prepare a series of *Italian Renaissance Novelists, text in Italian and in English, with notes* – small books of about 80 or 100 pp.;

[1] It is unlocated.

the same format, more or less, as the Fortini books – but not replica – not identical.

I have begun with the *Terza Cena* of Lasca.¹ It is a very interesting story, Lorenzo De' Medici – and about 60 pp, and quite proper. Get your old professor to write you a brief life of Lasca, and to make notes on the story – I will mention what I think should have a note, as I go on.

– The story of Lorenzo de' Medici and Maestro Manente. – It is important to start the series with an interesting and *not* indecent story. We can come on with the indecent ones later. I thought we would do Lasca in 3 vols. – three *Cene* – starting with the terza. This one won't take me very long. Let me know what you think.

There is great work going on for the *international suppression of indecent literature*. I enclose a cutting from the *Evening Standard*.² – Also – an incident. An Englishwoman saw a copy of *Lady C.* in a bookshop in Milan – went in to buy – man demanded to see her passport and *permesso di soggiorno*³ – the latter had only three days to run – woman said she was just going back to England – bookseller refused to sell her the copy. – I expect he was afraid customs might hold up the book and he might be cited as having sold it – and the League of Nations be after him!

DHL

4718. To Maria Huxley, [22 October 1928]
Text: Huxley 756–7.

La Vigie.
Monday, 22 October.

My Dear Maria, –

We've been here a week to-day. Frieda brought a *vile* cold from Florence, so I got it and have felt a rag of rags – but it's going. This isn't a castle or

---

¹ Antonio Francesco Grazzini (nicknamed 'Lasca') (1503–84) organised a series of stories in three 'Suppers'. DHL translated, and Orioli published in November 1929 in his 'Lungarno Series', *The Story of Doctor Manente being the Tenth and Last Story from the Suppers of A. F. Grazzini called Il Lasca* (Roberts A45). The story is of a macabre practical joke played by Lorenzo de' Medici on Manente. At the end of his 'Foreword' DHL announced two further volumes containing stories from the first and second Suppers; neither was completed.

² The *Evening Standard* reported on 16 October 1928 that the Home Secretary, Sir William Joynson-Hicks, 'might in the near future find himself obliged to deal with objectionable books', which the paper took to mean that he would prosecute their publishers. On 19 October the paper reported action by the Home Office to prevent the sale and distribution of Radclyffe Hall's *The Well of Loneliness*. The book had been printed in Paris; it was seized by the Customs but subsequently released; and the Home Office then acted to stop distribution. The report continued: 'The Continental edition may be seized and destroyed by the police . . .'

³ '*permission to stay*'. Cf. Letter 4716.

fortezza at all – but a thick defence-wall enclosing a cleared two acres or so of the crown of the hill – and all the enclosure just gone wild, wild lavender and little arbutus trees. The rooms are just built up against the defence-wall one storey – brick floors – quite nice. There are fireplaces and we burn lots of pine-wood – a great blessing. Outside all is pine forest and rosemary – we look down on green pine-tops and blue sea. A long *hour* up from the hotel – bathing place ¾ hour up. I've not been – Frieda has. It's quite nice for a time, especially the fires – and the Aldingtons are old friends. So is Bridget Patmore. We get on very well, and I'm the only disagreeable one. Mail comes Tuesdays, Thursdays, Saturdays. All food, all supplies must be brought from the mainland – when the boat comes. We'll probably stay till December – then where? – How's the house getting on? When do you move in? – We've had all weathers, from violent mistral to creeping hot fog. I'll be all right when my cold goes – those Italian germs! – I've begun Aldous's book, what a fat book![1]

No news. Have had practically no mail yet. Oh, Maria, if 100 frs. is enough, send a little stodgy cake and a few sweets – tea is a blank. Let the shop do the sending, don't you bother. Orioli wanted to ask Aldous if he had a little book to let him publish.

Let us know how it all goes.

DHL

4719. To Ada Clarke, [23 October 1928]
Text: MS Clarke; cited in Lawrence–Gelder 184–5.

La Vigie. *Ile de Port-Cros.* Var, France
Tuesday

My dear Sister

Well we've been here a week, and I've not written, because I had a cold, the regular Italian germ-cold, which Frieda arrived with from Florence, and handed on. But it's going away.

It's quite fun here – an old fortified place on the top of the highest hill of the island, but not a castle at all. Just an enclosed space, all gone wild, and smallish rooms on the inside, and outside a dry moat. There's an Italian manservant to fetch and carry, and he does all the housework except cooking – which the women share. Richard and Arabella are very nice – so is Brigit Patmore, a woman about my age, whom we knew in the old days. They are all busy doing literary work – and they go off to swim.[2] But it's an hour's climb up from the sea, so with my cold I don't go – we look down on the green island, all

[1] *Point Counter Point*, published in October 1928 (see Letter 4724).
[2] Aldington was writing his novel, *Death of a Hero* (published September 1929). For Brigit Patmore's recollection of DHL's reaction to their 'going off to swim', see Nehls, iii. 257.

umbrella pines, and the blue sea and the other isles, and the mainland ten miles off. It's quite nice – somehow doesn't move me very much. We are due to stay till beginning December, but I'm not sure.

Dorothy Warren is due back in London now – whether she's got married again or not, I don't know – but the pictures are hanging ready for the show, which is due in November now.

I hear from Emily there was a grand Fair – did you go? I guess it was a hullabaloo.

The post only comes three times a week, and not even then if weather is bad, so sometimes the letters take a long time. But Today I think it will leave all right – there's been no boat since Saturday. It's a lovely sunny morning, and a blue sea. But I wonder if we really shall stay long here. Now the Mirenda is given up, one is more restless than ever. I suppose we'll have to find another house somewhere.

How are you all? – and how is G[ertrude Cooper]? And how is poor Bertie sticking his school? And how are the miners working, now winter is near again? I do hope it'll be a good friendly winter all around, not a poisonous one.

Love   DHL

4720. To Laurence Pollinger, [26 October 1928]
Text: MS UT; Unpublished.

La Vigie. *Ile de Port-Cros*. Var. France
Friday

Dear Pollinger

I sent you the address on a p. c. two weeks ago – didn't you get it? Then I sent it to Miss Pearn – hope she gave it you. – I went and got influenza – my wife brought it me from Florence – and didn't care if the post never came again, or left. Am getting up today however, and feeling better. – Mail only comes three times a week – even then only when the sea's not risen – so if there are gaps there are gaps.

Hope you are well.

D. H. Lawrence

4721. To Giuseppe Orioli, [27 October 1928]
Text: MS UCLA; Unpublished.

La Vigie. *Ile de Port-Cros*. Var. France
Saturday

My dear Pino

Your letter today with bordereaux and cheques.

Yes, send Mrs Chambers a couple of copies and see if she gets them – at *our* risk, of course. I'll write her – but now she threatens to appear here.[1]

I have half done the Lasca story. Don't you like the idea of a series of Renaissance stories? – I sent *Escaped Cock* to America, but I expect it will come back.

I have been in bed all week with that flu cold – and two days hemorrhage and feel rather rotten. I don't think we shall stay here very long, I don't believe it suits me.

Yes, beware of Douglas limericks – I haven't seen *John Bull*: but that paper has always hated me.[2] – I don't suppose there will be any more orders for *Lady C.* for a while – till the booksellers have sold *their* copies!

Did you send Pollinger his four copies! No word from him.

Wish I felt better – this is worse than the Mirenda. – Frieda wants to go and live on Lago di Garda.

How is Carletto!

Love from both.   DHL

I've not written to London yet for the poems – seedy.

4722. To Else Jaffe, [27 October 1928]
Text: MS Jeffrey; Frieda Lawrence 279–80.

La Vigie. *Ile de Port-Cros.* Var.
Saturday

Dear Else

Your letter today, saying the Schwiegermutter is in bed. I'm awfully sorry, and do hope it's not much. I thought in Lichtenthal she wasn't well. Of course she is a heavy woman, and her legs are sure to suffer. Let us know how she goes on – and I hope she'll soon be up and about.

We are here settled in. But Frieda arrived in Lavandou with that fatal Italian Grippe, and of course I took it. I felt ill all last week, and have been in bed all this, with a very raked chest. Sickening! – The others are very nice and very kind. The Vigie isn't a castle at all – just a low thick defence-wall with loop-holes, enclosing the top of the hill – about as big as the Leopoldplatz –

---

[1] If DHL did write shortly after this date his letter has disappeared. He told Maria Chambers in December 1928 that the two copies of *Lady Chatterley's Lover* were in exchange for the $40 which she sent by cheque dated 24 September 1928 (recorded in 'Memoranda', MS NWU).

[2] Under the heading, 'Famous Novelist's Shameful Book', an anonymous writer excoriated DHL and his novel in *John Bull*, 20 October 1928 (see The *Critical Heritage*, ed. Draper, pp. 278–80): 'the most evil outpouring that has ever besmirched the literature of our country . . . the fetid masterpiece of this sex-sodden genius . . . we have no doubt that he will be ostracized by all except the most degenerate côteries in the literary world'.

and the inside all wild, grown with lavender and arbutus and little pine trees, and with a few rooms built against the inside of the wall.

[sketch][1]

It's quite pleasant, and comfortable, and we have big fires of pine logs in the open fires. Giuseppe is a strong fellow of 28, Sicilian. He fetches and carries and washes all dishes and makes fires. The women have only to cook, and they do it in turns. Joseph brings the food from the boat on a small donkey, Jasper – and we get abundance. The ship comes nearly every day – but post only three times a week. The climate is very warm – warm and moist. I am afraid that doesn't suit me very well. I don't know how long we shall stay. I have promised, till December 15 or 20. But if the warm-moist is bad for my cough, we shall leave soon. The others are really very nice and kind, it will be a pity if we have to leave them. And where shall we go?

The Brewsters are back in Capri. Inevitable.

I ordered the poems to Heidelberg. They look very nice.

We are on the top of the island, and look down on green pine-tops, down to the blue sea, and the other islands and the mainland. Since I came I have not been down to the sea again – and Frieda has bathed only once. But it is very pretty. And at night the lights flash at Toulon and Hyères and Lavandou. – But I don't really like islands. I would never stay long on one. – Frieda wants to go back to Lago di Garda. Vediamo! I am in abeyance.

Write and tell us how the Schwiegermutter is. Frieda says she feels worried – but it seems to me there is no danger, only it is painful and depressing. No peace on this dark earth.

Love from both.   DHL

I hope this letter will leave the island before next Tuesday – the next mail.

4723. To Martin Secker, [27 October 1928]
Text: MS UInd; Secker 113–14.

La Vigie. Ile de Port-Cros. Var.
Sat.

Dear Secker

Your copy of my poems today, and many thanks – looks very nice indeed, am pleased with it – any news about it?

Frieda came with the most beastly influenza cold from Italy, and of course gave it me. I felt so cheap – but better. It's fun here, in this old fortified sort of

---

[1] DHL provided a rough outline-sketch of the Vigie: a circular area bounded by a 'dry moat' and, inside the wall, a 'kitchen', 'small dining-room', 'tower', 'look-out', 'bedrooms', and a 'sitting room' adjacent to 'my bedroom'.

a place on top of the island, with only pine trees and sea below. It's about 2 hours crossing from Hyères – mail comes three times a week. There's an hotel, but nothing else, away at the little port – about a dozen fishermen. We are here with Richard and Dorothy Aldington – and Brigit Patmore – known them a long while.

Do send me two more copies of the poems – as Richard wrote yesterday.

Would you answer this man if you feel like it, and send him some books if you feel like it.[1] I cant bother.

You never sent those two books to Boshy – *Fantasia* and *Mornings*.[2] Why didn't you? Are they out of print? Is it well to leave them out of print?

I told the Coghlan[3] he could broadcast greetings from us both – hope all goes well.

D. H. Lawrence

4724. To Aldous Huxley, [28 October 1928]
Text: Huxley 757–8.

La Vigie, Port-Cros (Var).
Sunday.

Dear Aldous, –

I have read *Point Counter Point* with a heart sinking through my boot-soles and a rising admiration. I do think you've shown the truth, perhaps the last truth, about you and your generation, with really fine courage. It seems to me it would take ten times the courage to write *P. Counter P.* than it took to write *Lady C.*: and if the public knew *what* it was reading, it would throw a hundred stones at you, to one at me. I do think that art has to reveal the palpitating moment or the state of man as it is. And I think you do that, terribly. But what a moment! and what a state! if you can only palpitate to murder, suicide, and rape, in their various degrees – and you state plainly that it is so – *caro*, however are we going to live through the days? Preparing still another murder, suicide, and rape? But it becomes a[4] phantasmal boredom and produces ultimately inertia, inertia, inertia and final atrophy of the feelings. Till, I suppose, comes a final super-war, and murder, suicide, rape sweeps

---

[1] DHL's letter is on the verso of one to him (c/o Secker), on 9 October 1928, from Gérard de Catalogue in Paris (MS UInd). He was planning a series of articles in *Le Figaro* on 'les jeunes romanciers anglais d'aujourd'hui' and wished to devote one to DHL. However, since he had read little beyond 'The Fox' and *Aaron's Rod*, he wished to read more and asked if DHL would send copies of other novels, particularly *Sons and Lovers* and *The Trespasser*. Further, 'Si vous avez des details biographiques interessants et des articles qui vous ont été consacrés, et que je vous retournerai après lecture, je serai heureux de les incorporer dans mon "papier".' Secker's reply has not been traced.   [2] See Letter 4639.   [3] Unidentified.
[4] Huxley's text reads: 'of a'.

away the vast bulk of mankind. It is as you say – intellectual appreciation does
not amount to so much, it's what you thrill to. And if murder, suicide, rape is
what you thrill to, and nothing else, then it's your destiny – you can't change it
mentally. You live by what you thrill to, and there's the end of it. Still for all
that it's a *perverse* courage which makes the man accept the slow suicide of
inertia and sterility: the perverseness of a perverse child. – It's amazing how
men are like that. [Richard Aldington][1] is exactly the same inside, murder,
suicide, rape – with a desire to *be* raped very strong – same thing really – just
like you – only he doesn't face it, and gilds his perverseness. It makes me feel
ill, I've had more hemorrhage here and been in bed this week. *Sporca miseria.*
If I don't find some solid spot to climb out of, in this bog, I'm done. I can't
stand murder, suicide, rape – especially rape: and especially being raped. Why
do men only thrill to a woman who'll rape them? All I want to do to your Lucy
is smack her across the mouth, your Rampion is the most boring character in
the book – a gas-bag.[2] Your attempt at intellectual sympathy! – It's all rather
disgusting, and I feel like a badger that has its hole on Wimbledon Common
and trying not to be caught. Well, *caro*, I feel like saying good-bye to you – but
one will have to go on saying good-bye for years.

DHL

4725. To Nancy Pearn, 30 October 1928
Text: MS UT; Unpublished.

La Vigie. Ile de Port-Cros. Var. France
30 Oct. 1928

Dear Nancy Pearn

Your bunch today – my cold went – and became flue, but it's passing now.
The island is very silent and nice, when one can be up and about. I'll answer
you bit by bit.

1. I never had Mr Olley's of Sept. 27th. – so don't know how or why he
    wants me to alter 'Cocksure Women': Can't he alter it himself?[3]
2. I doubt if I could write about my uncensored Film – feel I haven't got
    one – but if anything comes I'll send it:[4]

---

[1] Cf. p. 326 n. 3.
[2] Rampion is the Lawrentian figure in *Point Counter Point* (cf. Letter 4747).
[3] Cf. Letter 4612 and n. 1. Later, 20 November 1928, Nancy Pearn told DHL that Olley did not
believe the article 'could be altered to suit them' (TMSC UT).
[4] Pearn had enquired on 9 October 1928 whether DHL was interested in an earlier invitation that
he should write an article for *Film Weekly*. The journal's editor had remarked: 'No doubt Mr
Lawrence could write a good article on the sort of film he would write or produce if there were
no censor' (TMSC UT).

3. I'll try and do an article for *Sunday Despatch* on 'What is Sex Appeal'.[1]
4. I don't mind the *Evening News* not printing 'Ownership' if they don't want to. I'll write some more little articles when I feel chirpy.
5. I'll have a shot at 'England as a man's country' for the *Daily Express*.[2]
6. I really like 2000 word length better than 1000, so I'll turn up something one of these days for *Vanity Fair*.

There – makes one gasp! – What a storm in very tin-pot kettles over *Lady C*.! Can't hurt me, as I've sold the edition.

ever   D. H. Lawrence

4726. To Laurence Pollinger, 30 October 1928
Text: MS UT; Unpublished.

La Vigie. Ile de Port Cros. Var.

30 Oct. 1928

Dear Pollinger

Yours today – calm sea! What a babbling of village idiots over *Lady C*.! I wonder if the Customs *did* really hold up any? Whose could they have been? – Orioli seems to have a complex about sending you copies. I'll ask him *again* if he sent. – Anyway it's too late to hurt me.

I'll make *Rawdon's Roof* a bit longer – I take it Elkin Mathews want it then. – I shall be glad if they don't, because then I needn't sign those copies, which will be a relief. So tell them they're let off if they will be.

I don't quite like Rich's way of handling me – he certainly seems to prefer Knopf to me. I don't see why books should be piled on liked that – I never thought contracts *added up* their promises of future books. I'm riled. See if Alfred ever gets three books out of me – just see! Nobody does anything about the poems in America – benissimo! I do nothing about anybody in America. Suo devotissimo[3] –

Thanks for that list of contracts – I'll keep it by me.

Hasta otra vez[4]   D. H. Lawrence

How tiresome Secker is! I sent a[5] list of the poems to send out to him – then he goes and sends the bunch to you. He's a liar too – on another point, however – with which I won't weary you just now. Will you please send a set to:

---

[1] The *Sunday Dispatch* had invited DHL to contribute to a series on the subject (Pearn to DHL, 11 October 1928); the resulting article was 'Sex Locked Out' (cf. Letter 4732).
[2] See p. 606 n. 1.   [3] 'Your devoted friend'.   [4] 'Cheerio.'   [5] a] him

1. Mrs Maria Cristina Chambers, 43 Hillside Rd. Elm Point. *Great Neck.*
   Long Island. N.Y., U.S.A.
1. Aldous Huxley. 3 rue du Bac. *Suresnes* (Seine), France
1. S. Koteliansky Esq. 5. Acacia Rd. St. Johns Wood. N.W.8.
1. Signor G. Orioli. 6 Lungarno Corsini. *Florence.* Italy

and please send the other two sets to me here. Sorry for all the bother.

                                                                    DHL

4727. To Giuseppe Orioli, [30 October 1928]
Text: MS UCLA; Unpublished.

                                        La Vigie. Ile de Port-Cros. Var.
                                                                 Tuesday
Dear Pino
    This is from Beazley to say he has just paid £5··2··0 to my account, for his
copies of *Lady C.*[1]
    Today I have a bunch of cuttings from *John Bull, Church Times* etc. about
Ladyship – saying she has been confiscated in customs.[2] Is it true? Whose
copies? Kot's?
    Did you ever send those four copies to L. E. Pollinger, Curtis Brown? – four
additional ones? He has not received them. *Please let me know.*
    Flue rather better, but still tiresome.
    This man, an American, wrote to Richard Aldington that he wanted a copy
of *Lady C.* and could dispose of ten others. But that was presuming the price
£2··2··0. You might write and ask him what he can do at £4··4··0 – and give
him the discount if he wants it.
        Walter Lowenfels, 16 rue Denfert-Rocherau, *Paris.*
Hasn't he already had a copy?[3] But send him a line.

                                                               Yrs   DHL

---

[1] DHL enclosed the letter from H. K. Beazley, Belgravia bookseller (MS UCLA):

   Dear Sir
       Many thanks for your card. being away on holiday I was too late for Baden. so have paid £5
   into your a/c as receipt herewith. It should be £5.2.0. so forward stamps which I hope will be of
   use.
                                                and Remain   Sincerely yours

[2] Cf. p. 598 n. 2; the alleged reaction by the *Church Times* has not been traced.
[3] Two cheques for $10 (22 August and 11 September 1928) are recorded in DHL's 'Memor-
anda' (MS NWU).

4728. To S. S. Koteliansky, 31 October 1928
Text: MS BL; Postmark, [Ile] de Port-Cros [. . .]28; Zytaruk 364–5.

La Vigie. *Ile de Port-Cros.* Var. France
31 Oct 1928

My dear Kot

Have I written to you since we are here, or haven't I? I've lost track. But Frieda arrived from Florence with that Italian flu, and of course I got it, and have felt bad these two weeks. But am a lot better.

I had your letter here – and yesterday, came something from *John Bull, Sunday Chronicle*[1] etc – what a tin-pot shindy! What fools altogether! But what about those customs confiscations? was it your copy? I hope no trouble to you, anyhow. How bored one gets by endless mob-stupidity. – But let me know. I seem to know nothing here – mail comes three times a week, when the sea is not rough. – Today it's a storm, so probably tomorrow no boat.

I should like it here if I had shaken off this cold. It is very quiet. Richard Aldington and Arabella and Mrs Patmore, and an Italian man to do the fetching and carrying – that's all. For the rest it is a fortified hilltop on an island covered with pine-trees. There is one hotel, one little port with eight or nine houses – nothing else but hills and trees, and sea and other islands and mainland ten miles or so off. The hotel is nearly an hour's walk. I have not been down since we are here. All being well, we shall stay till towards Christmas, then I don't know where.

I ordered you a copy of my poems – suppose you'll get them.

How are you? are the Farbman's back, and is there any news? *Where* does Murry want to go? Brett threatens to come to Europe – hope she'll go to him. We get on very well here – manage to get good food and all that. – I still haven't heard if Dorothy Warren is actually in London: Frieda might come in Nov. if she shows the pictures. I feel very indifferent to almost everything.

tante cose!   DHL

[1] Cf. p. 598 n. 2. On 14 October 1928 the *Sunday Chronicle* devoted a whole column in the centre of the front page to: 'Lewd Book Banned./Under Name of Noted Author./Printed out of England.' The report ran as follows:

A sensation has been caused in the literary world by the dramatic action which has been taken by the British Customs authorities against an astounding book, 'Lady Chatterley's Lover', signed by 'D. H. Lawrence'.

The *Sunday Chronicle* learns that copies of the book have been seized in the Customs with the object of preventing its circulation in this country.

Admirers of Mr D. H. Lawrence, the famous novelist and poet, are questioning whether he can possibly be the author of a book which the *Sunday Chronicle* has no hesitation in describing as one of the most filthy and abominable ever written; and an outrage on decency . . . It reeks with obscenity and lewdness about sex.

. . . Messrs Curtis Brown . . . told the *Sunday Chronicle* yesterday that they had no knowledge of the book except that slips announcing its publication were put into circulation from Italy . . .

4729. To Giuseppe Orioli, [1 November 1928]
Text: MS UCLA; cited in Moore, *Intelligent Heart* 392.

[La Vigie, Ile de Port-Cros, Var.]
Thursday.

I have nearly done the Story of Lorenzo il Magnifico and Maestro Manente, and next week I can send you the typescript. It would make about 70 pages of a book: quite a nice little book. I want you to decide whether you will announce a series of Renaissance Stories:[1] also whether you will print both Italian and English text, or only the English. But in any case you need an introduction on Lasca, about eight pages, and notes to Maestro Manente and other things. You might print a map showing Florence, Mugello, La Vernia, Vallombrosa, P'Ermo di Camaldoli.[2]

If you like to do this, I suggest you make it your enterprise, and give me 10% – I would do the book at 12/6 or $3.00[3] – in hard covers bound in parchment paper (or 15/- and $4 if you print the Italian text).

PINO ORIOLI.

will publish a series of Italian Renaissance stories, English (and Italian) text, the stories to be translated by D H Lawrence, Norman Douglas, Aldous Huxley and other well-known writers, with introductions by the translators and with notes and maps. The first number of the series will be ready December x – 'The Third Supper', by Lasca. Translated with introduction by D H Lawrence. Limited edition of 1000. Post free 12/6 or $3.00. (if you print Italian text too, you must charge more: 15/- and $4) –

Let me know what you think, and I will have it all typed out properly, the slips and all, for you to give to Giuntina.

4730. To Laurence Pollinger, 1 November 1928
Text: MS UT; Unpublished

La Vigie. Ile de Port-Cros – Var.
1 Nov. 1928 Tutti i Santi

Dear Pollinger

I have been looking through the *Rawdon's Roof* story, and feel very bored about it. I am so sick at the thought of signing 500 copies – I sort of can't get a

---

[1] See Letters 4717, 4721.
[2] All these places feature in *The Story of Doctor Manente* (see pp. 9, 29, 39, 87); they are explained in notes following the text.   [3] 12/6 or $3.00] 12/6 or $2.50

move on anyhow. Ask the Elkin Mathews people if they'll cancel the contract: or else, if they'll be content if I sign only fifty copies – I don't mind so many. If they'll accept that, I shall be able to do those five extra pages quite nicely, because I shall not feel so utterly bored by the thought of the signing business. Then they can have a full-length story and 50 signed, which by heaven, is quite enough for their £25. – But if they won't have this, they'll have to put up with the story short as it is – I shan't touch it.

D. H. Lawrence

4731. To Nancy Pearn, 3 November 1928
Text: MS Lazarus; Unpublished.

La Vigie. Ile de Port-Cros, Var.
3 Nov 1928

Dear Nancy Pearn

Here are proofs – and an article – will send more later.[1]

D. H. Lawrence

4732. To Nancy Pearn, 5 November 1928
Text: MS UT; Unpublished.

La Vigie, Ile de Port-Cros. Var.
5 Novem 1928

Dear Nancy Pearn

Here is the article on 'Sex Appeal'.[2] I made it 2000 words so it would do for *Vanity Fair* if they want it. And if the *Sunday Dispatch* or whatever it is wants it at 1500 words, they can cut it down to please themselves.

Hope you got proofs of the *Eve* story 'Blue Moccasins' and the other article.

Saluti   D. H. Lawrence

---

[1] As the letter following makes clear, the proofs were of the story 'The Blue Moccasins', published in *Eve: The Lady's Pictorial* (cf. Letter 4550 and n. 1). The article was 'Is England Still a Man's Country?' (cf. Letter 4725) which the *Daily Express* published on 29 November 1928 (Roberts C180).

[2] Cf. Letter 4725 and n. 1. 'Sex Locked Out' appeared in the *Sunday Dispatch*, 25 November 1928. It was separately printed from the *Dispatch* text in December 1928 (Roberts A44); it was reprinted as 'Sex Appeal' in *Vanity Fair*, July 1929 and as 'Men and Peacocks' in *Golden Book*, December 1929 (Roberts C179).

4733. To Herbert Seligmann, 8 November 1928
Text: MS PM; Huxley 759–60.

> La Vigie. Ile de Port-Cros. Var. France.
> c/o Curtis Brown Ltd. 6 Henrietta St. *London W.C.2.*
> 8 Novem. 1928

Dear Mr Seligman[1]

Miss Brett sent me your review of *Lady Chatterley* from *The Sun*. Sporting of you to do it! Stieglitz said you were going to. But I'm sorry you got put out into the cold because of it. I'm afraid it doesn't pay to stand up for me and my iniquities. But I am properly grateful – and every little helps. I shall send you a copy of my *Collected Poems*.

Do you ever see Thomas Seltzer? I think of him always with affection and a sad heart. I wish to God he had been able to prosper on me. But I'm afraid I'm not the the stuff prosperity is made out of. I expect little myself, and trim my sails accordingly, and get along well enough on what comes my way. – By the way, if you see Seltzer ask him if he'd let me buy the copyright of *Birds Beasts and Flowers*. I want to do my *Collected Poems* in America as in England: they are in such a scattered mess, my poems in America, I mean. Curtis Browns don't seem to be any help to me in the matter. Knopf won't take it up. So I must do it myself. And I don't even know who has the books. Seltzer has *Birds Beasts*. The Viking Press have *Look! We Have Come Through!* and *Amores* (I think it is *Amores*). I believe Mitchell Kennerley once bought sheets of *Love Poems and Others*, my first volume – but who has the rights now, I don't know. Then about *New Poems*, I don't know if they ever appeared in America at all.[2] So you see it's a mess. – But I have written to the Viking Press[3] – and I must

---

[1] Herbert Jacob Seligmann (1891–1984), author of *D. H. Lawrence: An American Interpretation* (Seltzer, New York, 1924), the first American book on DHL. He explained the background to this letter when writing to M. H. Black (Cambridge University Press) in November 1981. At the prompting of his friend Stieglitz, Seligmann ordered and received two copies of *Lady Chatterley's Lover* from Orioli, 'despite all banns'. His account in 1981 continued:

I spoke about the book to my friend, Henry Hazlitt, then editor of the New York Sun's literary pages and he gave me carte blanche. My review appeared in the early edition of the Sun on 1 September 1928 under the heading 'The Utterance of a Man' and the editors of the Sun were so outraged by my pollution of their pages that they took the unprecedented step of remaking the literary supplement to remove it in later editions.

Seligmann subsequently met Brett in New Mexico; he told her of the ill-fated review and its consequence – that he would not be asked to review again for the *Sun*; whereupon Brett reported this to DHL who in turn wrote to Seligmann.

[2] Seltzer published *Birds, Beasts and Flowers* (1923): Chatto & Windus published *Look! We Have Come Through!* (1917) and Benjamin Huebsch's American edn followed in 1918; *Amores* was first published by Duckworth (July 1916) and then by Huebsch (September 1916); *Love Poems and Others* (1913) – DHL's first book of poems – was published by Duckworth who sold sheets to Kennerley for his American edn; *New Poems*, published by Secker in October 1918, appeared in USA under Huebsch's imprint in 1920.   [3] The letter is missing.

approach Seltzer – I always feel so unhappy about him – not because I left him, for his affairs would have gone just the same, if not worse, had I stayed with him – but because of the great disappointment to him. Myself I don't expect money success so it doesn't matter. But a publisher has to have it.

Somebody sent me a letter from Lawerence Gomme, who is a bookseller in New York, in which he said he had seen pirated copies of *Lady C.* in Philadelphia.[1] I wonder if it's true. I've heard nothing. There was talk of a private edition in New York, but I've heard nothing of that either. – But I don't trust Gomme. He wanted me to send him fifty copies, at my risk – and he doesn't even pay for the six copies I did send, and that I know he received. So it goes – they take advantage of the Customs suppression not to pay for what they get. No wonder poor Seltzer was worried out of his skin.

Though it's no reason why I should worry you. But write me a line c/o Curtis Brown Ltd. 6 Henrietta St. Covent Garden, London. W.C.2.

And many thanks for your backing.

Sincerely. D. H. Lawrence

4734. To Earl and Achsah Brewster, [8 November 1928]
Text: MS UT; Brewster 184–5.

La Vigie. Ile de Port-Cros. Var.
8 Nov.

Dear Earl and Achsah

All this time I haven't written to you. But the cold Frieda brought from Florence developed into the regular Italian Influenza, and I was in bed feeling low. However, I'm better and moderately well. We've had great storms and torrents of rain, and the boat doesn't come out then there's no food – so we are leaving the island, God with us, next Tuesday. I think we shall only just go over to Bandol, on the coast between Toulon and Marseilles, for a little while, just to gather our wits and decide where to go. If I were a bit tougher I'd go to Spain. We *might* go to that coast near Biarritz – we might go to the Garda – God knows. I don't mind very much. – And what about you? What are you

[1] The 'Somebody' was Mabel Luhan who had received the following letter, dated 16 October 1928, from Gomme (TMSC UN):

I have just been shown an edition of Lady Chatterley printed and published in Philadelphia. The salesman who solicited an order from me would not disclose the name of the concern and I don't know whether it is a pirated edition. He informed me that it was authorized by D. H. Lawrence and was being published because of another reprint which had been pirated. I have not seen the pirated edition but he tells me that it was a photographed reproduction from the original . . .

doing? Have you found a house, and are you settling down happily to work a bit and see your friends and not bother? I hope you are – that's the best, anyhow. We can't have life just as we want it, so if we have space and peace and freedom and food, we ought to be jolly thankful, and possess our souls. So many people have so much less.

There's no news. – As I told you, the English papers wouldn't print 'Cocksure Women' – but the *Forum* in America bought it. I am expecting a copy of my poems now, which I shall write in and send you. 'Hymns in a Man's Life' has appeared.[1] And I have had the proofs of 'Blue Moccasins', with such illustrations you *never* saw – from *Eve*.[2] Now there's nothing – except that there was a great attack on *Lady C.* in two of the inferior papers in England – *John Bull* and *Sunday Chronicle*.[3] – The foulest and most obscene book in the English language. – I'll order you a copy at once, after that. – In this place I tried to paint a bit – no good – I merely wrote three little articles.[4] I don't care for islands, especially very small ones. I want to get on the mainland again. – Frieda's mother was ill – her legs, a lot of pain in them, had to be in bed. But she seems better. – Now I do hope you're settling and feeling your own selves. – I'll send an address. I expect Harwood is chirpy with the three pals.[5]

Love from us both: DHL

4735. To Maria Huxley, [8 November 1928]
Text: Huxley 758.

Port-Cros.
8 Nov.

Dear Maria, –

No, the island isn't good enough – storms, torrents, no boat, no bread, uncomfortable Vigie. No, no good. We are leaving Tuesday, D.V. – boat, that is, just going over to Bandol, beyond Toulon, for a bit. Will send address. – But where then? where shall we go for a little house to keep? Where? Do you think we'd like somewhere near Paris? – Forest of Fontainebleau perhaps – a

[1] See Letter 4635 and n. 3.
[2] Cf. p. 475 n. 1. There are two illustrations by 'Spurrier'. The first dominates the printing of the first two pages of the story in *Eve*: it shows Lina M'Leod, now Mrs Barlow, demanding the return of the moccasins from her astonished husband dressed in Arab garb, on the stage; its caption reads: '*Percy, will you hand me my moccasins?*' In the second, Percy, dressed in his pyjamas and totally bemused, watches his wife brushing her hair; the caption reads: '*He would sit there silent, watching her brush the long swinging river of silver.*'
[3] Cf. pp. 598 n. 2 and 604 n. 1.
[4] They were 'Sex Locked Out', 'Is England Still a Man's Country?' and 'Do Women Change?' (see Letter 4736 and n. 3).   [5] See Letters 3983 and p. 22 n. 4, and 4390 and n. 1.

bit higher up than you are? Do you think? Or must it be Italy – perhaps Lago di Garda, where we first started.[1] If you have a bright idea send a line *poste restante*, Bandol, Var. I do hope you're not so busy. Do hope the book makes *real* money![2] Do hope all well. Skies look sort of lowering.

Love,   DHL

4736. To Nancy Pearn, 8 November 1928
Text: MS UT; Unpublished.

La Vigie. Ile de Port-Cros. Var.
8 Nov 1928

Dear Nancy Pearn,

Here's a little article, 3 copies, for *Evening News* or anybody who wants it.[3]

Very stormy and wet here, and this poor old fort not quite weather-proof. So we are leaving on Tuesday and going over to the mainland. I'll send an address. And would you please tell the mailing dept. to hold my mail.

Ever[4]

4737. To Laurence Pollinger, 8 November 1928
Text: MS UT; Unpublished.

La Vigie. *Ile de Port-Cros.* Var.
8 Nov. 1928

Dear Pollinger

Thanks for yours about Cape and the poems. I shall try what I can do with the Viking Press and Seltzer, who hold the most important books, and let you know.

Terrific storms and torrents here, and this poor old vigie not quite sea-worthy, and not a loaf of bread on the island when the boat fails. So we'll have to go – just over to the mainland to Bandol, I expect – but I'll send an address. We leave Tuesday next: sea consenting.

What about the Elkin Mathews story?

Ever   D. H. Lawrence

---

[1] When DHL and Frieda first visited Italy together, they lived by Lago di Garda September 1912–April 1913.   [2] Cf. p. 596 n. 1.

[3] The article (acknowledged by Nancy Pearn, 13 November 1928) was 'Do Women Change?' It appeared (entitled 'Women Don't Change') in the *Sunday Dispatch*, 28 April 1929 (Roberts C185).   [4] DHL's signature has been cut from the MS.

4738. To Enid Hilton, [9 November 1928]

Text: MS UCLA; PC v. Ile de Port-Cros (Var), Et la féerie devient plus intime: Une Vallée verte invraisemblablement touffue L'Égarée sur la route; Postmark, Ile de [Port-Cros] [. . .]28; Unpublished.

Port-Cros.
Friday

Very stormy weather here – no boat for several days, and torrents and leaky roof! So we are all clearing out next Tuesday or Thursday. I expect we shall stay on the coast, though – perhaps Bandol, other side Toulon – do you know it? – I had your letter – *where* did you stay down here – on the Giens peninsula?

No news of the Warren.

Will write an address.

DHL

4739. To Else Jaffe, [9 November 1928]

Text: MS Jeffrey; PC v. [Ile de Port-Cros]; Postmark, [. . .]; Frieda Lawrence 281.

Port-Cros.
Friday

Such storms, such wind, such torrents of rain! And the Vigie, although quite *hygenic*, is not very *comfortable*. So we are all leaving next week – Tuesday or Thursday, as the sea permits. I think Frieda and I will stay in Bandol, on the big railway. – Am so glad the Schwiegermutter is better. Will write next week.

DHL

4740. To Giuseppe Orioli, [9 November 1928]

Text: MS NWU; PC v. Ile de Port-Cros (Var.), Ce ciel et cette mer, ces montagnes et ces grèves ont la même nuance de lumière transparente que l'Attique ou le Péloponese Voyageuses; Postmark, [. . .]; Unpublished.

Port-Cros.
Friday

No boat – no word from you for a long time – very bad weather – island, or rather Vigie too uncomfortable. We are leaving next Tuesday or Thursday – I expect we shall stay somewhere on the coast for a while – shall send an address. Meanwhile I do hope nothing has gone wrong.

I shall send the Lasca translation from here.

DHL

4741. To Emily King, [9 November 1928]

Text: MS Needham; PC v. Ile de Port-Cros (Var.), Un de ces tragiques couchants d'un rouge sanglant dont les nuées paraissent élargir la blessure La Fée de Port-Cros; Postmark, Ile de P[ort-Cros] 9.[. . .]28; Unpublished.

> *Port-Cros.*
> Friday

Had terrific gales and torrents here – the boat hasn't been for several days, which makes supplies difficult – and the poor old vigie won't stand really bad weather. So we are all packing up and leaving, either next Tuesday, or at latest Thursday. I expect we shall just go over to the mainland and stay in one of the little places by the sea – quite nice, they are. But I'll send an address. Hope all goes well.

> Love to you all   DHL

4742. To Ada Clarke, [9 November 1928]

Text: MS Clarke; PC v. Ile de Port-Cros (Var.), Ce ciel et cette mer, ces montagnes et ces grèves ont la même nuance de lumière transparente que l'Attique ou le Péloponese Voyageuses; Postmark; [Ile de] Port-Cros 9[. . .]28; Lawrence-Gelder 185–6.

> *Port-Cros.*
> Friday

Well the weather has bust up with a vengeance – such gales, such torrents, no boat able to come, no bread, and the poor old vigie none too water-tight. So we are all packing up and leaving – either next Tuesday or Thursday – as the sea allows us. I expect F[rieda] and I will just cross to the mainland, and stay on the coast a while – I'll let you know. – I had your letter and the photographs – very swanky the new camera! Hope G[ertrude Cooper] is keeping well.

> Love.   DHL

4743. To Jean Watson, 9 November 1928

Text: MS UT; Unpublished.

> Port-Cros. Var.
> 9 Novem. 1928

Dear Miss Watson

No, there is no reason why *Lady Chatterley* shouldn't be published in French and German, if the French and Germans want to do it. The Kippenbergs bought one copy. Anyhow, they can get others from Orioli.

> *Signor G. Orioli.* 6 Lungarno Corsini, Florence

but the price is now four guineas – Orioli bought the remainder of my stock – not many. But I'll write to him and tell him to let you have a copy at £2-2-0 – you write to him also, ordering a copy and telling him what I say: He's not very anxious now to sell them. I don't know why he never sent those four to Pollinger – unless the price.

Don't write to this address any more – we are leaving next week – the island too cut off, the vigie too *uncomfortable* in bad weather.

                                                      Sincerely   D. H. Lawrence
I'll send an addresss.

4744. To Morris Ernst, 10 November 1928
Text: TMSC NWU; Huxley 760–1.

                                        La Vigie, Ille de Port Cros, Var. France
                                                            10. Novem. 1928.

I have finished reading *To the Pure*.[1] I find it a curious, interesting, pertinent book, curiously moving. As the work of lawyers rather than literary men, it conveys an impression that no truly literary work would achieve. I look out with those unemotional lawyer's eyes, and have a queer experience. I am left feeling puzzled, uneasy, and a little frightened, as if I had been watching a great unchained ape fumbling through his hairs for something – he doesn't quite know what – which he will squash if he gets it. I see that weird and horrible animal, Social Man, devoid of real individuality or personality, fumbling gropingly and menacingly for something he is afraid of, but he doesn't know what it is. It is a lawyer's vision, not an artist's – but it is the result of experience in dealing with the Social Man. The book, in its queer muddle – for legal precision is artistic muddle – creates the weird reactionary of the ageless censor-animal curiously and vividly. It leaves one feeling breathless, and makes one realise the necessity of keeping a chain on the beast. For censorship is one of the lower and debasing activities of social man – that is obvious.

Myself, I believe censorship helps nobody; and hurts many. But the book has brought it home to me much more grimly than before. Our civilisation cannot afford to let the censor-moron loose. The censor-moron does not really hate anything but the living and growing human consciousness. It is our developing and extending consciousness that he threatens – and our consciousness in its newest, most sensitive activity, its vital growth. To arrest or circumscribe the vital consciousness is to produce morons, and nothing but a moron would wish to do it.

[1] *To the Pure: A Study of Obscenity and the Censor* (New York, 1928), by Morris L. Ernst (1888–) and William Seagle. According to Aldington the book was sent to DHL by Ernst, a lawyer specialising in libel, slander and copyright (Nehls, iii. 254). Cf. p. 548 n. 1.

No, the book is a good book – and the very effect of muddle which it has on me conveys most vividly the feeling of the groping atavistic working of the ageless censor, furtive, underhand, mean. Print this letter if you like – or any bit of it. I believe in the living extending consciousness of man. I believe the consciousness of man has now to embrace the emotions and passions of sex, and the deep effects of human physical contact. This is the glimmering edge of our awareness and our field of understanding, in the endless business of knowing ourselves. And no censor must or shall or even can really interfere.

Sincerely,   D. H. Lawrence

4745. To Caresse Crosby, 13 November 1928
Text: MS SIU; Unpublished.

Port-Cros. Var.

13 Novem 1928

Dear Caresse Crosby

I am distressed about this sheet.[1] The post is a one-eyed affair on this island, what between no boat and our henchman Giuseppe with his little ass and his vagaries – and your letter comes to my hand only this minute – and it's dated 30 October – veramente da piangere.[2] I expect it's too late to be of any use – nevertheless I now send the sheet, as you request – *post-haste!*

I got the two *Sun*s in their golden boxes: very gay and glorious. I like the book itself immensely, the print and the paper – very elegant and aristocratic and lovely. What fun to do it!

I wonder if you have sailed away! We leave here on Thursday – the island too impractical – I think we shall stay a while longer on the coast. I shall send an address: but c/o Curtis Brown Ltd. 6 Henrietta St. London W.C.2. always finds me. – I shall send you my poems to Paris – heaven knows where else you'll be.

Meanwhile joy go with you.

D. H. Lawrence

4746. To Baroness Anna von Richthofen, [14 November 1928]
Text: MS UCB; Frieda Lawrence 282–3.

Ile de Port-Cros. Var.

Mittwoch.

Meine liebe Schwiegermutter

Ich bin froh dass es dir besser geht. Du bist zu tapfer gewesen. Weisst du,

---

[1] Cf. Letter 4712   [2] 'really it's enough to make you weep.'

du bist jetzt schwer auf den Beinen, du bist nicht mehr ein leichtes junges Ding. Geh nur nicht so weit. Ich denke immer mit Weh an den Fischkultur – ein wahnsinniger Ausflug, und du *wolltest* es machen. Nein nein, sei nur weise und mild. Anstrengen ist nicht für dich. Wir gehen morgen fort von hier. Gott sei dank, das Wetter ist schön, blaue Himmel, blaues, stilles Meer: und so warm. Aber ich habe genug. Länger wie ein Monat möchte ich nie auf einem kleinen Insel bleiben. Als Erfahrung war es aber schön. Ich glaube, wir gehen nur bis Bandol, ein kleiner Ort auf der Küste, eine halbe Stunde von Toulon. Aber dort sind wir auf der grosser Eisenbahn, und nur eine Stunde von Marseille. Und wir können denken, wo wir wirklich gehen wollen, um ein Haus zu suchen. Wir wissen beide nicht, was wir wollen.

Man schreibt von Florenz, es regnet und regnet und regnet, furchtbar. Gott sei dank dass wir nicht da sind. – Das Buch meiner Novellen kam, mit Insel-Verlag *Almanach* und Mörike. Du weisst, ich breche nicht ab vom Insel? Nein, wir werden alle einen neuen Vertrag unterschreiben, sie zahlen mir fünfzig Pfund statt fünfunddreissig, und die Else kann immer noch übersetzen, wenn sie will. Das ist gut – es ist wirklich besser, nicht vom Insel zu Fischer zu gehen.

Ich schicke dir £5. – wenn du mehr brauchst, sage nur. Es ist mein Geld, ich geb' es dir freilich. Aber bitte zahle die Mark 10. für Frieda's Kleid.

Hat die Else meine Gedichte erhalten? zwei schöne Bände.

Die Brewsters sind wieder auf Capri – sagen es ist der Beste Ort der Welt. Schön wenn man es weiss!

Also ich schicke dir die Adresse gleich – Freitag oder Samstag.

Bleibe still und innerlich ruhig, dann werden die Beine schmerzlos gehen.

DHL

[Wednesday.

My dear Schwiegermutter

I'm glad you're better. You've been too brave. You know, you are now heavy on your legs, you're not a light young thing any more. Just don't walk so far. I always think with pain about the fish-farm – a mad trip, and you *wanted* to take it. No no, just be wise and gentle. Exertion is not for you.

We're going away from here tomorrow. Thank the Lord, the weather is lovely, blue sky, blue, calm sea: and so warm. But I've had enough. I would never want to stay longer than a month on a small island. As an experience, though, it was fine. I think we're only going to Bandol, a little place on the coast, half an hour from Toulon. But there we're on the main railway line, and only an hour from Marseilles. And we can think about where we really want to go, to look for a house. We don't either of us know what we want.

They write from Florence, it rains and rains and rains, awful. Thank the Lord that we're not there. – The book of my stories came,[1] with the Insel-Verlag *Almanac* and Mörike. You know that I'm not breaking off from Insel? No, we shall all sign a new contract, they'll pay me fifty pounds instead of thirty-five, and Else can go on translating, if she wants. That's good – it's really better not to go from Insel to Fischer.

I send you £5. – if you need more, just say. It is my money, I of course give it to you. But please pay the 10 Marks for Frieda's dress.

Has Else got my poems? two fine volumes.

The Brewsters are on Capri again – say it's the best place in the world. Nice that someone knows it!

Well, I'll send you the address at once – Friday or Saturday.

Stay calm and quiet inside, then the legs will stop being painful.

DHL]

4747. To William Gerhardie, 14 November 1928
Text: MS SIU; Gerhardie, *Memoirs of a Polyglot* (New York, 1931), p. 229.

La Vigie. Ile de Port-Cros. Var.
14 Nov 1928

Dear Gerhardi

I was amused by the Beaverbrook blurb.[2] But you mustn't grumble at his inconsistencies. The heart doesn't know what the liver thinketh, and the stomach speaketh unsooth to the mind. That comes of creating a newspaper

[1] Else Jaffe's translation of *The Woman Who Rode Away and Other Stories, Die Frau, die davon ritt* (Insel Verlag, 1928) (Roberts D78).
[2] Gerhardie provided a tortuous explanation of the background to this letter (Nehls, iii. 705 n. 19):

[DHL's letter] was in answer to my letter in which I pulled Lawrence's leg at the expense of Lord Beaverbrook, with whom my long friendship was clouded intermittently by his failure to live up to my conception of an unilateral friendship: which is to differ from oneself only in the friend's superior capacity to further one's own interests. The occasion was the inauguration of the Scottish *Daily Express* which carried in the Beaverbrook Press a full-page manifesto over the signature of Lord Beaverbrook, in which he claimed to have created his newspapers by invoking not his brain alone but other organs as well. I charged Lawrence with Beaverbrook's conversion to the Lawrence creed of the "complete man." That he should not see that work so humourless must invalidate its seriousness, prompted me at the same time to pull his leg at the expense of Aldous Huxley . . . Hence the wary but pathetic attempt on the part of D. H. Lawrence to be humorous at all cost, to dissociate himself from Huxley's portrait [of DHL as Rampion in *Point Counter Point*] and from his own involuntary caricature in the Beaverbrook manifesto.

with all your anatomy. The little toe, as you remark, has a small say all on its own. One could do an amusing skit on that. I wish *we* created a 'Monthly Express,' out of our various anatomies, to laugh at it all. Just a little magazine to laugh a few things to death. 'The Big Toe Points out the Point or Points in *Point Counter Point*.' – and so on. Let's make a little magazine, where even the liver can laugh.[1]

No, I refuse to be Rampioned. I am not responsible. Aldous' admiration is only skin deep, and out of the Mary Mary quite contrary impulses.

We leave this isle tomorrow – *I don't* like little islands. I suppose we shall stay a while on the coast here. We have given up the Florence house, and I am absolutely at a loss, where to get another. *Where* does one want to live? Have you any bright idea on the subject? Did you get a house west of Marseille, as you said? How is it there?

Send a line c/o Curtis Brown, if ever you want to. My wife sends her greetings, and tante belle cose.

D. H. Lawrence

4748. To John Clark, 14 November 1928
Text: MS UN; cited in Pinto, *D.H. Lawrence After Thirty Years*, pp. 46–7.

Ile de Port-Cros. Var.
14 Novem 1928

Dear Mr Clark[2]

A delayed answer to your letter, which comes on here. – Squire is a sniveller, he wouldn't have the pep to dance on my grave even if I'd got one – he'd only drone and sniffle through his nose.[3]

About *Lady Chatterley* – Smiths *did* import two copies! – If you write to
Signor G. Orioli, 6 Lungarno Corsini, Florence
I should think he could send you a copy, he bought up my last lot, and I believe his price is now £4. – if you can run to it. – worth it though. – I believe

---

[1] Gerhardie, writing to Nancy Pearn on 23 November 1928, dismissed this jocular proposal as 'a pleasant idea, but, of course, impracticable' (TMS Lazarus).

[2] It is presumed that 'Mr Clark' was John Clark, the export bookseller whose earlier letter is printed at p. 520 n. 1.

[3] (Sir) John Collings Squire (1884–1958), editor of the *London Mercury*, had reviewed DHL's *Collected Poems* in the *Observer*, 7 October 1928 (see *The Critical Heritage*, ed. Draper, pp. 299–302). The review begins:

Mr. Lawrence is not always a poet, but he is always himself. Good or bad, he is himself, and symptomatic of his time. Three-quarters of his poems must irritate either the man who is fastidious about expression and form or the man who dislikes crude generalizations about life as a whole or indiscreet revelations of the life of an individual. The fact remains that Mr. Lawrence, passionate, brooding, glowering, worshipping man, is undoubtedly a man of genius and big and fiery enough to eat a dozen of his merely clever contemporaries.

the book comes in to England all right – every copy has done, so far. If there is any hitch, write me *c/o Orioli* – not here. – Glad you like the poems. – Don't apologise anyhow.

Sincerely   D. H. Lawrence

4749. To David Chambers, 14 November 1928
Text: MS UN; Postmark, Ile de Port-Cros 15 NOV 28; Huxley 761–2.

Ile de Port-Cros. Var. France.
14 Novem. 1928

Dear David[1]

I hardly recognized you as J.D. – and you must be a man now, instead of a thin little lad with very fair hair. Ugh, what a gap in time! it makes me feel scared.

Whatever I forget, I shall never forget the Haggs – I loved it so. I loved to come to you all, it really was a new life began in me there. The water-pippin by the door – those maiden-blush roses that Flower would lean over and eat – and Trip floundering round[2] – And stewed figs for tea in winter, and in August green stewed apples. Do you still have them? Tell your mother I never forget, no matter where life carries us. – And does she still blush if somebody comes and finds her in a dirty white apron? or doesn't she wear work-aprons any more? Oh I'd love to be nineteen again, and coming up through the Warren and catching the first glimpse of the buildings. Then I'd sit on the sofa under the window, and we'd crowd round the little table to tea, in that tiny little kitchen I was so at home in.

Son' tempi passati, cari miei! quanto cari, non saprete mai![3] – I could never tell you in English how much it all meant to me, how I still feel about it.

If there is anything I can ever do for you, do tell me. – Because whatever else I am, I am somewhere still the same Bert who rushed with such joy to the Haggs.

Ever.   D. H. Lawrence

The best address is:
   c/o Curtis Brown Ltd. 6 Henrietta St. Covent Garden. W.C.2.

[1] Jonathan David Chambers (1898–1970), youngest child of Edmund (1863–1946) and Sarah Ann Chambers (1859–1937) whom DHL remembered with great affection at the Haggs Farm near Eastwood. In 1928 Chambers was a Lecturer in Adult Education, University College, Nottingham; he later became Professor of Economic History. (He may have sent a copy of his first scholarly publication: 'The open fields of Laxton', *Transactions of the Thoroton Society*, xxxii, 1928, 102–25.)

[2] The old mare, Flower, and the bull terrier, Trip, are similarly described in Chambers' 'Memories of D. H. Lawrence', *Renaissance and Modern Studies*, xvi (1972), 9.

[3] 'They are times past, my dears! how dear, you will never know!'

INDEX

No distinction is made between a reference in the text or in a footnote.
All titles of writings by Lawrence are gathered under his name.
For localities, public buildings, etc. in London, see the comprehensive entry under the place-name; all biblical references are collected under 'Bible'.
A bold numeral indicates a biographical entry in a footnote.

Index